MOSQUITO

MOSQUITO

GAYL JONES

BEACON PRESS

Boston

BEACON PRESS
25 Beacon Street
Boston, Massachusetts 02108–2892
www.beacon.org

Beacon Press books are published under the auspices
of the Unitarian Universalist Association of Congregations.

04 03 02 01 00 99   8 7 6 5 4 3 2

This book is printed on recycled acid-free paper
that contains at least 20 percent postconsumer waste and meets the uncoated paper
ANSI/NISO specifications for permanence as revised in 1992.

Text design by Charles Nix
Typeset in Nix Rift
Composition by Wilsted & Taylor Publishing Services

Library of Congress Cataloging-in-Publication Data

Jones, Gayl.
Mosquito / Gayl Jones.
p.   cm.
ISBN 0-8070-8346-1 (cloth)
1. Afro-American women—Southwestern States—Fiction.   I. Title.
PS3560.0483M67   1999
813'.54—DC21   98-27644

Mosquito is the "spiritual descendant" of Kate Hickman, a New World African character invented by Lucille Jones and the strength of one of her novels, Stop Dat Moda *(excerpts published in* Obsidian, BOP, *and* Callaloo*). Electra Lucilla Martin Wilson Jones (Lucille Jones, the Good Spirit) is the Spiritual Mother of Mosquito. However, Ray's Aunt Electra is fictional.*

—NZINGHA

CHAPTER 1

I WAS ON ONE OF THEM LITTLE BORDER ROADS IN South Texas, you know them little narrow roads that runs along the border between South Texas and northern Mexico. Maybe that Dairy Mart Road, probably that Dairy Mart Road, though all them border roads in them border towns looks alike. On either side of the border. Brownsville, Laredo, Del Rio. All them border towns. I usedta travel into Brownsville in Cameron County a lot because it one of them international seaport towns. That's when I was transporting electronics, apparel, and transporting for the shrimping industry. This that Dairy Mart Road, though. Your source for superior tanning products, one of them roadside signs say. It's got them Southern California types in they bikinis showing off they tans. Another roadside sign advertising cactus candy and got a picture of a buffalo and some cactus. I's got me a teacup I got from a trade show that have got a handle that is in the shape of a cactus and resembles that exact same cactus. I mean the handle of it ain't a ordinary teacup handle, it's a cactus, so when you holds the teacup you's got to hold the cactus. I think that that cactus is the archetypal cactus, 'cause I has seen more cactus like that in them ads than I has in the Southwest itself. I calls it Arizona cactus, but I don't know its true name.

Another sign advertising Brownsville as a tourist attraction. It tells you that Brownsville ain't just Brownsville, but it got all the amenities for tourism, that tourists don't got to go to Acapulco or even Tijuana, that they can come to Brownsville. I try to think of the Kiowa word for Brownsville, or maybe it the Kiowa word for Sweetwater I'm trying to think of. Sound like the name of somebody, like the names that they gives people in the South, though, that Kiowa word.

Am got a few of them cactus plants along Dairy Mart Road, though they ain't the archetypal cactus, I think it's Dairy Mart Road, and some of that poverty grass. I guess it called poverty grass, or maybe it pampas grass, 'cause it the Southwest, you know. I'm going to have to find out the names of these grasses and plants and trees, so's I can tell y'all what they is. I guess that's what I likes about the Southwest, though, the landscape. Well, I likes the people that I likes (the Perfectability Baptist Church would want me to say more about the likability of peoples and us commandments to love), but when you gets to the Southwest it got it own distinctive landscape, and you knows you's in a different country. You knows you's in the Southwest. Them mountains and the ranges and the deserts. Them trees, whatever they names is, starts looking like they's wearing Afros and then they turns into brush and cactus. I gots to get me a natural history of the Southwest, or at least a natural history of Texas. I be thinking why them native peoples don't got Afros in the dry tropics, 'cause in the East the leaves of them trees is broad and flat, then as you travels toward the Southwest, them leaves gets stingier, and then they becomes cactus or palms or them trees and brushes that looks kinda like them monkey puzzle trees. They's got flowering cactus and bushes, though, so's they's all kindsa colors in the desert. You's got the desert-colored desert and then there's desert flowers that is red and yellow, bright green, and orange-red, and white—I guess that a color—and sage green and bright red. I know there's what they calls buffalo grass and there's a weed that got orange flowers that attracts butterflies and there's a coyote bush. I don't know if it's named that 'cause it attracts coyotes. I know they's a hummingbird bush that supposed to attract hummingbirds, but I don't know if that the name of that bush. Desert shrubs and bushes and brushes and cactuses, Delgadina could tell you the names of all of them, and even the one she uses to make what she call Navajo Tea. And she knows the names of all the trees of the Southwest. I tells Delgadina she could be a natural historian, that she could write a natural history of the Southwest. But like I said, when you's in the Southwest you knows you's in the Southwest. When you's in the Southwest, you knows where you is.

Who amongst y'all knows the name of every tree? I might not know the names of them trees, but if you shows me a tree, I can tell you what part of the natural country it is from. I can tell you whether it from the East, the West, the Southwest, the South Central, the Midwest, the Southeast, the Pacific Southwest, the Northeast, or wherever you asks me. I might not know the names of them trees, but I knows them by better than they names. I even knows trees that is originally from the Pacific Southwest when they's in South Florida. Now if you tries to play me for a fool and tell me that that tree you's planted is a South Florida tree, I knows that you might have planted it in South Florida, but that its origins is the Pacific Southwest or even South Central. I might not know the names of them trees, but you can't play me for a fool about they origins. And them desert ain't like the desert sands in them Arabian lands, the Southwest desert is dotted with brush everywhere, little trees and bushes, like I said, or it the ranch country with broad ranges, ponds for the cattle and bales of hay. The Southwest is a landscape full of power.

I knows the Southwest. Traveling through some of them mountainous type regions in Texas and Arizona (when you's in Arizona you know why they calls it the redlands—I ain't signifying on the native peoples I'm talking about the color of the land itself; some people say the land that color 'cause of all the iron ore it got in it; them's the scientific peoples), though, you'd think you was still out East, I mean when you's up in them mountains, traveling them mountain roads, I don't mean them dry boulder mountains of Nevada up around the Hoover Dam, traveling they truck route, I mean them temperate mountains, 'cause they's got natural forests, of cypress and alligator juniper, of spruce, and fir trees, and white pine trees, I knows them 'cause they's similar to northeastern trees, 'cept they's southwest white pine trees not northeast white pine trees, then when you come out of them natural forests you's in the sparse landscape again, the flat country, the deserts, the ranges, them adobe-type houses with them flat roofs, the Southwest's own architecture.

3

They's got pyramidal-roofed houses in the Southwest, but them flat-roofed houses is the Southwest's own architecture. Them adobe-type houses that dots the landscape, and what I've heard people call them dog-trot houses, 'cause they ain't them elaborate-type houses. I guess they calls them dog-trot houses, 'cause they's just big enough for a dog to trot in them. I ain't like to call them dog-trot houses my-self 'cause they's human beings in them houses. Ain't got no balus-trades and bay windows and art deco and arcades-type architecture. Most of them is clay-colored, that clay mixed with straw adobe. Few of them got them red tile roofs. They is just Four Square houses. They is some native peoples that considers that Four a sacred num-ber. That that supposed to have something to do with they cosmol-ogy. I ain't know if that why they makes them Four Square houses. I was in this desert I calls the Chihuahua desert, though it was some other desert, traveling for 'bout eight mile and all I seen was them Four Square house. Nothing but them Four Square house. Some of them had things to distinguish them from the other Four Square house to show the personality of the owners of them houses. One might have a red tile roof, another a green tile roof, another might have a more elaborate-looking door, another might even have a arch above the door, one might have a little bay window, one might sug-gest more the Moorish, another more the Spanish, another even look like a little Hawaiian house, but they's all Four Square house.

Am got every kind of architecture in the Southwest, prairie styles and classical and colonial and renaissance and Victorian, and art deco–type modernity, but there's also the kind of architecture that people says, This the Southwest. McDonald's might be everywhere, but it ain't everywhere the same aesthetic. Here there's even Mc-Donald's that shaped like them adobe's architecture, and not the McDonald's architecture that in the East or Middle America or them south-central and southeastern states. And some little towns and villages all the houses that same adobe color or that same adobe architecture. You know, that pueblo architecture. I guess that the Mexican influence, or the Native American aesthetic, it ain't neo-classicism. Though I guess them cowboys claims it like they claims the Southwest for theyself. There's them real cowboys that rides the ranges and tends the cattle and sheep and mends the fences and car-ries them bales of hay and keeps the land irrigated, Mexicans and

Navajos and Zunis and Cherokees among the whites and "Okla-homa Africans" I calls the others, 'cause the first black cowboys I seen was in Oklahoma, and then there's them pretend cowboys that waves to the tourists soon's they enters them western towns. There's always a pretend cowboy on his saddle horse who doffs his cowboy hat and waves to me when I'm coming into Albuquerque. I don't travel that route through New Mexico now, though. I mostly travels just the route along the Texas border, along the Rio Grande. I likes to say that, though some of them roads don't exactly travel along the Rio Grande.

Me I'm pulled to the side of the road 'bout a hundred or so yards from the truckstop, de moda running, reading me some of my mail—letter from a friend of mine out in California, a brochure on Citizen's Rights, another brochure wants me to join the Republic of Texas which say it ain't the same as Texas itself, 'cause Texas it consider to be a independent and sovereign nation, not a state of the United States, but they is proclaiming they independence: "When you be-come a citizen of the Republic of Texas, you are still an American but you are no longer a citizen of the corporate United States; there-fore, you are a free Texan; the annexation of Texas to the United States isn't legal." I guess I can quote from that brochure; it ain't no confabulatory brochure neither; then it say something about the his-tory of Texans fighting for they freedom and independence from im-perial Mexico, got some photographs of neoclassical architecture, a lot of white people wearing the flag of the Republic of Texas; and them that ain't draped in the Republic of Texas flag is wearing ban-dannas made out of the Confederate flag. Maybe I'm being a little confabulatory, but I'm thinking how I got on they mailing list—a coupon for a free pizza, and this book I just bought at this flea market near the Galveston Bay. If any y'all been to Tijuana, y'all know the area. That's when I heard me this commotion in the back of my truck. Sounded like a coyote or something, or maybe one of them prairie foxes. I think they call them prairie foxes, don't ya? A lot of them prairie animals they just stick a prairie on the front of they name and they got the animal. They even got prairie oysters, though I don't know how they can have a oyster of the prairie. There's a band from the Southwest, I think, that calls theyselves the Prairie Oys-ters. I wonder if they's aphrodisiacs like them other oysters. That's

5

named after the Greek goddess of love and beauty, you know. I don't mean them prairie oysters, I mean them aphrodisiacs. That Aphrodite. Sound like the name of some African goddess, though, don't it? Wonder if them Africans got they own goddesses of love and beauty. Only gods and goddesses you hear about though is them Greeks. Or if it ain't the Greeks, it's the Romans. I heard of that Krishna though. He supposed to be the ideal perfect man amongst the true Indians. I wonder if them Africans got that ideal of the perfect man. Course the man's ideal of the perfect man and the woman's ideal might not be the same man. Same for the women. Course I've also heard them say that religion started in Africa, and that even them Greek gods and goddesses is really Africans disguised as Greeks. But everybody claims religion started with theyselves. The Perfectability Baptists even claims that they started perfectability. I prefer not to talk to y'all about Perfectability baptism, 'cause I'm only a member of the church and ain't no specialist in perfectability. The Perfectability Baptists, though, believes that the only true baptism is Perfectability baptism.

I ain't much of a natural historian myself, like I said, or a mythologist neither, but I do likes to watch them National Geographic specials, I mean for natural history, especially when they talks about the more exotic-type animals or make the ordinary beasts of the wilds seem extraordinary. They's even got a Animal Planet on cable, where the peoples learns that the planet belongs to animals as well as humankind. I know it ain't every race of peoples that thinks they's supposed to have dominion over everything, or absolute and arbitrary power. That Citizen's Rights brochure said something like that. I'm thinking how they got my name on they mailing list, 'cause I ain't on the Citizen's Committee.

And I just seen one of them shows on my pocket TV, which says animals can be as neurotic as human beings. Ain't saying I'm neurotic, or crazy neither, just that I found that interesting. And they says that them animals has dreams, has dreams the same as human beings. If y'all is amongst the people that wants to think it the dream what make us human, then you be saying that them animal dreams is less complex than human's dreaming. And they's got psychic ability, them animals and more developed than most human beings. Course

6

that don't mean them psychic animals is superior to humankind. That don't mean them psychic animals has the superior intellect.

Anyhow, I heard this commotion in the back of my truck, so I keeps de moda running, takes my flashlight and my stun gun outta the glove compartment and goes back there to look. I opens the back of the truck real careful like, shines the light in there, and then climbs up in the back of the truck. Y'all wants me to describe my truck? I prefers not to describe my truck. I'll explain to y'all why when I comes to why. Of course y'all will probably say it ain't logical, 'cause I's described myself and I's described everything but my truck—at least what to me is description—and y'all that don't already know me would know me anyhow. Still there might be somebody else on this route in the Southwest that resembles me. But I acknowledges y'all's question regarding the description of my truck. I knows that there is no doubt spies and informants amongst y'all that will go around to the truckstops anyway or ask some of the peoples in the union whether they knows me and has they seen my truck. How big is it, how many axles it got, how many tons is it, what color is it? I gots to tell y'all that the roof of my truck ain't the same color as the rest of my truck. So those of y'all that thinks y'all knows my truck to be one color don't know the fullness of my truck.

In describing my truck, I prefers not to describe my truck, which I sometimes calls my moda, after a book I reads. 'Cept moda my personal name for my truck. I ain't tell most peoples I calls my truck my moda, 'cause truck is most people's name for truck, so I calls it my truck. That don't mean that I ain't proud of my truck. I'm proud of my truck and I'm proud that I owns it. I'm proud that I'm an independent even though the peoples in the union knows me. I'm proud of how big my truck is. I'm proud of how many axles it got. I'm proud of how many tons it is. I'm proud of what color it is. I'm proud even that the roof ain't the same color as the rest of my truck, 'cause I got up on the roof and painted the roof of my truck myself. I ain't too proud of my truck, though, and I gots to tell y'all that I ain't too proud of it, 'cause the Perfectability Baptists believes that you can't be too proud of material things, and you's got to rise above that. The Perfectability Baptists combines traditional baptism with ideals of perfectability. They believes that the true nature of man and woman is to be perfect, or at least perfectable. But like I said I ain't no specialist in perfectability baptism, and don't claim to be no perfect Perfectability Baptist, and even my reasons for joining the Perfectability Baptist Church ain't perfect, and although I wants y'all to know all about my truck, I prefers not to describe it. I can describe everything but my truck, except for what I prefers not to describe. I knows that there is rumormongers amongst y'all that will probably go and tell the Perfectability Baptists that the reason I won't describe my truck is because I'm too proud of it to describe it. I still ain't going to describe my truck. And even if I do tell y'all the color of my truck, don't mean it's got to stay the same color. When I first got my truck I would sometimes repaint it different colors. Once I painted my truck a bright red and it were the most visible truck, then another time I painted my truck a dark gray. When I painted my truck a dark gray, you could see it sometimes at dawn and it look like it made out of steel. I even had some peoples that was calling my truck the Steel Truck, 'cause when they would see it at dawn it would look just like it were made of steel. Or I might mix them colors. I might paint the cab of my truck a bright red and the other of my truck steel, and then the roof of my truck I might paint even another color. But I can describe everything but my truck. Sometimes birds is attracted to my truck. Once they was a red-tailed hawk perched on my truck. I went into this truckstop and when I come out there was this red-tailed hawk perched on the cab of my truck. Another time one of them prairie falcon, another time a golden eagle, another time one of them vermilion-colored flycatcher birds. A lot of red birds likes to perch on the cab of my truck. The cab of my truck attracts other color birds—golden, blue, green, yellow and brown birds—but seems like it attracts more of them red birds or red-tailed birds and it ain't just when I paints my cab a bright red.

The birds they has got they own language. Anyhow, I think I hears this scuffling sound, but might just be me scraping my knees climbing and scrambling up the back of that truck, trying to hold on to both that flashlight and that stun gun at the same time. They needs to attach a flashlight onto them stun guns or a stun gun onto them flashlights, less they thinks everybody got the dextrosity, I means dexterity, of them circus jugglers. Or what them other circus crea-

tures? Not them acrobats. Them contortionists. They think everybody got the dextrosity and dexterity of them contortionists. Well, I
guess them contortionists they supposed to be acrobats too, but they
seem more extraordinary than them ordinary acrobats. Or like them
that do that yoga. Like my friend Delgadina she do that yoga. She
say that that yoga ain't just exercise, it a whole philosophy. Be saying
there's different types of yoga. Not that yogurt, 'cause that yoga and
that yogurt do got the same sound to them and a lot of the peoples
that does that yoga eats that yogurt. Ain't just the countercultural
neither, like it usedta be. That yoga and that yogurt is mainstream
today. Them yoga postures only makes you look like you's a contortionist, but you ain't a true contortionist.

    Beginning Yoga Postures is one of them books I's got myself. Am
got one of them solar-powered flashlights anyhow. Recharges it on
my dashboard. When I first got me that stun gun I felt like something outta science fiction, with my laser ray gun and shit like in
them science fiction movies, but now it just a ordinary utensil. And a
lot of them popular science fiction they just cowboys and cowgirls
except but set in the future, you know, 'cause I reads that science fiction along with them cowboy and cowgirl novels when I ain't reading romance novels and they be sounding like the same novel, except
but one be set in outa space or in some distant galaxy and the other in
the Wild West. I likes that science fiction with the girl heroes in
them as well as the man heroes. Them science fiction movies is like
comic books. They jokes about them Japanese science fiction movies, but that's 'cause they's colored peoples saving the Universe, and
they just wants to save the Universe theyselves. I mean, the pink
people. They just thinks they's white. And them that ain't white
plays once they gets to America. Peoples that is desperate somewhere
in they own little countries and America is the true dream. They
might be the niggers of they own little countries, like they say, but
they knows that part of the American dream is they ain't have to play
the Niggers in America. Like the man say on television on some talk
show, if they's white they gets to play full white; if they's peoples
with some color in them, they gets to play probationary white. Them
that can't play white in America or refuses to play white is the niggers. There is some whites that plays niggers for commercial or pro-

test purposes or to innovate or renovate white culture, but they is generally the marginal types. And, of course, they is also whites that plays white. 'Cause they don't know what white is.

And some of them stun guns, you can even buy you them leather holsters for them, or them plastic holsters, make it seem like you's in the real Wild West. And in that science fiction they uses them same metaphors as them cowboys. My ray gun, I mean, my stun gun don't have no holster. It one of them streamlined space-age stun guns, which I thinks is more prudent than them real guns. Some of them truckers, they carries them real guns like they thinks they's road warriors, or road cowboys, like in them Australian movies, but me I just buy me one of them stun guns, you know. But they's even women truckers who thinks they's road warriors. I seen one of them on that TV show *Geraldo*. But I remember that Geraldo bemused when one of them African-American mens talk about even the possibility of getting theyselves guns, and ain't bemused when the likes of Charlton Heston talk about the First Amendment rights to bear guns. As if ain't what's good for the goose ain't good for the gander. And all them suburban white women learning target practice. Even showed that on TV. Now if it were colored womens learning that target practice. . . . They be bemused as Geraldo, and be instituting some new legislation to make it against the natural law for the colored woman to bear guns. I mean, if it were a organized thing amongst the colored womens. I'm thinking if that Oprah got her a gun, or some of them mahogany starlets. I still prefers me my stun gun. They oughta outlaw all them guns, though, as a universal law. Course they say that means that only the outlaws got guns. And that means the official outlaws, the government outlaws and all them other legal outlaws as well as the common outlaw outlaws. Them outlaws that do they outlawing under the cover of law is the outlaws I'm talking about. They's the outlaws that oughta be outlawed. They talks about them outlaw nations, but every nation is a outlaw for its own interests. Delgadina say they ain't no such thing as law. That law is them that makes the laws. That law is discretionary, when it ain't arbitrary. But a lot of them treats them guns like they's amusements, though, and even go hunting for them prairie foxes. They has them prairie fox hunts like them Englishmen has they regular fox hunts. I seen a poster for one of them prairie fox hunts. Even seen a poster in Mr.

Delgado's cantina. The true patrons of Mr. Delgado's don't go to that prairie fox hunt, but there's a few agringados that joins in the hunt. And treating it just like it a sport.

First I don't see nothing 'cause they's these big yellow tins and drums and crates of industrial detergents. I don't cram the whole back of the truck with them big yellow tins and drums and crates of industrial detergents 'cause you got to have you space to move around in the back of that truck, plus them border patrols they always insists that they has space to move around. But anyway they's the kind of silence where you know they's something in the back of that truck. If it *is* a coyote or a prairie fox, or even one of them horny toads, what look like them baby dinosaurs, you know, like in them dinosaur movies, spiny, short-tailed lizards, with them horns projecting from they heads and probably they is modern-day dinosaurs like that Komodo dragon but they calls them toads, then it's one of them intelligent and cunning coyotes and prairie foxes or horny toads. I think them horny toads is only native to the Southwest, 'cause I ain't seen none of them horny toads till I was in the Southwest. But all animals is intelligent and cunning when they's hiding. Of course they says a lot of that intelligence and cunning is instinct. Like maybe that psychic ability is just instinct. Can intelligence be a instinct or instinct intelligence?

My favorite animals is them that changes color when they's hiding. And when they's dreaming? Like a lot of them ocean animals. They's got a lot more tricks than land-dwellers, except maybe them chameleons. What another name for them chameleons? They's got them another name. They's supposed to be Old World lizards, them chameleons, the New World lizards, they's supposed to have them another name. Whether you's talking about the Old World or the New World, a lot of them animals got theyselves another name. But them ocean animals, some of them even speaks by changing colors, they says. Them rays, some of them speaks by changing colors, I think, or maybe it's them jellyfish. They's supposed to have theyselves a whole language based on them color changes.

They showed them at Marineland in Florida, them rays and jellyfish, and this marine guide was talking about how that's they way of speaking, they form of communication, 'cause I be wondering why them marine animals keep changing color and think it just for camouflage. 'Cause most of the time they tell you when animals changes color, it's for camouflage, least all of them land animals. Few of them has color displays for mating purposes, but when they changes colors that's for camouflage.

Anyway, we was walking through one of them glassed-in rope-walks underneath the ocean surrounded by all them fishes and looked like some type of marine city. Like we was in some future world that was a marine city. And the marine guide he didn't call them by no ordinary names, called them Rajiformes or something, like they was not no ordinary marine fish, but name sound like some Indians from India. Raji. I call them true Indians to distinguish them from the Native Americans, though that don't mean the Native Americans ain't true people theyselves. Even they names for theyselves means people. Course there's still peoples in the South-west that treats them Zunis and Hopis and Cherokees and Navajos like they ain't true peoples or they comes to the Southwest to photo-graph them and calls them all Charlie Potato. I ain't know the names they calls the womens. But I did see a tourist photographing a Na-vajo man and keep telling him he look like Charlie Potato. I sup-pose, though, that Charlie Potato must be a famous photograph of a Navajo. I heard they ain't usedta let theyselves be photograph. I know Leonora Valdez don't let none of them photograph her. She a Navajo I met when I was in New Mexico when I stopped at one of them adobe McDonald's. She seen me climb out of my truck and took a interest. I believe she were on her way to the University of New Mexico. She a reservation Navajo but her name Valdez. She ain't let none of them photograph her. She don't even let her own peoples photograph her, 'cause they was some peoples from the American Indian College Fund in Denver, Colorado, that wanted her to send them a photograph so's they could use it in they advertise-ments for the American Indian College Fund, and she ain't even sent a photograph for that. She from a reservation in Arizona, and be tell-ing me about that reservation. A lot of the tourists when they'd come to the reservation, 'cause she work in a store on the reservation selling cactus candy, want to photograph her. She says that there's still people—she got another word she uses for white people—the tour-ists, when they travels through the reservation, thinks that they's just supposed to be tepees, not no modern houses. Some of us is poor as

shit, but we ain't in no tepees, she says. Some of us have got tepees,
for cultural purposes, and houses. Some Native American culture,
though, has always been houses, at least for centuries.

My route went through that reservation, so I knows the reservation she talking about. As soon as you arrives in Arizona, you's on the
reservation. You's at the Arizona Welcome Center and then you's on
the reservation. A lot of people travels through the reservation and
ain't even know they's traveling through the reservation. 'Cause a lot
of them don't notice the little road sign that says they is entering the
Navajo Reservation. If you ain't notice that little road sign that says
you's entering the Navajo Reservation, you ain't know you's in the
reservation. I remember I stopped on the reservation at this little gas
station to get gas and this couple from the East comes and asks me
where is the Indian reservation, or maybe they says Navajo, and I
says, Y'all is on the reservation. Is this the reservation? Yes. They's
on the reservation and ain't even know it. 'Cause ain't neither one of
them noticed the sign that says, You are entering the Navajo Reservation. Y'all's on the reservation, I says. And the fools ain't believe me,
of course, they asks the owner of the gas station—who a Navajo but
kinda look like a gringo—Where the reservation? They believes
him when he tells them they's on the reservation, 'cause he a gringo-
looking Navajo. His wife, though, a brown-skinned Navajo. And
don't none of y'all fool tourists be calling her no squaw, 'cause then
y'all learn the true meaning of squaw. If they's one thing I do know
is not to ask the wife of a native person if she is his squaw. Them
eastern tourists, though, they be looking around for tepees. They's
a trading post, but it looks like a regular store. It Navajo-owned.
'Cept it say trading post, that the only way you know it a trading
post and ain't a regular store, and probably the only reason it say
trading post is the tourists, if they's on a reservation, wants to shop
at a trading post rather than a regular store, though it probably were
originally a trading post. There's a tepee village where the tourists
can rent tepees, though, but most likely when you see a tepee on that
reservation, there's a white person staying in it—or that word she
uses for white—rather than a Navajo. Seem like she use the word *pa-
huska*, but I ain't think that a Navajo word. Maybe I heard another
Native American use that word for whites. Every colored peoples in
the world I knows about has they word for whites, and they word

for whites ain't have the same dictionary meaning as the word for whites the whites has for theyselves. Like one of them books I's read says, the whites they renames everybody. 'Cept that book ain't say them whites is renamed they ownselves by the peoples that they renames. Especially when them renamed peoples learns the true meaning of white, least as it applies to they ownselves and they peoples. Changing color, though, is that intelligence or instinct?

Whenever I'm anywhere in South Texas, traveling them roads, I thinks about them ancient cultures, wondering whether them mammoths, supposed to be the ancestor of them elephants, and them bison, supposed to be the ancestor of them buffalo, traveled these same roads. I thinks of them roads when they was still the roads for muskox and elk and brown bear. I remember hearing a poem where someone talked about the road like that, and took them roads back to they beginnings and what and who traveled on them before the modern peoples traveled on them roads. I thinks about this whole land when it were just the lands of the Kiowa, Cheyenne, Arapaho, Comanche, Apache and what Delgadina call the Clovis Culture before them. Sometimes I finds pottery in the desert which I collects and thinks were it made by them Ancients. I daydreams of myself sometimes, riding the prairies on a wild, Spanish mustang. I ain't know the full history of this land, but sometimes I hears pieces of the story. The fabled cities of gold, explorer-mapmakers, the California Gold Rush, Chief Peta Nocona, Comanche, Quaker Indian agents, New Mexico cattle rustlers who would masquerade as native Peoples, native rebels like Quanah. I ain't like to hear the white man's version, 'cause everybody know that. I likes to hear the other people's eclectic stories of the Southwest.

Leonora Valdez, the Navajo I met in New Mexico, asks me whether I wants anything from the McDonald's counter. I says Naw, 'cause I gots me my Coca-Cola. She goes up and gets her one of them salads—which seem like it a special southwestern-style salad—and comes back and sits down at the table. I didn't have the intention of staying in McDonald's that long, but now she's telling me that she seen several men climb in the back of my truck—a Indian—she use the word *Indian*—a black, and some type of clown.

Ah, I knows they's there, I says. I explains that one's a Navajo—seem like she would say Navajo since she a Navajo—the other's from

Oklahoma but is working one of the ranches in New Mexico and the other is a roustabout with a local carnival, 'cept sometimes he plays they clown and don't always take off his clown makeup. I always gives them a ride into Albuquerque, I says.

Ain't that against y'all's union rules? she asks. She wearing moon disk earrings, a silver and turquoise bracelet. Naw, it ain't just silver and turquoise, look like it got all kindsa things in it—silver, turquoise, gold, copper, little bits of iron, marine shells, quartz, coral, mica, I think it called mica. I heard of something called galena, maybe it got galena in it. It ain't that big a bracelet, but look like whoever made it try to put every metal and what you makes art with in that bracelet. You could probably go over the whole list of metals and what you makes art with and find it in that bracelet. She kinda remind me of a woman I seen in a book called *Mystic Women of the Southwest.* 'Cept it were paintings of women, not photographs, so I ain't know if she the model for any of them paintings. And kinda remind me of women I seen in paintings by a woman that Delgadina calls a "southwestern fantasy landscape artist." She say they is painters that ain't paint real landscapes, but paints fantasy landscapes.

Am got a union, but . . . Well, I'm a independent, I explains. Then I explains that them mens usedta ride into Albuquerque with someone else that works on one of the ranches. They usedta ride in the back of his truck sharing hooch, one of them open-air trucks. I usedta see them myself when I was coming into Albuquerque, this long-haired Navajo, the black cowboy, and the roustabout who were sometimes made up to look like a clown. They was always sharing hooch, and to tell y'all the truth, it all looked pretty low class; then once when I was at that same McDonald's I heard the man tell them that he couldn't drive them into Albuquerque and they was asking around for somebody to drive them into Albuquerque. Ain't nobody want to drive no long-haired Navajo, black Oklahoma man, and white clown into Albuquerque. I told them I'd drive them into Albuquerque, but I didn't want them to be sharing no hooch and spilling no hooch in the back of my truck. I usedta tell them I usedta see them in that open-air truck and how low class they all looked and told them how they ought to acquire a little race pride, and then I told them that they can ride in the back of my truck—I don't let nobody ride in the cab of my truck but me—that they could ride in the back of my truck as long as they didn't share no hooch back there, even if mine ain't no open-air truck I ain't want them to be sharing and spilling no hooch back there, and they's got to wait till they gets into Albuquerque to share they hooch, if they's got to share that cheap hooch. I likes Budweiser myself. They says, Yes ma'am, so I lets them ride in the back of my truck. And they don't behave as low class as they usedta behave when they didn't have no discipline. I mean they is disciplined men and ranch workers, except for the clown, who's a roustabout, that sometimes assumes the role of a clown, but ain't nobody look disciplined when they's riding in the back of a open-air truck and sharing hooch. To tell you the truth I didn't want to include the white clown in the back of my truck, but the Navajo and the Oklahoma black man vouched for him.

Hooch? asks the woman.

You know, liquor, from one of them brown paper sacks, you know, cheap wine or whiskey, you know.

I thought that's what you meant, 'cause you kept saying spilling hooch, said Leonora. Then I didn't know if you meant they was sharing a woman. I thought you were using that as some type of metaphor.

Naw, that's hoochie. I don't think that even they is low class enough to be sharing no hoochie in the back of a open-air truck. And they knows who I is and shows that they is got to be disciplined mens in my presence. Plus, they's all got wives in Albuquerque and I knows all they wives by name. So they knows they can't be sharing no hoochies in my presence. Men has got they own places that they can go to share a hoochie, but it ain't in the back of my truck. Men has they own places or creates they own places to do shit like that, but this truck is mine. And as for me myself I just drives them into Albuquerque. And them that thinks that I'm a hoochified woman has another think. I likes my romantic freedom, like the books say, but that don't mean I is hoochified, and I don't even take the same romantic freedom as the womens in the books I reads. 'Cause there is some hoochified women in some of them books, even them that don't believe theyselves to be hoochified. Well, some of them books you reads, these modern novels, they is perfect models for hoochification. But they is modern women and reclassifies hoochification as romantic freedom. I'm romantically free, but it ain't no hoochified

romantic freedom, and I believes in the old-fashioned kind of romance myself. Which don't mean I'm naive. Some womens gets
grown, or think they is, and they forgets Whose child they is. The
mens they helps me to unload my truck when I gets into Albuquerque. Them industrial detergents that is meant for the warehouse in
Albuquerque. Then I travels through Laredo, Brownsville, Galveston, Texas City, you know, I gots customers all along the Texas border. I travels through the whole Southwest, though. I ain't know
what it is I likes about the Southwest. Maybe 'cause I grew up on
them cowboy and . . . I mean cowboy movies.

You can say it cowboy and Indian, she says, taking a forkful of
salad.

I starts to tell her I was always cheering for them Indians myself,
but then she be thinking I'm just trying to brown-nose her, 'cause
she a Navajo. So I just drinks my Coke and don't say that. The cowboys was always the heroes, though, and you always got to know the
cowboys as individual people and the Indians was just Indians. If
they was individual Indians, they was always played by white
people. I think even Elvis played a Indian. Or they'd be white
women playing Indian women and they'd always be in the Pocahontas mode. I only seen one movie that weren't the Pocahontas mode,
a television movie about Crazy Horse, where the Native American
woman loving a Native American man. I know some of y'all knows
what I means when I says not in the Pocahontas mode, but a lot of
y'all I gots to explain.

Then I notices some whites come in McDonald's and look toward me and Leonora, like they is asking theyselves whether we is
wild or tame. Maybe I'm just thinking that, though, 'cause I'm
thinking about them cowboy and native peoples movies. The
whites they goes up to the McDonald's counter and orders something, then they sit in one of the booths. Then the clown peeks in
McDonald's and looks at Leonora like he thinks she's "wild and
gorgeous" like she Pocahontas 'cause I usually ain't stay in McDonald's that long, so I waves at him, then I tells Leonora that I gots to
drive these men into Albuquerque. She sits eating her salad and I
drinks my Coke and then gets up. Leonora wearing blue jeans and
one of them cinnamon-color blouses, the same cinnamon color them
Buddhist nuns wears, and she got Navajo ornaments on and that big

turquoise bracelet. She got a scarf around her hair with geometric-type designs and she got long, clean, black, straight and braided hair. I pictures her riding on a horse through the Arizona desert.

Please to meet you, she say.

Same here, Leonora. I starts to put a tip on the table, but then remembers this McDonald's and you ain't supposed to tip no McDonald's. I'm used to them truckstops where I always puts a tip on the table. You got you a way into Albuquerque? I asks.

Yes ma'am, she say, and stay there eating her salad.

You ain't hitchhiking, is you? I asks, still standing at the booth.

No ma'am.

I seen some of y'all college types out there hitchhiking, and I wants to make sure you ain't no fool.

She kinda smile. No ma'am, I ain't hitchhiking. I got me that jeep out there.

Ah, yeah. That's a nice-looking jeep. That your jeep?

Yes ma'am. She wipe the side of her mouth with her napkin. She sit up straighter.

Seem like I might have even seen that jeep when I was in Arizona, 'cause I remembers seeing a jeep like that and thinking it a nice-looking jeep, Arizona license plates, then I was noticing the jeep as I was coming in McDonald's and was thinking if I wasn't driving no truck I'd like a jeep like that jeep. That looks like a genuine Army jeep.

I got it at the Army surplus store, she say. She say she got it real cheap, otherwise she couldn't afford a jeep like that and would be having to hitchhike. Naw, girl, don't play that kinda fool. You is too gorgeous. Promise me you ain't going to play that type of fool. You got enough gas to get you to Albuquerque?

Yes ma'am. She straighten one of her braids and the geometric scarf. Then she take another nibble of salad. People that is new to the Southwest don't know 'bout the vastness of the land. I don't give her no lecture on the vastness of the land and all the undeveloped land between here and Albuquerque and sometimes they ain't another gas station for hundreds of miles or what seem like hundreds of miles. But she from Arizona and she know the landscape, so I don't lecture her on the landscape. I don't pick up hitchhikers, and the only reason I lets them undisciplined disciplined mens ride in the back of my truck is because I knows who they is.

As I'm going out the door, someone hands me a flyer that says, UNA UNIÓN FUERTE INCLUYE A TODOS. I folds up the flyer and puts it in my shirt pocket. The man that gives me them union flyers knows that I'm not recruitable, but he gives me them union flyers anyway. The mens is standing around the back of my truck, 'cause it hot in New Mexico, and the air-conditioning only starts when the truck starts and air-conditions the whole truck. They spots me and climbs in the back of the truck. One of them opens the skylight and I latches the truck. Then I unlatches the truck again and reaches in and one of them hands me they hooch, which I carries for them in my glove compartment till they gets into Albuquerque and helps me unload at the warehouse, then I drives them to the center of town and hands them they hooch. When they wives is waiting for them at the warehouse, I keeps the hooch. When they's on they own in town, I gives them they hooch. 'Cept sometimes I forgets to put the hooch in my glove compartment. When I forgets the hooch, some-times they drinks the hooch before us gets to Albuquerque; other times they keeps the hooch till we gets to Albuquerque.

Anyway, I takes the hooch, then climbs in the cab, puts the hooch in my glove compartment, and heads toward Albuquerque. I knows the black cowboy started to ask me if he could ride in the cab, but he knows I'm like that squaw when you calls her a squaw. I don't let nobody ride in the cab of my truck but me.

One of them rap on the cab. Who the gorgeous gal?

Your wife, I say, and keeps driving.

Why they be changing colors like that? I be asking, standing up close to the glass of that glassed-in ropewalk and be wondering what kind of glass that is, able to hold back the ocean. I'm talking about Marineland. Got to be a mighty powerful glass to hold back the ocean like that. I poke my nose up against that glass and be looking at them marine animals and some of them marine animals be looking back at me like they ain't never seen a African nose. I know it's my African nose they's looking at. I should call it my West African nose, 'cause them East Africans, most of them, they ain't got noses like that. Them Caucasians likes to claim the refined features for theyselves, and I know in them early literature they is them that claims the Ethiopians as Caucasians on account of them refined features. And even likes to refer to it as refined; otherwise broad features would be considered the good features to have, or the features of universal man and woman. I ain't think about a lot of that stuff my-self, though, till Delgadina start taking them courses in Cultural An-thropology and even got a course called the Politics of Race. She the one showed me that book that claimed the Ethiopians as Caucasians because of they refined features and they literary history. Because they is amongst the Africans to have a literary tradition. While she were taking that course, she would talk the politics of race, and how in some cultures people negotiates they identity. I have had people to even ask me if I'm African. Ain't mean I don't know who I am, though. You don't have to take courses to know who you are. Or who you is, neither.

Then one of them Rajiformes it swim up close to the glass and seem like it be wondering what kinda substance that is that hold back the ocean too.

That's their way of communicating with each other, say the ma-rine guide.

What they be saying? I asks, stepping away from the glass.

He be looking at me like I'm some ignorant and crazy woman, the marine guide not that Rajiform. He a slim young man with thick brown hair and got the physique of a swimmer and he nose even look aquatic. I guess that's how come they uses noses to stereotype people. They always uses the distinctive features of a people to stereotype them. And that makes it so you think that they's the norm. And then you have people that don't want to be who they naturally is, 'cause they's been stereotyped. The ruling peoples makes the norm into who they is and how they does things. Anything that diverges from the way they does things ain't the norm. Biko talked about that in that movie we seen, that movie about Steve Biko, the South African freedom fighter. Delgadina say he reminded her of el Ché, 'cept she say his real name Ernesto, Ernesto Ché Guevara. She say that her fa-vorite name, that Ernesto. 'Cause it mean earnest. But it also got a nest in it. What else she say about that Ernesto? Something about the CIA and the Bolivian government conspiring together. That's what I mean about them legalized outlaws. Every country got they legal-

ized outlaws, and ain't just the CIA and government outlaws. He
wearing blue jeans and one of them sweatshirts with a dolphin on it,
I mean the marine guide. I don't know what they be saying, er, I
don't know what they're saying.

Well, how come you knows they's communicating, and ain't just
camouflaging theyselves?

Delgadina were with me at Marineland, 'cause she the one convinced me to come to Marineland to learn about them marine animals, but she were just observing them marine animals, and reading
them brochures and the Marineland literature and weren't asking no
questions. She probably knew all them answers to them questions
about them marine animals that I were asking, 'cause she is always
taking courses. I seen the way the marine guide looked at her,
though, like he thought she were one of them hoochie women, you
know, the stereotypes they has of them women they considers exotic
looking. Like them Asian women, even them Asian-American
women. They's people just see a woman who to them is a exotic and
think she a hoochie, even them that looks high class. They be looking at her and thinking about "that sex thing." Ain't nobody think
I'm exotic looking. They might think I'm a nut. But not even no exotic nut.

He smooth back his thick brown hair and kinda hunch his shoulders, the Marineland guide. We have scientists who study them and
have certain generalizations about what their chromatics mean, I
mean, what their color changes mean, however only generalizations—that is, the general subject matter, but not the specific vocabulary. Professor Hauberk Honeyeater, the renowned oceanographer
and psychologist of color, has written a book on the subject, but it's
not for a popular audience . . . And then he show me Professor Hauberk Honeyeater's picture 'cause it on the brochure 'cause he one of
the Marineland advisers. He don't look like no honeyeater, though,
he plump and long-necked and look more like one of them bustard
birds.

Say what?

For example, what you see now is probably some sort of mating
ritual, he saying. When he mention that mating ritual them other marine tourists, they be sticking they noses up against that glass. Ain't I
said that sometimes them color changes is a mating ritual?

So you mean they be courting, they generally be talking 'bout love? I asks.

Yes, but we don't know the specific vocabulary. What color changes correspond to a specific vocabulary, a specific amorous word, that is.

Say if that turquoise mean yes? I read somewhere they's certain women when they's in a yes mood they puts on certain colors. Seems like I read that somewhere, or men thinks that certain colors means a yes mood. Seem like if there ain't a article like that, there oughta be one, in one of them *Cosmopolitan*-type magazines.

Yes, but not just these primary colors, the light and the colorant primaries, er, but. . . . He got them blue-green eyes the same color as the ocean. He look at Delgadina again like you would look at somebody you think is a hoochie woman, and then continue to lead us through the marine tour and introduce us to some more of them marine animals. Then when we's emerging from the glassed-in ropewalk, somebody hand Delgadina some literature on worker ownership of Marineland, 'cause I guess she must look like somebody that work there.

Changing colors, though, for them, then that gotta be both, seem like that gotta be both intelligence and instinct.

I flashes the flashlight again, and gets the stun gun ready—it ain't the kinda stun gun where you can set and reset the power on it like in the movies or on television, or like that *Star Trek*—and then I turns like I'm going out, and then I turns back, and then I sees the guaraches first, what I think they calls guaraches, them straw-type sandals, you know, ain't them traditional woven leather, and then I shines the flashlight on them guaraches. I think them sandals made of that straw. And they got some other fiber they make them sandals out of. That raffia. My African sandals made out of that raffia, supposed to come from one of them African palm trees with them large leaves, but I guess that a kind of straw. I got them from one of them little import shops when I was in Canada once. I don't wear them, though. I keeps them as art. Probably in that Old World Africa they call it raffia, but in New World America it's straw. And then they got that wicker that they makes chairs and furniture out of—is it raffia in the Old World and wicker in the New?—probably they can make them wicker guaraches, but I don't know whether them guaraches made out of straw or wicker or raffia.

I know you ain't no coyote, I says. Coyotes and foxes don't wear no guaraches.

'Cept maybe them human coyotes. And they's plenty of them human coyotes and coyote humans too. And I ain't talking about just them tricksters neither. They's biggish feet and biggish toes, but you can still tell they's women's feet. Slender ankles though. And them guaraches looks like they's full of bird guano or bat guano. My friend Delgadina she tells me about that guano, 'cause me I just calls it bird shit and bat shit myself. 'Cept when I first heard that word *guano*, I thought it was some kinda caviar. She say you can buy you that guano to use as fertilizer. And she the one told me 'bout them human coyotes too, Delgadina. Trickster stories she call them and nayatls or some shit, 'cause she say they's humans that can really change theyselves into coyotes and coyotes that can change theyselves into humans too. And that ain't just no imaginary tale either, it ain't just folklore, she say, 'cause they's them that say the nayatl is real and she even sculpted one of them looking part coyote and part human. All over Mexico people tell you them tales of them nayatl and probably be pointing out people and tell you they a nayatl. She even pointed one of them out to me, say in Mexico people say he a nayatl, and supposed to be able to turn into everything from a jaguar to a spider crab, but just look like a ordinary man to me.

He come into the cantina where she work and she say, You remember when I was telling you about them.

Yeah, I says, sipping on my Budweiser.

That one of them, she say. I ain't want to turn around and look at no nayatl, 'cause I ain't know what kindsa powers they has. And I ain't want no nayatl to catch me spying on him, so I ain't turn around to look immediately, but when she go over there to serve him, I kinda glance over there. He just look like a ordinary Mexican to me. But I guess that the power of them nayatls. They just is supposed to look like ordinary peoples.

They call it folklore, say Delgadina. She ain't talk nayatl while he in the cantina. But then some woman came in and the nayatl and the woman went upstairs to the little hotel above the cantina. But what's folklore but people's knowledge, people's learning? said Delgadina. She says the people the types of people that believes in them nayatl, they ain't always politically correct, but they's got true knowledge. They's got they own truths and knowledge. And sometimes they even starts rumors about people to say they a nayatl when they ain't. But she say she know for true that that's a true nayatl, though she ain't never explained to me how she know he a true nayatl; she ain't never explained to me that. But they's villages in Mexico where they starts rumors about people being nayatl, like they usedta start rumors about people being communists when they wasn't, like them Hollywood people.

Maybe the people that is real nayatl they don't even have no rumors about, I says.

She have sculptured a nayatl that she have in her apartment. She ain't no artist, though, Delgadina, and say that just a hobby. Or maybe she the kind of artist I heard somebody call a half-artist. But then maybe everybody got some degree of artist in them. Maybe some be one eighth of a artist or some shit or one sixteenth of a artist like with them musical notations. But then if you gotta be a artist, maybe it better to be a whole artist. Look like a whole artist make them guaraches, though they don't call people that makes guaraches artists. The more pure the art, I guess, the more they refers to it as art. 'Cause them guaraches looks like handmade guaraches, they don't look like no store-bought guaraches, no machine-made guaraches. Them smugglers, they call them coyotes too, don't they? Wonder if some of them smugglers consider theyselves to be true artists?

Don't look like no coyote feet, I says out loud, signifying, you know. You better come on outta there, gal, whoever you are. Them's guaraches, ain't they? Gal, this ain't no game of hide and seek. Though it might be a game of "hide" if you don't come outta there.

The guaraches they disappears behind the detergent tin and me I heads back there with my stun gun ready, 'cause ain't just mens that's dangerous, like the poet Guillen say, they's knife-toting womens too. And womens got as much coyote in them as mens, though from the point of view of the mens they got more. And from the point of view of the womens, the mens got more, 'cause that's just human nature, or how people maintains they sense of who they are, though everybody always likes to think that they's superior to human nature—coyote and chameleon and maybe even them prairie fox and that horny toad too. You know, how when the mens sings they blues songs they's always singing about how the women's done them wrong and when the womens sings they blues songs they's always singing about how the men's done them wrong. Don't know if there's a blues people talking about how they done each other wrong or how they done each other right. Or maybe that's just love. Though the best thing for the mens and the womens to do is what that other song say—If you don't want somebody peaches don't shake they tree. And that's for the mens and the womens too.

Gal, whoever you are, stop acting like a fool, and come on out from back there. Girl. Rascal. I know you ain't no prairie fox. And you shore ain't no chameleon.

I'm wearing them camouflage britches, you know, and one of them golf shirts, you know, them sporting shirts with the alligator on the pocket, except mine ain't got no alligator on it or crocodile neither, one of them bargain basement golf shirt. Got a kangaroo on that golf shirt, though I don't know if it were made in Australia. They call 'em golf shirt, but I don't play no golf. Delgadina, she like to wear them golf gloves, you know them gloves that got the fingers free, but she don't play no golf neither. And I ain't no chameleon neither. I beat on the top of one of them drums of detergent to scare her out of her hiding place. But it ain't like scaring chickens. She don't scare. One of them cunning womens. I shines the flashlight all along the back of the truck. Light don't bend around the corner but I does. I jumps around the corner. Then I shines the flashlight in her face, but she don't look dangerous. So I don't use my stun gun. In fact, she look right meek. It ain't the meekness of fear, though, but the meekness of someone that don't want you to think they some strange bad woman.

Course they's plenty of women don't care whether you thinks they's some strange bad woman—I guess not when you got no stun gun though. I usedta think I was that kinda woman, the kind that don't care whether they think you some strange bad woman. But not when they got no stun gun though. And stun gun don't have to be real. Stun gun can be a metaphor. Like Delgadina always talking 'bout them metaphor. I be thinking she mean a real hermit crab, for example, and she be talking about a metaphoric one. She be describing the real hermit crab, soft-bellied crabs that carries around they armor, or rather them hermit crab they carries around the armor of another crustacean, like them snail or them mollusk, 'cause them hermit crab they don't produce they own shell, not even like them spider crabs; they uses the shells of other creatures. That Delgadina she have got a obsession with knowledge. I guess so many peoples looks at her like she a hoochie woman she want to prove to them that she ain't. Or maybe it ain't to them she want to prove that she ain't, but to herself.

Anyway, she a twentyish woman with longish black hair—this meek-looking woman, not Delgadina—only thing bodacious-looking about her is that hair; coarse, long, rippling hair that she pushes out of her eyes, and she got big black eyes, them wide-spaced black eyes, intelligent-looking eyes, though, they ain't them dufous-looking eyes you always see in the movies and on television on womens like that, even them that supposed to be high-class and got them chaperones and shit, got them dufous-looking eyes, but her she got them intelligent eyes that she scrinch up in the flashlight and then I shines the light on that belly. And they ain't no wild animal eyes neither. I once heard eyes like that described as wild animal eyes. Overheard this man talking about this Italian woman—Italian, that pretty close to Mexican. I think the woman she from Italy in this movie, southern Italy, where the people almost looks Moroccan, 'cept the movie set in Germany though, and then this man he describe her wild animal eyes. Didn't look like no wild animal eyes to me, look like human woman eyes. One of them intellectual-type movies that Delgadina likes, 'cause Delgadina she say it be based on a German novel; me I always likes them action movies. But Delgadina she like them intellectual movies and even them noncombatant movies. The major American actors, though, they's them action heroes. But like I say, didn't look like no wild animal eyes to me, look like human woman eyes. Though they's some would say that wild animal eyes can be clever and cunning too.

But what I got me back there ain't no wily coyote or no prairie fox neither. What I got me back there is a pregnant Mexican woman. Though she look more like a girl than a woman. And twentyish to me is a girl. Her toes is bruised traveling in them guaraches, or them huaraches—is they guaraches or huaraches?—and her clothes and face and hair is streaked with sweat and dirty. She still squinting, so I turns the light back on that belly. That belly pretty big. She wearing them ragged baggy blue jeans—not them ragged baggy stylish designer rags them college girls wear looking like beggar's holiday, the kind that shows they knees and even they ass, they buttocks, I mean—and one of them horse-blanket ponchos, but you can still tell that belly big. All them girls in them colleges they wants to look like the working class, and I'm talking about them elite-type colleges, I ain't talking about just them working-class colleges. She look as much Indian as Mexican though and maybe even a little bit Chinese, but them Mexicans they's supposed to be the cosmic race. Like them Brazilians, they could call theyselves the cosmic race. Like all that talk about multiracialism. We's just a cosmic race. 'Cept nobody wants to identify with the African in the cosmos. That's how I read that multiracialism myself. Delgadina say them whites that's all for multiracialism just want to use the multirace as a buffer, you know. 'Cause somebody told them that in the next millennium the white people be the minority, so they wants as many people as they can to identify with them, rather than the other colored peoples. So now they's modifying they racial purity myth, 'cause it's in they best interest, so's they can coopt the multiracialists to play white. I ain't thought all that till after Delgadina start talking about it. Then she say she don't know whether they model be South Africa or Brazil. 'Cept that Brazil ain't no racial paradise; they just let more people play white than in America. I ain't think Delgadina be talking like that, but she does. I be asking Delgadina what she is and she say, I'm neither black nor white. Ain't that the same thing them multiracialists wants to say about theyselves. Course there's many multiracialists that's got Asian and Native American and every other race in them. America ain't just black and white. But there's still them that wants to portray America as just black and white. First they wanted to portray it as just white, then they wants to portray it as just black and white.

And you can almost see that baby kicking, like it want outta it hiding place. I know a few things about birthing babies, but I don't want her to birth no baby in the back of my truck. They always shows you them Mexican immigrants on television, mostly men though, scrambling up over that wall. I tries to picture her, pregnant, and scrambling over that wall they done built along the border. I don't know how she get in my truck, 'cause they's be bragging about putting up more and more patrols along the border and where they ain't got more patrols they's building more walls. Talking about that Berlin Wall and shit. Everybody supposed to be a Berliner on ac- count of that wall. Then everybody be celebrating when they tore down that Berlin Wall. *Ich bin ein Berliner.* Everybody be wanting a piece of that Berlin Wall. Don't know if they got a name for that wall on they own border. Be good if them Mexicans would build up that Mexico and then use that wall to keep the Americans out. Or the Norteamericanos. 'Cause we's all Americans. We's the Ameri- cas, so we's all Americans. Or we could call usselves Turtle Island- ers, like them Native American name.

I ain't from the Southwest originally. I ain't from one of them bor- der towns. I'm from Kentucky originally. Covington, Kentucky. So I guess you could say I'm from a border town—border between Ohio and Kentucky. 'Cause during the Civil War, they usedta call Kentucky a buffer state, talking about buffer, 'cause it a buffer be- tween the North and the South. Anyway, I was on my way to South- ern California like a lot of fools and I just settles in Texas City, Texas, and decides to go to one of them truck driving schools. I needed me a new air filter for my automobile and pulled into this gas station and seen me one of these truck driving school brochures. I seen them advertisements on television, but they ain't never enticed me, then I starts reading that brochure. I guess that's what they mean when they talks about direct advertising, them brochures. I even know a faith healer that uses one of them brochures. 'Cept she say she ain't no faith healer, it's just that other folks refers to her as a faith healer, 'cause that's the way that they can comprehend her healing powers. But even she know the power of direct advertising. When the mechanic was putting on the new air filter, though, I read the whole brochure and even called they 800 number. I don't think that faith healer got herself a 800 number though. The voice on the tape say that that school is a licensed school and they got them dual- control trucks. Y'all know, that mean that either the teacher or the student can control the truck. And then it tell you about experienc- ing the freedom of being your own boss and shit. Then they tell you if you's interested in the school to call a 900 number. Now that's just to get people's money. The 800 call is free, and then they tells you to call a 900 number, and then when you calls that 900 number they tries to keep you on the phone as long as they can so's they can get your money. It ain't really a scam, though, 'cause they say there's a lot of fools that only thinks they wants to be truck drivers, and they say that 900 number helps to pay for all the calls they gets from fools. So, anyway, I says the only word of Spanish I knows, *Buenas Buenas*. I mean, to the woman in them guaraches.

And she whisper what must be the only word of English she know, Sanctuary.

Say what, girl?

Sanctuary.

Or maybe she say it in Spanish, but it one of them words that sounds like English, so I know what she saying. Then I say something about her getting all that guano in the back of my truck. She must be think I'm talking Spanish. 'Cause guano do sound kinda like Spanish, and maybe it is derived from a Spanish word, 'cause a lot of them English words ain't English words. What the dictionary call etymology or some shit. Especially them Spanish words and English words that come from Latin is like speaking the same language. And then you's got a lot of English words that's Spanish, and ain't just taco neither. English language especially that American language that supposed to be a cosmic language, 'cause they's every other language in the etymology of America. Of course they's them that wants to make American a purified language, like them French purists, 'cause them French is supposed to be the most purified purists about they language, even them African writers who writes in French have commented about the purified purity of the French language, and thinks that them African writers that writes in English have got more freedom, and they's talking about the Englishman's English, but true American is every language. But I'm looking at them guaraches, and I'm thinking 'bout the first time I seen me a real Mexican. One of them dark-skinned Mexicans, not them televised Mexicans or even them Mexican movie stars, though I seen me some true Mexicans on a soap opera once, and hair as kinky as mine. And then I'm thinking 'bout the first time I seen me a real Hawaiian. And the first time I seen me a real Egyptian. And ain't at all like the American movies. That's 'cause they didn't want you to know that so many people in the world was colored, and even have the white people thinking that all the world look like theyselves. Like when me and Delgadina was in this bookstore and I started reading this book that had something to do with Negroes, 'cause at the time it were written we was called Negroes, and it was supposed to contain either a hundred or a thousand facts about the Negro, so one of the tales the man tells is about this white woman in the 1920s or 1930s who goes to vacation in Hawaii. So when she comes back to America, the people asks her, How'd you like Hawaii? and she answers that she like Hawaii well enough, 'cept them Hawaiians looks like niggers to me. I told my uncle Buddy about that story and he give a name to the man; I mean a name to the man that wrote that book. Me I was just reading the book, but didn't think to put a name to the man that wrote the book.

And then she say something else in Spanish, it kinda fast-talking Spanish, but ain't as fast as that Puerto Rican Spanish I heard once in New York City, though I thinks I hears, *Buenas Buenas* mixed in with her *muchachas*—yeah, I know me that word too. You hear you plenty of *muchachas* in Texas City. And *loco* and *loca*, I know me them, 'cause Delgadina she always calling plenty of people *loco* and *loca*. Fools in love soon grow wise, *loca*, I hear her telling one of them girls, quoting that song, you know. And then she be telling her to take love easy, quoting another one of them songs. You be thinking all them books she read, she be quoting more of them books, but I guess fools in love understand them songs more easily than books on romance. If some fool in love I don't think you quote Henry James to 'em. But they might understand some Dinah Washington song or Billie Holiday. Though this girl she don't look like no crazy woman. Maybe she been crazy in love like a lotta young womens.

I think maybe she one of them girls from the country towns, one of them Mexican country towns or one of them little Mexican villages. I starts to call them one of them sleepy villages, but I don't know whether them Mexican villages is sleepy or not, though in the movies they's always sleepy villages; every time the hero or the villain come into one of them Mexican villages it siesta time—siesta, I know me that word too, but I guess it as much English as Spanish; they have them they siesta, so they call them sleepy. Still there's businessmen and consultants that says that the Americans theyselves can learn from the siesta, that if some of them would take a little siesta every now and then it would increase they productiveness. 'Cause in the American mythology you ain't supposed to take you no siesta. But she look like she from one of them little villages and not one of them border towns or them storefront cantina girls, 'cause it ain't sound like that border town Spanish, it ain't no Tijuana Spanish, and it ain't Spanglish, which they tells me is a combination of Spanish and English. That Spanglish you can almost understand. It ain't called Spanglish though, they got they own Chicano word for it. Like some of them factory girls from across the border. *Comprendo.* I understand me that word too. And *bicho,* I heard me that *bicho* in New York City. I think that Spanish for bitch. I guess they's as many *bichos* in New York as they's *muchachas* in Texas City. Delgadina she be telling me not to call no Puerto Rican *bicho,* 'cause I guess that mean the same thing as bitch. And though them border town women they got intelligent eyes it that bold-eyed intelligence. Them kinds of freedom-loving women what ain't meek-eyed 'cause they ain't used to taking orders. Some of them womens looks like they used to giving orders, though they says the true freedom ain't to give orders nor to take them. 'Cause a lot of people thinks that freedom is they's supposed to start giving orders. That's why I likes the kinda job I got, 'cause I don't work for no company, I'm a independent contractor and ain't got to give orders nor to take them.

I says *Buenas Buenas* again and then I mentions all that guano on them sandals, them guaraches I mean. But maybe guaraches and sandals is the same thing, just got different names.

I returns to the cab and pulls up into the truckstop parking lot, then climbs in back again.

She start to rise up but I motions for her to stay behind the detergent drum, and her stomach's growling in its own language. Naw, ain't no coyote or prairie fox or horny toad that make that noise, them's honger pains. I just got beef jerky, so I gives her that. I goes to the cab of my truck and gets the jerky and my thermos and comes back. I sometimes keeps jerky in the back of my truck, but sometimes them mens when they helps unloads my truck, they think that jerky is to be unloaded or is a favor, so now I keeps the jerky I wants to keep in the cab of my truck. She got them strong-looking teeth that can eat that beef jerky. Look like some of them Africans' teeth I seen, them that chews them chewing sticks and chewing sponges, ain't them that uses toothbrush and dentifrice. I be wondering whether them Mexicans got they equivalent to the chewing stick. And I pours her some hot chocolate from my thermos. It beefy-flavored hot chocolate, though, 'cause I mostly keeps beef bouillon in that thermos. And I got me some of that trail mix, you know the kind you get from them mail order health food stores, but she shake her head at that trail mix, like she think it cattle feed. I keeps that trail mix in the back of my truck, 'cause ain't nobody want that trail mix. I starts to say, Good, sounding like that Sheriff Andy, or Andy Griffith hisself, but don't that *buenas* mean good?

Buenas. Buenas.

She gulp that hot chocolate down first, gulp down my whole ther-mosful like it stored energy and then she sucking on that beef jerky like it sugarcane candy. I know me sugarcane candy. And I got me one of them bottle water. She gulp that down. Got to water that baby too, and then gotta pee for them both. I peeks out of the truck to make sure I ain't see none of them patrols; I see a green and white Land-Rover and think it a patrol, but it just a Land-Rover; then I goes around to the back of the truckstop with her. I tries to think of them names. If I were a professional smuggler, I'd be called a coyote, and she'd be a pollo. Yeah, I remembers that from a Cheech movie I seen. 'Cept in that Cheech movie, they just put all these pollos in the back of a truck to bring them across the border. But you can't just put pollos like that in the back of a truck, 'cause of these border patrols. I guess they had false employment papers for them, 'cause that coyote made them peoples pay lots of money to smuggle them across the border. Maybe she paid a coyote to smuggle her across the border, then when she gets across the border she spot my truck and climb in. Delgadina know which Cheech movie I mean, 'cause she got every Cheech movie, even Cheech movies ain't nobody heard of, except maybe Cheech hisself. And them that made the movie. After I seen that movie, though, I was calling everybody that wasn't a Mexican a OTM—Other Than Mexican. You know how them whites likes to define peoples based on theyselves. If you ain't white then you's a nonwhite. Well, I be defining people based on that Cheech movie. And that's even before I met Delgadina. Them what he call them border classifications, though. Mexican and Other Than Mexican,

like them that he were referring to as "Chinese Indians." Y'all remember that scene where Cheech disguised hisself as cactus, trying
to get back across the border into the USA. He got stranded in Mexico without his citizenship papers, so he couldn't prove he was a
American, so he had to try to get back across the border like them
pollos. So in one of them scenes, he disguise hisself as cactus, then
them patrols disguises theyself as brush. He think he hiding in this
brush and it turn out to be one of them patrol's vans. He climbing
into one of them patrol's vans and think it brush. He trying to return
from Mexico, you know, to East L.A. I even got me a sweatshirt say
EAST L.A., and I ain't even ever been to East L.A. *Hola vato.* And I
knows how to order cerveza from that movie.

They's got a rear door to the truckstop restaurant where you can
enter just to go to the restrooms. I waits for her and then we comes
back, and I peeks to make sure they ain't none of them patrols. I see
something that looks like a patrol, but it ain't a patrol. It one of them
Land-Rovers. Then I motions for her to come and get back in the
truck. I helps her up in the truck and be thinking how she get in the
truck the first time. I knows somebody musta helped her up in that
truck. I don't keep my truck all latched up like some of them trucks.
I means it's got a latch on it, but the latch itself kinda easy to open.
Delgadina asks me why I don't latch my truck better, 'cause of all
them thieves along that route. She saw something on television about
them thieves along them truck routes. Or people that might want to
sneak rides in my truck. I tells her that I latches it as much as it needs
to be latched. Like I told you, there's a Navajo and a Oklahoma African and a roustabout that I usedta sometimes let ride in the back of
my truck, coming back to Albuquerque from they farm work, when
I was on that route. I don't think none of them thieves wants industrial detergents, though, I tells Delgadina, but she still be asking me
all them questions about the latch on my truck. I tells her seem like
them border patrols is always having me latch and unlatch my truck,
so that another reason I ain't keep it latched up the way some of them
trucks is latched up. I tells her I'm watching more for them border
patrols than them they says is thieves. What about sneaking rides?
she ask. Don't people sneak rides? I tells her I gives rides to several
of the peoples, 'cause I'm independent and don't got to go by the
union rules. 'Cept I ain't let nobody ride up in my cab with me,

they's got to ride in the back of my truck. I tells her about the Navajo and the Oklahoma African and the roustabout, and she be saying shouldn't oughta be giving them rides. I tells her that that were
just when I were on the New Mexico route. 'Cause they's too many
border patrol in South Texas, and they be thinking I'm smuggling
peoples. Then the union got they rules. And she even come out and
look at the latch on my truck. I be thinking whether she gots to do a
lot of peeing, 'cause I ain't know when the border patrol be wanting
me to latch and unlatch my truck. Least they says them pregnant
womens gots to pee for theyself and the baby too. I ain't never been
pregnant myself, but sometimes when you looks at them babies you
see wisdom itself.

She looking surprised, though, when I shines the flashlight on my
own face. You woman, her expression be saying. 'Cause she wasn't
expecting no woman to be driving that truck. And maybe no
African-American woman neither. I'm one of them deep-voiced
womens, but it still surprise me that she surprised I'm a woman. Or
maybe she have that image of Andy Griffith herself, 'cause I know
they probably show them reruns down there in Mexico. *Bueno*. And
him be sounding like Sancho Panza, 'cept he really a countrified
Quijote, and the deputy is Panza. But maybe she more surprised that
I'm African American. Or maybe she might even think I'm African,
'cause they's a lot of Africans in America, I mean true Africans. And
I've had people to mistake me for African. When I was in Canada,
though, not the U.S., I been mistaken for Kenyan and Sudanese,
though they got them African Canadians too. You know, a lot of
them fugitives that escaped up there to Canada. Them old slave refu-
gitives and them new African refugees. And one of them Portuguese
Africans. I been mistaken for one of them Portuguese Africans too.
Mozambique. They thought I had immigrated to Canada to escape
the civil war or some shit, 'cause they have them a lot of Africans that
come to Canada to escape the different civil wars. This man come
talking to me in Portuguese, African Portuguese, but that's another
tale. Don't sound like Brazilian Portuguese and don't sound like
Portuguese Portuguese; it's its own language. Naw, I ain't no African
immigrant, I says, I'm African American. Went up to Canada, you
know, for one of them trade shows. I'm addicted to them trade
shows. A lot of them Africans they eats with they hands, just like the

true Indians, but in some of them African and Mediterranean countries and in that India, I think it's that India, that supposed to be the
etiquette to eat with your hands, like they is even some countries
where people is supposed to slurp they soup and even burp. So that
all them etiquette books they writes for the Europeans and the
European-minded peoples they'd have to rewrite for the other peoples of the world.

Buenas Buenas, I says again, shaking that trail mix, and thinking
about that Portuguese African, but she don't want that cattle feed.
She kinda burps and puts her hand to her lips. Is that her burping or
that baby burping? Seem like somebody said something about when
you's pregnant, you's a woman carrying two souls. Your own soul and
the soul of another person. You ain't just carrying your own soul,
you's carrying two souls. Or if you's got twins or something you's
carrying even more souls than that. Least you's responsible for more
souls than your own. I sits down beside her in the back of the truck
and nibbles on some of that trail mix myself. I picks out some of the
apricots and coconut meat and peanuts but she still don't want that.
Or maybe it's the baby that don't want that trail mix. I stands that
flashlight up on the floor so's we can see each other at the same time.
I nibbles me some more of that trail mix.

She looking at that stun gun I got. She still got that meek look but
it mixed with inquisitiveness. She run her hand through the top of
her hair and it kinda stick up like one of them hoopoe birds. Then I
got a picture of them Mexican womens in the revolution, 'cept they's
holding stun guns. And one of them's a general. Us got us a woman
general in our own history, I start to tell her, though I know she
don't see that picture in my head. Ain't it Harriet Tubman they call
the General. Or that "Ain't I a woman?" woman, Sojourner Truth.
Naw, Harriet Tubman, that's the General. And I'm even picturing
her with a stun gun. Some of them fools don't want to continue north
but wants to go back to the plantation, and she just aim that stun gun
at 'em, and they gets to steppin' towards freedom. Or what they
thinks is freedom. Land of Canaan. The Promised Land. Course
they's many steppin' south now, say they's been in the Deep North
too long. Continuing south to Brazil though or Mexico.

This a stun gun, I says, and then puts it in my belt. I picks up the
flashlight but keeps it catercornered to her face.

She sucking on that beef jerky and just a-looking at me. Maybe she wondering whether I'm to be trusted. Least that's how I interprets that look. When you's African American—there's them that says they don't wanna be no hyphenated American, so I says don't hyphenate it then; but I yam who I yam and claims who I'd like to be—you gets good at that sorta interpretation, and when you's a woman too you's even better, 'cause you ain't just colonized you's precolonized and recolonized. I'm wondering if they's got them them stun guns in Mexico, made in Mexico or imported from the USA, then I'm thinking of that Frito Bandito with a stun gun. But Delgadina, she say that a stereotype. That Frito Bandito. And that Juan Valdez too. She say they protested that Frito Bandito, 'cause he a more obvious stereotype. How come that Juan Valdez gotta have a donkey and only the cowboys gets the horses? And reading to me about them stereotypes. That mean I ain't supposed to say them? I asks. "I'm a hongry outlaw, where's breakfast?" they be asking on this television show with Peter Coyote. And then Delgadina changed the channel to one of them National Geographic gorilla documentaries and Delgadina asking, I wonder what them gorillas are thinking? Then on another channel they be talking about the urban gorilla population. And on another channel be teaching them gorillas language. But then Delgadina's got books on them other types of guerrillas. She got that book by el Ché called *Guerrilla Warfare,* and she got another book, I think it a work of fiction called *The Guerrilla's Notebook.* I know I have seen a copy of *The Guerrilla's Notebook* and must be Delgadina's.

Sanctuary? she asks again.

And then she just sucking on that beef jerky. That bottle water, that beef jerky, them thermos, they the best invention. I got me one of them newfangled thermos I seen at this automobile show in Memphis, actually this trade show. One of them space-age thermos. I always shops at them trade shows, 'cause they's always got them newfangled inventions. And it's kinda like a circus or a carnival, except it's got all these inventions. They's got miniaturized spy satellites, quartz halogen flashlights, and computerized language teachers. Talking about that science fiction, a lot of them things you read about in that science fiction, they's got at them trade shows. People talks about that science fiction, but science fiction is now. If I were to go back in one of them time machines, bring the General, Harriet Tubman, to one of them trade shows with me—now, that would be science fiction.

I be thinking maybe she wouldn't have no use for none of them newfangled inventions, but she be saying, That miniaturized spy satellite, we can use that; I don't know about them quartz halogen flashlights, 'cause we's got to train usselves to see in the dark and by the light of the moon and the Northern star, I'm curious about them language teachers, but what else they got to help us to freedom now? 'Cause she means then, but she saying it like time all the same. And behaving like she don't even know she in science fiction. 'Cause she the General, you know. Then she notices one of the mens at the trade show. Who dat? I don't know, I says. She thinks 'cause I travels back and forth in the time machine that I must know everybody. Kinda look kinda like Frederick, don't he? That what you new Negroes call a Afro? Like I said, all time's the same to her. I tells her I don't know, 'cause I'm a Ethiopianist myself.

Sanctuary, I says, and nods at her, that Mexican woman, though I knows she means more than some place to hide.

I nibbles me some more of that trail mix, then I starts out of the truck. I can smell them border patrol even when I don't see them, so I don't open the door of the truck all the way. And I tucks that stun gun in my pocket, then puts it back in my belt, 'cause they might think it a real gun. They take a gander at the truck and I think they gonna stop and inspect it, but they don't, they just keeps heading north. But I can smell them border patrol, like it hunting season. And seem like they can always smell me, like it hunting season too. And always looking at me like I'm some kinda conspirator. Confidence woman or some shit.

What's your name? I ask the woman, calling toward the back through the little vent. And then I remembers another Spanish word. *Nombre.* Your *nombre?* I asks. And pretty good Spanglish, ain't it?

Maria, she says, sounding like she the Keeper of Names or something. Maria Barriga.

That Spanish got that trill in it. She trill them *r*'s. I can't do that trill like that, so I just says Maria.

I'm Sojourner, I says. Sojourner Jane Nadine Johnson. But they calls me Mosquito.

Them that don't calls me Mosquito calls me Nadine. Don't many peoples calls me Sojourner, though they's a few that calls me 'Journer. Ain't nobody calls me Jane, though. I ain't favored the name Jane myself till I seen that movie 'bout Miss Jane, y'all know, Miss Jane, and read the book too. 'Cause the only Jane I knew before Miss Jane were Dick's Jane. But after I read about Ernest's Jane—don't that even sound better than Dick's Jane—then I began to favor my name, though I still don't use it. Them names is something, though. I know somebody went to Africa and come back with the name Uthlakanyana. Now I know what Jane mean. But I don't know what that Uthlakanyana mean. And the fool didn't neither. Just know it African. Now I don't mind the people taking they new names. But you's got to know what your new name mean.

Mosquito, she repeat, sounding as if the word the same in anybody's language. But she say it more on the tip of her tongue than I says it. Mosquito. You don't say it like them Spanish say it, 'cause them Mexicans got they own Spanish. And then she try to say my first name but it come out sounding like Journal. She don't attempt to say that Jane or that Nadine. Juanita, that Spanish for Jane. They's plenty Juanitas in Texas City. Ain't all Mexican though. Even I been called a Juanita, though I was being mistaken for some other gal. I been even call by my true name and mistake for other peoples too.

I'm still thinking them border patrol circle back and inspect my truck, but they don't. I parks the truck beside the road and wait while the Mexican woman relieve herself. She keep darting her head around looking and pulling that bodacious hair out her eyes and looking like she think I'm gonna pull the truck off. I see one of them prairie foxes in the road—look like it guarding the highway. I guess they calls them prairie foxes. Then she scurry back into the back of the truck, the woman not the prairie fox. That prairie fox it scurry off the road. The woman she grab herself a handful of that wild mustard. I think it wild mustard. Then she put a little of that wild mustard in her mouth and start chewing. Maybe it the baby want that wild mustard. They knows what's good.

CHAPTER 2

Y OU LOOKS LIKE YOU'S BEEN SWIMMING IN THE
Rio Grande, I says, yawning.

We done both slept in the back of that truck. That bird and bat guano still on them guaraches, but it dry and caked. I take one of them whisk brooms I keep in the back of that truck and whisks some of that guano off the floor of that truck. We both sleeping against one of them drums of detergents. She's slept in her poncho, and I've slept using my horse blanket for a pillow. That horse blanket kinda look like her poncho, though, with them Aztec-looking geometric-type designs on it, except but it a blanket. One of them multicolored woolen blanket. I think it a Mexican horse blanket or a Native American horse blanket 'cause I bought that blanket at a thrift shop in one of them border towns. Mighta been made in China, though and relabeled Mexico. But a lot of them Mexican and Native American geometric designs is similar. And a lot of them geometric designs on them horse blankets ain't just geometric designs they also supposed to be a language, so even though me and her don't speak the same language her poncho and my horse blanket be speaking the same language. 'Cept I don't think she know what that language mean any more than I do. So them blankets they just be speaking to each other. This the New World? Yeah, Bo. Old World to me, though.

Sanctuary, she repeat, but say it almost so it sound like Thank you.

I returns to the cab. When we gets to the next truckstop, I parks, then climbs in back.

I motions for her to take off them guaraches so's I can whisk that bat guano off them, 'cause I don't want to be whisking them with her wearing them, but she won't take off them guaraches, so I just whisks the other bat guano out the back of the truck, peeks around to make sure there ain't no spies (don't have to be just border patrol to be spies), then grabs my purse and heads for the truckstop restaurant. This another truckstop, but they all resembles. I climbs back in the back of the truck with a thermos full of hot chocolate and omelet sandwiches from the truck stop restaurant. We can see each other more clearly through the crack of light from the door. I've park kinda catercorner to the other trucks at the truckstop, so's they can't spy in the back of my truck, and you don't know which of them truckers is spies for immigration anyhow, 'cause I know a lot of them truckers they's probably just pretending they's truckers but they's spies for immigration, or maybe they's real truckers *and* spies for immigration. Border patrols for free. Course them real border patrol they stop any truck they want to, don't seem like they would need extra spies.

First I gives her some of them Handi Wipes that I've done damp-ened with water and a little bit of that liquid soap, so's she can wash her face and hands from that Rio Grande. They got the best liquid soap in that little truckstop restaurant. The waitress she say it ain't nothing but dishwashing liquid but won't tell me the secret of which dishwashing liquid, 'cause I be asking her what kinda liquid soap that is 'cause I be wanting to buy me some liquid soap like that. Honey, that ain't nothing but dishwashing liquid. I can't tell you which dishwashing liquid 'cause I don't know myself. I know she just want to keep the secret of that dishwashing liquid. And then she be in there telling me she trying to train this Vietnamese woman im-migrant to work in the truckstop restaurant. I thought them Asians was smart people, she be saying. You'd think she's a Mexican. Ex-cept she don't use the word Mexican, she use one of them border town words for Mexican. Use the word *greaser*, I think, 'cause spic is New York. Maybe the woman is smart and just don't understand her type of English, I be thinking. 'Cause when you's in a foreign country, you can be smart and just ain't know the people's language. The waitress she be telling me the man who own the truckstop restaurant usedta be in Nam hisself and so that's probably why he hired her. I thought it was a doxy when she first come in here. A prostitute, you know. Plenty of doxies around here. They oughta learn English before they seek legitimate employment, the waitress be saying. She got all her legal papers, though, her working papers, her green card. Naw, she ain't none of them boat people, I don't know what kinda people she is. Think she was a refugee in Hong Kong. Naw, I don't know how she got over here. He was in the war, though, and now he's acting like a conchy. One of them conscientious objectors, but I calls them conchies. If it was me, I only be giving green cards to people what could speak English like a native myself, good English. Gotta speak good English to be in this country. She speak Vietnamese and some of that French, though. Them French never shoulda brought us into their Indochinese war. She speak a little English. Boss know what she's saying anyhow, even in Vietnamese, 'cause he was in Nam, like I said. We had us a Cajun in here th'other day from down there in Louisiana that knowed what she's saying in French anyhow, say she speak French like natural French woman, say she was raised in one of them French convent schools over there in Nam, so she can't be too dumb. French convent school my arse. Still I don't think them French shoulda got us into their war. I ain't never been to France myself, but I heard they don't even like Americans, I mean true Americans. And we saved their asses in two wars. We whipped the Germans' ass for 'em. Whipped the Japanese ass, though it was the Germans occupying their ass. We even saved some of the collaborators' asses, 'cause some of them escaped to America after the war. Shoulda let the Namies whip the Frenchies' ass, though. Course they'll tell you we were over there to save democracy's ass, but I ain't no moon calf. Boss asked me to show her the ropes, though, so I'm showing her the ropes. Maybe she just pretending to be a dolt. You'd think we was playing charades. And I ain't good at charades. But these Namies even speak a different language playing charades. I call 'em Namies 'cause the boss don't want me to call 'em gooks, ya

know. Thinks he's a conchy now. The Vietnamese woman's dusting
off the counter while I'm pouring chocolate in my thermos. You can
tell she ain't wholly Vietnamese though, but one of them Amerasian-
type women and don't look doltish to me. In fact, she looking like
she understand everything the waitress saying, like she understand
the language, but just don't speak it. The waitress motions for her to
get my sandwiches and she get my sandwiches and hand them to me.
Thanks, I says. Say yousa welcome, say the waitress. Yousa welcome,
say the woman. Then she say something in French that must be
yousa welcome in French. And I says, *Merci beaucoup*. Sometimes
she be talking to herself in that Vietnamese. I hope he ain't hired
him none of them crazies. What they oughta do before they allow
peoples into this country is to check they sanity, give them a psychiatric examination. Of course some of the things these people do that
is custom in they country seems crazy to us. But at least they can learn
them to speak clear English. I don't even think we's got any gook
psychiatrists over here. Some of these countries don't even have psychiatrists. 'Cause I don't think you can get psychoanalyzed playing
charades.

To tell the truth I were about to take that Vietnamese woman out
of there and put her in the back of my truck, though I ain't speak that
Vietnamese neither. Seem like I overheard her say something sound
like Fock yo, and sound like clear English to me. Anyway, the Mexican woman she washes her face and hands from that Rio Grande,
like I said. We call it the Rio Grande, but I heard that on the other
side of the border they call it the Rio Bravo, 'cause I seen me a movie
about the Rio Bravo. Our Rio Grande is they Rio Bravo. Or they
Rio Bravo is our Rio Grande. Ain't they a movie about the Rio
Bravo? I be thinking it a different river. I be thinking the Rio Bravo
a different river. Same river but different names. Like them people
got aliases and shit, different people be knowing them by different
names. Like a lot of these truckers got they CB radios, got they CB
radio names. They the same person but different names, or them
with them stage names, like that Tina Turner. But you be thinking
it her real name and it her stage name. I guess I'm kinda like that river
myself, though, 'cause they be people that call me Nadine and others
that wants to call me Jane but don't and a few that call me 'Journer.
Of course I ain't no river, I'm a woman. And them is all my real

names. Mosquito, though. That's what most calls me, like I said. Hey, Mosquito. Hey, ain't you that Mosquito woman? Ain't you that woman they calls Mosquito? I think them volcanoes in Mexico they got names like that too, 'cause them Indians they give them volcanoes one name and them Spaniards they give them another name. All them Latin American countries they's supposed to have them active volcanoes, except that Honduras. Anyway, she wipe one of them Handi Wipes through her hair too till it glisten and then she braid it. She take a little Vaseline out of her pouch and put it on the Handi Wipe and then rub it on her hair and then rub some on her lips. Her hair look longer after she braid it. Tangled and shit it look like shoulder-length hair but braided it almost waist-length hair. Still a bit of the top of it stick up like one of them hoopoe birds. I think they's called hoopoe birds. And she got them thick braids. And she wipe off them guaraches. And then she wipe her hands again. I whisks some more of that bat guano out the back of my truck and then wipes my hands on one of them Handi Wipes.

Sanctuary, she repeat when I gives her them sandwiches and pours her some of that hot chocolate. I rinsed the thermos out in the women's room so's the hot chocolate ain't got no more of that beefy flavor. I told you I got one of them streamlined space-age thermos, ain't I? Harriet Tubman, she be liking that thermos too. Though me I got used to that hot chocolate with beef bouillon flavor and sometimes even mixes them. Pours the hot chocolate in there when they's still beef bouillon. As for her, the young Mexican woman-girl, she bite into that omelet sandwich and sip some of that hot chocolate and then she show her teeth slightly which surprise me again they's so clean and white. Like I told you, I only seen them Africans with teeth that clean and white, them that chews on that bark, that don't use toothbrushes but has them chewing sticks. I seen me one of them chewing sticks when I was in Canada. I was in a immigrant African's apartment, went into the bathroom and didn't see no toothbrush and none of that dentifrice, just one of them chewing sticks and some of them chewing sponges. Ain't seen none of them chewing sticks before, but I'd read about them. That bark supposed to be made from some special type of tree. I don't know what kinda tree. Only African tree I heard of is the baobab tree. The sandarac tree. I heard of the sandarac tree. That supposed to be a African tree. But like I said,

I ain't no natural historian or no ethnobotanist neither. Be nice to
know the names of them African trees though. Most everybody they
be knowing the names of them African animals, them giraffe and
them gorillas and them lions and them wildebeests. Ain't even been
to Africa and know the names of all them African animals. Bet they
don't know the names of them African trees. And probably don't
even know the names of many of the African peoples. Know the
Zulu and the Masai and the Pygmies and the Bushmen. How many I
know? Ashanti, Hausa, Chagga, Kamba, Bundu. Know they names.
But wouldn't know a Bundu if I saw one. But them wildebeests can't
fool me.

We nibbles on them omelet sandwiches. Mexican omelets with
onions, green peppers, pimentos and jalapeños. Them jalapeños little too hot for me, though, but I figures she like them jalapeños being
Mexican. I ain't mean to stereotype her, though. Delgadina she be
telling me they's some agringado Mexicans likes jalapeños but don't
eat them because they thinks they be stereotyping themselves, like
African Americans that don't eat watermelon, and they don't eat
them tacos neither. They likes tacos but don't eat them. But she be
saying they's two kinds of stereotypes, though, them based on falsehoods and them based on some kinda reality, when they vulgarizes
another people's culture, so when people be running from them stereotypes based on some kinda reality a lot of times they be running
from they own culture, they be running from theyselves. Like in Africa, North and South, you see them women wearing them headscarves, 'cause that's part of either they culture or they religion. But
then in America they be stereotyping that, even the Africans themselves, and just be thinking Aunt Jemima or they be calling people
handkerchief head, and that's they own culture or they own religion. But they just identify it with slave culture in America. Delgadina says she knows this Mexican American who likes African-
American culture, or what he considers African-American culture—jazz and soul food and calls himself a Chitlins con Carne
Mexican. And what about a African American that likes Mexican
food? That truckstop restaurant specializes in them omelet sandwiches and got one of them salad-type bars with different omelet ingredients. You can even put them chickpeas in your omelets and they
even got them fruit omelets. So I guess whatever your culture, you

can make you one of them omelets. Ain't got no watermelon omelet, though. Delgadina she allergic to them jalapeños, but she eat them anyway. 'Cause they's her culture, I guess.

Sanctuary, she say.

We nibbles on them omelet sandwiches. She look like she hungry, but she still eat that omelet sandwich real dainty, she don't gobble it. She gulp down that hot chocolate, though, then she wipe her mouth on one of them Handi Wipes.

Again she make that Sanctuary sound like Thank you. Me I ain't no part of that Sanctuary movement, though I heard of it, 'cause I seen one of them documentaries on that movement on my pocket television, and knows what that Sanctuary mean. They be interviewing them Sanctuary workers and then they be interviewing some of them refugees. Some of them workers and refugees they be camouflaging and others they don't camouflage. I guess it depend on whether or not they need they innocence protected. Seem like they all be wanting they innocence protected, though. And I heard of that other Sanctuary too. I also heard that name Sanctuary when Delgadina she be wanting to take me to the opening of this new Nature Sanctuary. She be talking about her culture, but she ain't no stereotype. You don't see no Mexicans on television going to no Nature Sanctuaries. I mean, no Mexican Americans neither. I guess if they have them Sanctuaries for people they be having them Sanctuaries for nature too, and they probably got more of them Sanctuaries for nature 'cause that's how people are. If that Vietnamese women was a flower or even one of them flowering cactus plants, we wouldn't be saying, You gotta speak clear English. We be having sanctuaries for her, even cultivating her in her own garden. Well, maybe not that one. Probably only American flowers. Born and raised in the USA. Unless they's Native Americans, of course.

Anyway, this sanctuary suppose to specialize in the plants of the Southwest. This couple who were sponsoring the sanctuary, a couple named Powers, they suppose to be sponsors of sanctuaries throughout the country, Delgadina say. Wealthy gringos, though the opening of the sanctuary were multicultural, because this wealthy couple, philanthropists, always insists on having they sanctuary openings multicultural, even before everybody was using the word *multicultural*. They used to use the word *multinational*, but then multina-

tional started having too many imperialistic connotations. I remember standing at the refreshment table and listening to that couple,
though. A slim, suntanned, middle-age gringo couple, both in yellow bermuda shorts and paisley shirts, the woman wearing espa-
drilles, the man guaraches. Well oiled and wealthy looking. The
kinda gringos you see in Miami. Delgadina say you can tell people
who's rich on account of they looks well taken care of. She don't vilify the rich like a lot of working people, 'cause she say all the rich
ain't villains and all the working people ain't the good guys. But
them rich seem like they always likes to vilify the working people,
though, or say they ain't got no culture. Delgadina she be reading
this book about the working class in academia, 'cause she say they's
a lot more of the working class in academia now, and that's why
you's got this renewed Great Books movement, 'cause they don't
like the working class deciding what's great literature, not to mention women and minorities. They seemed a shy couple, though, the
Powers, except with each other. Delgadina say he made his money
in mechanical engineering. I don't see how nobody can make money
in mechanical engineering, 'cause that don't seem like a lucrative
profession, but she say he own some kinda mechanical engineering
company or some shit. He ain't a little man. He got the physique of a
man used to play football or some shit. I pictures him on the line of
scrimmage, like in them 1930s photograph, and some of them men
played with Jim Thorpe, you know, not Jim Thorpe himself but
them others, but she look like the only game she play is miniature
golf or pinochle.

Would you like some ice cream, Dickey? I think she say Duckey
at first, but it Dickey.

Every time we come to a new sanctuary you ask me if I want ice
cream, you know I don't like ice cream.

But this is fried ice cream, this is special Mexican ice cream. Try
some of it, Dickey.

I don't like ice cream. Plus, how can they fry ice cream?

Try it and see. I bet you'll like it. It's sort of like Baked Alaska,
you know. Well, you should try something, darling. Try some of
these nice Mexican tacos.

They don't look like Taco Bell tacos.

Because they're real Mexican tacos, and Taco Bell tacos are, well,

Taco Bell tacos, American tacos. Remember when we were in that nice little Mexican village, the one Sophia told us about, these are the kind of tacos they had. But I know you'll like this ice cream.

I don't like ice cream.

You've got so many dislikes, darling, how can I remember them all?

The sanctuary, it didn't look like a sanctuary, it looked more like a desert. I asked Delgadina how come it looked like a desert and she said it was because it specialized in plants from the Southwest. And told me that most of the cactuses flower. That cactuses blossom. I kept trying to listen to Delgadina telling me about them flowering cactuses and even their names, but I kept hearing Dickey and his wife. I didn't hear him say her name, but I kept imagining it was Jane, although Dick and Jane in the storybook weren't husband and wife.

And everything they have here is natural, Dickey, no artificial lakes like that other sanctuary.

I thought that was a real lake. Didn't they tell us it was a natural lake? Didn't Sophia tell us it was a natural lake?

I thought she told us it was an artificial lake.

No, I'm sure she said natural lake.

They oughta have an oasis, I told Delgadina.

But that would be artificial, said Delgadina, who seemed also to be listening to Dickey and his wife. They don't want anything artificial.

Try some of this fried ice cream, said Dickey's wife.

I don't like ice cream.

Remember when I used to be as pretty as that girl in the peacock skirt?

You were never as pretty as that girl, said Dickey. Though you could be wild and gorgeous when you wanted to be. Remember when we went to that Zulu village, and I bought you all those barbarous ornaments? All the women looked like they were wearing helmets and you tried to fix your hair like that.

I glanced around to see who was wearing a peacock skirt—and it was Delgadina.

Try some ice cream. Everybody likes ice cream. And this is fried ice cream. It's exotic . . .

Exotic? I heard Delgadina whisper, and then she told me the name of another cactus flower.

Delgadina wrote all that down in this notebook she keep. She call it her *cuaderno*. I don't keep no *cuaderno* myself. I remembers what the people said, but Delgadina put they descriptions in her *cuaderno*. She trying to be more descriptive, she say, but she ain't trying to be too descriptive. She say she trying to use description the way they uses it in them Mexican and Spanish ballads. She say she were named after somebody in one of them Mexican ballads, but she say she ain't nothing like the woman in that Mexican ballad, though. I remembers that woman commenting on Delgadina's peacock skirt. I remembers that woman commenting on me too. About me being statuesque. About me wearing one of those fantastic headdresses. That's what she referred to it as, not as a scarf but as a headdress. I just give her one of them steady glances, you know, like she know I know she talking about me, and don't mind talking about Delgadina and me right where we could hear her. Delgadina, she don't say nothing to them, she just tread proudly around the sanctuary, showing me the different cactuses and telling me they names. Sometimes she start strumming them glass beads she wearing. Seem like she strumming them, or touch them like they's holy beads. I'm a truck driver, like I told you, and the onliest African-American woman trucker on this route. They's plenty women truckers nowadays—though ain't that many in South Texas. Seen me a documentary on one of them women truck drivers, 'cause what supposed to be ordinary for a man supposed to be extraordinary for a woman. She be in her truck, one of them eighteen-wheelers, giving this interview on television and they's treating her like she ain't no common woman. In fact, they's treating her like she some kinda princess, some kinda royalty, which ain't no common woman. Princess in blue jeans and a sweatshirt. Stringy blond hair she tie back with a rubber band. Actually she got her hair in French braids—what I hear them call French braids, but I can't tell them French braids from them African braids—and then she tie them French braids back with a rubber band. I guess the French musta got that style from them Africans in France and then the Americans they be seeing the French with that style and be calling them French braids. Or maybe they know they African braid and just call them French braids 'cause they don't wanna call them African braids. 'Cause you know a lot of they clients wouldn't be wearing them braids if they call them African braids. I even heard some fool try to say it were the French that invented jazz. Now, if they didn't have the true musicians to tell it differently, everybody be saying them French invented jazz.

I asks Maria she still hungry. Course I don't know them Spanish words for it. But she know what I'm saying. She shake her head no and wipe her mouth again on them Handi Wipes. She kinda pat her belly, like she saying that baby he seem like he well fed too. Then she kinda lean back against one of them detergent drums. I rolls up my trail mix and puts it behind one of them other detergent drums, but nods towards it, so she knows if she want some of that trail mix she welcome to it. Then I just sits back against one of them detergent drums. That Maria her features kinda reminds me of them Mayans. I can't tell whether she a peasant or what. Her hands kinda got few blisters on them, but they ain't knarled sunburnt like the hands of them womens that works in the fields. They's dirt under her fingernails, but that seem like it from scratching her way across the borders.

Pierced earrings. I think I seen me them kind of earrings she wearing, that woman trucker, I'm mean, I'm telling y'all about that other woman trucker—them tiny slot machines and got movable parts like them real slot machines; you know, you buy them in them novelty stores. They especially got them in them novelty stores in Vegas. So them other novelty store they must import them from Vegas. Ain't one of them skinny blondes, though, but more on the full-figured side. I be wondering if that like one of them tabloid journalism shows where they sometimes get them a actress or model—gotta be one of them full-figured models—pretending to be the real woman, but she say she the real woman. Man, he be driving a eighteen-wheeler he supposed to be a ordinary man, just a ordinary working man, but woman, she be driving a eighteen-wheeler and she ain't no common woman. Like that woman I see sometimes on my route that wears her hard hat and works with them mens building them new highways. She be behaving like that job make her extraordinary, and she do behave a little more classy than them mens that works the same occupation. All them women they be talking 'bout that feminism. True feminism they be treating her like she just some common woman. That would be the true feminism. But then they's feminist that would say that when mens do women's work or traditionally women's work, it elevates the work. Like that American Gigolo. Most of the womens you see on these routes, though, is them waitresses at the truckstop restaurants, you know, and most of them's surprise when they first see me drive up in my truck and come into the truckstop restaurant. And ain't all them beehive-wearing womens neither. Every time you see one of them truckstop womens on television, they's always one of them beehive-wearing womens. In fact, most of them southern waitresses is most always them beehive-wearing womens. Beehive wearing and chewing gum. Delgadina say they's a Spanish writer that even wrote a whole essay about gum-chewing Americans. Los Estados Engomados. They's got some of them beehive-wearing womens, even chewing gum, but a lot of them is modern girls. Some of them even wearing them French braids. And ain't all them ignorant types neither. Some of them they be studying for they GEDs, and some of them they even be asking me about truck driving school. I carry around some of them brochures and sometimes I gives them to different womens wants to learn about truck driving school. I got a lot of beauty school brochures too, 'cause the same people that owns the truck driving school owns the beauty school. And some of them they be even more ambitious than that, be wanting to become legal secretaries or start they own businesses. One of them she be talking about learning that legal shorthand, you know where they be using them stenographer machines. They call them machine stenographers, 'cause that different from what they call that Gregg shorthand. I tells them it be better if they learns them computers, 'cause courts all starting to use computers, but a lot of them schools they still teaches that legal shorthand and stenography. They's even got classes that teaches you just how to transcribe that legal shorthand. Somebody else do the legal shorthand and then you transcribes it. She be showing me her textbook and it look like Greek. Well, them ain't the only womens you see on these routes, to tell you the truth—at night sometimes you spots womens sneaking in the back of these trucks. You know what kinda womens I mean, and ain't seeking sanctuary neither, or maybe they's some of them that do consider that sanctuary. Shouldn't say sneaking, 'cause a lot of them kinda womens don't sneak.

Come here, girlie.

I know one of them girlies. She tells people to call her Panza, but I don't think that her real name. Calls her tricks dinks. 'Cause I heard one of them other girls asking her if she want to have dinner and she say, Naw, I'm waiting for my dink. I think that Panza on her way to California too, or on her way from California and think them truck stops look pretty good around Texas City. I don't know them other girlies by they names, though. Got on them skimpy dresses and high heels and shit. And makeup so thick it look like a mask. A few beehive-wearing womens and modern girlies too. And more of them French braids. A lot of them is real statuesque-type girls too, who don't look any different from the Hollywood types. Only difference is they's in Texas City and ain't Hollywood.

Trucker that mistook me for Nadine musta thought I was one of them, 'cause I was crossing the truckyard to go into the truckstop restaurant one night and this man call, Nadine, is that you? I can hear the music from his truck. He listening to one of them cowboy-outlaws, you know them country music singers that considers they-selves cowboy-outlaws. They's got the gangsta rap, you know, but them country singers have also got they outlaws. Now one of my names is Nadine, like if you be asking the Rio Grande if it the Rio Bravo ain't it say yes, so's I answers, Yes, then realizes I ain't the Na-dine he mean 'cause he got this truck door swung open and curving his little finger, and so I says, Naw, I ain't Nadine, and I ain't Panza neither, and then I goes toward the truckstop restaurant and the next thing I knows this guy got hold to my arm and swung me around, then get a good look at my face in the light from that restaurant and say, Nadine . . . You ain't Nadine. I thought you said you Nadine. I thought you Nadine. I *am* Nadine, but I ain't the Nadine you mean, I says. I mean, I ain't *your* Nadine. Man he look real foolish but kinda intrigued too—or maybe that just my conceit—and then go back to he truck. One of them beaver-toothed men and kinda look like Paul Bunyan wearing eyeglasses. At least the Paul Bunyan of the storybooks. And then I'm trying to think of who else he look like in the storybooks. Most of them is real men but they treats them like they's mythological men. Don't look like John Henry though. And me I weren't even wearing none of them skimpy little dresses nei-ther, wearing same camouflage britches I'm wearing now. 'Cept I had taken off my jacket, and had on one of them tank tops, 'cause it a hot night. You know them accordion-type tank tops. Him looking like a fool though and probably wasn't even expecting me to be such a big woman neither. 'Cause I'm over six feet tall. When I come out of the truckstop with my sandwiches and thermos full of beef bouillon, I seen this woman climb up in he truck. Don't know if that were the other Nadine or not. Wearing one of them little tight-ass skimpy dresses they wears these days, even them high-class womens, and high heel shoes make her look like she walking on stilts. Even them hippopotamus-butt women—them Nile hippopotamus—likes them tight-ass dresses. And wearing that carnival makeup.

I shouldn't be saying that about them carnival though, 'cause lots of them carnival women that works in these carnival shows, they knows a few things about putting on that makeup, 'cause one of them women I met at one of them carnival she be talking about how she got to reinvent herself from them different carnival sideshows. She be saying that she play the Unicorn Woman, then she got to pretend she the Butterfly Woman, then she got to pretend she the Crocodile Woman, and she be telling me some of them makeup secrets like they do on television when they be showing you the makeup secrets of the stars. She got one of them little trailers just like a movie star trailer, except it a carnival star trailer and got all kind of theatrical makeup and carnival makeup and paraphernalia in that trailer. I was on my way to one of them trade show, and spotted one of them carnivals. They probably set up in front of the trade show so's they could entice folks to them before they got to the trade show.

Don't look a thing like this Nadine, I mean the broad in the skimpy dress—I can call myself Nadine 'cause it is one of my names. Don't look a thing like this Nadine.

That same trucker I seen again when I was at the circus watching them jugglers. That carnival, you know, whet my appetite for the circus. I know it was that same trucker. Didn't have Nadine with him, though, but the wife and kids eating cotton candy and butter popcorn. His wife ain't got none of them beehive hairdos neither; she wear her hair blond and straight and kinda old-fashioned like in them days when the white girls usedta iron their hair, 'cause you know they wouldn't be using no straightening combs. I always thought that was odd, right at the time when the white girls was ironing their hair, a lot of the African-American girls was kinking

theirs. I guess they both thought that they was being natural. And
kinda look like them that be studying for they GEDs, I mean the
woman with that old-fashioned hair. In fact, she kinda look like that
princess that they interviewed on account of her truck driving, but a
more slender figure. I don't think she drive no truck though, 'cause
he don't look like the kinda man be wanting his woman to be driving no truck. In fact, he look like the kind of man don't be wanting
any woman to be driving no truck. He glanced at me out of the corner of his eyes, though I don't know if he was mistaking me for that
other Nadine again, or whether he was remembering that I wasn't
that Nadine.

I'm munching on my own cotton candy and watching them jugglers and I'm listening to a couple behind me. You don't want a wife
you wants a quisling, the woman says. What's a quizzling? the man
asks. After the juggling act were the clowns. I'd been used to seeing
just men clowns, but this clown act had women clowns too. Acrobat
clowns. One clown and his daughter did trick riding, bareback on
horses, and then elephants. What's a quizzling? the man kept asking.
And then he says, You're a puzzling bitch all right. You prig.

What's a quizzling? I asks Delgadina when I got back from the
circus, 'cause Delgadina she say she don't like them circus. I think a
quizzling got to do something with puzzles myself.

Quizzling? That's why I'm a bartender.

But she still don't tell me what a quizzling is, and I'm still thinking it got something to do with puzzles. I looks the word up in the
dictionary, but the dictionary don't say a meaning that I think that
woman mean, so maybe she use the word *quizzling* but want it to
mean something it don't mean.

Course I seen the two of them again years later, the quizzling and
her husband, and she in one of them truckstop restaurants and done
discovered that other Nadine, but that a tale for her to tell. And him
still calling her a puzzling bitch, 'cause she don't look much like no
quizzling. And by then I know what a quizzling mean. But it seem
that one of her girlfriends, a certain Beatrice McDowell, had been
driving from Disneyland in L.A. back to Texas City when she spot
him and this other Nadine in one of them truckstop restaurants, so
when she get back to Texas City she call up the wife and tells her
where she can find her husband and this other woman, so she go

there to confront her husband and the whore slut bitch who insist she ain't a whore slut bitch but as much a lady as she, the wife, is, but like I said, that's another tale and a tale for her or the other woman that other Nadine to tell, 'cause I don't think husbands much tells tales like that.

Anyhow, the border patrol, like I said, they's almost always stopping me to see whether I'm carrying any of that contraband and doing that smuggling. They's caught some of them smugglers, mostly Mexicans, which ain't to say it's only Mexicans doing that smuggling, ain't just smuggling people and drugs neither, but some of them's smuggling parrots and even cactus and shit. Different exotic animals and plants. They's supposed to have a lot of exotic animals and plants and shit that's peculiar to Mexico. Delgadina roasted me some of them Mexican cactus. Taste pretty good with that salsa. Don't know if she roasted me one of them rare and exotic cactus, though, probably one of them ordinary cactus. She say in some parts of Mexico, during the dry season, they call that starvation food. Well, I guess to the Mexicans them plants and animals ain't exotic, even the exotic ones, but to the North Americans they's supposed to be exotic, like that woman calling that fried ice cream exotic. Well, I guess to them Spaniards they's supposed to be exotic, but not to them original Mayans and Aztecs and Olmecs, them original Mexicans. Like Delgadina be saying people ain't exotic to theyself, but they's exotic to other peoples, except she be saying them colonizers and shit they be trying to convince you to be exotic to yourself, to see yourself as exotic, and ain't see them as exotic. That Mr. and Mrs. Powers, it's us should see them as the exotics, like that Baked Alaska she be talking about. Baked Alaska sound more exotic than fried ice cream. To tell the truth, though, when I first seen that Delgadina, I be seeing her as a exotic, with all them glass beads she sometimes wear, and them skirts with peacocks and birds of paradise, but after she be lecturing me on that exoticism I stopped seeing her as exotic, but I do see that Miguelita as exotic. I tell you about that Miguelita later. But Delgadina she always be talking about that colonialism stuff and be calling us colonized and shit, be saying that women of color is colonized as women and people of color, where the gringa is only colonized as a woman. So us can't be the same kind of feminists as gringo feminist, if us consider usselves feminists at all. She be talking about that Alice Walker word *womanist,* but then she be saying that womanist ain't her culture neither, so she can't be calling herself no womanist neither. Then she be calling herself a daughter of Juárez, but then that don't express Chicana feminism neither. Then she say a name that I think mean the name of a Aztec priestess, but then she say that don't describe her modern self neither. Most of the time she be talking colonized I be colonizing me one of them Bud Lights or some of them pretzels or some of that salsa. I know all about that colonization myself. But Delgadina she see the world like that: who be colonizing whom. And she even talk about the colonized colonizers. That's the people that's colonized theyselves and still be colonizing other peoples, or it's them peoples that got a history of being colonized theyselves, but then when they's the rulers they starts colonizing other peoples. Of course when I said I'm gonna colonize one of them Bud Lights she be saying I don't understand that colonization, and I be saying she don't understand signification. Course there's some of them colonized people that wants to be colonized, like they say that Gibraltar. And then there's that economic colonization. She say that most modern colonization is economic. That's how the modern colonialists, the neocolonialists colonizes, she say. Then they can pretend they ain't colonials. 'Cept they knows who they are. Least them in power does.

I don't smuggle nothing. I do got me one of the nayatl that Delgadina made that I lets sit in the window of my truck. Instead of one of them Kewpie dolls I have me one of them nayatl. Sometimes I think if I had me one of them Kewpie dolls or one of them plaster of paris saints maybe them border patrol wouldn't consider me no smuggler. I knows I told y'all about them nayatl.

Delgadina, like I said, she sculpts them nayatl mens, but I guess they musta got nayatl womens too. I guess I coulda asked her to sculpt me a nayatl woman, but I guess she have just got herself a preference for sculpturing them nayatl mens, or maybe the tradition in Mexico is to sculpture them nayatl mens. I don't think that even amongst the Mexicans it's only the mens that can transform theyselves. Or maybe they got another name for them when they womens. But the proverb say that people is as hard to understand as a melon, which don't exactly make sense, 'cause seem like compared to human beings, a melon, even one of them watermelons, is pretty easy to understand. Unless it some type of metaphor, on account of 'cause a melon, even them watermelons, can't explain itself and shit. Now don't none of y'all come calling me no stereotype 'cause I'm mentioning them watermelons and signifying on 'em either, 'cause they's native to Africa, them watermelons. I got ostracized once on account of favoring watermelons, but I ain't going to tell y'all that story yet, and it wasn't on account of me letting nobody photograph me with no watermelon, neither. I know there's a rumor that whilst I was in the Southland sitting on my uncle's porch eating watermelon some white tourists from West Virginia seen me and took my photograph and it were reprinted as a postcard that were sold throughout the Southland, and even up North and became the cover photograph of a neo-African satire called *The Cosmic Pickaninny*. I've read *The Cosmic Pickaninny*, but I know for a fact that the cover photograph ain't me, nor am I depicted on any Southland tourist's maps. Y'all heard what I said about the Old World and the New World. Well, y'all can follow my logic. I'm talking about them smugglers now.

Anyway, some of them smuggles this exotic cactus. Cactus that's just supposed to grow in Mexico, though I don't know how a cactus can tell a border myself. Seem like a cactus that can grow in Mexico would cross the border and grow in the southern U.S. too, 'cause that supposed to been Mexico, what Delgadina she call Aztlán. I don't see how them cactus and them parrots knows borders. Don't even seem like them smugglers would even need to try to hornswoggle them border patrol to transport no cactus or them parrots neither. How a cactus or a parrot supposed to know Tijuana from Texas City? Like them ocotillo trees that grows in Mexico and the southern United States too; they don't know they's a border. Delgadina she say they's people that eats roasted cactus, like I said, and I be wondering how that roasted cactus taste, and then she go to one of them Mexican stores and buy some fresh cactus and then she roast it. We drive out to the desert and roast that cactus 'cause she say you can't roast cactus in no microwave and I be wondering why she buy that cactus in a store and ain't be roasting the pure cactus from the desert, but she be roasting that store-bought cactus. And she even take Miguelita out with us into the desert to roast cactus too. Miguelita she the crazy woman, but I tell you about her.

I seen me one of them parrot smugglers, though, one of them Mexicans. I think he be a Mexican. Border patrol had him spreadeagled
against he truck, and had them green and orange and yellow parrots
in them cages speaking Spanish. Sound like Spanish. Mighta been
Portuguese. Mighta smuggled them parrots up from Brazil where
they speak Portuguese, 'cause they supposed to have a lot of parrots
in that Brazil; in that Amazon they's people make a profession of being birdcatchers. They goes around the jungles of Brazil catching
birds and selling them in the cities. Don't know what make them
think they can smuggle talkative birds like that, though. Had several
birds in one cage, all colorful as orchids. Maybe they even smuggles
orchids. They probably smuggles orchids, them orchids that grows
just in Mexico. Maybe they call them helmet orchids. I've heard of
them helmet orchids. Or maybe they just peculiar to Australia. I seen
me one of them documentaries on Australia and they be talking
about them helmet orchids. Wonder if they got cactus in Australia.
Delgadina say her favorite orchid the peacock orchid. If they got a
bird of paradise orchid that be her favorite orchid too.

And a lot of them border patrol don't believe it my truck neither,
they be asking who truck this is and where my registration papers,
and this my own truck, ain't no company truck. And this ain't no
company truck hired out to me neither. I'm a independent contractor, I be telling them, this my own truck. Used to lease this truck
from a company in New Boston, Texas, though, but now it my own
truck. Always dreamed, though, of having me one of them custom-
made trucks from Kron International. This ain't no custom-made
truck, but pretty good truck. A lot of them drive them company
trucks. A lot of them in my union drives company trucks. I'm a independent but I still believe in the union. Course they say it ain't the
working man and woman's country anymore. That's what them Citizen's Rights brochures say. Course they ain't talking to me. 'Cause
them same people be saying it ain't my country neither. I been to
them trade shows where these companies they be trying to hire them
drivers, you know, and in the want ads they's always got companies
advertising for people to drive they company trucks. Some of them
they even be teaching drivers and be saying they teach you to drive
they company trucks for free, except you got to contract to drive they
company trucks. But that ain't no kinda independence. It be sound-

ing like that indentured servitude, except I guess them people they be learning theyselves a trade. You gotta learn yourself a trade. Even them white-collar people now is learning theyselves trades.

I thought of after getting me my truck driver's training maybe getting a job teaching other truck drivers, but that ain't no kinda independence either. I met me one of them what they call them industrial actors at one of them trade shows. You know, they learn them lines about how to introduce them new trade show products just like they be learning them a television or a movie script. That woman she be saying they's a lot of competition for actors at them trade shows, as much competition at them trade shows she be saying as the legitimate theater, and in fact she be saying they's actors that have worked in television, the movies, and legitimate theater that auditions for them trade shows. People know about them famous movie stars, but they's a lot of working actors that ain't famous. I usually just be listening to them people that gives them presentations about them new products and shit, but this one's a spliv so I be talking to her and shit. She one of them light-skinned splivs. She the first spliv I seen that look well taken care of almost like that Mr. and Mrs. Powers couple, Dickey and his wife, but her background ain't rich. She tall and slim and look like a model, in fact look like one of them splivs I seen on a soap opera, except on that soap opera they had her looking as plain as cottage pudding, but at the trade show she looking like a model. And wearing something look kinda like a space suit, 'cause I guess they wants her to look ultramodern or futuristic to hype they ultramodern and futuristic products. She be wearing her hair slick and straight and ain't no nap in it, and that the first time I seen a African-American woman, even one of them light skins, with ain't no nap in her hair either, or least look like it want to nap. I mean, they's straight-haired African-American women, specially them with Native American in 'em, but they hair still look like it want to nap or want to curl. And I mean hers ain't got a natural nap or a natural curl in it. She be saying how she learned how to understand her product, but she be saying a lot of them trade show actors or industrial actors, especially the ones that got aspirations for the legitimate theater they be talking about them products and don't understand the first thing about them, like some of them computers and new-age technology

and shit. A real intelligent young woman. She say she study that political science in college, though, and then she met somebody in a
theater group and got interested in acting. Say she thought she might
be interested in being a diplomat, why she study that political science, 'cause she seen that African-American woman who speaks
Russian on television, except she didn't learn Russian she learned
Chinese, 'cause they didn't teach no African languages, not even
Swahili, 'cept she wasn't sure if she wanted to be no diplomat in Africa, but then most of them classes she say you don't learn nothing
about international diplomacy just how to be a polemicist, at least at
the college she was attending, but then she like being around creative people and be saying they's something liberating about creative
people. Then she discovered there ain't many magnum opuses written for African-American actresses, or if they is magnum opuses they
gives the work to only a few leading African-American actresses, so
she got interested in the trade show circuit. They ain't no magnum
rpuses for trade show circuit actresses, but she least gets to learn
about modern technology. And she be saying how she learn about
her product even before she goes to audition, 'cause she say they got
to audition just like for them regular acting jobs.

Y'all got to audition? I asks.

'Cause I'm thinking they just hires them for they looks. We's
standing over by the Coke machine 'cause they let them stop and
drink Coke and go to the bathroom. Though she say sometimes at
them trade shows they don't even get a chance to go to the bathroom.

Yeah, we got to audition. I still sometimes audition for the movies,
but most of the time they don't have roles I want. There really aren't
any good roles.

They wants you to play a hoochie woman.

At first she looks at me like she's not sure what a hoochie woman
means, then she says, Oh, yeah, that, but even when they don't want
me to play a hoochie woman, as you say, there still aren't any good
roles. Or they want you just to be a starlet, but not a real actress.

I'm still looking at that hair that ain't even look like it wanna nap,
and I ask her where she from.

Vienna.

Naw, girl. You one of them Army brats?

But she ain't mean Europe, she just like to say that. I be thinking she from Europe, and maybe that explain why there ain't no nap in her hair, but she mean Vienna, Virginia.

Anyway, that border patrol be flashing they lights all in the back of my truck. He's one of them uniform-wearing border patrols. They got them plainclothes border patrols too. But seem like them border patrol all got the same flashlight. I ain't talking about when I'm carrying that Mexican woman. I mean other times when I'm in my truck. I don't even know how she sneaked in my truck, or maybe somebody paid somebody not to look in my truck. But other times them border patrols they's flashing they lights all in the back of my truck.

What's this?

Industrial detergents.

What?

Detergents.

Opening up them big drums and stick one of them dipsticks in them drums, make sure they's full all the way through with them detergent. He keep lifting that dipstick up and then plunge that dipstick back into that drum. Then he have me open up another one of them drum and he test it with that dipstick.

This ain't no detergent, he say. He put his hand in it, scoop it up and smell it. I think he gonna taste it too. Then he sniff at that detergent again like he one of them prairie foxes his ownself.

These detergents ain't for everyday peoples, I explains. They's for industry. Biodegradable. And them detergents they uses to sop up that oil on the beaches with. Like them oil spills they has in the Gulf all the time. These is industrial detergents.

And I be wishing I had me that intelligent young woman from that trade show, that woman from Vienna, Virginia, to explain to him about these industrial detergents. She be telling him about the sodium perborates or whatever the detergent got in it, or maybe it biodegradable 'cause it *ain't* got them sodium perborates in it.

All this industrial detergents?

Yeah.

Let me see your registration papers.

Yeah.

He look at me as if to say, You one of them wise-gals, ain't you? Like wise-guy, you know, except you a gal, 'cause I ain't say, Yes sir. 'Cause I ain't massa him. I believe in being polite to people, though. But some people they don't want polite. They want you to massa them.

CHAPTER 3

I DON'T KNOW NOTHING ABOUT THAT SANCTUARY movement, like I said, but I do know where they's this mission school run by this Carmelite nun, I think she a Carmelite nun, school that got mostly Native American and Mexican-American children and still look like it right outta the seventeenth or eighteenth century where they teaches them discipline and catechism and agriculture. Actually, I think it was the Indians taught the Spaniards agriculture, at least New World agriculture, taught them about that corn anyhow. In fact, supposed to be a lot of different foods, even medicines originates with the Native Americans, like Delgadina be saying a lot of that style that people think originate with the gringo cowboy that originate with the Mexican cowboy, but they's got another name besides cowboy. Anyhow, that mission school teach them how to be artisans and shit, 'cause they show something about that on television during that Columbus celebration; them old Columbus celebration they just be telling you about that Columbus, but now you be learning more about them native peoples, 'cause a lot of them natives peoples they don't celebrate no Columbus. Maybe Columbus discover the white man's America, but he ain't discover they America. And they America ain't even America. Got they own name for it. It look part fortress and part cathedral that mission school, but they says that in them days the cathedrals was fortresses and the fortresses was cathedrals, 'cause nothing but pirates and invasions in them days. Them conquistadors, though, they would always come with the Bible and the gun. 'Cept that Delgadina say them Aztecs they was conquistadors too. But that the way the history of the world is, she say. Like them cathedrals on the coast of Spain and on them little Spanish islands, I mean this mission school, cathedral, fortress.

So a cathedral it couldn't just be a cathedral, had to be a fortress too, had to have not only them cathedral spires but them thick walls and turrets like them fortresses and supposed to have as many soldiers in them cathedrals as monks and priests and holy men. And maybe some of them monks turned into soldiers during the invasion and after the invasion went back to being monks. A monkish soldier or soldier-monk. Course a lot of them monks in Asia they knows that kung fu. They exercises the soul and the spirit and the body at the same time. But a lot of them learned men in them days supposed to be monks, I mean them learned European men, like that Albertus Magnus and the Venerable Bede and that Aquinas. Maybe the learned men in every early culture is priests and monks, or they culture equivalent to priests and monks. You hear about a lot of them nuns being learned women, 'cause they be saying in them days if you want to be a woman and be learned, then a lot of them be joining them convents, 'cause if they becomes wives a lot of them wouldn't be able to continue with they learning, or they would have to learn just woman's knowledge, or knowledge that were acceptable for a woman to know, like art and music and dance and poetry, but a lot of the learned men they's monks too. Them that weren't monks supposed to be alchemists and shit. I don't know if there were any women alchemists, 'cause that's science. Delgadina she took her one of them courses in the Middle Ages and told me about them nuns and them learned monks and she the only Chicana there in that class and the professor be asking her how come she in that class about the European Middle Ages like a Chicana ain't supposed to be interested in Albertus Magnus and the Venerable Bede and that Aquinas,

though I be wondering how come she be interested in that Albertus
Magnus and the Venerable Bede and that Aquinas my ownself.
That Delgadina read somewhere about the Renaissance man and
want to be a Renaissance woman, but she be saying even amongst
certain other Chicanos and Chicanas they be saying she agringada
'cause she be studying about that Albertus Magnus and the Venerable Bede and that Aquinas and ain't even want her to read *Don
Quijote*.

And got one of them bell towers, that mission school. The whole
fortress look like it whitewashed till you gets upon it, then it look
like it been brushed with water from the Rio Grande or the Rio
Bravo. Everything that dirty whitewash except for that colorful mosaic walk full of turquoises and reds and golds. Maybe that Quetzalcoatl in that mosaic. Or maybe one of them other Aztec or Mayan
gods. Them Aztecs and Mayans now they got a different name for
the same god. Quetzalcoatl and Kukulcán they supposed to be the
same god. I think it Kukulcán. And they's other Native Mexicans
that got the same god and call him by yet another different name.
Maybe everybody that believe in one God got the same god and just
call him by a different name. Course there's people that's got little
gods. In this movie I seen this man say even a banana could be a god.
And then the white man ask him, How can you make a god out of
something you eat? And ain't they eat they God? Least in metaphor? Ain't that they communion? And there's peoples that say man
himself can be a god, or woman herself. For some they's got to pro-
gress spiritually to be a god, for others they's just natural god-men
and god-women. Or maybe there's one god but that one god is made
up of lesser gods. Delgadina she say she a monotheist, though. She
say she just don't like the idea of worshiping other people God or
gods. She a Catholic, think, but sometimes it seem like she treat
them saints like they's gods. Or maybe they ain't the same saints as
the Catholic saints. I ain't ask her much about her religion. I know
they's some type of religions that sound like some type of wine or
some type of feast. But every religion probably sound like some type
of wine or some type of feast. Unless it's one of them religions with
Science in it. But people don't like it when you talk about they religion. Or anything they make into a religion. Race, religion, and language. Them's the things that defines for people who they are.

That look like it outta the seventeenth or eighteenth century too, that mosaic, or maybe one of them earlier centuries. And got one of them gargoyles too swinging from one of them towers and one of them lion guardants. But that gargoyle it look more European than Aztec or Mayan.

Anyhow, I cross the courtyard where they's childrens playing and go up the steps to the main building. The door open so I goes in and knocks on the office door which got a sign on it that say KNOCK. And another sign that say the same thing must be in Spanish and another sign maybe in one of them Indian languages. Mixtec or something. I heard about that Mixtec. And one of them French doors, though I guess maybe it a Spanish door and look like one of them hand-carved doors. But them French they's supposed to influenced everybody all over Europe, that neoclassicism, so a Spanish door might be the same as a French door.

Come in.

She got one of them soft, high-pitched, gentle voices—kind that elementary school teachers has and peoples used to talking to childrens all the time, you know. Most of them, though, they even speaks to grownups with them voices.

This nun she sitting behind her big desk shuffling papers. Behind her's a wall of books, and to the right they's this huge window where she can look out into the courtyard where the childrens is playing. It look like a modern window, like they done cut it into the wall of the cathedral fortress in the modern era, or maybe enlarged a little window, 'cause I don't think they had no glass windows when that cathedral fortress was built and I do know them castles usedta have them little windows so's the arrows couldn't penetrate, when they try to aim they arrows at them little windows, 'cause you don't see any castles with big windows, 'less they's modern-day castles or them converted castles, 'cause in Europe they's supposed to have a lot of castles that they convert into hotels. 'Cause a lot of them Europeans they can't keep up them castles unless they turns them into hotels. I can't read the titles of them books but a lot of them looks like them books and manuscripts from the seventeenth and eighteenth centuries. They's supposed to had books in China, though, before they had books in Europe. The person invented paper a Chinaman, but Delgadina she be saying you don't call a Chinaman a Chinaman you's supposed to say Chinese. Unless you's a Chinese or a Chinese American then if you want you can call yourself a Chinaman, 'cause I know I seen this book she reading where this Chinese-American writer call hisself a Chinaman, and Delgadina got another book called *Chinamen*. If you look *Chinaman* up in the dictionary it be telling you to say Chinese man.

She looking all surprise when she see me come in there, the nun, like she ain't spied me 'cross the courtyard, and she even looking kinda like she think maybe I'm one of them knife-toting womens. I'm a stun gun–toting woman, I guess, but don't tote no knives, though I does like them Swiss knives, 'cause they always be having them newfangled Swiss knives at the trade shows and sometimes you can get you free Swiss knives at them trade shows. Wonder what sorta knife they use to hand-carve that door. I start to compliment her on that hand-carved door, like she done carved that hand-carved door herself. But maybe one of them Indian, one of them Native American, artisans done carved that door with one of them knives you see in them museums. She look out where they's childrens playing in the yard, like I said, and look up at that picture of the Pope she got on her wall, on the other wall across from the window, 'cause them wall of books is across the whole back wall, and another picture of a monk but one that look more like that Benito Juárez, who Delgadina want to be the daughter of, and another monk that look like that Pancho Villa, no not that Pancho Villa, that Sancho Panza in the storybook 'cause Don Quijote he supposed to be aristocratic but Sancho Panza he supposed to be the ordinary common man except Sancho Panza supposed to learn some aristocracy from Don Quijote and Don Quijote supposed to learn some ordinary mannishness from Sancho Panza and then she tell me this a mission school, like I don't know it. This a mission school, she say. I bet she even got some of the alchemy books amongst that wall of books. I be starting to ask her if there any alchemy books amongst that wall of books, 'cause I ain't never seen a real alchemy book.

This is a mission school, she repeat, like she talking to one of them elementary school childrens. And she straighten that hood she wearing, what they call a wimple. And she looking at me like she think I'm one of them elementary school childrens too, though like I told

you I'm one big woman. And she a kinda smallish one. She remind
me of one of them pilgrims in the storybook. Delgadina got a storybook from the Middle Ages with pilgrims in it, telling stories.

But ain't that kinda voice you mistake for anything but a woman's, though. Ain't one of them girlie voices some of them womens
has. Ain't one of them girlie voices, though she talking to me like
she talking to a girl. But she got one of them high-pitched voices, like
you could tune the upper keys of a piano with a voice like that.
Usedta have me a boyfriend a piano tuner—actually, he moved pianos but could tune them too. Hear people's voices like they keys on
a piano. A lot of them people they didn't mind him moving they pianos but didn't want him to tune they pianos. Like when Delgadina
she be studying Japanese, and I be listening to them recordings with
her, them Japanese women have them high-pitched voices like that,
and she be saying in Japan women have they own whole language,
and them womens they always uses more especially polite form of
the language than the Japanese men.

And then she give some fancy name for the school, the nun I mean.
I don't remember the name except it got plenty of saints in it. Maybe
them monks on the wall ain't just monks but saints too. 'Cept that
Sancho, he don't look like no Saint Sancho. Look a little too impish
to be a saint. No, not impish. Sly.

Yes, ma'am, I knows it a mission school, I says, then I realizes you
don't call nuns ma'ams. Yes, I know it's a mission school, I repeats.
That a real nice hand-carved door you got there.

I starts to ask her whether that monk is a saint too, but I don't.
Probably he the monk what founded this mission, 'cause they's
plenty of monks what founded missions, like them mendicant missions. Most saints, though, they says, begins as sinners.

Yes, ma'am, I know it a mission school.

Then she asks me whether I come there to apply for one of them
housekeeping jobs that they done advertised, and say that they already hired they housekeeper. I didn't come for no housekeeping
job, that's why I'm driving that truck, to get away from them housekeeping jobs. 'Cause every time they see me that's all they see me for
is to be they housekeeper. I don't tell her that, though. I got me a
girlfriend, housekeeper for one of them movie stars. Naw, ain't one

of them personal assistants, she a housekeeper. She the one try to entice me to come out there to California, to Hollywood. In fact that
the name of my piano-tuning boyfriend I told you about, my piano-
tuning boyfriend he name John Hollywood. John Henry Hollywood. Yeah, John Henry. And maybe even kinda look like the original John Henry. My girlfriend out in California telling me 'bout the
first time she seen a palm tree and the first time she seen a beach and
how at first she didn't know that woman she were working for were
a movie star 'cause she don't go to them movies as much as me and
Delgadina does. She don't know she a movie star, just think she one
of them socialite-type women till they at this movie studio and the
woman standing in front of the camera before she realize this a movie
star. When they first go in the studio she think maybe the woman
being a socialite and all maybe she own some stock in the studio or
maybe she the socialite friend of one of them movie stars 'cause a lot
of them movie stars got theyselves socialite friends, 'cause being a
movie star in the United States she say is kinda like royalty. The
people might be trash anywhere else but Hollywood. That her
word, ain't mine. I ain't tell y'all which movie star. She say that's
how come that movie star hire her, 'cause she ain't knowed that
movie star from Eve. And didn't come in there brownnosing her like
a lot of them other housekeepers she interviewed for the job. And she
didn't want none of them star-struck little girls, or none of them girls
fresh out of college can't get a job in their field so's they becomes the
housekeeper or secretary for some movie star, you know. Or none of
them ambitious little gals that wants to be movie stars they ownselves like in that movie *All About Eve*. She a bitch with other
people but she nice to my girlfriend. This is her talking. I think
that's on account of she insecure. A lot of these movie stars is inse-
curer than you'd think, Nadine. She call me Nadine. She likes to vacation in Scandinavia 'cause everybody there is blond, you know,
and so they treats her like a ordinary woman. 'Cause everybody
there is blond, you know, and good-looking by Hollywood standards. And it true, girl, 'cause more people turn they heads to look at
me when we's in Sweden and Denmark than they does at her. And
I'm thinking they supposed to be looking at her 'cause she supposed
to be this great beauty in Hollywood, but they's looking at me. And
I don't mean looking at me like they does in the States, but looking at

me like they thinks I'm gorgeous. Then the farther south we travels, down to the Mediterranean, the people turns their heads more to look at her and anything blond and looks at me like I'm just a common woman. In the Mediterranean, they considers the blondes the exotics, like in Japan. Except them Japanese knows who they own women are. They don't raise them blondes above their own women, like some other mens does. She supposed to make a movie in that Japan too. You oughta come to California and see the world.

Anyhow, the nun, she tug on her wimple. I said Naw I didn't come for no housekeeper job, and then I asks her if she know anything about the Sanctuary movement.

You know anything 'bout that Sanctuary movement?

She look at me a moment, look at me like she want to see my registration papers, or maybe my citizenship papers, even them border patrol don't look at me like I ain't no citizen, or like maybe I'm one of them sly, cunning and shifty-eyed citizens, but still a citizen, and then she lift her eyebrows, and then she put her fingers to her lips and then she write down the name of this priest and he address. She don't say whether or not he in the Sanctuary movement, she just write the priest name. And she sitting there with her finger to her jaw—she got them nice manicured hands; she ain't wear no makeup, though, but she look like she keep them hands manicured—and looking like she really is outta that seventeenth or eighteenth century, like this nun in this painting I seen once, and the sunlight from the window almost give her a halo like in them paintings by one of them Dutch masters or maybe one of them Spanish masters. And she don't ask me how come it's me asking about the Sanctuary movement or what concern that movement is of mines, but that how she looking. Her face got them strange proportions. She got that broad forehead, them inquisitive small eyes, kinda almond shaped, even inquisitive little nose, but full lips. They calls them Hapsburg lips when they's white people or Austrian lips. Seem like I read that somewhere. Most the nuns I seen in the movies and in them paintings always got them little thin lips. The odalisques and the voluptuous women got the full lips, but them nuns and the virtuous-type women got them little thin lips, 'cause I guess they associates them full lips with sensuality, which is the same as voluptuosity, but she got them full lips. Then her top lip it be sweating and she dabbing it with the inside of her sleeve. Talk-

ing 'bout strange bad women, she give me that look that want me to
know she a strange good woman. Or what the opposite of strange.
'Cause good women ain't supposed to be strange. Course in some of
them cultures they would probably think her a strange woman. And
she still looking like what concern the Sanctuary movement is of
mines.

But she do add, If you're really interested in the Sanctuary movement, this is the person to talk to.

And I starts to say I wouldn't be asking about the Sanctuary
movement if I wasn't really interested in the Sanctuary movement.
Like that professor in that class be asking Delgadina how come she
interested in the Middle Ages. I guess that New World, it be having
its own Middle Ages. She could study the Middle Ages in the New
World. Ain't have to study the Middle Ages in the Old World.

But I just thanks her and ma'ams her again and takes that piece of
paper, puts it in my shirt pocket and goes back to the truck. *Y'ain't
supposed to ma'am a nun, fool.*

But from the window I can see her talking on the telephone to
somebody and maybe it that priest. Maybe she warning that priest.
Be warning him about some spy or fool come asking about the Sanctuary movement. I watches the childrens play for a moment. Children, they be playing stickball and tag and airplane and whatever
childrens play. Cute as thunder all of them. Girls got them long
braids and boys them bowl-type haircuts. Maybe it that nun give
them that bowl-type haircut. Some of them childrens got them
Aztec faces, think that them Aztec faces. Seen that on that Columbus
show too. Them Aztec or them Mayan faces or them Olmec faces.
They talk about them Aztecs and Mayans and Olmecs like they's
just in the ancient world, but they's in the world today. And one little
girl she be wearing one of them colorful headdresses like them Mayans wear; they say them colorful headdresses supposed to tell their
lineage, almost like the colors in them headdresses a form of writing.
Lot of people when they think of them Mayan and Aztec and Olmecs, like I said, they think of the ancient world. But them Aztecs
and Mayans and Olmecs they's in the modern world too. Them Olmec faces they's almost look like my face. But they got that sweet
potato complexion. That yam complexion. They ain't playing that

Nintendo. 'Cept a couple of them kids sitting on the mission steps playing one of them board games—maybe Chinese checkers—or maybe them Mexicans and Native Americans got their own board games and maybe the real name of Chinese Checkers ain't checkers at all.

I'm itching to smoke me a cigarette, but I done give up tobacco. I'm allergic to that nicotine. I can still taste them jalapeño peppers, though. I wonder if you can dry them jalapeño peppers and smoke 'em. Delgadina say when she give up smoking tobacco, she smoke them herbal cigarettes made outta sage. Seen the recipe for 'em in some book. But that's still smoking.

And then she peeking at me out the office window, that nun, when I climbs into my truck. She peeking out the window and straightening her wimple. And then she comes to the door of the mission and calls all them children. I guess they's supposed to return to the classroom, 'cause it supposed to be a mission school. I grabs me my bottle water and swigs. It's that mineral water. Sposed to be that spring water from one of them springs like up at Saratoga Springs. But I seen a documentary on that bottle water too. Says that some of them is frauds, 'cause they fills up the water with that ordinary tap water and pretends that it pure, and a lot of fools buys it thinking it's pure water. I'm thinking 'bout California and that movie star. I know when I tells Delgadina 'bout this girlfriend and her being housekeeper of one of them movie star, Delgadina, she say, So-'n'-so? I kinda look like her don't I?

She do kinda look like her, 'cept her hair ain't blond. Me, I don't kinda look like none of them movie stars, not even them African Americans, not most of them leading women types, and wonder what it must be like when you's sitting in the audience and always be seeing people you kinda look like or even think you kinda look like. Well, in some of them African-American movies I spots womens that I kinda looks like, but then, they ain't playing the leading roles or what they call the love interest. Some of them is playing the girl-friend of the love interest. And sometimes the love interest is even playing white, you know what I mean, is playing the roles that's usu-ally played by the white women in the movies, and the dark-skinned girls they's playing the maid of the love interest, one of them light-skinned girls. Or the dark-skinned girl is the one that provides the comedy. I don't never resemble none of them womens that plays the love interest, white or African American.

Except once we come from this movie and Delgadina she says one of them characters reminds her of me. The movie is called *The Bear*, ain't no human movie, a movie from the bear's perspective, you know, and the human beings they's the outsiders, so Delgadina, she says, That bear reminds me of you, the way he stood up to that wildcat. You remember when that big drunken *gabacho* came in the bar and sat down at the bar and looked over and seen you sitting at the bar and say How come our cantina let a big nigger like you in the place.

Except Delgadina, she don't say nigger but the man he say nigger. And looking at me like I'm one of them bad nigger not one of them good one. Like he think that just gringas or Mexicans supposed to come in this cantina.

And you just give him that look, say Delgadina. You didn't even have to roar like the bear in the movie 'cause that look roared. Roar? That's what lions do. What do bears do? And then Miguel and Juanito brought you a beer on account of the way you stood up to that *gabacho*. Him, he was acting like it was his stage.

Say what?

She don't explain what she means, she just say, And then you give him that look and he left the bar and went and sat in the corner, that *gabacho*, and then I seen him trying to talk to Miguelita and then Miguel and Juanito bought you a drink. They're good *vatos*. But you remind me of that bear in that movie.

And then he be over there pestering Miguelita and be asking her what a nice white woman be doing in a greasers' bar and she be telling him she ain't a white woman, she a Mexican just looks like a white woman. They's plenty of white Mexicans that looks just like Miguelita, though most of them that frequents the bar is brown-skinned Mexicans. Then I hear her telling the fool I ain't a spliv I'm a Hawaiian, 'cause you know I told her that story I read about what that white woman call them Hawaiians. She just over there playing the fool or playing that *gabacho* for a fool.

I think she call them *vatos*, though, Delgadina. *Hola vato*. Yeah, I remember that from a Cheech movie. Miguel and Juanito, I mean.

Vatos or *gatos*. I think one of them from El Salvador and ain't Mexican, though. But if she call them good vatos, then to that man they must be bad *vatos*, eh?

I watches them children return to the classroom, except the nun she got to pull one of them little wayward boys by the ears, then I study my road map, backs the truck up, and pulls off in the direction of town.

CHAPTER 4

THIS TIME IT ME THE ONE SURPRISE 'CAUSE I'M
expecting a white priest and this a African-American priest.
Leastwise on television when they tells you about the Sanctuary
movement, they's always some white priest. Ain't even show no
Mexican priest. He look though like he maybe mixed with Mexican
or Native American or something, you know, the cosmic race, but he
hair kinky as mines. He got one of them broad forehead. They say
intelligent people got them broad forehead, though I don't think
people these days believe in that physiognomy as much as they used
to. Few people tries to classify people as primitive people based on
their physiognomy, but it ain't the same type of individual physiognomy where they study individual virtue or vice in physiognomy.
Like in one of them books I be reading in Delgadina's library, which
is what I call her bookshelf 'cause she got so many books on it, they
be saying where gap-toothed womens supposed to be lecherous, and
the gap-toothed womens I know ain't no more lecherous than any
other womens.

His complexion look like honey and gingerbread. He got them
kind of eyes look like them hieroglyphic eyes. I be sitting in this restaurant and hear this man trying to court this woman, be telling her

she got them hieroglyphic eyes, you know, like them Egyptians. You
got hieroglyphic eyes, he be saying, just trying to sweet-talk that
woman, but he look like the kinda man be telling every attractive
woman he meet she got hieroglyphic eyes. I guess them men they can
have them hieroglyphic eyes too, but I ain't about to tell no priest he
got hieroglyphic eyes or to try to sweet-talk him. I ain't no Catholic,
but he still a priest. Of course when I first seen my friend Delgadina
I be thinking she African American too, then she be telling me she
Mexican American, I mean, Chicana. She didn't just say she Chicana, but she be talking about Chicana and I realize she Chicana.
Maybe she ain't want me to think she African American so she start
talking about Chicana. You know signifying, 'cause she don't want
to come out and say, I ain't African American, if that's what you're
thinking. And I didn't think no African American be talking so
much Chicana, though Delgadina say she know this African-
American woman that specializes in Chicano literature and everybody be wondering why she ain't specialize in African-American
literature. Even Chicanos be wondering why she don't specialize in
African-American literature. Delgadina say she met her at one of
them conferences on Third World literature at the University of
Houston or one of them universities, and she was talking about Chicano plays. Even Delgadina say she be wondering why she so interested in Chicano literature and kinda suspicious of her. But she gave
a good lecture on Denise Chávez. I ain't ask her, Who Denise Chávez? Sound like the name of one of them labor organizers, though
she supposed to be a literary woman.

But like I said I'm expecting a white priest and this a African-
American priest. And he still looking at me suspicious like maybe he
think I'm one of them spies for the immigration department or them
border patrols.

Like I remember the first time I come to Texas City and I had me
this date with this fellow and I didn't know nothing 'bout no immigration, nothing, 'cause in the part of the country I'm from you don't
have you a large immigrant community, though there's a few Vietnamese and Spanish-speaking people, but they ain't enough of them
to be a threat to the so-called American values. We come in this
restaurant-cantina and I notice that a lot of the peoples they like
cleared out and remind me of them Western movie when the gun-

slinger come in or the sheriff, even them Clint Eastwood movies or that movie *Posse* I think that the name of it that Mario Van Peebles movie, and them gambler and bandit types clears out of the saloon, and even the gringa clears out, that Miguelita, and then later I mentions it to Delgadina, woman that work behind the bar, and she say he immigration department. The peoples they can smell that immigration department, she say, and me I ain't even ask him what he profession. We met at this trade show—actually he the one that pointed out the newfangledness of my newfangled flashlight. 'Cause I be standing up there saying this ain't got no battery, where you put the battery? I ain't talking especially to him but I'm asking out loud, This flashlight ain't got no battery, where you put the battery? The trade show in one of them huge armory-type buildings, you know, and I'm standing there looking at this flashlight and wondering out loud where you put the battery. I've heard of them flashlights got their own built-in generator and am thinking maybe it's one of them. He hear me talking to myself 'bout that flashlight and maybe he think I'm talking to him, or wants him to start talking to me, so he starts explaining to me about the newfangledness of that newfangled flashlight.

This a new solar-powered flashlight, he say. See, this is the solar cells, and shit like that. Now they got even newer-fangled flashlights that got they own built-in generators, like I said.

This solar-powered? I asks, picking up the flashlight, and he be explaining how it work, how the solar cells on it work, and showing me them solar cells kinda look like beehives, then he be saying how it space technology and the use of solar power in certain space vehicles that enable them to make that flashlight. The way he be talking about the space age I be thinking maybe he a rocket scientist. He a smaller-sized man compared to me but don't seem to be bothered by my height and size at all. You know, like some mens they be insecure about a woman taller than they is. He one of them wiry-type men, dressed casual in one of them windsuits and baseball caps, though he talk like a professional man, like a rocket scientist, and I be thinking maybe he a schoolteacher, maybe a science teacher, or a professional radio announcer. Say he from New Orleans, but couldn't get no job in New Orleans so he came west.

And he be kinda shaking my tree, you know. Just a little bit. I got me a pretty sturdy tree. But sometimes the mens can shake it, you know. And he of the attractive persuasion.

And then he talking 'bout that flashlight and solar power lead into him inviting me out to dinner—I thought he might invite me to a movie, but it's dinner—so I recommends this restaurant-cantina. 'Cause you know, I don't know the man from Adam though he right friendly, and they always advises you when you out on a date with somebody you don't know to date them in a public place, especially in the modern day and age, and most of the peoples I know in Texas City is in that restaurant-cantina. Turn out he a social worker not no immigration department, but them peoples they think immigration department. 'Cause the next date when we goes to see this movie I asks, You immigration department?

Why, are you an illegal alien? he jokes.

Naw, and then I tells him how the people in the restaurant-cantina clears out when he enters. Like in them cowboy movies in them saloons, even that Mario Van Peebles movie. I don't know if they got that stylized scene in that movie or not, though it seem like it in every cowboy movie. And he pretend like he ain't noticed it. Though he do say that he like Mexican food.

You know, like in them cowboys movies, I says. You know, them saloon scenes where the sheriff or even the outlaw come in and the peoples in the saloon clears out, except they's always one or two fools that confront the sheriff or the outlaw.

Naw, I'm a social worker, he say. A social psychologist actually. He says he works with a lot of Chicanos and Native Americans as well as African Americans. And then he go into detail about what a social psychologist is and shit and how he ain't a psychiatrist, and the difference between a psychologist and psychiatrist, 'cause a lot of people thinks he's a psychiatrist. Got his degree at one of them community colleges. And then he start defending the community college system and say how I oughta be more ambitious and return to college too, maybe one of them community colleges, 'cause the purpose of the community college is to educate the community. He be saying he ain't like some men that don't like ambitious womens. He likes ambitious womens. And to tell the truth he the first man I heard to say he likes ambitious womens, 'cause most of the men I know associates bitch with ambitious when it a woman. You know, they pronounces ambition so's you can hear the bitch in it, especially when they's talking to a woman.

I been to truck driving school, I says. It sorta like community college, I mean if community college supposed to educate the community. And I consider myself the community. I mean, I ain't the whole community, but you know what I mean.

He be telling me how aside from being that social psychologist he a amateur inventor, that's why he likes them trade shows, 'cause that one of his hobbies, inventions. Course I'm just a amateur inventor, a avocational inventor, and ain't attempted to put any of my inventions on the market. But I guess my profession is inventions too. How societies invent and reinvent themselves. And then he start telling me about this book called *The American Invention* or some shit, about how America itself supposed to be a invention. I heard that America supposed to be an experiment, but I didn't know it supposed to be a invention too. Say he working on a book his ownself about the sociology of identity and he have some theory of American identity he be trying to explain to me that he call the additive identity or want to apply the theory of additive identity to the social psychology of America but I ain't make hide nor hair of it. He say he also the author of a book on hospital racism and patients' rights abuse, which also another area of his expertise. He talk a little bit about that. From what he saying make it seem like when somebody go into a hospital, they's gotta have they lawyer, they own security force, maybe even they own private army to protect themselves from them medical men and women.

It's not just people of color, he says. But when racism and rights abuses converge . . . There's this group that sometimes sends in hospital spies. They pretend that they're patients and document their treatment or try to retrieve documents or copies of documents. That's usually after the abuses occur or complaints have been made, so the hospitals are on their guard. I consult with individuals on a wide range of areas where society, psychology, race, and politics converge.

You sound like Delgadina when she's talking human rights, I says. Some of them peoples sounds just plain crazy, though. I mean, they has positions of authority and pretends to be sane, but they sounds crazy they ownselves. It sound plain crazy, though. Naw it don't sound crazy. Miguelita crazy, and she ain't in no authority. What you talking about sound deeper than crazy. I believes you, though, 'cause they sounds just like them things Delgadina talks when she's talking human rights. It sounds just like human rights.

It's all human rights, he says. That's what it's all about, human rights.

He ain't immigration department he a social worker, I tells Delgadina. A social psychologist and a human rights advocate, 'cept he put everything in the category of human rights. I tells Delgadina how he didn't even seem to notice how the people in the cantina thought him immigration department, like in them Western movies. I mean, being a social psychologist. He say he ain't a psychologist for the individual person, he a psychologist for the whole society. He says he works with individuals, but he say that he really think of hisself as a psychologist for the whole society. And he says that America is a invention. I always thought it were just a experiment myself. And he writing a book on the sociology of identity and have also done some work in hospital racism and patients' rights abuses. I knows that they abuses mental patients all the time, like in the old Russia when they wanted to abuse people's rights they would pretend that they was locking them up for psychiatric reasons. He be telling me they does it here all the time. You know, when we were in here he be looking over at that Miguelita and be saying that she remind him of somebody that he were an expert witness for. He tell a story that sound something like *One Flew Over the Cuckoo's Nest,* you know that movie about them abuses to mental patients. He don't think she the same woman, though. He says he can tell me that story 'cause it in the public domain and ain't confidentiality. He be looking at her like he think she that woman. I knows he wants to go over and talk to her and see if she that woman but I knows if he do that the *vatos* be thinking she need to be rescued, you know, so I convinces him that that ain't her. Somebody named Tucker, though, he say her name, so it weren't us Miguelita, 'cause her name Miguelita Delgado. I ain't know her maiden name. But I just tell him her name Miguelita Delgado. I do ask Miguelita for myself whether her maiden name Tucker next time I'm in the cantina and she says, Sophie Tucker? So I knows she's crazy. But I ain't let him go over there 'cause them *vatos* too protective of Miguelita Delgado. He be telling

me a lot of stuff, a lot of different abuses he see in his profession.
'Cept he ain't a expert witness for the government types of people, he a expert witness for the individuals that is abused by the government and official types. The way he be describing them official
types, though, it be making me think of that movie we seen with
Denzel Washington where he playing the detective and be talking
about everybody peeing on his head and telling him it's rain. You
know that movie, *Devil in a Blue Dress*. About peeing on somebody's head and telling them it's rain. You is always telling me about
them human rights abuses yourself. I knows what you's saying but I
ain't always know what you's meaning.

You means they really does that? I asks him.

Yeah. I can't talk to you about the specific individuals. But that's
exactly the way it is.

So you ain't no social psychologist that works for no government?

No. I've testified in too many cases against them, so I wouldn't
get any government clearance anyway. I have a private consulting
company and I do work as an expert witness. I write books and I
work with individuals and do various kinds of research.

Just peeing on they head and telling them it's rain.

Say what?

So I tells him 'bout Denzel. And then he start talking to me about
Kafka, that the social psychologist book he working on now uses
Kafka as a metaphor for various essays that he's writing on social
psychology.

So you ain't like them regular-type social workers?

No. I have done that regular type of social work. Then I didn't
want to be part of the abuses, you know. The system. Then I started
becoming aware of a lot of official abuses, you know. I thought I
could work better with people on an individual basis, independent
of the government.

Delgadina she don't say nothing, she just look at me like she think
social worker or social psychologist or whatever and immigration
department they the same thing, even if he do claim to work independent of the government, that that just his way of trying to camouflage hisself. Plus she seem like she ain't like the interest he take in
Miguelita, though I be wondering what Miguelita got to do with

immigration. Even though I explains who he say he is, Delgadina still act like she suspicious of him.

I tries to tell Delgadina some of them other things that we's talked about and about him being a expert witness and about what seems like peeing on people's head and telling them it's rain, but she ain't act like she's interested or like I'm talking about ecology and environmentalism. 'Cept now even the civil rights peoples talks ecology and environmentalism now that they knows they's a connection with racism. They's even got they own environmental racism resources organization. So I don't talk to Delgadina about de facto coercion and none of that other stuff I were talking about with that social psychologist. I don't even give her none of them brochures he give me.

And them abuses is going on right in America. They's peeing on your head right here in America and telling you it's rain. Except when it's us own country, he say, the peoples just steps in line. Like when they was doing them medical experiments on them Tuskegee men. A lot of peoples remembers that. That them Herr Doktors over here in America ain't no different from them Herr Doktors over there in Germany, and a lot of them even wrote up they experiments in them medical journals, like it were monkeys they was experimenting on instead of men.

I orders me a Budweiser. Then I reads one of them menus that Delgadina got up at the bar. You can't order nothing that's on them menus; you's got to go inside the restaurant part of the bar to order, but Delgadina keeps them menus on the bar, so's to entice people to go into the restaurant and order something.

> German pancakes
> Prairie pancakes
> Mexican pancakes
> Oklahoma caviar
> Chocolate cheesecake
> Cilantro Chicken with Fettuccini

I ain't going to give you everything that's on them menu, except that Oklahoma caviar I don't think that that is real caviar. I be wondering, though, why somebody come in a Mexican restaurant and order German pancakes. And them Mexican pancakes is wheat tortillas 'cept some of them tourists buys more of them when they's referred to as Mexican pancakes rather than wheat tortillas. Then they's got a Mexican salad that's made with beans and corn and green beans and that cilantro. Some people that frequents the cantina ain't Mexicans or Chicanos, though, they's Native Peoples. And Delgadina knows all them by name. She knows them by name and she knows them by tribe. She can look at any Native American and tell you what tribe they is. Kiowa, Cheyenne, Arapaho, Comanche, Apache, Osage, Hopi, Zuni, Navajo, and she can even tell you if they is combinations of tribes. For example, if somebody a Kiowa Apache, she say, He a Kiowa Apache. I knows the Native Peoples from the Chicanos, except for the Native Peoples that looks like Chicanos, but I can't tell you the tribes of everybody. We's even got a Comanche Apache Arapaho Kiowa. There's one man that frequents the bar who say he a combination of Comanche, Kiowa, Kiowa-Apache, Osage, Cheyenne, and Apache Apache. He got this story about how his peoples—all them tribes—banded together to fight the white men before the Civil War. He say he originally from Wyoming, but he prefers South Texas. He say the only reason them white men made treaties with them Indians during the Civil War was so's it could free them to fight in the war. 'Cause them rangers and federal troops and soldiers and shit was fighting the Indians, so during Civil War the whites had to stop fighting the Indians and fight each other, so they made treaties with the Indians. Course the white claims it was the Indians that didn't honor them treaties, and the Indians I means the Native Peoples claims it was the whites. 'Cept I knows about all them treaties the whites ain't honored with Native Peoples, so I believes the Native Peoples claims myself. And he the one told me about Chief Nigger Horse. I thinks he signifying about me, you know.

I'm sitting there at the table with him, drinking my Budweiser, listening to his tales of white men and Native Peoples in the Southwest, when he say something about Chief Nigger Horse.

Say what?

That was the leader's name, an Indian leader in the Texas area. I ain't even remember what he said about Chief Nigger Horse, 'cause I just hear his name. Chief Nigger Horse.

I tells him that he can't just say that Native hero's name around just anybody.

Then he say a lot of glorified things about Chief Nigger Horse and say he can't change Chief Nigger Horse's name 'cause that his name. I would like to hear about Chief Nigger Horse and the white mens hunting him in West Texas and Fort Concho, Texas—I think he say something about Fort Concho, Texas, and a place called Hidden Canyon and a place called Buffalo Springs and about a small log cabin that he got in West Texas and about a town called Monterey that he call Ray Town, but seem like every time he say Chief Nigger Horse all I hears is Chief Nigger Horse. And even had me a dream about Chief Nigger Horse, 'cause it seem like some Native Peoples from West Texas has a movie or a documentary about they West Texas hero Chief Nigger Horse, but the West Texas Colored People's Association was picketing the movie on account of the *Nigger* in the chief's name, so the people wanted the movie to be renamed Chief Horse or Chief Colored Horse, 'cause this were a group of colored people that still referred to theyselves as colored, but the Native Peoples kept insisting that they couldn't change they chief's name 'cause that were his true name.

We don't mind you Native Peoples maintaining the true name of your great Native American hero, Chief Nigger Horse, and there is fools amongst us who is even pleased that he chose to use a adjective derived from who he supposed is us, otherwise he coulda called hisself Chief Honky Horse, and we don't believe that he hisself or his people that named him named him with evil intentions, says the president of the West Texas Colored People's Association, but it is just giving these old buffalo hunters, the white boys of West Texas, the excuse to say Nigger, why it even gives colored people, who have stopped saying Nigger in civil society, the excuse to say Nigger, why I have heard white boys who wouldn't dare say Nigger in my presence because they know I am the president of the West Texas Colored People's Association 'cause they know us West Texas Colored People ain't like them Other Colored People that ain't from West Texas. I's still got my great-grandpappy's Sharps buffalo gun and I knows how to use it, but even they feels free to say Nigger in my presence when talking about going to see the movie *Chief Nigger*

Horse at the West Texas Palace Theater, and a lot of them is going to see *Chief Nigger Horse*, not because they is so fond of Chief Nigger Horse, or even esteems him 'cause it were their own peoples that joined the hunt after Chief Nigger Horse was it into Hidden Canyon? I don't remember the exact history but it just gives these white boys the opportunity to say Nigger in civil society, even in the presence of them that ain't like them Other Colored People that ain't from West Texas. There is even them that says Chief Nigger Horse in my presence to try to signify that I am the Chief Nigger of the West Texas Colored People's Association rather than its president. We calls ourselves the Tenth Cavalry and the New Buffalo Soldiers, 'cept now we's an all-colored unit with no white officers, I'm the president, and I got a buffalo gun I uses. We might petition you Native Peoples, out of the esteem with which you are held in the Colored People's Communities Everywhere, there's even us who claims kin that ain't kin and wouldn't know a Kiowa Apache from a Navajo Apache, but if we hear any more of these white boys coming out of the Liquor Emporium talking about Chief Nigger Horse and his squaw, the one riding along with him on the Spanish mustang, at least in the movie, well, we ain't the colored people of your dreams, we's tough as a boot all hat and plenty of cattle do to run any river with big enough to hunt any bear and whatever else y'all white boys of West Texas likes to say about y'allselves.

Chief Nigger Horse, but not just Chief Nigger Horse, I travels all around Texas listening to stories about our leader. I mean, people know about Crazy Horse and Geronimo, our great leaders, but I also want to be able to tell people about, not just Chief Nigger Horse, but Lone Wolf and Stone Calf, White Shield, Big Bow, Tai-hai-ya-tai, Wild Horse, and Big Bow.

Them sounds like names.

What do you mean?

I tells him about meeting a woman named Leona Valdez, the first Native American I ever met, and how I be thinking she have one of them names like Wild Shield.

At first he looking like he know the name Leona Valdez, and then he looking like he don't know the name Leona Valdez, and then he looking like he pretending he don't know the name Leona Valdez. I'm thinking maybe they usedta be lovers in West Texas, or maybe

she even been to that small log cabin of his in the Hidden Canyon
or wherever.

You know Leona Valdez? I ask.

I know a Leonora Valdez, he say.

Maybe it Leonora and I'm thinking Leona, I says.

He wants to know when I met her and how. I explains to him I
met her when I was on my way to Albuquerque once and she were
on her way to the University of New Mexico. I explain that I don't
really know her. I tell him about her not wanting nobody to take
her photograph.

He looking like they's a story he wants to tell about hisself and
Leonora Valdez, but instead he tell me more about Chief Nigger
Horse. I gots to tell y'all that I ain't got that story from him about
hisself and Leonora Valdez, though I has heard about Peta Nocona
and Quanah and Quaker Indian agents and the Comancheros,
though I dreamt of them once, him and Leonora Valdez in a small
cabin in Hidden Canyon. They is together on pallets of buffalo
robes and they's making love. I ain't want to dream about them making love like that 'cause it make me seem like I'm one of them voy-
eurs, but that exactly what they was doing in that dream, 'cept he
were calling hisself Chief Nigger Horse and she were calling herself
Wild Shield. She mighta been calling herself the name of Chief
Nigger Horse's woman—I ain't going to say squaw—but I don't
know the true name of Chief Nigger Horse's woman. Chief Nigger
Horse Woman?

Then I'm sitting there drinking my Budweiser and seem like I'm
daydreaming, 'cause he start telling me about the symbolism of the
different colors that he wearing, except he ain't telling me and now
the drink he drinking that I thought were Mexican beer he telling
me is some kinda tea made from the bark of a tree.

The red shirt I'm wearing? he say. Red symbolizes war. It symbolizes my ongoing Spiritual Warfare with the white man.

He just say white man but he don't put white woman in it, but I
guess white man just a generic term that means white people in general, 'cept when I'm having that thought I remembers a book I seen
in Delgadina's library called *Sacred Revolt* and it say something
about how them Native Peoples at least the Native Peoples described in that book always treated them white women and chil-

drens differently, sometimes adopting them into they tribes. 'Cept what about the white women that is they enemies? 'Cause I remember reading this account by this white woman telling about her adoption which she called a abduction into the Native tribe and she sounded like they enemy. But he just say the word *white man* in my daydream, or what I think a daydream.

This white deerskin jacket I'm wearing symbolizes the potentiality for peace. But I consider peace only and always a potentiality, because I don't believe the white man will ever have peace with anyone, I mean any Native Peoples—when he say that Native Peoples it seem like he were including me and other nonwhite peoples and ain't just Native Americans—with peace on our own terms. Peace, maintaining our cultural integrity. Peace, maintaining our lands and the integrity of our lands. Peace, maintaining our own political autonomy. Peace, maintaining our own economic autonomy. Peace, maintaining our ownself hood. Peace, maintaining our own power.

He said a lot of peace maintaining things, but I just include them. Then he say he wear that white deerskin only for the potentiality of peace, 'cause he say he know who the white man is. That why he wear the red shirt. (I wears a red sweatshirt myself most the time, but I ain't know it symbolic of war. Course now I wears it for war knowing it for war, 'cause it got to do with my Spiritual Mother—but that a whole 'nother story.)

Red just for war? I asks.

Well, it can be a symbol for the Native Peoples as well, he say. Our collective Spiritual renewal, or it can be the symbol of war.

I always thought that white supposed to be a symbol for the spiritual.

Then he say the white feather he wear that look like it been dipped in brilliant red also a symbol for war. The white feather ain't dipped in brilliant red he say a symbol for peace. Then I sits there and drinks my Budweiser and looks at him. He got a broad, tan-colored face and high cheekbones and brilliant black eyes and a substantial nose that symmetrical and look kinda like a Roman nose.

What is your name? I ask.

Saturna. I'm named for my great-uncle. I only met him once, when we went east to Kentucky.

I starts to tell him that I'm from Kentucky, but he seem like he already know that.

We went to a little community near Warthumtown, Kentucky, out in the woods and met my great-uncle Saturna and his horse Chew Sue. He was an old, old man. When they had forced some of the Native Peoples off their lands west, the African-American communities in the area adopted him, or rather he adopted them, because he stayed pretty much independent in the woods around Warthumtown—I call it Warthumtown, but I heard some people also call it Wathamtown.

I starts to tell him that I know about a Saturna and his horse Chew Sue, but he seem like he already know that. 'Cept the ones I knows is ones in a book. The ones he know must be the real Saturna and his real horse Chew Sue.

An African American was supposed to have founded that town, but there were different peoples of color that also inhabited it, and some poor whites, and others whose race you couldn't determine. But I remember we went to my great-uncle's house in the woods. It was a small, square house with plaster walls. It was a perfectly square house with a chimney of red and white clay, a tile roof, an elaborate entry door that seemed to have ancient symbols of our people, inside a white deerskin rug, a buffalo rug, all the furniture made out of cypress. I remember that all the furniture looked symmetrical and had been designed and made by himself as was the house. His horse Chew Sue was an old, old horse that sometimes he tied to a cypress tree, other times he let roam free, other times he could even enter the house. I don't remember anything we talked about. We sat and drank a certain bark tea. I think I was taken there because they wanted me to meet the man whose name I have. Although in that area he was thought of as an ordinary man, except for the fact of being referred to as Saturna the Indian by the people in the area, in my family he is consider the symbol of resistance. Not from any warfare, but simply by refusing. He refused to come east. He came as far east as he wanted, until he found the land that he wanted, and the African American people of Kentucky that he wanted to stay among, the ones in the area of Warthumtown. He gave me a golden eagle and this.

He pointed to a eight-sided star made of some sort of fabric but the points of the star were painted to resemble feathers and each feather was dipped in bright red. He wore it where others might wear a bowtie.

He told me about his great-uncle making him sit upon the back of Chew Sue his horse like a kind of initiation. Chew Sue traveled with him into the forest and he didn't return until Chew Sue brought him back. In the woods he felt as if he were in a fantasy landscape, because it was so different from the deserts of the Southwest. But then while in that forest, sitting on Chew Sue, he found himself in the Chihuahua desert, then Chew Sue took him into the Chisos Mountains, then he was among the piñon trees of New Mexico, all places of the Southwest. He knew without being told that Saturna, although he had stayed in Kentucky near Warthumtown, had also traveled west with his people, that he had stayed in residence in Kentucky but could also travel west with his people, and view the West where his people were any time that he wanted, even though he stayed in Kentucky. Even though Saturna was an old, old man Saturna had lifted him onto Chew Sue when Chew Sue took him into the forest; when he returned he had climbed down from Chew Sue himself. He was the same-size boy but a different one. That was when Saturna gave him the golden eagle and the disk that he wore.

There are other things it seems as if he will tell me in the daydream, but then it seems I know them without being told. That he himself can enter the sacred spaces while still in the Chihuahua Desert and travel east or west or north or south, wherever his people are, and since he claims all the tribes for his people, he travels wherever they are. He doesn't have a tribe because he contains all the tribes and so cannot be admitted into just one. He knows Leonora Valdez because he knows all his peoples—he use the word *peoples* not *people*.

Is you a shaman? I asks, 'cause I's read about shamans.

I don't call myself a shaman. Some people call me one. I am a shaman for myself, a shaman without a tribe.

That's 'cause you's every tribe, I says.

Some people call me a knower. Some people call me a spirit talker, others a spirit listener. Then it seem like we's sitting there and I'm daydreaming about the Chihuahua Desert and we's watching birds

and he's telling me all about them birds of the Southwest, so I can't
see a bird in the Southwest and ain't know its name. He be showing me a group of birds and saying they is migrating up from Central America. He ain't tell me the name of them birds, but he tell
me the names of them others: orioles, sparrows, green-tailed towhee,
warbler. Then we's near a spring in the Chisos Mountains—we's in
some kinda mountains and I'm guessing they's the Chisos Mountains—and he shows me cactus and rock wrens. I be thinking the
cactus wrens oughta be in the Chihuahua Desert but they's in the
Chisos Mountains. He shows me hawks and falcons, a red-tailed
hawk and a prairie falcon, a golden eagle, some orchard orioles, some
red cardinals, a yellow chat, a mountain bluebird, a red flycatcher,
which is the same bright red as the shirt he's wearing, then we travels
into a canyon, which I says is Hidden Canyon, though I don't know
if it Hidden Canyon, and he shows me some canyon wrens, some
nighthawks, a lark, a brown towhee bird, a kingbird, a titmice
which he say a bird. We sits on one of them canyon boulders and a
stream appears. It's bank the color of the redlands of Arizona and he
dips in the bank and takes that red mud and paints my face with it,
and then we's back sitting in the cantina, and I touches my face,
'cause I thinks it's got that red mud on it, but it ain't. And he just
drinking his beer and behaving like we ain't been to the Chihuahua
Desert or the Chisos Mountains or even Hidden Canyon, and he just
sitting there telling me some more stories 'bout Chief Nigger Horse.

But it like when he say that Nigger in Chief Nigger Horse, it like
that word ain't got no power. Before when he said Chief Nigger
Horse, the Nigger in that Nigger Horse seem like it had so much
power to make me not hear none of the other things he were saying.
But now when he say that Nigger it seem like it ain't got no power in
that word, least no power over me in it. Or maybe he just be saying
that Nigger so many times.

Believe me, because I'm telling you the truth, he says. All I knows
is I'm sitting there drinking that beer and feeling like I's been resanctified. I says resanctified rather than sanctified 'cause of the Perfectability Baptist Church. When you first joins they church, you is
sanctified, but then there is times when you has to return to the
church to get resanctified. Since they ain't no Perfectability Baptist
Church in Texas City or anywhere in the Southwest I has to travel

East to get resanctified. 'Cept I'm sitting there drinking my Budweiser and feeling resanctified. Of course in true resanctification, you
ain't supposed to be drinking Budweiser, you's supposed to be
drinking some type of wine. Usually they has some type of sweet
wine, like Mogen David. I knows that there is them amongst y'all
that ain't going to believe me, even if I am telling y'all the truth, but
as soon as I has that thought 'bout needing sweet wine to become
truly resanctified, at least that being part of the Perfectability Baptist
Church resanctification tradition, I'm sipping on that Budweiser and
it's tasting like Mogen David Concord wine, then it start tasting like
Budweiser again. And Saturna just sitting there telling me 'bout
Chief Nigger Horse and Chief Nigger Horse's wife. Then he be
saying something about the other Saturna, be saying that he his
great-uncle, but he also think of him as his Spiritual Father. He say
he still go out near Warthumtown and visit with Saturna and Chew
Sue, though he ain't know if it Saturna and Chew Sue or Saturna and
Chew Sue's spirits, 'cause he say that they was old, old when he was
a little boy and were initiated by him into shamanhood. He ain't exactly explain it like that, but that the way I understands it. At first
his shoulder-length hair were on his shoulders, but now it in braids.
Then I'm in Brownsville at one of the tourism centers and a Native
American is walking around with a camera photographing all the
white people. He don't photograph no Mexicans or other colored
peoples, he just photographs the white people. Most of the white
peoples lets theyselves be photographed, 'cause it seem like to them
a novelty to have a Native American photographing them. Then I'm
sitting in the cantina again drinking Budweiser.

Remember the story of Chief Nigger Horse, he say.

Okay, I says, and sips some of the Mogen David–tasting Budweiser.

Remember the story of Chief Nigger Horse's wife, he say.

Okay, I says, and sips some of the Mogen David–tasting Budweiser.

Remember the story of Saturna's Resistance, he say.

Okay, I says, and sips some of the Mogen David–tasting Budweiser.

Remember the story of Chew Sue, he say.

Okay, I says, and sips some of the Mogen David–tasting Bud-weiser.

I think it kinda strange he be telling me to remember a horse's story, but I says Okay. Then I looks up and sees a truck that have got HORSES HORSES HORSES HORSES HORSES on it. It a sort of gray and white truck, and a African American is driving it. He got on a gray sweatshirt and a red baseball cap and he kinda remind me a little of my daddy, 'cept he ain't my daddy. He a kinda dark-complexioned man and first he kinda remind me of a picture of my daddy I seen when he were a soldier during the Second World War. A truly handsome young man in his soldier uniform and his hands with exactly the shape of my own, his long, tapered fingers, and then he look like my daddy as a elderly man. Looking like a combination of a African and a Mexican. And then he be dressed up and looking like he in the Mexican Revolution and then he be in the white apron he wear when he working in us restaurant, and then he be in the gray sweatshirt and red baseball cap and dark blue trousers and sitting behind the wheel of that truck—the truck is gray but the cab of the truck is white—that got HORSES HORSES HORSES HORSES HORSES on it. I ain't know if Chew Sue in that truck 'cause you can't see what horses in the truck, you has just got to believe that they is horses in that truck 'cause the truck say it got horses in it.

Then they is Africans and Mexicans and Native Americans crowding around that truck looking like they is admiring that truck. I remembers once when I first got my truck, and because of the novelty of a woman driving a truck, sometimes mens would come around to look at my truck and seem like they was admiring my truck, but that were only when I were a novelty. But they is all ad-miring the truck of the man that look like he my daddy and got hands in the same shape of my own. 'Cept they asks him questions about his truck that ain't nobody asked me about my own truck.

How does your truck make you feel?
How does it feel to be driving a truck like that?
How does your truck make you feel?
How does it feel to be driving a truck like that?
I ain't overhear what my daddy say to answer them questions, though I remember reading somewhere that some peoples likes

trucks 'cause it make them feel like they's riding high, others them trucks gives them visibility, others likes trucks just 'cause they's big, others 'cause they looks to have people admiring they trucks, and others has lots of other reasons for liking them big trucks. Then they's on one of them little roads in the Chisos Mountains—I be thinking that truck too big to be on one of them little dirt roads in the Chisos Mountains, but it ain't—and they's all following my daddy's—I be thinking he my daddy now although before I just be thinking he resemble my daddy, like a African-American man I seen once in a Mr. Goodwrench commercial on TV. I be knowing my daddy ain't on television be doing no Mr. Goodwrench commercial but it be looking just like him, be looking like him when he smiling at me, be looking like him when he want to tell me something of importance, be looking like him when he just say Sojourner Nadine— truck and it's just like in that Caribbean rap video where the people is following this big truck, 'cept the horse truck ain't as big as the truck in the video, plus the truck in the video have got lots of Caribbean peoples standing on the truck and it a open-air truck, and this truck have got HORSES on it but you has got to use your belief to believe that there is real horses in it and maybe even that it got Chew Sue in it. But these people, as they follows my daddy and his truck, is singing just like in the video. I think the peoples is named & Xstatic, I means the name of the Caribbean rap singers and they rap song is called "Big Truck."

I remember when I first heard that video I be in my truck sometimes and I just starts singing that song my ownself.

> Hold on to de big truck.
> Hold on to de big truck.
> Hold on to de big truck.
> Hold on to de big truck.
> Hold on to de big truck.

Then I be hearing us preacher saying, Reverend Wolf of the Perfectability Baptist Church of Memphis saying, I knows that some of y'all has got the spirit so deep, that y'all is drawing y'all strength and y'all spirit and y'all wisdom from a well so deep that y'all thinks that y'all is crazy. Every time I resanctifies people they thinks that they is crazy. Y'all ain't crazy, y'all is just resanctified. Then the peoples starts singing. I knows the people ain't supposed to be singing no rap song, but instead of singing 'bout de river or even de well so deep, dey's singing 'bout de big truck. Hold on to de big truck hold on to de big truck hold on to de big truck hold on to de big truck hold on to de big truck. Resanctify.

Then I'm sitting there in the cantina trying to remember something I learned about jazz. Something I heard in one of them documentaries or read somewhere. It ain't say that jazz is in a warfare with classical Western music, but it say that jazz is a music in conflict with classical Western music 'cause they is the opposite of each other in scales, intervals, and chords. They say that they is even jazz musicians that don't even use Western notation system anymore that that is just how much they considers they music in conflict with Western classical music and how much they wants to free they music from classical Western music. They's got they own scales, they own intervals, they own chords, and they don't need Western music to tell them of the intellectual complexity of they own music, nor do they judge the intellectual complexity of they own music by how much it resemble classical Western music. They might judge the intellectual complexity of everything else, even they language, by how much it resemble the Western traditions, but that ain't how they judges they music.

I know I read it somewhere, about that jazz music, 'cause if I heard it I be remembering all of it, so I musta read it somewhere. Be saying every jazz musician is a composer 'cause that what jazz is. Them classical musicians they's got to interpret the music, they has got to interpret the music the way them classical composers have wrote that music for them to interpret it. But them jazz musicians they composes it as they plays it. They might all be playing "Chitlins con Carne" but they gets to compose it for theyselves. I be wondering if it be possible to tell a true jazz story, where the peoples that listens can just enter the story and start telling it and adding things wherever they wants. The story would provide the jazz foundation, the subject, but they be improvising around that subject or them subjects and be composing they own jazz story. If it be a book, they be reading it and start telling it theyselves whiles they's reading. For example, if they gets to a part of the book where I talks about my daddy, say if I was the storyteller, then they ain't just have to read about my daddy, they can start talking about they own daddy or other people daddy or even they Spiritual Daddy or if I be talking about my real mama or my Spiritual Mama, if I be the storyteller my-self of such a novel, they could start talking about they own real ma-mas and they Spiritual Mamas and maybe they own mama and they Spiritual Mama is the same mama or anyplace in the novel they wants to integrate they own story or the stories of the peoples they knows, so they be reading and composing for theyselves, and writing in the margins and ain't just have to write in the margins, 'cause I ain't wanting my listeners to just be reserved to the margins, but they writing between the lines, and even between the words, and be add-ing they own adjectives here and there, and if I ain't described some-thing they wants described, they be describing it they ownselves, and be composers they ownself. And they ain't even have to read the novel word for word 'cause they be as much creators of the word theyselves. And they ain't even have to name the peoples same as I names them. Maybe they's got they own names for the people. Like maybe I have a character name Nadine like myself and they be say-ing Nadine that ain't the proper name for that woman. And they be saying us want to name her something other than Nadine. Course I ain't want nobody to just name me who they wants, even if I were a character in a novel. But some peoples is like that. They names you who they wants anyway. I ain't know if I wants them peoples to be changing names, though they can compose around the themes, but they could still bring they own multiple perspectives everywhere in that novel, and they own freedom.

Then I'm still drinking that Budweiser and trying to remem-ber something that Delgadina said. We were looking at something on television, I think BET or a talk show, and somebody was talk-ing about the growing popularity of African-American literature amongst white readers, and then Delgadina starts saying something about because they have figured out now that they can put African-American literature into the category of Entertainment. That before writing books was considered a European intellectual achievement and just mostly white people could read and write or during slavery when it was criminal for blacks to even know how to read or write. So then she's saying something about only those types of books that whites can put into the category of entertainment are popular, novels, autobiographical writings, popular essays, mostly about race or white man done us (or me, for those writing from a personal rather than a collective ethos) wrong scenarios, poetry, but that ain't the same as building an intellectual literary tradition. Plus, now the white man considers the sciences and technology the intellectual arena so it's okay to be a little more generous about literature, that is a certain type of literature that don't provide no intellectual competition.

I figure when they figure how to commercialize Chicano literature and put us into the category of Entertainment, we'll get some popularity. Well, there are some publishers who are publishing more Chicano-oriented books and books in Spanish, but that's mostly because of the numbers of Chicano readers. We aren't as popular as African-American writers with white readers, though. And mostly we're published by little publishers, like E. D. Santos.

I know that that is true 'cause I remember that us school went to this big auditorium at one of the white schools and we gave readings and Monkey Bread—she's the one I told y'all about who works for the movie star in Hollywood—read a little poem that she wrote, 'cause she were considered to be the best by us English teacher. Myself I thought it were the best little poem amongst the peoples that read including the white students from the white schools. Monkey Bread didn't get the prize, though, but I remember that one of the judges at the table that were all white—they allowed the black schools to enter students in the contest but not to be among the judges. They got to judge the students before they come to what was considered the real contest. I mean, all the little colored schools got to judge the students from their own schools, but then when it came to the real contest, there were only white judges. But the white judge says to Monkey Bread that she a good entertainer and although Monkey Bread didn't claim the prize for being the best poet, she claimed the prize for being the best entertainer, and that wasn't even supposed to be a legitimate prize, even in the real contest, but because Monkey Bread was in the contest and her poetry was so legitimately good that they had to acknowledge the goodness of her little poem, and even though they didn't give her any of the real literary prizes, they created a special category of prize for Monkey Bread that they called the Best Entertainment Little Poetry Prize. And

there is still colored children in the area that they gives the Best Entertainment Little Poetry Prize but not the Best Poetry Prize or even
the Best Little Poetry Prize. I remembers that before when all the
prizewinners were getting their pictures taken and Monkey Bread
was the only little colored child in the group, I overheard someone
say, You ought to hear her. She's a good little entertainer. She gives
a good little performance. And I thinks that now they even allows students—not just colored students—to enter the new category
called Entertainment Poetry, as if it were a whole new genre. (Some
people will say that Monkey Bread invented that genre because of
her protests; I don't remember Monkey Bread protesting; nor was
the little poem she read a protest poem.) Anyway, the judges, they
calls the new genre Entertainment Poetry 'cause they ain't want to
call it Colored People's Poetry, and it wasn't Protest Poetry.

It is only colored people's childrens that wins the prize in that category, though. I ain't known them to win in any other categories,
even though the school ain't as segregated. When they seemed like
one of the colored people's childrens was going to win in one of them
other categories, them people invented yet other genres—the Best
Entertainment Lyric Poem, the Best Entertainment Haiku, the Best
Entertainment Narrative Poem, the Best Entertainment Sonnet,
even the Best Entertainment Free Verse. They retains the epic and
have decided not to create a category called the Best Entertainment
Epic. Even now when I hears of people of color winning literary
prizes, even on television, and not some little auditorium in Covington, Kentucky, I wonders if they is only the Best Entertainment Little Literature Prize, only the white judges that distributes most of the
prizes is more subtle than when Monkey Bread won her Best Little
Entertainment Poetry Prize, 'cause at least they told the colored girl
the truth. (Monkey Bread likes to tell people, when showing them
her poetry prize, the confabulatory lie that the *Little* in the name of
her prize is named for Malcolm Little before he become Malcolm X.
Even though there ain't no chronological logic in that confabulatory
story about the origins of her little poetry prize, there is peoples that
believes it. There are even those who credit Monkey Bread with being the first colored people's child in Covington, Kentucky, to write
a protest poem. But I'm here to tell you that the poem she wrote was
not a protest poem at all, but was even of the dubious title of "Why

I Likes Little Black Sambo." Needless to say, it was a substitution poem and not the poem that the English teacher had originally approved of to be read before the white judges. The poem that the colored school approved for reading was called "Chicken Soup with Garlic":

> My mama makes the best chicken soup with garlic
> And the bestest sweet potato pie
> Would I lie?

Of course there was a bit of controversy about whether she should use *best* or *bestest*; they decided because she was a child she could use *bestest*, because didn't even the children characters in Mark Twain use *bestest*; they were sure that the white judges would realize that the colored children were taught better English and that *bestest* was there because it was the best word for the little poem. They wished that their colored children would write longer poems with longer lines, though, because they were sure that the white children writing for that contest had written longer poems with longer lines. Monkey Bread said she liked writing poetry that the audience had to answer. In the colored school whenever she read that poem, the colored students would answer Yes, but once when a white superintendent was visiting, and Monkey Bread was sent to the front of the class to read her poetry, they answered No, because they didn't want the white superintendent to doubt the credibility of colored people. None of the children actually expressed that formally, nor had our teacher told them to say No, but I just think that they instinctively knew to say No in front of a white person. I was the only person to say Yes and the other colored children looked at me, so I changed my Yes to No. But the truth was I had tasted both Monkey Bread's mama's chicken soup with garlic and her sweet potato pie, and though they is good, I can't truthfully say they is the bestest. Plus, when I thinks about that poem I thinks why it ain't consistent, 'cause she do use *best* in the poem's first line, so how come she ain't use *best* in the poem's other line, or use bestest in both lines of the poem. And sometimes when Monkey Bread would quote that poem to peoples she would change other different words in it. Sometimes she say "My mama she make the best chicken soup with garlic" instead of "My mama makes"; other times she say "My mama make"; other times the poem say "the bestest chicken soup" but "the best sweet potato pie." And I be thinking that ain't like no poetry I've heard, 'cause all them other poems if them poet say it one thing, they's got to read it as that thing and say all the words as they is in the original poem, I mean unless they revises the poem. But I remember when Monkey Bread would read that poem, she would have it written the way I told y'all it is, but she would change the language in it just like I says, 'cept she would consider it to be the same poem. And garlic don't even have to be garlic in her poetry, 'cause in some of her versions of that poem the garlic is chives.)

That Native American with all them Indian tribes in him, I would dream about him again, years later, when I was in Cuba, New Mexico. I ain't know if it a daydream or a dream. He would come to me playing his wooden flute, one of them wooden flutes that some Native Peoples plays they music on. He be playing traditional music on that flute, then I go with him to what look like some type of fantasy landscape—I knows about them fantasy landscapes. I thinks it be the Chisos Mountains, but it some type of fantasy mountains. It be dawn in them fantasy mountains; it be in the Southwest, and he show me this steel horse riding. He call it the steel horse, I think 'cause it the color of steel. I ain't say it a horse made of steel, but he call it the steel horse and it just be riding, it seem like it be riding all over the nation and all over the world. It ain't got nobody riding that horse. This horse be leading itself. It be riding in real landscapes all over America and the world. It be dawn on that fantasy mountain. And Saturna, he be playing that flute and be calling that the steel horse, or he say Steel Horse, and it be riding everywhere. I ain't say it a wild horse 'cause it be a self-disciplined horse, but it discipline it ownself. It be dawn on that fantasy mountaintop, but it be like we is inside a sacred space and time watching Steel Horse ride and the music he be playing be sounding like that Steel Horse galloping everywhere. Watching that Steel Horse galloping I be thinking about Revelations first and then Revolutions. And then I'm in a room he call the Wisdom Room and I'm reading from a book he call *The Wisdom Book*. I ain't just reads it silently, I reads it aloud.

What's the name of your social psychiatrist? Delgadina asks. Or social psychologist? Is he a psychiatrist or a psychologist?

I's sitting up at the bar, like I said, though I's thinking about Sa-

turna (once I did ask Delgadina whether he a shaman, that Saturna
that sometimes come to the cantina one always wear that red shirt
and white deerskin, and she say she don't know, but she do know the
Hoyas who is his family—his name Saturna Hoya—and they is all
strange types so they could be shamans or he could be a shaman, but
they don't belong to any tribe; some of them make sculptures out of
copper, iron, and silver in the shapes of bears, foxes, deer, beaver,
panthers, even ground squirrels and other kinds of animals), drinking Budweiser, and looking at that menu and wondering who comes
into a Mexican restaurant and orders German pancakes. I'm thinking about that cantina in the Cheech movie and wondering if they
serve German pancakes. Then I'm thinking 'bout the Cheech cantina got a pool table in the cantina, and also got musicians in the cantina. I be wanting to ask Delgadina 'bout the archetypal cantina, but
us talking about the psychiatrist or psychologist. I know they's a cantina named El Turko's, 'cause people say the owner look more like a
Turk than a Mexican, where they's got them pool tables and's got
them musicians that calls theyselves Bigotes, which is they names
'cause they's all got theyselves whiskers. They's also a cantina that
call itself California Gold Rush, but it more a cowboy-type saloon
than a cantina. They's also a cantina called Comancheros named after them Mexican bandits, 'cept Delgadina say they wasn't bandits,
they was merchants, it's just that they was merchants that traded with
the Native Peoples, the Comanches, that's how they got they names
Comancheros, so the whites would call them bandits. But I remember all them cowboy movies that ain't got Native Peoples in them,
they's got them Comancheros selling rifles and whiskey to the Native Peoples. Thing about that history, it depend on who tell the
history whether somebody a bandit or a merchant. I knows a lot
of white merchants is bandits, but they gets to call theyselves merchants. This cantina got a mural. I be thinking they be a Texas or
Mexican scene with cactus, but somebody painted musk-ox, elk,
and brown bear. I guess they's some cactus for scenery.

I think he a psychiatrist and a psychologist. 'Cause he ambitious.
I think he both, I say, talking about that psychiatrist or psychologist.

I tells her his name. She look like she interested in that name more
than whether he a psychiatrist or a psychologist. I goes to the bathroom and when I comes back, she writing in her notebook. I told

y'all she always writing in her notebook. Then a *vato* come in and she serves him a drink, then she come back to the bar and writes in her notebook.

You didn't tell him nothing about Miguelita, did you? she asks.

Naw, just that she Mr. Delgado's wife. I didn't want him going over there bothering her, 'cause she crazy, and then I knows how these *vatos* like to protect her, and them thinking he immigration and shit, I don't know what they be doing seeing him talking to Miguelita. He mighta been a expert witness for her like he say, 'cause I know she crazier than shit. She need somebody to expert witness for her. I couldn't be no expert witness for nobody myself, 'cause you don't know the monkeys from the men.

Say what?

That just a expression they uses in the Perfectability Baptist Church. I ain't know why they uses that expression, since they believes that people is perfectable. But maybe they means that although they believes that people is perfectable, it don't mean that they is knowable.

Is that your church? ask Delgadina.

Well, I tells peoples it's mine. And I does believe in perfectability. Though I ain't sure if Perfectability baptism is superior to traditional baptism. And I didn't get Perfectability as a child. As a child I were a traditional Baptist. I didn't become a Perfectability Baptist till I become a adult. They don't allow no womens to preach. The reverend, though, say that if they did allow womens to preach that I am the long and preachy type of womens that they might allow. He says that us womens can preach as much as we wants and become as perfectable as we wants, they just ain't going to allow us in no pulpit.

I wanted to become a nun, said Delgadina. But what I really wanted to be was a priestess.

I don't say nothing. I sips my Budweiser, then I thinks about them thinking that social psychiatrist immigration.

I never heard that expression monkeys and men, though, say Delgadina. Then she be saying something about her Catholic priest not being so colorful in his metaphors as Baptist preachers; she says her Catholic priest tends more towards intellectual abstractions than metaphors. I went to Catholic school and was taught by nuns. I still sometimes visit a nun who was one of my teachers. I used to think that I would become a nun, like I said, then, I knew it wasn't a nun I wanted to be but a priestess. I told the nun who used to be my teacher and she says it's only, you know, because I wanted to have power in the church, and I didn't think that nuns had any real power in a mas-culine church. Then she starts talking about the difference between worldly power and spiritual powers, that the lowliest nun can have spiritual powers. Then she say that expression again about monkeys and men, then she write something in her notebook.

At least to anybody in that cantina they the same thing, I don't mean monkeys and men, I mean, social worker, social psychiatrist and immigration department. I don't know if them social workers is spies for the immigration department, though, even them that claims they's independent social workers. And Delgadina look like some-body them immigration be spying on. The blouse she wearing got one of them mandarin collars she got in a thrift shop. She got them thick eyebrows that always look like she comb them up, but she be saying her eyebrows seem like they grow that way. She say when she a little girl, though, she be having them real delicate eyebrows. I give her one of them patients' rights brochure and she stick it in the pocket of her skirt. She fixing somebody one of them margaritas and her specialty is margaritas with mandarin oranges. You know, they even got salsa made with them mandarin oranges.

But I also wanted to be a lady rancher, said Delgadina. I remem-ber once when we left Houston and went to this ranch, I was a little girl, and saw this lady rancher, she was a gringa, though, but then I dreamt of owning my own ranch, not some little apartment in a place like Texas City. I'd have my own ranch, my own Spanish mustangs, saddle horses, cow ponies, wild stallions, mixed breed, all kinds of horses, Longhorn cattle. She was a gringa that owned that ranch and I didn't know why we went out there to that gringa's ranch, except maybe my father was looking for work there or something, but I remember liking that ranch better than the city of Houston. Most of the men that worked on that ranch weren't family-type men like my father. They was mostly single men that worked for her taming horses and taking care of the Longhorn cattle and mending fences, you know. We had this Ford automobile. My daddy went up and talked to the lady rancher and then came back and got in the Ford automobile and drove us all back to Houston. I don't know why we

ever went to that ranch. And she didn't even have a typical ranch
style house, she had one of them ornate type of styles of architecture,
you know. I was used to them dog-trot houses in Houston, well,
they've got classical houses in Houston, but when you see your first
really ornate architecture, every other type of house is, well I won't
call people's houses dog-trot houses, but that was the first time I saw
a house with all these gables and spindlework and different colors
and textures and painted siding and patterned shingles and chim-
neys and porches and bay windows.

That sounds like you's describing a plantation, I says.

Does it? Well, it was a ranch. Except for the house. But it was a
working ranch, though, so maybe my daddy was trying to get a job
on that ranch, and then she saw all his family with him and explained that she didn't hire family-type men. I don't know if that's
why we went there at all, that's just what I imagine. All I know is
Daddy drove us to that ranch in his Ford automobile, went and
talked to that lady rancher, and then drove us back to Houston. So
for a while I wanted to be a lady rancher. And the thing about those
ranches, Nadine, a lot of those ranches you've got everything on
those ranches. A lot of those ranches have got their own stores, their
own barber shops, their own stables, well, of course they've got their
own stables, and women that work on them that do nothing but the
laundry. Men have to go into town if they want liquor though, 'cause
you can't buy liquor on those ranches, at least the one I worked on
in the laundry. The one I worked on didn't have a lady rancher,
though. But I'm not going to tell you that story. Well, there was this
group of Comanches, you know, they sorta reminded me of the wandering bands of Comanches that you read about, except these are
modern Comanches, you know. I'd formed allegiances among them.
I wasn't lovers with any of them, I'd just formed allegiances. I had
more friendships among them than with any of the women on the
ranch, and so people started rumors about me. I don't know if it was
one of the other women who worked in the laundry, or the ranch
owner's wife. I had this idea that I'd work in the laundry, doing the
women's work, you know, but at the same time to learn all about
ranches and about the horses, and these Comanches they knew more
about ranching and horse breeding than anybody else on the ranch.
I liked them the best as people, but they were also the best ones on

that ranch for me to learn from. But I guess the other women on the ranch just saw me as a woman, you know, I mean you know what I'm talking about, I am a woman, but as a woman I wasn't supposed to be spending all of my time with these Comanches, and at first even they weren't convinced of me until we started developing friend-ships, you know, allegiances. I hadn't told anyone my real age either, I pretended I was older than I was. That was before I went east, so I was still a teenager, but they thought I was in my twenties, maybe my early twenties, 'cause I always looked and acted older than my age, I mean I looked my age, but I was the sort that could tell people I was older than my age, and they'd believe me, they'd just say you look young for your age. The Comanches knew my age, so none of them took advantage of me, they didn't make a Lolita out of me or anything, you know. But then the rancher's wife told me if I was to stay on the ranch, I couldn't keep my allegiances with the Coman-ches. She didn't express it like that, because she thought that they had made a Lolita of me. So I decided not to stay on the ranch, be-cause I wouldn't give up my allegiances with the Comanches. I didn't learn all about ranching that I wanted to learn, but I do know how to ride a wild Spanish mustang. Not any wild Spanish mus-tang. But they had this wild Spanish mustang on the ranch, and it wouldn't allow anybody to ride it but the Comanches or me. The white men or women couldn't get on that mustang. No one but the Comanches or me. And there's Comanches that said that horse could understand human language. It didn't talk human language, but it understood human language, except it only understood Comanche. If you said something to it in Comanche, it knew what you were say-ing. Maybe it knew what you would say to it in English, but it would only acknowledge Comanche. I don't know if it was true or not, but I'd see some of them Comanches talking to that horse and he'd nod sometimes and shake his head other times, and when those Coman-ches wasn't sure if that horse would let me ride it they talked to that horse and he let me ride. Maybe those Comanches talked to that horse and told it not to let any white people ride it, or maybe that horse decide who it would let ride for itself. I remember once them Comanches teased me with that horse. They brought that horse over to me and said something to the horse in Comanche and the horse nodded and the Comanches laughed. They said something else about me to that horse in Comanche, the horse shook its head and the Comanches laughed. I didn't know what they was asking that horse, but then later they explained to me that that was their initiation with Comanches that came to work there. I wasn't a Comanche, but they would ask things like, Is he as dumb as he looks? and the horse would nod yes, things like that, as a kind of joke among themselves. So they were asking the horse those kinds of questions about me. 'Cept I didn't know none of their Comanche. Didn't none of them try to Lolita me, though. And we had an allegiance. There were others that tried to Lolita me when I was on that ranch, but it wasn't the Comanches. 'Cept the ones that tried to Lolita me didn't know my age. That wild Spanish mustang came to my rescue when one of them was trying to Lolita me, and that's when the rumors started. They kept the wild mustang on the ranch, though. 'Cause of them Comanches. And they was supposed to have the best horses on that ranch, on account of that Comanche knowledge. You know, the Comanche knowledge of horses.

What the name of that horse? I asks.

What you mean what the name of that horse?

You know, like horses got names. Copper Bottom, Harry Bluff, Big Nance, Tomoleon, Sir Archy?

Uh, I don't know the name of the horse. Uh, yeah, I remember, because I thought they were talking to the horse, even when they were saying his name. I mean, they were saying his name, but it sounded like talk. Tai-hai-ya-tai. I don't think it's Comanche. It might be Comanche. But that's what they named that horse. Before they said anything to it, they'd say Tai-hai-ya-tai. I remember that there was one woman there, one woman that the Comanches respected. I won't say that they respected me, because they knew my age. She was not the rancher's wife, but it was the woman who wrote the names of people who came to work there. Otherwise she kept to herself and seemed sort of a hermit. But when new people came to work, she sat at this table, and she did this when I came to work there. She asked merely this question: What is your name, or what is the name you want to give? That was the only question she ever asked and the only thing she ever said to anyone. I remember that, because I had never been asked that by anyone. I am told that among certain guerrilla groups that is the question they ask everyone. But I'd never been asked that question. Anyone who asked me my name always asked me my name to learn my true name. But to have some-one tell me that I had the choice of telling them my true name or only the name I wanted to give.

What name did you give? I asked.

My true name. But besides the Comanches and the wild Spanish mustang, I most remember being asked the question of my name. She did not join the other women in making me leave that ranch. . . . Well, first the ranch owner's wife gave me a little envelope with the moneys that were owed me, and when I wanted to see the ledger with the amount of the moneys that were owed me, we went up to the table and the woman handed her a ledger which said the amount of the moneys that were owed me. I thought the ledger would con-firm the amount that the ranch owner gave me, but instead, it made her have to give me additional money. The woman at the table her-self said nothing, for she was asking new hired people questions.

What is your name? asked the woman when the ranch owner's wife was standing near the table. Or the name you wish to give, she added, when the ranch owner's wife was out of hearing, or was at a distance where she could pretend not to hear.

We just date each other for a little while, though, me and this so-cial worker psychiatrist psychologist, and I never did get to see any of his amateur inventions or understand his theory of the sociology of identity. He ain't invited me to his apartment like some mens do. They invites you to they apartments and even cooks meals for womens. Usually we eats out or goes to the movies or dances, 'cept he talks, even though he looks like he'd be a good dancer. He talk to me about them different kinds of human rights abuses, 'cause he preoccupied with his profession, at least in his conversations with me, and he talk about how the people disguises they human rights abuses under different disguises. He don't act like he trying to recruit me to join no organization, though. Then seem like everything he say to me, I be using the same expression, Just peeing on your head an' telling you it's rain. I be explaining that that from the *Devil in a Blue Dress*. Or I be saying, You can't tell monkeys from men. I be explaining that that from the Perfectability Baptists. Or I be saying some kinda proverb or expression like that. Some of them proverbs I ain't know they origin, though. Or I be saying, You is right to become your own independent man. That ain't no proverb, though.

Sometimes we would even go to them trade shows together, 'cause we has got the same addiction. He say whenever he ain't being a expert witness or a consultant in social psychiatry or working on his research in social identity that he likes to go to them trade shows. Or if he ain't doing that he working on his own inventions. Reason we stopped dating, though, 'cause he be start telling me how I shouldn't be driving no truck and shit like that. I lets him ride up in the cab of my truck when we goes to one of them trade shows, and I even tells him that he the first person I have allowed to ride in the cab of my truck. I be thinking he going to say something good about that, but then he say, You know, Nadine, I don't think you oughta be driving a truck. He be telling me I'm a remarkable woman. He be telling me how he like my personality. And about how I should be more ambitious and shit. Whenever a man be telling a woman she should be more ambitious, for some reason, I always hears the *bitch* in that word, like I said. You shouldn't be driving no truck, he be saying. You should be more ambitious.

We was riding in the cab of my truck coming back from a trade show near Galveston. You know I thought I had found somebody to go to them trade shows with. And he a intelligent man that know more about them trade shows than the trade show people theyselves. And know more about them trade shows than me myself. I'm a ignorant woman in a lot of things, but I knows about them trade shows and I knows about driving my truck.

I guess for him the idea be for me to be a secretary or a schoolteacher or maybe work in a bank, pushing them papers. Course I gots to work with different kinds of invoices, you know. I knows about them invoices and I knows how to entrepreneur. But he don't consider that as ambition. And he say he ain't like a lot of men that tries to sabotage ambitious women.

I'm not trying to sabotage you, Nadine, he say. I tells him to reach into my glove compartment and get me some of my beef jerky. He get some forme and some for hisself. 'Cause there's a lot of men, he says, chewing on that beef jerky, that don't like ambitious women. But he ain't one of them type of men. Least at first he talk about that

ambition. About how he likes ambitious women and especially ambitious African-American women. And then he be saying that don't
none of us need to be acting like that Madonna to show usselves ambitious, that we can be civilized and decent women and still be ambitious. He say Madonna can be wild, but in a African-American
woman that kinda wildness is just thought barbarous and just con-
firms the stereotype.

That's what I like about you, Nadine, he saying, chewing that
beef jerky. You're a decent woman, and you're ambitious to learn.

I hope I ain't the biggest bitch you know.

Say what? he asks, chewing that beef jerky.

When peoples say ambition I always hears the word *bitch*. Then
I thinking about Delgadina. She say when she was going to school in
Houston that she was in love with this boy, this young man, this
vato, and somebody went and told him that she was in love with
him, you know, so this *vato* says, Delgadina? I wouldn't be going
with Delgadina. She's the biggest bitch in the school. And she said
there was also a group of people in the school who usedta call her
agringada, you know, 'cause sometimes she likes to talk like a gringa,
you know, their idea of a gringa, when she wants people to know
how intelligent she is and not to treat her like no hoochie woman. So
whenever anybody says ambitious I think bitch. You know Delgadina, the bartender at the cantina where us had our first date.

He looking like he trying to remember who Delgadina, then he
nod, then he look like he thinking he thought she were a hoochie
woman, then he say how the African-American woman have got to
tread proudly in the universe, and that people can't identify freedom
with license or decadence. I ain't know whether he say that 'cause he
think Delgadina a licentious-type woman and he ain't want me to
pattern myself on Delgadina.

Freedom is responsibility, he say.

I ain't dispute that, I say. You's right. I know I's got to be more
responsible.

Freedom ain't just responsibility for yourself. You've gotta be responsible to and for others too. Especially our people. You remember
that old song "Respect Yourself." When we respect ourselves we're
respecting each other as well.

I ain't dispute that.

Then he tells me some more of them abuse stories and each time he tell one of them stories I be saying, Peeing on your head and telling you it's rain.

They tried to get me to write one of their official reports he said. That's when I decided I just wouldn't participate in the system anymore. 'Cause I knew the official report was a lie.

Trying to pee on your head and tell you it was rain, ain't they? Or trying to get you to pee on other people's heads and tell them it rain. You's right not to participate in that. If I peed on anybody's head myself, I'd tell them it was pee, I wouldn't tell them it was rain.

But you wouldn't pee on anybody's head in the first place, Nadine, he says.

I think everybody pees on somebody's head. It's just whether you tells them it's pee or tells them it's rain. I would like to think that I'm perfectable enough not to pee on nobody's head. Course there's them that pees on people's head and ain't know they's peeing on they head. Like that Miguelita that you thought was some crazy woman that you thought you knew, if Miguelita was to pee on somebody's head, she would think it was rain her ownself. So if she told you it was rain, you would have to explain to her that it was pee and ain't rain. And then if you told her it was pee and ain't rain, she might stop peeing on you. Least that's the Miguelita us in the cantina thinks she is.

When we gets back from Galveston, we don't go to the cantina, 'cause if they be thinking he immigration, then they might start thinking I's immigration. We go to one of them little nightclubs in Texas City and he's drinking gin and tonic and I got me a Budweiser. I keep waiting for him to ask me to dance, specially when they plays the tango music. I knows I'm a little bigger than him and he might not want to be on the dance floor with me. But when you dances the tango it don't matter who bigger than who. Specially that tango that I calls the butt-out tango. Where you don't tango upright but the woman kinda pokes her butt out. Delgadina when she ain't learning intellectual subjects got her a tango class and have taught me the difference between the café style, which I calls the butt-out tango, and the salon style, where you tangos upright and looks classical, and then there's different modern- and old-style tangos, and even military-style tangos. She say she ain't got her a master teacher of the tango, 'cause you's got to go to Argentina to get you a master teacher,

but she say she got a pretty good tango teacher. So when they's playing that tango, I wants to show him what I've learned, but he prefer to talk than dance. While he talking, though, I'm kinda daydreaming I'm doing the tango with him, and that we's in one of them
tango clubs in Argentina. And while he talking, it like his talking
got a tango base to it. Then I'm daydreaming I'm tangoing with
John Henry Hollywood.

Did you know John Henry, there's a whole social history to the
tango?

Naw, I didn't know that, Nadine.

Delgadina say when military rule come to Argentina, they prohibited the tango.

No, I didn't know that, Nadine.

I'm an ignorant woman in almost everything else, but I knows
how to tango.

Why you keep calling yourself ignorant, Nadine? He pulls me
toward him for a kiss. You's a big sweet.

I tries to hear the tango base in every music while John Henry
dances like a master teacher.

Freedom.

Seem like he say something again about freedom ain't being Madonna freedom and something about how they's gotta be some kinda
immitigable rules to African-American womanhood. Either that, or
he say they ain't no immitigable rules to African-American womanhood. He say another word but it sound like *immitigable* so that's
what I remembers. I'm trying to listen to him talk and listen to that
music at the same time, listen to them tango rhythms, then they's
playing rap music and I'm trying even to hear the tango base in the
rap, or the rap base in the tango. Seem like it Queen Latifah singing,
or one of them female rappers rapping in the background, and his
male voice talking in the foreground, and don't it sound good, 'cause
he got one of them deep-type voices, and I likes them deep-type
voices, then it seem like Queen Latifah singing and she jump to the
foreground and he rapping in the background, and then it seem like
they voices blends into song.

I kinda liked hearing him talk that talk, though, except I didn't
understand how you could tread proudly in the universe, though,
unless you's on *Star Trek*. Maybe that Whoopi Goldberg when she

were on *Star Trek* could be up there, and she ain't playing the role of no plebeian neither, treading proudly in the universe, but seems like you's got a lot to do to try to tread proudly right here on Earth. Course I know he means that as a metaphor and that we's got to see beyond the stars usselves. 'Cause y'all needs to be more ambitious.

And I know you're ambitious, Nadine, because of that steady glance you give a man, well, not just a man, but everybody. Some of my colleagues thinks African-American women are too ambitious and greedy and self-seeking, and even those that aren't ambitious are greedy and self-seeking. And that's an African-American man I'm talking about. Those aren't the African-American women that I know.

And then as if on cue there's someone singing in the background. Some woman singing about the rent. Some woman singing about how a man gotta have a job if he want to be with her.

But he act like he ain't hear that singing. And then he be talking about how even womens got to invent themselves too, especially the African-American womens, but then it be sounding like it him want to invent me and not me myself. I do like that idea of me treading proudly in the universe, though. Then he just say I shouldn't be driving no truck. And then he say something about my language. First I think he gonna say something about how he don't like my language. How I gotta clean up my language and start talking like them secretaries and schoolteachers and bank employees. But then he say he do like my language. I know he's dating me and all that, but just 'cause a man date you don't mean he like your language.

You know, before I met you, he said, I thought people that talked like you, you know, who used the vernacular, so to speak, although I use some myself every now and then, were unintelligent people, but with you, your intelligence shines through, even though you speak corrupted English.

He said corrupted English or corruptible English or maybe even incorruptible English. I ain't sure what he say, but I know he talking about my language. What that have to do with my intelligence? I'm asking. 'Cause I ain't exactly sure what he talking about myself. 'Nother reason I liked that movie that me and Delgadina seen with that Denzel Washington, 'cause he was talking my language. *Devil in a Blue Dress.* 'Cause I told Delgadina that that the first time I seen

a movie where somebody was talking my language. I mean, the one
that was actually telling the movie, narrating the movie, and not
just somebody in the movie. I didn't much like the women in that
movie 'cause they didn't seem like true women to me, even the one
supposed to be the central woman and love interest–type woman,
but that Denzel Washington was talking my language. And ain't
nobody say he ain't play the role of a intelligent man. But I'm still
thinking about that treading proudly in the universe, though, 'cause
I ain't never had nobody to sweet-talk me like that. Now I likes to
be called intelligent like any woman, even whilst I'm telling y'all
I'm ignorant, but I ain't never heard no man to talk to me about
treading proudly in the universe. 'Cept telling me I shouldn't be
driving no truck. He be my almost perfect idea of a man 'cept telling
me I shouldn't be driving no truck.

I tell Delgadina what he say, 'cause I want to hear what she got to
say about a man that your almost perfect idea of a man 'cept for telling you you shouldn't be driving no truck, so she say, You've got your
own mind, Mosquito, but that's some sweet-talk, I mean about the
universe. I never had a man to tell me that either. Course the sweeter
talk for me would be for a man to tell me I'm intelligent. Not that I
need someone else to tell me who I am, but you know what I mean?

I think she's gonna tell me what I hears other women say, you
know, defending themselves from the tyranny of men, how they
don't put up with mens telling them what to do and what not to do
and all that, but she don't say that. I know there's plenty of men that
done told her that she shouldn't be bartending and shit, and not just
Chicano men either, but every man, and I know she's still bartending. And she's still dating who she wants to, and even dating some of
the same mens that tells her she shouldn't be bartending. I call that
Delgadina freedom. That man talking about Madonna freedom.
Well, I call that Delgadina freedom. Me I didn't stop dating him
neither, but I just keeps driving my truck and then so he the one decide he don't want the sorta woman stay driving her truck when he
think she oughta be more ambitious than that.

If I were of another generation, he said, I don't think I'd be a social psychologist.

You be a doctor or a lawyer?

No. Something that would tell me better who I am or who I could be. For my generation, it was important that we work with people, you know. I didn't go to one of the traditional black colleges that would've shown me other possibilities, more of the essence of who I am. The little community college I went to, we were either political science or sociology majors. I was lousy in political science, so I took sociology. I won't say I was lousy in political science . . . I don't have the logic of a politician . . . I know you shouldn't be driving a truck. . . .

Maybe he ain't mean it the way I hear it. Maybe he just mean that driving a truck ain't the essence of who I am. But it seem like once he got that idea he just keep telling me that ain't who I am. And so when he say, You shouldn't be driving no truck, me I just ignores that. I gots to drive my truck. I gots to. Even if he don't think that's the essence of who I am or who I could be. 'Cause that's something I knows I gots to do. It always makes me wonder why people, and ain't just mens, that always wants to try to make you stop doing the very thing you gots to do. I mean, if the thing's a evil thing, you's got to stop doing it. That's why they's got moral and civil and all kindsa laws for human beings. 'Cept doctors, if what them brochures say is true. But if the thing ain't a evil thing, but it's something that you gots to do. I don't know why you gots to do it. Maybe it's the closest thing you come to to what freedom mean. Your own idea of freedom. And don't nobody want freedom for you. Not the true thing. And I ain't talking about license or decadence. I'm talking about freedom, the true thing.

I don't know whether he say I shouldn't be driving no truck 'cause he don't see it as my essence or if he want me to stop doing my freedom thing. Course mens don't always mean the same thing when they tell a woman she shouldn't do what mean freedom to her. Some means women shouldn't be doing they freedom, others means *they* womens, they own womens, shouldn't be doing they freedom, and others means just you yourself. Course when you's married people you's got to have the same freedom ideal. But marriage is a unity and it's got its own logic. Talking about the logic of political science. Marriage, it got its own language. I think it just the peculiarity of being human to want to colonize somebody else freedom idea. And I mean when that freedom idea ain't a evil thing. Delgadina got her own thoughts on that freedom idea. I guess that bartending for her is freedom idea. Delgadina one of them people you don't have to ask nothing, 'cause she's always telling her opinions. Delgadina, she one of them real opinionated womens, you know. I gots my opinions, but I ain't opinionated. I tells my opinions, but you still gots to ask me what I mean.

So what did you say to him when he say you shouldn't be driving no truck? asks Delgadina, scratching inside that mandarin collar.

Nothing.

That's 'cause you want him to keep romancing you. Or, what's that expression you like to use, Mosquito? Shaking your tree?

I don't say that that's the truth. And about that shaking somebody tree. Maybe it depend on what kinda tree the man shaking. Maybe you don't mind a man shaking your peach tree, but you don't want nobody to shake your banana tree. You know what I mean? I just orders me another Bud Light. Nibbles me some of them pretzels and peanuts on the bar. Some of them corn chips. Some of that salsa with the mandarin oranges. Itching to light me a cigarette. Or ask Delgadina for one of her sage cigarettes. But she stopped smoking even those. Y'all know, her herb cigarettes. I ain't talking 'bout that marijuana y'all.

I used to be like that too, say Delgadina. When I was in my twenties. And she pour the Bud Light in my glass and go take another order and then she come back. She still looking like she in her twenties to anybody ain't know her age. She wearing one of them really feminine-type blouses with smocking on it. It one of them mandarin-type blouses with the mandarin collar, like I said, and all but it got honeycomb-type patterns on it, kinda remind me of them solar cells. I'm always wearing them sweatshirts myself, but she's always wearing them real inventive-type blouses. That ain't to say I don't consider myself as feminine as her, it just we's got different styles, you know. And what look like them Native American sand paintings. I mean, she got on that blouse. Or them aborigine sand paintings, though them aborigines they's Native Australians. She say she embroidered it herself, though, 'cause she really artful. She got another blouse she done embroidered a tree on it. Soapbark tree, she call it. She don't embroider no ordinary tree, got to be a soapbark tree. Women has got they own peculiarities too. I guess to embroider a ordinary tree make her think she a ordinary woman. Course I don't

see nothing wrong with being no ordinary woman myself. They's
got them a whole symphony for the common man, but when the
woman want to write the symphony she be wanting it to be for the
uncommon woman. Like them people that wants to identify with
the kings and queens in Africa. Now they might be identifiable with
them African kings and queens, 'cause a lots of them were captured
in warfare and sold into slavery, and that's by Africans us ownselves.
That's the history that us don't like to tell about. And they's still selling them into slavery if them stories is true. Course when people does
wrong theyselves it don't exonerate the other peoples from they
wrong. But every people is like that. That's why they's got they hero
songs and stories—the idea of who they is. I might be descended
from a king or queen myself, or some of them African noblemen and
women. But what if I ain't? Seems to me if you's a true African, you's
just as proud if you's descended from the common African man or
woman. They's some of us that's descended from them European
kings and queens. Them that wants to talk kings and queens.

Anyway, Delgadina she give me one of them embroidered
blouses, too, except with me one of them boabab's on it and one of
them sandarac tree, 'cause she be saying they's African trees. Don't
go talking about my African tree now, I wants to say when she starts
talking African trees. She the one told me about this tree called the
monkey puzzle tree. I think she be signifying when she be talking
about that monkey puzzle tree. And I be asking if that a African tree,
and she be saying it a South American tree, but it sound like a African tree on account of that monkey in it, but I guess they'd got monkeys in South America, 'cause that's the tropics. Then she talking to
that man in Spanish and I hear the words *loca* and *loco*. I don't know
whether they talking about that crazy gringa or whether she calling
the man she talking to *loco*. He got one of them oversize mustaches
and wearing him a polo shirt and dungarees. He look kind of Indian
as well as Mexican—I mean Indian from India, one of them rajahs.
Got a kind of lean face and thick dark hair, a lean and muscular man.
She talking to him and scratching inside that mandarin collar. I guess
she been eating some of them jalapeños, 'cause like I said she allergic
to them jalapeños. I know about that loco weed. I remember Delgadina and me was sitting in the municipal park and she picked up
this weed and started chewing on it. She know a lot about them

plants and know which plants is eatable and which ones is medicinal. She might be chewing on one of them plants. She also one of
them container gardeners. She grows different kinds of plants and
herbs in them containers, you know.

That loco weed? I ask.

Naw, it's wild mustard. Yeah, that's 'cause you want him to keep
romancing you, she say, scratching inside that mandarin collar.

I might want romance but I don't need it, I says.

That's a good one, Mosquito, that's a real good one, she say, and
then she grab this little notebook she keep under the bar and jot it
down. You a wit. I like wit.

I ain't never heard myself call no wit before, no whole-wit, but
she taking one of them creative writing class at night at this community center and she always jotting down shit like that. She say she the
only one in that writing class that know the different names of trees
and plants and flowers, though. 'Cause the other ones they just call a
tree a tree. She the one jot down all that shit them powers be saying,
that Dickey and Tea Biscuit—I don't remember him referring to her
as Tea Biscuit, but Delgadina got that in her notebook—and that's
how come I remember all that shit them powers be saying, 'cause she
let me read it in her notebook. You know, all that shit about the fried
ice cream. She even put a monkey puzzle tree in one of her stories.
She a real nice gal, though, that Delgadina. Grew up in a mixed
neighborhood in Houston and knows how to socialize with all sortsa
peoples, all different cultures and races, and can talk all sortsa
people's talk. I likes folks like that, though I ain't like that myself. I
socializes with *some*. And seem like the older I get, the fewer that
some get. When I tell Delgadina that she one of my few acquain-
tance, she say, Mosquito, you ain't no elitist, are you? I know she joking, but I still ask, What that got to do with it? 'Cause Delgadina she
always talking about the community this and the community that.

Delgadina she taking that creative writing class at the community
center and she also been talking about going to detective school. I'm
the one give her that brochure on detective school, and she say my
going to that truck driving school influenced her to maybe try that
detective school, and maybe that give her a sense of possibilities. Of
course, me I'm thinking it that movie we seen about that detective.
'Cause after I seen that movie about that detective that's when I got

them detective brochures. Not that I ain't seen movies about detectives before, it just this a movie about a African-American detective. I mean, private investigator. Before that creative writing, she took one of them acting classes. Is that ambition enough for you? 'Cept I know that ain't what he mean by ambition. But like the song say, everybody want to be in show business. I tell Delgadina what that man say about greedy and she say she intellectually greedy but she don't think she greedy greedy. Intellectual greediness, she say, ain't the same thing as them other kinds of greediness. When she were taking this acting class, I did go with her to see one of them plays. Luis Valdez, I think she say the name of the playwright. Yeah, that Luis Valdez, 'cause she be saying he also a filmmaker and he supposed to be a important Chicano playwright and not just a playwright but a true *vato* and I don't know what she mean by true *vato*. But maybe that like when African Americans usedta call someone a race man or race woman. 'Cause that's supposed to mean you's for the people. 'Cept somebody say they's always a newer Negro, so that a lot of them race men and race women. . . . Well, you know what I mean. 'Cause a lot of them people that thought of theyselves as radical in the 1920s and 1930s, in the 1960s, for example, they was the old Negro. They's always a newer Negro. I don't know if them *vatos* is like that. And she ain't just look at the play like a lot of peoples, she be jotting things down in her notebook. Be saying maybe she write her a essay on that play, 'cause Delgadina like that. The play it were in English and Spanish, enough English so's the English-speaking people could understand it, enough Spanish so's the Spanish-speaking people could understand it, though the English sound kinda like Spanish, or at least it be more of a jazzed-up English than a lot of the English you hear, or maybe jazzed-up ain't the right word for that English. I don't know if you should say Chicanified English. Or maybe Mexicanized English. But Chicano and Mexican ain't the same thing, say Delgadina. Heard plenty of *locos* and *locas* in that play too. And gringos they ain't called gringos they's called *gabachos*. 'Cause I be asking Delgadina what a *gabacho* and she be saying that's a gringo. I like that English they be speaking, I says. Kinda remind me of that Cheech, you know. I think I seen me one of them Luis Valdez's films, 'cause I think that Cheech were in that. That Luis Valdez he supposed to have founded a famous Chicano theater company. I like that play, though it ain't my culture. But then I'm wondering why people have to like they own culture. Them with dominant cultures, though, it seem like they's freer to like or not like they own culture 'cause people ain't say of them they just imitating someone else culture.

They got a African-American theater group at that community center too, she say, and ask me why I don't try out for *The Tale of Uthlakanyana*. She had to write that *Uthlakanyana* down for me. Seem like I heard that name before, or somebody name that name? *Tale of* who? *Uthlakanyana.* Don't sound like no African-American play to me. That kinda sound like that Eskimo, that Inuit language, don't it? Or maybe that Africanized English. Say what? *Tale of* who? *Uthlakanyana.* Yeah, I do know me somebody that went over there to Africa and come back with that name. And ain't know what it mean.

I peeked my head in the door and seen these African Americans dressed up like Africans, but Africans in the New World. Ain't real Africans. They own versions of Africa, African-Americanized Africans or some shit, but I guess that ain't no different from the Europeans in the New World looking like they own versions of Europe and be European-Americanized Europeans and one woman in some of them New World African clothes she spy me and point to me and say, That's Yo. We've found Yo. Least I think she say Yo, but I duck my head back out the door before she could grab me and try to put me in that play. I be telling y'all I'm a big woman, but that woman in that theater she be looking like a giant compared to me. And I be thinking of that nun pulling that little wayward boy by the ears, and be imagining her pulling me up onstage by the ears and calling me Yo. Now I know what that Yo mean in Spanish, but she saying it like it a name. And she one of them big African-American women, bigger than I am. But she got on these African clothes, like I said, and they makes her look more majestic than me in my sweatshirt. And she one of them Africanized African Americans. You know one of them real pretty African print skirts you tie around your waist and scarf she tie around her head but them Africans don't call it a scarf matching that print skirt, but that blouse she wearing it look like a ordinary American blouse, though. And wearing some type of sandals kinda look like them guaraches of Maria. Maybe made out of

that raffia fiber. I be saying them Africans they have they own type
of guaraches; Delgadina she say they ain't guaraches they huaraches
or some shit. Delgadina she don't know who Yo is neither, though,
'cept Yo she say in Spanish it mean I. But in Africa it must be some
kinda name. And them young hip-hop people they got them they
Yo. They be saying Yo, except I don't think it the same Yo them Africans be talking about. 'Cept that Yo must be one of them universal
languages.

Delgadina she always going to them plays and she got a string of
them novels behind that bar too. And ain't them modern romances.
She might read a paragraph or so from them novels here and there
when she ain't busy bartending. She likes them novels about people
that does things. One's about some kinda botanist in South America
and she say she herself wanted to be a chemist in high school but the
teachers steered her to the vocational track and not the college track.
Well, you gotta be a little bit of a chemist to mix drinks for some of
these suckers, she says. And I use chemistry in my container garden-
ing. One of them novels about a cannery worker. She say she herself
usedta work in a cannery, usedta can smolt, that young salmon.

You remember that Susan Sarandon movie where she would rub
lemons all over her arms. You know that movie *Atlantic City*?
That's me after working in that fishery.

Delgadina she don't usually like them working-class movies,
though. She say it ain't true, 'cause she be always taking me to them
working-class plays. I don't know what kind of stories that Delgadina write, though. I know she got a lot of them literary-type novels
too. Them Henry James–type novels and intellectual-type novels
and shit. And a lot of them Germans, that Mann and that Goethe.
She say she dream one time she were that Goethe. She like all them
Germans, I think, 'cause they supposed to be the most intellectual.
The French is intellectual, but she say the Germans know how to
combine intellect with a good story, and she don't think the French
tells good stories, least not them new novelist types, but I always
thought that were supposed to be the point of them new novels, least
from what Delgadina said another time about them French. She say
once when she was in high school she wrote a story about a Chicano
descriptive geometrist—I think they call them geometrists, don't
they?—and all the people did when she read it was laugh. 'Cause,

you know, she being a Chicana and a woman, and like she ain't supposed to write stories about no descriptive geometrists and only them
Europeans is. Even the Chicanos in the class laughed, 'cause they
themselves ain't supposed to write no stories about no descriptive
geometrists. And even have me dreaming I'm a descriptive geometrist and working them theorems. I ain't know what they mean outside the dream, but inside the dream they's freedom to me. Inside
that dream, working them theorems is what I gots to do.

Delgadina, though, she say she stopped writing stories for a long
time after that, but she think just 'cause she a Chicana don't mean she
just gotta write them working class–type stories, 'cause they's
got Chicano intellectuals and academics too. And I be wondering
whether they be laughing at a book about a African-American descriptive geometrist and be saying that ain't realism.

What's smolt?

You know, that young salmon. The fishermen catch it when it's
migrating. Young salmon when it's migrating from the fresh water to
the sea. Supposed to be a real delicacy or some shit. I never tasted it
myself. I canned it, but I never tasted it. I like salmon, though. I
mighta had some smolt, just didn't know it was smolt.

And she got a book called *The Adventures of Monkey*. When
she be reading that, I think she be signifying again, but it a Chinese
novel of maybe the sixteenth century or something like that. 'Cause
she ain't just read them modern novels. It about some intelligent and
magical monkey. And then she got her a copy of *The Arabian
Nights*. I thought it supposed to be a children's book, but she say
anybody that want to can read it, like *Don Quijote*. She say her
creative writing teacher recommended it 'cause it done influenced
everybody from Chaucer to Cervantes. She say a lot of that humorous and fantasy-type adventures and shit in that *Don Quijote* book
is on account of being influenced by the Moors in Spain. That *Don
Quijote* book I thought that was a children's book too, but she say it
ain't. And then she tease me about being her Panza, and be saying
she always wonder what that *Don Quijote* be like if Sancho Panza
wrote that book. 'Cept ain't even Don Quijote wrote that book, so
how could Sancho Panza write it? I asks.

Naw, that's everybody's book, she be saying.

It that Susan Sarandon movie, though, make her wanna study acting, 'cause when we come outta that movie she be saying, I kinda look like her, don't I? Except she be saying there ain't no good roles for Chicana womens in them movies, except some seductress. But she say that there ain't good roles for Chicana womens in a lot of them Chicano mens plays either, say Chicana womens they be having to write they own plays. She be saying how mens is always telling womens they don't like the mens in women's book, but then it's okay if the womens don't like the womens in they books. 'Cause I ain't seen no womens in a man's book I liked myself, 'cept I still likes the men's books. Well, I ain't say that. 'Cause I do likes that Miss Jane. But I'm still wondering how come her know all that social history in that book? 'Cause I'm thinking I be writing me a book and ain't no social history at all in it. But then everybody ain't Miss Jane. Thinking about that poem now. Look at that gal shake that thang / We cain't all be Miss Jane. Course that ain't what that poem say. That's just my version of that poem. And it don't rhyme.

Then she be talking about that Denise Chávez and some of them other Chicana women playwrights. There's a whole lot of Chicana women playwrights that I ain't heard of. But she ain't write no plays herself, though, just them stories. I kinda look like that Susan Sarandon, don't I? she be saying, but then I learn she be saying that about every movie star. Sean Young. I kinda look like her, don't I? Then she say the name of another actress. I kinda look like her, don't I? Then she say the name of another actress. I kinda look like her, don't I? I ain't going to say the names of them actresses myself, 'cause y'all think she a fool, 'cause them actresses don't even look like each other. They's all gringa actresses, though. 'Cause they's got all the world's peoples identifying with them in they movies. Movies supposed to be the biggest American export, movies and entertainment. I even likes them movie stars myself. Them Italians, though. Them others that reminds me of them Italians. Or them that plays Italians. Y'all can name almost any Italian actor or actress, though mostly the actors, and put them on my list of favorite actors and actresses. She be even thinking she look like that Kim Basinger, though, except for that blond hair. And probably the truth is she do kinda look like all of them. Like I say, them Mexicans they's the cosmic race. The first time Delgadina say *cosmic race* I think she say *comic* race. And I be telling her the Mexicans they ain't no more comic race than any other race. And she say *cosmic* race. Only person she don't say she kinda look like is when we go see one of them Whoopi Goldberg movie. But the truth is, she kinda look like that Whoopi Goldberg too, except she more yam-colored than that Whoopi. 'Cept for them yams in Africa. I don't know what them yams in Africa look like. Maybe them African yams looks like that Whoopi.

You still thinking 'bout that detective school? I asks to direct her from talking 'bout that romance. I be thinking about that Don Quijote, Denise Chávez, Italian movie stars, and the cosmic race and she still talking about that romance. Still saying I wants him to keep romancing me. She leans her elbows on the bar and looks up at that disco globe. She got kinda ashy elbows, but the rest of her is buttery. I be telling her about aloe for them elbows, then remember she the one told me 'bout that aloe.

Yeah, I'm thinking about it, she say about that detective school. They give me one of those personality profiles, you know, and say I got the personality for it. To be a private investigator. Yeah, they say I got the talent for it. I enjoy my creative writing class, though, but it ain't practical, you know. I don't think there's many publishers that's interested in Chicana literature. Course I could publish myself, found my own little Chicana publishing companies.

Why it gotta be little? I ask.

You right. I'm thinking as us as a minority, you know. But why you got to have minority ideas? You right. But now I'm thinking about that private investigating though. You gotta have something practical. Even that little brochure you give me. If some of those people had them a private investigator. . . .

Yeah, I says, and grabs another one of them pretzels. I'm thinking of that metaphor of peeing on people's head and telling them it's rain again.

And then she start ribbing me about that romance again. Ain't nothing as impractical as romance, she say. And then she jot her own line down.

Anyhow, I tells that priest my name and we shakes hands and he says that the Carmelite nun already told him about me. I spent so much time telling y'all about Delgadina, y'all probably forgot about that priest. But that's the way true stories is. I want to ask him whether he

a Jesuit or a Benedictine or one of them Franciscans or do they have
Carmelite priests and he keep talking and he ask me what he can do
to help me and what it is I wants to know about the Sanctuary movement. Of course he talk real proper. He ain't real soft-spoken, not
that kinda proper, he got a forceful, aggressive-type voice, but he got
him one of them proper types of vocabularies. If y'all's from the
South y'all knows what I means by proper, and his office it surrounded by all kinds of them theology books and stuff. He sounds
like a man of education, although in the South you can be a man of
education and ain't talk proper. Ain't got more books than Delgadina, but they's a different type of books, and look more like them
ancient-type books. I know Delgadina read some of them sixteenth
century novels, but they's printed by modern presses. But these looks
like they's even printed back in the sixteenth century theyselves. He
got a smaller office than that Carmelite nun, so I can read some of
them titles, but a lot of them's in Latin. 'Cept there's a few modern
books.

What can I tell you about the Sanctuary movement? he asks. And
he behave about his mustache like that Carmelite nun behave about
her wimple; he pull on it like he straightening it, or so I'll know it a
real mustache.

I ain't sure how much to tell him 'bout that woman that hiding in
the back of my truck, but I knows that she can't have her baby in the
back of that truck and her belly pretty big. I've heard a lots of Mexican womens come across the border just when they's ready to have
they babies so's they can have they babies in the USA and make
them legal and get all the advantages of being a legal citizen, 'cause a
lot of them immigration people they be talking about changing that
law, especially in them border states, and I'm thinking that's how
come her swim the Rio Grande pregnant. That's the way them
people do; when they don't like some law, they changes it. There's
moral laws that people can't change, but them other laws is changeable. And there's even them that tries to change them moral laws, or
puts them in a different context. But ain't the law always them that
controls the law? And Delgadina she say that too, and she tell me
how she have a complaint against some gringo and they ain't even
take the complaint, and then they be telling her their statistics and

then we be listening to something on the television and they be telling their statistics and she say bullshit.

And this man be saying, Well, does that mean because they're
more complaints against minority policemen that minority policemen are not as good policemen?

That's not the point I'm making, the point I'm making is that
there are the same amount of complaints against the nonminority policemen, except for the nonminority policemen they handle
it informally, not officially, you know administratively, whereas
with the minority policemen they handle it formally. You know with
the nonminority policemen they feel more comfortable handling it
informally.

Do you hear that bullshitter? Delgadina is saying. That's what
I'm telling you about statistics. When I had that complaint against
that gringo, they wouldn't even take my complaint. So that bastard
don't even get on the books. Informally, my ass. Then the son-of-
bitches'll read you their statistics and make you think you're a criminal people. You ain't a criminal people. They just don't tell you
the truth. And don't tell themselves the truth either. And bastards
like them are off the books, handled informally, you know. 'Cause
they're more comfortable handling each other informally. Like that
cop show we saw. Gringos and all that drug paraphernalia. Well, that
cop treats them like they're just pranksters. Informally. If they was
vatos . . . That gringo, they wouldn't even take my complaint. . . .

What gringo? I'm asking.

And she ain't tell me.

What gringo? Every gringo. 'Cept maybe Miguelita. But even
she knows how to play the gringa.

Course she ain't literally swim the Rio Grande or the Rio Bravo
'cause that part of Texas you can cross the border walking. Anyway,
I think if the baby legal that mean she legal too, but I don't know
them immigration laws. I think it just make the baby legal.

You in the Sanctuary movement? I asks.

He don't say whether he is or he ain't. They's a reddish tint to his
brown complexion. Actually he one of them type of men of color—
not light-skinned—but can be almost any type of man of color he
tell you he is. Like a lot of them mens in Brazil. And I even seen Afri-

cans his complexion, especially from that Cape Verde off the coast of Africa, which surprise me as much as when I seen my first Hawaiian his complexion. I guess some of them Cape Verde Africans that color, though, on account of them Portuguese. Just like them Brazilians. But they's still natural Africans.

But I can tell you what you want to know about it, he say. Why are you interested in the Sanctuary movement?

I ain't interested in it myself per se, I says, but I knows somebody what is. I would prefer not to be here inquiring about the Sanctuary movement, 'cause I got some industrial detergents I'm transporting and I gots to have them at the warehouse. But I'm a truck driver and I . . .

He sits up straight and narrows his eyes at me and straightens that priestly collar and then he straighten his mustache again. He be straightening his collar and his mustache, just like that nun with her wimple, 'cept he a manly priest. I'm thinking about being in that restaurant-cantina again and them people's clearing out when I come in with that fool. Now why I say fool? Just 'cause us ain't dating no more don't make him no fool. Just 'cause he ain't think I'm ambitious enough—even with the *bitch* in it—don't make him no fool. Just 'cause he don't want me to be driving no truck don't make him no fool. Plus, he ain't that much a fool, 'cause a lot of them little mens they ain't secure enough to be dating no big womens in the first place. So why I say fool? When I seen him again in one of them shopping malls in Texas City he have with him one of them little bitty womens, though, shorter than him and a decade younger than him, maybe a secretary or schoolteacher or some shit. I think he be pretending like he don't know me, but he say, How you, Nadine? But he don't introduce me to the girl, though she looking at me like one of them koala bears, but I guess she figure we ain't old lovers or nothing 'cause I don't look like his type and since I'm wearing my brogans which make me look even taller than I naturally am. Maybe she figure I'm one of them peoples he met while he doing them social psychiatry surveys, you know, 'cause I guess them social psychiatrists got to study individual peoples too, 'cause it individual peoples that makes up societies.

Delgadina kinda a social psychiatrist her ownself, though she ain't got no degree in it. She a social psychiatrist of the Chicano and

Mexican personality. She were discussing with me with subject of hermeticism or hermitism. She be talking about something she call hermitism. She ain't named it herself, but she know the meaning of it, 'cause she be reading some book on Mexican psychology, she always reading them books, she talk about the people's knowledge and the people's learning, but always be reading them books, 'cept she don't trust that book, she say, because she be saying it depict Mexican psychology as pathological and she be saying that Mexican psychology ain't no more pathological than any other people psychology for a developing nation anyhow and maybe that hermit crab be a metaphor for it, that hermetism. She say you can take anybody culture and depending on the way you talks about it, you got yourself a pathological culture, like when you listen to them Europeans talk about American culture, and they ain't just meaning the minorities neither. Or when them Japanese talks about American culture. Or when anybody that ain't American talks about American culture, I mean them intellectual types.

I remember 'cause when she started talking about that hermetism, we was sitting in one of them little cafés. Sometimes she like to go to this little café that have these outdoor tables. I think it kinda remind her of a French café. So we was sitting there and she start talking about hermetism. I gots to tell y'all about Delgadina. 'Cause I know a lot of y'all be hearing she Chicana and y'all be thinking Rosie Perez or even María Conchita Alonso or some of them others that have the Chicana flavor to they voices. Delgadina she sometimes have a Chicana flavor to her voice, but she ain't possess it all the time. I think that because of the kind of community she grew up in Houston, where she heard every type of peoples speaking. Sometimes when she talking she be sounding like a gringa, other times she be sounding kinda like me, and other times she be sounding like Rosie Perez or María Conchita Alonso. I thinks that peoples refers to that as multilingualism, 'cept she be speaking English, 'cept she be speaking the same language. I ain't know if Delgadina know she always changing her way of speaking like that. I know she know about that multilingualism, though, 'cause she be telling me that her folks in Houston when's they's talking about everyday things or talking religion they talks in Spanish, but when her daddy is talking business he talk in English, when he talking politics he talk in English or

Spanish, or he mix English with Spanish, then when he be talking love talk with her mama he be talking Spanish. He be changing from Spanish to English depending on what kind of subject he talking about. 'Cept Delgadina herself she be talking English, but be talking different types of English. Course she be talking Spanish with them people in the cantina that speaks Spanish, but when she be talking English she be talking different kinds of English.

When she be talking intellectual stuff she be sounding almost like a gringa, then when she be talking everyday stuff she be sounding kinda like Rosie Perez or like María Conchita Alonso—they's movie actresses—or she be sounding like herself which is a Chicana flavor that's her individual ownself, and sometimes when she be joking sometimes or kidding with me about something or specifying or signifying sometimes she be sounding like me. I gots to tell y'all that, 'cause otherwise y'all be thinking I ain't know who Delgadina is. Course me myself I'd kinda like to hear her be talking intellectual and be sounding like Rosie Perez or like María Conchita Alonso. I guess she talk intellectual in Spanish, but I ain't know that Spanish.

Anyhow, I knows he, the priest not the social psychologist fool, thinks I'm maybe one of them spies for the immigration department, and I guess in these border towns they's got plenty of spies and informers for the immigration department like during wartime or something. 'Cause Delgadina be reading me one of them short stories be talking about how people behave during wartime, and she be saying that how it seem like certain minorities behave with each other all the time. I guess she be saying certain minorities, 'cause some minorities behaves better with each other than others. And maybe she ain't sure what kinda minority I am and don't want to start no war. Signifying, you know. Well, I guess they always got them they border wars. Anyway, Delgadina be telling me about some of these gringos that go out along the border with they hunting rifles and actually do hunt Mexicans trying to cross the border and set traps for them too. I ain't seen none of that myself, from my truck and all, but she say that it the truth. She gets along with all sortsa peoples, like I says, 'cept maybe gringos that acts like gringos. She say gringoism ain't a color, it a state of mind.

How do you know about the Sanctuary movement? he asks.

I seen this documentary about it on TV. I got me one of them pocket TVs I got at this trade show. Actually, they was talking about this immigration lawyer, 'cause she was like trying to get this Cuban woman outta jail, you know, 'cause they didn't know what to do with her, this Cuban woman you know, so they like just locked her up, like they just lock up a lot of these immigrants, you know, 'cause—I don't mean them detention camps I mean they put this Cuban woman in jail. Seems like in different parts of the country they has started locking immigrants in jail that they don't know what else to do with, you know. I prefers not to be inquiring about the Sanctuary movement myself. I don't think they should put them in jail, though, I mean just because they is undocumented.

He still narrow his eyes at me. They them hieroglyphic eyes like I says. So I just comes out and tells him my story, or tells him about that Mexican woman. Does this woman need an immigration law-yer? Here's a list . . . He takes out a list of immigration lawyers from his desk drawer. First, he unlocks the drawer, though. Now his desk, one of them antique mahogany desk, almost as big as that Car-melite nun's desk which make it look too big for this little office. Im-migration law is. . . .

Naw, she need a midwife. And ain't no woman actually. Well, she a woman. But look more like a girl, though, I says. I guess she done come across the border so's she can have her baby in the USA. She the one asking about Sanctuary.

And where is this woman? he asks, returning the list of immigra-tion lawyers to his desk drawer. Then he locks the drawer again.

I looks around to see if he got any books on that immigration law but I just see these theology books, like I said. I figure they theology books, 'cause most of them in Latin. And books got them Latin names on them: Arnobius, Lactantius, Africitas and names like that. You can tell them Latin names. Like that Albertus Magnus. And few books on the history of the Southwest. Now them is in English. And got a few books in Spanish too. Got a book on Mexican cook-ing. And coupla that looks like they must be detective novels. I be thinking a priest be embarrassed to have them detective novels in his office. Actually, when I was thinking about trucking school, like I said, I was reading on them detective schools too, but me I ain't no detective. I didn't take none of them talent profiles, though, like Delgadina. But them detectives is always going around interviewing all kindsa peoples, then they wears them disguises and shit. And you gotta be a good actor to be a good detective. But I guess that like hiding—except hiding in plain sight. Ain't that one of them detective rules anyhow?

She out in back of my truck, I says. I carry industrial detergents and she hiding back behind one of them drums, you know, one of them tins of detergent. Industrial detergent, you know, come in these big giant tin drums. She out in my truck. Look like she swam the Rio Grande. I would prefer that she had not climbed in my truck after she got across the border, though, and had climbed in somebody else's truck, but she is in my truck and is going to have a baby. Delgadina was telling me about the latch on my truck, but I ain't never had no smugglers to smuggle theyselves into my truck. I'm kinda new to this border route, though. I settled in Texas City, but I usedta travel through New Mexico and Arizona and Nevada, but now I gots me suppliers and peoples that wants supplies in South Texas. In fact, Delgadina told me about them new peoples that wants my industrial detergents. I kinda likes staying in South Texas, though. I sometimes travels to different trade shows, though.

Is her name Delgadina?

Naw, it Maria. Delgadina the cantina woman. I mean the bartender in the cantina.

Where is your truck?

I tells him where I park it.

Not there, he say, and he tell me where to park the truck where the truck ain't conspicuous. Where that truck can hide in plain sight, I guess.

And so I parks it in this little alley in back of the cathedral—alley so little I got to park up on the sidewalk—and when the priest come out he ain't wearing he priest clothes, but look like one of them mens that loads and unloads my trucks at the factory docks and ports and shit and he carrying a flashlight, one of them old-fashioned-type flashlights, and I opens the back of the truck and he climbs in there, no stun gun or nothing, and he goes straight back there, but whispering something in Spanish, not Spanglish, so's he won't scare her, sounding like peoples does when they gentles a wild or skittish horse, 'cept in Spanish, and then him and that pregnant Mexican woman—I think I hears *muchacha*—they starts talking back and forth to each other in Spanish. He asks her questions and she gives him answers and I guess she give the right answers and then he start feeling her belly, not like no horse, though, and behave like him gentling that baby too, and then he help her outta the back of that truck, and he lead her in the back of the cathedral. But he don't let me go in there with them, he wave at me to stay out in the alley, 'cause I guess they's hiding places in there and he don't want me to know where they are.

You better stay out in the alley, he say. Got a voice sound kinda like that piano tuner boyfriend. John Henry Hollywood. I told you about my piano tuner boyfriend. Fact I heard his voice, then heard his name, before I seen the man. Me and my California girlfriend was sitting in this bar, you know, before she decided to go out to California, when we was still in Covington, Kentucky, though John Henry from across the border in Cincinnati, and we hear this voice and she say, That sounds like John Henry Hollywood. And then she call him by his nickname. Hello, Snooker. At least I think she be calling him Snooker, 'cause when she introduce him she introduce him as John Henry Hollywood and she always be calling him John Henry Hollywood. And you know I got to meet anybody name John Henry Hollywood, and so she introduces me to this old friend of hers. We dated each other for a while, like I said. I asked him if he wanted to come out to California with me, but he weren't too interested in California, but then I figured he the sort of man want to be doing the asking he ownself; now if he had asked me to come out to California, we might be in California, but like I said, I started out to California, but just decided to settle in Texas City. He name John Henry Hollywood, but he ain't show the slightest interest in that Hollywood. One of them manly voices, though. His voice it be somewhere near them deep keys. Them keys you play boogie woogie with. 'Cept you ain't supposed to be looking at no priest and thinking 'bout that boogie-woogie.

He start inside with the Mexican woman, and then he come back and explain, like he gentling that skittish horse again, that it for my own good that I don't know where they are, and then he lead the Mexican woman-girl into them hiding places. But I knows it also because I figures he don't trust me, though he trust the Mexican woman enough to give the Sanctuary. All he know it could be her

the spy for them border patrol peoples, pregnant or not. And Delgadina she say they's Mexicans that spies for them too. Ain't just the
gringos. She get real passionate when she be talking about them
Mexicans that spies on other Mexicans, though she be pretty passionate when she be talking about them spies for immigration department. Passionate don't just mean amorous or lustful like I always
been thinking it mean. 'Cause one of them men come in the cantina
and Delgadina be saying something about him being a passionate
man, and I be asking her if they boyfriend and girlfriend for her to
know him to be a passionate man and then she be looking at me like
I'm a fool, then she realize it 'cause I only know me one meaning of
that word *passionate,* and then she get out her dictionary and let me
read the full meaning of the word. Then after I read it she explain
that he passionate about the rights of undocumented workers. She
ain't no alien herself, no undocumented worker, like I say, she born
in Houston. And she talking like the African Americans they the
gringo too, and in the Southwest they's African Americans that looks
at them Mexicans and Mexican Americans like they's second- or
even third-class citizens, 'cause that gringoism a state of mind, but
that social worker–psychologist him ain't no gringo. Well, I guess
from my description of him you know he ain't no gringo. Still it seem
like the true spies they be the innocent-looking peoples, gringo or
not, they don't have no sly-eyed spies. They gotta look innocent. Me
and Delgadina, us couldn't be no true spies, 'cept when I was a
young girl, people be telling me I have them innocent-looking eyes,
even young woman that Maria age. And Delgadina she got them
young photographs of herself where she got them young-girl innocent eyes and them photographs taken in Houston, 'cause I can tell
the Houston skyline and I know she from Houston. And she ain't
no immigration department spy neither, if that what y'all thinking.
'Cause they's plenty we both knows is aliens—or pretty much guess
that they is—and they ain't been turn in. I still sees them in that
restaurant-cantina. Unless maybe they's all spies, you thinking.

   After he place her in the hiding place he come back out to the alley
still in his dungarees and then he thank me for bringing her to them.
Looking just like them mens that loads and unloads that industrial
detergent at the dock. Still holding that old-fashioned flashlight.
   She calls you *"mujer buena."*

What's that?

Good woman. It means "good woman."

Oh, yeah?

He still looking like he don't know how much he should trust me, though, *mujer buena* or not. Still I ain't as sly-eyed as some womens. I know *buena* mean good, so *mujer* that must mean woman. I wonder if they got sly, hieroglyphic eyes. He thank me again and looking like he want me to get off the premises, *mujer buena* or not. But he do give me he telephone number. He fish in his pants pocket for some paper, then he used this little bitty pen to scribble his number on it. He real secretive looking about it. I guess them Sanctuary workers got to be real secretive peoples, carrying around them little bitty pens and scraps of paper and shit. And I be thinking about them spy movies where that spy eats that paper, but most of them spy got that photographic memory, though.

Here's a telephone number in case you want to get in touch with us again. He saying us and them and we, he ain't saying himself.

This your telephone number? I asks, but I know it ain't the same number the Carmelite nun give me.

I puts it in my shirt pocket, a pocket that's already bulging with a Bic pen, a stick of beef jerky, a pretzel, chewing gum and a little notebook. He say it ain't the number of the cathedral, but don't say whether it he number, and say if I have any more questions 'bout the movement—just say movement don't put no Sanctuary in there—or if I have anymore peoples for them I should call that number. I starts to ask him again if that he number but I don't want to act no fool. I tells him I might have some questions about that one Mexican woman and that baby when she have it, but that that were a fluke them being in my truck and that I don't intend to be bringing them any more them contraband, and that I don't have no real interest in the Sanctuary movement. If all them borders was free you wouldn't need no Sanctuary movement. But I guess all them borders can't be free borders. That Canadian border, though, when I went up to that trade show, they just wave me into Canada. And of course anybody from Covington can cross the border into Cincinnati.

He don't say nothing. But then while we standing there this man he come in the alley. Long-haired type with his hair in a ponytail. He a Mexican I think. Or maybe a Native American. Another one of them cosmic-type men. Him and the priest they shake hands. The eternal revolutionist, the priest say, or something like that, then the man he go into the back of the cathedral. Then the priest he look at me. What is your real name again? he asks.

I ain't remember telling him my real name, but I tells him.

Sojourner Jane Nadine Johnson. But they calls me Mosquito.

You don't look like no Mosquito to me, he looks but he don't say it. But then he looking, first person looking at me like he think I might look like that Sojourner. Got them masculine hieroglyphic eyes, like I says, but them thick lashes remind me a little of them Indonesian eyes. One time I went to see this troupe of Indonesian dancers with Delgadina, 'cause she a cosmic woman her ownself, and they uses they eyes to dance too. Well, anyhow like I'm saying, he's looking at me like I oughta be Sojourner. And got them Indonesian-type hieroglyphic eyes. I guess eyes can be hieroglyphic and Indonesian too. Plenty look at me like they thinks I might be that Nadine. And since I been grown ain't nobody looked at me like they thinks I might be Jane. But him he looking at that Sojourner. You don't look like no Mosquito to me, he say.

And don't I know it, 'cause I'm one big woman. And he a pretty big man himself. And don't look like nobody's priest. Thanks, Mosquito, he say, and we shaking hands.

He got them big-man hands. And don't got them manicured fingernails neither. Got them scraggly fingernails. And him looking at me like I'm Sojourner but calling me Mosquito. Mosquito, he repeat my name, but still looking at me like I'm that Sojourner, or just might be that Sojourner. Even that John Henry Hollywood be looking at Nadine.

I climbs in the truck and he waves his hand and that old-fashioned flashlight helping me to back outta that alley. In them dungarees, like I says, he don't look like nobody's priest. Leastwise not to me. Don't look like nobody's priest or monk or friar neither.

CHAPTER 5

DELGADINA TAKES THE MAN'S ORDER AND HE whispers something to her. I guess they be talking to each other in Spanish. Yeah, I can kinda hear they Spanish. I know when she talking Spanish. I always know when Delgadina talking Spanish, 'cause they's even certain *vatos* she only talk Spanish to, and almost talk it like it a language of love. Or like it they own communion language. Like when they's having communion together they talks Spanish. Otherwise they talks English. I ain't know whether Delgadina consider English or Spanish her first language, but I know she consider Spanish her sacred language. I ain't been with her to mass, but I knows she probably say them prayers in Spanish. I can repeat a lot of them Spanish words but I ain't know what they all mean. I know I hear her refer to him as Chico. He ain't the one she call Cheech, though. He a handsome man with a large mustache and one of them valentine-shape faces and longish, tapered nose. He wearing cowboy clothes, or I should say them *vaquero* clothes, 'cause Delgadina be saying them cowboy clothes is originally *vaquero* clothes 'cept them cowboys claimed them for they own. Peoples always likes to say that they is the originators of this and that. Like they is them that don't like Elvis, 'cause he ain't the originator of his own music. People can't originate everything they has. They just has to make it they own. I ain't know a culture that have originated everything it has. But what determine the strength of a culture is when it make what it have its own. Like that jazz. It a original and originating music and it make every musical influence it own. He kinda remind me of that Frito Bandito in the commercials, though, but I always tries to see beyond that Frito Bandito. I think they banned that Frito Bandito, ain't they? And that Juan Valdez. You know, the Juan Valdez in that commercial. They got that Juan Valdez, though he ain't a bandito. But every time the gringo in the commercial sees that Juan Valdez he standing with his donkey. He Colombian, though, not Mexican, but it the same Juan Valdez everywhere. You know, like Delgadina says about them stereotypes. Probably gringos who come in this cantina they just see that Frito Bandito or Juan Valdez or them other stereotypes. They don't see the real Mexicans and the real Mexican Americans. And they sure don't see the true Mosquito. Every time we see that Juan Valdez, though, Delgadina starts talking to the television screen in Spanish, or whenever there's a Latino drug lord or Latina whore or other stereotype on television, she starts talking to the television screen in Spanish. Even though there's Latino drug lords and Latina whores she say that's still a stereotype when that's all you see on television is drug lords and whores. And probably them people see Delgadina talking to that television screen, they still just see the stereotype, 'cause that the nature of the stereotype itself. 'Cause even the people that ain't it is it, 'cause that's the only way them others has of perceiving the people is via the stereotype, like in that novel *Invisible Man*. That still my favorite book. And Delgadina got that in her library. I guess she be saying some of them scatological words, but in Spanish. She shakes her head and says something to him in Spanish, the handsome man with the mustache. She be saying that there's a lot of Chicanos that just see theyselves as the stereotype themselves, and if you ain't that stereotype they got of theyselves, like she ain't the stereotype of the Chicana, they be saying you ain't a real Chicano or Chicana. She be saying that's how the dominant culture enforce that stereotype by having the people see themselves as the stereotype. Not just the dominant culture seeing them as the stereotype, but having them see themselves and each other as the stereotype. And even when they ain't see themselves as the stereotype, see each other as the stereotype. That's what she say is dominant culture control.

Like the way you talk, Mosquito. All the people hear is the stereotype. You know, the southern Negro. To tell you the truth, sometimes when I'm listening to you, it's sorta like when I was taking this course in African-American literature and we had to read slave narratives by women who were slaves in the Old South, and sometimes when I'm listening to you it's kinda like those old slave women might sound, if you hear them talking. You even resemble some of those old photographs. I remembers seeing an old photograph of a slave woman, big like you, and wearing a bandanna like you like to wear when you're not wearing your braids, and she was working in the cotton fields. It's like when I'm somewhere and people look at me like they think I'm supposed to start dancing the fandango. I know sometimes when we're shopping or that time when we were at the art gallery and you started talking to me, the people that didn't know you were looking at you like you were the stereotype rather than who you are. I wanted to say to them, This is Mosquito, she's not who you imagine she is. But maybe I was thinking I didn't want them to think I was with the stereotype, you know. I wanted them to know that you were more than they imagined you to be. I started seeing you as they saw you, you know, not as I imagined they saw you, but I know those people, I know what they see when they look at you, 'cause I know what they see when they look at me. I don't give a shit what they see when they look at me, 'cause I know who I am. Or like when we were at Marineland and you started asking that man all those questions. And I saw the way he was looking at you. I coulda answered those questions for you, 'cause I usedta want to be a marine biologist. So you can ask me anything you want to know about marine animals. The reason I didn't become one is I couldn't imagine going out on those marine expeditions with all those gringos. I started taking an oceanography class but then they started talking about going on these expeditions and I didn't want to go on expeditions with just these gringos. Nothing but gringos in that class, and they were treating each other like comrades. You know, when you see them on those expeditions, they're like comrades. They're like comrades. So I just went and bought all the books for the class and would study them, you know. You didn't have to be asking that gringo all those questions. You coulda asked me.

I said nothing. I sipped my Budweiser. I wiped my mouth on one of them cantina napkins that got a cactus on it.

And then I didn't feel free.

What do you mean?

You know, I didn't feel their kinda freedom just to go out on a ex-pedition and study marine animals. Like I know this, actually she's an African American, she's a botanist and environmentalist, but she didn't feel free to be a botanist and environmentalist until she could connect it with liberation, you know. Environmental racism and also trying to do something about the desertification of Africa, you know. Now she calls herself an ethnobotanist and ethnoenvironmentalist, you know. I've got one of her books on ethnobotany. Like if I could connect being an oceanographer with Chicano liberation, you know. I didn't think of them as comrades either. They were just free to go out and study marine animals, but I was sorta like that botanist. I guess I envy that gringo freedom. But it's kinda like during a war. You wouldn't just study botany during a war unless you could connect it with the war effort. Like all those scientists they weren't just doing their independent research during the war, they were working for the war effort. When people usedta use the war analogy I usedta think it wasn't exactly like a war, but it is like a war. Like I can't even go out and collect my wildflowers without some border patrol wanting to see my identification. Those people who think it's not a war, and that America's not a war zone, just don't know who they're dealing with . . . And I know who you are. They don't hear what you're saying. Sometimes I don't hear what you saying myself. I don't hear all that you're saying myself.

I know you don't mean that, Delgadina. I don't mean about the war, 'cause I believes you when you says that. I knows America. And I knows that some of them patrols ain't even official patrols. They is just ordinary gringos who has decided that they is going to control they own borders, like they thinks that y'all ain't human beings but prairie foxes. The real border and the border as a metaphor. Even the cultural border. I knows that there is plenty of metaphorical and cultural borders and they patrols them. And I patrols my own borders. There is a border I allows you to cross, Delgadina, but I don't allow that Miguelita. I likes Miguelita, crazy gringa, but they is borders I wouldn't allow her to cross. I knows that I's got to take that right myself, because I knows that I has rights that the United States is not bound to protect. I knows that from elementary history that they made that famous decision in the middle of the nineteenth century and is still making it. I forgot all about that decision, but then when you was taking that course in the politics of race, I was reading one of them books of yours and read again about that decision. It is the same America. So I has to protect my own borders. That's why I am ambivalent about the border, but I knows about the war. They is people who thinks I don't know about the war 'cause I don't all the time talk racism and I likes watermelon. But I knows about the war. I knows America like I knows myself. I knows if the colored peoples of the world writes they view of history it is a different history. Even when I reads the Native Peoples' view of history in them books that you has yourself, Delgadina, the whites is all liars and rogues, and the ones that ain't is the exceptions and not the rule. Of course they claims that they's is the objective history and us history is us subjective view. But I knows them Native Peoples in them books of yours is speaking the truth and more than the truth. They's this Oklahoma African I knows and that's his favorite expression. I speak more than the truth, Nadine. I usedta think that you couldn't speak more than the truth. But when I reads them Native Peoples speaking, they sounds like they is speaking more than the truth. I means about not hearing all I'm saying.

Naw, I don't mean that. I hear what you say, Mosquito. But you know what I mean. When I talk with more of a Chicana flavor to my accent, all the people hear is a stereotype. The stereotypical Chicana, not just that I'm speaking English with my own flavor, my own innovations, my own accent. I can sound just like a gringa when I want to. And I can sound just like you. Not exactly like you, but I can sound like you if you were from Houston. I mean, I can sound like the African Americans from Houston. I can sound like almost any kinda people. But then there are people who when they look at me, and not just gringos, think I'm just supposed to sound like Rosie Perez, you know. I can talk like Rosie Perez, but that's when I want to talk like Rosie Perez, but it's not just because some people think

I'm supposed to talk like Rosie Perez. I like the way Rosie Perez talks, but that doesn't mean we all have to sound like Rosie Perez. And a lot of people just hear her as a comedian, they don't hear what she's saying. So she only gets to play certain roles. I guess that's what I don't like, just having to play certain kinds of roles. Either roles controlled by my own people or roles controlled by the gringo. Sometimes I think you're the only one who knows who I am. But even you don't know who I am. 'Cause sometimes when I start sounding like a gringa, or how people think only gringas are supposed to sound, or start sounding like an African American from Houston, you start looking at me like you don't know who I am. Sorta like when Sancho starts sounding like Don Quijote. I remember when we were reading that book for one of my classes, and some of the students said that Cervantes was inconsistent, and I was the only one in the class that knew that he was deliberately making Sancho to sound like Don Quijote and even Don Quijote like Sancho. I don't have to just be Sancho, or Sancha. Or if you study the different women in that book. I could play the roles of all the women in that book.

Delgadina ain't no licensed Indian trader, but sometimes she put upon the bar pictures of things that you can buy from Indian traders. I be thinking why she got that upon her bar, 'cause it a cantina, but whiles I'm talking she straightening them pictures of silver and turquoise jewelry, Navajo rugs, sand paintings, Kachina dolls, different arts and crafts, turquoise, coral, Navajo pottery, concho belts—I thinks they's concho belts. Somebody send her them pictures and sometimes she puts them on the bar. You can order right from them pictures 'cause they's got the order forms. Perhaps she or Delgado gets a commission when they sells some of them things that is on them pictures. I know you can sound like me. 'Cause I know you hear everything I'm saying. I hears everything people say and sometimes I hears what they don't say. Sometimes I am even like them peoples that calls theyselves remote hearers. I ain't got the gift for remote viewing without a telescope, but I has got remote hearing. And sometimes I can hear what peoples don't even know that they is saying. I can hear what peoples mean. Sometimes I knows what peoples is meaning even when they is speaking foreign. Or speaking what is foreign to me but familiar to them. I knows the language of love in anybody's language. And I knows when people is using language for sacred possibilities and for healing purposes. I knows the language of warfare and the language of profanity. I knows the language of profanity even when it ain't profane. I knows the language of discipline and self-control. I knows the language of African women talking power when it ain't even in a language that I know. Well, I was watching a documentary and these African womens were talking power in a language I didn't even know, and then when the African woman told us what it meant in English I already knew: She said that they was talking about power from within, and how you can have power with people rather than power over them. Most people wants power over people. But these womens was defining their own ideal of power and Africans working together to solve the problems of Africa. I likes that ideal of power myself, but it seems that that would only work in the African world amongst the African theyselves, and maybe only amongst the African womens theyselves, for I've been almost everywhere in America and I knows power. I ain't been amongst the European powers, but my daddy has when he fought in the war and so has my uncle Bud. I knows that the European ideal of power is having power over peoples. They is the conquering types of people and it is conquering that they celebrates as virtue. And mens theyselves forms they own conquering race and celebrates its virtue. Yes, there is some powers that you has to fight, like they say, fight them powers. They is powers that only understands power as power over people, so you can't fight they definition of power with your definition of power, 'cause they ain't comprehend your definition of power, and everybody comprehend they definition of power. Power is power, though. And then they is the Pacific powers. That is why they wants to make China into they new enemy, and everybody talking about China, and I has even had people to ask me what I know of China, because they ain't want to be conquered by that new power. I conquers myself, and disciplines them that rides in my truck, and them that rides in my truck has got to work together with me or I works together with them. They has got to stay out of my cab. Perhaps that is the flaw of my character that needs perfecting. But I draws power from within and from my peoples and from the perfectability in Perfectability Baptism. I can't point to anyone I've conquered but plenty I've disciplined. Unless they's other people's children. Or them I learns discipline from my ownself. I wouldn't be talking to you if I didn't think you heard everything I'm saying. And even if you don't hear everything I'm saying, 'cause I don't know if any natural person can hear everything somebody's saying to them, at least you know I'm talking to you, and you don't even have to say I hear you like that man on TV 'cause I know you hear me. Now that African-American woman on there don't say that, 'cause she knows peoples knows she hears them. Monkey Bread say she is in South Africa now, though, and the Daughters of Nzingha is celebrating her for leaving the plantation. Might be a plantation there in South Africa, though. And you know us can run plantations. There is plenty of us usselves who knows how to run plantations. The white plantation owner claims that his the more efficient plantation, though.

Delgadina says nothing, then scratches her elbow.

Say what? What I'm saying, Mosquito, is that when people meet you who don't know you, probably to them you just seem to confirm the stereotype. You ain't exactly no invisible woman, but you know what I mean. I'm sure I see as much of the you that I want you to be as the you that you are.

She straightens a photograph of a concho belt, you know them pictures on the bar.

My natural self.

She straightens a photograph of a Kachina doll. Then Delgadina she say something in Spanish, and maybe it the same as saying natural self in Spanish. Then she say something about Langston Hughes. She say I kinda reminds her of people she's read about in Langston Hughes. Then she say something about a man who call hisself Simple. A *vato* comes in, she says *Hola vato* and goes and serves him some beer and then comes back to stand behind the bar. She asks me whether I wants another Budweiser. I says Naw, thanks. She wipes her forehead with her apron and leans on the bar.

I knows Simple and I likes Simple, I says, but I ain't say simple self, I says natural self. But you has still got to discipline the natural self. And the natural self has got to be like jazz, 'cause there is complexities in America. I knows that Hughes' Simple is a complex man, but he calls hisself Simple, 'cause they is peoples that don't understand simplicity unless it is named. Me I thinks that Simple is as sim-

ple as the Invisible Man is invisible. Me, whenever I says the word
natural I thinks about Africa, and elephants and hedgehogs and
pygmies. I knows I ain't supposed to put pygmies in the same category as them elephants and hedgehogs. And I knows I ain't supposed
to put elephants and hedgehogs before mentioning the pygmies. I
has always put the pygmies above the elephants and hedgehogs, and
I is always giving people the address of the Pygmy Fund to save the
Efe pygmies. Ain't I give you the address of the Pygmy Fund? I
knows that the elephants and hedgehogs needs salvation, but there is
everybody else to tell you about the elephant and hedgehog salvation
and the funds for they salvation. I think that even you, Delgadina,
has told me about elephant salvation and the salvation of the San Pedro River, 'cause them birdwatcher friends of yours is always watching birds on the San Pedro River. And even you thinks that every
pygmy is the same pygmy. There is some of your birdwatcher friends
that knows the names of four hundred species of birds and one hundred species of butterflies and thinks that every pygmy is the same
pygmy. They goes to the equatorial Africa even to watch birds and
knows every African bird—they's birdwatcher but they even knows
every minnow and snail and salamander on the San Pedro River—
and they thinks that the first pygmy that they meets is the only
pygmy in Africa. It don't matter if they is in the Cameroon or Zam-
bia and Zaire or anywhere in Africa. I knows there's the Tswa and
the Twa and the Mbuti of the Ituri Forest. In fact, I didn't even
know about the Efe till I learned about the Pygmy Fund. And
there's several other pygmy nationalities. I've never been to Africa
but there is so many documentaries on the African continent that I
sometimes thinks I inhabits Lake Tanganyika and the Ituri Forest
myself. Sometimes I thinks I knows Africa from the west, the southeast, the east, the north, the south. They is pygmies they calls the
true and unmixed pygmy, who must be the shortest people in the
world, and there is them that is just pygmoids, like Monkey Bread,
who has they height but the culture of America. There is probably
pygmy American or American pygmies, but most of us ain't know
our tribe. The Mbuti pygmies in Zaire in the Ituri Forest, them is
the pygmies that most of the television documentaries is about. I
only knows as much about them as I hear, but there is books you can
read about them. They ain't only pygmies on the Learning Channel.

I gots to find out more about that Pygmy Fund myself and whether it's for true pygmies. They say the best funds is them that teaches peoples to fish. I knows them pygmies already knows how to fish, though. 'Cept they might be trying to teach them to fish like Europeans fish. I knows that them Europeans is fishing fools. They even makes movies about fishing and television shows and builds houses just to fish in. For them they is something sacred about fishing. They even fishes like that man you read to me say about Americans chewing gum, like it a act full of poetry.

Un acto lleno de poesía, say Delgadina. That the Spanish I hears. But y'all that knows Spanish gots to say what it means. Delgadina say that supposed to be a famous Spanish essay about gum chewing. 'Cause for Americans chewing gum is just natural, but that Spaniard he wrote hisself a whole comic and cultural essay on the art of American gum chewing and what it say about popular American culture. Y'all that ain't read that essay has got to read that essay. Even y'all that is interested in the subjects of race and class and culture can find something in that essay on chewing gum.

I knows how to fish, I says.

But I still be thinking he look like that Frito Bandito, though, but that's why they got that Frito Bandito so you be thinking every Mexican a Frito Bandito. To tell the truth, when I first come in this restaurant, I be wondering which the Frito Bandito myself, though I ain't tell Delgadina. When she returns where I am she says that the man wanted to know whether I'm an immigration officer. I start to tell her about that Maria but decide not to. She got that bodacious hair too, except but it shorter hair than Maria's. Look kinda like Sean Young's hair, you know, the actress. Except in them early movies that Sean Young have that long hair, like Maria, when she used to play in them B movies and kinda look like a Chicana. Lotta them gringa Americans look like Chicanas, 'cept you know they ain't Chicana. If somebody tell you they Chicana, then you be looking at them like they Chicana. And you be having different ideas of who they are and they possibilities. That's how come some of them changes they names. And they even gets to play roles with different possibilities. Now how that man think I'm immigration? And them border police, I just seen men border police, but maybe they got women border police. I think I heard about some woman that goes along the border with them mens hunting them Mexicans. I don't know if that's a true story, though. And all them border police they ain't just gringos either, they got them some Mexicans or Mexican Americans, probably even African-American border police, but it seems like it's mostly them gringos that thinks I'm smuggling.

I remember once when one of them border patrols stopped me I started to say I ain't smuggling nobody but myself. Course I didn't say that, I just showed my license and my registration papers. I had to get out of my truck and open the back of my truck. Didn't have no Maria in it, then, but he was making me feel like I was some kinda smuggler, even though I knew I weren't. Then I be thinking about them fugitives and them good and bad slaves. Remembering something I'd heard about them good and bad slaves.

When Delgadina taking that course on the politics of race, she be talking about how that matter of race suppose to complicate the matter of goodness. Like in the old days. Ain't a good slave supposed to be bad and a bad slave supposed to be good? And what about them good and bad masters? There be some slaves talking good master this and good master that. And even heard somebody say that only good masters can make good slaves. A good master makes a good slave, that's what they said. I mean, that you got to be a good master in order to make people into good slaves. But what they mean by good master, and it the same thing a slave mean by good master? But then others be saying if slavery itself is bad, then there can't be no good masters. Then Delgadina be talking about Gypsy culture in Europe, and be calling the Gypsies the niggers of Europe. But then them Europeans makes a lot of peoples they niggers.

To tell the truth, when you first came in here, when you first come into this cantina, that's what I thought you were, Mosquito. I thought you were immigration, because aren't many African Americans come in here. Some of the tourists come in here, but not many African Americans from the area. They go to the restaurant for the Mexican food, you know, like the ordinary tourists, some Texas natives, they'll order the tacos and fried ice cream and chajitas and shit, but they don't come into the cantina. A few drunks come into the cantina. And not too many women come in the cantina either, chica, unless they're *putas* and you don't look like a *puta*. At least you don't look like a *puta* to me, though some of the men think you're a *puta*.

Even Mr. Delgado thinks you a *puta,* so Miguelita say she thinks. I
told her to tell him you aren't. But you know how men are. Every
woman's a *puta* to some man. I don't think there's a woman who
hasn't been thought a *puta* by some man, you know. Every woman's
got her *puta* story, believe me. Gringos come in here to slum, you
know, and you weren't acting like you were here to slum. And I
know you're no *puta.* So I thought you're immigration. Or one of
them social worker–psychologists, she jokes. Signifies. Then I'm
talking to you and I know this is your first time in Texas City. And
on your way to Glamourtown. Well, I'm glad you decided on Texas
City. I like Texas City myself.

Sometimes when I watches Delgadina in Mr. Delgado's I'm
thinking why she ain't have her own cantina and be calling it Delgadina's, 'cause she know all about that cantina. I ain't seen that Mr.
Delgado boss her or nothing, 'cause like I said I ain't even seen that
Mr. Delgado. I ain't seen Mr. Delgado to boss Delgadina, but I ain't
seen Delgadina to boss nobody either. I suppose if they was someone
else working the bar with her, one of them might be the boss to the
other. Or maybe that Mr. Delgado trust Delgadina to boss herself. I
remember I even thought that Delgadina name were Delgadina Delgado and that Delgado's were Delgadina's, but then they put the sign
up that say Mr. Delgado's to make sure, I guess, that peoples know
they's a Mr. Delgado. I ain't seen Delgadina to give nobody orders,
except a few drunks that needs to be give orders, like she be telling
them that they's had enough to drink. They's times when she don't
serve me no more Budweisers, though usually I knows not to drink
too many Budweisers my ownself. But I knows they's women, probably womens just like Delgadina herself, sees they freedom in giving
orders, in being the manager, the boss. Course some will say that a
woman's management style is different from a man's. Even that
movie about them working women suggested that the female management style were different from the man's, and they had that work-
sharing environment rather than that competitive work environment. But I heard me about this one town in Mexico where it the
womens that rules, though I don't know whether that a real town or
a imaginary one. I think it were even Delgadina that told me about
that town, so it must be a real town in Mexico, where it the womens
that rules. 'Cause I didn't read about it in the newspaper. That ain't

true freedom neither, though. I ain't thought that much about that freedom myself, what it true meaning is, but if I thinks about it, probably that be my ideal of what freedom is. Ain't to give orders nor to take them. Course, you's still got to belong to the union, though. If you's a workingman or woman. You's gotta be organized. 'Cause them others is organized.

Like I said, Delgadina she refuse to serve this *vato* any more liquor, not the *vaquero*, but this other *vato*. Instead, she bring him a cup of coffee. The restaurant serve all kinds of Mexican and Chicano foods, chilis and tortillas and fried ice cream and chajitas, like I said, and not that Taco Bell Mexican food, and it sells them soft tortillas, which Delgadina says is real tortillas. Authentic Mexican tortillas she say is soft, ain't like them Taco Bell tortillas. I know, I says, 'cause I overheard that couple at the nature sanctuary, that Dickey and Tea Biscuit, least Delgadina's notebook say that her name, be talking about them authentic Mexican tortillas and then I heard that other couple be asking the waiter why they tacos don't taste like them Taco Bell tacos, 'cause them fools be thinking that them Taco Bell tacos is the real tacos. And they be thinking the real authentic tacos ain't real tacos. And a lot of them even likes them Taco Bell tacos better than the real tortillas. I already know about them tortillas, I says, them authentic Mexican tacos. Y'all knows the difference between tacos and tortillas, don't you? Tortillas is the wrapping for them tacos. They's all pancakes. They don't serve no food in the bar, though, except you know that bar-type food, corn chips and pretzels and them tortilla chips and peanuts and them you get free when you order a drink, and you don't have to keep ordering drinks to get free food like in some of them cantinas; you order you a drink and then you can eat them tortilla chips and salsa. I think Mr. Delgado, he the owner of the bar, do that 'cause a lot of them *vatos* is unemployed and just got that migrant work. 'Cept Delgadina say there's other Mexicans and Chicanos that ain't agringada that come in there, 'cause she know one of them *vatos* an architect or some shit, though she say ain't many middle-class Chicanos that come in that cantina, though a lot eats in the restaurant section with the tourists and gringos. Sometimes she got dishes of different kinds of salsa on the bar, though. Ain't just salsa made with tomatoes and green peppers and jalapeños, but got papaya, pecan, and wild mushroom salsa. She say you can also put peaches and plums and any kind of exotic fruits in salsa. A lot of that salsa she makes herself. I told you about that salsa made with them mandarin oranges. They be calling them Mexicans and Chicanas the cosmic race, I guess that salsa a cosmic condiment or cosmic salsa.

Borracho, I hear her say. *Ebrio.* But she call him that in a joking, friendly way. He come in there all the time and he trying to sell her his Harley-Davidson. He tell her she'd look good on a Harley-Davidson. One of them Softail Harley-Davidson. But I ain't sure whether he call it a Softail for signifying or whether they really got Harley-Davidsons named Softail.

Don't pretend you don't know I'm in love with you, I heard him say. I thought I heard him ask.

Y su señora?

Ain't he the one trying to sell you that Harley-Davidson? I ask when she come back to the bar. Say what? she ask. I thought I heard him trying to sell you his Harley-Davidson. I ain't tell her I also thought I heard him say he in love with her, 'cause he be saying that in English. Or maybe he be saying something to her in Spanish and I just think that's what I hear. He be talking to her in Spanish, but that Harley-Davidson he be saying in English and that Softail he be saying in English. Then she say he trying to sell her his Harley-Davidson.

But she say he ain't the same one as the one trying to sell her that Harley-Davidson, and of course I don't say it is him or the one that be saying he in love with her, 'cause I don't want her to think I thinks all them Chicanos looks alike. When I showed her that picture of John Henry Hollywood, though, even she be thinking she know him from Houston. And when I tell her he ain't from Houston, she still be saying he look like somebody she know from Houston. And be surprised when I tell her he my old boyfriend, 'cause she be saying he don't look like my type or I don't look like his type. Standing at the bar scratching inside her elbows from eating that salsa 'cause she allergic to them jalapeños in that salsa and telling me he don't look like my type and I don't look like his. I starts to ask her what sorta man she think's my type, and what sorta woman she think his type, but a *vato* comes up to the bar and orders some drink and they start talking Spanish, but I kept thinking, He's just her sorta man. He must be her sorta man. And she must be his sorta woman. And then I hear her telling him, Learn to be the master of yourself. Even the gringos aren't masters of themselves. They conquer everybody else, but not themselves. If they'd learn to conquer themselves, they wouldn't have so long a history of so many peoples complaining about they behavior. There's this little village in Mexico where whenever they see a gringo coming, they hide. They just hide. Can you imagine? A whole village of people when they see the gringo coming, they just hide. 'Cause they know who they are. 'Cause they know who the gringo is. Every time we forget who they are, don't they always remind us? I don't hide when I see the gringo coming, though. But I know who they are.

But Delgadina she say she don't like to talk about the gringo, what the gringo doing. She says in a lot of her stories the gringo ain't even in them. 'Cept there's some stories you can't write unless the gringo's in them. She say the gringo like you to spend your energy thinking and talking about him and what he doing instead of use your energy for what you doing.

Like that little village I'm talking about. They hide from the gringo, but when the gringo leave they little village, they go back to they village and do what they doing. And they got one of the nicest little villages in the whole of Mexico. I tell everybody about that little village except the gringo. We's got to keep them safe from the gringo. We's got to keep at least one little village safe from the gringo.

Then I ain't sure whether she telling me about a real little village or a little village in one of her stories or a little village in her imagination. Maybe she telling me about a metaphorical little village in one of her stories or her imagination. Cause I be thinking seem like they's more fictional logic in that story than true logic. 'Cause what if the gringo decide he stay in that little village? They have to go and confront the gringo. They either have to ban him from they village or figure a way to integrate him into they village. Or some other logic of how to deal with that gringo. I know what she mean, though. I'm such a big African, I ain't hide from them gringos. Though I seen some of them hiding from me.

He kinda look like Nat Perrison, I says.

Say who?

Man this woman usedta write and tell stories about. She would write one story about him and then she retell his story in another story. So he might appear in several stories, but he the same Nat Perrison. Kinda look like a *vato*, except African American.

Oh, yeah?

Then she go wait on another table. I'm thinking about them little villages in Mexico. Sometimes they shows them little villages on television, when them anthropologists goes into them little villages to study the people. They showed one of them little villages where the Spanish-looking people are the aristocrats and the Indian-looking people or the mestizos are the commoners. In some of them villages the Indian-looking people questions they status and starts rebellions, but in others they just plays the Sancho Panza to Don Quijote and don't question theyselves being Sancho Panzas.

Oh, yeah? she ask again when she come back to behind the bar.

Yeah, I says, though I ain't sure if she saying Oh yeah to the conversation she having with me or Oh yeah to one of them other conversations, 'cause she be talking to me then she be talking to one of them *vatos* or Miguelita, then she come back and be talking to me.

She get a Mexican beer, the one with that Indian-sounding name, though she be saying they a beer factory in Mexico with that Indian-sounding name, and open it and I glances at that *vaquero* but he looking at Delgadina now and Delgadina take that glance and throw it back at him 'cause they always be some man in that cantina who want her for a love interest, and then she take that beer over to the gringa, then she come back and wipe off the bar again. That *vaquero* he looking at the gringa now, and then one of the other mens say something to him and must be telling him who the woman is, that that Mr. Delgado woman, the owner of the restaurant-cantina woman, that her name Miguelita, and that she ain't no *puta*. That beach towel one of them Acapulco towels, though she say she ain't never been to that Acapulco. She say she been to Mexico, even to that little Mexican village where the people hide from the gringo, and she like to go to them little Mexican villages the tourists don't know about, especially them gringo tourists. She say they a lot of them little villages in Mexico that the tourists don't know about, and she say in one of them little villages she say they was referring to her as the gringa—not the little village where they hide from the gringo but another little village—and she be trying to explain to them that she ain't a gringa, she a Mexican American, a Chicana, but they still be referring to her as the gringa. She say in that little village all the people look like Olmecs, them ancient Mexicans. So to them she a gringa. But in most of them other villages she say they be thinking of her as a Mexican, but from America, even that little village where they hide from gringos, though she be saying there's some that still consider Texas to be a part of Mexico. She be telling them she from Texas. And to them that still Mexico. 'Cause like I said it people that make them borders. I bet Texas don't know it ain't Mexico.

The gringa? I ain't really told you about the gringa. The crazy gringa. I mean I've mentioned her name Miguelita and kinda told y'all about her, about her being a crazy woman that even the social psychiatrist psychology know a crazy woman, you know, Miguelita, though he think she a crazy woman named Tucker and she a crazy woman named Miguelita Delgado, but I ain't exactly told y'all about her. They's only three of us womens that frequents this cantina: Delgadina, 'cause she the bartender, the gringa and myself. Occasionally one of them *putas* comes in the cantina, but they don't frequent it, 'cause Mr. Delgado discourages the presence of *putas* on his premises. Sometimes Delgadina gets her broom and chases them out, other times she just say whores gotta work too. She kinda ambivalent about that whoredom, like a lot of womens, though I guess there's a lot of mens ambivalent about that whoredom, too, but Mr. Delgado ain't ambivalent about it at all. There's another rumor about Mr. Delgado, that he finds other employment for them *putas* so's they don't have to be *putas*, but I don't know if that's a true rumor. I ain't never met that Mr. Delgadino myself, I mean Mr. Delgado, but he the one put the sign in the window NO SOLICITING and that mean whores too. When I first seen the gringa I thought she was one of them gringa whores from South Texas, though, but she ain't, she the wife of that Señor Delgado who owns the cantina, like I said. Always sitting in the corner of the cantina drinking that Mexican beer. Gotta have that Mexican beer. Not no Bud Light for her, always that Mexican beer or pulque or one of them margaritas. She don't even drink that German beer, and this cantina got plenty of German beer, 'cause Delgadina be saying a lot of Germans settled in South

America after the war, and Mr. Delgado don't import the German beer from Germany he import it from South America. I ain't never seen Señor Delgado myself, like I said—I calls him the invisible Chicano—but everyone know she his wife. At first Delgadina say she didn't like the gringa, or maybe just the fact of Señor Delgado he marrying hisself a gringa. She never liked to see the good ones marrying them gringas or even them Mexican or Chicana womens that looks like gringas or tries to look like gringas, 'cause she say a lot of the good ones that don't marry gringas be getting them Mexican women or Chicanas that looks like gringas, though it seem to me a Mexican woman that naturally look like a gringa, got as much a natural right to look like a gringa as them that look like the Native Mexicans, I mean as long as they ain't got that gringoism state of mind. The bad ones treating every woman like some *chingada*—seem like I heard Delgadina use that word for whore—they should marry themselves gringas in her opinion. The ones who know how to treat a woman should get themselves good Chicana wives. They's plenty of Chicanas that's wifable women, she be saying. But a lot of the good ones, she say, likes to get theyselves them gringa wives or as close to the gringa as they can get. And she be talking about one of her favorite Chicano movie and television stars, got him a wife who look like a gringa, though she Chicana. One of them blond-haired Chicanas. And you know she be sounding like she want that man for herself, or want a man like that to want a true Chicana like herself. And you know she be sounding just like them African-American womens when they be talking about them African-American mens getting themselves them gringas. 'Cause I know my girlfriend out in Hollywood be telling me how a lot of them Hollywood types be marrying gringas or the lightest thing they can get. Or can afford, 'cause that's Hollywood, you know. That why she say she like her that actor Denzel Washington—Delgadina say it his name I likes, 'cause I don't say it like a name, I says it like a metaphor—cause he got him a real African-American woman, but then I be thinking can't them light ones be real African-American women too? It must depend on what the mens motives is, if they's genuinely in love. 'Cause that love got its own logic. And maybe it just her seeing them with the lightest thing they can get that ain't gringa and they's in love. They tries to put that Denzel with the lightest thing they can get for him, she said, but he a true man with his own true mind about a woman. Leastwise that who I thinks he is.

Denzel, Denzel, Denzel, I says to Delgadina. There's a Denzel Washington movie. You want to go see Denzel?

I don't think Denzel movies is all that, she says.

This *Devil in a Blue Dress*.

Okay, she says. You don't say Denzel like it a name, though, you say it like it a metaphor.

Metaphor for what?

I don't know. Whatever Denzel means to you, I guess. I like Edward James Olmos, he's my favorite actor and person, I've even written him a fan letter, but I don't say his name the way you say Denzel. The day they forget who Denzel is, you still be saying Denzel.

Cause Denzel is Denzel.

Then she go with me to *Devil in a Blue Dress*. Delgadina watches the movie, but she don't behave like she think it all that. Me I thinks Denzel is all that. After the movie I goes into the bathroom, and there's some other women of color in the bathroom talking like they think he's all that. Then one of them starts talking that talk that you sometimes hear women of color talk.

Now I ain't the kind of woman to say that our mens can't have every type of womans they wants, from Swedes to Eskimo womens to Indians from India to them in Hong Kong, just like that James Bond, but you know what I'm saying, girlfriend. How come some of our mens places all the world's womens above usselves when he's got all the world's womens in his own womens.

That wasn't a white woman, that was a colored woman. Girl, sorta like those Creoles in New Orleans. You weren't watching the movie. She's a colored woman, but just a high-toned type of colored woman who looks like a white woman. In fact, I saw her in a movie where she played a white woman. Some of the other people watching the movie thought she was a white woman. I know she plays a lot of roles that are reserved for white women.

I know she's playing a woman of color. We's all the world's womens in usselves, I mean in ourselves, that's what I'm saying. Now I know you know what I'm saying, Nadine.

When she says Nadine, I wants to peek out of the toilet stall to see who this other woman named Nadine, but I just stays in there and listens. And to tell y'all the truth the woman talking to Nadine kinda reminds me of Monkey Bread, the kinda way Monkey Bread talk.

But I likes me them men my ownself who likes women that don't conform to the Hollywood aesthetic, and that got they own aesthetic. I think that Denzel, at least the Denzel I thinks I know, have got his own aesthetic. That's 'cause he seems to me like a man who knows who he is. 'Cause he could have him some of them hoochie Hollywood women. Course there's people who'll think I must ain't got my own aesthetic for liking Denzel so much that I turns him into a metaphor. I'm reading this book on the African aesthetic and what it says is that most of us New World Africans still have a mulatto aesthetic.

I ain't the only one thinking of Denzel as a metaphor, I'm thinking. I wants to see who them womens is, but when I gets out of the stall, Delgadina standing there putting on some lipstick. I wants to ask her if she heard them women talking about Denzel. She still looking like she ain't think the movie or Denzel is all that.

I'm thinking that the woman that played the love interest in the movie kinda look like a combination of Delgadina and Miguelita, the crazy gringa. But after Delgadina discovered the gringa was sorta crazy, she began to feel kinda protective toward her, in fact most of the peoples that frequents the bar feels protective toward her, say Delgadina. I guess that why that man be explaining to that new *vaquero* who wife she is. She ain't just any gringa *puta*, they be saying, she Mr. Delgado's wife. She weren't originally crazy, or rather when Señor Delgado first married the woman she were only in the first stages of some kinda psychosis, say Delgadina, except but Señor Delgado didn't know that, he just in love with the woman, I guess 'cause she didn't behave like none of them other gringas, didn't have that gringoism state of mind. She supposed to be a daughter of privilege, say Delgadina, but when Señor Delgado met her she were selling them slave bracelets and biker jewelry out on the Avenue. Like a lot of them gringa rebels. But Delgadina say she used to work as a tour guide or translator or some shit in Paris, not Paris, Texas, but Paris, France—I be telling Delgadina they got a Paris, Kentucky, too—and a real daughter of privilege. But even being a daughter of privilege, she don't act like none of them other gringa. 'Cause even

Señor Delgado, she say, used to think a gringa a gringa till he met this gringa. Especially these Texas gringa, who got they own history of gringoism. She say they's even African Americans in South Texas that's got they own brand of gringoism, like I told you, and she be saying that another reason she knew I wasn't from South Texas. Then after they got married she developed more and more of her psychosis. Delgadina don't call it a neurosis like a lot of them gringa womens, she say when they got psychosis they always call them neurosis, especially them daughters of privilege, but she call this a psychosis.

I think she was in one of them abusive relationships, says Delgadina. I mean before she met Mr. Delgado. 'Cause Mr. Delgado tender toward her. I think she's Mr. Delgado's first wife, though he's much older than she is. Though some people say he has a wife in Mexico. But I think she's his first wife. Anyway he seen her selling that biker shit and them slave bracelets and she wasn't acting like the ordinary gringa, you know. I think it's that more than Miguelita herself that he's in love with, the fact that there's a gringa who's not a gringa, you know.

Of course, he'd say he's in love with her. But I don't think it's Miguelita myself. I think she's a metaphor for the possibility of what gringos and gringas could be like. I don't mean the craziness in her. But the Miguelita that transcends her craziness. There's people say that racism is a form of insanity it ownself. And 'cause it's a form of insanity you gotta treat it like you treats other forms of insanity. Course the people that has it thinks they's sane. And like other forms of insanity the people that has it don't even know they's got it. Or they denies they's got it. Or they invents other words for it. 'Cause they don't recognize it for what it is. Course there's them that's got it and proud of it, you know.

But then, like I say, they got married, Mr. Delgado and this gringa Miguelita, honeymooned in Mexico, then returned to South Texas, and then she started developing this psychosis. Ain't no paranoid psychosis or nothing like that. It kinda like a split personality, except the other personality is more of a alter ego or some shit, say Delgadina. She know all about them alter egos 'cause she say in her creative writing class they always be creating them alter egos. One character she be saying might be a alter ego for another. 'Cause she

be saying nearly every story they read for they creative writing class
it got a alter ego in it, don't matter what culture the story is, seem like
they's always a alter ego. Say the alter ego might be a main character
or a minor character. I ain't never been to none of them creative writing classes, but she did take me to one of them poetry readings or
some shit, and then they had one of them receptions for the poet. I
was thinking that it would be a Chicano or Native American or even
a African-American poet, but it was a Welsh poet. But that Delgadina. She even the first one read me about the Wife of Bath and in it
own English, which is true English but ain't modern English.

What she say now?

Talking about her husbands, calling them worthy men.

Anyway, this gringa she have her a alter ego. Her name is Mickey,
but her alter ego name Sophie. Delgadina be saying Sophie is Mickey's alter ego. Except Sophie, Delgadina say, is also a real person,
'cause she have seen letters from a real woman name Sophie, some
French woman, 'cause the letters is postmarked all the way from
Paris, France. They in French and sometimes that Mickey even read
them to her. She know a little French, 'cause I even seen that Delgadina herself trying to write some poetry in French, but that Mickey
translate them into English, them letters from that French woman I
mean. She ain't read none of them letters to me, that Mickey, so I
can't verify that her alter ego Sophie is based on a real woman name
Sophie. And Delgadina she be wondering whether that Mickey talk
to Mr. Delgado about that Sophie as much as she do to everybody
else. But that alter ego, she be saying that be like if she were my alter
ego or I were her alter ego. And she be saying that sometimes a character is the alter ego of the author and not another character. And I
be wondering whether an author can be the alter ego of a character,
and she be saying maybe in what they call that metafiction, which
she say is fiction about fiction.

But peoples in the cantina don't call her Mickey now. Ever since
they started feeling protective toward her they be calling her Miguelita, which mean I guess the same thing as Mickey except but in
Spanish. And I think it mean Little Mickey 'cause it got the *ita* on it,
like that *vatito* it mean little *vato*. And Delgadina say that her real
name Mickey, that's why they don't call her Miguela but Miguelita,
plus Delgadina say she more a Miguelita than a Miguela.

I've heard drunken *vatos* that don't know who she supposed to be to call her other names. Pancha or Panchita Chapopote. Or maybe she the kinda gringa that reminds me of other women.

I don't know about that Pancha or Panchita Chapopote, but I know about that Sophie—not Sophie Tucker—cause sometimes when I ain't talking to that Delgadina I take my Bud Light to Miguelita's table. Everybody that sit down at that table she start to telling them about her alter ego, that Sophie, though like I said I don't know if she be telling Mr. Delgado about Sophie. In fact, she mostly never tell anybody about herself, it mostly always about that Sophie unless telling them about that Sophie is telling them about herself, like in the storybooks. Miguelita's a smallish woman with big bluish-green eyes—Delgadina says they're contacts—and yellowish blond hair and it look like her hair been colored to get that yellowish blond, though Delgadina say she a natural blond. And it ain't that straight blond hair, it that kinky and wavy-type blond hair. She's slender but her cheeks are plump, her chin plump and rounded and although she must be in her thirties, maybe the same age as Delgadina, she look like she still got her baby fat. She kinda remind me of a cartoon.

Then Miguelita start talking about them wines. She doesn't even know the difference between a Beaujolais and a Bordeaux, so I say how can you be a French woman, Sophie, and don't know the difference between a Beaujolais and a Bordeaux, that seems like a contradiction in terms to me, so I sent her the *ordonnance des vins*. You shouldn't be French and not know the *ordonnance des vins*, you know, that's almost like being Catholic and not knowing the catechism. I'm going to ask Sophie if she knows the catechism. The *ordonnance des vins*? Oh, you know, Mosquito, like with oysters and fish you can have Muscadet, Quincy, Alsace, Chablis; with liver a good Sauterne, Jurançon or Montrachet blanc, a Gewürztraminer; with red meats, a Pauillac, a Margaux, a Vonay, Nuits-Saint-Georges; with cheese, Pommard, Hermitage, Musigny, Pomerol; with patisseries, that's pastries, ice cream, and then you got you your sweet wines: Malvoisie, Muscat, Grenoche; with poultry and your white meats, a Saint-Amour, Saint-Estephe, Saint-Julien, Saint-Émilion; and then you got to know which ones to serve *frais* and which ones *chambre*, that's room temperature. It's all very complicated, Mosquito, and of course that isn't even your whole *ordon-nance*. I'm not going to bore you with the whole *ordonnance*, but everyone should know the *ordonnance des vins*, certainly every French person should know, certainly Sophie should know. I mean she doesn't even know a Bouzy's a champagne. And I'm teaching Delgadina the *ordonnance des vins*, though you don't much need to know the *ordonnance des vins* in a Mexican cantina. But I keep tell-ing Sophie she ought to be more like Delgadina. Delgada's real bright for a Mexican.

Delgada?

That's her name.

You mean Delgadina.

That's her little name, but Delgada, that's her true name. And she's real bright, I don't mean for a Mexican, I mean she's real bright, our Delgada, she's real bright. Sophie says Americans always think that she's Mexican, not just when she's in America but when they meet her in France, and she has to keep telling them that she's French. In England they always know she's French. The English rather see the French the same way we see our Mexicans. French women who resemble English women are always thought the most aristocratic.

A couple came and sat at the booth behind us. Miguelita scratched the tip of her nose and turned as if she were talking more to them than to me. The man look like a gringo, but she woman look kind of Italian, or like one of them Mediterranean womens. Mi-guelita is a small woman with a lot of kinky blond hair. A lot of white womens with hair like that straightens they hair, but Mi-guelita keep hers kinky. I likes that she keeps her hair kinky myself. I think the kink is natural, but I ain't know whether the blond is nat-ural. She got a creamy-type complexion, blue-green eyes, a small nose, and full lips. They's kinda irregular full lips that makes her look like a cartoon character or a comedian, at least about the lips. Usually she wear a pink-type lipstick, though her natural lips is pink.

I was traveling through France with an English woman, Jane, and she kept pointing out the quaint and cute little French villages, just like we do our Mexican villages. And when you see English movies about France they seem to always be set in these quaint little French villages and the French behave just like our Mexicans behave, though to most Americans we think of the French as aristocratic and intellectuals, except of course for the French in America, the Cajuns. But to the English, certainly Jane, the French are sort of like our Cajuns or the way the French in Quebec are to the English Canadians. It's all social status, Mosquito. France is England's Mexico. I can go into Mexico and they don't give me any trouble crossing the borders. I can go back and forth across the Mexican border whenever I want. We think of the English as Europeans, but they don't think of themselves as Europeans, they think of themselves as English. As Anglo-Saxons.

Delgadina come and take the couple's order. She give them a menu. I ain't see her give others menus, 'cause most of the *vatos* know what on the order. Then she tell them they must want the restaurant and not the cantina, then they takes the menu with them into the restaurant.

When I was in France, I learned all the wines, you know, of the different regions, red and white wines of Bourgogne, wines of the Southwest, I mean, the French Southwest. I really bowled them over when I first came back to the States, you know. I spent some time in northern New Mexico before I came to South Texas, one of those university towns. Then I was at the University of New Mexico because of the pueblo architecture.

Does you know somebody named Leonora Valdez? She at the University of New Mexico. She a Native American woman, though, and don't like to be photographed. I met her when I usedta have me a route in New Mexico, Arizona and Nevada. A reservation Native American, you know, from Arizona.

But Miguelita, she just continue with her conversation. We had a wine identification contest and all I identified was a Vosnes Romance 1979, but that was better than even this professional wine taster. Sophie's really bright, but I always tell her you can't be French and not know your wines, Sophie. They don't serve wines earlier than 1975 in some circles, you know. I got to work on Savoie and then the Côtes du Rhone wines. When I was in France, I worked with this master wine taster. I drank the Tokay and the fool kissed me and he could tell right away it was the Coteaux Champenois Blanc and not the Coteaux Chapernois Bouzy Rouge, and he couldn't tell by the color either, because he didn't even look at my mouth when he kissed me, but don't tell Mr. Delgado I told you about that kiss. It was all by taste . . . You know, my friend Sophie, even when she was a child men used to find her sensual. They used to want to cuddle her. She's got these almond eyes that slant a bit upward, you know, almost like Asian eyes, but a nose that turns a bit toward her mouth. She looks a little like me, actually, except she's French, and she's got sensitive lips, slightly irregular, you know, like what's that movie star? But that makes them all the more interesting, and she's always wearing different-color lipsticks, you know, turning her lips into peaches, apples, plums, tangerines, strawberries. She used to run from men who wanted to cuddle her until she turned eighteen, and then she started running toward some of them, but only the ones she wanted. She's the sort of woman who can be everything, I mean the men can see whatever they want to, you know, whatever they want to see in her. But don't tell Mr. Delgado I told you so.

The couple return from the restaurant and sit in the cantina. Then Delgadina comes and takes their order. Then she give them another menu, 'cause they forgot the menu they took with them into the restaurant.

He kinda reminds me of that general. . . .

What general?

I think she talking about the man in the couple, 'cause she be looking towards them, like she talking to them.

I was at this villa in France, some of my friends own this villa in the South of France, and they're very cosmopolitan, you know, they're like royalty actually they're so wealthy, so there was this general or something from one of those Latin American countries, I think he was in exile or something, anyway he was sitting there looking like a general, but I didn't know anything about the fool, so I went over and said, You sitting there looking like a general, and he said, I am a general. Well, I was embarrassed to say the least, and now of course I'm always seeing his pictures in the magazines. And I was thinking he looks just like Mr. Delgado or Mr. Delgado looks just like him. I didn't see him at all before, but all Latin American generals look the same to me. Just like Mr. Delgado. They'd had their revolution and so he was in exile, not Mr. Delgado, not Señor Delgado, but the general. He was trying to get a job as a consultant with the French military. He tried to get a job with the German military, and then he was trying the French military . . . If you could live anyplace in the world where would it be, chica?

I don't know. I've got this friend out in Hollywood who wants me to come to Hollywood. Her name's Monkey Bread. That's her nickname, though, not her real name. I kinda like Texas City, though.

Texas City's a dump. Well, it isn't exactly a dump. But Cougar, British Columbia, that's supposed to be the most beautiful place in the world. I've got an old boyfriend from Cougar, British Columbia. Don't tell Mr. Delgado. Sophie, of course, thinks Paris is the most beautiful place in the world, but with Paris it's the beautiful things . . . You know, there are people who know.

Know what?

There are always a circle of people who know. And know they know. And they are not us, Nadine. They are conspirators. And they are not us, Nadine. They are not like us, Nadine, or Delgadina, or Monkey Bread or Leonora Valdez. Or even Jane, even though she's an English woman of privilege, she's not true privilege. Sophie, I know Sophie is Sophie. But even Sophie can't imagine those people who really know and know that they are the people who know.

Say what?

Can you imagine? There's the rest of us, and then there's this circle of people who know. I wonder what it would be like to be among the people who know. And know they know. The people of privilege, real privilege. The people of real privilege, nobody knows who they are. And if they know them, they don't know who they really are. Can you imagine? They are the people who know. They are the people in power, real power, Nadine. And not people who we imagine are in power. I think I met one of them once. But I didn't know he was one of them. No one else would know either. They'd just think they were meeting an ordinary man. Sophie thinks I called her a whore. I can't imagine calling another woman a whore. I don't think women call other women whores.

Yes they do.

Do they? I only thought men called women whores, I mean the women they can't control. Whenever a man can't control a woman, she's either a whore or a bitch. But I can't imagine calling another woman a whore. Delgadina says you can't be a Mexican without saying *puta*, but they've got another word for *puta, chinga* something.

She sip on her Mexican beer. Like I said, she don't drink nothing but them Mexican beers. Or sometimes that pulque. That cactus juice. I guess you can call it cactus juice, 'cause supposed to be the fermented juice from some type of cactus. Or sometimes them margaritas.

The couple order themselves margaritas, then they gets up and take the menu with them. Maybe they just likes them menus, 'cause they's got South Texas plants and trees and flowers on them. Delgadina paint them menus herself and sometimes even draws little maps of South Texas on them, so's peoples knows exactly where the cantina is, you know, so's to advertise the cantina, and maybe they is tourists and thinks that they makes good souvenirs of South Texas and us cantina.

CHAPTER 6

H E KINDA SOUND LIKE THAT MAN THAT PLAY JAMES Bond, I mean the first James Bond. Kinda look like him too. I mean the elder James Bond. I don't mean the young James Bond, but the elder James Bond. Delgadina have showed me a book of his poetry with his photograph on it, and also she got a recording of him reading poems. We ain't gone there in my truck, but in a Land-Rover that she sometimes rents when she ain't want to ride around in my truck. I ask her why she don't buy that Land-Rover, but she say she prefer to rent it.

That's 'cause he's Welsh, she say, as we climb out of the Land-Rover. That Land-Rover looks like the kind that peoples rides in when they's in Africa on safari. Whenever I gets in and out of Delgadina's rented Land-Rover I feel like I'm supposed to be in Africa on safari. In fact, the khaki trousers and blouse that Delgadina is wearing do kinda make her look like she on safari. She even got her a khaki-colored safari hat, but she leave that in the Land-Rover.

The hills around the house are covered with palm trees and cactus plants. It looks more like a part of Arizona, though, than Texas. Beyond the house they's a full moon and hills that looks like sculptures or stone cathedrals or fortresses. Sorta like the scenery in them cowboy movies that they makes in Arizona for the landscape. I'm climbing out of the Land-Rover feeling like I'm on African safari, stepping into an Arizona landscape, which ain't Arizona but Texas. Them is them edible types of cactus plants that people uses to make cactus candy.

The grass is buffalo grass, the kind of grass you ain't have to mow. The house also got a little garden of wildflowers, a red bird of paradise and some butterfly weeds. Orange-red and orange flowers. Them type of cactus with the bright red flowers. Red and golden columbines. Some of them Navajo tea shrubs—I think they's called Navajo tea shrubs—and desert marigolds. Other types of Texas prairie wildflowers.

What's that type of cactus? I asks Delgadina.

Claret cup cactus, say Delgadina. Those are my favorite cactus. Their pods are sweet and edible. I think they're the most beautiful cactus. Their bright red flowers.

Delgadina lead me into the garden of wildflowers, telling me the names of some of them other wildflowers and different prairie bushes. She know all they names. Coyote bush the name of one of them bushes. Yucca and jojoba, wild hyacinth and chocolate flowers.

Chocolate flowers?

Smell them.

They smells just like chocolate, although they's yellow. 'Cept the centers is brown. Maybe they gets the chocolate aroma from the brown centers.

I call that the hummingbird plant. I don't know it's name myself. That's sage. She's got herbs mixed in with the wildflowers. You should know these plants, though, because I've got some of them in my container garden. Wildflowers don't belong in containers, though. If I had me a ranch, I'd have me a garden like this. Free all my wildflowers from their containers. That's buffalo grass.

I know.

How you know?

I just knows it's buffalo grass. I ain't know how I know. I just knows it's buffalo grass.

I like her receptions, say Delgadina as we leaves the garden and goes up the stone walk to the adobe ranch house. This ain't really a ranch, but the house in ranch style. All you can eat, I hear someone

say behind us, then, I thought I knew you. Then when we's inside,
there's someone else reading a poem. It ain't the Welsh poet but some
student poet. Delgadina say that student poets gets to read they
poems there. Say the student poet, And this poem is entitled "Penn-
sylvania Dutch." It ain't sound like no poetry, though. It sound like
the poet reading prose.

> Yesterday, we went up the hill to the store,
> and you asked me if I'd seen Pennsylvania Dutch before,
> and I said no,
> and so we went inside, and
> there were pumpkins,
> with cartoon characters painted on them.
> The woman who owns the place has an artist son,
> you said.
> And then farther back, there are plaques
> made of iron,
> and little skillets,
> and big iron keys.
> You ask me if there's anything I like.
> When I say no, you buy me anyway a plaque that reads,
> The hurrieder I go, the behinder I get.
> I buy you two candy sticks, a lemon and a wintergreen.
> Our window clouds when it rains.
> Your hands are on the table.
> There are hints of reconciliation.
> Nothing big.
> A few words over a cup of tea.

Bravo, say the Welsh poet. There is people sitting around on the
floor and on the chairs and couch. The couch is made of that beige
velvet. In fact, a lot of the furniture is that beige type of velvet, and
it really don't look like no ranch house–type of furniture. There's a
few vases that look like they's imitations of them Ming vases from
China, a sculpture that looks Mayan, another sculpture that look
like it African, but it got what look like braids draped on it, and then
there's some of that modern-type sculpture. The carpet is one of
them thick beige carpets that match the couch. I look around to see
which one her Community Center teacher, 'cause she don't come

and introduce herself. They all looks like teachers, except for them that looks like students. Except they's them modern-style educated people that wears blue jeans and tries to look like peasants. 'Cept there's a few true working-type people, 'cause that Community Center caters to everybody in the community, and it's a multiracial group of peoples; it ain't just one type of peoples. Delgadina don't introduce me to nobody but the Welsh poet, though, and to tell y'all the truth she behave like he the only one that there. She kinda wave at some of them other peoples that sitting around on the floor listening to the poetry, but she don't go sit on the floor to listen to no poetry. We stands near the door talking to the Welsh poet while a few people is commenting and asking questions about the poem. I remembers all them questions but they don't seem like they's got nothing to do with poetry.

What is the symbolism of the iron and the pumpkins and the cartoon characters? somebody ask.

Are you trying to say something about art or love?

I think it would be a better poem if you had a different title.

I wants to tell the student poet that that poem don't sound like no poetry 'cause it ain't got no rhymes in it, or at least don't sound as musical as I think poetry supposed to sound, and thinks maybe it might make a better story than a poem, and how I would like to know a little bit more about them peoples in that poem, but the Welsh poet who a poet and must know poetry have already say Bravo, and them peoples is already asking questions and making comments about it as if it is poetry, so I ain't say that sound more like prose than poetry. Like that man say in one of them books that Delgadina got, what ain't poetry is prose and what ain't prose is poetry. And I also wants to comment on the title, but I believes it a good title, 'cause it make us think how come that the title and ain't got no different title, and then the student poet smile shyly, you know one of them shy student poet-type smiles, and the shy student poet answer them questions, and the Welsh poet think it a poem and seem like everybody think it a poem and ain't nobody question that maybe it ain't no poem, and then the Welsh poet he heads toward the buffet table, fills up two glasses with punch from the punch bowls. Brings them to Delgadina and me. I shake my head no, but Delgadina takes hers, and he drinks the other one. But they's acting like they's known each other a long time, and they's drinking at the same time. They's drinking from different glasses but acting like they's drinking from the same glass.

When will you be back to America? ask Delgadina. That's the only reason I came here, because of you. I didn't bring any poetry to read.

I don't know. You know, my wallet was stolen in New York. Right now I'm nameless, I guess.

He got a lot of thick dark hair and look like he maybe twenty years older than Delgadina. He kinda one of them distinguished-looking mens, but they seem like they's a kind of wildness to him, like he's distinguished looking but ain't exactly tame. Seem like he can be real humorous and playful when he want to be and distinguished when he want to be.

You couldn't be nameless, she say.

How've you been? he ask. He come real close to her when he talk and seem like he ain't noticed me.

Okay. Delgadina kinda step back from him and point toward me. This is Nadine. I want you to meet Nadine.

How're you, Nadine?

Okay.

Then he start talking to Delgadina again and stand real close to her. I didn't know you'd be the student, he said. She said she had a student at the Community Center she wanted me to meet. I didn't know you'd be the student. When you came in she said it was you. Well, I should have known there's only one Delgadina. But she said another name.

I'm still looking around to see who the teacher. A few of the poetry peoples is looking in the direction of us, but most is listening to the new poets that's reading and asking them questions. I ain't going to quote y'all no more of that poetry 'cause it ain't sound like poetry to me. Ain't none of it got no rhymes in it. I knows it's modern poetry, but seem like a poem if it ain't got no rhymes in it, it's got to have music. I know they's Navajo poetry that ain't got no rhymes in it, and everybody's poetry ain't got no rhymes, but the poetry that ain't got no rhymes in it have got music.

Juárez. My husband's name. I mean, my ex-husband's name. I still use my ex-husband's name.

Did you get married?

Yes.

Whoever he was he wasn't good enough for you, Delgadina.

Delgadina said nothing. She sipped her punch, then she said, I wasn't good enough for him. Then she looked at me, then she said, I don't think we were good enough for each other. He's got a new wife now. Someone named Eden. Which is the perfect name. I call her Eden Pride, but it's really Eden Prine. Eden Juárez now, though. He's a sculptor.

Oh, yeah? the Welsh poet say and then he look like he want to ask more about her ex-husband but he don't. Well, I can't imagine anybody being good enough for you.

She look like she want to say Not even yourself? but she don't. She sip her punch, and then they looks like they's sipping from the same glass again. Then they listen a little bit to the student poets, then they look at each other.

I starts to tell them I don't like that phrase, that peoples should just be good for each other. Be talking about being good for each and ain't be talking who good enough for whom. I starts to say that about people being good for each other and good to each other.

Never been to the Southwest before, say the Welshman, then looks at me. Y'all got to remember that this man look almost like the elder James Bond, so y'all can imagine who it like looking at me. I likes James Bond. Course I ain't no Bond girl. Uh, we met on the east side of the Thames. New London. Galway Square. Delgadina said that would make a great setting for a play, *The Chicana in Galway Square*. He kinda laugh, one of them rugged, Welshman laugh. I tries to remember another movie I seen James Bond in when he wasn't playing James Bond. I means Sean Connery.

I ain't going to tell y'all that Welshman's name, though. To tell y'all the truth, while we's standing there, I'm thinking whether he got all his documentation to say that it okay for him to be in America. They's probably got special documentation for poets, though, to let them come across different borders to give readings and shit. I'm thinking this man look like a man can cross any borders and ain't nobody going to ask him for his documentation. Then I'm imagining I'm one of them border patrol, and I'm asking him for his documentation. Instead of handing me his documentation, though, he hand me a book of poetry.

Somebody else up there reading some poetry that ain't poetry. I gots to say though that that Welshman's poetry sound like poetry 'cause it got music in it. Some of that poetry that we listened to on them recordings, and got a lot of repetition in them and a lot of different images and music and even some of them got rhymes. He sound like the kind of poet that when he write poetry he must read it aloud to hisself or have other peoples read it aloud to him. Even his voice kinda sound like poetry, 'cause you know how us Americans is about them voices that sounds like Sean Connery.

He talking to me, but now he looking at Delgadina again and I'm wondering who this Delgadina, 'cause this a whole other Delgadina. I mean, this the same Delgadina, but I ain't know she ever been to New London. Delgadina have told me how they came naming the New World for the Old.

We'd come to hear the American poet. What is his name? I don't even remember which American poet it was now. But you know, Delgadina, the one who wrote the poem about people who never talk to each other.

They only talk in their sleep, said Delgadina.

Yes, I thought that was the most fantastic line I'd ever heard. Oh, I mean it's quite an ordinary line, but rather fantastic. I like the American language, but I don't much like modern American poetry. I don't know if he'd written the poem yet. Had he written the poem yet?

No, he was telling us about a poem he was writing.

Yes, I remember. After hearing him, you were wishing that you were a poet. But you were a poet. I'd read your poetry, Delgadina. But then you thought of it only as an avocation I suppose, but when you heard him read you wanted to be a poet. I didn't know whether it was because you thought he was so good or thought you'd be better. Young poets always have that conceit. When I read some of my poetry now, I see the look I get. From young poets who believe poetry is supposed to be, well, what they've been taught poetry is supposed to be. Not about ordinary things and ordinary people.

Your poetry isn't about ordinary things and ordinary people.

Because they're about my own people, and to you, I suppose, we're exotic, mystical. I mean, the true Welsh. Our own natural selves. It's always delightful to see you, Delgadina. And you know, Delgadina wasn't even one of my students.

What? I asks. I wants some Budweiser, but they's just got that punch.

I thought she was a student because she was always up at the college where I was teaching.

I worked in a factory in New London, that's in Connecticut. I ran away from Houston. Actually, I was going to go to New York, but New York seemed too fantastic, and then when I was in New York I overheard some college girls talking about returning to school in New London, so I got on the train with them. I pretended I was older than I was and got a job in a factory, you know. Then I'd go up to the college. All the students were older than me. I used to sit in on different classes, you know. And then she's talking to him. I always liked your classes best. Everybody else played the gringo with me except you. You treated me like an intellectual equal.

The Welshman said nothing. I wasn't sure if Delgadina's interpretation was the same, though, as his interpretation.

I thought Delgadina would explain what she had said, but she ain't. I tried to imagine Delgadina the intellectual equal of a Welsh poet when she a teenager and he twenty years or so older than her. I was thinking maybe she mean something other than intellectual equal but just say intellectual equal.

They told me you were a townie. That's a marvelous American expression, isn't it? He looked at me. Do you know what *townie* means?

Yes, I said. Them college towns. Everybody that ain't college people they calls them townies.

Yes, said the Welshman. I think that's a rather marvelous expression.

It's not meant to be marvelous, said Delgadina.

I thought you were one of the students there. I knew you weren't like any of my students, but I thought you were a student. Then when you told me you weren't a student . . . What would you like, Nadine?

Uh, talking to me? They got any Bud Light?

Let's go in the kitchen.

I follows them in the kitchen, though I ain't sure whether he just want to be with Delgadina. Maybe he ask if I wanted anything so's I'd go over to the table and get me some punch and he could be talking to just Delgadina. Yeah, that probably why he be asking me that. I starts to stay in there and listen to that poetry, but most of it don't sound like no poetry to me. But we's in the kitchen and he's looking in the refrigerator for Bud Light, and they's Bud Light in there. I'm thinking they ain't gonna be no Bud Light in there, and then I can let just him and Delgadina be in there, but they's Bud Light in there. I should say he ain't exactly acting like her old lover or nothing. But he is kinda acting like he her old lover or something, or maybe somebody who wanted to be her lover, or maybe wants to be her lover now that she's older than a teenager. But now I'm drinking my Bud Light and leaning against the counter and Delgadina, she and that Welsh poet sitting at the table talking.

Mark and Galway were the subjects of the evening. You brought up the name of LeRoi Jones. He was LeRoi Jones then, wasn't he?

Yes, he hadn't yet changed his name. It's just that everybody was acting like such gringos except for you. Maybe it's just I'm not your history. But you were the only gringo I ever met that didn't treat me like gringos treat me. I think there's something about me that just brings out the gringo in a gringo.

They thought you were black, said the Welshman. You wouldn't let me explain to them that you weren't.

Why should you? And anyway, I felt like LeRoi Jones was my poet too. I would have brought up a Chicano poet if I'd known any Chicano poets in those days. I didn't know any Chicano poets. If it was now I'd've said Alurista. So I mentioned LeRoi Jones, 'cause they were talking like poetry was just themselves. When I mentioned him, you were the only one who said, Yes, let's talk of him. The others acted like they didn't even hear me. I wanted to be the Chicana poet. I didn't call myself Chicana then, but I wanted to write about growing up in barrios in Houston.

Delgadina didn't exactly grow up in no barrio 'cause she had all kindsa people in the neighborhood she grew up in. But I ain't say nothing. Or maybe she did grow up in a barrio before she moved into the neighborhood with other Chicanos, blacks, Asians, Native Americans, whites.

I could relate to your poetry, but that's because you're Welsh, I guess, you know, growing up in those mining towns. Working-class Welsh. I mean, you write classical poetry, it's got a classical sound to it, but you know what I mean.

She sat on the edge of the table. Did I tell y'all he got me my Bud Light. I'm standing near the counter drinking it and he's standing near Delgadina.

Yeah.

And you didn't play the gringo with me. And you didn't shit me. You didn't shit me.

Why didn't you let me tell them you weren't black? he asked.

Delgadina didn't answer. She got up and reached for my Bud Light, sipped some, then gave it back to me. She sat back on the edge of the table. He towered near her. She was looking real pretty and made me think of one of them Bond girls. 'Cept the one that she kinda looks like played the villain. Anyway, they's talking about her poetry, though. About when she was a teenager pretending she was older working in that factory and sitting in on classes and trying to experiment with poetry and even writing redondillas and trying to write about the Chicana experience in America and trying not to write poetry that just shitted people and trying to write poetry that didn't have no category. You know, they's having one of them kinda conversations. I'm mostly drinking my Bud Light till Delgadina says, Somebody asked me whether I wrote as a black woman.

I tried to tell him you weren't black, said the Welshman.

I didn't want to play that, said Delgadina. Well, if it was South Texas, it wouldn't have made any difference. 'Cause we're niggers in South Texas ourselves, but I saw how the other Latinas there played it, and I didn't want to play it like that. I preferred them to think I was black than play it like that. I can put on any accent I want.

They said nothing. Then they were talking about some black girl who had worked as a junior diplomat at the U.N. and had gone to that school and had a nervous breakdown. I don't know who they was talking about. I guess she was supposed to have been somebody real intelligent, educated in Europe and shit, then returned to America and discovered she was just a nigger. They ain't used that word, but that's what they was talking about.

She was always preoccupied with people treating her like an intellectual equal, said Delgadina, as if she ain't just said that about herself. She went to schools in Germany and shit and was supposed to be top in her classes, and those German schools aren't supposed to be bullshit schools. So she didn't really know what America was. So she wanted to go to college in America. It was during the so-called Revolution, so she thought she ought to return to America. She thought she knew America most from the newspapers and books, but then she discovered the true America. She supposed to be in and out of asylums even now. My ex-husband knows her, actually. Because they sometimes exhibit in the same galleries in New Mexico. I haven't seen her myself since college though. We were sorta friends, but then she had her nervous breakdown and transferred to another school.

In Europe, I mean in Germany? I asked.

Somewhere else in America. I think she tried to start her own personal revolution. That was the first time they put her in an asylum. And like I said, she's been in and out of asylums. She has this magnificent protector of a husband, though, because she still does her art. I hear rumors, though, but I don't want to talk about all that. Imagine being her, I mean the top schools in Germany and shit, then coming to America and all people see is nigger. I guess it would make you crazy. Naw, I wouldn't play that. They wanted me to play their game.

Let's see what they've got in here, says the Welsh poet, getting up and going to the refrigerator again. Ham, potato chips and celery. No salad. Potato chips in the refrigerator? Rolls. No butter. We can have some hot, unbuttered rolls.

She's got a microwave, said Delgadina.

No, we've got to heat these properly, my dear.

He start taking things outta the refrigerator. And putting them rolls in a pan so's to heat them in a regular oven. I'm still leaning against the counter, sipping the Bud Light and wanting to hear more of their story. The kitchen's a low-ceilinged room, though the rest of the rooms in the house, least the front room, got high ceilings and look like a house maybe built back in one of them other centuries and in the style of them Spanish who come to the New World. A fat gray cat comes in the kitchen and look like it sleeping, then it springs up and runs back in the living room. You can hear the sounds of poetry from the living room, or what them peoples thinks is poetry. A teenage-looking girl peeks in the kitchen. African-American girl with braids in her hair, but she don't come in the kitchen.

You said your purpose would be to create mediums, to write neither poetry nor prose.

Yeah.

But that black girl, when did she have her first nervous breakdown? I asked.

At that party. You know, the reception for the poet. We were talking about that. I brought up the name of LeRoi Jones. But she was there seeming like she was having some kinda nervous breakdown even then, listening to those gringos.

I was thinking that she was having a nervous breakdown. She kept talking to herself. I had to go back to New York and then I was on my way to London, and then to my own country. But I remember she kept saying she wouldn't let the man get by with it. When he asked you whether you wrote as a black woman? She didn't attack him, but she looked as if . . . He called her paranoid.

She was making all the gringos nervous, you know. Except for you. But then you, it's not your country. It's not your history. And some of them were pretending they didn't even notice her, you know. Like she was invisible. And kept talking about poetry.

And what did she do? I mean, when I had to go back to New York? Did she have a nervous breakdown then?

Yes, of course. I don't think people really knew she'd had a nervous breakdown, though. She spotted her religion teacher. She started to major in Religion, you know. I'm not sure what she was majoring in. It wasn't Art, either. She wanted to be a sculptor, but she wasn't majoring in Art. Was it Chinese? Sociology? I know it wasn't Sociology, because her interest was the intellectual subjects. And the languages, she took a lot of language classes. She already knew a lot of languages, though. Not just German. And she went over and said, "You've grown a mustache." And he said, "I've been with Brahman." I think that's what he said. Something like that. And then she started talking about sculpture. And she and her religion teacher talked about sculpture. A dark-haired man who sort of reminded me of Freud. But a young Freud. And they talked about Africa. And she was doing some really nice stuff, really avant-garde. She was much older than me. Like I said, she went to another school and tried to start a revolution. Now I sometimes see interviews with her, you know, where people interview her for the art magazines and she says, Revolution yourselves, or something like that. She's start telling people to revolution themselves. I've heard rumors, though, about her. Not her insanity. But that she and her husband actually finance revolutions.

Sean get up and reach in the oven and get out the hot rolls and put some on a plate for me and some for himself and Delgadina and get us some ham and cheese.

Delgadina got up and went to the bathroom, and her Welsh poet looked up at me.

The last time I saw Delgadina, she thought I'd forgotten her. But you don't forget Delgadina.

I stood at the counter and nibbled cheese and rolls and looked at Sean till Delgadina came back from the bathroom.

I can't say how you delight me, he said. You're poetry itself.

I thought Delgadina would glow in his compliment, but she looked at him with amusement. She had toilet paper stuck on her shoes. 'Cept she didn't show embarrassment like most people with toilet paper stuck on her shoes. Delgadina got that toilet paper off, put it in the trash can, then she spotted a metal lady sitting on the windowsill with her hands on her hips. She picked her up. There was a bell underneath her skirt that went *ding*.

She's a bell, said Delgadina. She's a bell. I thought this was just some kinda doll. But she's a bell. Then she started singing that rap song that say, Ain't nobody's hero, but I wanna be heard.

Would you like to have a bell under your skirt? I asked.

Naw, said Delgadina. But she looks proud enough to be a bell.

They's looking like they just wants to talk to each other, or I imagines it, and I takes my Bud Light and goes into the front room. There's some space on the couch, so I sits on the couch and listens to that poetry till they almost convinces me it is poetry. I musta gone to sleep, though, 'cause Delgadina call my name and I wakes up.

Nadine, come on, she say.

I gets up and starts toward the kitchen 'cause I thinks it polite to say something to her Welsh poet.

Come on, Nadine, say Delgadina.

What?

They's still reading poetry.

Come on.

When we get out near the cactus that they makes candy out of she say, A gringo's a gringo.

She still ain't told me what happened with her Welsh poet, so I can't tell y'all why she say A gringo's a gringo. But to tell y'all the truth I didn't believe that tale about intellectual equality myself.

He try to kiss you? I asks, when we gets near the Land-Rover.

She don't say nothing. We gets in the Land-Rover. I wants to ask her all kindsa questions about that Welshman. I do know for several days she ain't even say nothing to Miguelita. Then she start talking to Miguelita again. I wants to tell Delgadina she ain't the only woman to think a man respect her for her mind and find out the truth. Course I ain't speaking for myself, I just means other womens that I's heard about. When a gringo gets mixed in with intellectual equality, even a non-American gringo, it makes for a different story.

I ain't got no tale about no Welshman, but I do wants to tell y'all more about John Henry. That night, though, when we got back to Texas City, some strange African-American woman knocks on Delgadina's door. I'm thinking that that's that crazy woman she were telling the Welshman about. The woman got some sort of papers that look like some kinda government-type forms. I think I seen her somewhere before, but then after she bring the papers, Delgadina say she want to go out to dinner, so I'm thinking maybe we'll go to some Mexican restaurant but instead she go to some Italian restaurant, and I orders a pizza and she orders a side order of french fries, lettuce and tomato salad, oil and vinegar dressing, tuna salad sandwich, a large Coke, a glass of water with no ice. Anyway, Delgadina go to the bathroom and then she come back. And I'm thinking I ain't never seen her with a glass of water with no ice in it. And then after a while she gets up and goes to the bathroom again, and I'm thinking maybe it that punch that she drank at that gathering, 'cause she come back to the table and then go to the bathroom again, and I'm sitting there playing with the selection meter on the jukebox 'cause they got one

of them jukeboxes on the table, and I ain't thinking about Delgadina
I'm thinking about one of my old boyfriends. John Henry
Hollywood.

You wants to go someplace and have a pizza or something, Nadine?

I'll go, but I'll drink water. I don't want no pizza. I'm too fat. If I
don't order something, will you feel uncomfortable?

Go on, order something, Nadine. I got the money. I got me a lot
of piano-tuning jobs, so's I got the money.

Really? I didn't know you was getting too many jobs to tune pianos around here. Before you said as soon as you showed up there
was a lot of peoples didn't want you to tune they pianos.

They's colored people with pianos, he said. Anyway, I told you I
got me a job up at the college now tuning they pianos. You know, for
they music students.

I thought that colored college had just one piano.

Naw, they's got more than one piano, Nadine. You know a whole
college have got to have more than one piano. And then some of they
music students have got they own piano. Thing is when some of them
college students sees me tuning the pianos, they wants me to play and
I got to tell them I tunes but I don't play.

You know how to play the piano.

I know I know, but if I be playing piano for all the fools that
wants me to play piano, I wouldn't be able to tune no pianos. Then
there's them that uses the music room to talk revolution. I was trying
to tune the piano and they was in there talking about revolution.

I ain't asked him what they said about revolution 'cause the waitress was there. She straightened her apron, took the pen from behind
her ear and ask us what we want to order.

You could tell that she kinda fancied John Henry, 'cause I ain't
known a woman to be in his presence that ain't. She looking at him
as much as she taking the order. 'Cause if I do say so myself that man
is a model for the other John Henry, the John Henry of legend. 'Cept
he tunes pianos.

I'll have some french fries then, and a Big Mac, and a Coca-Cola,
a large Coke, and one of them fried apple pies . . .

This ain't no McDonald's, Nadine. What you ordering a Big
Mac for? asked John Henry.

I mean, a hamburger, medium, and some kinda apple pie.

We's in the Galileo Club in Covington, which is a African-American-owned restaurant. I ain't know why they name it the Galileo Club. Us owns a restaurant usselves, like I mighta told y'all, us Johnsons is restaurant owners, but when I dines out I likes to patron other people's restaurants, though when John Henry were courting Monkey Bread he would sometimes bring her to us restaurant, which ain't got no fancy name.

I'll get it straight in a minute, the waitress says.

If you want to play something, I got the money, say John Henry.

Naw. I don't want to play nothing, John Henry. You's better than a lot of them on the jukebox. How come you's just a piano tuner?

I likes to tune pianos, Nadine. Anyway, they's a lot of folks that plays piano. I likes to tune them. I likes to make them something better. Plus I don't think I plays better music than the music that is played. Not if you been to Kansas City. I been to Kansas City and heard me some good and true piano playing. I am the man to tune pianos and I'm the best piano tuner they is.

Oh, yeah?

Yeah, I am. I knows I am. Well, I am the best piano tuner in the Covington region. And I got to tune some of the best piano players' pianos when I was in Kansas City. I was sitting in one of them clubs watching them having one of them jam sessions, you know, where they begins with just a few people playing and then them other musicians comes and joins in. One of the piano players saw me sitting there and asked me was I a musician, you know, 'cause a lot of musicians comes to that club. He thought maybe I was too shy to join in. Then I tells him I ain't no musician myself, I'm a piano tuner. Well, come here, boy, I needs a piano tuner. Then them other musicians they stops playing and watches me whilst I'm tuning that piano. Then they starts playing the jam session again and that man say that piano got the best tuning that it's ever been tuned and even suggests that maybe I should set me up a shop there in Kansas City. And don't believe my age when I tells him that I'm still a teenager and us is visiting in Kansas City, but I just wanted to come to that club because I have heard about it as being a legendary club. But he tells me whenever I wants to come to Kansas City, there is plenty of musicians there, piano players that's pianos could use some tuning.

We can go back to my apartment and listen to some tapes. What you like to hear. You like jazz, don't you?

Sure, I likes jazz. Anything you do.

John Henry got one of them basement rooms. I gots to tell y'all he ain't no teenager whilst we's in that apartment, he a grown man. I walks around in the room and he's got some of his piano tuning instruments on one of them tables, though he mostly just needs him that tuning fork. I picks up that tuning fork but I ain't know how peoples can tune pianos with just a tuning fork. He ain't got no piano in that little apartment his ownself, but there's a club down the street where he can sometimes go to play the piano. He don't play it for the peoples, though. Sometimes he go there and play it for hisself. Then we sit down and talk. He go back in the bathroom, and then he come back and turn on some jazz, and it that real avant-garde-type jazz, and someone in it seem like they's reciting poetry. I ain't remember what that poet say, but it sound something like:

> I'm here and my hereness is now,
> and my nowness is here
> and so
> from your there and your other.

Kinda surprise me that John Henry be listening to that avant-garde-type jazz, but he say that when he was in Kansas City some of them musicians got his address and some of them still sends him they music when they records it. And even new musicians he ain't met sometimes sends him they music. One of them say, To the best piano tuner in Kansas City, and he ain't even in Kansas City, he in Covington, Kentucky.

Then we's sitting on the couch together.

You want some Coca-Cola? he ask. You ain't afraid of me, is you?

Naw, John Henry.

What's kindsa things you like to talk about? he ask.

Me and John Henry we talks about all kindsa things, but you know when he ask me what kindsa things I likes to talk about, I ain't even know.

All kindsa things, John Henry. I likes to talk about all kindsa things.

We sits there and holds hands, you know. Then John Henry turn on the TV. We holds hands watching television. Then he say, I thought you wouldn't want to go with me. I mean, me once being Monkey Bread's man.

I ain't say nothing. Then I say, Monkey Bread don't play that. I ain't know why I say that.

I thinks the whole world of you, Nadine.

I say nothing.

Sometimes I feels this anger, you know, Nadine. I just feels it and feels it. Then I gets to tuning them pianos. I don't know what I'd do with that anger if I didn't have them pianos to tune. And then when I looks at you I feels.

I ain't say nothing. I'm waiting for him to say what he feels, but he just say he feels.

I thinks I'm in love with you, Nadine. What do you feel about me?

I feels, I says. To tell y'all the truth he the first grown man ever told me he in love with me. Though when he were a little boy he told Monkey Bread he were in love with her. I once asked Monkey Bread why her and John Henry stopped going together and she say, 'Cause I don't feel like I'm my natural self with John Henry. I don't feel like I can be my natural self with John Henry. I mean I could be the kinda woman that John Henry want, but it ain't the kinda woman I natural am.

She kept going with him, though, till she decided to go out there to Hollywood and asked him to come with her, and he didn't want to go to no Hollywood. Say he rather stay in Covington or go out there to Kansas City. Fool Monkey Bread thinking he mean Kansas City, Kansas.

I don't mean that Kansas City, Monkey Bread, I means where the musicians is.

I feels like I'm my natural self when I'm with you, John Henry, I says, and then we cuddles. I know some of y'all wants to know more about that cuddling, but I don't play that. And some of y'all might be a little too young to hear me talk about some of the things we was doing or to be doing some of the things we was doing.

Then I'm imagining I'm in the kitchen with Delgadina and the Welshman, nibbling that cheese and biscuits, and the Welshman say, Lawdy Miss Clawdy, Delgadina, you sho looks fine. And you

know ain't no Welshman going to be talking like that. 'Cept Delgadina wearing a skirt like the woman with the bell, and the Welshman try to raise up her skirt to see if they's a bell under it. 'Cept Delgadina as proud as the woman with the bell and ain't let him raise up
her skirt. Just to kiss you then, my sweet delight, say the Welshman.
Then someone in the other room say, Is y'all going to just read poetry? Where's the music? Come on, Nadine.

So that's how come you was so friendly when I first come in the place.
Spying on me, I says, when Delgadina come back from bringing Miguelita her Mexican beer.

She shrugs. Yeah, spying on you. But you know there's still one
thing about you that makes me suspicious.

What?

You never tell me none of your childhood memories. I always tell
you about my growing up in Houston and shit, and you even know
about me running away to New London.

I don't know all about that, I says.

Well, you know enough about when I ran away.

When did you come back to the Southwest?

When I discovered you don't run away for independence, you
make your independence where you are.

I'm thinking that ain't true, 'cause there's plenty of them refugees
that has to run away for they independence. They's others that tries
to make they independence where they is, and others got to run away
for it. Then I'm thinking about them first Europeans that run to
America for they independence, then made they own independence
at the expense of other peoples' independence. Then I be thinking
other thoughts about that independence.

But I never hear any of your childhood memories, say Delgadina.
Even some of these drunken *vatos* I don't know be telling me about
their childhoods. It's like you sprang grown or something. Like in
that mythology, that woman springs grown from the head of Zeus or
some shit.

Ain't I told you any childhood memories?

Naw. 'Cept you said that friend of yours in California, that Monkey Bread, you and her been friends since girlhood, but I ain't heard
no childhood memories. And you told me about that old boyfriend

of yours, that John Henry that looks like this guy I know from
Houston.

I shrug. Well, we been friends since girlhood, me and Monkey
Bread, used to pal around together when we were girls, used to go
fishing and shit. Grade school, high school, you know. We used to
go up to the college together, 'cause she knew a lot of them college
boys. I don't mean when we was in grade school, I mean when we
was in high school. I don't mean in Covington. One of her boyfriends usedta go to Kentucky State. Then she went with John
Henry. 'Cept she usedta go with John Henry when they was childrens, then she went with other boyfriends. Then she runs to Hollywood. Running from one Hollywood to another. Then after she
runs to Hollywood I went with John Henry.

Say what?

I tell her, or rather remind her, that that John Henry name Hollywood. John Henry Hollywood. Say he the first man who ask my
girlfriend to marry him, then the next thing I know she want to go to
California, to the real Hollywood. I tell her some more about me
dating that John Henry Hollywood for a while.

At first I didn't know whether I should date him, you know. So I
writes to Monkey Bread and she writes back and says, Girl, I don't
play that. 'Cause you know how some women is, when they stops
dating a man, they still considers him to be theirs. I know when I
was in this club, I met this jazz musician and she told me about her
ex-husband's ex-wife. Say after she divorced this man, his ex-wife,
who had divorced him herself comes in the club and tells her she's
gonna kick her ass for divorcing the man that she herself had divorced. They's some fools in this world. Didn't come after her when
she married her ex-husband, but after she divorced him she say she
going to kick her ass. Say she is still running from that woman. I ain't
know what kinda possession that is. Say the woman follows her from
gig to gig. Say she can't understand it herself. Monkey Bread don't
play shit like that.

That still you as a grown woman, she say. You ain't even told me
about any childhood boyfriends. I've told you about plenty of my
boyfriends when I was a girl.

I never had any childhood boyfriends 'cause I've always been
sorta big and the boys all like those little girls, you know. I was al-

ways taller than all the boys, you know. Monkey Bread, though, usedta have a lot of boyfriends when we was growing up, though. One of those cute little women that the boys like. But I think even John Henry Hollywood she consider her first real boyfriend, though. But I was shy too, tall and shy, so you know how boys are.

I think you just sprang grown, Mosquito. I mean, even all the books I read, the fictions, there're chapters where people tell their childhood stories. If you were a book, there'd be no childhood stories. I think you just sprang grown, Mosquito. Either that or you're a spy they forgot to give your dossier with your childhood memories, she joke. But I guess if you were a real spy you'd make up some childhood memories. They always have spies memorize their whole histories.

When Delgadina say that I be thinking what Delgadina told me her ideal type of novel. It would be a novel where you could read any chapter when you wanted to and where you wanted to read it. After you read the first chapter and got introduced to the principal charac-ters, you didn't have to read the novel chapter by chapter. Ideally, you didn't even have to start reading the beginning first. For her that the ideal novel, the ideal way of telling a tale. Course when you's lis-tening to a tale it ain't as simple as reading it. 'Cept if you got you one of them tape recorders, you can listen to the tale anyplace in the tape, especially them newfangled tape recorders. When you's talking to people, though, you can tell them anywhere in the tale you wants to tell them, and you don't even have to tell them all of the tale. And then they can ask you questions and have you clarify.

I start to tell her again about that Maria, then I tell her about my folks who own a restaurant in Covington, Kentucky, and how I usedta wash dishes in that restaurant when I was a girl but was al-ways too shy to come out of the kitchen. It my shyness give me the reputation at school of a loner, and even when I stop being shy I still have the reputation of a loner. Like me and my friend Monkey Bread be sitting on the bank of that Kentucky River fishing and be watch-ing them riverboats and them houseboats and she be asking, Mos-quito, how come you such a loner?

And I be giggling 'cause here I am sitting on the riverbank fishing with the fool and she be asking, Mosquito, how come you such a loner? And then I tell her, that Delgadina, I mean, about them min-

iaturized spy satellites I seen at this trade show, 'cause her talking
about spy be reminding me of them spy satellites. You know, they
like spy satellites except but they for everyday people, you know.
You oughta see all the new surveillance technology they got.

She get a bag of pretzels from underneath the counter and pour
more pretzels in my bowl, gazing at the restaurant-cantina, almost
like she wondering who a spy, then at Miguelita, sipping her Mexican beer, like she wondering if she a spy, then take her another order.
Her breath smell like cloves. She a bartender woman, like I said.
And then I be thinking that I heard or read somewhere that bartending Mexican-American women supposed to be a stereotype. Or
maybe it bartending Mexican women supposed to be a stereotype.
But then they be plenty of bartending gringa women but they ain't
supposed to be a stereotype.

Bartending Chicano women, that supposed to be a stereotype, I
says, 'cause I remember when I first heard or read it I be wondering if that Delgadina know she supposed to be a stereotype. I don't
think no truck-driving African-American woman supposed to be a
stereotype except that stereotype that supposed to make a African-
American woman not have no femininity, and I know I got femininity and womaninity too.

She prefer Chicana to Mexican American, though, that Delgadina, like I said. Chicana, I think that supposed to be more political
or more politically correct, like they be saying now. I don't know
what she say Chicana supposed to be. But anytime anyone call her
Hispanic she correct them and say Chicana and anytime anyone call
her Mexican American she correct them and say Chicana. She even
be correcting Mexican Americans that be referring to themselves as
Hispanic instead of Chicano or Chicana. Like when we was watching this Chicano comic on television who kept saying Hispanic she
kept saying to the television screen, Chicano. Every time he say Hispanic she be saying to that television screen Chicano. He one of her
favorite comic, so she say Chicano more sweet than if he somebody
else be saying Hispanic when they should be saying Chicano. She
even wrote that fool a letter explaining why he should be saying Chicano and not Hispanic, 'cause the next time I seen his comedy act he
be saying Chicano. And he even say Hispanic and then correct him-

self and say Chicano. She say it important to know who you are and to also know who you want to be.

Do I look like a stereotype? she ask, taking the towel and wiping off the counter again. African-American girls fishing on a riverbank, ain't that a stereotype?

I know she start to say colored girls. 'Cause I heard her say colored girls before, but I ain't correct her. And then in Covington, Kentucky, they be thinking she a colored girl her ownself, 'cause in Covington them that ain't white is colored.

And you got flashing eyes, that another stereotype, I says. You know, the flashing-eyed señoritas, that supposed to be a stereotype.

I got lightning eyes, she say. And that peacock skirt that probably a stereotype too. I try to picture her fanning that skirt out and dancing the fandango. Or one of them Mexican dances.

And all y'all supposed to be "women of questionable virtue," like us.

Oh, yeah?

I just thought you was the amiable sort, I says, about her friendliness I mean. I take one of the pretzels and chew. It one of them big pretzels, not them little stingy pretzels.

She lean toward me and her breath smelling like them cloves. I *am* the amiable sort, she say. But my virtue ain't to be questioned.

I ain't sure what she mean by that, but I tries to say something witty, like, Well, I won't question your virtue, then, but that only sound half-witty, so I just sips my Budweiser. And gets me some of them tortilla chips and that salsa. She allergic to that salsa, like I said, but she get her some of that salsa with the jalapeños. And then she saying again how she could tell when she first met me I ain't from South Texas or the Southwest either, 'cause she be saying a lot of African Americans they be treating Mexicans and Chicanos just like them gringos like they's second-class or even third-class citizens, and I be treating her like she a first-class citizen, so she figured I must be from some part of the country where they ain't many Chicanos. And then I be thinking about some more of them Chicano comics that me and her watches sometimes on television. Ain't but several Chicano comics that's regulars on television, so y'all probably know which comic I mean. I be thinking about the one that keep calling hisself

Hispanic and she keep correcting him and say Chicano, but correct him sweetly, you know, 'cause he her favorite comic, like I said, but then I be wondering what the difference between that comedy and that stereotype 'cause it seem like a lot of that comedy depend on the stereotype, like a lot of that Cheech comedy seem like that depend on the stereotype. And I be wondering what be making that Cheech different from the stereotype of the Chicano, 'cause it seem like a lot of that Cheech humor be the stereotype of the Chicano. Lot of that Chicano humor, though it remind me of that African-American humor, 'cause a lot of that depend on the stereotype and a lot of times you can't tell the difference between the comedy and the stereotype. That Cheech he one of my favorite comics though, but I ain't tell Delgadina when I first come in this cantina I be seeing that Cheech everywhere. He look like Cheech, I be wanting to say when she come back from waiting on a table, but I don't want her to think I think all Mexicans and Chicanos looks like Cheech. But he one of my favorite comics, though, that Cheech. And I even be imagining that Mr. Delgado look like Cheech.

Even Mr. Delgado don't question my virtue, she say, and be looking at that Miguelita, and I'm imagining that Cheech standing up at the bar sipping my Bud Light and questioning Delgadina's virtue, and then she take that little notebook of hers from under the bar and scribble something. 'Bout spies maybe. Wonder folks ain't suspicious of her, she always be scribbling in that little notebook. And it ain't no nondescript notebook neither. She done embroidered it with some type of Mexican scene with desert palm trees. That ain't the stereotype, though, I tell her, Mexican-American women scribbling in notebooks. Unless they counting up the figures for some monte bank game, she say. And then she say the same thing in Spanish; at least I hear the word *monte bank*. I don't ask what monte bank is, I just figures it's some kinda gambling. I wait for her to list the ways I fit the stereotype—my big mouth, for example, my African nose—but she don't. And I guess women like me supposed to have flashing eyes too, except comic flashing eyes, not seductive ones. Unless we the mulatto type, who suppose to be just seductresses, and I ain't the mulatto type, though I'm told that's a classification for mules, not women. Mulatto supposed to be an original classification for the mule. Course they's mulish women. And they even got this word for

women sounds like mule—muliebrity. But the mulatto that supposed to be a young mule, I think. That a Spanish word, 'cause they
supposed to have words for every kinda mule. In English a mule a
mule, but Delgadina she say in Spanish they got a word for she-mules
and he-mules too. And then she be asking me how come I'm so curious about that Spanish, 'cause I ain't even ask her what her name
mean in Spanish. And then I almost be telling her about that Maria.
But them mulatto women they's always depicted with having more
femininity, though, they always allows them to have they femininity. And that's probably why them mens that likes the mulatto type
likes the mulatto type 'cause they be thinking of them as more wom-
anly, more feminine.

You know, you oughta take advantage of learning some Spanish,
she say. Even Miguelita knows Spanish. She knows Spanish, French,
Italian, German. She's teaching me a little Italian and German. I already know some French. From high school, you know.

I know *bicho,* I says.

Yeah, don't everybody. But don't you be saying no *bicho* to no
Puerto Rican, though. In New York, they think I'm Puerto Rican.

In New York, they even think I'm Puerto Rican, say the imaginary Cheech.

Anyhow, now I'm chewing pretzels and she's scribbling in her
notebook. I think she's going to tell me some tale of calling a Puerto
Rican *bicho* in New York City, but she don't. Maybe she scribble
something about calling a Puerto Rican *bicho* in her notebook. And
I'm thinking 'bout that muliebrity. Where I heard about that muliebrity? Probably Delgadina, 'cause she always got that dictionary
out too, for her writing class, looking for metaphors, she say. Me, I
don't think you supposed to look for no metaphors in no dictionary.

You a Catholic, ain't you? I asks. 'Cause, you know, a lot of Mexican Americans they be Catholic, like they be Catholic in most of
them South American countries, and I be wondering what the
difference between that and a stereotype. Probably ain't all Spanish-
speaking people Catholic, though seem like they all Catholic, and
them Italians, and them Portuguese, them Brazilian and them Portugal Portuguese. Seem like somebody said about ninety percent of
them Portugal Portuguese is Catholics. Then if you make a Portugal
Portuguese a Catholic, that be a stereotype?

She scribble in that notebook, probably something about spies, or maybe about calling a Puerto Rican a *bicho* in New York City, and then she scratch her ear and bite the tip of her pen. It ain't none of them Bic pens neither, it one of them oversize psychedelic-looking pens. So it ain't like she trying to hide her scribbling. I guess if she a real spy she be trying to hide her scribbling or have one of them little bitty pens like that priest or maybe the real spies they be scribbling in plain sight. But nowadays they got all them electronic spy equip-ment. And maybe that pen really a tape recorder.

Naw, but I know plenty. Why? she ask. Most of the people in this cantina is Catholics.

I was just wondering if they's Carmelite priests or just Carmelite nuns.

She scratch her nose with the butt of her pen. I be thinking some of that psychedelic color rub off on the tip of her nose but it don't. She scratch her nose again with the butt of that pen, then chew on the pen's tip. I think there's just Carmelite nuns. You a strange bird, Mosquito. How come you think about that? Why you think up a question like that? Her eyes is as inquisitive as that Carmelite nun's, 'cept they's big inquisitive eyes. She got pretty eyes, but she ain't got them hieroglyphic eyes, like that Father Raymond, that Sanctuary priest, though I've seen a lot of Mexicans and Mexican Americans —Chicanos—with them hieroglyphic eyes.

Naw, they's this Carmelite mission school that's on my route, so I was just wondering. They's a Carmelite nun, so I was just wondering if they's Carmelite priests.

She look at me a moment. Her inquisitive eyes, they's full of amusement too. She tell me she don't have a lot of women friends. Actually, she say I'm her first woman friend. She a kinda smaller woman than I am, but she say if Mutt and Jeff can be friends, then we oughta. Though she the first one start talking 'bout us being friends, 'cause I be saying, This Delgadina, my bartender. And she be saying, This Mosquito, my *amiga*. In fact, any *vato* that come in the bar that I ain't met yet, she be introducing me as her *amiga*. I mean, *vatos* that she herself know already. And even one *vato* named Vato, like in that play we seen, or maybe she just be calling him Vato like it his name or maybe it just his nickname. Course I don't know if a non-Chicana is supposed to use the word *vato*, so I don't use the word *vato*, though I sometimes says *hombre*. But I think only a Chicano supposed to use that word *vato*.

That's Our Lady of Mount Carmen Mission. It was founded by a Carmelite monk or friar, I think. They got Carmelite monks and friars, anyhow. Must got Carmelite priests. I don't see why they wouldn't have Carmelite priests if they got Carmelite monks and friars. Though I don't think they've got any Jesuit nuns, though. But I ain't Catholic, like I said. She run her hand through her black hair and scratch the corner of her little upturned nose. It a small nose and a broadish nose at the same time. And she got tiny moles on the side of her face. All beauty marks. A nice gal, like I said. Maybe thirtyish. Her eyes could be fawn's eyes.

Naw I ain't Catholic, she say. But I know plenty that are. And plenty that think they are. Even Miguelita the gringita thinks she is. But she been a Buddhist and a Hindu too. I think she's reading about the Islamic faith now. And she flirts with a lot of them cults too. Her and Sophie, though I think she flirts with more cults than Sophie. You know, they's got thousands of cults. I know Sophie's a Catholic. She pour herself a soda and drop in a spoonful of that Neapolitan ice cream. She sip some of it, then she look like she standing on tiptoe but I know she putting her shoes back on. Sometime she kick them off and go walking around behind the bar barefoot, and other time she kick them back on. She act like she feel free behind that bar. Me working behind a bar like that I don't think I'd feel no kinda freedom.

She run her hand through her hair again, sip some of her rainbow drink, and then go take another order. She chat with the man and then she chat with that Miguelita and I be wondering if that Miguelita be telling her about them wines or if they be talking Catholicism and then Delgadina come back where I am.

He says they got Jesuits and Franciscans and Benedictines and Dominicans but he don't know no Carmelite priests, just Carmelite nuns. Even the true Catholics say they don't know if they got Carmelite priests, though plenty of Jesuits and Franciscans and Benedictines and Dominicans. But he say they got Carmelite monks and friars, though, like I told you. Our Lady of Carmen Mission School, he say he used to go there himself, so he know they got Carmelite nuns. You want to know anything about Our Lady of Carmen Mission School or them Carmelite nuns you ask him. That Miguelita she say they got Carmelite priests, but you know that Miguelita. Hey, that's a pretty good pickup line, though, or at least a good line to keep a conversation going. I mean, you asking me about that Carmelite priest. That Miguelita makes my notebook more than anybody, though, and that crazy *vato* from across the border, the one I call Cheech. And then she reach for that notebook of hers. She ain't only scribble in that notebook but you can see them caricatures too. Got plenty caricatures of that Miguelita. In fact, nearly every *vato* that comes in the cantina she does a caricature of them, but of course she doesn't show them the caricatures. Maybe she even got a caricature of that Mr. Delgado, but like I said I ain't never seen Mr. Delgado, so I wouldn't know his caricature from those of them other *vatos*. She got interested in them caricatures on account of them caricaturists at them art and craft festivals and I think she's as good a caricaturist as them at them art and craft festivals, except she don't like to show people they caricatures. They got them computerized notebooks now, you know. I seen one of them at the trade show. And I be telling Delgadina about them computerized notebooks. And you don't have to be one of them computer literates neither, they say. She be reaching for her computerized notebook, they be thinking she really a spy then. All them modern technology. I don't think Delgadina that fascinated with them computerized notebooks, though, 'cause I be showing her a catalogue with all them computerized notebooks that I got from one of them trade fairs. 'Cept them real spies they probably wouldn't be scribbling in no notebooks, computerized or otherwise, 'cause they be having them photographic minds, like I said. Sometimes I think that Miguelita got herself a photographic mind, though, some of that shit she be telling about that Sophie, and all that shit about them wines, seem like you got to have a photographic mind to remember all them wines, and then that Delgadina be talking about all them languages she know.

It Our Lady of Carmen Mission School, say Delgadina, scribbling in that notebook.

I don't think it Our Lady of Carmen Mission School though 'cause the name the Carmelite nun give me got plenty of saints in it. And Our Lady of Carmen Mission school ain't got no saint in it. Of course I don't say none of that. I just reach for some more of them pretzels and some more of them tortilla chips and salsa and have Delgadina pour me another Bud Light. She pour me the Bud Light and then she scribble some more in her notebook and run her other hand through her hair. Then she sip her rainbow drink made with that Neapolitan ice cream. She scratch the inside of her elbow on account of that salsa she eating. Then she scoop up some more of that Neapolitan ice cream and put it into her drink. Then she eat some more of that salsa and tortilla chips. In the restaurant section you can buy you that fried ice cream. You can get it made with that Neapolitan ice cream or any ice cream. I be asking Delgadina how they make that fried ice cream. She say they don't really fry that ice cream, but she ain't told me how they make that fried ice cream. Though she be saying some of them gringas they be wanting their fried ice cream made with yogurt rather than ice cream. That Delgadina she a slender woman to be always munching on that ice cream, though, and she also keep cereal behind the bar, that high-fiber cereal that she nibble on with her fingers. Maybe it the high fiber in that cereal that keep her slender, and she always be waiting on them tables, 'cause she the bartender and the waitress, at least in the bar section, the cantina section, 'cause they got them other waitress and waiters in the restaurant section. She got them tapering fingers. She one of them brown-skin Mexican Americans, like I said, the kind that you could mistake for African American till they tell you that they Mexican American or speak with they brand of English. She just got her a Houston accent, though, 'cept when she talk that Spanish and maybe she be talking that Spanish with a Houston accent, 'cause I guess that Spanish got as many accents as English. I know Delgadina went to wait on one of them *vatos* and she be saying he from El Salvador or maybe one of them other Spanish-speaking countries and she be saying she don't understand his Spanish and have one of them other *vatos* to translate his Spanish and he be speaking Spanish. And sometimes when she be talking to one of her *vato* friends she use some Chicanized English, like that Cheech, at least like that Cheech in the movies, though the *vato* she call Cheech he don't look nothing like the movie Cheech; he look more like one of them other comic. But they got Mexicans and Chicanos of all kindsa colors and people like Delgadina that why they call theyself the cosmic race.

I ain't never heard nobody talk about African Mexicans, though, but I know they had that slavery in Mexico same as the U.S. and a lot of them Africans that didn't escape to Canada escaped to Mexico. I even heard tales of Africans jumping off the slave ships headed for the United States and swimming to Mexico, 'cause they abolished that slavery in Mexico earlier than in the States. I don't know if they ever had that slavery in Canada, though. Delgadina she be telling me about these people supposed to be a mixture of Indian and African that fought in the Mexican Revolution and telling me about all the women that fought in the Mexican revolution and how for the first time they felt free. But most Mexicans she be telling me is mestizos which is a combination of Spanish and Indian. That the closest she come to admitting she got any African in her own ancestry, though she don't come out and say so. Anyway, she got them high cheek-bones, the kind I heard somebody say once was so high they reach the ceiling. That supposed to be the Indian in the Mexican. The Native American. But somebody say you ain't supposed to say Native American. You supposed to say the kind of Native American. If they Apache, you supposed to call them Apache. Like if African Americans knew they tribe, then we be Zulu Americans and Ashanti Americans and Hausa Americans and Thonga Americans or whatever, like on the National Geographic, but in America, though, all them tribes they all mixed up, though. Talk about the melting pot. That the African melting pot. Talking 'bout America the melting pot, that Mexico maybe that the true melting pot. I start to tell Delgadina that Mexico that a truer melting pot than America, but she still scribbling in her notebook. But Delgadina, she say in Mexico they got they pure Spaniards too. Mexicans that look just like Miguelita. Peninsula people or something. I ain't sure what they call them. But Delgadina she say there ain't no pure Spaniards. Mexico, she be saying, be kinda like Cuba, but they be talking about Afro-Cubans and like I said I ain't heard them talk about Afro-Mexicans. And even Delgadina don't be talking about no Afro-Mexicans. We was watching some African tribe on TV when she start telling me about them Native American Africans fought in the revolution, but she ain't admit to that African in her ownself. Sometimes they's Native Americans that comes in this cantina, but most of the time I be thinking they're Chicanos, and some even got Chicano names, but Delgadina be saying they's Native Americans. Some's Native Mexicans, though, and some's Native North Americans. She be telling me one of her first boyfriend in Houston a Native American. And be telling me the Chicano's Atzlan is they Turtle Island. Except the whole of America is Turtle Island. She say the whole of America them Native Americans calls Turtle Island, or I read that somewhere.

Or "pure" Americans, either, she add when she be telling me about they ain't no pure Spaniards, I guess on account of them Moors in Spain. She say racial purity a myth or some shit. You're from the South, she says. You oughta know that racial purity's a myth.

I'm from the South, but I ain't from the *Deep* South, I says.

I been in Kentucky, she say. I was in this town in Kentucky. I thought these people in it were white, and they were telling me they were black. It was like being inside somebody's fantasy. That's when I knew for sure that racial purity's a myth. And then they thought I was jiving them when I said I'm a Mexican, you know. If I was jiving them, then they was jiving me.

She take some of that spritzer that they spritzes the drinks with and spritzes her hair and then rub her hands through her hair again. Then she spritzes her rainbow drink. She wearing a T-shirt and blue jeans under that peacock skirt—'cause that peacock skirt fan out, you know, and you can wear it over things underneath. She got her a locker in the back room of this restaurant-cantina. She always keep her a change of outfit in that locker 'cause sometimes she be spilling drinks and shit. And sometimes she say she get sweaty and funky and want to change her clothes. And then sometimes she go to her classes at the Community Center straight from work and be wanting to change her clothes. She ain't no wild woman mixing them drinks like them boys in that bartender movie, though. I mean, she don't put on a show for the folks mixing them drinks. We both of us likes to shop in them consignment shops and surplus stores, though. She always spritzing her hair and face, 'cause she say it get hot and steamy behind that bar. And the heat and steam from the restaurant also come into the bar. And you can be smelling all that good Mexican food in the cantina, and some of the *vatos* that prefers the cantina, they go in the restaurant, but then bring their food back to the can-

tina, though Mr. Delgado prefers them to eat in the restaurant section, but there's too many gringos and tourists and shit in the restaurant section for a lot of them *vatos*. You wonder why she be wearing
that peacock skirt over them blue jeans, though, when it so hot and
steamy in that bar.

She go wait on another table, then come back and start scribbling
again. Like I said, she taking one of them creative writing classes at a
Community Center and say her teacher want her to keep that notebook. They always having classes at that local community center
and Delgadina say she want to improve her mind. Or maybe she just
signifying for me to take some of them classes so's I can improve my
mind. She don't tell me I need to be more ambitious, though, just signifies. They have this documentary on the TV too about the difference between men's language and women's language. They be saying
that men's language commands or some shit while women's language
suggests. Even little boys in they play they be bossing people around
and telling them what to do, while little girls in they play they be
suggesting and insinuating and signifying. They say them little girls
start playing with them little boys they don't play with them long on
account of that boys' language. Course they's bossy little girls too,
but that supposed to be mostly boys' language. Maybe that's why
women men don't consider wimps they considers bitches.

That Delgadina she overhear something and start to scribble,
then she serve somebody else a drink and then come back and scribble. Some of the scribbling in English, some of it in Spanish. She say
she let me read it again, before she turn it into the class. Scribbling in
that notebook. . . . She got a corn raised on top of one of her finger
where she scribble so much. I never seen a corn on anybody's finger before. She got one of them corn pads on her finger. From all
that scribbling in that notebook. Say the teacher read them a little bit
of Chekhov's notebook and Henry James' notebook and Goethe's notebook—I think that Goethe got a notebook—but say they
shouldn't try to imitate Chekhov or James or Goethe, 'cause this the
New World and the modern world. Delgadina try to get me to come
to that class, but I don't. I do buy me a notebook, though, like I said,
but I buy me a little notebook not one of them big notebook like
Delgadina. And I don't write no conversations in my notebook, I
writes words like muliebrity. And sometimes I drives Delgadina to

that class, but then I waits in the truck. I never did like no classroom. That's why I like that truck driving school, 'cause they don't teach truck driving in no classroom and they got them dual-control trucks. Delgadina say that they's all adults in her class, so sometimes they meets in a bar.

Least we used to, she says, but now the teacher is teetotaling, you know, so we meet in the classroom. Detective school, though, that's more practical. I told my writing teacher I was thinking 'bout detective school and showed her that brochure you give me on detective school, you know, the Cosmic Private Detective Agency School, so she says, why don't I combine the two things. She says I can go to detective school and still write stories. I think she even said that she knows the man that owns that school and he's supposed to be really brilliant. Says that if I'm going to become a detective Mr. Cosmic Bigbee is the best detective to learn from. Says she even knows the man who taught him detecting, a private investigator, Mr. Jo Jo Cushoff of New York, I think she said. Their original name, she said was "of Kush" but when they come to America, they became Cushoff. I could go to New York and learn from the master himself, but she says that Mr. Cosmic Bigbee is a brilliant man himself. She's a really good teacher, you know, I mean my teacher, and it seems like every time I mention somebody she knows them. I don't remember any good teachers like that in high school. Least not my high school. Just a bunch of agringadas. Gringas and agringadas.

Agringadas?

That's Mexicans or Chicanos that the people think are more gringo than the gringos.

I guess for the gringos and gringas they's good teachers, but not for Chicanos and Chicanas. Least not my high school. This teacher she always be calling me Jim-énez and my name ain't Jim-énez it's Rodríguez.

I thought your name Juárez.

That's my ex-husband's name. I keep that name, because it's more me than my own name. But my maiden name's Rodríguez. And I correct her and she still look at me like Jim-énez and Rodríguez the same thing. You know, like that play we saw where this woman call herself Jim-énez. And she's supposed to be my advisor and shit and keeps calling me Jim-énez. And then I correct her

and she be calling me Rodríguez for a while and then she start calling me *Jim*-énez. I think every Chicana's *Jim*-énez to her. She's supposed to be a regular lush, though. I mean the Community Center
teacher. She's teetotaling now, though. Maybe detective stories, you
know. You know, she thinks I could go to detective school and then
write detective stories. She's kinda impressed with my writing, you
know, and thinks I might be able to write good detective stories. In
fact, she wanted to see my brochure and jotted down the numbers
and shit.

A she? I dip a tortilla chip in some of that mandarin salsa.

Yeah, why?

I just imagined a he. And I seen you walking outta the Community Center with a he once. A Mexican, I mean, a Chicano. Thought
that was the teacher.

Uh, er, naw, we all adults in that class. You probably seen one of
my classmates. There're several Chicanos in that class, but I'm the
only Chicana. Sometimes she has us work on projects together, so
maybe we were discussing a class project. You know, when I first
went in the class, she had us like all sitting in this circle, you know.
Like, nobody knew who the teacher was. Like, we was all waiting
for the teacher to come in. Like, talking shit, you know, how you
talk shit when the teacher's not in the classroom, and then time for
the class to start, she like just starts talking, introducing herself and
shit, like everybody like thought she was just a member of the class.
And there we were just talking shit, you know. And then there we
were looking like fools when she up and starts talking and we realize
she's the teacher. I think she just does that, you know, so's she can
hear the sorta shit people talk. But still that's a good idea, you know,
go to detective school and just have the detective shit enhance the
writing, you know. I think she like intends to do that her ownself.
Go to detective school, I mean.

Yeah, I says, and plunges my hand in the bowl for some more pretzels. That's a good idea. Detective school. You'd probably make a
good detective.

Then I'd be advertising in the Yellow Pages and shit. I don't
think that the Cosmic Private Detective Agency School advertises
in the Yellow Pages, though they's on the Internet, at least according
to this brochure.

THE
Cosmic Private Detective Agency
SCHOOL

———

The Cosmic Private Detective Agency School is based in Texas City, Texas. It is a private Private Detective Agency School serving the South Texas area. The owner, Mr. Cosmic Bigbee, is a Harvard graduate in Mathematics and Computer Sciences and the former student of the famous New York Detective Jo Jo Cushoff (or Kushof). Mr. Bigbee has had many years of investigative experience in not only the South Texas area but worldwide. He has both national and international contacts and his students are employed nationally and internationally as private detectives. Unlike other detective schools, the Cosmic Detective Agency School teaches via independent conferences and is considered the most outstanding and professional Private Detective Agency School in the South Texas area.

Although some consider Mr. Cosmic Bigbee merely a "computer detective" because of his use of computer, database and electronic resources, he is more than the conventional "computer detective." At his school, you learn all of the ways of obtaining the information you need about anyone at any time. At the Cosmic Private Detective School you learn conventional and unconventional national and international techniques of surveillance, including aerial and surface surveillance, background investigations, corporate investigations, countersurveillance and counterstalking techniques, document searches, acquisition of documents, electronic debugging techniques, electronic searches, national and international databases, photographic and video surveillance techniques, credentials verification, industrial espionage (consultation & prevention), witness location as well as other modern and avant-garde private investigative techniques not listed here for security purposes.

Although a private Private Detective Agency School, the Cosmic Private Detective Agency School has a network of affiliates worldwide, all expert investigators. All initial consultations with Mr. Bigbee are free. Once you have graduated from the Cosmic School and are certified by Mr. Bigbee, you can be sure that you are one of the best private investigators in the world.

Note: Although certified by Mr. Bigbee, all certified agents must earn their clients' trust.

State of Texas License Number PI 46444

All students are taught on a confidential and personal basis. There are no classrooms at the COSMIC PRIVATE DETECTIVE AGENCY SCHOOL. Mr. Bigbee teaches via independent conferences only.

You may now apply to the COSMIC PRIVATE DETECTIVE AGENCY SCHOOL on the Internet.

Cosmic Bigbee
Cosmic Private Detective Agency School
The U.S. Intelligent Community (This is not the CIA or FBI)
Private Detectives for Hire
PO Box 444
Texas City, Texas 77590
(800) 236-CPDA

E-mail: Cosmic@bigbee.com

Cosmic Bigbee is president of the N.W.A. (New World African) South Texas Association of Private and Protective Agents.

References
Jo Jo Cushoff Detective Agency (New York)
Detective Book Publications
N.W.A. Legal Investigations Association
N.W.A. Legislative Committee
N.W.A. PI Licensing Board
N.W.A. Private Couriers Association
N.W.A. Private Investigators Institute
N.W.A. Security Auditors Association
N.W.A. Unconventional Investigations Network

Consultation
Cosmic Bigbee is available for free initial consultation. All consultation is confidential.
Fees for the detective school are available on request.

Say what? I try some of that tropical fruit salsa. This tropical fruit salsa is good. I didn't know people made salsa with bananas and, you know, tropical fruit.

I was looking through the Yellow Pages to see how detectives advertise. I mean those that are not just advertising a school but advertising themselves as private investigators, you know. Most of them are men's names, though, and I didn't see any women's names. They musta got women detectives. I know they got women detectives, they must got women private detectives, I mean. I did see a few Hispanic names, though. Maybe I won't even call myself a detective, maybe I'll call myself an investigative consultant or some shit. Delgadina Rodríguez, Investigative Consultant. Mr. Bigbee is a consultant. Seems like if his is such a certified school, though, that he would be in the Yellow Pages. But if my teacher says she knows him that's certification enough for me. Or be like that broad on television, that Jessica Fletcher. Wouldn't it be neat, though, if Rita Moreno played her a modern female private detective role like that, you know. Kicking ass. And she'd have womenfriends, though. You's the first person I heard say womenfriends instead of girlfriends. 'Cept I heard somebody say womenfriends on television, so a lot of people must be start saying womenfriends now, though you're the first person I heard to say womenfriends. I know you got it from them friends of yours in California, but you's still the first person I heard to say something about womenfriends. And we can say manfriends too. We don't just have to say boyfriend, we don't just have to say somebody is our boyfriend. If we say womenfriends or womanfriend then we can say menfriends or manfriend. Maybe if we start saying womenfriends and menfriends we'd be more men and women amongst us. Let the little boys and girls say boyfriends and girlfriends, 'cause we's men and women, ain't we? But I'd rather like to see her using her mind instead of just kicking ass, I mean, Rita Moreno, you know, I'd rather like her being one of them detectives that uses intellect and reasoning. If I wrote a detective story about a Chicana detective that's how I'd write it, have her using intellect and reasoning, but I don't think the people be wanting that kinda Chicana detective, though, 'cause they be thinking she ain't a real Chicana, you know, even Chicanos be saying a Chicana ain't supposed to use intellect and reasoning. I mean, she can still use her intuition,

'cause all detectives use their intuition, but I want her to use her intellect and reasoning too. Yeah, I'm thinking about detective school.
I want to have my free initial confidential consultation with Mr.
Cosmic Bigbee about his detective school, but I want to learn more
about detectiving myself first. I want to learn about detectiving before I go to detective school.

I know some of those other schools, at least in the Yellow Pages,
start you off, though, doing background profiles and skip tracing,
then you can specialize in domestic or civil or criminal shit, then
there's a lot of detectives these days that just uses computers, you
know. All they do is just sit behind a computer and get all their detective work done, depending on what you specialize in. The other
detective schools, though, have classrooms and I have enough classrooms at the Community Center, so I'd kinda like to attend a private
detective school that is taught in independent conferences. Miguelita says she knows a detective like that that just uses computers and
shit. It ain't like Raymond Chandler and shit. I asked her whether
she knows Cosmic Bigbee, but she says she don't. Then you gotta
learn all about these miniature cameras and listening devices and
for a bonus for signing up for the class, they give you one of these
tape-recorder pen sets. It looks like an ordinary pen, you know, but
it's really a tape recorder and shit. With the new technology and
shit. . . .

She goes to take a order, then come back and uncap a Bud and a
clean glass, then returns. That peacock skirt of hers is riding up like
the tail of a peacock. Women wear the peacock skirts but it's the
male peacock got all them pretty wings. Yeah, I'm thinking that Rita
Moreno would make a good detective. Last movie I seen her in,
though, she were in one of them movies where the hero or the villain
comes into this sleepy Mexican village and that Rita Moreno she a
songstress or something in this saloon, and she got them flashing
eyes. The stereotype señorita, probably a *puta*. Or if she ain't a *puta*,
you supposed to think *puta*.

But I think you oughta take this writing class, Mosquito, 'cause
we like keep these notebooks, you know, then she has us like writing
and rewriting one story, not a whole string of stories. I thought we'd
be writing a whole string of stories, you know. But she like believes
in revision, so we like write and rewrite one story and keep these

notebooks and shit. But she's like got this thing for revision. She says like writing is mostly revision. Re-vision. Get it? Sometimes she talks this metaphysical shit.

What's metaphysical?

You know what metaphysical is.

Naw I don't.

Sure you do.

Naw I don't. What does it mean?

You might not know what metaphysical mean, but you know what it is.

She serve another drink, talk a little bit to one of them *vato* who making a play for her, and then come back to the bar. You know, all that real abstract shit. You know that ontology- and cosmology-type shit. Whatever is beyond physics, that's supposed to be metaphysics. Ta meta ta physica or some shit. . . . You know, Aristotle and all that shit. I mean, it's this ordinary shit, and then it starts sounding metaphysical and shit. But mostly she gives you a lotta concrete tips you can use to write stories. It's a real interesting class. Of course, it was more interesting when she wasn't teetotaling and shit. You know, she comes into class kind of tipsy it's a more interesting class. Everybody in the class says the class is more interesting when she's tipsy. And she ain't as metaphysical when she's teetotaling. And she pegged me for a bartender right off. I don't know how she did, but she did. I guess if you a lush you know bartenders. Or maybe she's even been in this cantina. Or probably 'cause Budweiser is my perfume.

She spritzes her hair and face, then wipes her face with a towel from behind the bar, the same towel she uses to wipe off the bar. Budweiser and cloves, I'm thinking, is her perfume. And then Rita Moreno flashing her eyes at the hero or the villain, when this *vato* making a play for her come up to the bar, except he ain't a gringo like in this Rita Moreno movie. And then in this movie the Mexican men they always want to fight the hero or the villain. The cantina woman she always want to love him, and the cantina men they always want to fight him. Maybe that what she mean by all that ontology and cosmology shit. But them gringos they always got the same cosmology. Seem like them gringo movies, even when they on them planets of the aliens, always got the same cosmology.

She say something in Spanish to this *vato* that let him know that she ain't interested, and then she say, Anyway, I finished writing in this one notebook if you wanna take a gander at it. She says we can keep as many notebooks as we wanna. I let you read this one, though, 'cause it's got my story in it.

Your story?

Not my story, a fiction, an imaginary story.

Oh yeah?

But that *vato* he a persistent *vato*, he back over here trying to make a play for her again. But she's as resistant as that *vato*'s persistent. And me I still be wanting to tell her about that Maria hiding in the back of my truck, but I just sips my Bud Light.

CHAPTER 7

'M SITTING IN MY TRUCK READING DELGADINA'S
notebook, reading this story about some woman who can turn into
a coyote and she turn into a coyote during the Mexican Revolution
and travel back and forth across the border helping them revolutionaries, then they's snippets of barroom conversations, mostly in Spanish, except for that Miguelita and some of that shit that I be saying
asking her about whether they's Carmelite priests, and then they's
another tale about growing up in Houston and always being mistaken for a spliv and how she's always gotta tell people that she's Chicana, then they's a idea for a story, it ain't the whole story just a sum-
marization of a story about a Mexican coming into this sleepy
southern town in the USA and these gringo men wanting to fight
him but the gringo women want to love him, that gringo cosmology
only it's reversed, you know, 'cause in them gringo stories the Mexican women and all the world's women really always be wanting to
love him, but they mens they always be wanting to fight him, and
then they's some more of her conversations with Miguelita and Miguelita telling her that shit about the wines and how a real bartender
got to know the concordance of wines . . . and then there's things in
Delgadina's notebook that don't sound like Delgadina:

I do not know what he feels, though. He is very careful not to show me what he feels. We cannot find words for each other, though I talk to him. The airy words that fly from lip to lip, flighty demons, and end up saying what they don't mean.

It will be different when I meet him this time.

Sometimes when I'm with him I feel like walking or listening to music. There is no sense of the real or the unreal. Should I be in Latin America? Would I find my true self there? Ah, these are just the spirit's attempts at self-justification, when one should not try to justify self.

When I'm with him, sometimes I say things I don't mean. Words that are just words and have no connection with real meaning, words that are not lying, because that hurts no one else, words geared to . . . what? Let me say what I mean to him, what I want to say, let me speak as I will.

He is all the men I've ever written of—no, I should say dreamed of. He's all the words I've ever looked at, all the sounds that letters make, all the reveries in waking, all the thoughts of a day. And eyes that make me . . . who I am? No, no, no, no. You make yourself who you are.

But I just loved sitting there, hearing his conversations about what is for me the Old Country, the other America, sitting there, even saying nothing, listening. He knows things. He knows people. He knows who he is. He knows who we are. And each word I did speak, I could feel he knew their intimate meanings. Do I only imagine his mysticism? But we are of a mystical race, though some would say that we are no race at all.

His office is like a garret, small and windowless on one side, the entrance side. The palm trees wall off the distance and seem as thick as green hedges, not palm trees.

Take that chair. It's the only decent one. I appreciated the letter you sent me when I was in Chiapas.

But in Spanish, in Spanish. I sat in the chair by the window. And his notepad.

I see you've read your Guerrilla's Manual. *Learned a lot about how things are done.*

Yeah, but not to do them. How does an artist become a revolution-ary? Or a revolutionary an artist? Everyone can't be a guerrilla.

We must leave the plantation. That's what one of my African-American friends says. Leave the plantation, Delgadina.

But suppose one of our own people owns the plantation?

Leave the plantation, Delgadina.

Intellectually I know what to do. Ah, I just keep thinking about us in the early years, you know. When we were children.

Before you ran off to see the country, and discovered it wasn't your country.

But it is my country. Because they see you another way doesn't mean that's the way you have to see yourself.

You have a beautiful character. Your letters. The things you think.

You're always so far away, and then when I get your letters, you're so close that I can touch you.

Touch me now.

Our eyes are always moving, from our faces, back again, to each other's eyes, catching gestures, thoughts, and resting silently mo-ments. But never really resting until they find an unuttered word.

You oughta come see the other America. Who you are stays the same. Only your impressions change.

No, he didn't say that. I can recall the words, but he didn't say them. They were the words he meant. I was there when we said things and when we said nothing. But even saying nothing had itself an intimate meaning. We reveled in each other.

I read and I think too much. You can't be a revolutionary and just think.

He showed me a manuscript, notes that he keeps, and said I should keep a notebook. He must have felt it too. The mystical. The tranquil. Does he come here to this other America to be tranquil? Which is his America? Which is his true America? He won't tell me who he is.

On his shelves, books about faraway places. Not just the Ameri-cas.

I crystallize experiences, thoughts. Things that impress me rever-berate in story form. Therefore, this notebook of my impressions is not how things happened, or even why, but it is a word, or a moment, or a gesture, range of thoughts and feeling, that reverberate as a story.

My feelings for words are unexplainable, even when writing in a language that I feel is not my own. Things impress me creatively rather than analytically. That's not true. If I say that they'll think I'm a stereotype. I can analyze. For years now I've been puzzled by that purely conscious logic that breaks structures down into fragments. But I analyze by writing stories. I see a whole book in a word. These are building structures. I analyze creatively. Does Mosquito catch me brooding?

I am exiled in this America.

Except for Mosquito and some few others, I find myself more often searching out ways to be alone. Eating alone, being in my apartment alone, getting up earlier than the other apartment dwellers, being alone. Now there are night noises, the sound of a clock, the steady hum of all the sounds the night takes on. Voices, music, a rap, a ring. Bedroom noises. Love and kisses. Restless noises. Street sounds.

But him? Where in the other America is he now? Sometimes I imagine he's coming into the cantina, and when he does come, is it really him? Do all vatos look alike? Glimpses of him sometimes. I think it's him. It's that I feel so who I am around him, so relaxed around him. Does he come here to feel that way with me? And could we be that way in the other America? The other Americas. I feel that I don't need to say anything to be understood.

He watches me as I look from one corner of the garret to the next, from the shelves of old books, mostly in Spanish, some in Quechua. The sloping ceiling, his notepad, returning to the old books, to the window, to the palm trees. His eyes seem to express a whole world of thoughts. That time he told me his dream about the old gods waking up, the gods before the conquerors. He wondered whether all over the world the native gods were waking up again. And then he read a poem, he said, and someone else had the same dream. Another native. He wondered whether I had had a dream such as that one. Were other natives, in other places, having the same dream?

What are you writing, Delgadina?
You know. Nothing.

when I see her scurrying along the street with this shawl with
them Aztec designs on it—Maria, not Delgadina or Miguelita—and
then she standing in the window of this dry goods store where they
sells wholesale dry goods, you know, and then she go in there and
buy some different-color material and I'm stalking her 'cause I think
that her but I don't want to look like no fool and embarrass myself.
And all that nonsense about all Mexicans looking alike, you know,
so I don't want to ask if she Maria. Might be Maria, but another Maria. And she be saying, Yes, I'm Maria, like that fool asking me if
I'm Nadine and I'm saying, Yes, I'm Nadine. And she be saying,
Yes, I'm Maria, who are you? *Soy Maria, ¿y Usted?* So I'm standing
at the door window of the dry goods store watching. And the store
owner he cut off yards of different color material for her. And I watch
her haggling over the price of that material. And the dry goods man
he looking at her like she speaking Greek or Hottentot and he look
kinda like a Greek himself the owner of the dry goods store. I ain't
sure that Maria. And then when she come out she catch my eye and
she say, *Mujer buena,* and I thinks maybe she mistaking me for
somebody else, and then she say, Mosquito, and then she laugh and
say, *Buenas buenas.*

Maria Barriga, I says. I still can't say all them trills, but that supposed to distinguish the natural Spanish speaker, the ability to say
all them trills.

And she say, That right, you remember *mi nombre.* You remember my name. She say that Mosquito on the tip of her tongue, you
know, like the natural Spanish way of saying that Mosquito. I think
that the natural Spanish or the natural Mexican way of saying that
Mosquito, though Delgadina say that Mosquito like any American
from Houston, though when she be talking in Spanish she be having
them trills. She ask me if I'm still driving that truck, that *camión.*
That Maria Barriga. Yeah, I says as we scurrying along that street
and she holding the bundle of material like it a baby too. But she
ain't pregnant now, though, but she still got some of that plumpness,
like women who've had babies. And she tells me how she done al-

ready had her little baby, he a boy baby, *un hombrecito*, but she done name him after me. And then she say something in Spanish. Something sound like coyote, but now I know she saying something 'bout *calle*, telling me which street is her street. She still wearing them guaraches, but she dressed more American in dungarees and a sweatshirt. She still wearing her braid and got one of the barrettes with a little koala bear on it.

Mosquito? I asks 'cause I thinks she name him after my nickname, 'cause that the only one of my names you could rightfully call a boy, though I guess a boy could be name Sojourner too.

No, no Mosquito, she say. I name him you true name. I name him Journal. I name him Sanctuary too. I name him Sanctuary Journal Ramírez.

Ramírez? I thought you name Barriga.

She laugh. She punch my arm a little bit. I no give my true name, Mosquito. You know I no give you my true name. In Spanish, *barriga* that mean belly. I call myself Maria Belly, 'cause I no know if it good to tell you my true name. But then I learn you to be trusted, so I give my true name. She spy up at me, see if I'm angry 'cause she lie about her name. That little koala bear looks like it's winking at me. I think of that new girlfriend of my social psychologist friend with her koala bear eyes. That's cool, I says. You a real jokester.

Next thing I know we turning in the gate of this little house. Neighborhood they calls the barrio. A lot of them barrios they got names, just like them barrios in Mexico, they names them barrios in Mexico, but I don't ask her the name of that barrio. You want to come in? she ask.

This your house? I ask.

Sí, sí, mi amiga.

It a little house, but got a big porch. Porch look almost big as the house. Reminds me of one of them southern porches. I seen a porch like that in New Orleans once and they got porches like that in Covington, too, them long porches with them swing on them. I hold the screen while she open the door. This the kinda porch you could put a swing on, but ain't no swing on it, and ain't no hammock on it either, though I don't know if Mexicans puts hammocks on they porches, or maybe that's Brazil, 'cause I remember in one of them magazines seeing a hammock on one of them Latin American porches; where Americans would put a swing they had them a hammock. I think that Brazil where they got them hammocks. I don't know if it the Native Brazilians, them Indians that got them hammocks or other Brazilians have them hammocks. And Maria, she ain't wearing no Mexican clothes, like I said, she wearing blue jeans and a sweatshirt. But maybe blue jeans and a sweatshirt is as much Mexican clothes as American clothes. And that long braid of hers swings when she walks. That koala bear barrette looks like a little girl's barrette, not a grown woman's barrette, though, but I guess grown women can wear barrettes like that.

Little girl sitting in flowered chair holding the baby. Well, maybe a teenage girl. Look like little girl to me, though. She more Native American looking, though, than Maria. She look sort of Mayan with them Mayan features and Mayan eyes, and she wear her hair in a braid just like Maria. And Maria got one of them Jesus on her mantelpiece, except her Jesus look Mexican, and her mantelpiece kinda remind me of this mantelpiece I seen in one of them Cheech and Chong movies. When Maria come in she say hi to the little girl, then she dump the materials she done bought at that wholesale dry goods store on the table that got other cloth and sewing stuff and yarn and needles and handmade dolls on it and she take the baby from the little girl and say something in Spanish or Mexican and then the little girl say something to her in Spanish or Mexican and then go out the door. Maria she say the little girl from Chiapas and don't speak English. They's handmade dolls all lining the walls too and got little dresses on the girl dolls and shirts and trousers on the boy dolls, the *hombrecitos*. Men and women dolls. Mexican dolls and gringo dolls—*gabacho* dolls—and even African-looking dolls here and there.

She look out for him while I shop, she say. This you namesake. This S.J. She lift up the baby and hold the baby up for me to kiss. I take the baby. I always been kinda awkward with babies, and ain't had no children myself, but this a pretty baby. But like the little Mayan girl, he too look more Native American than Maria. And maybe even African too, but I don't say so, 'cause after reading that Delgadina notebook, about not wanting people to mistake her for no

African American, I be thinking Maria not want me to say her little baby remind me of a lot of little African-American babies with his reddish-brown complexion and curly hair.

This a pretty baby, I says.

Muchas gracias.

Of course I don't tell her that my name ain't Journal, either, it's Sojourner. But if she hear the word *journal* that's okay. Then she take the baby from me and put him in his crib. She got all these whirligigs dangling above the crib 'cause they say shit like that help to make intelligent babies. Padre Raimundo gave me these for a present, she says, as if reading my thoughts. He says they make intelligent baby. He a real good baby. *Muy bueno.* And he a smart baby too. He already a smart baby. Eh, baby? ¿Eh, *hombrecito?* ¿*Eres indio, verdad?* Y *muy inteligente. Bueno e inteligente. Yo sé lo que es y lo que puede ser.*

Of course I didn't know what them Spanish words meant in them days. And I don't know whether she calling him intelligent and good 'cause she think he already intelligent and good or she want him to become intelligent and good. Then she sit down at the table and show me her patterns. They's patterns for making dolls and patterns for making doll clothes. I makes dolls, she say, and show me one of her little Mexican dolls. Some of them are doll dolls and others are puppet dolls. She lift up one of them puppet dolls and show me how it dances in the air, just like a real store-bought puppet. I be thinking of them Sambo dolls when she be showing them puppet dolls. But she got puppet dolls of all races too, like them doll dolls. She give me one of the doll dolls and say I can keep it in my truck. Thanks, you really good. You very talented. You really learned English really quick too.

I learn English from reading the *muñecos.* I make the *muñecos* and I read the *muñecos. Muñeco,* it mean doll. *Muñeco,* it mean comics. She show me her collection of comic books. Got all kinda comic books, *Superman, Dick Tracy, Nancy,* and lot of them kinda comic books. Even got them Mexican comic books and I be wondering if I could learn that Spanish from them comic books the same as she learn that English. Lotta them comic books look like collector's items, 'cause a lot of them comic books is collector's items nowadays. I don't know if she know they's collector's items, though.

Maybe a lot of her Mexican friends and her trade them comic books around and learn English from them. I sit for a while watching her make the *muñecos,* cutting out the patterns and then sewing the material.

You got a real cottage industry, I says.

Say what? she ask.

Say what?

That I no learn from the muñecos. That I learn from Mosquito. Would you like something to drink? Would you like Coca-Cola? I have hot chocolate. You like hot chocolate?

No thanks, really I gotta . . . I rise.

I got some salsa verde. You want some salsa verde?

No thanks.

I know what you like. I got some salad with nuts, with green tomatoes, with cheddar cheese, with corn kernels, with green onions, with red chilies, with green chilies, and with garlic too. You like that?

Probably her version of my trail mix. No thanks, really.

Jalapeños too. I know you like jalapeños. You no like habanero, that too hot even for Mosquito.

No thank you. *Muy bueno.* I mean, *muchas gracias.*

Almond and cucumber ice cream?

Say what?

We both laugh.

You know I read they makes jalapeño paint?

What?

Paint they make with jalapeño. Barnaby Ban.

What?

Barnaby Ban. No, Barnacle Ban. It supposed to keep barnacles off the hulls of ships. Not cause pollution. I read about that in newspaper. I read the newspaper to learn the English too. About this industrious designer he discover you can make a paint out of jalapeños and put it on the hulls of the ships to keep the barnacles away. Say it repel the barnacles but don't pollute the water. Hot chocolate?

Hot chocolate?

I know you like hot chocolate.

Maybe I'll take a little hot chocolate, I say. I sit on the couch and watch S.J. play with his whirligigs. He a pretty baby. Little darker

than Maria, like I said, with curly black hair. *Indio*, I think that
mean Indian. Maria returns with the hot chocolate and a plate of
what look like little green tomatoes spread with cream cheese. I nibble one of them. It tastes a little like apples. These are good.

You want some banana shortcake?

No thanks. I finish the hot chocolate and rise. You make very
good hot chocolate.

I see you again?

Yeah, sure.

I name him Journal, she say. He a real good baby. *Muy bueno.*

Sí, sí, muy bueno.

You learn from *muñecos, verdad?* You have telephone? Can I
have your telephone number?

Yeah, sure.

Muy bueno. You are *mujer buena.* Father Raimundo will want to
know that I have seen you.

Who is Father Raimundo?

Padre Raimundo, the priest you brought me to. We talk all the
time of Mosquito. You know Padre Raimundo. *Sacerdote.*

Oh, yeah.

But I do not name my baby after Mosquito. I name him after your
true name.

I go over to Journal and say his name, Journal. He look at me like
he know that his name. He look at me like he know that his true
name. I kisses him. He put his little hand around my finger, then he
reaches towards some of the colorful mobiles above him. Maria got
them colorful mobiles dancing above him.

Do you have baby, Mosquito? I think you seem *madre.* Do you
have baby?

Do I have baby? No, I don't have any babies. I don't have any
babies of my own.

I know she waiting for me to tell her what I thinks about babies
in general, 'cause I know she know what I thinks about her baby in
particular, us Journal. I know I ain't have to tell her what I thinks of
us Journal.

Sí, sí, muy bueno, I says. *Hombrecito.*

I buy one of the dolls from Maria in addition to the one she give
me 'cause this one reminds me of the gringa, and when I go back to

the cantina gives it to Miguelita. At first she looks at the doll like she's afraid of dolls, and then she says that the doll looks just like Sophie, exactly like Sophie, and I'm thinking the doll looks exactly like Miguelita.

She looks just like Sophie, says Miguelita.

I started to buy a doll for Delgadina, but she too inquisitive, and the next thing I know I be telling her about that Maria, maybe even taking her to the barrio to meet that Maria and that S.J.

CHAPTER 8

IT AIN'T NO FANCY GOURMET RESTAURANT AND
ain't no greasy spoon either. Actually, it's one of them pizza joints
with a miniature jukebox at every table. Italian food, but it a Mexican that owns the joint, though. Delgadina and me been in this restaurant after that poetry reading so I know it's a Mexican that owns
the joint, 'cause she be talking to him and be asking him why he
don't serve Mexican food and he be saying that he didn't start making a profit till he start serving that Italian food, though she be saying
he could serve Italian and Mexican food, but he be saying he prefer
to specialize in Italian food, plus he be saying he prefer Italian food
to Mexican food, and he makes better pizzas than he does tacos, but
most people when they come in the Italian restaurant they be thinking it a Italian that own the restaurant and he kinda look like a Italian if you don't know he Mexican. Anyway, he take a couple of napkins from the dispenser and give me a couple. I tell him about it
being a Mexican that own this Italian restaurant and not a Italian.
Oh, yeah? he say. Well, they've got pretty good Italian food. I'm
wondering if I should play one of them jukebox tunes. Ain't no rap
on 'em, though. Ain't no Italian music either, or Mexican music.
Mostly 1970s disco music. Donna Summer on there. Disco cowgirl?

Somebody be saying she like that country music and supposed to be making her a country music album. Me and Delgadina seen her on one of them talk shows and she an artist too. Delgadina say she like her art, but say it kinda remind her of German art, and then she be looking through one of her art books and show me some of that German art that look kinda like that Donna Summer art. I ain't remember the name of that German art, though, but it look a lot like that Donna Summer art, so I be thinking she must be a real artist if her art look like that German art. I starts to play me some of that Donna Summer, then I looks at the menu, decide what I wants, then glances up at him. I don't want any pizza or lasagna or none of them Italian sandwiches, them hero sandwiches, though I likes Italian food. I be wondering why they calls them hero sandwiches. When he called me about us meeting he asking me whether I likes that Chinese food. Then he ask if I likes that French food. Then he ask me if I likes Mexican food. Then he asks me if I likes Greek food. Then he ask me if I likes Japanese food. Then he ask, What about pizza? So I says sure. I likes all them foods, but he the one keep suggesting one food after another. That Chinese food, that Mexican food, that Greek food, that French food, that Japanese food, everything but that African food. I know in that Paris, France, they supposed to have a lot of North African restaurants, a lot of them Moroccan restaurants, 'cause that Miguelita she been to Paris told me about them, but I don't think they even got any North African restaurants in South Texas. He invited me to lunch, but we comes a little bit after lunchtime, though, so the pizza joint ain't so crowded. Few people sitting at scattered tables and booths chewing on them pizzas or that lasagna or them sausage and cheese submarine sandwiches which is a specialty of the place. Mostly students from the local college. Seem like for them college students they be putting that new music on them jukeboxes. One of them chomping on a pizza wearing one of them nose rings. Seem like them college students be demanding that they update them jukeboxes with that rap music, but they don't. Or maybe that because nowadays they carry they own jukeboxes in they ears, them Walkman radios and even got them miniature CD players.

Father Raymond. Is it Raymond or Raimundo? I asks, leaning towards him. Like I told you, he got them hieroglyphic eyes.

Raymond, he say. Actually, it's Frederick Raymond. Frederico
Raimundo I'm also called.

Oh, yeah. I ain't never had lunch with no padre before, you know.
No real padre. I was at this costume party once this dude dressed up
like a padre. You know, you couldn't imagine somebody coming to
a costume party dressed up like a nun, but here this dude dressed up
like a padre. Frederico Raimundo. I been studying a little of that
Spanish. 'Cept that Mexican Spanish it different from that Spanish
Spanish, so the person teaching me is teaching me that Mexican
Spanish. I grabs me another napkin, 'cause with that Italian food you
needs more than a few napkins.

I'm impressed. You got a good accent. Actually, a lot of people
think I'm Mexican. I'm part Filipino and part African American.
The more mixed up you are the more you discover, as someone said,
that race is a myth. He peeking at them tunes on that jukebox too,
but he don't put no quarter in to play none of them tunes. And I be
wondering if he know the difference between disco and rap music
anyhow. I start to ask him what he think about that rap music, which
supposed to be a controversy. Then he look at me, his thumb riding
his jaw. Then he scratch his mustache. And then he kinda tug on his
mustache, again like he making sure I knows it a real mustache.

Oh, yeah? Race don't seem like much of a myth to me, I says.
Somebody say pure race a myth, say racial purity a myth or some shit,
but race ain't no myth. It seems pretty real.

In the U.S., I guess. But the more you travel . . . especially in Europe and the Caribbean and even Africa. In even Africa you learn
the myth of race, and all of those islands off the coast of Africa.

You been to Africa?

He nod before he answer, then he glance around at them college
students, notice that girl with the nose ring. I thinks he going to comment on that nose ring, Africa in the New World, but he don't. In
fact, I start to say Africa in the New World, but he's talking about
the other Africa. Yeah. It's rather disillusioning, modern African I
mean. I have this Caribbean friend, though, a school chum actually,
who whenever she comes to the States is always pointing people out
to me and is asking what race they are. People whose race would be
unquestioned here in the United States, you know, in the Caribbean
are considered white. And it always surprises her that I don't iden-

tify myself as white, as "colored" as I am. It's really enlightening, actually. Especially when you see people who look like you but would never imagine they have any connection to Africa. Like in Brazil, for example. Or even people who look like Europeans but would never imagine that they have any connection to Europe. Sorta like in New Orleans. Go to New Orleans and you'll learn the myth of race.

I don't tell him I've been to New Orleans to one of them trade shows. I even got me one of them brochures for an international trade fair in Brazil, though I ain't been to Brazil. My friend Monkey Bread, though, she been to Brazil with her movie star. And though she ain't said race a myth she be saying she don't know who white and who ain't in Brazil. And don't you be coming to Brazil assuming that colored people is colored, 'cause here a lot of colored people is white and a lot of white people is colored. I just ask, What's the Spanish word for race?

La raza.

Everybody got a word for race, I bet. If everybody got a word for race it can't be no myth.

I don't know if everybody's got a word for it. I spent most of the time in the African cities, among detribalized Africans, but I'm sure among certain remote tribes, they probably don't have a word for race.

Just tribe, I says.

He lifts an eyebrow and looks at me but don't say nothing.

Yeah, maybe some of them people that ain't never seen no other race. Maybe they ain't got a word for race, I says. And maybe where they just got one tribe, they ain't got a word for tribe.

He play with them condiments on the table and glance out the window. I think he's going to talk more about them African cities, but he don't. I try to imagine us in one of them African cities, 'cause they don't show that many African cities even on them educational channels, but that white girl with the nose ring at the other table let me know I'm in America. I be wanting to ask him if he been to the Ivory Coast, 'cause I heard that the Ivory Coast ain't as disillusioning as some of them other parts of Africa, that they supposed to be really progressive economically and politically on the Ivory Coast, but he don't talk no more about that Africa. He look at that

girl with that nose ring, though, and I be thinking he going to comment about her but he don't. I starts to ask him whether he got a lot
of African friends, maybe them intellectuals, and starts to tell him
about a African I met once, except up in Canada. I even starts to tell
him about Delgadina, 'cause she comes the closest I know to a intellectual, besides hisself. 'Cept when you thinks of intellectuals you
usually thinks of the elite and I don't think that Delgadina would
consider herself one of the elite working in that cantina, though that
Miguelita she supposed to be elite, I think from one of them New
England states, though she's spent a lot of time in Europe, and always be talking about Europe and know all them European languages, so probably that why Delgadina be calling her a gringa rebel
when she be selling them slave bracelets and that biker jewelry.
'Cause I be wondering why she call her a rebel 'cause she don't seem
rebellious, but somebody said that insanity supposed to be a form of
rebellion and maybe her psychosis is a form of rebellion. We's sitting
at a table by the window. I'm imagining us in New Orleans or Brazil
or Africa, then I'm watching the waitress at the woman with the nose
ring's table treating her like she just any ordinary girl, 'cause she
probably used to them college crowd, even that exotic-looking college crowd, then the waitress come to our table, take the pen from
behind her ear and ask us what we want to order. She even behave
like she used to us, and don't even seem to notice he a priest and all,
except maybe she think that he in costume. Neither one of us orders
pizzas. I orders a burger and fries and so do he.

   This ain't none of them fancy sandwich hamburgers is it, with
them little toothpicks?

   The waitress, she chewing gum. She chew her gum a little bit,
scratch behind her ear with that pen, and then say, No, ma'am. She
wearing one of them slave bracelets and some of that biker jewelry. I
be thinking she bought that biker shit and that slave shit from that
Miguelita when she were selling that shit on the boulevards. Speaking of stereotype, I guess that waitress she a stereotype waitress of
that younger generation. She ain't Mexican or Italian. She look kind
of Irish maybe, with them green eyes and reddish-blond hair. She
smells kinda like chicory or it the odor from the kitchen. Here you
can order chicory instead of coffee. And a lot of the college crowd
they orders that chicory.

Then I'll have one of them hamburgers, I says. I don't much like them fancy hamburgers, you know, that they put on rye bread and different-type breads and serves with them little fancy toothpicks. I prefers them hamburgers on a bun, you know, just the common hamburger. I been to a lot of these little pizza joints and can't remember if this one serves them fancy hamburgers or the regular hamburgers. But she assure me that they don't have none of them fancy hamburgers.

You got any of that new salsa-style ketchup? I know it a Italian restaurant, but I be thinking 'cause a Mexican own it maybe he got that new salsa-style ketchup. But that hamburger, ain't that American food? Or maybe in a Italian restaurant they be serving Italianized hamburgers. But this probably ain't real Italian pizzas either, though, probably Americanized pizzas or maybe even Mexicanized pizzas, since it a Mexican that owns this pizza joint. I don't think the hamburger is American anyhow though. Ain't that hamburger German? 'Cause they got that Hamburg, Germany. I know in them German restaurants you can buy you them hamburger steaks and they supposed to be named after Hamburg, Germany. Maybe even them hot dogs is German food, though America claims them.

No, ma'am, just regular ketchup. We got some of that new salsa style salad dressing, though, ma'am, if you orders you a salad. That ma'am that ain't too stereotype for someone wearing biker jewelry though.

I just have the regular ketchup. You can bring me a salad, though with salsa-style salad dressing.

Ketchup and mustard's on the table, ma'am. She pop her gum.

Oh, yeah. I shoulda known that, fool, 'cause he been sitting here playing with the ketchup and mustard.

Rare, medium, well done?

Well done.

Him, he order medium rare and order him a salad but with Italian dressing. Both of us orders that Coca-Cola, gotta have that Coca-Cola. Even in them Chinese restaurants you can order you that Coca-Cola. Still, it strange to be having lunch with a priest, like I said. I ain't no Catholic or nothing, but still it strange to be having lunch with a priest. 'Cause whether you Catholic or not a padre a padre, and I guess they's a whole mythology about them padres too. A

padre a padre. Course I don't know if they's as much mythology
about them padres these days with all them scandals and shit about
them padre—like there was in them old days, and all them romanticized movies about them priests, and you wouldn'ta imagined none
of that shit they be talking about them priests in them days, and not
just them priests. Course you don't know if all them tales about them
priests is the truth, 'cause I heard one of them Catholics be saying it
kinda like a modern-day witch-hunt. Delgadina, she explained to
me about that romanticized, though, 'cause me I thought it was the
same thing as romantic. 'Cause she be talking about how she didn't
want her stories to romanticize the Chicano and me I be saying I like
to read a Chicano love story too 'cause I likes me them love stories
and be saying that not just Anglos—I be calling 'em Anglos 'cause
she be saying Anglos—has love stories and I be interested in other
people love stories too and then she explain to me that romanticize
that ain't the same thing as romantic, though a lot of them scandals
be saying they romantic priest too, that not just them ordinary men is
romantic, but them priest too, though that supposed to be a contradiction in terms. And I told that to my girlfriend in Hollywood,
'bout Delgadina always gotta explain shit like that to me, and she be
saying I shouldna oughta let that Delgadina patronize me like that,
and I be trying to explain to her about that Delgadina, 'cause with
that Delgadina it ain't patronization. I don't have to go to that Community Center to improve my mind—you improving my mind, I be
telling Delgadina. Signifying, you know. And my friend in California, though, she be saying I shouldn't show my ignorance in front
of that Delgadina, 'cause no wonder people thinks colored people is
ignorant—she say colored people—cause one colored person show
they ignorance people be thinking every colored person is ignorant
and the smart and intelligent colored people they always supposed
to be the exception rather than the rule, and be saying how if she
don't know something in front of her movie star, she don't show her
ignorance, she just look it up in the dictionary or the encyclopedia,
'cause that's what the dictionary and the encyclopedia is for. She be
saying all that shit, you know, just on account of me saying Delgadina explained me that romanticism.

The waitress bring our orders, the padre and me. She bring them
ordinary hamburgers like I likes, but she got them fancy dishes with

the scalloped edges. He put mustard on his hamburger and I puts ketchup on mines. That salsa-style salad dressing is good. They could bottle it and call it a ketchup.

How'd you get the name Mosquito? I mean, you're a . . . He put one of the napkins on his lap and put the other underneath his glass of Coke. I just keeps my napkins on the table, and lean into my plate when I eats. That way any ketchup that drips drips on my plate. I ain't sure if that the etiquette way to eat or not, though. Big woman? I asks.

He pick up one of his french fries and chew. Yeah. He bite into his hamburger and some of the juice squirt onto his mustache, hamburger juice and mustard. He grab another napkin and wipe off his mustache. Then he eat some of his salad. He got some of that Italian salad dressing on his mustache and wipe it off with his napkin. Didn't know padres had mustaches either, like I said, or maybe that's monks. He got him a mustache look kinda like Santana's mustache and you know that ain't no fake mustache. He don't get all the mustard off his mustache, but before I can tell him they's still some mustard on his mustache, he wipe his mustache again and then look at the reflection of hisself in the glass. Then he look at me, the real me, not my reflection in the glass. Leastwise what I think it the real me. I glances at the girl with the nose ring. She pick at her nose ring and then pick at her nose and then she chomp another slice of pizza.

Well, a lotta kids used to tease me about the name Sojourner, you know. Of course, even a lotta kids, even African-American kids, they never heard of Sojourner Truth, you know. You heard of Sojourner Truth? Yeah? So anyhow I didn't like being named Sojourner, you know. So anyhow I got sting by this mosquito and my hand swoll up 'cause it turned out I'm allergic to mosquitos, you know, signifying, like my friend Delgadina she allergic to jalapeños, and probably them habanero peppers too, I guess everybody they allergic to something. I'm also allergic to nicotine, that's how come I quit smoking. I read this book on allergies, it's really enlightening actually, like when you scratching your neck there, you could like be allergic to that mustard, you know, maybe not the mustard itself but some of them additive ingredients, you know, you could be allergic to that turmeric or that paprika they put in that mustard or maybe even to that mustard seed it ownself, but they got a lot of vitamins in that mustard, though, that vitamin A and vitamin C and that niacin, even got calcium and iron in mustard, and it's supposed to be better for you than all that mayonnaise 'cause it ain't got all that cholesterol, but anyway, so everybody, all the kids at school, just started calling me Mosquito, like a joke, you know, 'cause I'm the furthest thing from a mosquito. Then a lot of people just starts calling me Mosquito 'cause they thinks that's my name Mosquito. Lotta people thinks that when I was young I was a little bitty thing, you know, one of them little bitty girls, and that's why peoples started calling me Mosquito, you know. But I wasn't no little bitty thing, I always been big. Was a big girl and a big woman. Kinda shy, though. A lot of people they be surprised at that, 'cause they thinks if you big you ain't supposed to be shy. In fact, I don't remember ever being called a little girl, though. She a big girl, they always be saying, and now a big woman. Of course when you a big little girl, you still a little girl. But I remembers going to the movies and they always be making me pay the adult ticket prices 'cause wouldn't none of them believe I'm a little girl. That's when I be about twelve, you know. This friend of mine, she out in California now working for a movie star, she come in the movies they know she twelve 'cause she look twelve, but me they be making me pay the adult ticket. And one of them ticket-taking women she be asking me ain't I too old to be wanting to go see one of them cartoon shows, now though they got these cartoon movies for adults, but in them days the cartoon movies they was for childrens. And a lot of them be thinking I'm a teenager running around with this twelve-year-old girl, but me and Monkey Bread we be the same age. That my friend's nickname Monkey Bread. If it were the modern day they probably be spreading some rumor 'bout us, me a big teenager, so they thought, be running around with this little twelve-year-old girl, but I were a twelve-year-old my ownself, just look like a teenager. Then when I got to be a adult, though, I'm still a big woman and all, but most people they be thinking I'm younger than my age. In fact, before she moved to California people be thinking Monkey Bread older than me. 'Cause this mutual boyfriend of ours he be asking me if I'm really Monkey Bread's age and don't believe me when I say we's the same age. We started in the same elementary school together, the same first grade. 'Cause when you a adult and big you can look young, but when you a child and big you always looks older than your age.

Hmmm, he say. He sound like he humming. I'm waiting for him to ask me my age, but he don't. He just look at me and humming like he think maybe he one of them mosquitos—naw, that a bumblebee hum—and then we just sit there eating them hamburgers and I'm leaning toward my plate, letting that hamburger juice drip on my plate and trying not to show too much ignorance, signifying on my Hollywood girlfriend. The padre he eat some of that salad and get that Italian dressing on his mustache. Didn't I tell you with that Italian food you need a lot of napkins. He lick it with his tongue first, like a ordinary man, and then wipe it with his napkin. I thinks people be gaping at us, me sitting with a padre and all. And me not being no nun. The people they not gaping at this padre and this ordinary woman eating hamburgers, though, they mostly just be eating they pizzas and that stringy cheese. Be making me wish I done ordered one of them pizzas. Then I be thinking of me and that padre at the circus or one of them carnivals and him buying me cotton candy. I be thinking of introducing him to my carnival friend or taking him to the circus, but he a padre and probably wouldn't appreciate the circus or that carnival woman be sitting there in her trailer telling him about how she can transform herself from a Unicorn Woman to a Butterfly Woman to a Crocodile Woman just by using the right makeup, but he a padre. And then I be thinking maybe 'bout us at the Kentucky Derby, but I don't remember seeing no padres at the Kentucky Derby. Then I be thinking about him up on horseback and them priest robes just a-flying in the wind. 'Cept, like I said, he wouldn't look like no padre except for that collar. And that mustache don't look like no padre mustache neither. *Bigotes,* that the Spanish word for them. Maybe it just them white priest that don't have them mustache, like I said, but even him the first colored, the first African-American priest I seen except for that African-American priest I seen on television the one adopted that boy and be advising African Americans to adopt more childrens. I picture him with a nose ring, this padre, and then I'm one of them African womens wearing a nose ring, them tribal African womens, not them detribalized ones. And then I'm wondering whether that celibacy a myth. I guess if you ain't a true and orthodox Catholic you can have a thought like that. But whether you a true and orthodox Catholic or not, like I said, a padre a padre.

I glances around at some of them people eating lunch, and that girl with the nose ring again, but they ain't studying that padre and me, and it just me preoccupied with that padre and me. I watches that girl with the nose ring lifting salad with her fingers, then she wipes her mouth with the back of her hand and ain't even using none of them napkins, and if it were a colored person doing that it would be ignorance.

I guess you know why I wanted to talk to you, he says.

I raise my eyebrows. How come?

The movement. We could use someone like you.

Now I'm chewing on my hamburger and dipping the bun in some of that salsa dressing, so I don't say nothing right off, but I does look at the padre like he a fool, and I don't think that no true and orthodox Catholic would be looking at no padre like he a fool. Of course, this man he ain't no fool. I nibbles on a french fry. My truck, right. Like I told you, Padre. With Maria, that were a fluke, you know, her hiding in my truck and all. I thought it were a prairie fox or one of them coyote or one of them horny toads, I mean horn toads, and then come find out I got me a pregnant Mexican woman. I ain't interest in no Sanctuary movement, you know. Ain't the slightest interest. I'm just a trucker. Maria, her hiding in my truck and all, that were a fluke. Plus, the border patrol they's always inspecting my truck. I don't know how come they didn't inspect it when I was carrying that Maria. That was just. . . .

Naw, he ain't no fool and I ain't no true and orthodox Catholic, so we just looks at each other. He still got some of that Italian dressing on his mustache, but I don't reach across the table and wipe it off for him like I would if he's a ordinary man. Finally, he realize he got that Italian dressing on his mustache and wipe it off his ownself. And I'm picturing him on horseback again with them priest robes just a-flying in the wind and me a African woman with one of them nose rings. 'Cept I don't think them priests rides horses and I don't especially comprehend the aesthetic of them nose rings. I think they rides donkeys or mules, though, them priests.

I don't mean carrying anyone across the border or even close to the border, he say softly. He dip one of his fries in mustard and chews. I mean, we don't want you to bring anyone across the border.

Say what?

Someone sit down at the table behind ours and so he's silent. We finishes our meal just chatting about the weather. Then I asks him who this Africitas.

Who this Africitas?

Africitas? What do you mean?

One of them books in your office. Name Africitas. Who this Africitas?

Oh, Africitas. And then he be telling me about how a lot of them early Latin writers was Africans and how they was a lot of Africans writing in Latin. Africitas of Apuleius and then some other Africans whose names I don't remember.

I mighta liked Latin if I knowed that.

You took Latin?

Yeah, in grade school we all had to take Latin. They told us all 'bout Virgil and Horace and Cicero and Petrarch and shit, and how everybody used to write in Latin and shit, all them Europeans and them English they all usedta write in Latin, but they didn't tell us about no Africans writing in Latin and I didn't know about no Africanus.

Africitas.

I mean Africitas.

Africitas. Yeah, all the scholarly work used to be written in Latin. Bacon. Newton, even Dante he wrote his scholarly stuff in Latin. The *Divina Comedia*'s in Italian, though. A lot of creative writers started writing in the vernacular. But scholars didn't use vernacular, they used Latin. The Jesuits . . . The Dominicans. The Dominicans used to be more scholarly than the Jesuits. That's why they still use Latin names in science, you know, for scientific terms, I mean.

And they usedta have a lot of wandering monks in them days, didn't they?

Yeah. He gives me a curious look. I studies the little lines in the corners of his eyes. And he's got a mole or a freckle on his chin.

I remembers I had to write some poetry in Latin. I don't remembers none of that Latin now. I remembers what I read aloud and learned to remember but I ain't remembers none of that written

Latin or that poetry. I was better at Latin than English, because I would obey the rules for Latin. I likes to make my own rules for English, 'cause it the language I speaks myself. I remember us had a history teacher who would make his own rules for history, because he wouldn't teach the history that was taught in the history books, or he would say that that was not the whole history. My favorite class, though, was Latin 'cause I got to play the scholar, which I didn't get to play in none of my other classes. But I remember this little boy he brought this nasty poem written in Latin, he wrote it hisself, you know, and everybody knew about this poem, you know, and we all thought that the teacher was gonna like whip him, you know— cause they whipped kids then—or send him to the principal, but she didn't. She be like telling him it a good parody and shit and how like a lot of them wandering monks would like write these bawdy and licensed and blaspheming poetry and shit. And she were a colored woman schoolteacher, too, 'cause they had them that segregation in Kentucky when I were in school, that's why it would surprise you that they didn't tell you about no Africans writing Latin. But she didn't whip him, she called it a parody and licensed.

Licentious.

And so we's all waiting for him to get his paddling, though, and she be praising him and shit and be asking him where he learn about parody. I think that's just 'cause he be the best Latin student and everybody be picking on him, you know, so then, he decides he'll try to win everybody over by playing the bad boy, you know, and then the teacher she don't want to believe that her best Latin student—the one that won the school Latin prize, 'cause even them colored schools in them days would give you a Latin prize, just like in that Dublin book, that James Joyce, you know, be talking about his character winning the Latin prize—is a licensed fool, she rather believe he a parodist. Anyway, I remembers we all usedta give usself Latin names and shit. Just put the *us* on us name and we think that make us Latin. Even Monkey Bread. Like that Africanus.

That's a very astute analysis.

Say what? But if I'd heard about that Africanus Africitas I woulda liked Latin more. Seem like that being a colored school they be teaching you about Africans writing in Latin, don't it? You woulda thought it being a African-American school they woulda taught you about Africans, but they didn't. But we be using the same books as them white schools in them days, and they be giving us they secondhand books. The white schools they be getting the new books and we be getting they secondhand books.

What did you write about in your verse?

Aqueducts and courtyards and shit. To come to think of it, I guess you gotta be pretty good in Latin to write licensed poetry. You don't have to know shit to write about aqueducts and courtyards and shit. And then I be telling him about that priest at that costume party. Then we leave the restaurant and cross the street to the municipal park. Sitting down on one of the benches, he start trying to recruit me again. But Maria, that were just a fluke, her hiding in my truck, I repeats. I ain't interested . . . I mean, I'm interested, not to say I ain't got no social conscience and shit, or ain't ambitious, but I'm just not a joiner of movements, you know.

We help all sorts of people. The Mexicans, for sure. But also Haitians, political refugees of all sorts. Conscientious objectors even. Not just the Third World. Well, I guess anyone who needs to be a refugee sorta becomes part of the Third World, you know. We're sort of like a modern Underground Railroad. In fact, there's a book I'll let you read called *Sanctuary as Metaphor: The New Underground Railroad*. I'm not the mainstream Sanctuary movement, though. Even those who wrote those books wouldn't know about me. I do like to refer to us as the new Underground Railroad, though, for historical reasons. I'm only one of the conductors on that railroad. The cathedral is only one of the many stops on that New Underground Railroad. Stops on it may be cathedrals, farmhouses, ordinary houses, motels, hotels, restaurants. Anywhere can be a stop on our railroad.

That restaurant a stop on your railroad?

No. I'm just giving you examples. A conductor on our railroad could work in that restaurant, though. A conductor on our railroad could have any type of employment.

He take a book from out of his priest's robes and give it to me. It one of them pocket-size books, so I puts it in my pocket. Then I takes it outta my pocket and scans a few pages. It be talking about the Immigration and Naturalization Service movement against a lot of them Sanctuary workers and seem like there be a lot of scholarly-type people in that movement: philosophers and theologians and historians and shit, and then they got some quote by a famous writer: Sanctuary is a human being. Any human being is a sanctuary.

Look like this a interesting book, I says.

Then there be another quote that say Sanctuary is a dream. How can sanctuary be a dream and a human being too? But maybe that Sanctuary can be whatever you wants it to be. And then the book even got poetry in it:

> Let us all rise up together
> Let us call out to everyone!
> Let no one group among us
> Be left behind the rest.

I reads it out loud to the padre. That the Communist Manifesto, ain't it? I heard about that. You a communist? Is y'all communists.

No. Actually, that's from a very old book, a Mayan book, called the *Popol Vuh*. It's much more ancient than the Communist Manifesto. It's sorta like the Mayan Bible. It's idea is that there shouldn't be superior or inferior peoples.

But you're superior to me, I says.

You're talking about knowledge, not essence, not potentiality.

Well, whatever . . . This seem like a interesting book and it written in a style you can understand anyhow. I was reading *Feeding the Guerrillas*, though, and I just got the image of them other gorillas, you know, like them documentaries on television. But they has documentaries on television of them guerrillas all the time. Yeah. Warriors. Fighters. Sometimes we use gorillas as a code word ourselves for the other type of guerrillas. We might talk about feeding the gorillas when we really mean for someone to feed the guerrillas, or something else that has to do with the guerrillas.

Like that book *Gorilla, My Love*. If that was y'all it would mean *Guerrilla, My Love*.

He looked at me. Yeah, something like that. Actually, we do do something very much like that. With books, I mean. We've also been experimenting with something similar to Navajo code talking, you know.

Say what?

Actually Native American code talking, because a lot of Native

American tribes were code talkers during the first and second wars. Choctaw code talkers, Comanche code talkers, Navajo code talkers, that's something you don't read about in the history books. In fact, I've been trying to find a history about them, or thinking of writing a history about them myself. But I think a Native American would be best at writing such a history, if one isn't already written. I know it's not in any of the standard histories.

I know, 'cause I still ain't know what you's talking about.

Well, during World War Two, for example, the Germans learned how to decipher all of the codes, so they used a Choctaw to send a message in Choctaw, and so the Germans weren't able to decipher it. The code talker would take the English message, translate it into Choctaw, but not only Choctaw but a special coded Choctaw, and then when the message was sent it would be retranslated into English. The Germans never could figure out what the messages meant. It worked so well during the first war that someone decided to do the same thing during the second war, and so they had Comanche and Navajo code talkers.

That sound like a confabulatory history.

He said nothing, then he said, Yes, because people don't read about it in the official history books. I've even told Native Americans about code talkers and they themselves had never heard of them. I know some people who are the descendants of the code talkers, so they know about them. I'm sort of ambivalent about them being referred to as code talkers, because the whites who developed codes and whose codes were used aren't referred to as code talkers.

Yeah, they's intelligence people or whatever.

Posah-tai-vo, that was the name the Comanches used for Hitler. What that mean?

Crazy white man.

I gots to remember that. *Posah-tai-vo*. They got any word for crazy white woman?

I don't know Comanche. I just know that. We want to try to develop something similar to use in addition to the other codes. Some people want to use Navajo, but even though code talking isn't known generally, among the government people, there are surely people who know of or remember the code talker, so we might use another language, probably some obscure language. But it has to have a syntax as complex as Navajo and complex tonal qualities, you know.

Yeah, they is a lot of history they don't teach, ain't it? I thinks they is even a book that claims to teach the history that the other history books don't teach. And I don't even think that that book teaches that history. What we has to do is to just tell the peoples the histories that the books ain't teach. Well, whether I's a Navajo or not, I's going to tell people about the Navajo code talkers. 'Cept when I tells people any kinda history they thinks it's all confabulatory, so maybe it is better for the believable peoples to tell about the Navajo and other Native American code talkers and to put them into they books. I is sho going to call some *Posah-tai-vos* everywhere they is, 'cause it ain't just the word for Hitler. I just wish I knew the Comanche word for all the crazy white peoples, 'cause I don't limit it to the mens amongst them. There is Hitlerish womens I knows for sure. I don't like to talk about other people's childrens. But if I was still a child, I would ask you they names as well, 'cause although. . . . Well, I will limit it to the crazy white mens and they crazy womens and other Hitlerish peoples. . . . I does know one Comanche word, *uru*, which I think mean thank you. Or it kinda sound like that. Least that how it sound, like *uru*. 'Cause I knows a Comanche truck driver named Little Coyote. He don't know no Comanche 'cept *uru*. They calls him Little Coyote, but it's like calling me Mosquito. I know the Navajo word for yucca, that's *tsah-as-zih*. Sometimes when I'm driving my truck I meets peoples and learns little bits of they languages. Little Coyote and me we ain't on the same route now, though, 'cause he travel around Arizona and New Mexico and Nevada, where I usedta have me my route, and he a true Comanche. I just be thinking about Little Coyote, but I ain't think of him as Native American, though I knows he Comanche, 'cause he grew up amongst the cowboys, so that kinda more his culture, though he know who he is himself. He know he Comanche. He say he be knowing more Comanche if his people hadn't had to stop speaking Comanche, 'cause they went to them schools where they made them speak English. 'Cept they kept one Comanche word. He say sometimes he use that word and it ain't mean thank you, though. He say it mean thank you, but because it the only Comanche word he know, he sometimes got to use it to mean other words than thank you. Sometimes when he use it it might even mean the same thing as *posah-tai-vo*. One time I come in this truck stop in Nevada. Little town got the name of a Colorado town, but it in Nevada. I come in the truck stop and he's saying *uru*, he just keep saying *uru*. Something with one of the locals. He ain't tell me what the scene was, but I know that *uru* ain't mean thank you. How you, Nadine? he says when I sits down with him. Sometime he call me Nadine, other time he call me Mosquito. *Uru*, who *uru*? I be asking, or saying that word that sound like *uru*. He tell me it mean thank you. But he say he ain't use it to mean thank you. He say it the only Comanche word he know, so it got to contain the meaning of every word. So that *uru*, it might mean thank you in ordinary Comanche, but the way that Little Coyote and his people have transformed that word, they have made it into the most powerful word in the universe, 'cause I ain't know of a word to contain every word. Most words is they own word, or they is other little words and meanings, but they ain't every word. I be thinking somebody else the first Native American I met, but it Little Coyote. But I ain't think of him as somebody to meet, 'cause he somebody I knows. Least whiles I was on his route. Not no lovers, though, I mean, 'cause he has him a Mrs. Little Coyote. 'Cept the way he describes her she ain't no Little Coyote neither. He transport furniture, I mean Little Coyote. Italian classical furniture, English, Italian Renaissance, seventeenth century, modern, you know, different styles. I remember he was transporting some bookcases, and one of them was supposed to be from a seventeenth-century sailing vessel, from a captain's cabin. It was supposed to be a real expensive bookcase. All the others was modern, but this were a seventeenth-century bookcase. He ain't tell me, but when I looked at that bookcase I knowed it was from a slave ship. I ain't knowed if it was seventeenth century or some other century, but I just knowed it was from a slave ship and ain't nobody have to tell me that bookcase from a slave ship. He hisself called it a sailing vessel, but I knowed it was from a slave ship. Little Coyote was transporting it to some wealthy people that had ordered it, so I ain't told him he were transporting the bookcase from a slave ship. Or maybe he know hisself and ain't want to say that. He the one showed it to me though, 'cause when we went out he say Mosquito, then he say he want to show me this seventeenth-century bookcase, 'cause it is more intricate you know than the modern-type furniture. Then he opens the back of his truck and shows me that bookcase, and we both lets each other call it a sailing vessel, though I knows we both knows the true nature of that sailing ship. But what we talking about? I looks at the little book.

Anyway, this section, he say, pointing out the section in the book, is about this group of Indians, of Native People, whose tradition and culture and even religion are based on corn, but they're not allowed to plant corn because their government claims that they use the corn to feed the guerrillas, the rebels who want to overthrow the government. Instead, they force the people to grow cotton. A group of us— you saw one of them, Alvarado, in the alley behind the cathedral . . .

The one you called the eternal revolutionary.

Revolutionist. Anyway, we tried to petition the government, but all governments respond the same. They don't see their own abuses of human rights—people who are part of their own history of abuse, you know. The book I've given you is considered a pretty subversive book. I know what that subversive mean.

Good. Anyhow, they planted subversive and compromising literature on us, Alvarado and myself, called us communists and political propagandists and had us deported . . . But these people, the ones who want simply to return to growing corn, they're descended from the world's first poets, first artists, first astronomers. People talk about the Chinese. But these people, you might call them the Chinese of the New World.

And treated like shit, right? I heard somebody else say the Africans supposed to be the first poets and artists and astronomers. One of them African-American poets that was reading at the Community Center. Everybody want to be the first.

He comb his fingers through his hair. I notice he got a gold band on his little finger. I know them nuns wear rings, mean they married to Christ, but I didn't know them priest wear rings. I don't ask him about that ring though. Right, he say. Anyway, Alvarado, he speaks Quechua and a lot of different languages, so he does most of our interpreting . . . We didn't go there to politicize the people. But, to quote someone from that book that I gave you, the masses have always been instinctively revolutionary, the common people, you know. As I suppose most of the ruling classes are instinctively non-

revolutionary—which I prefer to counterrevolutionary. And everybody has their own language. Intellectuals everywhere, no matter
how "revolutionary" always tend to speak the same language as the
oppressors. Even I myself was schooled in the language of the oppressors. The language of the oppressed has always been a different
language. But, like I said, we weren't there to politicize the people.
But people know that truth is *them*, not their oppressors. That's why
all governments want to turn people into things. People instinctively
know political falsehoods, even those who spout them. The small
political falsehood, people tend to know anyhow. It's the bigger ones
that often people accept. Like that there's such a thing as an illegal
alien. As Elie Wiesel asks, How can a human being be illegal? But
I'm sure you don't want to hear any speeches from me. The reason I
wasn't sure of you in the beginning is that we're trained not to trust
strangers and especially strangers who come and ask about the Sanctuary movement. You're saying now that you're not interested in the
movement, but then you were showing a great deal of interest. We
break the law, after all, you know, even though we break it in the
name of conscience, in the name of what we feel is our integrity.
People trust the state, but the state doesn't always tell you what's
true.

Texas?

The state, I mean, the government.

Oh, you mean like the State Department?

Sorta. Not just transporting them but *encouraging* so-called illegal aliens is a crime, you know. Anyway, every one of us has been
spied and informed on . . . Sounds like something outta that movie.

What movie?

Nineteen eighty-four.

You should read the book.

Yeah, it seem like a good book, I says, indicating the book he's
just given me. I puts it back in my pocket.

I mean *Nineteen eighty-four.*

Oh, yeah? They made a book outta that movie? I gotta tell Delgadina they made a book outta that movie. We seen it on her cable
TV.

You'd better tell her that they made a movie outta that book.

That's clever. You a revolutionist too, like your friend Al? Alvarado. Actually, he's a psychiatrist. Actually, he's a licensed psychiatrist, but photography is his avocation.

Yeah, I seen a documentary on them refugees. Says that they has got all kindsa psychological problems and shit, you know. When they was describing them refugees I was thinking of us people, 'cause I knows a lot of peoples even in us community in Covington, which is where I'm from, where they behaves just exactly like them refugees. This is they country, or it supposed to be, and they is behaving just like them refugees. I ain't mean them refugee immigrants that they prides theyselves on and tells us to be more like, like them Koreans, I means them that has the psychological problems.

In the refugee communities and detention camps.

Yeah, that's what I'm talking about, Father Ray. I seen me a documentary on that. They was talking about self-destructive behaviors and psychopathologies that's the exact word they used 'cause I remembers all them documentaries. They was even comparing them to minority groups and oppressed peoples and talking about they different manias and calling them hyperactive and even paranoid fools, 'cept they didn't use the word *fool*.

The book explains all that. Every time we bring a new group of refugees, Alvarado interprets and helps them with whatever psychological problems are brought on by the status of being not just a refugee, but an illegal refugee. That's what's *his* kind of guerrilla warfare. To keep people from being self-destructive. He interviews them and writes up their stories and a psychological profile so that we know how best to work with them. Not just to help them establish themselves in America or work with them on various kinds of legal defense.

Yeah, I knows. All that they have in them documentaries. I ain't even have to read no book to know that, Ray. I don't have to hear no pamphlet talk to know all that, 'cause all that is in them documentaries. I ain't seen you on television, though.

We keep away from the media, our group.

Yeah, I can tell you everything you needs to know and wants to know about them refugees. I ain't saying that I knows them better than they knows theyselves, but I knows them at least as good as them documentaries knows them. Well, if I was a social worker or some shit, I would treat us peoples like refugees, 'cause they is so many of us who is self-destructive towards usselves and each other. I ain't saying that we all is like that. They said in that documentary, though, that them refugees was especially destructive towards they own group, meaning other refugees.

That's all in the book I just gave you.

I know, Ray, but what I'm saying is I ain't have to read no book to know it, 'cause them documentaries. . . .

The book tells you more than the documentaries. . . .

Refugees, at least among usselves, should build a harmonious community. That's what I learned from them documentaries. The book teach me that?

It teaches you everything that's publishable about the Sanctuary movement. For security reasons, of course, even the book can't tell you everything. All of our strategies are not in those books, of course.

I ain't never understood y'all revolutionaries to write books on y'allselves. Y'all writes books and gets on television and expresses y'all opinions and a lot of y'all even tells y'all's strategies and I'm thinking is this revolution? Course I heard one woman say that true revolutionists is peacemakers. But then other peoples believes that revolutionaries is soldiers and all revolutionary soldiers has got to know what side they is on. I believes I believes in revolution at least the way they describes it and all them oppresses and abuses they describes, but everybody can't be no soldier.

Everybody can be a soldier, I mean, there are different ways of being a soldier.

I knows I ain't no soldier. Even them oppressors, they ain't make everybody a soldier. Even amongst the oppressors everybody ain't no soldier.

Think about it, Mosquito. Aren't they? Don't they conform to what I've said about different ways of soldiering? They work for the cause of oppression in their own different ways, even those who don't believe themselves to be oppressors.

But everybody can't be a soldier.

Some people transport the refugees, others do different work with them. We have some their only function is just to help the refugees start businesses, for example. Since they can't get green cards, we try to set them up as independent contractors—you know, like cottage industries. A lot better than being exploited in sweatshops, you know.

Yeah, like Maria's dolls.

He lift his chin and scratch at a little shaving bump on his jaw. Yeah. Of course all that's subversive. But we call it a constructive kind of guerrilla war. Sometime I'll show you this video we have. It's called *An Act of Subversive Love*. I bet you didn't know that love could be subversive, eh?

I guess I kinda instinctively knows. Talking about aqueducts, I mean that Latin I remembers about them aqueducts. I know y'all remembers all them Latin lessons and the history of them romance countries that talks about all them aqueducts. The municipal park look like it trying to build a aqueduct, actually it one of them fountains that they like to put in them parks. They don't just build them ordinary fountains now, a lot of that water uses computers, you know to choreograph the water. It a nice fountain. A few of them students done left the pizza joint and sitting around the fountain reading books or chatting.

He laughs. He looking at the fountain too and at that nose-ring girl who taken her shoes off and walking in the fountain water. People who have a tradition that tells them those who win are good have a different way of seeing the world. *An Act of Subversive Love*, he repeat. Like they say, America loves a love story. It's just America wants to control what sorta love story and whose love story. And the lovers gotta always . . .

What?

We don't protest, we resist. It all has to do with reality, Mosquito, and authority, and who decides reality and who decides what's legal and illegal. That's why international law is important, my good friend. Perhaps we're violating national law, but I don't believe we're violating international law. The law of humanity. Like one of our Sanctuary workers says, We can take our stand with the oppressed or we can take our stand with the oppressors, or rather, with organized oppression. We can be collaborators or resisters.

You sound like you's preaching. I don't mind preaching, 'cause I'm a member of the Perfectability Baptist Church. I likes to preachify myself, but I don't like to get too preachified. Anyway, the Perfectability Baptist Church just allows mens in the pulpit. Delgadina,

I told you 'bout Delgadina, she don't like preachification, when it's other people preachifying. But what's a collaborator? I knows what a collaborator is, but what do y'all mean by collaborator? You know, 'cause everybody got they own meaning.

He don't hear me or he don't want to answer. Maybe he ain't like me saying he sound like he preaching, 'cause that ain't his idea he have of hisself. But I's always been kinda attracted to preacherly talk myself. Of course that don't mean I'm attracted to every preacher or everything that's being preached.

I don't mean to sound like I'm preaching, he said. Usually I don't talk about the new Underground Railroad, I just do it. I answer questions at our strategy meetings, and help to formulate strategies, but I don't recruit, and I generally don't even answer questions about what we do. I suppose a collaborator is the opposite of a resister. How do we resist? Simply by helping people to avoid being captured. We resist in other ways, of course.

Yeah, well, that's good. But I ain't the sorta person for that, joining any Sanctuary movement. I guess I'm a resister myself.

He didn't say nothing. He looked at the fountain. Or if y'all wants to call it a aqueduct. He scratched the tip of his nose and looked toward the restaurant, then looked at me. I looked at some of them peoples on the street. That one of them streets in Texas City that gots everybody on it—Native Americans, African Americans, whites and other ethnic Americans, Mexican Americans, them that ain't Americans, them that's pretending they's Americans. A Native American woman in a oversize T-shirt and Bermuda shorts and carrying a copy of a newspaper looks toward Father Raymond and me. She looks as if she wants to say something to Father Raymond but she don't. She do sit down on the next bench, though, and unfold that newspaper and starts reading. It ain't no Texas City newspaper. Look too big to be a Texas City newspaper.

It's good and all, padre, y'alls new Underground Railroad, 'cause I am a fan of the old Underground Railroad that us history teacher Mr. Freeman taught us about. It weren't in the history books but he taught us about it outside the history books and got into trouble with the school board for it, 'cause he were supposed to only teach what were inside the books. But them highway patrol and all they always harassing me, you know, so I wouldn't be any good for bringing people across the border anyhow. That Maria, that was just . . . Well, you oughta get you someone that the border patrol don't harass. 'Cause them border patrol, you know, they always harassing me. And probably a lot of them border patrol people they ownself doing a lot of that smuggling and shit. They had a documentary on that, so I knows as much about that as I knows about them refugees. But they always harassing me, them border patrol. They see this big woman and think I'm smuggling. . . .

I said we don't want you to bring anyone across the border. He seem like he were kind of angry me talking about smuggling or me having different perceptions of what he saying than what he saying.

I just finished paying on my truck, own it, ain't leasing it no more. I'm too much of a loner for all this Sanctuary business. I would prefer not to be in y'all's Sanctuary business. I ain't no soldier. I might look like a soldier, 'cause once somebody told me I looked like one of them Amazons, you know, them warrior women and shit, but I ain't no soldier. At least that ain't the idea I has of myself. But them that knows me ain't surprised by my resistance at all. Even my schoolteachers usedta say that I resisted learning more than I learned, except for my Latin teacher. I myself thought I learned more resisting learning than learning. To tell you the truth, I learned more about history resisting history than learning the history that even Mr. Freeman wanted me to learn. I even knows more about the English language than they thinks I knows.

He looked at me and scratched his forehead. He smiled but said nothing. He looked at the fountain.

As I was saying, we don't want you to carry anyone across the border, Sojourner. We want you to carry them within the border.

Say what? I lean forward and pick up some wild mustard and start chewing. I looks at that woman with the newspaper that don't look like no Texas City newspaper. She look up at me and then continue reading her newspaper. Soon as she sat over there, though, Father Raymond start to speaking a little softer.

The people that we rescue often need to be moved from one hideout to another hideout until we can get proper papers for them.

I got work, I says in my same voice. He nudges my elbow and we walks toward the fountain. The woman look like she wants to rise up and walk towards the fountain with us, but she stays sitting on the

bench, reading her newspaper. She do kinda look toward the fountain. Then she take out one of them little radios and start listening to
her radio whilst she reading her newspaper. I gots to get me one of
them little radios. I gots me a pocket television, but you ain't always
wants to look at no pocket television. I gots to get me one of them
little radios, but I wants the newest radios that they sells at them
trade shows.

I can't be darting from one hideout to another, I says. You know
the fondest thing for me is my truck. I can't just be riding anybody
in my truck. I ain't a fool for my truck, though. Anyway, how you
know you can trust me?

We know.

Been spying on me, huh? You have been spying on me, ain't ya?
Well, I ain't never been spied on before that I know of. Seem like if
they have them laws against stalking, they have them laws against
spying, and what about them private detectives and shit?

Think about it, okay? To tell the truth, we don't usually recruit
new people. I certainly don't recruit anyone. I guess that's why you
think I sound like I'm preaching. To tell the truth, that's one thing
I've never been accused of—being a preacher.

You's a priest, though, ain't you? You's got to preach to be a priest
when y'all has mass and takes confession.

Yes, but that's different.

I've always thought of you priests as more glorified preachers,
though, on account of the Catholic Church being such a old church.
I mean a older church in being a church than for instance the Perfectability Baptists which is a new church and even new to the Baptists, 'cause they's a lot of Baptists that ain't never heard of the Perfectability Baptists. They's heard of the perfecting Baptists or even
perfect Baptists, but they ain't heard of the Perfectability Baptists.

The woman who I be thinking some spy gets up and goes into the
restaurant. We go back and sit on the bench. I can see her through
the restaurant window ordering a pizza. She take the radio out of her
ears but continue reading the newspaper.

We're not really the mainstream Sanctuary movement, if you can
call the Sanctuary movement mainstream. We recruit very few people. But you've proven your ingenuity.

Mi ingeniosidad.

Bueno.

Spying on me and shit. I mean, excuse me, Padre, excuse my French, but you know what I mean. But, you know what I mean. I mean, it's crazy, y'all trying to recruit me and shit. I mean even if you don't recruit and thinks preaching is recruiting. I'm still a resister. Who am I? *¿Quién soy?* I mean, even if I didn't intend to, I might compromise y'all. You know what I'm saying? I likes to talk to everybody that I likes to talk to and I might say something about the new Underground Railroad that might not meant to be told. I might resist to tell things, believing that by not telling them, I'm being a perfect conductor on y'all's new Underground Railroad, and then I might tell things that ain't meant to be told. *¿Comprende?* Plus, like I said, them patrols thinks I'm a smuggler. And being the Amazon that I am, people are always noticing me, even when they don't know it's me, or even thinks I'm another Nadine. Them that knows I'm Mosquito knows I'm Mosquito, but there's always peoples that thinks I'm another Nadine. You need you somebody inconspicuous and shit.

I think you're trustworthy. And he looking at me like he looking at that Sojourner, like he ain't looking at none of them Nadines, or Mosquito or Jane, but looking at Sojourner. I think that what first attracted me to him, I mean for a priest. You can be attracted to the personality of a priest and ain't mean that you ain't know he a priest. And there ain't many peoples that knows I'm Sojourner, or even has got that potential of being Sojourner, even them that knows that's my true name. And plus I know all that preachification ain't the true him.

Yeah, maybe I should join y'all's movement. You know, them border patrol they's always harassing me and shit, like I said, and I ain't carrying no contraband, you know. When Miguelita and Delgadina and me went to Marineland they harassed me and Delgadina but didn't harass Miguelita 'cause she one of them white girls who can go anywhere she pleases. They harassed me and they even made Delgadina get out of the Land-Rover and had to make sure that she were a citizen of the Americas. Miguelita was sleeping in the back of the Land-Rover and they pretended they wasn't harassing her 'cause she was sleeping, but Delgadina called her name and woke her up.

She woke up and seen us being harassed and they still didn't harass her.

Who's Miguelita?

Miguelita Delgado. She a white girl but she married to a Mexican American. Or maybe he's a Mexican. But she can go anywhere she pleases. She did get deported from Switzerland somebody said—it's just a rumor and I ain't know that story and Delgadina don't even know it—but she can go anywhere else and the borders is free for her.

How did she get deported from Switzerland?

Well, the rumor is that when she were going into Switzerland from France she seen the Swiss border patrols hassling these Africans and they let the Americans and French and others cross the border with just showing they passport, and all even African Americans had to do was to show they passport, but with them Africans they makes them open all they luggages and empty all they pockets and turn they pockets inside out, and for some reason that Miguelita decided she were going to say something to them Swiss about why they was hassling them Africans when they wasn't hassling any other nation-alities, even African Americans of the same color. So she started preachifying to them and the Swiss deported the fool. Least they sent her back to France. That's the rumor. I don't know whether it's a true lie or a fabricated truth.

He don't say nothing. He look like he want to hear some more true lies or fabricated truths. Or maybe he want to hear more about Miguelita.

She one of them white girls that can go anywhere, I said. She could probably even get back into Switzerland if she would just go along to get along. Me they hassles in us own borders, 'cause I think I brings out the gringo in peoples. And them that is carrying contra-band they don't harass. And if that documentary is true, they should start harassing they ownself, and they's probably more smugglers smuggling up in Canada than down in Mexico, 'cause they be talk-ing about how them Canadians always be crossing the border and buying up shit that cheaper in the States and I'm sure some of that shit is contraband, but I guess they don't call that smuggling 'cause that's a free border, like if you was to smuggle something from Texas

to California, or from Covington to Cincinnati. But as long as y'all
don't send me across the border with none of y'all contraband, yeah,
'cause I don't want to be none of them collaborator . . . I hope y'all
don't mind no phony in y'all's organization, though.

He pulls at his mustache and then scratch underneath his collar.
What do you mean?

Cause I still ain't interested in no Sanctuary movement, and I will
resist y'all if y'all tries to make me do what I prefers not to do. Not
that I don't have no social conscience and shit. I mean, excuse my
French, I likes you and Maria as individuals. I mean, my being more
interested in showing them border patrol sons of bitches, excuse my
French, thumbing my nose at them border patrol, you know what
I'm saying?

Exactly.

¿Exactamente?

Muy bien.

How come y'all wants a woman like me anyhow?

What do you mean a woman like you?

I mean, you know, just an ordinary woman. Working woman.
Trabajadora. Working-class woman. I mean, I thought people in the
Sanctuary movement was members of the intelligencia and shit or
those rich—excuse my French. I'm ignorant about everything except driving my truck and them industrial detergents and I do know
something about Latin and general science, a little bit about history,
but from my own interpretation, I knows a little Spanish which I
been learning, and I do know almost everything I've heard on them
documentaries on television, 'cause I got myself a pocket television,
I knows the English that I don't resist to know, I knows how to
dance the Argentinean tango, and I knows the difference between
Taco Bell tacos and real tacos, I ain't no songstress but I have sung in
a play and I can recite poetry if it rhymes, I knows a little Italian
'cause I knows some Italians who is as much colored as they's Italian,
I knows something about entrepreneurship and could run a restaurant if I had the desire to, I reads and writes, I has hidden talents and
I likes to reflect on people and ideas, and I'm addicted to trade
shows, so I knows a little bit about every newfangled invention. You
know what I'm saying, like on television, they always be saying
about women like me, She ain't no rocket scientist. Well, you know

what I mean. I ain't no rocket scientist. Delgadina don't like to hear me say I'm ignorant, 'cause people will overhear me saying I'm ignorant and feel justified in stereotyping all colored peoples as ignorant. I knows that there is brilliant colored people. I got sense enough not to tell everybody I'm ignorant. I just tells the people that is bright enough to know that christening myself as ignorant ain't christening the whole race. I mean, I wouldn't put my ignorance in no book for everybody to read. I honors my race, if I don't celebrate it as much as Delgadina celebrates Chicanoism. I thinks the best people ought to represent the race, and them's the people I wants to represent me. I don't want nobody to confuse me with no representative of us race or to use me to prove they theories of inferiority. I agrees on some things with the ex-colored man, but I still considers myself colorful. I ain't shitting you, Ray, excuse my French.

Father Raymond he don't say nothing, he just laugh. I figure he have read *The Ex-Coloured Man*, his theories on race, and his preachifying. I remember reading that preachifying, though, and thinking why they keep all that preachifying in that book, because it seem like to me it would have been a better book without all that preachifying.

You're a jokester too, ain't ya? asked Ray, and seem like he speaking like me, then he speak in his own proper voice. I don't know when you're putting me on, you and your French. You don't have to be a rocket scientist . . . As for the intelligentsia, there are people of all classes in the Sanctuary movement. We have a few rocket scientists and members of the elite, but there's plenty working-class people too . . . And working class don't mean you ain't intelligent, you know . . . Well, I'll be in contact.

Okay, Padre. And don't expect me to be no Vista Volunteer.

What?

I look across at the restaurant and at the Native American woman eating pizza. She still reading that newspaper. And now she got her radio back in her ears.

I mean, I might move some of them suckers from one hideout to another, but I ain't the Vista Volunteer type, if you know what I mean. I ain't no goody-goody.

Yeah, I know. He winks at me.

Hey, Father Raymond.

What?

You know, the Spanish word for Mosquito is *mosquito*.

Yeah, I know. It's a diminutive of the Spanish *mosco* which means fly and from the Latin *musca*. There're people in Honduras and Nicaragua called Mosquitos and mosquito's a language too.

You talking 'bout race being a myth. Well, it seem like to me that language is a myth too. I mean, mosquito being the same everywhere and shit. Well, I gots to get back to my truck.

We shake hands and I walks toward my truck which is parked around the corner from the restaurant. The road the restaurant on ain't wide enough for my truck so I had to park around the corner. When I'm turning the corner, I glance around and see the Native American woman leaving the restaurant and going toward Father Raymond. I ain't stand there to spy on them, though. I goes and gets in my truck. I be thinking she a spy for somebody else. But maybe she a spy for Father Raymond hisself. Then I realizes I knows that woman. Leonora Valdez. Least I thinks it Leonora Valdez. You know, the reservation Native American woman that told me she were on her way to the University of New Mexico. Were she scouting me then? I can't confirm to y'all it her, or confirm that I have seen her since I seen her hurry out of the restaurant and hand Father Raymond that newspaper.

CHAPTER 9

WHERE IS SHE? ASKED FATHER RAYMOND. HE WAS standing talking to a woman who looked like one of those professional types and was carrying a briefcase. We were in the basement of a farmhouse, a large-size basement that looked like one of them warehouses where I unloads when I'm transporting industrial detergents. They's standing near the bottom of the stairs leading up into the farmhouse kitchen. I'm standing over by a table of refreshments, mostly sodas and bottled water, no Bud Light. You ain't supposed to drink out of the bottle, though, 'cause they's large-size bottles. You's supposed to drink out of the plastic cups. They's also got one of them juicers where you can make your own juice. I watches as some of the Sanctuary workers comes and makes they own juice. One of them makes carrot and apple juice. You can also make pear and apple juice, a juice with parsley and celery, and other kinds of juices. I watches them make the juices, but I just gets me a Coke. I knows about that juicer, though, 'cause Delgadina got herself one of them juicers and say that it makes pulp-free juice and she's got a lot of different fresh juice recipes and menus. I think she say that that apples and pear juice is supposed to be good for digestion and

regularity. And they's even supposed to be a combination of juices
that is anti-aging juices. I think she say that that is parsley and carrot
and apples or maybe it's beet and apple and parsley and celery and
carrot. I know that she herself is always drinking them combination
of juices. They's got some recipes next to the juicer. I knows that that
juice is good, though, 'cause Delgadina made me some of that carrot
and apple juice. And she don't peel them carrots and apples neither.
She just put them in the juicer with they seeds and stems. And they's
got cinnamon sticks near the juicer. I just thought they was some
kinda red sticks, but then I picks up one and it smell like cinnamon.

Anyway, the woman Father Raymond's talking to, she has on
a beige business-type suit, but there's a multicolored silk scarf
wrapped around her head. She's a African-American woman. I don't
know whether the scarf's wrapped around her head for religious or
historical reasons or to make a fashion statement. Seem like I seen her
picture somewhere in a magazine, one of them African-American
magazines. You know where they publishes the pictures of certain
African Americans and tells you what they does. Usually they is the
elite type of African Americans, and they wants you to know they
accomplishments, so that you won't think that all African Americans is singers and dancers, on welfare, or the criminal personalities.
The minority peoples is always trying to prove they ain't the stereotype. Seems like they spends so much of they time and energy trying to prove who they ain't. I spend a lot of time myself wondering
who people is. I knows who I thinks people is. But who you thinks
people is ain't always who they is. Sometimes people ain't even who
they thinks theyselves is. I always wonders who us peoples would
be if we didn't have to always prove who us ain't. Usually in them
magazines, though, they is people in the financial world or they's engineers or scientists or they is in professions that is not traditionally
associated with African Americans. They might be in entertainment
if they has they own production company or is something like a entertainment lawyer. It's like they's got rules for who they puts in they
magazines. But I guess all them magazines has got rules for who they
puts in the magazines.

One of them African-American television personalities who
usedta be in the soap operas said that when she were in the soap operas she read one of they rules that the central hero or heroine had to

always be white. I don't know how she got a copy of them rules, or maybe she were at one of them production meetings and got a copy of them rules. Seem like the producers of that soap opera would have known not to let her get a copy of them rules. Maybe these days they don't write that in the rule book. For some of them television shows, though, it is probably just the unwritten rule. Like that movie called *Powder*, the hero of the high intellect and all them powers had not only to be white but the whitest of the white. They had theyselves a intelligent-seeming African-American doctor, though, and he were a nicer-seeming gentleman than some of them others, but they probably only allowed him to be there because they had the whitest of the white for the superior intelligence and to represent the highest evolution of mankind. He was one of them white albinos. I went to school with a African-American albino, but people treated her like a rather average-seeming girl, and she didn't have any peoples calling her out of her name; they just treated her like a ordinary-seeming girl. I sees her sometimes when I returns to Covington. All her childrens is brown-skin childrens, ain't none of them no albinos. And one of them mens told one of them other mens, I didn't know anybody could be too white for you. Maybe the man in the movie thought he were saying something about racism, but it seem like the point of the movie were just that: that nobody could be too white. 'Cause they give him all the powers and all the intellect and he even had a girl in the movie to call him beautiful. And what else he have? He supposed to represent not only intellect but humanity, 'cause he supposed to be more human than anybody in the movie, and to be able to read people's thoughts and motives and the thoughts behind the thoughts and the motives beyond the motives. And what else he have? He the whole mythology of the ideal self. But then if he be anybody but the whitest of the white man people be saying the story weren't credible. Them Kabuki peoples, though, they powders theyselves like that. I seen a Japanese woman once while shopping at the grocery store and she had her face powdered up like that. And they's African tribes that powders theyselves like that. Delgadina sometimes kinda powders herself like that. She always wears a little lighter powder than her own complexion. I ain't know who started that tradition amongst them peoples. As for them magazines and they rules, I know the first time I seen Oprah it were in *Essence* mag-

azine, and that were before she become the Oprah that everybody
know. She were still a teenager, but I believe she were the youngest
local television personality, that were before she became international. Or maybe she just look like somebody I seen in a magazine. I
mean, this woman with the scarf around her head. Or maybe I just
imagine I seen her in a magazine, 'cause she look like them peoples
that I have seen in magazines. Seem like I seen that woman that
wrote that play for colored girls with a scarf just like that on her head
in one of them early photographs. Of course this ain't her. Monkey
Bread collects them *Essence* magazines and have got copies of them
from the time we was teenagers. The only *Essence* magazine I's got
is one with Alice Walker on the cover of it. And I's got another Alice
Walker magazine picture where she sitting up in a tree. I likes to collect them magazine pictures more than I does them magazines. I
wants to make a collage with them.

El centro. The detention camp. Concentration camp I call them.
Didn't your cousin write a book about her? the woman look like one
of them magazine pictures say.

It wasn't about her, said Ray. It was about someone like her. At
least she claims it's a work of fiction, but you know my cousin. I
never can tell whether she's writing true fiction or fictional truth.
Anyway, she's not the only guerrilla woman in Latin America. Now
she's writing romance novels. My cousin, I mean. Rather witty satires of the romance genre. But maybe that's because I know my
cousin. The reviewers review them as real romances. Or maybe they
are real romances.

And still a great beauty. I mean, the guerrilla woman. She's our
age.

Yeah, said Ray. Come over here. Ray spots me standing near the
wall, drinking Coke from one of them plastic cups, and motions for
me to come over. Well, I won't introduce you, but you should be
able to know each other when you see each other.

How are you? the woman said to me and I stood with them. Ray
wasn't wearing his priest's robes but had on blue jeans and a
sweatshirt. 'Cept the way the woman talking to him you know she
know he a priest.

We were classmates, actually, the woman said. Oh, everybody
knew she was from one of those little Latin American countries

somewhere, but you know. And that they were having some sort of revolution. We had our own Revolution, or so we thought. I always wonder now what she thought about us and our so-called revolution ... I didn't actually know she'd been a guerrilla, Ray, but I knew they were having their revolution. And then your cousin wrote that book and I knew it couldn't be anyone else but her, because of her going to school in America and then returning to her country to fight in their revolution. I remember she and I and your cousin and one of the other girls were sitting in the cafeteria, and then she got up and then this other girl says, She's got as much booty in her as us. You know, on account of she got to play white at that school, even though she's got as much of Africa in her as most of us. I don't think she was playing white myself. Maybe the whites were treating her white 'cause of her Spanish accent. 'Cause she ain't a part of their own history of oppression. I mean, we were in New England. And what does New England have to do with Mexico? If we were here in South Texas, she couldn't've played white. I'm not as dumb as I look, she joked. Am I as dumb as I look? she asked me. Do you think I'm as dumb as I look?

You don't look dumb at all to me, I says. I starts to tell her that she looks like the types of African-American womens I see in the magazines, I mean the African-American magazines.

Don't let my garb fool you, she joked.

I didn't ask the woman's story. Probably she's got a story like most African Americans, where the people's thinks they's the stereotype. I remember Delgadina was reading this book about the history of American literature or something about American literature by some famous essayist in American literature or American literary history, so Delgadina stopped reading the book, and then I asked her why she ain't continued reading that history, and then she say it 'cause he mentions some stereotypical African-American student in that book. That's all she said. He mentions some stereotypical African American. I think it be something about the Chicanos, but it ain't. Maybe when they ain't no Chicanos in them books, she identifies with us. 'Cause everybody got to have a space somewhere for they identity, so I guess she figure the same ideas they be having about African Americans they be having about her Chicano peoples, so's they's gotta spend most of they time proving they ain't as dumb as the stereotype. I figured she must have her a story like that. Delgadina got a story like that. She say she almost wanted to become a schoolteacher. But then she was in one of them classes. She sat in on a class being taught by a Chicana, and one of them gringo bitches asked this Chicana what her qualifications were for teaching that class. They never ask them gringo teachers that, you know, but she thinks 'cause this is a Chicana, she can just ask her right in her class what her qualifications are. I could see myself trying to teach some of those bitches if I was a teacher, and every semester I'd be trying to prove I ain't as dumb as they think I am. That Chicana professor she told the gringa bitch her qualifications, but me I woulda told the bitch who she herself was.

I wouldn't've told the bitch my qualifications, said Delgadina. I started to ask the Chicana teacher how come she told that bitch her qualifications when she probably didn't ask none of her white teachers that. She ain't reply, she just started saying how she was glad I was in her class. 'Cause you keep me civilized, she said. I thought it was strange her telling me that, that I was the one in her class that kept her civilized. I think she meant civil.

Naw, I think she know what she meant, I said.

I wanted Delgadina to tell me more about her Chicana professor, but she didn't. She said some other things about the gringa bitch for asking that question that she wouldn't've asked to any gringo professors, and it sounding like she was specifying, you know. If y'all don't know what specifying is, y'all's got to read Zora Neale Hurston and about that woman she call Big Sweet. Monkey Bread say when she first read about Big Sweet, she thought about me, 'cept I don't specify people like Big Sweet and I ain't like Big Sweet, except perhaps that Big Sweet a Amazon type of woman. Anyway, I wanted to know the woman's name, I mean the new Underground Railroad woman, but of course I knew that was against the rules. I liked her 'cause she was wearing a scarf like me and didn't care if nobody thought she was Aunt Jemima. Maybe a glorified Aunt Jemima, but still Aunt Jemima.

Anyway, these peoples at the new Underground Railroad they's talking revolution. I mean, Ray and the woman with the scarf. She still talking about that guerrilla woman. I goes and gets me another plastic cup of Coca-Cola and then comes back and listens to them.

Everybody talking about the revolution and they were having
their own revolution . . . One of those little Latin American countries . . . I mean, that's how a lot of Americans thought of them, like
they were all the same country . . . Like Latin America was just one
big revolution.

Then they's talking some more of what Delgadina call polemics,
which is something like politics. I guess somebody's got to talk that
kind of talk. Delgadina talks that talk all the time, 'cept she says
when she's writing stories, she tries to find something else for her
characters to talk about, 'cause she says in stories political and polemical talk ain't as interesting as other types of talk. What if you's
got characters who's political and polemical peoples? I asks. Ain't it
being true to them to have them talk the kind of talk they would
most naturally talk. Seem like you wouldn't be true to them types of
characters if they ain't talk that politics and polemics. You can have
them talk a little politics, little polemics, she says, then you's got to
get on with the stories. It's like stories about intellectuals, she says.
You can have them be true to themselves, but at the same time you've
got to put them into an interesting story. They've got to be interesting people as well as intellectuals. In fact, I've written stories about
intellectuals that readers don't even know are intellectuals, 'cause
they never say anything intellectual. I usedta know somebody like
that when I worked in this little college town. The only way I knew
she was an intellectual was because everybody said she was an intellectual, she was supposed to be this woman of a superior intellect,
but I never heard her say anything intellectual. Or maybe that's just
because she was talking to me. Well, she had all these books on intellectual subjects.

I try reading the Germans and the French, but if I wrote stories
like that, even like Hoffmann, no one would find them credible.
Then it would just be imitation German or French intellectualism.
Russian intellectualism is different because the stories themselves are
so interesting, the characters. In fact, this intellectual I was talking
about, her favorite authors were the Russians. And the Spanish mystics. Spanish mysticism, the Spanish mystical writers. And Cervantes, you know. I've been reading a book that imagines what Cervantes' novel would have been like if Sancho had told the story rather
than its being written from a third-person perspective. You know, if

it was Sancho's story and Sancho is telling us about himself and Don Quijote. But that's the archetypal relationship of the novel.

I know she was here legally as a student, says the woman in the scarf. I guess she coulda gotten legal status if she'd stayed in America then, but not now, as a subversive . . . They act like they think she'll come to America and start a revolution. Where's *el centro*?

California. I've got a map of where it is. I can give you the map. Also, I'll give you the name of the Latino group out there.

Ray kinda combs his fingers through his hair. He got a lot of that thick, kinky, wavy hair I told y'all about. I wants to comb my own fingers through that thick hair of his, but you know I ain't gonna do that.

Where've you been, Ray? ask the woman, looking at him like she's noticing him for the first time. You look like shit. Well, you still look good. Is it okay to tell a priest he looks good? I ain't Catholic, so I guess I can say so. Even when you look like shit you look good. Don't he?

Yeah, I say, though I don't feel like it really my conversation. I think that woman just wants to talk to Ray his ownself, but Ray look like he want me to stay standing there. We's in the basement of somebody's house, somebody on the new Underground Railroad, I think.

I was down in Mexico with this group. We got deported, say Ray. He comb his fingers through his hair again and then scratch the top of his head.

Some shit! What?

Yeah, the other Ray, Ray Mendoza, Al, and me. They knew I was an American citizen, but the other Ray and Al they thought had falsified documents, so they didn't want to deport them back, so we all had to insist even on being deported back to America. Even when we proved Al was an American citizen, they still tried to keep Al in Mexico.

I ain't gonna describe it all to y'all, but the way Ray was describing it it was like something out of Cheech and Chong, you know one of those Cheech and Chong movies, but without the marijuana. I mean, the way he was describing the whole scene at Mexican immigration, and the woman he was talking to she was laughing like it was supposed to be some comic story, though I don't believe the

truth of it were a comic story. They were with some group of refugees
or trying to work with some group of refugees and got deported back
to the USA. I mean Ray, the other Ray and Al and the others. I don't
know them myself, but I've heard people talk about them. Or
maybe I've met them and just ain't been introduced to them. The
woman tells Ray he oughta write a story about that, 'cause the only
stories you hear are about Mexicans getting deported from here. I
think Cheech did a movie where he got deported back to the States,
but you know what I mean. What was interesting about that story,
though, were he didn't make them Mexicans sound like the fools
and fool's fool, like a lot of them people that tells they Mexico
stories, but you be thinking that Ray and Cheech Ray Mendoza and
Chong Al the fools, which I know for a fact they ain't.

I'm sure there are a lot of American fools that go down there and
get deported, said the woman. Not that you and Al and the other
Ray are fools. Didn't Cheech Marin make a movie like that?

You know, I'm thinking all that but I ain't want to tell Ray he
sound like he telling a Cheech and Chong movie, but that woman
she mention Cheech Marin.

Koshoo's converting his barn for some of the refugees, so we were
down there trying to negotiate with the government, explained Ray.
You know, the real government, not the one everybody thinks is in
power. Anyway these were supposed to be a special group of refugees, so we couldn't just smuggle them here. Well, we didn't have
anyone to smuggle them. And then the borders are getting tighter. So
we wanted to negotiate them out of Mexico.

I know what you mean, said the woman. You was negotiating
with the real people.

Yeah, Ray said. And then we found out that even they didn't have
the right to negotiate with us.

I know what you mean, said the woman. Somebody else in power
down there that we don't know about. What do you know about it?
the woman asked me.

She doesn't know anything about it, said Ray. She's not involved
with us in all that. Don't ask her about that. I know what he means,
'cause he ain't involved me in crossing them borders and trying to
prove to them peoples that I'm a true American. I know I be down
there acting like I'm in a comic movie myself. Then he said to the

woman. So they didn't want any Americans down there, any American citizens, I mean independent of the American government negotiating, so they deported all of us back to America. You want a Coke or something? he asked the woman. Then he asked me if I wanted another Coke.

Naw, thanks, I said. No thank you. Since when has Koshoo become a gentleman farmer? You said you wanted to bring them to Koshoo's farm.

He's always had a farm.

I didn't know that. I ain't seen Koshoo in years. I know we usedta correspond and he was talking about us owning farms then. That we oughta be using our money to buy farms. Specially us splivs from the USA still talking about our forty acres and a mule and wanting reparations and shit. . . .

What about reparations? They talk about reparations for everybody else. What about reparations? I ask, 'cause I've heard everybody talking about that. I even seen one of them talk shows on television talking about reparations.

The woman is still talking to Ray, though. She kinda look at me when I says something about them reparations, like she saying this her and Ray's conversation, then she starts talking to Ray. Maybe it ain't that expression, but that the expression I reads. Then she look at me again as if to say that that ain't the true expression that she meant and that she talking to me as much as to Ray, and then she say, looking from me to Ray, Use some of that Cadillac money to buy your forty acres and a mule. . . . We oughta reclaim a lot of that land, though. . . . You hear stories all over the South, like in Mexico, during the revolution, a lot of the peasants' land got confiscated, you know, 'cause a lot of the people didn't have documents showing that they were the owners of the land, or the people in power falsified a lot of the documents, so's they could take over the people's land, lotta that happened in the South. . . . Instead of buying Cadillacs we oughta reclaim our land.

You know that's a stereotype, Ray jokes. He goes over and gets himself a Coke. Says something to another one of them refugee workers, look kinda like a stereotypical Mexican, wearing them white pajama-type clothes and guaraches, and then he come back where we is.

Is it? asks the woman. Everything stereotypical ain't a stereotype.
Like Langston Hughes usedta say. I think he said something like
that. Him or Claude McKay. Naw, I think Langston Hughes. I
know somebody that had Langston Hughes for a teacher. Can you
imagine having Langston Hughes for your teacher. Well, I guess you
can have him for a teacher, just read his poems and stories. Course
they's writers that ain't at all like the stories they writes. Least people
don't expect Langston Hughes to be no Simple, even when he's writing about Simple. Suppose Langston Hughes had written about Simple but give him his own vocabulary, you know?

Ray didn't say nothing. I starts to say something about it look like
Ray were standing over there talking to a stereotype, but I don't.
I likes Langston Hughes, but I ain't know nothing to say to that
woman about him. I knows the poems and I knows something about
his characterization of Simple. I could recite Simple, but I ain't.
They think I'm crazy standing up there reciting Simple in the pres-
ence of them refugees. And then maybe they ain't know it Simple
I'm reciting and think it me personifying Simple.

Well, some stereotypes got some basis in reality, one of my professors usedta say. I'm talking about a African-American professor.
Had us reading one of those poems about Aunt Jemima. Reclaiming
Aunt Jemima, you know. 'Cause when you go over there to Africa
you see a lot of women wear headscarves. I mean, as part of their culture and tradition and even for religious reasons. Then they come
to America and they's supposed to be Aunt Jemima. But in Africa they's true women. He started showing us pictures of African
women all over the world wearing that headscarf, and then even
started showing us Eastern Europeans and Mediterranean women,
women all over the world wearing that headscarf. So he had us reading this poem about Aunt Jemima. I didn't know why we had to
read a poem about Aunt Jemima, but he said we were reclaiming the
stereotype. They had taken something that had a basis in our reality
and perverted it into a stereotype and then we ourselves perverted it
into a further stereotype. Anyway the Cadillac ain't just a Cadillac,
the Cadillac is anything, the Cadillac is a metaphor for anything. . . .
Instead of buying Cadillacs we oughta buy back our land. . . .

How come we have to buy it back? If the land was ours, how
come we gotta buy it back? Ain't that reparations? I ask. 'Cause I

heard them talk about reparations on all them talk shows. When they wasn't talking about a apology to the peoples of Africa, they was talking reparations. I don't owe you people a apology for slavery, said one of the women. I didn't enslave you people. I don't own you people. And what about Reconstruction. I'm from the South. Some of y'all owe me a apology for Reconstruction.

That's because you don't know the true history of Reconstruction, said one of the people.

I know about as much of the true history of Reconstruction as I need to know, said the woman. And then I think the woman is about to say something about affirmation action when there's a commercial.

The woman looks at me and starts talking to me now. I mean the woman with the silk headscarf. Well, there's no way you can prove a lot of those documents were falsified. . . . Then she starts talking to Ray again. I mean you could say the land was yours, but then they'd go to the documents and the documents say it ain't, and you can't prove them documents are falsified. . . . That's how the system works. . . . Either they'd point to the documents or they'd say they ain't no documents. . . .

She do say they *ain't* no documents. I know some of y'all be telling me she ain't say that 'cause she supposed to be a cultured and educated woman, but she do say they *ain't* no documents.

That's how they use their literary tradition—they go by what's written down, not by what people say, even if the people falsified them documents. . . . But every African-American family in the South has got the same tale, part of their family history and folklore. Call it folklore 'cause it ain't written down . . . You be with somebody in Georgia or somewhere and they say, Look at that land over there, that usedta be us family land, and then they be telling you they history. . . . 'Cept they ain't got the documents or the documents they do got is falsified. . . . So Koshoo thinks we oughta all buy farms. . . . Koshoo ain't from the USA. . . . Every time I'm in the South people tell me the same story. I hear the same story when I'm in Mexico or Brazil. . . . Do you think y'all try to go out there to the detention camp. 'Cause I don't know if we can free her by legal means. . . . I mean, Ray, we can go out to *el centro*. I can talk to the Latino group, 'cause they seem like a well-organized and reliable group of people from what I hear, but I don't think we can get her out of *el centro* by legal means. And the people who remember her as the general's girlfriend don't want to liberate her from *el centro* anyway.

Ray looks at me like I'm not supposed to hear what they're saying. Then he doesn't say anything, and the woman doesn't say anything. Then Ray kisses her on the jaw and touches my elbow and he goes up the stairs. Somebody else in the basement comes up to us and starts talking to the woman with the briefcase. She a African-American woman too. She wearing her hair in them braids, though. She 'bout the same age as the woman with the briefcase. I can't tell if they's my age, though, or older than me.

Girl, you's looking like you's in love with that man.

First I think she's talking about me but she's talking to the woman with the briefcase.

I know you ain't talking about Father Raymond, says the woman.

Y'all could be in love. You hear all them stories these days. People think they's new stories, but they had stories like that back in the Middle Ages in Europe or I guess wherever they had priests. In the Middle Ages those holy men had girlfriends. They had all sorts of famous people claiming to be the children of holy men.

Don't joke about Father Raymond, says the woman.

Do y'all see the scene we had?

What scene? me and the woman asked at the same time.

I call her the girlfriend of everybody, everybody who's a general and the ones the general want her to spy on. She's here as a refugee and somebody recognized her and started a ruckus. Had to get Father Raymond to come and calm down everybody. He didn't tell y'all about that?

Naw. He told us about getting deported, I said.

I know about the guerrilla woman, but I didn't know they had a scene here, said the other woman. He just told us about getting deported from Mexico.

Oh, yeah, him and Cheech and Chong down there in Mexico. I told the fools not to go down there. I mean, Father Raymond might have been an effective negotiator if he didn't have Cheech and Chong with him.

Don't talk about Al or the other Ray, now. They ain't no Cheech and Chong. Even Cheech and Chong ain't Cheech and Chong like in the movies.

About the guerrilla woman, when we brought her here, some-body knew her and pointed her out and says, Don't think I forget, I don't forget. Then some of the others who were in the same revolu-tion joined in. We got her out of here, and then the fools who were transporting her to California got confiscated and she's in *el centro*. I told the fools they oughta take her north to Canada.

I'm supposed to go out to *el centro*.

Naw, not you. Ray and Al and the other Ray. I don't think they trust you, girlfriend, 'cause you knew each other in school, and y'all be talking shit and get her deported or some shit. They're sending somebody out there they can trust.

Who said that?

You talk too much shit. Talk shit to me. Don't talk shit to Ray if you want to be trusted.

Are you going out there?

Naw. I wouldn't trust myself at *el centro*. Not with the guerrilla woman. Somebody they really consider a subversive. I mean, most of these refugees here wouldn't start no revolution. I mean, not here in America. But she's on their subversives list. I think some spy is following me about. So I told Ray I can't smuggle none of his true revolutionaries. You know these old spies gotta have jobs. You know that poem about the old spy? I remember reading that poem in school, about some old spy from the FBI, during the days of deseg-regation. . . .

Shhh. . . .

I heard you're being reassigned?

Yeah, Miami. Who say Ray don't trust me? I know you're bull-shitting me. Koshoo's designing some new brochures about thumb-nail size that can't be easily confiscated. So I'm going to be giving everybody copies of those brochures, you know, so they'll know their rights. A lot of them they don't even know they've got rights, you know. And the government isn't going to tell them their rights. I'm talking about our government. Who say Ray don't trust me?

Koshoo? Is that his real name? Girl, I thought I was saying his code name. . . . Girl, if you're going to talk shit, don't talk shit in front of Ray is what I'm saying.

He's the only one we're allowed to name. . . . He's got contacts everywhere in the world, so he can go to just about any country. . . . Anyway, Ray says he's getting one of his guerrilla lawyers to represent Koshoo. Ray trusts me. I know he does.

Legal guerrillas? Say what? What's a legal guerrilla? I asked. Seem like I heard about legal guerrillas.

People that the government and the official sorts can't coopt, said the woman with the briefcase. 'Cause a lot of these lawyers are cooptable. I know Ray trusts me. I might talk shit sometimes, but that don't mean I ain't trustworthy. Plus I know enough not to acknowledge the fact that I already know the guerrilla woman if that what Ray wants. I know enough not to go to *el centro* telling everybody all the shit I told Ray. I wasn't talking shit, was I?

I didn't say anything, 'cause I wouldn't know if she was talking shit or not, plus I didn't hear all the shit she was talking 'cause she was already talking to Ray when I come down to the basement and heard them talking shit, then I went and got me a Coke, and I didn't come over to where they was talking till Ray indicated for me to come over there, so she mighta been talking shit, except I wouldn't know what Ray considered talking shit 'cause they was talking about somebody I didn't know.

Yeah, said the other woman. You think they're working for you and they're working for the government or some other official type.

'Cept ain't nobody supposed to call them though. . . . You can't just call one of Ray's legal guerrillas. You got to get word to Ray that you need one of them. . . . They publish their own literature, but you can only contact them by contacting the people that contact you . . .

Are you a guerrilla lawyer? You look like a lawyer, I told the woman who looked like a lawyer.

Naw, girlfriend. I ain't no lawyer. Actually, I help with various documents, but Ray says you're not involved in all that. I make sure all our documents look like the real ones. I supposed I can tell you that. I know Ray trusts me, 'cause he wouldn't have me making sure all our documents are real.

I know the only reason she tell me that much is Ray say it okay to tell me that much about what she do, 'cause these people has got rules. And maybe that ain't really what she do. Maybe she just telling me all that to camouflage what she really do. Or maybe she just talking shit, like that woman say, and ain't to be trusted.

We've got a whole list of code words we can use. Code words and code names. I sorta don't like to use the words *code word* because of them.

Who? I asked.

Who do you think them is? she asked. All their code words for people like us. Or for people not like themselves. I remember they usedta have a song during the Second World War—"People Like Us." You know, defending the world for people like themselves.

Telling your age, said the woman who denied being a guerrilla lawyer. I bet Ray trusts me more than he trusts most people.

Girl, Ray don't trust nobody. Well, he trusts people as much as he trusts them. Anyway, I mean, I saw it in a movie. One of those movies made during the war, about this group of American musicians, European-American musicians. So they had this girl singer, I guess they usedta call them then, singing about "People Like Us" while the band was playing, you know. No satire meant at all in that song. They really believed that shit. You know, one of those sweet-voiced girl singers, not like the girl singers today. Then they were sweet-talking a lot of people into thinking they meant them in that song. Sweet-talked a lot of African Americans to fight in their war.

My uncle Buddy Johnson fought in that war, I says. And we were fighting Hitler—Nazism—that was different. I surprise myself talking to them women about my uncle Buddy Johnson and that war but I was talking to them like I always knew them and belonged amongst them, and that ain't the truth for me and most people I don't know shit about.

Yeah, but the Nazi aesthetic, I heard somebody call it. Lotta European Americans they still believe in the Nazi aesthetic. What's the Barbie Doll, even Madonna and Madonna wannabees, nothing but the Nazi aesthetic. You have a few of them questioning that Nazi aesthetic, but most of them, most of them want blond-haired, blue-eyed children. Like I was listening to these two white women, one had this little girl, this little blond-haired girl and the other white woman was telling her how pretty this little girl was. Now if this little girl had had dark hair and brown eyes but the same features, this woman wouldn't be calling her a beauty at all. They call a few dark-haired women beautiful, but mosta them still gotta have blue eyes. So, anyway, this woman with the little blond-haired girl says, Yeah, she is pretty. I hope she stays blond, though. I hope she's not a false blonde. You know, 'cause a lot of them are false blondes. They're blondes when they're babies, but when they grow up their hair turns dark. That's what I mean by the Nazi aesthetic. Even though they were over there fighting them Nazis and that so-called Aryanism. . . .

Well, you have some people that question it, like Naomi, that Beauty Myth woman, you know, said the woman that denied being a guerrilla lawyer.

Yeah, but they didn't always question it. You can read African-American literature, even from the very beginning, and we were always questioning it. I mean, there were a lot of people who supported it, I mean their idea of beauty, so you've got books like William Wells Brown, where the heroine's gotta resemble a white woman to be called beautiful and valuable . . . but you've always had other writers questioning it. It's a recurring theme in African-American literature, the beauty theme, the European-American myth of beauty. You just now got European Americans questioning it. . . . Even a lot of those blondes in Hollywood. . . . Some of them even allow themselves to have red hair now. They don't all gotta be blondes. . . . I mean if you're a true blonde, like that Nordic woman who's in our group, but if you're a blonde on account of somebody else's aesthetic. . . . I mean, you can be who you wanna be as long as you got your own aesthetic . . . Like a lotta them blond rappers, seem like they're just signifying on that . . .

. . . Pretending we're writing Ray an ordinary letter, you know, to our cousin Ray—that's why I don't think she his real cousin—and then include those words in the text of the letter. I know Ray trusts me.

Course he keeps changing the code words . . .

. . . Or pretend we're having an ordinary conversation with him, but then the code words are there. Anyway, they're trying to rule her as immoral to get her deported, but Al's putting together a psychological profile, you know, of the psychology of refugees, even legal refugees. I'm not sure what he calls it . . . not sexual hyperactivity. . . . Who else don't Ray trust? I know Ray trusts me. I know he does. I don't talk shit. Here you are talking shit and talking about me talking shit. Look at these refugees looking at you, girl. You're supposed to be a exemplar and talking about me talking shit. Girl, you just like you were when we was at school. Everybody would be talking about the revolution and you'd get up and do your comedy act. Talking about me talking shit. I thought you would at least go to New York and become a comedian and ain't play these little comedy clubs around South Texas.

I know who I am, said the woman. I ain't know if she a true comedian like the woman say though. If she do play the little comedy clubs around South Texas, I ain't seen her act myself.

I goes upstairs to the bathroom 'cause of that Coke, look around to see if I can find Ray upstairs, then when I comes back to the basement they's still talking. They's talking about somebody. Maybe they's talking about me but pretending they's talking about somebody else. I go over and get me another Coke, but I can still hear them talking. I ain't going to say they's talking shit, though. Or maybe it's just they's used to hearing the same conversations all the time, whereas a lot of them conversations I'm hearing for the first time, except for when they starts saying some of them kindsa things that Delgadina have already said. I know I have heard Delgadina to mention the State Department and the Soviet Union and China. You know I feel a little like that jazz musician. Say he was playing a jam session with these other musicians, then he got to go take care of some business, when he gets back they's still playing the same song. Since I figure they still be playing the same song, I go upstairs again and search for Ray. I ain't find Ray, but I see Alvarado in a little room that look no bigger than a closet. He got a computer in that room, and there's a Asian-looking woman in the room, but he ain't talking to her he talking to somebody on the phone. When he see me, he motion for me to come in. I nod to the Asian-looking woman, who sitting in a little chair near the computer, but she ain't working the computer. I think she a refugee. Alvarado motion for me to sit down, so I sit down in one of the other little chairs. At first I'm thinking the Asian woman the one that work at the truckstop, but that ain't her.

We both sitting there ain't saying nothing whilst Alvarado talking on the telephone.

No, I can't tell you who we are, where we are, when or how we'll assist you, or what our strategies'll be. No, I can't tell you who we are. I can just tell you we'll assist you. No, that's not us. We don't allow our people in the media. Well, some of our people are in the media as individuals, as citizens, representing themselves, or maybe different organizations, but not representing us. We don't allow our people in the media. No, I can't tell you who I am either. But we've reviewed the documents you sent us. Yes, it is our ideal form. One of us will get in contact with you, okay?

He put down the phone and looked at me, then the woman started saying something to him in French.

Why don't you ask her these questions? said Alvarado, handing me a sheet of paper.

I don't know no French, I says. The paper in English, though.

She understands English. You ask her the questions in English, she'll answer in French, and I'll translate into English. It's all being recorded. I ain't want to be recorded. The truth is I prefers not to ask them questions, but he be asking me to ask them questions. I ain't want to say I prefers not to ask them, so I looks at them.

What is your name? I asks the woman, 'cause it say that on the paper.

Da hieu. My name Nguyen Smith. I try speak English.

Tell me about yourself, I says. I ask her all them questions that on the paper. 'Cept when they write up the report it don't read like what on the tape recorder, 'cause they just writes up her answers to them questions.

I am girl daughter of Mr. Joe Smith and Miss Ko Xuan Truyen. I am half African American and half Vietnamese. Return beginning. Born Saigon 1970. Mr. Joe Smith and Miss Ko Truyen separated during war and I grow up French convent school. Mr. Joe Smith find me bring me America 1988. Convent school I study seamstress. I no dumb woman. I no speak English, but I speak excellent French. I speak excellent Vietnamese, my native language. Nuns say I speak impeccable.

Here in America I meet Mr. *Il a fait impression.* Like man I see in

movie picture show. Play true American. *Aussi, il me porte intérêt.*
I no come America make revolution. Mr. begin court me. I here
America. Free say yes. I say yes. I like very much. He ask marry me. I
like very much. We marry, live Keeneland country, Kentucky. Mr.?
Homme blanc. Him have many horse. Colt, stallion, filly, foal.
Many Thoroughbred. Horse colors. White, gray, black, brown,
red-brown. People say he crazy. In Vietnam, people say I ugly. But
here America they say I beautiful. Mr. Joe Smith he say no like me
marry Mr. Say he no like Mr. Him work factory Richmond.

At first Mr. nice nice, like man in movie picture show. Teach
Nguyen ride filly. Learn horses. Learn buy horses. Buy English
horse. Buy Arab horse. Buy Turk stallion. Buy Hausa horse. Buy
hybrids.

Have two babies Mr. After have babies Mr. say he no longer
wanna be married Nguyen. Mr. take Nguyen before judge. I no understand. I say I fit keep babies. Mr. Joe Smith say I good girl, say I
raised convent school not streets Saigon. Mr. Joe Smith say all good
things. Mr. Joe Smith say I all good things. Mr. say I no speak good
English. Want babies learn good English, be American. Say babies
grow up Vietnamese brack. Say he don't want he babies hang on
street corner and learn cultural differences. Mr. Joe Smith hire lawyer take Supreme Court. Say challenge Mr. I know this no story. I
say Vietnamese brack culture very valuable culture. I no know if Supreme Court rule in favor Nguyen. I know Mr. not like man Nguyen see in movie picture show. I think Mr. Joe Smith true American.

I ain't read the file, then, I just ask them questions and she answer
them in English and keep saying she not a dumb woman, that she
sound like a dumb woman 'cause she don't speak English, but she a
intelligent woman in her own language. Then after I ask her them
questions, Alvarado take her to another little room and Ray come in
that little room and ask me what I'm doing there, and I tells him that
Alvarado want me to ask a Vietnamese woman some questions, and
he asks what kind of questions and I tell him, and then he listen to
the tape recorder for hisself, and then he jot down some notes. I ain't
want him to hear me ask them questions, 'cause I'm supposed to fill
in some of them blanks myself and I know for one of them I asks,
Did you grow up in blank? And I'm supposed to say Did you grow

up in Saigon, 'cause I'm supposed to fill in the blanks myself, but that woman she a intelligent woman so she know I means, Did you grow up in Saigon? and she fill in the blank for herself and say yes she grew up in Saigon until Mr. Joe Smith come and bring her to America. But she be seeing men like that Mr. in all them picture shows and she be thinking he real self the self in them movie picture shows, but then she learn what he true self. So they's supposed to be getting their legal guerrillas to work with that woman. Ray take some notes, like I said, while he listen to that tape. Then the phone ring and he be talking to someone on the telephone.

What's his girlfriend's name? asked Ray. Yeah, they knew her from the revolution, so the person who was supposed to transport her to Canada refused to. They said they wouldn't forget even in America. Yeah, I know, yeah I know, yeah I know, yeah I know, man. Naw, I didn't go to the meeting. Talking, you know. Gave her a beer, though. Koshoo bandaged her arm. Naw, he ain't the one usedta be a medical student. Say what? What do you mean say what? Anyway, so we took her to Koshoo's farm, but some of the guerrillas wanted to follow them there. And especially the man that kept saying he didn't forget, that he wasn't so stupid not to remember. We had to rescue her again man. I've got her at the cathedral now. At first I thought they were some instigators with the CIA, man. Yeah, man. I know who she is. Like I told them, they're in America now and this is a different revolution, if you want to call it a revolution. Do you print well? If you do, then you can work with Koshoo on the documents. I mean you have got to be an artist, though. Don't bullshit me. Maria? I gave her some of the tapes and she translated for us. Yeah?

He put the phone down and looked at me.

Our Maria? I asked.

What? He scratched the tip of his nose.

Is our Maria working with us? I asked.

Oh, yeah, well, yeah. She knows this Native American language, Quechua, and we needed her to do some translating. One of those Mayan languages, I think. They were just saying the same thing, though. What were they saying? He looks at his notebook: Don't believe the government officials, don't believe the military people.

They wouldn't tell us anything about themselves, just that. Listen, it's better if you don't ask me who's doing what, you know.

I just heard you say Maria.

I shouldn't have said Maria. She isn't exactly working with us. I needed her to do some translating. She wanted to get involved, you know. But her little baby needs some babying right now. He's still a baby.

He's so cute, ain't he?

Yes, he is. I went by there and she introduced me to him. I took her those tapes, you know, the Quechua tapes. She does some magnificent, really magnificent work, you know, I mean the dolls. It's better that you don't ask too many questions, though, not of our people.

I know, you said they might be Nicodemuses.

Yes, even if you do think someone is with us, and you're not sure, don't ask them questions.

Alvarado wanted me to ask questions.

That's for our interview. We have to interview some of the people. But those are the documented people. Those are the official interviews. Well, we have our official files on the people that we assist.

So if them immigrations comes snooping, you's got them documented peoples you helps.

Right.

I kinda liked asking them questions, asking that woman who she is and everything.

Yeah, well, Alvarado shouldn'ta had you do that.

I kinda liked it, you know. 'Cause before I just seen these people. I ain't know nothing about them. Is y'all going to help that woman to prove that she is a woman of culture and substance?

Ray said nothing. He laughed and scratched the tip of his nose, but he said nothing.

Ah, Ray, I knows that's prohibited. I didn't mean to ask you that. I knows that who is or who ain't in us movement and who is possibly involved is supposed to be kept as a question unless they is peoples that you have introduced to me, and I ain't even supposed to ask them they names. I gots to remember everything that's prohibited. I been reading some of it aloud so's I can remember what's prohibited. Seems like y'all has got so many prohibitions. No wonder you says that y'all ain't the mainstream Sanctuary movement, 'cause I don't think them peoples has as many prohibitions as y'all. I know even that book you give me to reads gives the names of some of them people. Seem like them peoples would know a woman of culture and substance even if she don't speak no good English. And I know she speak better English than any of them speak Vietnamese, nor French neither.

Ray don't say nothing. But he look like I'm discussing things that is prohibited. I be sitting there imagining him with Maria and her baby, though. I be imagining coming in and Ray got Maria baby and he kiss Maria baby and say something to Maria baby in Spanish, and then he put Maria baby back in the crib, and then he say something to Maria in Spanish and then he say something to me in English.

Ray looking through some folders on the desk. I notices a big book bound in black leather. They ain't no writing on the outside of the book. It about a couple of inches thick. I reaches for the book but before I can open it Ray takes it from me and puts it on the other side of the desk. Seems like I has seen that book before. I ain't know what kinda book it is that Ray ain't want me to read it. I be thinking it some type of wisdom book. I ain't know why the word *wisdom book* come in my thoughts. Being bound in black leather it also remind me of some type of Bible, 'cause they is Bibles that is bound in black leather, 'cept them Bibles usually is gilded and announces theyselves as Bibles. I knows what some of them folders got in them, 'cause they is writing on the outside. They is also a filing cabinet that has writing on the outside:

Immigration and Naturalization Forms
Applications for Nonresident Alien's Canadian border crossing
Immigrant Applications for Special Immigration
Applications for Employment Authorization
Visa Waivers
Applications for Naturalization
Applications for Asylum
Citizenship Applications

Fingerprint Charts
Sample Green Cards
Employment Papers & Authorizations
Employment Letters
Sample Visas
Affidavits of Support
Petitions
Adjustment of Status Applications
Supporting Documents
INS Submissions Addresses
Sample Forms
Booklets
Guides to Citizenship Examinations

I got some phone calls to make, Mosquito, say Ray. Why don't you go downstairs and talk to the gals till we get the people ready that you're supposed to transport.

Okay, Ray, I says. Then after I transport them me and Delgadina going to see Denzel Washington.

Say who? Deznel?

Denzel Washington. He a big movie star. I gots to get you to come to the movies, Ray. He one of the handsomest movies stars they is.

Deznel?

Denzel. He's a African-American movie star. You gots to know Denzel. Maybe you seen him as Malcolm X. I likes him in every movie. There is better actors I have heard. But every star ain't the best actor. 'Cept Delgadina's favorite is Edward James Olmos. She comes to Deznel's movies 'cause I likes him. I mean, Denzel. You's got me saying Deznel, and I knows the man's name. He's almost as handsome as you is, Ray. Monkey Bread is still a fan of Billy Dee Williams and when us were in Covington were the president of the local Billy Dee Williams fan club. He looks like he wants to ask me some more questions about Deznel or Denzel but he don't. He scratches the tip of his nose and turns the tape recorder on. Then he dials a number on the telephone, Mickey? Yeah, we were thinking if you could maybe rent a Land-Rover or something? Yeah, the people that we have can't forget the revolution. Did he say that he knows her? I didn't know your husband was in that revolution. I thought he was Mexican. Yeah, I guess a Mexican doesn't have to fight just in Mexico's revolutions. He talking to some woman name Mickey but looking at me, like he still thinking 'bout Deznel or Denzel, like he thinking what I favors about this Deznel or Denzel. I ain't really thinking 'bout Denzel, though.

He puts down the telephone and looks at me. On the walls they is maps and photographs of different areas of the Southwest, mostly areas around the border. There's also a map of the San Pedro River. I'm thinking of when I first met Ray and then when he were trying to recruit me for the new Underground Railroad or whatever the name of these people. I calls them Ray's people myself. I'm thinking listening to him were kinda like listening to the Learning Channel, but better, 'cause sometimes when I'm listening to the Learning Channel they teaches me what I already knows, but when Ray were telling me about the code talkers that weren't something that I already know. Then I be thinking about being a little girl and listening to Monkey Bread talking. Sometimes I ask her, Monkey Bread, who taught you that? And she be saying, Ain't nobody taught me, I just knows. Seems like they's a flowering tree in this room. Sometimes I has images like that. I remember once I was in Delgadina's apartment and I had this image of the Brazilian rain forest, and then she shows me some new books that she have ordered and one of them is about the Brazilian rain forest. I's got this image of a flowering tree, so I puts my little red bird up in that tree to sing in it.

I knows a woman name Mickey, I says. 'Cept her name Miguelita, which is the Spanish word for who she is, and she a crazy gringa that the wife of Mr. Delgado who own Delgadina's cantina, I mean the cantina where Delgadina work except but it Mr. Delgado's cantina and they's crazy bosses 'cause they don't boss nobody but to tell you the truth I think that Mr. Delgado is a nayatl and that he has taught that crazy gringa the art of transforming yourself 'cause that what nayatl means except I don't think they transforms theyselves into peoples I think they transforms theyselves into other men and womens, and that's how ain't nobody seen that Mr. Delgado and wouldn't know him if they did see him 'cause he be any man he want to be, 'cept Miguelita allow people to see her as her true self, 'cause that true self is crazy as shit, so people only think they knows who the real Miguelita, that's what I thinks myself. Sometimes Miguelita travels around with me and Delgadina in Delgadina's Land-Rover and we been to Marineland and to New Mexico and to Galveston. Delgadina just rents that Land-Rover, though. I says, Delgadina, why don't you buy you that Land-Rover, 'cause I know Mr. Delgado paying her enough to buy her that Land-Rover, and what he don't pay her she gets in tips, but she prefers to rent that Land-Rover.

He looking at me like he still thinking about Deznel or Denzel.

So what I think is the mens that come in to try to court Miguelita, especially them that think she a *puta*, which is the Spanish word for whore, is really Mr. Delgado transformed into other mens, 'cause some of them mens even calls Miguelita by other names, like they knows her but knows her by different other names. So I thinks that Mr. Delgado has taught her the art of being a nayatl and I think that's why she loves him myself, 'cause he has taught her the art of transformation. I don't know if Mr. Delgado thinks she's crazy. Maybe Mr. Delgado is the only one who knows she ain't crazy or believes she ain't as crazy as everybody else thinks she is. 'Cept they is crazy bosses that don't boss nobody.

He looking at me like he still thinking about Deznel or Denzel.

Delgadina don't boss peoples, but she do a lot of specifying.

What's specifying mean? He kinda lean back in his chair and look at me. The chairs and writing desk is old-fashioned-looking mahogany and looks like they was manufactured in the American Colonial period. He look at his notebook and I think he going to write that word in his notebook like Delgadina likes to write words in her notebook, 'cept he don't write that word in his notebook, nor do he write *Deznel* or *Denzel* in his notebook. I can tell what in that notebook. He ain't write *Deznel* or *Denzel* in it. Part of the notebook he write, "The Spiritual Mother Project" and then in another part of that notebook he write "El Despertador Mexicano." Get a copy of their Declaration of War and the *Lacandona Jungle Chronicles*. Then it just be notes, then it seem like what be a article or a translation from a book:

Today the guerrillas are saying, Enough is Enough! They, who consider themselves to be the descendants of the true builders of the nation, are speaking to the people of the Mexican nation, to the people of the Mexican government, and to the people of the world. They are speaking from the jungles of Lacandona. They are speaking from the mountains of the Mexican Southeast. They are speaking from the remote little villages. Today the guerrillas everywhere are saying, Enough is Enough!

What about specifying? he's asking, but then the phone rings.

Yes, we've got the newspapers. The newspapers? *Proceso, El Financiero, La Jornada, San Cristóbal de las Casas.* Yes, we sent someone there to interview some of the Zapatistas. Yes, we know, but we told them they didn't have to give us their true names. I've been doing some translating. No, someone else is putting together all the documents, the Declaration of War, you know, the interviews with the rebel leaders. All the moneys are supposed to go to support the Zapatistas. To get the ones out of jail who are in jail, to support the ones who escaped. . . . It's a controversial book, but we have distributors for controversial books. . . . Well, about the Zapatistas, the Mexican government. Okay, this is as much as I can tell you. They have someone who can provide them with logistical support. Even we have people who can provide logistical support. People have to fight their own rebellions. They don't want us to fight their rebellion for them. People have to liberate themselves. . . . No, it isn't just a story, they do help finance revolutions, but they have to know who the revolutionaries are. I told you, it isn't necessary for them to give their true names. The government knows that if they attract enough support they could possibly defeat the government militarily. But it's not enough to defeat the government militarily.

He paused for a moment and looked at me. I thought he wanted me to let him talk on the phone in private, so I got up and started out the door, but he waved for me to stay seated. I sat back down. He listened to what the person on the phone was saying, then he said, The modern guerrillas, they're not like the classical guerrillas. Well, you can read what they have to say in the book. They're not like the classical guerrillas. I mean you have the classical guerrilla struggle with military weapons, but that's only one of a process of struggle. I can send you a copy of the book on liberation theology. Also, there are some documents that we received from the Clandestine Revolutionary Committee that have already been translated. No, they've already been interviewed. Juárez? Well, now they want to get their message not to the government, because they know what the government is, but to the people that they refer to as people of civil society. People that they call the people of honor in civil society, you know. I can't tell you their names. No, and anyway, we haven't asked them their names. We don't ask them their names. What do they want? They want what everyone wants. Free and democratic? Well, it always amazes me how people understand freedom for themselves, but when someone else talks freedom, they put these pretenses that they don't understand what the people mean. The French, for example.

Indochina or Algeria or Africa, I said, like I was on the phone with them. Ray looked at me but said nothing. Then he was talking to the person on the phone again.

Everybody understands freedom when it's themselves. I'm in conference with someone now, but we'll send you the literature, the documents. The women have their own manifesto. They say this revolution isn't going to be like the others. They've written up something they call "Women's Law." Yes, well the guerrillas, at least the ones I know, are listening to what the women have to say. They might not agree with everything. But you have to listen to the women's voices as well as the men's or you don't have a true revolution. No, you can't just have contempt for a woman's voice because it's the voice of a woman. In fact, if you read the documents that's one of the complaints of the guerrillas themselves, the Zapatistas, one of the reasons they're saying Enough is Enough! The women have to negotiate power with them. I mean, they're fighting the same revolution, but the women know that they have to negotiate their own power. I have my own theories of power, but it's their revolution. No, no, no, no, no the money goes to. . . . Then it'll be sent to the Liberation Army. Me? I'm involved with another Declaration of War. . . . *Dzeh Dibeh-yazzie Dzeh Mosai Than-zie Gah Wol-la-chee* . . .

As he was talking that strange language, he handed me some folders. He didn't exactly say what he wanted me to do with the folders. But whenever peoples gives you folders like that they wants you to put them in alphabetical order, so I puts them in alphabetical order:

Ant
Bear
Cat
Deer
Elk
Fox
Goat
Horse
Jackass
Kid
Lamb
Mouse
Owl
Pig
Rabbit
Sheep
Turkey
Ute
Victor
Weasel
Yucca
Zinc

I don't get to put everything in alphabetical order before Ray reaches for them folders. I ain't know why them folders has got the names of mostly animals on them. First I'm thinking they all has the names of animals on them and then they's Victor and Yucca and Zinc, which ain't animals. I supposes that Ute is a animal, though I has heard womens with the name Ute. I wonders if them is the nicknames of the peoples that works with Ray. I ain't opened them folders to see what in them, I just puts them in alphabetical order. I be thinking they be a mosquito on one of them folders but they ain't. I be thinking who the peoples they has nicknamed Jackass and Weasel, though, or maybe them peoples has called theyselves Jackass and Weasel. Or maybe they is just codes that ain't the names of peoples.

Fight the power
Fight the power

Fight the power
Fight the power
Fight the power

I'm walking in the woods with my mother.
Red bird, Mommy.
Yes, I see it.
It was talking to me, Mommy. It said Fight the power, Mommy.
No, it didn't, Sojourner.
That's not a talking bird. There are talking birds in the world. But that's not a talking bird. That little bird's not a talking bird.
Yes, Mommy, it was talking to me, Mommy. Fight the power. It was talking to me, Mommy.
That little bird didn't tell you that. You've got to fight the power. But that little bird didn't tell you that.
A little bird told me.
Years later I would see that little red bird again. It would turn into a white dove and then back into a red bird. A talking bird and with the powers of transformation. And I would see it again, riding on the back of a horse made of steel.

He put the phone down and then he say, Specifying? I be thinking after talking all that about true revolution and liberation and declarations of war he forget what we's talking about, but he ain't.

I knows what it says, but I don't know what it means, I says. I means, I knows specifying when I hears it. But I can't tell you what it means.

He looking at me like he still thinking about Deznel or Denzel. Like even after talking about revolution and liberation and declarations of war, he still even thinking about what us said about Deznel or Denzel. Explain to me about specifying, he says.

Well, when Delgadina specifies she takes peoples to they origins and then some. She has specified me and even Miguelita when we does something she don't like. So you know that she specifies everybody else. Some of them mens that comes in that cantina thinking she who she ain't gets specified. She takes them to they origins and tells them things about theyselves they don't need or want to know. I knows every flaw they is in my character and every flaw in my character's character, because she have taken me to my origins and told me all my flaws.

What does she consider your flaws?

I think he going to say something about Deznel or Denzel, but he don't.

Well, she say for one thing that I subdues myself in the presence of men.

Subdue?

You know, that I subdues myself in the presence of men. She give what she call the political and social interpretation of who I am. And say that I don't want none of y'all mens, especially y'all mens of color to confuse me with no matriarch, so I subdues myself rather than to be my true self.

Do you? he ask.

I ain't even know what no matriarch were till she told me that who I ain't, or that ain't who I wants y'all mens to confuse me with. Well, I did know that a matriarch were sorta like them African-American womens that usedta play in them movies and that the wife of Kingfish were considered to be a matriarch, but I didn't know what a true matriarch. I told her that I subdues myself in the presence of love, which is true, 'cause the Perfectability Baptist Church of which I belongs says that you is supposed to subdue yourself in the presence of love. Or if they don't say it, it sounds like something they would say, or at least that the way I interprets something that they have said.

Is he still thinking about Deznel or Denzel? He looking in his notebook. Then he's looking in some of them folders that have the written interviews of them documented peoples.

I subdues myself in the presence of love, but the Perfectability Baptists says that mens and womens is supposed to do that. I tells Delgadina I can specify myself, but she's a specifying woman so she likes to specify everybody. She have specified Miguelita and if you'll specify a crazy woman then you'll specify anybody. I have seen her to subdue herself when she don't want nobody to think she a hoochie woman, 'cause when we went to Marineland she didn't ask the marine guide no questions. She subdued herself in the presence of our marine guide. I bet she knew more answers to them ques-

tions about them marine animals than that marine guide. She subdued herself so's he wouldn't think she were a hoochie woman, and
he thought she were a hoochie woman anyway. But when I subdues
myself that's a flaw.

Ray look like he still ain't sure what I means by specifying. They
is a lot of peoples like that. They is developed when it comes to everything else, but they has to be taught specification. I'm thinking
how would Delgadina specify Ray and starts to invite him to us cantina. But I wouldn't want Delgadina to specify Ray in front of me.
She could specify him to hisself. I be thinking what she would say
of Ray. I know she would want to paint him with a little more humor, little more playfulness, 'cause she know the whole history of
humor and playfulness in the African-American traditions. But that
her idea of Ray. Me I'm just in awe of his perfectability.

He look like he start to say something and then the phone ring.
He see someone in the hall and call Ray! I think he calling hisself,
but know you can't be sitting in no chair, see yourself in the hallway,
and call yourself, not if you's no natural man. Then I realize it the
other Ray he calling. The other Ray come in and answer the telephone, and Ray hisself he starts reading documents.

I'm still thinking about him, my Ray, and Maria and Maria baby
and thinking if he the kinda man that baby babies, whether he talk
baby talk or talk man talk to them babies, then I goes back downstairs and them gals is singing the same song. Might be singing 'bout
me. While they's talking, though, I'm thinking about Maria and
Maria baby and Ray.

Then I goes downstairs and they's singing the same song.

I think she's a spy for the State Department. . . .

You think everyone's a spy. . . .

You know those old spies gotta have jobs, now with the Soviet
Union. . . .

They're looking towards China now, girlfriend.

When they starts talking about China, I comes back over to
where they is again.

Talking about that jazz musician. Years later when I ain't no
greenling no more and am running my restaurant in Cuba, New
Mexico, them women of the new Underground Railroad comes into

my restaurant orders some Mexican beer and some Spanish-style paella and they's still having the same conversation.

Anyway, she's working with some Refugee Policy Group in Washington. You know, the ecologist. I don't know what that has to do with ecology though, unless it's human ecology. She calls herself an ethnoecologist. You know, the old chestnut about joining the system to change it. I don't believe that bullshit. The people I know who join the system become the system. Think she's trying to develop some sorta medicines from cactus. . . .

Now, though, I'm thinking 'bout Ray and Maria and Maria baby, and Ray asking Maria to translate them tapes. How he know she know that Indian language? I'm thinking. That Quechua. That the same as quiche? Ain't I hear somebody say quiche? Quechua? Ain't somebody say that Alvarado know Quechua? If Alvarado know Quechua he ain't have to have Maria translate that Quechua. Seem like he know them people be saying the same thing over and over again. You ask them who they name? They say the same thing. You ask them where they born? They say the same thing. You ask them why they want to come America? They say the same thing. You ask them is they documented or undocumented? They say the same thing. You ask them to fill in the blanks, they say the same thing. He know they saying the same thing. He just not know the same thing they be saying. So he go to Maria's he say, Somebody say you know Quechua? Who that somebody? Koshoo? Alvarado? The other Ray? Then he meet Maria baby.

Yeah, didn't we all say we wasn't going to join the system? I know, when they were having those Summer Jobs Programs to keep the kids off the street, she got a job with the Police Department, the Detective Bureau. . . .

Really? I asks. I'm sitting down at the table with them, drinking one of them Mexican beers that our restaurant imports from Mexico. I ain't going to tell y'all too much of that story.

He meet Maria baby. He baby Maria baby, but he talk man talk, he don't talk baby talk. Who else I hear say that about babying baby. I didn't baby y'all when y'all was babies and I ain't going to baby y'all now. That woman standing at that bus stop. Her little girl want to be babied and she say that. I didn't baby you when you was a baby and I ain't going to baby you now. But he say it okay for Maria to baby her baby, but he be talking man talk. He let Journal hear man talk.

And the fool telling everybody about it, and there was folks said she was a spy then. . . . I knew she wasn't a spy, because a spy wouldn't be telling everybody she spent the summer working at the Police Department, Detective Bureau, and wouldn't be no botanist. . . . But you know they were giving a lot of kids those kinds of jobs. . . . Keep them from rioting. . . . 'Cept a lot of them they was giving them jobs wasn't the rioting type anyway. . . .

You talk that shit when you're in school, then you join the system.

He let Journal hear man talk. I knock on the door and Maria say come in and I open it and Ray in there lifting up Journal and talking to him man talk. And Maria sitting at the table listening to them tapes.

What are they saying? Ray ask.

They're saying the same thing over and over again, Ray.

What exactly? Ray ask, and he holding Journal and talking to him man talk.

Some people manage to stay free, I says, reaching for them choco-late pretzels that I puts on every table.

But I see a lot of women my age with children, and I don't have that responsibility, says the comedian, who still playing them little comedy clubs in South Texas though sometimes she comes out to New Mexico. But to them I suppose I'm selfish. You still hear that. That women who don't have kids are selfish. Or if you can't have kids yourself, adopt them. I guess you's gotta have the revolution-aries and then you's gotta have the types of people that. . . . That guerrilla woman ain't got no children, does she? But we can't all be guerrilla women.

Still talking about that guerrilla woman, though I think she in Canada now.

The refugees are still my children, I says. I mean, they ain't all children. But y'all know what I mean. I know y'all know what I mean? she asking me.

Yeah, they says.

Other people's children can be us children, I said. And I starts to tell them about Maria and her baby, but I don't trust these gals with Maria's story.

Cathy she's still trying to have kids, I hear, say the one that still won't tell me whether she's a guerrilla lawyer, though I know who she claims she is and still wearing that silk headscarf, looking like a glorified Aunt Jemima, I don't mean the stereotyped Aunt Jemima, I mean the reclaimed Aunt Jemima. She's in one of those fertility ex-periments. She's got this Chinese doctor, though. Ern thinks she's enough kid for him, though. Call the fools by name. They ain't in our group. Bourgeois bastards. Cathy pretends she ain't bourgeois. Cathy's descended from those free blacks. Slave-holding blacks. Pretends they was abolitionists.

One group of them was slave-holding free blacks and another group abolitionists, 'cause you did have a lot of free blacks that was in the abolitionist movement. It wasn't just a white people's move-ment. There're trying to rewrite the history of the Civil Rights movement. Seen on TV where they's supposed to have another movie like that, some white woman in the South fighting for colored people's rights. . . . And you wanna make a movie about colored people, I mean African people fighting for their own rights. . . .

Maybe that's why Cathy's so ambivalent. Cathy and her little group of cosmopolitan Negroes. What's that Hughes usedta call them. The Niggerati? Negro Litterati. Negro internationalists.

We should be international. Not just provincial. We shouldn't just be a provincial people. That's what they want, just to keep us think-ing we're a provincial people, and they're the universalists. That their perspective is the universal perspective. They claim for their provincial perspective universality. We're a universal people. We're more universal. 'Cause we don't think everybody's supposed to be like us.

Ray and Maria and Journal. And Maria saying she'd like to do more for the Sanctuary movement, the new Underground Railroad, and then Ray saying that Journal needs to be babied and she's got those dolls and he be telling her how magnificent her dolls are. He be telling her how magnificent her dolls are. But she be knowing he Father Raymond. She know he Father Raymond. What's that word they have? Sacerdote. She be knowing he a priest.

We just think we're supposed to be like them, joked the other woman. You know what I mean.

Yeah, but you know what I mean. 'Cept Ern is sweet. He's really sweet.

Who's Ern? I ask. They's always talking about Cathy and Ern and other peoples I don't know.

Oh, those are people you don't know and don't want to know, said the woman who still deny being a guerrilla lawyer.

Ain't he, though.

Ain't he from Minnesota or somewhere? Farmer's boy. I mean, man. I mean he's a man, but you know what I mean. Acts like a southern gentleman, though, but with a northern accent. Well, not the white southern gentleman type of southern gentleman. We've got our own southern gentlemen. Don't mean you's gotta take nobody's shit. Some people think being a gentleman mean you gotta take people's shit. Them's the sorta people I like, that don't take other people's foolishness. I mean, he takes Catherine's foolishness, but that's love. Cathy ain't take nobody's foolishness.

'Cept she wants everybody to take her foolishness. I know a lot of peoples who's like that. I guess I'm like that myself. Course nobody ever thinks that their foolishness is foolishness. I make my foolishness rational, like everybody else.

When she say that, I start thinking about that Big Sweet in Zora Neale Hurston's book. Ain't it say something about her not taking other people's foolishness. Seem like it say something about her not taking other people's foolishness. Or being a lady, say the other woman. Let me tell you about Lady Day. . . . That's the kinda lady I'm talking about.

I loves Lady Day, I says. Sometimes I plays Lady Day music in my restaurant. Other times I plays Mexican and bordertown music. Sometimes I plays jazz, I means them musician jazz, not them jazz singers singing jazz.

Maria knows he's a Sacerdote. Yes, padre, she says. Yes, but I would like to do more for the Sanctuary, padre. Yes, padre. I understand what you are saying, padre. Thank you, padre. I am pleased that you like the dolls I make. Ah, yes, I name him Journal, you know. You say that is not her true name? I think she say Journal, I name him Journal. No, padre, I do not want to name him Pedro. And

do they do the Argentinean tango. Do they tango like the Argentin-
eans tango? Yes, padre. But I'm not from Argentina, padre, I'm from
Mexico. And what if I ask Maria? But he say I shouldn't ask Maria.
If she translate for them, then maybe she don't want people to know
it. Sacerdote Guerrero and he could be like them Sacerdotes Guerre-
ros that Delgadina talks about. Warrior-priests because in some of
those Mexican nations they would have them, priests and warrior
and wise men. Sagaz. When Delgadina wanted to buy that native
Indian jewelry, she was talking about how it looked like what the
warrior priests usedta wear. And I guess they had warrior priestesses too. She rented a Land-Rover and took me and Miguelita with
her. She didn't want to go in my truck, and Miguelita didn't want to
ride in it, so Delgadina rented a Land-Rover and we went to Santa
Fe. I didn't think Mr. Delgado would let Miguelita go to Santa Fe. I
don't know why I thought that. That she'd ask him and he'd say no
she couldn't come with us to Santa Fe. But Delgadina wanted to see
the Loretto Chapel and the miraculous staircase that was supposed
to be built from a miracle, and then she wanted to go to all the art
galleries on Canyon Road. I think her ex-husband exhibited in some
of those galleries. If she found any of his work she didn't point them
out to Miguelita or me. We didn't go to all the hundred galleries, but
we went to a good many of them galleries, even Miguelita. Then we
all bought some of that Native American jewelry. That wasn't sold
in the galleries. The Native Americans lined one of those streets,
and all the jewelry had to have something to verify that they was
authentic. Delgadina said a lot of they so-called crafts was better
than a lot of the art she'd seen in the galleries. Then she said a lot of
other things about the rules that them Native Americans had to
abide when making they jewelry. That it had to all be handmade
and made by themselves in they own houses, and it couldn't be
made in no factories. Miguelita she ain't say nothing, she just go
around with us to the different galleries and the different Native
American jewelers. She ain't say nothing till we go to one of them
restaurants. It a Mexican restaurant, but it ain't no cantina.

We orders different Mexican foods, but to tell y'all the truth I
wanted some French toast. They's got French toast on the menu, but
I don't want to be no fool to go into a Mexican restaurant and orders
French toast.

We got us Indian jewelry and you tried to find your husband's art, I says. What else us going to do?

Don't you like New Mexico? asked Delgadina.

I likes New Mexico. But seem like you spent all us time looking for your husband's art.

I didn't say I was looking for my husband's art. I said he usedta exhibit on Canyon Road. I like art galleries.

Yeah, but you wanted to go to every one of them galleries.

She's still in love, said Miguelita.

You don't know what I am, said Delgadina.

Well, we've got ourselves some valuable acquisitions, said Miguelita, eating her refried beans.

Yeah, this is fantastic, said Delgadina about some of her jewelry. It makes me look like a warrior-priestess.

I thought they just had warrior-priests, I said.

Well, where there are priests there are priestesses, she said. They might call 'em nuns, though. They don't call 'em priestesses anymore.

One must not scorn love, said Miguelita.

We're not scorning love, said Delgadina.

One must not scorn love, said Miguelita.

When we returned to South Texas, Delgadina took Miguelita to the cantina and then we went to her apartment. She went to her bookshelf and started thumbing through some of the pages.

I knew I heard that, I knew I heard that, she said, opening one of the books. She showed me something that she herself had underlined in one of Freud's books on dreams. "One must not scorn love as a curative power for delusion," it said.

That's Freud she were quoting, I said.

I don't know if she was quoting him, said Delgadina. I don't know if she knew she was quoting him, but I knew I heard that. Or maybe it's something her psychiatrist told her, quoting Freud.

I'm surprised that Mr. Delgado let her come with us to New Mexico, I says.

She just crazy, Mosquito.

She ain't say what she mean by that. Maybe she mean that even though Miguelita crazy don't mean she ain't supposed to have no rights and privileges. And Mr. Delgado must know that Delgadina protective towards her. Ain't I told y'all who they is? I be wanting to talk about New Mexico, but once Delgadina get that Freud, she start to reading him. I turns on the television whilst she reads Freud. Then she underlines something and shows it to me. One forgets nothing without a secret reason or a hidden motive, it say. I ain't know why she show that line to me. Maybe it just a line she herself like and want to show it to me, or maybe she think it got something to do with me myself. Anyway I watches television while she reads Freud.

But then, in the basement of that house, amongst them refugees, them womens that I been holding a conversation with goes upstairs to the bathroom or to look for Ray or Alvarado or the other Ray and then I'm standing by myself. I'm thinking 'bout Ray and Maria and Maria baby and Delgadina and Miguelita and Mr. Delgado and I'm listening to them other Sanctuary workers, but I don't go over and join none of them others. I wish I had asked them women about them code words, though. I'm wondering what them code words of Ray's is 'cause ain't nobody told me nothing about no code words, though I guess all secret societies got they code words, but they's Mexicans, Haitians and assorted other refugees crowded in the basement of this farmhouse. They's talking about a barn, but this ain't a barn. It one of them large-type basements with them pipes running along the walls and ceilings, but them pipes kinda remind you of that modern art. Most of the refugees are huddled against the wall, mostly silent, though sometimes you can hear snippets of some of them languages: French, Dutch, Spanish, them Creoles, Hindi, Chinese, some of them African languages, I guess that Swahili, maybe Hausa and Ibo. They ain't all migrant workers and peasants and shit, a lot of them supposed to be schoolteachers and engineers and even architects and shit. The Sanctuary movement workers is in the inner circle of the room, talking shit, as Delgadina would say, except but I can't make hide nor hair of the shit they're talking, except the gossip-type shit. I ain't know none of them people talking. Then the two women, the one denied being a guerrilla lawyer and the other woman, come back downstairs, but they don't come back where I am but stand talking to each other, but I can still hear their conversation. Delgadina call some of that type of conversation polemics and political debate, but I likes hearing every type of conversation myself. Lotta times, though, they says that type of conversations don't belong in stories. I always wonders about that, 'cause people has them types of conversations, even them intellectual debates. Even Delgadina has intellectual debates. She says, though, I ain't heard no true intellectual debates, 'cause she ain't yet had the opportunity to debate with true intellectuals, 'cause ain't many of them that frequents her cantina. Delgadina say one time somebody introduced her to some people as the Chicana bartender-intellectual except she didn't know whether they were joking or not. One of them is talking about smoking something called kif, something from North Africa, but most of them is talking politics or martial arts.

I were expecting to find a lot of revolutionary slogans on the basement wall but there ain't. Ain't no revolutionary slogans and no revolutionary posters either. I guess because if this place is raided or some shit by them immigration authorities they don't want them to find no revolutionary slogans. A nationalist and a revolutionary's not the same thing or doesn't have to be the same thing, I hear the woman in the peacock skirt say. When I first seen her, I thought it were Delgadina but it ain't. I be thinking they at least have some revolutionary art or posters on the wall, though. But like I said, them Sanctuary movement workers is in the inner circle of the room, talking shit, even that metaphysical shit. Most of them refugees they be looking like they don't understand hide nor hair of the shit either; I don't mean to say shit. Excuse my French. And some of them refugee workers they be looking like they trying to outrefugee the refugees in the way they be dressing, in them torn dungarees and do-rags and shit, and these ain't even college girls. Trying to play the peasants and the exotic types. One of them even nibbling on that kinda bread they call peasant bread.

There aren't any generals here, say the one nibbling on that peasant bread. I think it called peasant bread; it called either peasant bread or Indian bread. That peacock-skirt-wearing woman in them guaraches. Though Ray comes the closest to being a general. If we got anybody that comes close to being a general that's Ray.

Anyway, like I was saying, I think every government's a kakitocracy of sorts—is it kakitocracy?—you know, ruled by the most unprincipled people. She's apolitical herself, but I guess even apolitical people can have political opinions . . .

Some of them Sanctuary workers drinking Coca-Cola and some of them drinking that chamomile tea and some of them other herbal-type teas, 'cause one of them come offering me some of that herbal tea. Most of them refugees they be drinking that Coca-Cola 'cause they know what that Coca-Cola is. They got them this television commercial where this refugee don't understand English but he understand Coca-Cola, like it a universal language. I guess it a universal language, 'cause I don't see none of them refugees drinking that chamomile tea and none of that other herbal tea. Some of them Sanctuary workers looks like they workers for the State Department and others of them, like I said, wearing them blue jeans and them do-rags. One of them Sanctuary worker looks kinda familiar, then I realizes she one of them people I seen at one of them craft festival that make pottery and stain glass butterflies and even stain glass octopus with them suction cups except they ain't real suction cups, they's stained glass suction cups and she make a lotta different animals out of that stain glass.

I seen that stain glass artist before, 'cause Delgadina she be interested in that stain glass and be asking that woman how you become a stain glass artist and whether they's any courses you can take to become a stain glass artist, and that woman be talking about how she cut the glass into these different shapes first, and then she stain the glass, and then she glue the glass to make these different animals and a lot of them exotic-type animals 'cause she got them stain glass kangaroos and platypus and koala bears and kingfishers, and then Delgadina she be asking the woman where her studio is 'cause the woman she got a studio like a real artist. And then they even be talking to each other in Spanish 'cause this woman like has been to Mexico or something to study pre-Columbian art or some shit, 'cause Delgadina she be saying she can see the pre-Columbian influence in that stain glass and shit, and they be talking about it like it real art, and Delgadina buy one of them stain glass butterfly 'cause that her favorite animal. The woman she be saying her favorite, though, is her stain glass spider monkey. And then they be talking about something they call border art which supposed to be different artist conceptions of the idea of the border. And the woman she look kinda like one of them kingfisher her ownself, you know them kingfisher birds, 'cause she a little blond woman and her hair kinda look like the feathers of a kingfisher bird and she got them stain glass objects hanging all around her booth and look like wind chimes. And I be studying that octopus and be wondering how she can make stain glass look like it real suction cups.

What's border art? I be asking Delgadina, while we walking along through the maze of craft booths, and she carrying her stain glass butterfly and I'm carrying a handmade broom. Occasionally she stop in front of some of them other craft booth, especially them leather crafts and them craft jewelry. There's a girl there selling them slave bracelet and biker jewelry that she handmade herself, but it ain't that Miguelita. Kinda remind me of that Miguelita 'cept these is handmade slave bracelets and biker jewelry, and Miguelita would buy hers from one of them jewelry wholesalers in New Mexico and then resell them. This one be saying her slave bracelets and biker jewelry is handmade and like art and be telling me I'd look good in one of them slave bracelets and Delgadina she would look good in that biker jewelry. And then there's a Native American got his spears and shields and turquoise-type jewelry. He one of them Navajo 'cause Delgadina say some of them symbols on them shields is Navajo symbols.

You know, different artists from both sides of the border, their response to the idea of the border, the real border and the border of the mind. But border art can be anything, it can be a painting or sculpture or music or even a story. You can even write a novel and call that border art. Anything that uses the real border or the border as metaphor is border art. But the concept of border art don't just have to be the Mexican-American border, though, it can be any country that has a border with another country.

That woman she a Chicana or a gringa? I be thinking, as Delgadina tries on some of that biker jewelry, then she try on the slave bracelet. I don't try on none of that shit myself. I'm holding that handmade broom and still thinking 'bout that stain glass octopus, and wondering whether that woman a Chicana or a gringa, and thinking maybe she a blond Chicana, 'cause they got them blond Chicanas. Or maybe she like that friend of Delgadina's in Houston she be telling me about, telling me how this woman friend of hers in Houston always be wearing her a blond wig 'cause people treats her

better when she got on that blond wig and don't know that she Chicana, like that Turkish movie Delgadina and me seen take place in
Germany and this Turk be treated like shit when they know he a
Turk, then when he bleach his hair blond to look like one of them
Aryans they be treating him like a gentleman, and then when we
come out of the movie Delgadina start telling me all about that girlfriend of hers in Houston who would do the same thing, put on that
blond wig so's that people could treat her like a lady. So when I first
seen that stain glass artist I be thinking that that Delgadina girlfriend
from Houston and maybe she decided to bleach her own hair blond
instead of wearing them wigs.

When she hand the slave bracelet back to that woman 'cause it
too expensive and we come away from that booth, I be asking her
whether that stain glass artist a Chicana or a gringa.

A gringa. But not all gringas are gringas. Gringoism a state of
mind.

Like the border a state of mind.

Exactly.

Except the border ain't a state of mind, I be saying.

Exactly.

I be thinking that stain glass artist kinda remind me of Miguelita,
though I knows she ain't Miguelita.

Abyssinian, she says she's Abyssinian from Abyssinia. As crazy as
a loon, the woman in the peacock skirt is saying. She takes a map out
of her skirt pocket. Where's Abyssinia? I can't find Abyssinia on
this map. What language do they speak in Abyssinia? Oh, she must
mean Ethiopia. Abyssinia didn't that usedta be the name for Ethiopia.

I'm still standing there waiting to find out which refugees I'm
supposed to drive and where. One of the men sitting at this little
gambling table offers me a chair so I sit down. I call it a gambling
table 'cause they's several of them Sanctuary workers sitting at it
playing chess. They's dressed like working-class men but they's
playing chess and don't sound like no working-class men:

They're not revolutionaries, they're pedagogues. Anyway, they
were attempting to overthrow the government. . . . Not a coup a
putsch. . . . Who's the greenling?

We call them greenlings, the new Sanctuary workers, the one who offers me the seat explains, then he moves one of his chess pieces. Coup or putsch, he's still gotta find a job here. Ray thinks he can become an independent contractor doing topiary work. Before the revolution, he was a student in astronomy, studying galactic noise or intergalactic noise. . . . He moves another chess piece, then looks around at the refugees. It's all about the American dream, man. . . . I don't think America's ever been Al's dream, though. . . . We're all Americans, they're just the other Americans. . . . Or we're the other Americans. He's a chameleon, though, that Ray. He says he can go anywhere in the world and they think he's one of them. He was telling me about New Guinea. . . . Thinks she's the Grand Pan-jandrum.

Who?

You know who. Bet she's sweet on somebody.

Then I'm looking at one of them refugees who's looking at me, eagle-eyed, East Indian looking, then he's studying them men play-ing chess, on what ain't a table but a kettledrum turned into a table. And I be thinking maybe he a spy and not no true and orthodox ref-ugee at all. But I guess them refugees can have that furtive-eyed in-terest 'cause they be in a New World and America it be like for them a whole new planet. 'Cause they be calling them aliens anyway, even some of them Sanctuary workers, they be using the word *alien* some of them and others they be saying undocumented workers and others they be saying refugees, but most they be using that same metaphor for them aliens from outer space. But I still be thinking he a spy, though. But then he ain't looking at them Sanctuary workers any more furtive-eyed than I am.

When I first come in the basement, the woman in the peacock skirt come up to me asking me if I speak English and then be asking me what country I'm from, and then one of them other workers who kinda look Japanese but sorta dark-complexioned who that Koshoo they be talking about be telling her I'm Nadine. That's Nadine, he say. Oh, you're Nadine. Maybe that's why them Sanctuary workers talking what sound like that code, though, 'cause they don't know who a spy. How come they be trusting all them refugees to be true refugees anyhow? Them Sanctuary workers they be telling you not to trust strangers that show too much interest in the Sanctuary move-ment and that same advice in that book that Father Raymond give

me, and a lot of them same recruiting arguments they got in that book
too. But I guess all them Sanctuary people they use them same recruiting arguments, and be talking about how them refugees is migrants and be talking about how you shouldn't criminalize migrants
and about them people that have the border mentality and them that
don't. Some of them refugees, though, they be looking at the Sanctuary workers like they think it them that the aliens. I'm still listening
to them chess players:

Anyway, so that's what Roosevelt said about Somoza—sure, he's
a bastard, but he's *our* bastard, right? You know how to play chess,
greenling? he's asking me. Standing up there trying to look like Sojourner Truth or what's her name? Naw, I don't mean you, greenling.
Yeah, she's joined the Sanctuary, wearing this kerchief and shit, like
I said, trying to look like Sojourner Truth. I met her at the Quijote
Center. So, like I'm saying, the problem is that people allow their
governments to tell them what to believe—or the voice of authority.
But when you know the voice of authority is lying. Today too many
people know the voice of authority for the liars that they are. That's
why people don't trust authorities anymore. I mean government
officials, congressmen, doctors, lawyers. They know them for the liars they are. . . . People have to be the means to their own salvation. . . . I belong to this international consumers group. Naw, she's
waiting for some new refugees. Are you waiting for some new refugees?

Yes, I answer.

What's your name, greenling?

Chito Chiton.

We're all Chito Chitons here. And old revolutionaries. Some of
us were on different sides in the revolution, but . . . I mean in our
different countries' revolutions, but we're . . . *¡Hijas de puta!* Chingada! As soon as I get my working papers, as soon as I get my freedom papers, muchachos. . . . Race? So he asks me my race. In my
country, you never ask a man his race. Race is a North American
myth.

Then that woman, that Grand Panjandrum, find out I'm waiting
for the new refugees, tell me to wait against the wall till they decide
which refugees I'm supposed to drive and where. Then she herself
stand near that kettledrum that them men done turned into a chess

table and then come to me again telling me my assignment, that I'm to drive them—some of them refugees—to another farmhouse. You know, one of them big ranch-type farmhouses; she describe the farmhouse and then take a map out of her peacock skirt, must be another map 'cause the other map she have were a world map and this a Texas map and show me where it is on the map, but she make me memorize where the farmhouse is and what it look like—I guess in the old days farmhouses like this used to be the big house, like the plantation big house, but in this part of the country they didn't call them the big house or plantation neither, they call them the hacienda or some shit. Yeah, I think they call them the hacienda, but they still the same plantation. But they got a Spanish word for plantation too. I guess that just *plantación*. That hacienda that just a farm, Delgadina say, *hacienda* that just the Spanish word for farm. And farmer that a *hacendado*. Still that sound fancier than farm. When you say you a *hacendado* instead of a farmer. And they have them they slaves and *peones* working the land. And some of them haciendas they got them slave cabins, except but they put them migrant workers in them cabins. Them migrant workers is the *peones*. 'Cause every group they always be wanting to make somebody into the *peones*. Like them ex-slaves when they returned to Africa they be making the native Africans into they *peones*. And like that Portuguese African he be talking about the elite Africans. I guess they be making the other Africans the *peones*. And he be talking about what he call them detribalized Africans. And the elite Africans they be moving into them colonialist houses and shit and supposed to like them Mercedes, 'cause every group got to have they *peones*. Like that Delgadina she be telling me about that African filmmaker be satirizing all that about them Africans and they Mercedes, but she be saying she likes his films 'cause he don't just show the African jungle he show the urban Africans too, like that woman be talking about that man doing that series on the African cities, 'cause when most people think about Africa they don't think about them cities, and they always be more interested in them animals than they is in them human beings. And like I said they know the names of all them animals and don't even know the names of them human beings. Lotta them animals they's got they own language, though. People think 'cause they don't speak the human languages, they ain't got no languages. 'Cept the woman that own this farmhouse she ain't no fancy socialite elite-type woman. She look more like she mighta been one of the *peones*. She a sorta plump woman and look kinda Eastern European, like one of them Eastern European refugees, but somebody say she Dutch. I don't know if she a illegal alien herself or not. And I can't make out the accent of hers. If it is Dutch, I don't know. It a strange-type accent. That detective school that supposed to teach people different types of accents too. That Delgadina she pretty good with accents. I wonder if that Dutch a easy language to learn. Dutch supposed to be kinda like German, except it ain't German. But she ain't got no Dutch name, though. Then somebody else say she Dutch and Indonesian. The secret word for everyone is Chito Chiton. We've all got the same name: Chito Chiton. And that Portuguese African he want to give me one of them African names that mean the beautiful one, but I think he kidding. And he don't want me to call him no Portuguese African he just want me to call him African. 'Cause he be saying if I call him a Portuguese African that the same as colonialism. He speak Portuguese, though, as well as his tribal language. He say when he ain't in Africa or Canada he in Brazil and be telling me about all these ex-slaves who came from Brazil to Africa and from Africa back to Brazil. He say that he could claim to be Brazilian as much as he could claim to be African. And he be talking about the Africanization of Brazil and he be telling me about these towns in Brazil where he be in Brazil and think he still in Africa. And he be saying how they got towns all over Latin America like that, even Mexico, and he be saying he been in them towns and think he still in Africa. But, like I say, that another story about that Portuguese African, that African, 'cause he should have his own whole story. But one of them refugees kinda remind me of him and I be looking at him when I first come in the basement, 'cause I be wondering if maybe that him. He wearing a vest and spectacles and look like he should be one of them Sanctuary workers, but he don't look like he recognize me, though, so I don't figure it that African. And I don't ask nobody what he name, 'cause we ain't supposed to ask them refugee name, and I think they gives them new names anyhow.

You think you can remember that? the woman in the peacock skirt ask.

Yes.

Are you nervous about taking these refugees?

No, I ain't. I's got my own citizenship papers. Them refugees is them that looks nervous. What'll they do if they catches me smuggling?

You call this number. Do you have Ray's private telephone number? And you know about some of the patrols?

Yes, I remembers everything. I's got Ray's private telephone number. Do they put me in jail if they catches me smuggling?

You just call that number. I'd ride along with you, but they know me. If they see me riding with you, the patrols would be sure to stop you.

They always stops me, but Koshoo say the people's supposed to have they own documents. As far as I know these is farmworkers, and if I'm harboring illegal aliens I'm harboring them unknowingly. It Koshoo's farm itself that asked me to transport these peoples.

Ah, yes. Okay. Well, if they stop you, then you just show them your own registration. These are farmworkers, okay. They have their papers, okay. I was thinking you'd be transporting the other refugees, the ones that no one would mistake for farmworkers. Do you want me to get someone to ride along with you?

Naw, I don't allow nobody in my cab. I mean nobody I don't know. And I don't know none of these peoples. 'Cept some of them do kinda look like peoples I know. Some of them even looks like peoples I've seen on documentaries. I ain't saying they names, though, and ain't telling nobody who they is.

She return the map to the pocket of her peacock skirt, and then when them refugees that I'm supposed to transport is account for the woman in the peacock skirt lines them up and I can sorta tell why that man be calling her the Grand Panjandrum, whatever that is, even though she be wearing them guaraches just like some of them refugees. But you can tell she one of them elites, just trying to look like a refugee. Too old to be a college girl, though. Y'all know that singing group, the Fugees. That's why they call themselves Fugees, on account of them refugees.

The refugees, though, they don't all get in the truck at once. The woman in the peacock skirt act like a lookout. She peek out the door of the farmhouse, and then she motion for them one at a time to get in the truck. If they go too fast toward the truck she sorta holds them

back and then motion for them when they supposed to go toward the
truck. They's as many refugees as they's crates and bins of industrial
detergents in my truck, so's each has got his or her own crate or tin
drum of industrial detergents to hide behind. Though this ain't near
the border, and the border patrols just checks my truck when I'm on
that border road. But like Father Raymond said I don't have to carry
none of them refugees across the border. At the next farmhouse papers are being made up for them and they will be given new names
and they be given bags with food and powdered milk and hygiene
stuff. But we all be name Chito Chiton. Even I must not tell them
my true name is Sojourner. My true name Sojourner, I be wanting to
say but I gotta say I'm Chito Chiton, that way they know I'm the
one they're supposed to trust. How come them say my name Nadine
if we all supposed to be Chito Chiton? Maybe they don't know the
rules they ownself. 'Cause they sho said Nadine and they say that
Koshoo name.

You refugees' transportation? ask the man. It the other Ray.

Yeah, I says. He hand me a map, a rolled-up newspaper and some
documents.

Thanks, I says.

You know the Koshoo farm? he asks.

Yes. And I ain't nervous. 'Cept I am a little nervous 'cause that
woman told me not to be nervous. I ain't never been nervous of them
patrols. But now I'm the smuggler that they have always accused me
of being. 'Cept I ain't smuggling for myself. I'm smuggling for these
peoples. And I ain't smuggling things, I'm smuggling peoples. And
I ain't crossing nobody's borders but my own. I must be kinda nervous. They's calling these farms, but they ain't just farms, they's
hideouts.

Have you ever been arrested?

No, but I have seen it on documentaries. I got Ray's private telephone number and the telephone number of y'all's legal guerrillas. I
gots all the maps I needs, but I already knows the area. I knows
where that farm is. I've seen that farm on my route, but I ain't know
it were a stop on nobody's Underground Railroad.

I'll ride out to Koshoo's with you, he say. I've got to pick up some
documents. Naw, you don't have to drive me. I just remembered.
We've got the Land-Rover. You know the route?

Yes. I just told you I knows the route. I might be a little nervous 'cause that woman asked me is I nervous and that's the power of suggestibility. I wish she hadn't signified on being nervous, though. I'm trying to think what Delgadina, well, she ain't no new Underground Railroad person so's I can say her name, what she taught me about yoga so I can triumph over the power of suggestibility. But I knows all the routes in South Texas. In fact, I could conduct y'all's refugees to Arizona, New Mexico, and Nevada, but I would prefer not to, and Ray have said that I can join the new Underground Railroad according to my own preferences. Koshoo the brown-skin Asian-looking man. I knows him.

I still be thinking they uses the name Koshoo and Al and Ray and the other Ray but ain't supposed to say the names of them others. Or maybe everybody else a Nicodemus and they ain't no Nicodemuses. Ray say they's coupla kindsa Nicodemus. They's the Nicodemuses that don't want you to know they names, but you can know they works with the Sanctuary, and there's the Nicodemuses that wants you to neither know they names nor that they works with the Sanctuary.

I ain't had to read them maps, 'cause like I said I knows all the routes in South Texas. And the curious thing is I ain't stopped by none of them patrols. I seen a patrol, one of them patrols who have stopped me, but even he didn't stop me. He look like he going to stop me and then he spot that man in the Land-Rover who look more like a illegal alien and smuggler than I does myself, so he stops him, and I continues on the route to the farmhouse. I ain't know whether that part of they strategy, though. To get a alien who look more like a alien and smuggler than me so's I can have a free route. 'Cause they knows they's only one patrol for this route. When I gets to this other farmhouse, the Asian-looking man, Koshoo, is there. He leads them refugees into the basement of his farm, except the door that leads to the basement is camouflaged so that if you didn't know there was a door to the basement, you wouldn't know there was a door to the basement or that the farmhouse even had a basement. Then he shows me his art studio, which look like a ordinary art studio and have a skylight. Then we go into another basement, but ain't the same basement where he led the refugees, and I be thinking how many hidden basements his farmhouse have and be

thinking that maybe they's a whole lot of hidden basements, then I
be thinking about Ray's cathedral and be thinking if that have a
whole lot of hidden basements, and be thinking why Ray more secretive about the hidden basements in his cathedral than Koshoo
about the hidden basements in his farmhouse. I be thinking why
Koshoo ain't no Nicodemus, but I knows I'm prohibited from asking questions, so I lets him tell me as much about hisself as he wants
to say.

I finds out that Koshoo a true artist, that he a art artist but that he
also work with the Sanctuary movement making all kinds of documents and papers. I finds out he a true artist, a art artist who can do
any kind of papers. He a brown-skin man, like I said, but look kinda
Asian and kinda African, but I can't tell he nationality. He speak
English without no accent, though. He that same Koshoo, but they
don't introduce me to anyone by name, and I be wondering why
they be gossiping about people by they true name. And how come
that peacock-wearing woman be calling me by one of my true name,
like I said, 'cause I know she be saying You're Nadine? or maybe she
think Nadine ain't my true name, maybe somebody told her that my
code name Nadine and that ain't my true name, and supposed to be
calling me Chito Chiton anyhow.

This Koshoo, if he name Koshoo, he kinda speak English with
a accent, but it a American accent, one of them ordinary American
Midwestern-type accents, not no Asian accent and not no African
accent. Got a ponytail and hair sorta kinky and sorta straight, and he
wearing one of them goatee. He just sit down at this desk and with a
ordinary pen he can make any kind of papers. Well, he got different-
color pens, but they all them ordinary-type pens. Least the first time
I seen him he have one of them ordinary pens, then I see him again
he be having one of them computers that got them graphic designs
where he can draw with this ordinary pen, but then it put what he
draw on the computer screen, then after that he got him one of the
scanners and the pen too. But then that first time I seen him he just
have him one of them ordinary-type pens. Anyhow, I'm waiting for
a new load of Chito Chitons and watching him make up these papers
with one hand and holding this telephone under his chin with the
other hand. I don't understand all of what he say, but I just tell you
the way I hears it, and it don't exactly sound like he just talking shit.

I be wanting to scribble some of what he be saying in my notebook,
but don't want them to think that I'm no spy:

Yeah, a bullet in her arm, he be saying. She came across the border
with a bullet in her arm. Yeah. Anyway, so they're insisting she's a
economic refugee and here the woman has a bullet still lodged in her
arm. Al's trained as a medical doctor, so he took it out. Then somebody recognized the woman, one of the refugees. Some of them are
staying at my farmhouse. My other farmhouse. . . .

He say a lot of other stuff that y'all don't have to listen to. I likes
to listen myself, though I don't know all that he's talking. He's talking about someone from the INS and Ray and *el centro* and old lovers and the Haitian Refugee Center and Miami and something else
about lovers and more about the woman with the bullet in her arm
and Ray and economic refugees and revolutionaries and people who
consider themselves revolutionaries and computers and Form I-274
and G-28 and making some G-28s. . . .

Green cards? Now, you've got to tell them what their rights are,
because if you give them any kind of packet, anything written down,
the officials just confiscate it, you know. Because they don't want
them to know what the immigration law is. Knowledge is power.
Well, they'll tell you it's political propaganda. Like when Ray and
Al were deported. I think Ray's the only American I know to be deported from Mexico. Most Americans don't even know what their
own immigration laws are. They break their own immigration law
every day. The Refugee Act of 1980. . . .

Then he's talking about somebody from the U.N. "If they're
criminals, then what's their crime?" he asks the person on the other
end of the telephone.

Yeah, she's the new one. Name? You know I'm not gonna tell you
her name. . . . Like your friend says, What's a sanctuary but people,
people themselves? Because a bunch of them come in with this coyote that led 'em right to the INS. From El Quiche, I think. Say,
someone said you speak Quiche, do you speak Quiche? Well, Al
probably speaks Quiche. You don't know which coyotes to trust and
which not to trust. Yeah, she's one of our scouts. . . . Naw, you
wouldn't know her. A friend of Ray's. Peck Canyon? We're trying
to get some more legal representatives. Well, you can convert your
garage, can't you? Naw, that's her whole thing—she just counsels

refugees. . . . I can't be talking to you and get these free papers. . . . Well, I didn't knowingly harbor an illegal, that's the point. So that's why I decided if the sons-of-bitches was going to bring charges against me for *unknowingly* harboring an undocumented worker, I'd start *knowingly* harboring them, or at least using my talents to create free papers for them. That's what you call real art.

He put up the telephone and then that woman they call the Grand Panjandrum, I think it the one called the Grand Panjandrum, though any of them women could be the Grand Panjandrum talking to him. I know some of y'all wants me to describe her, but if I describes her some of y'all authorities and government-type peoples and officials might know who she is. Course some of y'all might already know who she is. Just might be more concerned now about what them Chinese is doing. I mean, the peoples in power. Them others, they's patrolling the border. Some of them is patrolling the music. But some of that music, some of them lyrics, maybe they needs to be patrolled. Do true musicians patrol theyselves? Like Delgadina say, freedom don't got to mean decadence. Course they's people see everybody else culture as decadence and ain't they own.

Then that woman with the briefcase and the one denying that she's a guerrilla lawyer, the one they call the Grand Panjandrum, comes over where Koshoo is. So what have we? she asked.

One of the refugees recognized her, so people thought a war would break out here. Different sides in the same revolution, you know. They're in a new country, but they can't erase their own history. . . . We oughta charge fines ourselves for shit like that . . .

What's your fine?

Two hundred and fifty dollars.

The charge?

Being a co-conspirator to bring in illegal aliens. . . . My ideal world, where people can enter and reside in any country's against the law. It ain't practical. But no Utopia's practical. Civil disobedience is. . . .

The elite do it all the time. What about the deportation papers?

They tricked them into signing voluntary deportation papers. I speak their language but I don't write it. You're supposed to write it in their language and then translate it into English. Cathy's faxing me Form I-274. Told me a lot of shit. They should call it INS brutality. Of course they're not going to call it INS brutality because they're aliens after all. Cathy's still calling the detention camps con-centration camps. We're putting these scrambler devices on all our telephones . . .

They can unscramble anything these days. They know who we are. . . . You make sure Cathy's faxing you the right Form I-274. Sometimes they change the forms on us, you know, so they detect whether or not it's false documentation.

Anyway, Cathy's at their deportation hearing. Political asylum they're trying for. Coercive sons-of-bitches, though. It's de facto co-ercion. She's filing an asylum petition.

Well, the important thing is to get them outta the corral.

Concentration camp. . . . You know the one they gave political asylum?

Who?

The one usedta be a soldier in Guatemala, part of the regime. . . . Hey, greenling, you wanna Coke? Give the greenling a Coke, some-body . . .

Coke? That's fucking Yankee imperialism, eh? . . . Who's got the *U.N. High Commissioner for Refugees' Handbook?*

. . . Every nation violates international law when they don't think that international law is in their national interests. Anyway, so Cathy's documenting the human rights violations at the refugee camps. . . .

. . . We've already bonded him out from the detention center. . . . You know anybody speaks Quechua? I thought Al spoke Quechua but he says he doesn't.

No.

Do you speak Quiche?

No, I says.

We're waiting for Al, so he can translate. . . . We need us a peace-maker . . .

What?

The refugee community. It's like any minority community, you know. You know, you've got to keep the people from destructive be-havior. Well, I've mastered the psychopathology of refugees. Ru-mor, gossip, aggression, mania, hyperactivity, you know. Paranoia.

Everybody thinks you're a refugee.

I am a refugee. What supplies we need?

Corn, wheat, beans, sugar, cacao. . . . And we need someone who understands this other Brazilian dialect.

She's the greenling . . .

No, I don't mean her, I mean the Brazilian . . . She was jailed when this group of workers took over some beach in Rio, I think. Well, they didn't really take over the beach, they just came onto the beach. And you know when a group of the poor come onto the wealthy people's beaches. Well, she keeps saying *Secuta aqui.* Yeah, Al figured out that she's says *Ecuta aqui.* Listen. She thinks we all understand her. She calls me *Chiol.* I think that's *senhor.* Not *señor.* Whatever the Portuguese is. Isn't it *senhor?* I know Spanish is *señor.* They say she's the leader, playing this little wooden flute. *Afofie,* they call it, leading the other workers onto the beach. No, they speak their own special dialect of Portuguese, sorta like African Portuguese. Mozambique, you know. Anyway, no one can make hide nor hair of it. She got as far as Acapulco on her own. Sure. No, I thought she was one of the Haitians at first . . . *Estou fugitiva* . . . Name's Almeida Bastiao . . . Sounds like *bastard,* don't it?

The rich don't have borders, all the borders are open for them. Do you think the rich are respectors of borders? The rich don't have borders. They talk that patriotism shit for the common man so's they can keep him in their control. That's what the very rich do anyhow, like this play by the Molettes, *Noah's Ark,* where they say, The people who are really in power have no allegiance to any country. . . . They are above the law of any one country. There is no such thing as that, not when you're talking about people, I mean, it's all a question of power. . . .

You know they just keeps talking them polemics, which I knows ain't interesting conversation. I gets me one of them Coca-Colas and drinks it. Course that woman talking about *Noah's Ark* kinda glances at me and looks like she wants to build some polemics around Coca-Cola. But them people ain't different from Freud. They say that Freud turned a hat into a sexual symbol. So I guess if Freud can turn a hat into a sexual symbol, peoples can turn Coca-Cola into politics.

CHAPTER 10

COMES UP FROM THE BASEMENT OF THAT OLD house, it a big farmhouse in pueblo style with one of them long flat roofs, you know that pueblo style, and I'm thinking about *Noah's Ark*. I ain't going to describe that farm too much for y'all. Course there's a lot of farmhouses in that pueblo style, and even if y'all goes to Koshoo's farm, it might not be the same farm. I think they just calls that farm Koshoo's farm. I think they's talking about a play named *Noah's Ark*, though, ain't the biblical Noah's ark, I go over and stands by my truck. I wants me a Bud Light, but I can't be drinking no Bud Light. Them Coca-Colas might not be politics, but they ain't as satisfying to me as that Bud Light. After I gets through transporting these Chito Chitons, then I gots to transport my industrial detergents, then maybe I can get to the cantina, get me some of them pretzels and that salsa. Delgadina got some of them new chocolate pretzels. I might get me some of them. Order me my Bud Light. If Delgadina is busy with her customers, I might read me one of Nefertiti Johnson's new romance novels. Delgadina don't think much of them, but I likes them myself. I think they oughta make movies out of them. Them whites mens and womens is always romancing each other. Somebody say that supposed to be a pen name

for one of them African-American women writers that writes Literature, but when she writes them romances she writes under the pen
name of Nefertiti Johnson. Ain't none of us Johnsons, though. Monkey Bread writes her fan letters. Every time she read a new Nefertiti
Johnson novel she writes her them fan letters. I ain't no drunk, I just
likes me my Bud Light. Some people says I gets that from my uncle
Buddy. His real name Buddy Johnson, but they would call him Bud
on account of his name and on account of him liking that Budweiser.
I usedta see him when I was a little girl growing up. He the one John
Henry usedta think he the sorta man he'd like to grow up to be, you
know. Least that what he told me one time when he found out that
Uncle Bud were my uncle. He fought in the Second World War, Uncle Bud, stayed in Paris for a while, come back to the States, stayed
in Kentucky for a while, then went up north, went up there to New
York, then went up there to New Jersey. Rumor is he returned to
Paris, but I ain't know that for a fact. I know he usedta tell a tale
about a Unicorn Woman he seen once at a carnival. Some peoples
said it were a tale he would just tell the childrens, other peoples said
it were a real Unicorn Woman and even a colored "Unicorn
Woman" which were the name we were referred to in them years,
others said he was a drunk and a nut—I know for a fact he weren't no
drunk, although he liked him his Budweiser—and others like John
Henry, who were nothing but a little boy, considered him to be the
ideal type of a man. 'Cause there were something about him that
would make you know he were his own man even in them segregation days in the South. I usedta wonder myself why he never told us
no segregation stories, 'bout being segregated over there in the
Army, or even about when he usedta travel throughout the South,
and even in Memphis, looking for that Unicorn Woman he'd seen at
a carnival once and which became his ideal for a woman. I ain't
know whether it were a true fiction, a fictional truth, or a plain lie
myself. But I does know I would like to go over there to Douglass
Park and listen to them tales he would tell, every time he would
come back from one of his journeys to try to find the Unicorn
Woman. Then somebody said he started hunting up a real woman
that he'd met over there in Memphis. But he were a curious man.
Big, gingerbread-colored man. I ain't going to say he were my ideal
for a man, 'cause he were my uncle. Then he went up north and ain't

nobody know his whereabouts. Us got a few letters from him postmarked New Jersey for a while. Even I got some letters from him,
but when he wrote to me he'd pretend he weren't a true man and
would sign his letters New Jersey Woolly Rabbit, and pretend like
he were a New Jersey Woolly Rabbit writing to me, and he would
always have some little proverb about the rabbit for me. Like he'd
say, Never pick up a rabbit by the ears. When I was a little girl I
usedta imagine I'd grow up and go searching for him my ownself,
you know, become my own private investigator and go searching the
world looking for my uncle Bud. Then I just grew up and developed
a preference for Bud. Least that's what peoples says.

Anyway, I'm standing over there by my truck thinking 'bout Bud
Light and Uncle Bud, the New Jersey Woolly Rabbit, when a
African-American woman—I think she African American—wearing a kerchief, a flannel shirt and hiking knickerbockers comes out
of the new farmhouse and introduces herself as Chito Chiton, then I
opens the back of the truck and she lead the people into the basement
of that farmhouse, another one of them hacienda-style farmhouses,
maybe built in the nineteenth century or even eighteenth century.
She the complexion of Delgadina with them high cheekbones. Then
I'm thinking maybe she one of them modern-type of Muslim
women I seen once at a rest stop. I got out of my truck and seen these
Muslim women. They was wearing they traditional Muslim scarfs
on they heads, you know. But instead of wearing them long robes
they was wearing long-sleeve shirts, 'cause they's got to cover up
they arms, long blue jeans and them sneakers. They keeps themselves covered up with the modesty of the Moslem woman, but
they's got on them modern-type clothes, and they's putting food out
on one of them picnic tables. Funny thing is they glances at me and
I'm dressed up looking just like 'em. I know they ain't think I'm
a Moslem woman, getting out of that truck, but I am dressed up
to look just like them. People says part of us ancestry supposed to
be Moroccan, though. So maybe it ain't just my name Sojourner
that make me sometimes dress the way I does. In the New World,
though, we's Catholics and Methodists and Baptists, Witnesses for
Jehovah, and even some Christian Scientists amongst us. I think the
New York Johnsons has even got a few Buddhists, Muslims, and
Ethiopianists (or whatever they call themselves).

Seem like the only time I'm asked my religion is when I'm amongst people of the older generation, my uncle Buddy's generation. They always asks you what church you's affiliated with, and you's got to be affiliated with somebody's church, otherwise you's a heathen.

What church you's affiliated with, Nadine?

I used to tell them none till I realized I was embarrassing my own people. And them Elders would look at you. You know how them Elders looks at you. 'Cause being affiliated with somebody church is fundamental. Now I tells them the Perfectability Baptist Church in Memphis, Tennessee. Which is the true church that my uncle Buddy Johnson usedta go to whenever he were in Memphis, which might be a true fiction but it ain't no fictional truth.

Who the pastor out there? I mean the Perfectability Baptist Church in Memphis. I been to Memphis but I ain't never heard of no Perfectability Baptist Church.

Reverend Wolf.

And I knows that for a fact. 'Cause Uncle Buddy usedta say they had at least three Reverend Wolfs in Memphis, and even usedta tell a confabulatory story about all them Reverend Wolfs, so I know he's got to be pastoring somebody's church.

The farmhouse look like it been freshly painted, and I be wondering if it that paint made with jalapeños Maria be telling me about, but naw, that barnacle paint, for the hulls of them ships. Maria she be talking about that barnacle paint they paint the hulls of ships with, supposed to be more ecological than that chemical paint. Jalapeños and some other-type pepper. And suppose them barnacles starts to liking the taste of them jalapeños? How does they paint the hulls of ships, though? I guess they must have them scuba divers. They can turn them little ships upside down and paint the hulls, but what about them big ships? That African I met in Canada come over to the New World on a ship, and he told me when he were traveling on that ship he had him a dream about them early captured Africans making that voyage across the ocean to the New World, but him he a free African. Of course weren't all them Africans in the New World captured Africans; you always hear them tales about them captured Africans, but they's a lot of them free Africans in the New World, and not all of them abolitionists neither, some of them they be owning they own slaves, but you don't hear many tales about them free Africans in the New World. And they be saying even today they's plenty places in the world where that slavery ain't abolished, and they's even supposed to be the equivalent of slavery in the New World and including America. Delgadina be saying when she were in Houston she worked in this women's shelter and she be saying they's a lot of the equivalent of slavery with a lot of them womens, and they even be womens who's got to escape just like them refugee slaves and them rebel slaves. And some of them mens they even be keeping them women prisoners or the equivalent of prisoners, and they be all kindsa races and classes, and not just them low-class women but them middle-class womens and even some of them wealthy socialite types. But in his dream he said he were one of them early Africans. He say it a lot different coming to the New World as a free African and coming in chains. But he be saying them refugees smuggled to the New World probably be riding in them ships just like them captured Africans. He say, though, when he were invited to eat at the captain's table, he couldn't bring himself to sit at that captain's table, 'cause he kept thinking of the slave ship captain he seen in that dream. I'm thinking about that African I met in Canada, when somebody open the door of the other side of the truck and I'm thinking it's him, I must be daydreaming it him, that African, when I turns around it's Father Raymond climbing inside. Except I guess I'm supposed to call him Chito Chiton, so I says, Hello, Chito Chiton. And he says, You can call me Ray.

Ray, I mean Father Ray. But then he take the collar off and he say he ain't no real padre. Didn't I tell you he don't look like nobody padre to me? Him and that mustache. And me be telling him about that costuming priest. You know, I be telling him about that priest at that costume party, or rather that ordinary man come to the costume party disguised as a priest. And I be saying how I couldn't imagine no woman coming to a costume party disguised as a nun. Maybe he be thinking I'm signifying and shit or be suspecting he ain't no real priest. Y'all heard that tale about the signifying monkey.

I knows I has told y'all I don't let nobody ride in the cab of my truck, but that don't apply to Father Ray. I mean I ain't about to tell Father Ray he can't ride in the cab of my truck. Well, I don't tell Father Ray he can't ride in the cab of my truck.

He take his priest collar off and open his shirt collar and say he riding back to Texas City with me. He scratches at the stubble on his chin. He got one of them strong-type chin. He scratches he mustache. He done trimmed he mustache a little, but it still look like that Santana mustache. I turn on my radio trying to find some of that Santana-type music, but the radio playing rap. I likes me that rap too, but I don't play it loud like it supposed to be played. Course I don't always understand what that be saying, though. That man be saying he can't decode that jazz; I can't decode that rap. Unless it like what Delgadina be saying about that metaphysics. I might not know what that rap say, but I know what it mean. Which I guess better than them folks that don't know what it say or what it mean. Of course like jazz, they's different kinds of rap. Probably they even got that metaphysical rap, and then they got that rap with them dirty lyrics. I heard somebody be calling them type of lyrics ghetto expressionism, but ain't everybody in the ghetto be talking that dirty-type language 'cause a lot of them so-called high-class types they be using a lot of them expletives in they language. They always associates them expletives with the common people, though. Lot of them people they be saying they don't understand the lyrics of that rap, but then they be understanding the dirty lyrics. When the lyrics is dirty, they be understanding it 'cause they be talking about wanting to censor that rap. So how come they be understanding the dirty rap lyrics and ain't understand the ordinary rap? Or even the metaphysical rap, if they's such a thing as metaphysical rap. And I be listening to that rap and ain't understand most of them lyrics whether they's dirty or ordinary or metaphysical but be asking how come when the lyrics dirty, them that wants to censor them lyrics be understanding the rap then or understand it well enough to want to ban it. But then them other lyrics, they be saying, I don't understand that rap. I don't understand if them lyrics talking dirty or not, and then I be wondering whether I should be playing that rap, but then he ain't no priest. And then I be wondering whether you can have them dirty lyrics in rap and still be metaphysical or whether metaphysics just supposed to use a certain type of language.

Why you looking at me like that? he ask, then he turn that rap up just a little louder. I be trying to listen to see if there any of them dirty lyrics, but I don't understand that rap. Maybe he be thinking my truck be bugged or something, so he want to play that rap for them that can't decode it. Then he change to one of them jazz stations but keep the music kinda loud. Now I likes me that jazz. Sometimes them jazz lyrics is dirty, but when it is it that double entendre signifying dirty. 'Cause I remembers meeting this woman horn player, spliv like me in one of them jazz clubs in Houston. I buys her a drink and be telling her she the first woman I ever met that play a horn, and she be telling me I'm the first woman truck driver she ever met. She be saying a lot of people especially the mens tells her she plays horn like a man which supposed to mean she a real good horn player, like they be saying that Tina Turner sing like a man. That Tina don't sing jazz, though, she sing that rock. Anyway, we be talking about the difference between high-minded and funky-butt jazz, me and that woman horn player. I thinks she call it funky-butt jazz or some shit. She say she play all kinds of jazz, though, play that intellectual-type jazz and play that funky-butt-type jazz, can play jazz for the intellectuals and the common folk. I be telling her I really likes her jazz but I'm surprise she a woman.

Jazz ain't got no gender, she be saying, or some shit like that. And she be saying she kinda surprised that the hicks in Texas likes jazz anyway. Don't they like jazz everywhere? I be asking. Crazy broad, but I guess you gotta be kinda nuts to play good jazz. Maybe even great jazz. We be talking about jazz and then we be talking about glamour-town. That what she call Hollywood: Glamourtown. Then she improvise a tune she call "Glamour-town." And I be telling her about me having me a boyfriend named Hollywood. And be telling her about my girlfriend out in Hollywood and how she usedta go with that John Henry Hollywood before I went with him. And she looks like she be jotting that name down in her head, like she didn't know there could be a person named Hollywood.

'Cause I gotta get used to you not being no real padre, I says. They don't got no laws about impersonating and personifying a padre, does they? He turn up that jazz a little louder, again like he maybe think that truck be bugged or something. It play that jazz that "Chitlin con Carne" the name of one of them tunes and I be thinking about Delgadina she be telling me about that Chitlin Con Carne Mexican and I be telling her they's a jazz tune called "Chitlin con Carne" and he probably named himself after that jazz tune, then there another jazz tune something by Bird and something called Lazy Bird and then I thinks something they call that third-stream music which suppose to blend classical music and jazz, or be classical music except but use that jazz improvisations, so I guess that why they call it that third-stream music and wonder what that first-stream music supposed to be, I guess that be classical, 'cause they be calling theyselves the first world. But the most versatile music is that jazz. Playing that jazz you supposed to be able to move freely in everywhich direction, or rather that jazz music supposed to be able to move freely in everywhich direction. What that that woman say about jazz, something about being free to be yourself? Another one of them prairie foxes. Prairie oyster, that's what Delgadina advises for them hangovers. A raw egg in any liquid swallowed whole. And I be thinking she means a real oyster of the prairie. I be thinking that prairie oyster a real oyster of the prairie. I drink too much of that Bud Light and she be telling me I need one of them prairie oysters.

Is you is or is you ain't my baby? someone is singing as we turns off the farm road onto the highway. A lot of that wild mustard along that highway, but ain't the same border road I picked up that Maria on. Least I thinks they calls that wild mustard. Delgadina the natural historian know all them wild plants: wild ginger and wild vanilla and wild mustard. I guess they names them like that 'cause they supposed to smell like those things except but be wild. Delgadina she the natural historian. In them story she write she got all them plants and shit, be describing them plants and shit and cactus and what kind of cactus, if it a rattail cactus she be telling you it a rattail cactus and me I just be saying cactus, but she be saying in them stories you gotta have a lot of details, but all them cactus look alike to me, except she say that's 'cause I ain't from the Southwest, 'cause if I were from the Southwest I'd know them plants as well as she, and then she be describing them chicken and don't just say chicken but tell you what kind of chicken they is, know a Cochin China chicken from one of them bantam rooster and she know all of them tree, be describing them cocobolo trees. And don't just tell you the name of the cocobolo tree, but when she get through describing that cocobolo tree you think you know the cocobolo tree. 'Cept you gotta be in the tropics to find one of them cocobolo trees, 'cause they ain't native to the Southwest. And she even know the plants and animals of the oceans and they names. They's some cactus along the highway, some of that starvation food. I don't know if it rattail cactus, though.

Who the woman in the kerchief and them knickerbockers? I asks. That your girlfriend?

What? He listening to that jazz. The jazz loud like I said, but he lean forward like he be trying to hear the jazz inside the jazz. He scratch he nose and look at me. Say what?

The woman in the do-rag and them knickerbockers. That your girlfriend?

I don't have a girlfriend.

Your wife then? I asks, 'cause she look like what that Delgadina call wifable. I ain't never heard nobody but Delgadina use that word wifable. Ain't even in the dictionary, though they got *wifehood* and *wifedom*.

Nor wife either, he says, tugging on his mustache, then scratching it. I can see him out of the corner of my eye. She's just one of the Sanctuary workers.

That's 'cause they all thinks you a real padre. You have you plenty of girlfriends if they didn't think you was no real padre. 'Cause that fellow that come to that costume party plenty of girls they be dancing with him 'cause they know he ain't no real padre. Maybe some of them they be fantasizing about being the girlfriend of a real padre. Anyway, you hear all them stories in the tabloid even about them real padres. But even in the Middle Ages they usedta have tabloid stories like that. Except they didn't call them tabloid stories. Except but they supposed to be celibate, them padres. But maybe that why some of them girls be fantasizing about them. We got anymore Chito Chitons to pick up on the way back to Texas City? Watching him scratching his mustache make me start itching. I scratch my side, then my chin, then my nose. Then put both hands back on the wheel.

No.

Someone called you the General. I heard one of them Sanctuary workers they be calling you the General. One of them say you the General. Woman in that peacock skirt, I think.

Oh, yeah?

So you the head honcho.

We ain't really got a head honcho. We're egalitarians. We don't

have a hierarchical type of group. It's more like a mosaic, or a collective, I guess. More like a council of leaders, but anyone can lead or
coordinate. Sometimes I coordinate the Sanctuary workers. Our de-
cisions are made democratically. He take a small paperback book
out of his pocket. Here's another book on the Sanctuary movement
that might interest you.

Thanks. I nods towards my glove compartment. He put it in my
glove compartment. They's some letters in there from Monkey
Bread. I know he be glancing at them like he think they might be
love letters, then he put the book in there on top of them letters. The
new book is just called *Sanctuary.* You already recruited me, though.
But for a organization so secretive as y'all's, y'all got a lot of books
about y'allself. Seem like if y'all such a secretive Sanctuary movement wouldn't be all them books on y'all.

Like I said, we ain't really the mainstream Sanctuary. The mainstream Sanctuary thinks that the more they're known the safer they
are. That's why most sanctuaries declare themselves. We're more
like what they'd call the Nicodemuses of the movement. We don't
declare ourselves, though there are certain ways that we're known to
each other.

Say what? What's a Nicodemus?

The ones who believe the more secret we are the safer we are. In
that handbook you'll find a list of sanctuaries that declare themselves
as sanctuaries, though. The immigration authorities know about
them and occasionally decide to make a move on certain sanctuaries
and certain Sanctuary workers, I suppose when it's politically expe-
dient and to set an example, I mean whenever there's a new ruckus
about immigration and our immigration policies.

Yeah, like now when I go to some of these warehouses to get my
industrial detergents, you know, they be asking me to show them my
green card, like they be thinking I don't look American enough for
them, and I be telling them I'm a citizen. Even one of your Sanctuary
workers, she be thinking I'm a refugee. They didn't use to be asking
me to show my green card 'cept like you said when they's a new
ruckus about that immigration and shit. I just tell them I'm a citizen,
show my license and my registration papers, I mean at them warehouses where I get my industrial detergents, 'cause I don't want to
make no ruckus and compromise y'all's movement. One of them

jokester fools be telling me that no true American be having them string of names like I got and be saying my real name must be Salvadora Natalia Juanita Hijo de Juan or some shit he made up. When I was up in Canada, I met this African that give me a African name that mean the beautiful one but fool that I am I didn't write the name down, so I don't remember what it is now. He just keep calling me that name, though, that mean the beautiful one. I mean, in his country and language, it mean the beautiful one. 'Cause I ain't considered that much of a beauty in my own country and language, though mens have always found me kinda attractive and I've had my share of boyfriends. Except when I was little, I was kind of shy, though, you know, so I didn't have any boyfriends till after high school. He a Portuguese African, the one name me the beautiful one, but I don't think it in Portuguese, I think it in one of them African languages.

One of your boyfriends? He scratch his mustache and look out at them wild mustard. I think they wild mustard.

Naw. I met him in Canada at one of them trade fairs. Thought he was a Canuck, though he told me you ain't supposed to call them Canadians Canucks. I overheard somebody calling them Canucks and thought it was just a name, you know. But I guess everybody they got names you ain't supposed to call them.

There are a lot of African names that mean the beautiful one. He loosen his collar some more. I wonders if he one of them smooth-chest men or whether he got lotta hair on his chest. I thinks he gonna tell me some of them African names that mean the beautiful one but he don't. Maybe he don't know them neither. Maybe he just know of them African names but don't know them. And I think he be surprised somebody be calling me the beautiful one too, but he ain't.

So if you ain't a padre what are you?

Usedta be a immigration agent, and then I realized I was on the wrong side.

That say love. Talking about that subversive love.

What do you mean?

I ain't know what I mean. I think I overheard Delgadina one time says something about subversive love, or maybe read it in one of her books. I glances toward him and then back at the highway. Man on a Harley. Wonder if it's one of them Softail Harleys. Man wearing one of them leather jackets got a peacock on it or a lyrebird. Funny with them birds, it's always the male birds got all them beautiful feathers and be spreading them beautiful tailfeathers out when they courting. When people realizes they's on the wrong side it's always 'cause they fall in love with somebody that's on the right side. Leastwise in the movies.

He laugh for a moment, then pull at his mustache. I'm still wondering if that one of them Softail Harleys. Starts to ask him if he know anything about them Harleys. Then I pictures him in his priest's robes riding one of them Harleys. And then I pictures him as a lyrebird. And then I be wondering if he got that hair on he chest, he got that soft hair or that scratchy hair? That hair on he head it kinky and wavy, but I can't tell if it soft. And I can't tell if that mustache soft neither, though he still be pulling on it and combing it with his fingers. Actually, you're right. Actually, I did fall in love with somebody on the right side.

She still in the States? I be thinking maybe she one of them other Sanctuary workers. But I thought most of them supposed to be citizens. Maybe some of them started out as refugees theyself, though, then when they become citizens they be helping the other refugees.

Naw. Deported. El Salvador. She lives in Mexico now, though. Mexico City.

I takes some beef jerky outa my shirt pocket and offers him some. He shake his head. I bites off a piece of it and puts the rest back in my shirt pocket.

That's beef jerky, he comments. I thought you's chewing tobacco.

Naw. Gotta have my beef jerky. So why ain't you in Mexico City with her? I asks.

I did go down there to find her, but when I found her she was with another guy.

So that didn't push you back to the wrong side?

One of them hitchhikers. Guy on the Harley pick up the hitchhiker, who climb onto the back of the Harley. Think it a girl hitchhiker. Maybe that the Harley's softail. Girl with the nose ring. I'm sure that's the same nose-ringed girl we seen in the restaurant.

Like in the movies, right? No, it didn't. I'm not even sure it's her that pushed me to the right side.

I bet that pushed on your buttons, though, didn't it? Seeing her with some other guy? Or maybe seeing you pushed on her buttons. I don't pick up me them hitchhikers. You don't know if they might be mb and dtk.

Say what?

What my friend Delgadina call mad, bad, and dangerous to know. She say that the name of a play, though.

Isn't that Lord Byron?

Delgadina just say that the name of a play.

I think it's Lord Byron. Or Lord Byron quoting Lady Caroline. I think it's Lord Byron quoting Lady Caroline.

I don't know about that lord and lady, but Delgadina said it's the name of a play. An Australian play. Or a Austrian play. Perhaps the playwright is quoting Lord Byron quoting Lady Caroline. They be talking about satire in her writing class at the Community Center, you know, so her teacher, she like be reading to them from this play by that title, some Australian play or Austrian play, but it sound more Australian than Austrian, though, 'cause them Australians they supposed to be a signifying people. Me I be wanting to know more about the original Australians, the aboriginals, but whenever they be having these documentaries on Australia, they be showing you the other Australians, or they be telling you about the aboriginals like that dreamtime, or they be interested in them Australian animals like them kangaroo and shit, I guess since you ain't a real priest you don't have to excuse my French, but they not having them speak for theyself, you know, the aboriginals, and be showing you them drawing on these caves and shit. Anyway, so since then we be sometimes pointing out different peoples, you know, that we thinks is mb and dtk. Oh, yeah? Course not everybody ranks as all three. And they's even mad good peoples. But mad good peoples can also be dtk. She also be calling them by they Spanish name, though, she be calling them *buenos locos* or *locos buenos*. Her boss wife is kinda *loca*, we call her the crazy gringa, but she be calling her a *buena loca*, though. When he first married her, though, Delgadina be thinking she might be one of them dtks. But me I thinks everybody's got a little of that in them, that dtk, otherwise they wouldn't be human beings, you know. So how come you disguised yourself as a priest?

At first because a lot of the people trust me better, you know. . . .

'Cause most the people you work with from Catholic countries,

I bet. 'Cause a lot of them Latin American countries they Catholic countries. But I seen them Hindu refugees and some of them Bud-dhabists, though.

Buddhist.

Buddhist. Didn't I say Buddhist?

Naw, you said Buddhabist.

I mean Buddhist, 'cause one time Delgadina be talking about how she want to become a Buddhist 'cause I think one of her favorite rock stars is a Buddhist, not a true and orthodox Buddhist I mean from the country of Buddhism, but one of them British Buddhists like in the sixties when a lot of them rock stars had they gurus and shit, you know. I think even Tina Turner a Buddhist, ain't she? So Delgadina she be thinking of becoming a Buddhist or something. I be asking her who this Buddha. I know who the Buddha, but a lot of times I likes to know what Delgadina got to say about things. She say he a great teacher. She get these interests, you know, and be tak-ing these courses at the Community Center and at the community colleges and shit to improve her mind, and I guess to improve us mind 'cause she be telling me all the same shit she be learning, not that it's shit, you know, and then she be like interested in these mys-tics and prophets, you know. She even know about Sojourner Truth, you know. Know more about Sojourner Truth than I do, and I'm named after her.

What does Sojourner Truth have to do with Buddhism? You probably instinctively know more about Sojourner Truth. But what does she have to do with Buddhism?

I scratches inside my ear. We's on a little border road. Red ferns that look like red sticks. I think there's some of that wildflower they calls a wine cup, I think. It's got wine-colored, cup-shaped flowers. You see it everywhere in Texas. The prairies, the woodlands, all along the road. Delgadina knows the name of that wildflower. She say that that wildflower can grow and thrive anywhere. I guess that why it a wildflower. Naw, with mystics and prophets, I mean. She say she like to read about African-American history 'cause it help her to understand her own history, both being colonized people and shit. I mean, Delgadina. So she be telling me that if Sojourner Truth weren't a slave and a African woman and shit they probably be call-

ing her a mystic if not a prophet on account of them different religious and mystical experiences she be having. Maybe she even be
Saint Sojourner.

My aunt Electra, some people say, is a mystic and prophet.

I don't understand that mysticism myself and that enlightenment,
though Delgadina be enlightening me all the time. She be telling me
I ain't no ignorant woman, I just don't know a lot, which to me sound
the same as ignorant.

The Harley turn off the highway onto one of them narrow dirt
roads leading to a farm. It ain't none of them farms that I been taking
them refugees to, though.

You're not an ignorant woman. You don't look like an ignorant
woman. You look too cunning and clever. I think you're a trickster,
a jokester.

I know what a jokester is and a trickster, too, so I'll accept that as
a compliment, though I ain't sure you can be both a jokester and a
trickster. What I do know I know from trade fairs. I mean, what I
knows of modern knowledge. The best trade fairs is in Taos and
Santa Fe, New Mexico. Or maybe I just thinks of them as the best
trade fairs 'cause Delgadina told me them Comanches usedta have
they trade fairs in Taos and Santa Fe. I mean, in the old days before
they sent them to the reservations and they usedta do trading with
different peoples. For all I knows the Native Peoples started the
trade fair. I don't know the full history of the trade fair, I just knows
I likes them. They ain't just trading silver conchos and leather boots
and woven grass mats, though, but all kindsa modern electronics.
And they's all kindsa people at them trade fairs. Delgadina, though,
she a wild woman. And a signifying wild woman. You know what
signifying mean, don't you? . . . Well, you instinctively know what
it mean. But that Delgadina she a wild woman. I like me them wild
women. I ain't half so wild as I seem to some. I don't mean wild in
the bad way I mean wild in the good way, 'cause wild that ain't the
same as mad bad and dangerous to know. She got one of them peacock skirts. You ever seen them peacock skirts, yeah you have 'cause
one of your Sanctuary workers got one of them peacock skirts, 'cept
it's the male birds got all the beautiful plumage, you know, like them
sunbirds and them peacocks and them lyrebirds. This musician
woman I know she told me about them sunbirds and Delgadina she

told me about them lyrebirds. I been thinking about getting me a peacock skirt, but I look like a fool in a peacock skirt. Well, maybe I wouldn't look like no fool in a peacock skirt, but I probably feel like a fool in one of them peacock skirts. The female peacock—

There's no such thing as a female peacock.

Say what?

The female is called a peahen.

Oh, yeah? Well, how come them women wear them peacock skirts then? I guess 'cause it the prettier bird. What we talking about? Oh, yeah, you being on the wrong side and shit. . . . But I guess a padre's a padre. Even if you a Buddhabist. 'Cause all them religions got they padres, though they don't call them padres.

. . . Even when I was on the wrong side I always admired some of the people, you know. Sorta people who act on what they believe.

Long as what they believe is right, I says. And long as you believe what they believe is right, 'cause I guess a lot of them immigration agents acting on what they believe. But then they got what you call the state behind them. The state be saying, I got your back, so it pretty easy for them to act on what they believe, I mean, when they believe the same thing the state believe. I been thinking about what you call the state. But all them type people they always call them the right. Except nowadays it hard to tell who on the right. Like them bikers type, a lot of them on the right, when in the old days people like them bikers be on the left, you know. I guess you can't have no nose ring and be on the right, though, or maybe you can. How come folks like y'all ain't called the right? Why we let them appropriate the name of the right for theyselves when maybe the people on the left is the peoples who's right? I looks at him askance.

What? he asks.

Maybe I wouldn't trust you myself if I didn't think you was a priest and all, and I ain't Catholic, no true and orthodox Catholic anyhow. I got this girlfriend in California that joined this group call themselves the Daughters of Nzingha. She the one wrote me them letters you seen in my glove compartment. She supposed to be a African queen, you know. I don't mean my girlfriend from California, I mean that Nzingha. Got themselves a African-American woman for a priestess too. I be telling her that it sound like some kinda cult to me. She be saying they call theyselves the Daughters of Nefertiti, then they changed it to Daughters of Sheba, now it be Daughters of Nzingha. She want me to join, but I be telling her I don't join none of them cult. She be telling me they priestess look something like me. I been a Jehovah Witness and a Methodist Episcopal, though. But to tell you the truth, even in the beginning, you didn't look like nobody priest to me, no true and orthodox priest. And you don't look like no true and orthodox immigration agent either, to tell the truth.

Oh, yeah? What do I look like? he ask.

I don't tell him. I just pull off the highway. Some of that wild mustard.

So why'd you stop? he ask.

Cause I can't kiss and drive at the same time.

CHAPTER 11

I KNOW Y'ALL THINKS I'M CRAZY, BUT ALL THE
time we's making love, Ray and me, I can still hear them peoples
talking 'bout them refugees and other peoples. We's making love
and I'm hearing conversations. Which don't mean we ain't making
good love, but them womens is still having they conversation. I'm
thinking if whether one of them patrols is going to come, saying Ray
darling and still hearing them people's talking about the new Underground Railroad, thought they ain't exactly just talking about the
new Underground Railroad. I'm trying to think more about me and
Ray, and us loving, but I'm still that jazz musician and them womens
is still saying they same song. I says Ray darling and listens to them
at the same time.

. . . I've got a couple of martial arts teachers. One's Chinese, the
other looks like that giant in Norse mythology. What's the name of
that giant? The one that guards the well of wisdom. . . . The Grand
Panjandrum thinks we oughta buy ourselves an island and turn it
into an independent country where refugees from all over the world
can come. . . . Middle-age radicals. . . . But the point is it's America
they want to come to. But at least it's better than detention camps,
you know.

. . . No fascists, dictators, or imperialists allowed.

. . . We need somebody who speaks Quechua.

. . . He'll probably try to free her. She's his old girlfriend, ain't she? The guerrilla woman. Somebody said she was or maybe they're mistaking her for another one. Like all Latinas look alike, you know. Who, the one playing chess? Name's Ray Mendoza. Not our Ray. I know that ain't Father Raymond. I think he's from Chiapas, though. She usedta be his girlfriend too. Spying on him for one of her generals. Or maybe she was spying on the generals for them?

Who's his old girlfriend? I'm asking, 'cause we's making love, like I'm saying, and I'm listening for them patrollers and I ain't want them to be talking about his old girlfriend.

You ever been to Mexico? I ask Ray.

You know I have, he says.

You know, Ray, I ain't never been across the border to Mexico. Well, once I was in Mexico and didn't know I was in Mexico. Seem like Delgadina was in her Land-Rover and knew some secret route into Mexico, but I ain't sure if we was really in Mexico. I travels along the Mexican border, but I ain't never been into Mexico, I mean, knowing that I'm in Mexico. You know the typical American attitude toward Mexico? You know us typical American attitude toward Mexico.

He look like he more interested in kissing me again than talking about Mexico. I hear something I think might be a patrol, and I grabs toward my jeans and bra, but it ain't no patrol. Then I hear a honk that sound like the honk of a member of my union. I still calls it my union, but I gots to tell y'all about my union.

What? asks Ray. He sits up against a detergent drum. I tells him I'm a Trojan woman, like that commercial, and then I starts talking about Mexico again.

What I'm saying is I ain't never had that typical American attitude towards Mexico myself, even before I met Delgadina. I ain't know why I always liked that Mexico. I ain't never been to Mexico, like I said, but I have never had that typical attitude toward Mexico. Us family history say that some of us Johnsons originated in Mexico, that we was originally Mexican Africans, then if that is true history then maybe that's why I's never had the typical American attitude towards Mexicans. I know I don't look like no Mexican, but family history say that there's a little Mexican in me.

A Mexican can look like anybody, say Ray. Mexicans are like Americans. They are Americans. The other Americans.

I know that's true, 'cause some of them refugees they tells me is Mexican don't look like them Mexicans on television. I ain't even told Delgadina about me and Mexico. Delgadina she always talking about the typical American attitude towards Mexico, and she even got them posters on her wall that was made by the Americans during the war years, you know, when they was enticing them Mexicans to come to America to join they *bracero* program. The Americans they-selves, they's the ones started encouraging them Mexicans to come to America when they needed them to work the American farms and do that other work for America during the war.

Ray looking like he know all that history, like he more interested in loving than talking Mexican history. I thinks I hears another pa-trol and grabs toward my jeans. Another one of my union honk. They probably knows what us doing, 'cause I ain't got my white flag up. I knows what they's doing sometimes when they's parked by the side of the road and ain't got they white flag up. Another one of my union honk.

Hey, Nadine.

That's one of my union. They's all jokester. 'Bout Mexico, though, Delgadina showed me a book she got in her collection that were published by the American State Department that were en-couraging Americans to learn Spanish and Portuguese, for Brazil, you know. It were written for Spanish-language teachers and busi-ness peoples. I told Delgadina I were interested in learning Spanish and she give me one of them books published by the State Depart-ment or one of them government type of books, you know, where they teaches the diplomats foreign languages, 'cause she say them is the best books for learning languages and even spies and military peoples learns to speak languages from them books, but anyway, like I'm saying, they couldn't do business in Europe during them war years, so's they had to do business in Mexico and Latin America, so during the war years them other Americas wasn't invisible 'cause they needed them, but after the war years Mexico and Latin America become invisible again. They looks toward Mexico and Latin America when they thinks they needs them, like with the Pacific Realm and European commercialism and shit. You gots to get somebody like Delgadina to explain all that though. You would like Delgadina, Ray. Except she only likes mens who treats her like she is they intellectual equal, though.

What I'm interested in doing, Mosquito, is—

I ain't going to record for y'all all his sweet-talk. Ain't Delgadina said something about Americans sweet-talking the Mexicans in those days? Ray sweet-talking me, and I'm still hearing them women singing they song. Or them jokesters honking, or trying to listen for them patrols.

Hey, Nadine. Honk.

I ain't even that sociable with them fools, but them honking like that be making Ray think I knows all them mens on a personal basis.

They belongs to my union, I explains. They's just peoples that belongs to my same union. You know what jokesters some of these union peoples are.

. . . Yeah, we're the ones who started the *bracero* program, one of the women is saying. I calls them jazz musician womens, 'cause every time I hears them, they's continuing the same conversation.

We? ask the other one.

Well, you know what I mean. When the men were at war, bringing workers up from Mexico. I met this Mexican flier when I was in Mexico. Had their own squadron during that war. A friend of mine's working on a movie about his squadron. You know, like that movie about African-American flyers. . . . You know, the one with Cuba Gooding, Jr.

. . . You remember when I was talking to Ray and I says, Castro's Cuba and Amanda Wordlaw says it ain't Castro's Cuba, it's Cuba's Cuba, it the People's Cuba. . . . She was down there trying to get an interview with Castro, though, you know when her daughter, Panda, was in that gymnastic shit, the Americas games or something. . . . She's some kinda scientist, I mean, Panda, but she's also a gymnast. I remember I saw an interview with Panda on one of those sports shows and ain't nobody said nothing about her being a scientist as well as a gymnast. So I'm talking to the TV asking them to ask her about her being a scientist or mention something about her being a scientist, but they just wanted to maintain the fiction that she was just a gymnast, you know.

What kind of scientist is she?

I don't know. She made the American gymnastic team, but she's a scientist, that's her profession. But whenever I see any articles about her, I mean, in the mainstream media, they just talk about her gymnastics. Like you wouldn't even know how intelligent she is. They just want to maintain their fiction, you know. So, anyway, Amanda Wordlaw. They can maintain any fiction they want about her, 'cause she's a nut. Anyway, she was down in Cuba trying to get an interview with Castro, and he didn't know her from Pooka, plus she don't write the kinda books that somebody like Castro would be familiar with anyway. . . . You imagine Castro reading some shit like *Don't Let Cowgirls Fool Ya*. It's a satire, it don't even pretend to be the Great African-American Novel or even the Great African-Un-American Novel. And I know he don't read them romance novels she's writing. I think it's called *The Goodest Gal in Tulsa*, or some shit. I think there's some Cubans in it, I mean the cowgirl book, but he still wouldn't be reading shit like that. It's more like tabloid journalism except in a novel. Seems like I was reading somewhere in an interview where she was talking about how in her early novels she was like using the different popular forms but putting them into fiction. So you've got tabloid, soap opera, and the movies and shit. But most readers, if you're using tabloid journalism as a motif, they just read tabloid journalism. This motif shit. The interview sounded more intelligent than the novels, though. Now if she were Alice Walker or somebody. . . . I mean, Castro might have given her an interview.

She got the same initials as Alice Walker. . . . I mean, Amanda Wordlaw.

Oh yeah? I met Alice Walker at graduate school. I mean, she came and gave a reading. I can't claim I know her. I know Amanda Wordlaw, though. I can use her name. She ain't our group.

I know another Amanda Wordlaw. Seem like there's another Amanda Wordlaw.

I don't know. I think she writes some of her shit under pseudonyms, but she's the only Amanda Wordlaw that I know.

I'd heard that she was sweet. Maybe there's a sweet one and a bitch and they's got the same name. I met her when I was down in the Caribbean, in Nassau. My people's from the Caribbean originally, the Wisdoms.

I know some Wisdoms in New York.

Yeah, they's my people. We's everywhere, though. All over the world. In Quebec we call ourselves La Sagesse but it's still the same Wisdoms. I guess I can mention their name, it ain't my name. My last name ain't Wisdom.

The men, though, in some of them books. . . .

But we've gotta have our books, we women have gotta have our books. 'Cause we ain't in they's. I mean, I likes a lot of they books, you know I loves *Invisible Man*, I loves a lot of our men's books, but we ain't in them. I mean the true us. Claude McKay's got some of us in his books, and Ernest Gaines got some of us.

Miss Jane, he got Miss Jane. Course the mens wants to see theyselves, they wants to see they whole good selves. They wants to be Marcus Garvey or Malcolm X or Martin Delany or Noble Drew Ali. We can't all be Noble Drew Ali.

Who he?

He's somebody Ray's always talking about. I think I heard Ray talking about him. I heard somebody talking about him. Somebody like Garvey, I think. Anyway, so the State Department's telling the people another one of its lies and they're buying it. . . . Well, I think they're going to try to free her from that detention camp.

Free who from what detention camp?

His old girlfriend, you know, I'm talking about the guerrilla woman. Well, rumor is she's his old girlfriend. . . . A group of artists are getting together to put graffiti on that border wall. . . . I don't believe nothing the government tells me. It ain't just our government, I think every government's. . . . Who are you? the woman asks and's looking right at me.

Shhh. . . . Don't ask her who she is. She's one of Ray's new people. You're one of Ray's new people, aren't you?

Yes, I says. And I kinda likes that name for myself. I mean, amongst people that ain't supposed to know my real name.

So anyway, Ray wants us to read this book on guerrilla law. . . .

I'm thinking about them legal guerrillas. I know where I heard about them legal guerrillas. The first time I heard about that guerrilla law, I were with Delgadina. She were going to buy some new books, so I went along with her, and I guess somebody had told her the name of the book that she wanted 'cause she went straight to the law section. She lifts up a big book by somebody called Gabriella Juárez and it called Guerrilla Law. It a big book maybe a thousand pages, and then they another book beside it called *The Adventures of a Guerrilla Lawyer*. I ain't know if this the same guerrilla law they's talking about. I ain't even thought about that till they starts talking guerrilla law.

Gabriella Juárez? I ask.

What? asks Ray. What do you know about Gabriella Juárez? He raises up.

The women were talking about guerrilla law. They said you had your own group of legal guerrillas.

I don't want to talk about legal guerrillas, says Ray.

I ain't read her book myself. Delgadina got a copy of that book though. He kissing me and ain't want to talk about Delgadina or Gabriella Juárez or them legal guerrillas. But them women they's still having that conversation inside my head. I'm like that jazz musician and they's still singing that same song.

Yeah, Ray tells everybody to read her books. She's from Mexico City, I think, was one of that group of students, you know. Educated at the Sorbonne in France and then got her law degrees from the University of Mexico and then from Harvard University. Practices what she calls guerrilla law. In the Americas.

Now she's working in the USA.

We need us a lot of guerrilla lawyers here in this regime. Shit. Somebody oughta do a teleplay about her, about this group of guerrilla lawyers. Put something intelligent on TV. And they're keeping all the documents for us and for all the different people whose rights have been abused. Ray likes to tell this story about Brazil.

What about Brazil? I asks. I mean, I ain't ask Ray, but them women inside my head they's talking Brazil now. About how the first thing the Brazilian authorities did when slavery was abolished was to destroy most of the documents or as many of the documents as they could. Of course, there were too many accounts that they couldn't destroy—people who had been there. People who had the story of Brazilian slavery in their memory. The stories that people told about slavery. The people who had already written books about it. A lot of those journals that a lot of people from Europe kept when they came to explore the Americas and to explore Brazil and then they would publish a lot of those journals in Europe. American authorities, I mean the USA America, Norteamericanos, 'cause it's all America, I don't think ever destroyed any slavery documents. The masters wrote the history books anyway—it had been a crime for slaves to read and write! 'Cept in Kentucky and Arkansas.

I'm from Kentucky, I said. It might ain't been a crime, but it were the custom. 'Cept I usedta hear a tale 'bout one of the Johnsons who was a soldier during the Civil War and he usedta know how to read and write and he usedta write letters for the other colored soldiers, you know, the ones that joined the union, 'cause they saw theyselves as fighting for they own freedom in that war. Some of us Johnsons was named after him, 'cause his name were John, and so we is his descendants. Somebody told me that Johnson were my slave name, but we was named after that John. We changed us name after Emancipation to the name of that John, so's it wasn't a slave name, it were a Emancipation name. You know, you know like Monkey Bread, that's my friend in California, she once told me us should change us names to some Swahili names telling me my name were a slave name. Or us should have African names. Aw, y'all, I ain't supposed to tell y'all my name. Well, they's so many Johnsons you ain't gonna know which Johnson I is. Don't tell Ray I told y'all my name.

They pretends they ain't heard me say my name, and goes on with they own story. Anyway, so the master's tale was that of Rhett and Scarlett. The southern gentleman and the southern belle. They hadn't done anything wrong. Southerners even today have that myth about their own history. I think people of Linda have always known the true America, the reality of America as opposed to all that idealistic shit. I mean, we believe the ideals, but we know it ain't never applied to us. So when those fools start saying American values they hear one thing and people of Linda hear another thing. But those people, you know. Believe all that Rhett and Scarlett shit about themselves, want to be Rhett and Scarlett. You's even got Northerners wanting to be Rhett and Scarlett. Like they've turned a lot of them old plantations into inns and shit, and a lot of them Northerners likes to stay in them old plantations, and they've even converted them former slave cabins into guest houses and a lot of them fools likes to stay there and pretend, you know. And even got colored folks waiting on them and shit, pretending they's in the South Befodewah. And I even overheard one of them women that owns one of them former plantation talking about how them people just loves to come there.

Honk. Honk. Honk. Honk. Hey, Nadine.

Got them servants and shit. They likes that shit. Everybody serving they funky-butts. Like in those old movies. You know those old movies. Whether they's in Asia or Africa or anywhere in the world. Got everybody serving they funky-butts. That's the way the world supposed to be. And when the colored people ain't in the movie, they women is serving they funky-butts. I was going to say that the women that don't serve they funky butts is whores. But even the whores are there to serve they funky-butts. I mean, their funky-butts.

Course she calls them servants and don't mention that other history. Just talking about how people just loves to come there and pretend it's Befodewah and Emancipation. And a lot of Northerners. The Union won the war, but the South, the Confederacy, won the propaganda, least when it comes to the slaves. Of course, you've got the depiction of them other Southerners, the poor Southerners, the so-called white trash and the neurotic types. The hillbilly stereotypes and shit. But them ain't noble Rhett and Scarlett. Slavery was a shameful history but one the slaves should be ashamed of, not themselves. And, of course, they convinced many of the slaves, the former slaves, to be ashamed of that history—so that the masters could tell it the way they wanted it, and the slaves, or former slaves—or so they thought—wouldn't tell it at all. And they's still got they Rhett and Scarlett images. . . . They really believe that shit. We don't romanticize ourselves enough and all they do is romanticize themselves. . . . I mean, even their so-called realism, when it's about themselves, is romanticism. That's why they prefer Rhett to whoever he played in *The Misfits*. . . .

Somebody said she started her a cult out there in California, Nzingha I mean. . . .

It ain't actually a cult. . . . I think they's a bunch of satirists myself.
I've read some of their literature, and I don't even know if they're a
real organization.

Hey, Nadine. Honk.

I knows about Nzingha, but I ain't say nothing to them women.
They's just talking and Ray kissing me and I wants to tell Ray that I
told them women my name, but maybe Ray know I told them my
name. Maybe one of them women already told Ray I told them my
name. I told them my name. I just told them my Johnson name. They
ain't know my whole name. They ain't know my whole name till
years later when Ray say it okay to tell them my name. But then him
loving me and I ain't want him to think I'm a fool and talking shit
and ain't obeyed all they rules, but when they started talking that
woman deny being a guerrilla lawyer and that woman supposed
to be a comedian in them little comedy clubs in South Texas when
they starts talking about it being a crime to read, I couldn't help but
think of us ancestor who could read and write and usedta read and
write for them other coloreds who couldn't read and write, sorta like
them scribes. But them Sanctuary workers, them new Underground
Railroad peoples, they's all races and all classes too, not just them
African-American women that I'm listening to. I'm that jazz musician and they's singing the same song. And Ray's kissing me and loving me. And even them they's looking at me like they think I'm some
kinda spy. But even though they be mostly speaking English, it
kinda sound like one of them foreign languages. This ain't no foreign
language. Love. Then I hear some of them same words I heard from
Father Raymond, call me Ray, darling, about the ruling classes and
revolutionaries and oppressors, call me Ray, darling, and aliens and
the state and, call me Ray, darling, not trusting strangers, call me
Ray, darling, especially strangers who comes asking about the Sanctuary movement and the new Underground Railroad. Call me Ray,
Darling.

Tell me about her, I says, rising up, calling him darling but still nibbling the soft hair on his chest. His mustache is scratchy, though.
We's still in the back of my truck and's pulled over to the side of the
road. Seem like it the same road that I first met Maria on, but I can't
tell y'all that for a fact 'cause all them border roads is alike. I hope

none of them border patrols don't come checking for no contraband. I wishes we was at my apartment, though, or his, and I was sipping me some Bud Light. Or even one of them Mexican beers. We us-selves could be in Mexico City or staying at one of them Mexican haciendas. Or be in one of them Italian villas like you reads about in the novels. I think in the Afromance novel by Nefertiti Johnson—we ain't the same Johnsons—the one called *Valentino's Kiss,* they's staying in one of them villas in Italy. And I know a lot of y'all be imagining y'all's at the Plaza in New York sipping champagne. I likes me champagne, but to tell y'all the truth I prefers Bud Light. I knows I'm supposed to prefer champagne. This ain't no commercial for Bud Light, 'cause us can prefer what us wants to prefer. I know there's a lots of us that is more champagne womens than we is Bud Light gals.

Her? he repeats.

The woman you were in love with. The one in Mexico City.

You're a strange one, he says. He sits up straight against one of the detergent drums, my horse blanket hugging his knees. Here we've just made love and you wanna hear about the other woman.

Yeah, why not? What's the Spanish word for strange?

Extraña. Rara. A stranger is an *extranjera,* that is a woman stranger. A man *extranjero.*

I rises forward and kisses him again and say Yum. I nibbles his mustache, then leans back against another detergent drum. He sit up even straighter, leaning against his own detergent drum. I reaches up on top of one of them drums and takes a beef jerky from my jacket pocket and offers him one. He take a bite of the beef jerky and chew, then he say, Very good. *Muy bueno.*

The woman, the kiss, or that beef jerky? The jerky.

And what about the woman. Very good?

Very beautiful. A newspaper woman.

Honk.

Oh, yeah? That's almost a rocket scientist. I mean, compared to me. I leans forward and kisses him again. Yum.

Comparison's a petty demon.

Say what?

Just some quotation. Some Russian writer. I forget who.

I scoots up next to him and takes some of the horse blanket. I nibbles a bit of his chest hair. It taste like coconut. That coconut oil. Not scratchy like his mustache. Probably Chekhov. Delgadina read that Chekhov all the time. Say her teacher say they don't think as high of him in that Russia though as they does in the States and Europe. To them Russians he sposed to be just some ordinary writer, you know, maybe even mediocre. But to them Europeans and the Americans he like the start of modern literature and shit. She read to me some of that Chekhov, some oyster story. You know this story about some little boy that ain't allowed to eat oysters, 'cause only adults is allowed to eat oysters. Sounded like a pretty good story to me, but Delgadina say to them Russians he supposed to be mediocre. Delgadina say her teacher always use that Chekhov, though, to teach the story. Except but she don't just use that Chekhov, 'cause she say storytelling is universal, and she have her class read stories from all over the world, and she one of them multiculturalist, you know they always be talking about that multiculturalism, so she don't just have them read European stories like when I were in school. When I were in school multiculturalism just mean Europe. You read you some stories from England, some stories from Spain, some stories from France, some stories from Italy, some stories from Germany and that be multiculturalism. What you think about that multiculturalism, I mean the real multiculturalism? And they's that other one, that Afrocentrism? Can someone be a Afrocentrist and a multiculturalist? But the only multiculture we had when I were in school were them haiku. You be reading all them European stories, then instead of reading Japanese stories or even Chinese stories you be reading them haiku. You know them haiku? They teach that haiku in college too, don't they? I ain't been to college myself, though my girlfriend and I drove to that Tuskegee Institute 'cause we all the time be hearing about that Tuskegee Institute. My friend Monkey Bread she went to culinary school and were working with me and my folks for a while in us restaurant, they owns this little restaurant in Covington, Kentucky, you know, and then she decide to go out there to California, Monkey Bread. How she get the name Monkey Bread? I ain't know how she get the name Monkey Bread. I gotta ask her how she get that name Monkey Bread, I just always call her that Monkey Bread. Everybody call her that Monkey Bread. But I like me them haiku, though. We read them from this book called *Poems You Can Eat*. I don't know why they call them eatable poems, though. And I remember that teacher who teach us them haiku, colored teacher, 'cause we had us that segregated school when I were in school, she put on one of them Japanese puppet plays. But everybody they got them puppet plays. But that petty demon that probably Chekhov be talking about petty demon. I remember one of them haiku about water birds.

Naw. Not Chekhov.

And?

And what?

Your girlfriend. Yum.

Newspaper woman, broadcast monitor, public opinion analyst, propaganda analyst.

Honk.

Rocket scientist. And speaking of cunning and clever. . . .

Got in trouble with the government—with *el jefe* anyhow—because she's too honest and opinionated for them, too "liberated," and had to flee the country. Now she's in Mexico, like I said, has a shoe repair shop. Shoe and saddle repair shop.

I'm still thinking about that comparison's a petty demon shit. And I be thinking ain't she too cunning and clever to repair shoes and saddles, but then she be a refugee in Mexico. And a lot of them refugees when they come to them new countries, the rocket scientists they ain't always rocket scientists in the new countries. Because a lot of them countries that got rocket scientists they be reserving them rocket scientist jobs for they own nationalities anyhow. And then a lot of them refugees they don't know the language. But I guess if she from El Salvador—he say El Salvador?—she be knowing Mexican.

I'm not in love with her now, if that's what you wanna know, he say.

I nibbles the hair on his chest some more, then I rises and leans against another detergent drum. Seem like to me he a little too quick to protest about that and maybe he be telling himself not me. Anyway, they says that love is as hard to understand as a melon. True love, I means. True and orthodox love. So she's with this other guy, right? I asks, reaching for some more beef jerky.

Yeah, Mexico City, like I said. Actually, they specialize in repairing saddles. . . .

Honk.

You spy on her or have someone else spy on her?

He don't answer. He get another piece of beef jerky. Actually I was in Mexico for a conference on Latin America when I thought I saw her. I followed her to this saddle shop. I knew it was her, of course, but I . . . then I saw her with this new guy. A Mexican friend of mine, a journalist actually, who has his saddles repaired there told me all about them. Well, as much about lovers as there's to tell. She's quite happy. A perfect love, *un amor perfecto*, it seems. Stepping into that shop, he says, is like stepping into Eden. He's married to a bit of a ogress himself, a beauty, but a bit of an ogress. So he says, but when I met her she didn't seem like an ogress at all, my friend's wife, I mean. My friend's a journalist but an amateur poet, and so he talks like that, you know, about Eden, I mean. They mend shoes and saddles in the back room, the lovers, but shoes and saddles aren't all that's mended there. She's still the same woman, mixing love and . . . I don't want to call it politics, for politics, *el político*, is more often talk than action. I didn't reveal myself. But yes, knowing that she's found her Eden, so to speak and at the same time's still committed, you know, still engaged. . . .

Engaged? I mean, like the French *engagé*.

Ain't the French engaged the same as the English engaged?

It's just another word for committed. Yes, that pushed my buttons, I mean, that she's still the same woman. Or better. Or no doubt a better woman. I can't imagine her turning into anyone's ogress. I don't know if seeing me would have pushed any of her buttons. When I saw her new lover I just didn't reveal myself. . . . But I'm not in love with her now. I love her, the old cliché, you know, but I'm not *in* love. And I suppose there's still some aspect of me she loves, though I didn't reveal myself.

I tries to picture her, his old lover, but can only see one of them Latin American heroines of them B-type movies on television or in the movies about them Latin American revolutionaries. Revolutionary women or *soldaderas* Delgadina calls them. And she kinda look like Bianca Jagger, though, or maybe even Delgadina herself. Except her hair longer than Delgadina's and she a little lighter-colored Latina. And her name ain't Delgadina. Manuela maybe and she be saying, *Vamos. A librarnos de estos gabachos,* like in this play I seen with Delgadina, and she saying whatever that Spanish word for them imperialists and shit. And she a revolutionary and intellectual heroine, like this woman Delgadina be praising, 'cause Delgadina she be telling me about this woman giving a lecture at the Community Center. A revolutionary and a intellectual. Lecture on the Chicana. The lecture in Spanish though. You should come and hear her lecture, Juanita. Sometimes Delgadina, she call me Juanita. Then she remember the lecture in Spanish 'cause this woman though she know English she refuse to speak English 'cause she one of them linguistic nationalists or something, Delgadina say, and even when she give her interviews she always insist on speaking Spanish, though she understand and can speak English as well as anybody. Clever and cunning.

I was married once, I says.

Honk.

Oh, yeah?

Them's just my union, Ray. Somebody musta radioed the others 'bout me being parked here, 'cause this ain't even some of them jokesters normal route.

Honk.

He lift a eyebrow and chew that beef jerky. He got lashes thick as his eyebrows. I'm trying to picture him and that Bianca or that Delgadina. But I don't see the real them, I sees the stereotype them with flashing eyes. With them stereotypes, though, Delgadina say you can always find people that fit them stereotype, and then there be other people that be running from that stereotype. She say they don't know who they true self is 'cause they be trying not to be that stereotype. And Delgadina's wearing her peacock skirt, which she spread open like the tail of a peacock. And I be wondering again why they don't have peahen skirts, and that be because only the male peacocks, only the peacocks, is beautiful. But she ain't wearing blue jeans under that peacock skirt; she just be wearing that peacock skirt; and she ain't be wearing any drawers under that peacock skirt either. And maybe I be thinking not of the true Latina woman but the stereotype Latina woman.

After we divorced, I set out for California, you know, but got only as far as Texas City. Well, I didn't set out for California immediately. Monkey Bread, she had them California dreams first, then she wrote me this letter telling me all about that California and enticing me to come out to California, you know. I had me a boyfriend for a while, on the rebound Monkey Bread calls it.

Think he's gonna ask me about my ex-husband but he don't. Or about that boyfriend on the rebound, but he don't ask me about that boyfriend either. He just chew that beef jerky. That Jungle Jerky. Wonder why they call it Jungle Jerky. I guess on account of that alliteration. What I oughta do is get me one of them machines where you can make your own jerky. They got machines where you can make your own beef jerky, 'cause I seen some of them at one of them trade shows, even before they put them machines on the market. I'm still thinking about that Latina woman, though, and that comparison a petty demon shit. Ain't in love with him now if that's what you wanna know. And ain't on the rebound if that's what you wanna know. And maybe he on the rebound from that rocket scientist woman. But making love don't mean you lovers. I like Texas City, I says. I don't dream about that California much. My friend Monkey Bread she in California and she still have California dreams.

But making love don't mean you lovers. And that Delgadina she be saying you can even stereotype love. Well, first she be talking about them stereotypes, how stereotypes give people they picture of reality and condenses people, 'cause they's so much more possibility to people than them stereotypes, so she say even when the person ain't that stereotype of them, like she be talking about how this psychology class she took at the community college—she took her a psychology class at the Community Center after I told her 'bout that social psychiatrist, you know, 'cause Delgadina is that sorta person —and then she be saying how if you tell somebody that somebody is crazy then that's what they see, and the teacher like did this experiment by telling the class a certain person crazy and then asking them to observe what they saw when this certain person came into the classroom and then like things that be like ordinary human behavior, like scratching your nose with your pen, the students they be seeing as a signal of neurosis in they evaluation, like if I be telling you I'm neurotic you like be seeing neurosis everywhere, in like even what I'm telling you now and even in the way I'm telling it. That's how a lot of them people like stays in the psychiatric system, 'cause one psychiatrist evaluate someone as neurotic and every other psychiatrist be seeing that neurosis even when it ain't there. Which don't mean that there ain't some real crazy people the same as there can be real peoples that conforms to them stereotypes. Like that Miguelita. When she first come telling me that we be thinking maybe that Miguelita ain't really crazy. And then we both be saying it at the same time, Naw, that b—— is crazy. Same way she say if they tell you somebody is cruel or a liar or lecherous or a drunkard or impudent or profane and shit, that's what you see or hear even if they ain't them things. She be saying that that the same power of the stereotype. And she be saying you can also stereotype people as the ideal of they culture, so that even if somebody is treacherous or lecherous, you be seeing them as the cultural ideal—so you be seeing the hero or the heroine. And them people might not be the hero or the heroine at all, but she be saying a cultural ideal is sorta like a myth but ain't the same thing. Like that nun and this padre disguised as a padre and even Delgadina I be seeing my own picture of reality, the stereotypes that I got in my head, of course she be saying you can modify the stereotypes in your head, like when the teacher be telling the students that the person ain't crazy after all. And then the same things they be seeing as crazy they start seeing as normal and sane. But she say ain't just people can be stereotyped, even that cantina be stereotyped, even my can of Bud Light when I'm drinking Bud Light, even this Jungle Jerky. And even conceptions people has of them abstract things, like love. 'Cause it that love set me to thinking about that stereotype anyway. And I be asking her how you stereotype love, but she ain't answer that, then one of them *vatos* come in and she go over to his table and ask for his order, and then I never do ask her how you stereotype that love.

Yeah, got as far as Texas City, I repeats. Got me a housekeeper's job, you know, till I could accumulate enough dough to go to truck driver's school, then I leased me this truck, made all the payments, and now it's mine.

Honk. Hey, Nadine.

I starts to tell him more about that friend of mines in California, how Monkey Bread working for that movie star. Instead I tells him about them beef jerky–making machines. Course I don't know if my own jerky would taste as good as this Jungle Jerky. But this is good 'cause it ain't have a lot of them additives and shit. And then I almost tells him about my ex and his Tasmanian aboriginal girl.

Half-aboriginal anyhow. Half-aboriginal he be saying but she identify with the whole aboriginals and then he be telling me about the
original Tasmanians and how they be hunting them for sport like
Delgadina be saying they do some of them aliens that come across
the border and be hunting them for sport. And just like them people
on them safaris in Africa hunts for sport.

Come over here, he say.

I slides over next to him and we leans against the same drum. I'm
trying to remember that haiku about them water birds. And I'm trying to think what that half-aboriginal girl look like and maybe even
she look like Delgadina. 'Cause a lot of them mestizo races kinda
look alike. Them haiku poems, though. I be asking the teacher why
they call them haiku poems you can eat, maybe 'cause they bite-size
poems. She be saying how them Japanese, though, they got they own
aesthetics, which she say mean idea of beauty, and has that haiku like
them paintings where they don't paint everything in detail like that
poetry it don't describe everything in detail like with all that detail
like you got in them European Baroque-type paintings with all that
description and shit in them paintings and poetry, and then she be
reading us something from this Japanese painter named Mitsuki or
Misuko or Mitauoki who be advising his apprentice painters not to
paint anything in full detail 'cause the best way to express the meaning of a painting, he be saying, is to put as few descriptions in it as
possible. But by descriptions he don't mean word descriptions, she
say, 'cause I be asking how can you put descriptions in a painting.
Not word descriptions, she say, painting descriptions, and be talking
about how them good painters don't put in all the details and describe everything and where them master painters puts in even fewer
descriptions than them good painters. Them master painters is able
to put in as few details as possible in they descriptions and yet they
meaning in them paintings is more manifest which is probably what
that Delgadina mean when she say you don't have to understand that
metaphysical to know what it mean. But Delgadina she like them
luxuriant descriptions, she always like to put them luxuriant descriptions in her stories.

You look like one of them African sculptures I seen, I say.

Oh, yeah?

Honk.

When I seen me my first African sculpture I be thinking 'bout that Japanese aesthetic of not describing everything in detail, 'cause that Portuguese African I met at the trade show be saying they's this museum in Toronto with African sculpture and he take me to that museum and I just be looking at that sculpture and be thinking that sculpture kinda look like me and now I be thinking that sculpture kinda look like him, like Raymond. 'Cept we ain't no sculpture. Yum. Ashanti, Dahomey, Benin, Yoruba, Fulani, Hausa, Ibo, and even pygmy sculpture from Ituri.

You talk about cubism, you talk about impressionism, you talk about your artistic audacity. . . .

Me I don't talk about them things, but if he say I talk about them things I just let him. All the fresh ideas, all the originality, you find in this sculpture here. Original and traditional at the same time. It is ancient and modern at the same time. And it is modern without being decadent. It proves that modernity does not have to be decadent. Or dishonest.

Sculpture of wood, ivory, metal, shells and beads, leather, masks and pottery. We's standing near that sculpture, then we's sitting on one of them benches they's got in the museum. We's sitting near them sculptures, though, and he's still talking about them.

You a sculptor? I ask. 'Cause seem to me somebody know all that about sculpture got to be a sculptor theyself.

No, Beautiful, I am a geometry teacher. I always have my students come here to study the African sculpture, you know. Those who do not understand the geometry and those who think they do. All the geometry you can find in these sculptures. Look at these eyes, Beautiful, shaped like diamonds. And look at these masks, Beautiful. You African Americans talk about jazz. Even the rhythms of the jazz are here. In my village, not just our medicine men and women but our keepers of the peace wear masks like this one. You know nothing of Africa? But you must learn, Beautiful. What are you but an African in the New World. I look at your face, Beautiful, and I see the Fon and the Kimbundu.

Say what?

He touch my face like he a sculptor. Ain't I say he a sculptor? He call me that name that mean beautiful again.

The Fon. A tribe, or rather I must say ethnic group. For Africa is an abstraction, Beautiful. Many who think they know Africa know only an abstraction. We Africans have our ethnic groups the same as the Europeans. They have their Italians, French, and Dutch, and British, their Portuguese. We have our Ashanti, Yoruba, Fulani, Hausa, Fon. . . . I am a pan-Africanist, but we still have our Ashanti, Yoruba, Fulani, Hausa, Fon. . . .

We rise and enter another museum room. More displays of African art. I thought there'd be one small room of African art, but the whole museum is devoted to it. Well, not the whole museum.

What's this? I ask. I start to pick up the art, but the display says, DO NOT TOUCH.

A mancala board. An African game board. I don't know how it's played myself. I believe it is a very ancient game. And here's surrealism. Speak of surrealism, here it is. I come here to this cultural richness, this confident geometry, even the humor in these sculptures, when I want to feel restored to a sense of not just wholeness but normalcy. Not to feel racially superior to the Europeans or to feel inferior to them, or to learn that the Bishop of Hippo is an African or to learn about medieval African kingdoms, but just to be my normal human self. But to also have a cosmic sense of who I am. To know that we Africans are not just on the cultural border or in the cultural margins. I am a dissident and disillusioned African in exile. But speak of the modern world and you must speak of us. If you are African, every day they try to invade your self, not just the Europeans, the colonialists, I speak of now, but even sometimes your own rulers, when you have your nominal freedom, our *independence*. See these overlapping planes, each plane is a self—this one is the essential self, the transcendental self. Don't let anyone invade your essential self, your transcendental self. Them or us. We're both of us, Beautiful, exiles in the New World.

I am not sure which them he means or which us.

I be thinking he a strange man. He take me around to that museum, he tell me about his Africa, he call me the beautiful one but he don't try to court me or nothing. And I didn't try to court him either. Exiles in the New World.

I didn't expect I'd be no contrabandista though, I says. That ain't contraband you carrying, is it, *mi general*? You know, like that old Mae West line? Is that contraband?

It must be, he says, as I lean toward him for another kiss. Yum. Smell of coconut and lavender.

Honk. Hey, Nadine, you want to give me a ride to Albuquerque. Ah, I forgot, you got to belong to the union.

I gots to tell you about them union peoples, I say. Yum. I gots to tell you about them union peoples. I mean, they ain't all jokesters, some just likes to harass me 'cause of the union. I gots to tell you about the union. A lot of them thinks I changed my route because I ain't in the union. Although a lot of that is a pure fabrication, Ray, the truth is . . . What motivates them is . . . What I'm saying is they just has a total disrespect for my independence. . . .

But Ray say he just thinking about us own union now.

On us way back to Texas City, I see some of them fools lined up at the truck stop and I honks at them. Ray don't look in they direction. Few of the fools is sitting in the picnic area eating they lunch and waves at me. I gots to pee, but I don't want to stop my truck in the same area of them fools, so Ray and I stops at the next truck stop, then we drives back into Texas City. I lets Ray off at the cathedral, then I goes to the Community Center, 'cause Delgadina putting on one of them Chicano plays. I asks Ray if he wanted to come to the Chicano play.

Where?

Community Center. Delgadina directed the play. It a play by a Chicano playwright. She always does what she can do to promote Chicano literature, even if it just promoting it to me. She been advertising the play around the cantina, though, and even got some of the cantina patrons, I know the one she call Cheech, to perform in that play. She wanted me to play one of them roles, 'cause although it a Chicano play, they's got roles in it for representatives of every race. I read the play and I likes it but I told her I'd rather be in the audience. She tried to persuade me, you know, 'cause Delgadina can be real persuasive, you know, 'cause she took a course in the art of being persuasive, but I used a line on her that I learned from Cayenne Goodling from Memphis who belongs to the Church of Elvis. In fact she is the only colored woman I know to belong to that church. She also belongs to the Perfectability Baptist Church, which is where I met her, but she don't believe there is any contradiction in belonging to

the Perfectability Baptist Church and the Church of Elvis. But anyway I told Delgadina, quoting Cayenne Goodling, quoting Elvis
and says, The show is in the audience, not on the stage. So that per-
suaded her not to persuade me to be in that play. And she is making
better use of the audience than she would have made of us when she
thought the show was just on the stage.

Of course, y'all know I'm saying all that to try to persuade Ray to
come to that play, but he say that they's work he's got to do for the
new Underground Railroad so he don't come with me to the play
but goes into the cathedral. I parks around the back where he told
me to park before so I ain't conspicuous. I wants to ask him to give
me a tour of his cathedral, but I ain't asked that. I watches him go
into the cathedral. I ain't know if he fully believe me about them
mens and the union. Seem like fools is always doing that to a woman.
Them fools don't wave and call my name and honk at me when I'm
alone in my truck, but wait till I gets me a man I'm trying to impress,
and they pretends I knows and associates with every man in South
Texas. And to tell y'all the truth, I ain't even the same Nadine most
of them thinks I am. I don't want to explain to Ray too much about
them, though, 'cause then it be sounding like I'm protesting too
much.

I goes and parks in front of the Community Center. I knows
where they theater is, so I goes straight there. Lotta peoples I've seen
in the cantina is there. Miguelita she there. I be thinking she there
with Mr. Delgado, but she just there herself. Them that ain't in the
audience is on the stage. Delgadina she on the stage. When she first
give me the play to read, I thought she would not only be the director
but play one of the roles, but she said she didn't want to play none of
the roles but just be the director. I know why she onstage, 'cause I
knows Delgadina. As the director of the play, she feels that it isn't
enough just to have the people come and watch the play. Although
she herself feels that the play is understandable, she don't trust the
audience to understand the play, or maybe she trust us to understand
the play but believe, nevertheless, that a play such as that one deserve
a lecture about itself.

So before the play begins she is standing onstage in front of the
curtain and is talking about the play. I starts to go sit next to Miguelita, but to tell y'all the truth, although I talks to Miguelita in the

cantina and have even traveled with her and Delgadina into the desert to eat roasted cactus, been to Marineland with her and Delgadina (she refused to go see the marine animals but stayed in the Land-Rover), have been with her to various parts of Texas, New Mexico, and Nevada, I decides to sit next to some Chicano I don't even know. I think it Cheech.

Cheech, I thought you was supposed to be in the play.

Chica, my name's Pedro Alfonso Bueno.

Rubén Sierra's *La Raza Pura* is a satire of the melting pot, Delgadina is saying. She wearing her favorite peacock skirt and one of them white blouses with lace on it.

So some of the jokers in the audience, even Pedro Alfonso Bueno, start playing games with her like asking her what's a satire, 'cause they kinda think that she was underestimating their own intelligence.

One of them even say to her, Hey, Delgadina, why you underestimating our intelligence?

But Delgadina actually think they didn't know what a satire is, so she explain to them what a satire is. I ain't gonna explain to y'all what no satire is. And those of you that don't know what a satire is can ask Delgadina.

So after she lectures about the play, we watching it. It's a play with a lot of scenes, but the scenes melts one into the other, 'cause the whole way the play is made is like the theme of the play itself. I mean, the theme of the play itself is reflected in the way the play is made. And then they's even reprinted Sierra's stage notes, which explains that one scene should lead into the other as quickly and as honestly as possible. I be wondering how come he got that *honestly* in them stage notes and I be wondering how scenes can move honestly. 'Cause seem like *honesty* one of them words that people uses with people. But I guess scenes in a play can be honest.

I got to tell y'all about that play, 'cause it's about America. 'Cept it's about the American myth, the American myth of race that say that they's racial, cultural and social purity in America. Naw, that ain't what it's saying. It's saying that the myth of racial, cultural and social purity is supposed to be the basis for prejudice in American society. I know all that 'cause I ain't just seen the play or heard Delgadina's lecture, but she let me read a article she wrote about it. She sent the article to one of them little literary magazines but they returned it back to her 'cause ain't none of them heard of Rubén Sierra and didn't consider him mainstream. Or maybe it was because her own article didn't appeal to the mainstream. Or maybe they didn't believe she was a true Chicana and might have accepted the article, even though it didn't appeal to the mainstream, if they thought it was written by a true Chicana in the true language of what they considered to be the true language of Chicanoism.

I got to tell y'all that the play by Rubén Sierra is a true play and ain't the product of my own imagination. I ain't sure whether Rubén Sierra would want me to converse with y'all about his play, though. Delgadina says I ain't allowed to quote from it, 'cause you can't just up and quote from a play without getting the permission of the author for the use of his or her Intellectual Property. However, she says it's okay to tell folks about somebody's play or your own interpretation of it.

So anyway what the play got in it. It got a agency that call itself the All-Purpose Racial Agency which Delgadina say is somewhat reminiscent of Louis M. Valdez's Honest Sancho's Used Mexican Lot and Mexican Curio Shop in *Los Vendidos*. What the play is is a inventive satire that exaggerates the ironies of racial and ethnic prejudices. Delgadina refer to it as a hypothetical play but one based on the real world. It a experimental play in the way that it mixes the different scenes, that is it mix stage scenes with film and slides and video and soundtracks which Delgadina say reinforces, introduces, explains, or comments on the action. It a mingling of dramatization and statement, and Delgadina say it like most Third World plays— she use the words *Third World*, though I thinks they's got another phrase for theyselves now. But she say it like most Third World plays in that it challenges us conception of dramatic form. There is also the sense, say Delgadina, I mean when she's lecturing about that play, of the mingling of the "orature" in modern technological society with the "orature" in Chicano traditions. Course they's a lot of people just come to see the play and ain't want to hear Delgadina talk about the play, or intellectualize it. A lot of them is polite and listens, but then I hears others say things like *agringada* or whatever the Chicano word for that, which I think means they thinks 'cause she up there intellectualizing that play that she trying to act like a gringa.

Edward Said has spoken of the "monocultural myth" of American society and this play debunks that myth. Written from the "Chicano perspective," it is likewise universal in its inclusion of the whole of American culture in its nonconventional panorama. . . .

Hey, Delgadina, I like you better when you're tending bar. Let's see the play, chica. . . .

Yeah, but. . . .

I'm in love with the Chicana girl. Come here, Delgadina, chica. Chica chica chica chica chica.

He gets up and looks like he's trying to do the rumba or the samba and starts making conversation, except it sounds like a poem:

> I went down to Argentina and all I learned was to tango,
> But it was the real tango.
> Rumba, rumba, rumba, rumba,
> Samba, samba, samba, samba
>
> I went down to Brazil and all I learned was to samba,
> But it was the real samba.
> Rumba, rumba, rumba, rumba,
> Samba, samba, samba, samba
>
> I come back to America to do the New York rumba,
> 'Cause I can't go to Cuba and spend no American money,
> Rumba, rumba, rumba, rumba,
> Samba, samba, samba, samba
>
> This rumba ain't the real one
>
> Chachachachacha

So, anyway, Delgadina comes and sits with the guy who tells her he's in love with her and they do something that looks like the tango, which I think is a part of the play, then they sits together and watches the play, and like I said they's got these signs that reads ALL-PURPOSE RACIAL AGENCY, RENT-A-RACE. And then somebody distributes newsletters to everybody in the audience, and I think some of them Rent-a-Race advertisements is in them newsletters. Of course, it's a confabulatory newsletter and ain't a real newsletter, and you can't really go to some of them places and rent yourself out as a model of the race. They's even got a Samba in that newsletter that kinda look like myself. Then there's a film and some musical pieces that accompanies the film. Then there's different agents for the racial agency that appears onstage. I know what some of y'all thinking, that this is just a confabulatory play or the play written by Delgadina, but it ain't, that Rubén Sierra a real Chicano playwright and his play a real Chicano play. I know a lot of them ain't known to the general mainstream American audiences and I ain't seen none of they plays on Broadway. Anyway, so there's a scene between an Anglo boy and a Chicana girl that's in love. I know y'all seen them types of scenes. I can't quote y'all none of them words in that play, 'cause y'all got to see that play for y'allself. Plus Delgadina say you can't just quote from anybody play, and even she herself had to write to the dramatist for permission to put on that play. I don't even know whether I'm supposed to talk about that play or even tell y'all about the All-Purpose Racial Agency Rent-a-Race. 'Cept Delgadina say you can tell people about a play, but you just can't quote from it without permission. What about them press releases and them manifestoes, I mean them that ain't confabulatory? I gots to ask Delgadina. But somebody say something about how prejudice can be financially rewarding, except I heard Delgadina say that sometimes when prejudice ain't financially rewarding they's less of it, but then when it's financially rewarding again they's more of it. I guess like them talking about Mexico during the war. But I think it's one of them advertisers in the play that says that. And then there's also a Chicano boy in the play that is in love with a Anglo girl, and I'm wondering how come they ain't no scenes where they's Chicanos in love with each other. And I wants to say, Don't let them Americans play you and make you think you's just supposed to be in love with some Anglo girl, but then I realizes it just a play, and anyway can't he be in love with who he want? 'Cause I ain't sure myself whether he in love with her or he just being played by that ideal of American womanhood, and what supposed to be beautiful? Anyway, they parents disapprove of they relationship. The Chicanos don't want the Chicano boy to love no gringa and the gringos don't want the gringa girl to love no Chicano. And the Chicano boy say how he usedta tell hisself that he wouldn't marry nobody but a Chicana, but then he love that girl.

Start the love, I hear one of them Chicanos say. And then I hear one of them say he don't think that boy love that gringa girl neither he just think she high class 'cause she gringa. He think she high class, but that just a lie, he say, and make me think about that Elvis.

That when Maria and Journal come in and Maria sits beside me with Journal. Journal climb into my lap for a little while during the play, then he climb back into Maria's lap. Pedro Alfonso Bueno say something to Journal in Spanish. Journal look like he watching and understanding the play.

Then on the stage they's some more of them films and recordings that comment on the society and the couple, and then there's a bigoted Gringa that comes to the ALL-PURPOSE RACIAL AGENCY because she's giving a small dinner party for about 200 people and she don't want anyone to think she prejudiced, so she comes to rent some Chicanos to attend her party, 'cept she don't even call them by they names, she say. Your . . . people. So the agent for the All-Purpose Racial Agency shows her a Linda chart to make sure they have exactly what she wants. So they's got Tijerina Off White, Acapulco Gold, Chávez Beige, Fuentes Tan, González Brown, Chicano Cream, Plain Old Brown. So this gringa woman she selects several from that Linda chart: that Acapulco Gold, that Gonzales Brown, and that Plain Old Brown. Then after the Linda selection, she got to select the type: so they brings her a number of different models. They's Frito Bandito, the Jaime Bond Secret Agent, the Juan Frijole, they's the Greaser type, and they's the *Vendido*. So the agent characterizes them types: One will eat all the dip, another seduce all the women, another entertain with the guitar, then the peasant type will sit in the corner and make tortillas, and the Greaser will insult everyone at the party. Seem like them types is in everybody race. I'm kinda thinking I likes the Jaime Bond Secret Agent type myself, though I realizes he supposed to be a stereotype and ain't just a type. And also the Gringa got the choice of not being too obvious about having herself a integrated guest list so's she can have the Vendido model who "looks like a Anglo but smells like Messkin!" Can I quote that? So the Gringa, she decide on two them types, the Jaime

Bond Secret Agent and the *Vendido*. She ask the agent to charge it to her BankAmericard and then the agent reminds her of the company's motto. I ain't going to tell y'all the company's motto, 'cause I wants to persuade y'all to see that play for y'allself.

Anyway, they's more movie slides and more monologues and they's Jenny, the gringa girl's conversation with her parents about that Jorge business 'cause that the name of the Chicano. They's satire in that play, but it's also about real prejudice. But like I said y'all's got to see that play for y'allself. And it also got something to say 'bout the Anglo justice system. Other scenes has got songs and poems in them.

Then they's this other scene that got a bar in it. Delgadina say that bar scene got to do with the relationship between economics and racism. But anyway this the bar scene: Jim who a Anglo and Carlos who a Chicano come into this bar. Jim buy them a beer and is charged forty cents for each beer. So anyway this friend of Jim's say he don't like spics, which he word for them Chicanos. I always thought that the word for Puerto Ricans, but he use that for them Chicanos. I guess it the word for anybody that spic Spanish. So while they's having that conversation, a black—they didn't call us African Americans when he wrote that play—enters and is charged forty-five cents for the same beer that Jim paid forty cents for. So Carlos says to the Black that he'll buy him a beer. I ain't know whether it Bud Light. So the bartender charges Carlos fifty cents for the same beer he charged the black forty-five cents for and Jim the gringo forty cents for. In the meantime, while that scene is going on the All-Purpose Racial Agency is still selling races, you know, 'cause it one of them parallel-type scenes, you know like they have in the movies, 'cept this a play. And they's working on different slogans with various advertisers.

MARTINEZ GET ANGLOCIZED. I think that one of them slogans. That plays makes everyone a object of satire, people of every race. It Jorge's uncle who Delgadina refer to as the moral center of the play. He got something to say to Jorge and Jenny about love, 'cept I ain't remember exactly what he say to them about love. 'Cause I be thinking he going to say something to them about politics and he come talking 'bout love. Maybe he say you's got to love. I ain't remember exactly what he say, I just know he wisdom got to do something with love. I know that's what they call wisdom talk, 'cause every play got to have a scene where somebody talk that wisdom talk, 'cept the whole play itself wisdom talk. Then when the play ends they's this taped dialogue and it ask. Well I ain't gonna tell y'all what that taped dialogue ask, 'cause y'all's got to see that play for y'allself. And like Delgadina say I can't be quoting y'all all that play. I ain't even sure whether Señor Rubén Sierra would want me to be telling y'all about his play. Delgadina say that that taped dialogue supposed to give what she call the essence of Chicanoism. And the essence of Chicanoism ain't none of them stereotypes about the Chicano, it all of them good things that every group of people wants to think about theyselves. The gringo think he all them good things. But the essence of Chicanoism and probably the essence of everybody race all them good things. They is meaningful and sincere and proud and loving and what else? But like I say, you's got to see that play for y'allself. A Chicano is a Americano. What I think that play mean by that is that what Delgadina call the archetypal model of the American—all them ideals that them Americans has of theyselves and the good people, I mean them white Americans 'cause we's all American—is that that really the model of any race and not just them Anglos that appropriate all that goodness for theyselves.

This play combines realistic, stock and hypothetical scenes to show that the monocultural or melting pot a myth of the American society. . . .

So what the play saying, Delgadina?

That we're not made differently from anybody else.

Is that what the play's saying, Delgadina? I think you're made different from all the Chicas I know. . . .

I don't, replied Delgadina.

So what's the play saying, Delgadina?

About self-definition, self-identification, the need not to be afraid to be who you are, to be yourself, even in a multicultural and multiracial society . . . like the other play we saw, it's about the need everyone has to define themselves and not to be defined by others, the need everyone has to tell his or her own stories. We Chicanos have to know ourselves, and to know each other, and to know others. It's the same theme that other Third World peoples have, whether it's presented in surrealistic or realistic or mythic or symbolic portrayals. Reality is always open to interpretation and imagination. This play explores both the Chicano's inner nature and the nature of society. Even we have different and even conflicting conceptions of reality and human possibility. You remember that other play we saw, with the *soldado*, the one about the revolution that changed the role of Mexican women in Mexican society. There were not just *soldados* who followed their husbands and lovers which the Americanos want to tell you about, but also those who were revolutionary leaders themselves, like La Negra. . . . You know, I'd like us to put on that play by Estella Portilla, not La Negra, I mean one of Estella Portilla's plays, so you *vatos* can see more plays from the Chicana perspective, Chicana writers who are not merely "camp followers" but leaders too, I mean leaders of the creative imagination, the revolutionary creative imagination. . . . We Chicanos must understand ourselves by any means necessary—legend, history, stories, plays. . . . All playwrights in some manner have the role of the *vate*, the seer, and the *curandera* or *curandero*, the healer, in our learning who we are and what is real and in recreating in us a sense of possibility. . . . I'd like us also to do one of Alurista's plays, the great Alurista, there's this mythopoetic play of his in which myth, history, metaphor, poetic image, imagination and reality occupy the same time and place. Some of you have read Alurista's poetry, *Nationchild Plumaroja* and *Floricantom*, but this play, I think, is of epic dimensions. It's both an assertion of the Mexican-American, the Chicano complex cultural identity, Spanish, Native American, even African, and a critique of Anglo-American manifest destiny and exploitation. . . . And we've got to put on another play by Valdez. . . . Does anybody know anything about the deer dance of the Yaqui? I need someone to choreograph. . . . And someone to play the Council of Elders. . . . And Quetzalcoatl. . . .

And Pepsi-coatl and Coca-coatl. . . .

Soy noble y sincero.

But who are you, Delgadina?

I'm who I am.

I looks around and sees Maria and her baby Journal still in the audience. I goes back over and starts talking to them. I wants to introduce them to Delgadina, but I know that Delgadina, she be asking me all kindsa questions about them, and then I be telling her everything about them. I think Delgadina be asking me who they is anyway, but she don't. Anyway, seem like everywhere Delgadina go, there's some *vato* trying to court her.

THIS AIN'T NICODEMUS

I think Maria's there to see the play, but she ain't. Or rather, that ain't her true purpose of being there. She starts telling me 'bout her cousin being in jail and that they's going to deport her. Course I thinks she just wants me to go with her to some local jail, but the next thing I know I'm lying to Delgadina telling her I got a job to transport some new industrial detergent across the country, then Maria and Journal and me gets in my truck and heads towards Middle America. I starts to ask Delgadina if she wants to go with us to Middle America, but Delgadina and that guy are standing in the hallway kissing, and Delgadina look like she was trying to teach him how to do the real rumba and not the New York style. I was still wondering how come he couldn't go to Cuba. Then I remembered they was always changing them Cuban laws about Americans going to Cuba, and the new law was that you could go to Cuba but you couldn't spend no money there. At first I thought that that was the same as saying you couldn't go to Cuba, 'cause how could you go to Cuba and not be able to spend no money while you were there. Then I figured the people would have to change their American money for somebody else's money, maybe German money, before they got into Cuba. Well, didn't the poet say it was only American money that he couldn't spend? I mean, the guy making poetry out of conversation.

The reason Maria's cousin got throwed in jail was because they didn't have no detention camps in Middle America. There weren't as many illegal aliens in Middle America as in South Texas and the Southwest and when they did find one, they didn't know what to do with her, so they throwed her in jail. Plus, they didn't know what kinda illegal she was. They thought she mighta been Cuban, and the State Department policy then was that Cubans was supposed to be processed into America, and they had to send for somebody from one of them states that was usedta dealing with illegal aliens, and to even import an immigration lawyer, 'cause there weren't any in Middle America that knew anything about the immigration laws.

They had a small Spanish-speaking community, but they were mostly migrant workers who worked on the farms during harvesting seasons, and most of them just migrated to other areas. But somebody just happened to ask this woman for her papers. And it was discovered that she wasn't a citizen, nor did she have any papers to justify her being in America. Did kinda have an accent. Somebody said it was Spanish. Somebody said it was Portuguese. Somebody else said it sounded kinda Italian. They took her to a place people referred to as Little Italy, but it turned out to be Irishtown. Then one of the professors at the university said it was Spanish, 'cept it sounded like low-class Spanish, he couldn't fully understand what the woman was saying. And when she spoke English, he couldn't fully understand her English. Well, she was an illegal alien, so they couldn't just let her go free. Somebody suggested that they put her in the women's wing of the state asylum. That didn't seem the thing to do 'cause she seemed pretty sane. They might be crazy peoples in the state asylum but they was all documented citizens. They did have a Texan who thought he belonged to the Republic of Texas and was a free and sovereign citizen, but even he were a documented citizen and a United States American even if he thought hisself a Texan. They thought he might understand her Spanish, though, but when she started talking it to him he started saying something about imperial Mexico and how the Texans had gained their freedom and independence. In fact, he thought he was still in Texas, till somebody told him it was Middle America. Didn't nobody understand her Spanish or English, though, but she did seem sane. But it was illegal to be an undocumented citizen, so one of the documented citizens, one of the true Americans, suggested that she be put in jail till somebody could adjudicate what to do with her. So they put her in jail and forgot about her.

I ain't sure what made them remember her. Maybe the jail had a new jailkeeper that decided to check her files to see what she was in for. Maybe she got the phone call that was everybody's right to have and called somebody that spoke her brand of Spanish. Maybe she got a letter out to somebody via of someone else who was in that jail and knew the true meaning of America, or at least had their own agenda in regard to them jailers even if it wasn't to defend the rights and freedoms of Maria's cousin. Maybe she got the visitor that it was everybody's right to have because they heard some rumor that there was somebody in jail that didn't belong there, even if she were an undocumented human who happened to be jailed in Middle America. Maybe one of the other prisoners learned her brand of Spanish which I know now to be Spanish spoken with a Quechua accent and concluded that this was somebody who was no criminal and didn't belong there. Maybe one of the other prisoners who knew something about legality or who believed that they had more of an obligation to the human community than the community of any one national, including Middle America, started asking questions. The next thing she knew she was being visited by an immigration lawyer from South Texas named Linda Chong. It surprised her that this Asian-American woman understood her brand of Spanish and even her brand of English, both spoken with what I know now to be a Quechua accent. The Asian American was a well-groomed woman that kinda reminded her of a high-class Mexican. But her name was Linda Chong and she was an Asian American, actually a Chinese American, and expert immigration guerrilla-lawyer.

She was there to prove that Maria's cousin's arrest was illegal. That even though she was an alien and stranger in a strange land among strange people dressed in strange clothes she still had certain inalienable human rights. She couldn't just be kept in jail and forgotten about 'cause the citizenry didn't have a clue.

That's when Maria's cousin got her first telephone call to Maria, and Maria and her baby Journal got in my truck and we drove out to Middle America. I thought Middle America would be put on trial for their inhumanity and crimes against the humanity of Maria's cousin myself. (Maria herself always says I starts sounding like a preaching woman whenever I tells people the story of her cousin.) In fact, we couldn't even get proof of how long they'd kept Maria's cousin in jail or even that they'd kept her in jail. Linda Chong the expert immigration guerrilla lawyer tried every legality to get copies of the documents to prove that they had illegally kept Maria's cousin and it seemed that the documents on the arrest of this undocumented human had disappeared. Linda Chong the expert immigration guerrilla lawyer was made to sign papers. Maria was made to sign papers and even show her bank statement. And I was made to sign an affidavit testifying that Maria was who she said she was and that Journal

347

was her natural baby born in America. They made copies of all the papers, documents, and affidavits we signed but still did not produce any documentation on the arrest of Maria's cousin. Years later I tried to get copies of copies of my identification and the affidavit I'd signed, and even they'd disappeared. Except for Linda Chong's copies which somebody said weren't legal because the seal of the Middle America wasn't on them. And when I tried to explain to them what had happened with Maria's cousin, that she had really been arrested and illegally detained and jailed in Middle America (since then they've probably made it legal, like changing the immigration laws for them Cubans), they started looking at me like I was the one giving false information. I know my papers was on file with somebody, though. But everybody claims that nobody with none of my names really signed no papers, documents, and affidavits for Maria's cousin or anybody else, and then they starts looking at they Wanted posters to see whether I'm naturally wanted in any of the Natural United States or even other states in the natural Americas.

We'll institute a complaint on false detention, said Linda Chong. Then she starts talking about illegal detention, illegal arrest, malicious arrest, malicious detention, vindictive arrest, vindication detention, reprisal arrest, reprisal detention, false arrest and detention without excuse in law, arresting with malicious or vindictive intent or as a reprisal, produces complaint forms addressed to government officials, members of Congress, members of international human rights organizations, mentions abuse of process and abuse of power, criminal abuse of process, obstruction of justice, dilatory and unlawful peremptory actions to delay charges and complaints against themselves (sometimes I'm not sure if she's talking about Maria's cousin or another case she's working on against other Middle Americans), conspiracy and breach of political ethics and protocol, withholding of evidence, including the documentation of the original arrest of Maria's cousin, perjury, malice in law, coopting of the political system to do their dirty work against an undocumented alien that they didn't have a clue about (this ain't exactly her language, but it's mine when I retells this story), suppression of Maria's cousin's free speech, intimidation, use of the political and legal system to even try to intimidate her, Linda Chong, expert immigration attorney and guerrilla lawyer. Then she starts reading various statutes, some

is immigration statutes and others is from the Constitution, the Bill
of Rights, the Declaration of the Rights of Man and Woman, the Divine Rights of Man and Woman, or whatever them other declarations of the rights of humanity, citizens and noncitizens. She also
quotes from various ethical, moralistic, humanistic, and religious
and spiritual codes of ethics, and even unwritten divine codes of
ethics. I don't know if she a Buddhist, but seem like she were even
reading something from the Buddhist Bible. She even recited they
own Golden Rule. And even reading from a draft document called
"Laws of Electra" or "The Electra Laws." I know she was using
all them legal terms with those people, though, and a lot of them was
looking at her like they ain't never seen a Chinese woman neither or
a Chinese-American woman speaking Middle American and wanting to know whether she herself a documented citizen. I want to see
all the documents. I want photocopies of all the documentation.
What's your name?

I didn't arrest her, ma'am. I'm just an ordinary officer of Middle
America and the southern commonwealth. There's just no documentation. There's simply no documentation. You'll have to speak
to Detective Brad Doy or the social worker, Joby Herrington. Is that
her name? Herr something. I think it's Herrington. I'm just a low
man on the totem pole. He's shitting you, I said. They're shitting us.
You can't detain a person and not have documents on them. That
is obstruction of justice, just like you said, Lawyer Chong. They is
shitting us. They is playing us for fools. I knows I am a fool, but I'm
still a American. And the thing about being a American is that you
gets to choose who plays you for a fool. Them that votes does it every
election. And them that don't vote does it every time they watches
television, or a movie, or listens to the radio, or reads a newspaper
or magazine or tabloid or listens to whoever they listens to. I'm a
fool and I have played for fools, but I'm an American, and I gets
to choose who plays me for a fool, and I chooses for these people not
to play me for no play. They is playing us for fools.

The officer looked at me like he was trying to figure out whether
I was indeed some kinda fool and furthermore one of the fools,
played for a fool, or not fools at all persons of colored persuasion
you-know-what-we-really-call-them on one of their Wanted posters. Then he was looking at me like my very presence was against

the law, or oughta be against the law. He was tolerating Linda Chong 'cause she at least looked like a professional woman and them - modern - minority - except - they's - a - majority - in - China - remember-all-them-human-rights-violation-they-puts-prisoners-to-work-Asians-has-at-least-made-contributions-that-we-know-of-here-in-Middle-America-to-the-world. He might prefer to see her in a kimono or thong bikini. Course I ain't know what he really thinking. But I do know when somebody looking at you like they thinks you's against the law and just your very being in the world.

He's shitting us, I repeated. Chong!

That's obscene communications ma'am, he said. That's against the law here in Middle America.

Jesús, María y José, said Maria.

You're obscene communicationing us, I started to say. I mean he wasn't using the language of obscenity, but wasn't his meaning obscene? And they was lying. They was playing us for fools. Or maybe they hadn't kept documents on Maria's cousin. Maybe because they didn't know what to do with her because of her being an illegal and undocumented alien, they hadn't kept documents on her. Maybe they thought she wasn't even human, because an illegal and undocumented alien of the nonwhite persuasion, so they didn't have to document detaining her. She wasn't even human and wasn't even supposed to have any rights that they were bound to respect. They could just throw her in jail. Wasn't no American anyway. Not people like themselves. I tried to remember what Andy had said to Kingfish and started to tell them that they was boozling us. Maybe they wouldn't know what I meant by boozling and so they wouldn't consider that Obscene Communications, even though they, or peoples like them, had had Andy to say that to Kingfish. That didn't mean that they recognized boozling as part of the English language, though.

She can work with me in my doll factory, said Maria. She can work with me in my doll factory. I've got a doll factory. I make my own dolls. I'm not rich, but I'm a woman of resources.

I bet you are, said the officer, looking at her like he thought *doll factory* meant something other than a doll factory, you know, like a doll factory were a metaphor for a hoochie factory, like that Hollywood madam.

Now you know I'm looking at Maria, 'cause her English sound

good. She got the accent of the Southwest in it, the accent of South Texas, and her own Mexico, but sound good. You would think she been in America speaking the American English longer than any of us Johnsons, except those of us who were born in Indiana and the ones that fought up in Canada on the side of the English during the Revolutionary War 'cause they promised they would free them. I think they called theyselves Lord Dunmore's Revolutionary Blacks. Of course they wasn't considered revolutionary heroes by them that fought the English on the other side in the Americas and didn't promise freedom to nobody but the peoples exactly like theyselves, though the blacks that fought to help free the colonists from the British was played for fools, thinking that if they helped win that war they'd win their freedom in America. What I'm saying is that Maria sound like she know English better than us Johnsons except for the Indiana and the Canadian Johnsons.

And she showed them one of her dolls, which kinda looked like a Aztec god.

Shango! I says.

I know my client's rights, said Linda Chong. 'Cept she said it in lawyer's language and started talking about democratic principles. And there's certain things she wouldn't talk to them about at all. I know she was a real lawyer, and a specialist in immigration, and one of them guerrilla lawyers, 'cause them guerrilla lawyers always has certain things, certain strategies that they don't talk about at all.

Then a man appeared. The officer was looking at him like he wasn't sure who he was. He started talking about rights and immigration law and seem more like a specialist in immigration law than Linda Chong. I thought maybe he might be one of them Haitians when I first seen him but he talked with more a American than a Haitian accent. I'd heard, though, that there was Haitian lawyers among Ray's guerrilla lawyers. Then I thought he was some sort of private investigator. He was there for our benefit and I figured he must be one of Linda Chong's associates, because Linda Chong gave Maria, Maria's cousin, Journal, and me a card that said Linda Chong Associates, Immigration Law, however it didn't identify her as a guerrilla lawyer, 'cause guerrilla lawyers can't identify themselves as guerrilla lawyers, you's just got to know they is guerrilla lawyers and can't be coopted. The officer started looking like a kinglet. And then he just looked at the man who a independent man of Linda, that's why I assumed him to be a Haitian or some person of Linda with they own country before he spoke with the accents of America with contempt.

And then there was a lot of men running around looking like wild men, looking excited, but they still maintains there were documents and maintained that it was within their legal rights according to the what seemed like newly right there and then formed codes and stat, utes of Middle America and southern commonwealth legalism, though they wouldn't admit to what they had done. Then they looked like they had called in reinforcements.

Shango!

Speak to me in a civil tone, the officer said, surrounded by his rein, forcements, some officers looking like hisself and others in plain clothes.

Shango!

Tone sounded civil to me and extraordinary diction. I still thought maybe he must be one of them Haitians or a man of Linda from some independent country other than America, though he spoke with the accents of America. And a associate of Linda Chong's, although he didn't give me no card saying that he were a Linda Chong associate. The officer just looked at him with hostility.

I waited to be introduced to this man of Linda who seemed to have his own independent country. But Linda Chong didn't make no introductions. She took out some kinda portfolio, and then she and the man of Linda who seemed to have his own independent country started talking.

Shango!

The officer just looked evil and then him and his cohorts huddled. They was men and women polices and I guess there must've been some social workers amongst them. One of the women looked like a huge Fraülein I'd seen in a German movie. Another one was diminu, tive. There were not only whites, I gots to be truthful, but people of the colored persuasion among them. I believe, though, that they only went and got people of the colored persuasion when they saw that the people there to rescue Maria's cousin include people of the colored persuasion, and so they also wanted to prove that they also had

people of the colored persuasion among they cohorts, to try to furthermore prove that they were the typical and stereotypical Middle
Americans of the southern commonwealth that we presumed them
to be and made sure that we saw they had someone-you-should-
hope-to-resemble-at-least-they-can't-say-that-we're-racist-with-
this-more-than-token-defenders-of-Middle-American-and-the-
southern-commonwealth persons of the colored persuasion to help
them tell their version of the story about Maria's cousin and how
rather than being jailed against her will she willingly went to jail in
Middle America of the southern commonwealth rather than return
to her poor old can't drink the water you better bring bottled Mexico with all them wild Mexican bandits, drug smugglers, and corrupt
police and government officials. Control the border! Contact the
president of Mexico and force him to control the border! Build a
wall along the border of Mexico just like the wall in China which is
the only manmade wall on earth that can be seen from the moon!
Clean up them barrios along the border! The Rio Grande is shallow
only four feet deep there's too many Mexicans crossing over they
must think it's the Jordan! We needs more federal agent immigration
patrols and border patrol chieftains from Brownsville to Tijuana!
Control the border! Control the border! Control the border! Control
the border! We ain't got no border here in Middle America of the
southern commonwealth, but like every true American we knows
that even our borderless border has got to be controlled! Then I pictures them strutting like John Travolta in that movie, strutting
around the police station. They don't sing the same song of the Travolta movie, though, they modifies it:

> You can tell by the way I boogie my boogie
> I'm a border patrol border patrol
> You can tell by the way I boogie my boogie
> I'm a border patrol border patrol

Shango!
And then one of the I-might-not-be-who-they-think-I-am persons of colored persuasion stands out from the group, singing, like
that rap modification of that song, I think the one by the Fugees, one
of them young men that sings with the Fugees:

Can't stop the shining
Can't stop romancing
Can't stop the shining
Can't stop romancing

When they finally released Maria's cousin, she looked worn, even sick, her hair frowzy. She had pretty hair like Maria's but it was all frowzy. It was kinda lighter than Maria's, though, kinda light brown and more delicate. She was tan and real pretty, well, you could tell she was pretty, looked kinda Mexican and kinda Navajo and kinda Native Hawaiian, like them true Hawaiians, not them in the movies. She said something that sounded like *kuokoa*. Which made me think of Hawaiian, 'cause that word kinda sounded Hawaiian instead of Spanish. Or maybe it me thinking she said *kuokoa*. She was wearing some nondescript prisoner's garb, or maybe the garb that they give people when they release them. I didn't know Maria's cousin, so I didn't know how she looked before her detention. I do know that later when talking to Linda Chong, Maria would detail what seem like hundreds of ways that her cousin seem transformed from being jailed in the Middle American southern commonwealth. I know she didn't look at any of the officers, the ones in strange clothes or the ones in plain clothes or the social worker even the persons of colored persuasions and even the man singing can't stop the shining can't stop romancing can't stop the shining can't stop romancing that was standing there. She didn't even look like she wanted to look at us, or even her cousin Maria, even though we were the ones who'd come there to rescue her. Later Maria told me when she saw her cousin. . . . Well, she said her cousin looked like she'd been in somebody's hell. Which made me think of something that Delgadina said when somebody come into the cantina once. She knew the person from Houston, I think. She said to him, You look like you been through a season in hell. What have you been doing, abusing your liberty?

'Cept it was these people who had abused Maria's cousin's liberty. Linda Chong kept talking to them in legalese, and I said a few more things to them in Mosquito language, and the man of Linda who seemed like he had his own independent country spoke to them in what sounded to me the true accents of a true American and Maria

talked about herself as a woman of resources and even Journal said,
Jiba jiba jiba jiba jiba, and seem like the only documents that was
produced was the ones we had to sign. Maria's cousin, though, refused to sign anything for her own release. She looked at the people
asking her to sign like she didn't trust none of them. Then she said
that word again that sounded like *kuokoa*.

I ain't gonna tell y'all what else Maria said, what she felt like doing to those people that had detained her cousin. What she said
wasn't in no legal language, it wasn't in Mosquito language, it wasn't
in the true accents of a true American, not the confabulatory American that most Americans think is America, nor in her woman of re-
source good English, nor in Journal's Jiba jiba jiba jiba jiba. I think
the language she spoke was Quechua, but it was the Excuse my
French type of Quecha, said by the kind of person who says they
French without excusing it. But she did say that she thought her
cousin looked like she'd been drugged or brainwashed or something. We stayed in a motel for a few days so's Maria could coax her
back to health, but all the time we was kinda paranoid. 'Cause them
people mighta known that they mighta had some responsibility even
for the human rights of immigrants. So we wasn't really sure what
them people might do. They mighta had some people fooled, but
I'd heard they lies for my ownself. When you hear they lies for your
ownself, even if they's government and official peoples and peoples
of authority, then you know who they are.

In the motel, I watched Maria try to coax her cousin to health. I
didn't know what she was doing but it seem like she was mixing poetry and music and song and dance and chanting and even long talks
that reminded me of Delgadina when she was having them intellectual debates with some of them people who'd come into the cantina
and seem like they wasn't surprised that a bartender would engage
them in intellectual conversation. And anytime anybody ask her has
she read something she answers yes.

Have you read *Trotsky in Exile?* someone asked.

Yeah, sure.

And I thought they's talking about the races.

I say something about the races. I means the horse races and that
man talking to Delgadina look at me like he think I'm a fool. Delgadina she don't say nothing, then they continues talking about

Trotsky. And that man still looking at me like I'm a fool, like he don't know why Delgadina would befriend a fool. I drinks my Budweiser and listens to them talking about Trotsky. Then I realizes he somebody that gots to do with the Russian Revolution or one of them revolutions.

Then I'm thinking about Monkey Bread. One time I'm sitting in the Galileo Club in Covington and she come in singing something about Jim Dandy. She was singing that song "Jim Dandy to the Rescue," and then she be telling me about going out to Hollywood and want me to come with her.

Jim Dandy to the rescue, Jim Dandy to the rescue, Jim Dandy to the rescue. Then she pretend she got one of them slide trombones, and ain't saying the words but making her voice sound exactly like it a slide trombone. I ain't gonna sing all that song, but y'all knows the music.

Come on, Nadine, and come out to Hollywood. We can get us some good jobs out there in Hollywood, Nadine. We oughta go out to Hollywood.

I don't want to be no movie star, I says.

People don't go out to Hollywood to just be movie stars. And I'm just talking about jobs that is legit, Nadine. I ain't talking about that documentary we seen on Hollywood. I mean, there is legit jobs in Hollywood. Hollywood ain't just the movies, Nadine. I wants to go out to Hollywood. I told John Henry he oughta come with me to Hollywood 'cause they's plenty of musicians out there that needs they pianos tuned, but he want to stay in Covington or go to *Kansas City*. I told him if he go to Kansas he might as well come to California. He must think I'm a fool. He means the musical *Kansas City* and I'm thinking Kansas City in Kansas.

But that Maria she looked like, well, I couldn't tell whether she was a madwoman or a saint the way she was coaxing her cousin. I think she might have even sang a healing song to her in Quechua, 'cause it wasn't the Spanish language, and then when her cousin started looking like the possibility of improvement, we headed back to Texas. Least Maria said something to make her laugh. And I ain't seen her laugh at all after her detainment. I ain't know whether it was Maria told her a joke or just being in the presence of someone who valued her.

356

Going back to Texas, Maria and her cousin rode up front and
Journal in a baby's seat, 'cept Maria would sometimes ride in the
back with her cousin and sometimes up front with Journal and me
'cause there wasn't room for all of us up front and also 'cause the
closer we got to the Southwest the more them highway patrol started
looking at us with suspicions, but when I was just there with myself
and Journal they believed Journal was my baby, though one of them
thought I'd adopted a little Navajo baby and tried to find out
whether there was a law against a baby riding in my truck, but I as-
sured them that I wasn't transporting any goods, and not being a
member of the union I didn't have to abide by they rules. They
checked the back of my truck but both Maria and her cousin had
their papers. They suspected the papers was forged, but they was no-
tarized, and they had other illegals that didn't have no papers at all
heading for the borders, so we got back to Texas City.

Linda Chong didn't come back with us to Texas City riding in
my truck but had her own jeep, she said. She never introduced me to
the man of Linda who seemed like he was from his own independent
country, so I can't say for sure he was one of her associates, or
whether he was one of the guerrilla lawyers, or whether he was one of
Ray's group. Or just his own person who seen the abuse of us rights.

I ain't tell y'all what Maria's cousin's name is 'cause I ain't seen it
written. Maria told me her name, but even that sounded like *kuokoa*
to me and I didn't want to keep asking the woman's name 'cause I
didn't want to express my ignorance. And it wasn't really necessary
for me to know her name. I was just glad with Maria and Journal and
Linda Chong that she was free. I don't know how much Maria paid
Linda Chong, but I myself didn't see any money change hands. I
guess I could have learned her name from them papers that Maria
had to sign on her behalf. Everybody else was examining them papers, but I just seen she kinda look like Maria, so I figured she Maria's cousin so I ain't need to be examining no papers. Like I told you,
I signed affidavits stating that I knew Maria and that she a woman of
resources and that I knows Journal and that he born in America. I
ain't understand none of what she said, though, I mean Maria's
cousin. And her and Maria talking so fast Spanish or Quechua or
Quechua-accented Spanish or Spanish-accented Quechua I ain't understand a word of that, and when they's talking English they's talk-

ing so fast I ain't understand a word of that neither. Only person I did understanding going back to South Texas was Journal, and he kept saying Jiba jiba jiba jiba jiba, which I knows now is both his baby word for rebellion and his baby word for my name.

Now y'all know I ain't one to do much talking to babies, but I talked to that baby, from Middle America of the southern commonwealth all the way back to South Texas. I didn't do no baby talk, though. And he didn't seem like the sorta baby to expect no grown woman to be baby-talking him.

Maria's cousin went back to Mexico, but had to be cured of America. Least that's the story I hears. Then Maria be telling me she ain't know where in Mexico her cousin, or if she stayed in Mexico or went to some other country.

This is Nicodemus, he be saying.

I'm at Father Raymond's, I mean Raymond's apartment, except he back to being Father Raymond now 'cause I gotta pretend with him that he a real priest and he introducing me to some of them Sanctuary workers. I already seen a lot of them in the basements of them farmhouses, but I ain't been introduced to them. This time he introduce some of them by they real name, at least by they real first name, and me he introduce as Nadine. He ask me whether I want him to introduce me as Jane or Mosquito or Nadine and I says Nadine. He don't ask me whether I wants to be introduced as Sojourner, though, or maybe he think Sojourner too unusual a name to stay secretive whereas Jane or Nadine or even Mosquito could be anybody's name or nickname. Anyway, Raymond he got him a nice apartment with a lot of what they call that eclectic-type furniture, some of it modern, some of it antique, some of it American and English, other of it Asian and African and Mexican and probably that pre-Columbian. I heard somebody talk about that international mind, maybe he got one of them international minds. Look like the apartment of a man who either do a lot of traveling around the world or got friends who do a lot of traveling around the world. And he got one of them tall, African-looking drums in the corner near the writing desk—maybe one of them talking drums—and some tapestries and furniture that might look like that Oceania-type furniture, and a lot of it be made out of eclectic fabrics too, silk and raffia and glass and velvet furniture and tapestries and shit. But it ain't no crowded apartment, though. It sound like it crowded with furniture when I describe it but it ain't. He introduce me to that stain glass artist. Like I said I remembers meeting her with that Delgadina but she behave like she be meeting me for the first time. And I be introduced to some of them other ones. We ain't introduced as Chito Chiton, we introduced by our own first names, like I said. I won't tell you any of they names, though, even they first names, I just call them Nicodemuses. They Sanctuary workers, but ain't none of them come out and declared theyselves. But that Nicodemus I seen that Nicodemus, 'cause he the one were a refugee. The one look like a East Indian. The one he look like he spying on everybody, but I guess he must be a spy for them Sanctuary workers; probably they mix him in with them real refugees so's he can tell them if any of them refugees is spies. Least I guess that who he is. But like I said they's as many different kinds of them refugees as they is them Sanctuary workers, 'cause some of them refugees is ordinary working peoples, even peons, and some of them's members of the elite and they's artists and intellectuals too. Father Raymond he be telling the refugee Nicodemus—I think he say he name Nicodemus—about my encounter with that Mexican woman, and turn out he ain't East Indian at all but just look East Indian. A spliv like me but who grew up in Hawaii. And you got different personalities too. You got some of them goody-goody types and you got some of them cynical types and you got to have you a range finder for all the types of people in that Sanctuary movement, whether it the mainstream Sanctuary movement or not. Raymond he got one of them dolls on his writing desk and I'm sure that one of them Maria Barriga I mean Maria Ramirez dolls. And he also got him some of that stain glass art.

I'm kinda shy-shy with all these different peoples, all different, so I be over there near that antique writing desk looking through Father Raymond's books. He got a modern bookshelf full of all these books in different languages and books on everything from economics to politics to religion to language itself and got a whole lot of books on Africa. Got a larger variety of books in his apartment than at the cathedral. Or maybe a smaller variety of books, but just ain't in Latin like most of them books in the cathedral. And above that writing desk he got framed words not pictures. One a advertisement for

something called the Bandung Conference and another the Preamble of the Society of African Culture.

It a real preamble, but where the preamble say just *mens* somebody scribble *womens*. Where it talk about "men of every philosophical, political and spiritual tendency in the cultural field,"
somebody have add *women*. Then he have him a quotation from
someone which say, "We can take our stand with the oppressed, or
we can take our stand with organized oppression." And then they's
another quotation from another someone that say, "Protest is speaking; resistance is acting. . . . To protest is to say you disagree; to resist
is simply to flatly say no." I ain't know whether I'm to tell y'all the
names of them peoples so I ain't name them, though they is named in
various Sanctuary literature of the mainstream Sanctuary movement.
And then they's that quotation again from the *Popol Vuh*:

> Let us rise up together,
> Let us call to everyone!
> Let no group among us
> be left behind the rest.

Some of them titles of them books on Africa includes *Principia of
Ethnology, The World and Africa, Africa in the Modern World,
The African Abroad, An Introduction to African Civilization, The
Vai Language, or an African System of Writing*. I didn't know
they's any African systems of writing. I opens that book but it look
like some type of secret language. And then I be especially interested
in the title of one of them African books: *The Leopard's Claw: A
Thrilling Story of Love and Adventure from European Castle
Through the West African Jungle, Disclosing a Deep Insight into
the Quality and Spiritual Influence of African Social Institutions
and Conditions, and Revealing a Profound Psychic Interpretation
and African Inner Life, All Clustered About the Mysterious Function and Significance of the Leopard's Claw*.

I be wanting to read a book with a long title like that, and I be
standing there thinking about the African jungle, but seem like
every time I be thinking about the African jungle Tarzan and Jane
and Jane's daddy and some other man that I just calls Bwana in that
jungle. And then there is two kinds of Africans I has a choice of be-

ing. There is the tame ones that is always on the side of Tarzan and Jane and Jane's daddy and Bwana and the ones that leads Jane and Jane's daddy and Bwana through the jungle; they don't lead Tarzan through the jungle 'cause Tarzan supposed to know the jungle better than the Africans knows the jungle they ownselves and knows all the animals in the jungle better than the animals knows theyselves he don't know Cheetah, though, as well as he thinks he do and them animals is always coming to Tarzan's rescue when he ain't rescuing hisself. Then there's the wild Africans, the untame Africans, who always has bones in they noses or uses bones for they jewelry. Anyway I'm thinking all that while trying to read about the "profound psychic interpretation and African inner life, all clustered about the mysterious function and significance of the leopard's claw" when somebody say, There's Alvarado. Al.

Now I know I heard that name Al. I look around to see where Al, but they's talking about that drum.

What kind of drum is that?

Ashanti, I think.

Ain't Ray part Mohawk too?

No, Polynesian, I think, or Filipino. . . . These chicken wings are good.

Ray has the luscious most beautiful eyebrows in the world, doesn't he? I mean, for a priest.

I hope there ain't any wheat in this barbecue sauce. I'm allergic to wheat.

Give you hives?

Naw, more than that. I have a toxic reaction to wheat. What's the chemical?

I don't have any allergies.

She's allergic to love.

I'm not allergic to love. I love love.

The provost had a reception for me at this plantation. However, I wasn't told it was a plantation till I was already there sipping punch and eating Cheez Whiz on toast. Then the provost asks, What do you think of our plantation? One of his ancestors was put in prison, though, for helping a fugitive slave escape. . . . I call them the new niggerati. I'm an African American, I can call them what I want.

Now, if you were to call them the new niggerati. . . . Anyway, Amanda Wordlaw's writing a book called *A Natural History of Afro-Mexico*, which deals with the African presence in Mexico, from the slaves who jumped slave ships to seek refuge in Mexico to others who traveled south to Mexico rather than north to Canada. . . .

Some friend of Ray's. . . .

So anyhow that's how they got the land from the people. They reclassified it so that it seemed like it was the least valuable land when actually it was the most valuable, the most tillable. So that's how the colonialists originally got the land for themselves. . . . But everyone's like that. They can only imagine freedom for themselves. Like the French and their Resistance fighter heroes, but impossible for them to imagine freedom for the Algerians during the Algerian War or to see themselves as the Occupation. . . .

Or in Indochina.

Exactly.

Everyone rationalizes their oppression to make themselves seem moral, but like this friend of mine says, Reactionaries are the same everywhere. . . . But the problem with that kind of private investment is it continues to exploit the people because it only invests in raw materials . . . and that's what distinguishes the undeveloped world from the developed world, raw materials or manufactured goods. . . . Anyway, that's what I mean by economic colonialism.

What are you gals gossiping about? asks Al.

We're not gossiping. Why is it when women talk politics it's still called gossip? And when men gossip it's called politics?

Anyway, so this truant officer came from the Bureau of Indian Affairs school and took me to school. And we were like reading these Dick and Jane books when I'd been hearing stories of Tseitsinako, the Thought Woman. . . .

You're not full Indian, are you? You look like a half-breed.

Ignore her, she's a fool.

'Cept when she says that word, she glances over where I am. I'm still standing over there at that antique writing desk. When, I opens one of the books entitled *Africa*, one of the Nicodemuses come over to antique writing desk. He look at the *Africa* book first and then he look at me. He wearing dungarees and a sweatshirt, his hair tied back in a ponytail. Must be a style among a lot of them Sanctuary workers.

Hello, I'm Al—Alvarado. Do you remember me?

He extends his hand and we shake hands. Yes, I know, you's the one had me interview that Vietnamese African-American woman. Juanita, right?

But your nickname's Mosquito.

Yeah.

Would you like some wine, chica? It's from Jerez. I'm from Jerez originally by way of El Salvador, by way of Guatemala, by way of Honduras. . . . Ray always has these gatherings so's we can get to know each other. I usually don't come to them myself. To tell you the truth, Juanita, he say, calling me the Spanish version of Jane— the first to call me any kind of Jane—the more I get to know some of these fools, the less I want to work with them for any kinda cause. I respect Ray, though.

No, thanks. I got me my Bud Light. I motion to my Bud Light on one of them coasters on the edge of the writing desk.

Now y'all know I likes Alvarado ever since he had me interview that Vietnamese African-American woman, but when anybody be talking about getting to know fools, I ain't sure I wants to talk to them, 'cause then they be getting to know me for the fool that I am. Suppose Alvarado get to know me for the fool that I am and then ain't want to work with me for the cause?

Anyway, so he's got a new identity. He used to make them for draft dodgers, I mean conscientious objectors. Making new identification is not as profitable as you might think.

What's that you're reading?

Some book on Africa. It's just called *Africa.* I'm kinda surprised that Ray got so many books on Africa.

He push my glass of Bud Light over and sit down on the edge of the writing desk. We're all Africans. The first men and the first women. *Mi abuela* insists that we're Indo-Hispanic, but trace us all back far enough we're all Africans, and all *negritos.* You know in my country it has always been against the law to inquire into a man's ancestry, or a woman's, and in yours it is against the law not to.

What is your country?

All of Latin America. I'm Mexican, but I think of all of Latin

Americas my country. I think of every Latin American as my coun-
tryman.

I wants to say "and countrywoman" like that person that scrib-
bled "and women" on that preamble. I kinda don't know what to
say to Alvarado, 'cause I don't want him to get to know me for the
fool I am. I mean there's them that knows me for the fool I am and
still likes me, but Alvarado seem like the kinda revolutionary that
don't suffer no fools.

I heard Father Raymond call you the eternal revolutionist, uh,
revolutionary. Why?

Because he is a *pensador moralista* and thinks I still have my revolutionary ideals.

Don't you got your revolutionary ideals? I asks. I gots to ask that
man questions even if it do reveal me for the fool I am. I sits the *Africa* book on the writing desk and sits on the corner of the writing
desk.

Alvarado ain't as tall as Ray, and I kinda ain't want to tower over
him whilst we's talking. He ain't no little man, but he ain't as tall as
Ray. He got him a mustache and a high, broad forehead. There is
something kinda cunning in his expressive black eyes, though they
seems also like they is the eyes of a idealist, but a idealist who is also
a realist, 'cause he seem like he been everywhere in the world, maybe
a disillusioned and jaded idealist.

And then as soon as I'm thinking that he saying it.

Ray wants to think that at least one of us isn't disillusioned. Ray's
disillusioned, but he continues the revolution. He's dubbed me the
Eternal Revolutionist but I think that's really a description of himself. To tell the truth, if Ray wasn't in this revolution, I'd just go back
to photographing revolution. That's how Ray and I met, when I was
photographing a revolution. I was never a revolutionary my ownself.
I would just document revolutions, photograph them, photograph
revolutionaries.

Well, some of them revolutionaries needs to be documented and
photographed. I mean, they needs people to document they revolutions. I mean, you know what I mean. Do you know what I mean?

He nodded and said nothing. I was thinking that it meant that he
knew now that I was one of the fools. He went over and got him a
cup of wine, asked me again if I wanted any. I was sitting on a corner

of the desk, ashamed of being a fool, when I looked up and he was standing beside me drinking wine.

He offered me some kinda biscuit and I nibbled on it.

My grandfather, he was saying, is a child of the Mexican Revolution of 1910. *Yo soy revolucionario*, he's always saying. He still sees himself as a revolutionary. That's how he defines himself. He was only a child during the revolution, but he still thinks of himself as a revolutionary. I've photographed child revolutionaries in various countries. They always seem like the purest.

I know this woman she got her a baby she got a little costume she sometimes put on him that make him look like a little baby Che and that make him look like a baby revolutionary.

Maybe he's the only true revolutionary amongst us, said Alvarado and laughed. He sipped more of his wine and offered me some. I drank from it, then gave it back to him. He leaned against the wall.

Ray lets almost anybody join us. Some of these people belong in a carnival sideshow. And some of these privileged. I don't think the privileged can be true revolutionaries. I think true revolutionaries must be the workers or the peasants. What do you think?

I ain't know. Seem like to me that true revolutionaries can come from any group or class.

When I met Ray I was in this migration of El Salvadorans seeking refuge in Honduras and Guatemala. Ray was down there. I don't know what he was. A lot of people thought he was CIA or some shit. Then when I met him again it was when we were both part of the Sanctuary movement. I think he was in El Salvador for love. I mean, as opposed to the CIA, you know.

I don't say nothing. I don't know if he probing me to see what I'll tell him about Ray.

Maybe they is testing me to see if I'm loyal to Ray or to they revolution. I don't say nothing.

I work mostly Texas now, he says. Sometimes California. Sometimes they send me to Chicago, Boston, New York, Washington, you know, to interview people.

I'd also heard that he supposed to be some type of psychiatrist, but I ain't tell him what I've heard about him.

Does you still photograph peoples? I asks.

No. I don't photograph people anymore. But, you know, traveling from one revolution to another, I know different languages, I understand different kinds of people. I've just come back from Chiapas. I'm working on the Chiapas Project.

I ain't say nothing. I ain't know whether I'm supposed to ask about the Chiapas Project or just let him tell me what he know. I knows this got to be some kinda test to see if I'm loyal to the revolution.

Perhaps a rebellion is a better name.

Say what? He saying something about rebellion, but I ain't want to ask him exactly.

I was saying that perhaps rebellion is a better name. I was tempted to photograph again, in Chiapas, I mean. I'm disillusioned, but I have my uses. I know some medicine, I know some psychology, I know some diplomacy, I know some law, I know about filing asylum petitions, and I'm good at organizing.

That's kinda like me. I'm ignorant about everything except what I know. I don't exactly mean that. Well, you know what I mean.

Yeah. He nods and sips his wine. He go over and get some more of them biscuits and comes back and gives me some of them. I sips some more of that wine from his glass, but I don't get me no wine of my own. I still got my Budweiser sitting in the coaster.

Sometimes refugees appear at my door, and I give them lodging. I've got a little adobe house out in the desert. You need to know where it is. I won't draw you a map. Will you remember?

Yes, I says.

He tells me exactly where it is, but I ain't going to tell y'all.

We're all *negritos*, says Alvarado.

And then I knows that *negritos* the code word if I brings any peoples to his lodgings. Then we's just standing there conversing with each other. I ain't tell him too much about me, though, 'cause I still believes he the type of revolutionary that don't suffer fools. So I'm mostly listening to Alvarado talking about his grandfather being a child of the Mexican Revolution. I can hear the other Underground Railroad peoples behind him talking, and then one of the women looks towards me and Alvarado and starts singing, Is you is or is you ain't my baby?

The bughouse, didn't I tell you?

I got to explain to y'all the origins of the "fool that I am" expression, at least as I knows them. Monkey Bread first wrote me a letter saying, The reason that I still loves John Henry is he knows me for the fool that I am. Then when I started dating John Henry I writes her and says, I understand why you loves John Henry, 'cause he knows me for the fool that I am, and still loves me. And then she wrote me a letter saying, My star knows me for the fool that I am and still asked me to be her personal assistant. Then she wrote me another letter saying, The reason I trusts the Daughters of Nzingha is because they know me for the fool that I am. Then I wrote her a letter saying, I don't believe the Daughters of Nzingha really know you for the fool that you are. And she wrote me a letter saying, Nzingha herself knows me for the fool that I am and still wants me to be a Daughter of Nzingha. Then I wrote her and said, I don't believe that Nznigha knows you for the fool that you are. And then she wrote me a letter saying, Nzingha, fool, not Nznigha. You think every time us gets together us supposed to have a *nig* in us. The Daughters of Nzingha. Then she wrote me a letter saying, Nadine, I think you really are the only person that knows me for the real fool I really am, and I'm the only person that knows you for the true fool that you are. Then, after watching the Oprah Winfrey show with some other womenfriend members of the Daughters of Nzingha, she wrote me and says, I know we is fools, Nadine, now you know if anybody know how much fools we is it's me, but I don't think, even knowing us for the fools that we are, that we's as fools as some fools.

Alvarado, the eternal revolutionist, is talking to someone who look like that Carmelite nun but in plain clothes, yes it is the Carmelite nun 'cept she in plain clothes, when Raymond come over. I'm still standing near the writing desk reading. This book ain't about Africa, though. A wild book by somebody named Clarence Farmer. Some kinda satire. I'm reading what he has to say about immigrants. And they's a group of brochures there that say something about patient's rights. Now I heard of that before. And then I see a bundle of documents that got written on them the Electra Project. I wants to open that bundle of documents but I don't. Then I see a folded letter. I can only see the top of the letter 'cause of the way it's folded.

Dear Ray,
    I'm writing to you about Our Spiritual Mother.

Then I can't read any other lines of that letter. However, it's sitting next to the documents that says the Electra Project. I don't know if it got to do with that project. I be thinking Father Raymond know all sorts of people. I don't know whether that a cathedral project or a project with the new Underground Railroad. I be thinking how Ray be able to be my lover and fulfill on the demands of the revolution. I know I ain't no type of revolutionary myself. All I does is transport them refugees. I do know that some of them refugees is revolutionaries in exile from they countries. I do know that some of them is even revolutionaries that has fought on different sides of the same revolution. I knows enough Spanish and few of them other languages now to know when I'm transporting them and they points at each other and say, I don't forget, meaning they don't forget what them other revolutionaries did on the other side of the same revolution.

    I'm trying to transport them to refuge in America so I says, Y'all is in America now, and I don't want y'all to start no revolution in the back of my truck. *Comprende?*

    And sometimes they is so intent on not forgetting that I's got to transport one group that fought on the same side in the revolution and then transport the other group that fought on a different side in the same revolution. But most of the time when I tells them not to start no revolution in the back of my truck, they don't start no revolution in the back of my truck. They still tells each other, though, I don't forget. Or sometimes they says, We don't forget.

    And if any y'all starts a revolution in the back of my truck, I ain't gonna forget none of y'all neither, I says. This is my truck. Now I'm going to transport y'all to refuge like it is my commission to do, but I remembers every one of y'all. I ain't involved in y'all's rights like Father Ray, so I don't mind transporting y'all to the immigration itself.

    Now y'all know I ain't going to be transporting them to the immigration, I just tells them that. But it is true that I ain't as involved in they rights as Father Ray and Alvarado and the other Ray. I just transports them. I still takes an interest in the rights of Maria and her baby, though. And the more I learns about Father Ray's projects, I takes interest in other people's rights. And then like everybody else I's got my own rights to defend. But that don't mean I gots to tolerate no revolution in the back of my truck.

Y'all can wait till I gets y'all to Koshoo's farm, and then y'all can revolution there, I says, and then offers them some trail mix or beef jerky.

I saw you talking to the Eternal Revolutionist, say Raymond. What were you talking about?

Why you call him the Eternal Revolutionist? I says. But to tell the truth he's kinda making me feel like I'm defending my own rights right now. You know, him asking me about my conversation with some other man. Except he ain't asked it exactly the way some other mens asks it. Maybe he thinks that Alvarado wants me to get involved in more people's rights than he think it my capacity to become involved with. I ain't tell him that Alvarado told me about his adobe house in the desert, 'cause then I'm thinking maybe that ain't no lodging for them refugees and maybe he just want to get me out to his house in the desert. Then I decides better not to go out to that house in the desert 'cept Ray tells me that it a stop on the new Underground Railroad. Then I'm wondering if Alvarado think Ray a real priest. Didn't he think he in the CIA when he first met him? And what he say about Ray being in El Salvador for love? Or maybe he signifying on us making love? I'm wondering now if Ray told him about me being a Trojan woman like that commercial and then Ray telling him about us lovemaking and then about all them men in my union—I got to tell y'all about my union—and maybe he really do think I'm that Nadine they calling Nadine and think I know all the men in South Texas and then telling Alvarado about me and even if they is revolutionaries they's still like men and maybe they's like them men in *Carnival Knowledge* talking about women. *Carnal Knowledge,* fool, not Carnival Knowledge. Maybe Alvarado is just there playing me and ain't got nothing to do with testing to see if I'm a loyal revolutionary. Then I'm standing there thinking about Alice Walker. I'm thinking these is revolutionaries and ain't none of them asked me that question that revolutionaries always asks them that's

new to the revolution. I'd have to tell them about my stun gun. I'd
have to tell them I gots me one of them newfangled stun guns from
the trade fair in Galveston.

I'm thinking all that whilst I'm waiting for Ray to ask me what
reason Alvarado gave for why he call him the eternal revolutionist
but he don't. I starts to repeat that line about comparison being a
petty demon. Then a woman who look like the daydream of Raymond's former girlfriend or even some El Salvador lover come over
and start talking to him in I don't know what language. I don't know
what they saying. Then she go over to the buffet table.

What did she say? I asks.

About English lessons, he says.

English lessons?

Yeah. She's a mathematician in Indonesia, but here she works in a
factory because she doesn't know English well enough, so we're getting her some English lessons.

You know Indonesian? Y'all be talking Indonesian?

Yeah. Actually I'm Filipino, African American and Indonesian.

Oh, yeah? I thought you already told me that. Or somebody told
me. You one of them multiracialists?

There are some places people get to decide what race they wanna
be.

I'm thinking how in the old days African Americans usedta always be telling people what all they had in them wasn't African,
most be talking about that Indian in them, that Native American,
then they got so they just be boasting about being African, and then
they be telling you again what all they got in them, except now most
of them includes the African. And some of them even includes the
African before they includes everybody else. In fact, I remember
when us was in grade school, me and Monkey Bread, and they asked
us what we had in us and ain't nobody say African. Of course, I said
Moroccan and Mexican and Cherokee, but that still ain't say African. I mean Morocco in Africa and they's Moroccans my color, but
that still ain't say Africa itself. Others in the class was mentioning
Greeks and Italians and even Irish.

I do know when I said Mexican I heard somebody say, Mexican
from the west coast of Africa.

I do know when I said Cherokee I heard somebody say, Chero-kee from the west coast of Africa.

So that just made me start calling more people as my own.

Italian from the west coast of Africa.

I said Italian 'cause you know I likes them Italian actors and ac-tresses. As far as I know, I ain't got no Italian in me, though.

Greek from the west coast of Africa.

I said Greek 'cause I know how us peoples likes to claim them Greeks, all them Alpha Beta Gamma sororities and fraternities.

Irish from the west coast of Africa.

I played with my classmates a little bit, though I didn't mention Africa myself. To tell the truth, I think I'm the only person who heard that person chanting that every time I said some new group of people. I kept claiming everybody's people as my own people, even the Russians and Swedes and Dutch, till the teacher say, Hush, Na-dine.

Since us was a segregated classroom of all colored childrens I thought it would be a lesson in ancestry and that the teacher would ask us how come none of us didn't claim Africa. In fact, I thought the teacher would praise me and say that of all the childrens, even Monkey Bread, I come the closest to claiming Africa, even if it was Morocco. When somebody asked the teacher, teacher said, Ah, my people's all Creole from New Orleans, got Indian in us, and a little Cajun, though.

'Cept when she said Creole I thought she still mean colored till we got outside of class and Monkey Bread explained to me that in Louisiana Creoles didn't think of theyselves as regular colored people and that they had they own community and that us teacher's people had settled amongst the colored people in Kentucky because in Kentucky they didn't make the same distinction amongst colored peoples as in Louisiana.

We's all niggahs here, say Monkey Bread. I was waiting for one of y'all niggahs to say something about Africa.

Didn't you hear that little boy?

What little boy? I didn't hear none of y'all niggahs say Africa. I know I ain't said Africa myself. I was just waiting for one of you other niggahs to say it first. Anyway, when I started to say Africa,

Miss La Sagesse thought that I was trying to be you and told me to hush just when I was ready to call Africa by name. What I shoulda done was said Africa first. And then named my Greek and Italian and Seminole. Course us people claims to be more Italian than anything else. You know how us niggahs is.

And I gots to tell y'all the truth, it weren't a white person the first person to call me niggah, although plenty of them looked niggah at me, it were Monkey Bread the first to call me niggah by name, although it were in a collective context.

Anyway, I'm talking to Ray.

Alvarado say that where he from it against the law to ask people what race they's from. It against the law to ask people they origins.

He lift an eyebrow but say nothing. He ain't say which of them races he call hisself, though he look like a man who know who he is.

Another rocket scientist, I says. Your friend.

She's just someone I'm helping to get English lessons.

Teach her yourself?

She come up to him again and I hears the word *guru*. And words that sound like *radjin* and *pintar* and *elok*. *Guru datang*, say Raymond. Then she point to me. She holding a small chinette plate from the banquet table with one hand and pointing to me with the other. *Orang Amerika? Orang asing? Orang Amerika*, he reply.

I hope y'all ain't calling me no orangutan, I says, looking from one to the other. And maybe that's another reason he a good Sanctuary worker, I'm thinking, not just disguised as a priest, but maybe because almost anybody can see theyselves in him.

She's asking me if you're an American.

Oh, yeah? An American orangutan?

Apa? ask the woman.

Ape? I asks.

She's just asking what kind of American you are, he say.

He tells her. *Besar*, she say.

I know what that *besar* mean in Spanish, but I don't know what it mean in that Indonesian. They ain't talking pidgin Indonesian, though, them's just the words I make out. And I knows in Spanish *besar* has something to do with kiss, but I don't know what it means in Indonesian. I'm still thinking about comparison's a petty demon.

She's very beautiful, I says when she go to join a group of others. Maybe Indonesian speaking.

Oh, yeah? In Indonesia, she's really considered rather ordinary-looking. There are many Indonesian women far more beautiful than her.

Then they's a beautiful people, I says. They's a lot of women wouldn't mind being that kinda ordinary-looking. But comparison's a petty demon, like you said.

Where's your apartment?

Raymond is telling me that the reason he's brought her here is because the other refugees from her country they don't trust her. As he talking I'm thinking of first opening my apartment door and seeing them standing there. At first I think it's that Indonesian woman, her hieroglyphic eyes and his and her with this scarf wrapped around the lower part of her face like them Mediterranean-type peoples, and the next thing I'm thinking is that's her, that's *la mujer*, that's his lover from the old days, the rocket scientist, and then when they gets inside she take that scarf off and put it in this tacky bag she carrying, and don't look like the kind of bag no woman of mystery be carrying, and he ask whether they can spend the night here. They's a guest bedroom in my apartment, so I says yes, but him he say he'll sleep on the couch. He in his priest's clothes, and he behaving like sort of her protector.

Her she holding tight to that tacky bag and's wearing combat boots with what look like them palazzo trousers and a sweatshirt, I think they calls them palazzo trousers, them real wide trousers, and look incongruous with them cowboy boots and sweatshirt, and she ain't wearing them stereotype of Latin American women-type clothes, though I know she Latin American. Her she don't say a word and I figures it 'cause she don't speak English. She look Latin American, though, like I said. He don't tell me her name either. I ask him her name, but he don't say *la mujer* name and I shows her where the guest room is and where the bathroom is and I gives her a extra pair of pajamas, though they's too big for her and she got to roll the cuffs and sleeves up, and gives her a fresh towel and washrag. I don't got no extra toothbrush, but I see her take out a toothbrush from that tacky bag and some clean underwear, but it that clean underwear that them Sanctuary workers gives them.

When I go back in the living room, Raymond sitting on the couch with his arms thrown back along the couch, and he rise and look like he want to kiss me, but I waves him away with her in the house and I still don't know if that he old girlfriend. I got one of them couches they advertises in the newspaper as Western-style couch, but it got the same Mexican colors—reds and turquoises and yellows and them same geometric-type patterns—in it as that rebozo of Maria's and that scarf of *la mujer*. I ain't got as much eclectic furniture as that Raymond. It eclectic but it mostly American eclectic. Then I makes him and me some hot chocolate and then we's in the living room drinking that hot chocolate and sitting on my Mexican-style couch and talking and he start to kiss me again, but I says naw not with *la mujer* here. He won't tell me her name, though, but he don't mind telling me her story. She in with a group of them refugees but then one of them refugees from her same country and same village point her out to the others and tell her tale to them and he decide for her own protection to bring her here. She were staying for a while with some others, but the refugees got wind of it, and so he decided for her own protection to bring her here.

How do I explain her? he saying. One of the general's concubines, one of many generals' concubines. I don't know her own story my ownself, but I hear, overheard, the man who pointed her out say that she takes up with every strong man that comes along, you know, takes up with every tyrant. And I gather from some of the talk, the gossip about her, that she's much older than she appears to be because there's more than one generation of strong men, more than one generation of generals, more than one generation of tyrants. He look around at my apartment while he talking and I be hoping he don't think it tacky. This apartment don't look like you, he say. But he don't say what a apartment of mines suppose to look like.

I explains that I don't spend that much time in my apartment, so's you can't say much of my personality's here. I don't tell him so, but I got that rent-to-own-type generic furniture and even rent-to-own TV, except for some of them things that I've picked up at the flea markets and thrift shops. And I got a lot of doilies on everything, though, 'cause I been reading this novel with a doily-maker in it so I bought me some doilies. Doily-maker not dolly-maker like that Maria. And I got a few of them oil paintings of the Southwest on the wall, you know them landscapes, and also them portraits of Native Americans, you know, the kind of paintings that you buy at thrift shops, and garage sales, and them roadside market stands in the Southwest.

Most recently she was the concubine of one of the members of the secret police, but now finds herself a refugee. She spied and informed on others and then found herself spied and informed on. She thought she'd make a fresh start here in this country, but one of the other refugees knew her. We're hoping maybe to transport her to Canada.

The woman, draped in a blanket, come into the living room. She holding the blanket like a rebozo and running her hand through her hair. Waves and waves of hair, like the dream of Raymond's lover. She come and sit in the armchair, one of them rent-to-own armchair.

Would you like some of this hot chocolate? I asks. Ask her if she want some hot chocolate.

I'll take some hot chocolate, she say, and I will tell you my story my ownself. She wait while I pours her some of the hot chocolate. She drink almost half of it before she start telling her story. Some of the hot chocolate spill on her rebozo-blanket and she lap at it like a cat, then she dab it with her napkin. The man who pointed to me and some of the others, they only know the old me, they only pointed to the old me. They do not know the me who has been a long time a worker in the refugee camps, the detention camps. She sip some more hot chocolate and then look at Raymond. She mostly look at Raymond, but only at me when she explain the meaning of some of them Spanish word. I saw you, señor, first when you came to our refugee camp. You were with the hombre from Amnesty International and your friend the other hombre, and I was one of the ones packing the medicine kits. But it is the old me that they know, the one who some of the villagers call La Loba, the wolf woman, and some of them claim that they have seen me turn into a wolf. But it is *la loba* and *el lobo* in their own selves. *La loba* of their own imagination. Or the metaphor for our own country. I come from a very hard country. The tyrants are hard, but the people are also hard when they think you are not one of them. But it is true. There are those even in your group, señor, who do not like to hear me talk like this, *compañeros* and *compañeras* who do not like to hear me talk like this, for they say it feeds the stereotypes of Latin America, that it feeds the prejudices, but not for those of us who know who we are, who have learned who we are. But it is true, the only men that I always attach myself to are the strong men—the strong-armed men you would say, for the strong men are not always the strong-armed men. As for him, the one who pointed me out, he tried to make love to me himself before he joined the popular forces and fled to the mountains and when they were routed from the mountains by the government police he fled here. I saw you and your friend, señor, the one who gave the speech, the Eternal Revolutionist you introduced him as, but when he introduced himself he called himself a peacemaker, not a pacifist, but a peacemaker, who said the act of making peace, the art of making peace is more difficult than the art of making war. In that part of the world those who make peace are considered *cobardes*, cowards, you see, but he does not seem like a *cobarde*. He is no coward. I thought it would be him to take up for me, but it surprised me, señor, when it was you who came to my defense, or rather brought me to safety. I was not surprised when that hombre found me at my first hiding place, for he is a tenacious *diablo*, a tenacious devil. Do not let all those who join the popular forces convince you that they are the innocent ones, señor. It does not surprise me, señor, that you've come to my defense again, and brought me again to safety.

She sip more of that hot chocolate, look toward me, then back at Raymond. Now she talk only to Raymond.

At first when I was thrown out of the refugee camp, because someone thought again that I was the old me, I almost returned to being the old me, to practice the old vices, to go with another of the strong-armed men, for there are some of us, señor, who practice vices like other people practice virtues. I'm not a *católica*, señor, so I can say so, and I can see with you, señor, that one does not have to be a *católica*, but then I did not want to be the concubine of any more of the men who relish the art of war, and I decided to come north. I cannot be a peacemaker my ownself for there is always someone who sees the old me and uses it to wage war. But like everyone of my country, I have always had dreams of freedom. Even the tyrants have freedom dreams, you know. Except their idea of freedom is to control others, denying the freedom to others. *Una pájara mágica* that is what one of my *generales* called me. I call them all *generales* but every strong-armed man thinks he's a general. Every strong-armed man believes himself a general. But me? A magic bird. Wouldn't anyone prefer to be called a magic bird than a wolf? Though they say wolves aren't as bad as we make them out to be. But if I am a wolf, then I'm a sheep in wolf's clothing. She sip her hot chocolate, spilling more on her rebozo. I notice that her lips is slightly bruised, and I be wondering if one of them men have given her a beaten or tried to kiss her too hard? She dab at her rebozo with her fingers and at her lip with her rebozo. I gets up and goes in the kitchen and comes back with a napkin.

It was when I began to write, señor, that my strong-armed man began not to trust me. It was only *escritura* for myself and not for the public, but he discovered one of my notebooks and began not to trust me. *Mi escritura más que mí actividad con* the refugee camps. *Pero no me gusta hablar de mí.* I don't like to talk about myself, señor, but I know you have heard all the others talking and I heard you yourself to talk about me and there are so many stories of what an ogress I am and so I wanted to tell you that I am no longer my old self but my new self. *Pero el arte de la guerra es menos importante que el arte del amor.*

She speak Spanish and then translate it after she speak it, so I ain't got to translate for y'all. 'Cept that thing she say about the art of love and war she ain't translate that. It mean something 'bout the art of war being less than the art of love. 'Cept it sound better in Spanish than English, and it seem like it got a more significant meaning in Spanish.

La loba, no es más que una leyenda. It's no more than a legend that bit about me turning into a wolf, you know. A legend or a metaphor. But in my country sometimes the people cannot tell the difference between the legend or the metaphor or the reality, and sometimes they are even all the same thing. When I was at my youngest and most beautiful and with the strongest of the strong-armed men, someone started a rumor that I turned into a wolf.

But *la mujer* do look wolfish with her tousled black hair and piercing black eyes, sly wolf's eyes, and sipping her chocolate. I asks her if she want more of the chocolate but she say no and then she go back into the guest bedroom. Then I get Raymond one of them blanket and make up the couch. I think he gonna try to kiss me again, but he don't.

She remember you but you don't remember her? I ask.

He say that there were many women in that refugee camp fixing medicine kits. I think he going to say more about this one, though, or how she reminds him of the other one. Then he over looking at my bookcase. I'm kinda embarrassed 'cause I ain't got the sorta intellectual-type books that he got in his office. I gots a lot of romance novels by Nefertiti Johnson. I's got my favorite novel which have got romance in it but ain't all romance. I ain't got no political books about Africa, but I has got one of them travel guides to Africa. I gots me a Swahili book. I got me a book from Consumers International. I gots me some other books, but I don't think that they is Ray's types of books. I got a novel that I calls a Mosquito-crafted novel, 'cause it the kind of novel I might want to write if I wrote novels. But mostly they is popular novels and science fiction novels and Westerns and some of that detective fiction. I also got me some novels by some of them African-American authors, though most of them was given to me by Delgadina. Although Delgadina weren't the one to introduce me to African-American authors, she the one to sustain my interest, her and Monkey Bread.

This looks interesting, say Raymond, turning the pages of one of them African-American novels. That the one my favorite novel. It were given to me by the author herself.

You can borrow it if you wants to. I would give it to you, but it's the only copy I been able to find. It's about a little town in Kentucky, like a lot of little towns in Kentucky I know about myself. Delgadina say it kinda like a Utopia, though, 'cause ain't no real little towns like that, and especially when this story supposed to take place, in the 1920s and 1930s.

They's realistic-seeming people, and a lot of them people is like peoples I know myself, but it still kinda a Utopia. Actually the woman that wrote that book I usedta visit her when I would visit my cousins in central Kentucky and she were a neighbor woman of theirs. She give me that book. I don't believe that she would trust me with the only copy of that book, but that is the only copy I knows about. That's my favorite book.

Ray picks up the book and looks through it like he interested. I ain't know whether he interested in the book itself or because it a book I say I been trusted with. He do look like he reading it, though, and ain't just looking at it to be polite 'cause I's said it my favorite.

I keeps rereading that book, and I knows them people in that book as well as I knows myself and a lot of them better than I knows myself. They's Saturna the Indian—they called them Indians in them days—they's Olga and Kate and Charley Hickman and Nat Perrison. I knows about a true Nat Perrison, but that's a fictional Nat Perrison and is what she refers to as a retold story 'cause that story of Nat Perrison gets retold in other novels and stories and even in one of her plays. They's Mag and Leola and John Branurn. They's fictional stories in that novel but they's like real stories about real people I knows.

I know there's those of you that believes that my bookshelf is confabulatory, 'cause I don't seem like no literate woman, but my little bookshelf ain't near so confabulous as that of Delgadina's and even Delgadina she were still surprised to see the books on my bookshelf—the book about Olga and Kate and Charley Hickman, the book about *Gulliver's Travels*, the book about *Alice in Wonderland*, Alice Walker's novels and poetry, *The Portrait of a Lady*, *The Harmless People*, *The Communist Manifesto* (I found that abandoned at one of the truck stops and the woman that owned the truck stop said it didn't belong to nobody so's I could have it), *The Year of the People* (I got that at a flea market), Edmund Spenser's poetry, *The Woman's Guide to Confident Home Repair*, *2,000 Years of African Poetry*, *Egyptian Love Poetry*, *The Buddha's Favorite Disciple and Other Stories*. She imagined that the only books I had in my possession were the ones she gived me and not the ones I gived myself. The books that she herself wanted to read were the one about Olga and Kate and Charley Hickman, *The Woman's Guide to Confident Home Repair*, and *The Buddha's Favorite Disciple and Other Stories*. I kinda didn't want to lend her them books, 'cause I knows how peoples is about returning books. They asks you to lend them a book and they thinks you's give them the book. I kinda reluctantly loaned her them books, but she returned them all to me. And said she'd liked all them books. She'd ordered her own copy of *The Woman's Guide to Confident Home Repair*, but claimed that she were unable to find any copies of that Olga and Kate and Charley Hickman novel, or that books of short stories called *The Buddha's Favorite Disciple and Other Stories*. Though that Buddha book started her to talking about the concept of the disciple and also that disciple were derived from discipline. She said she remembered when they was at Catholic school they'd put on a play about Jesus and his disciples and she'd wanted to play one of the disciples but was told she couldn't play no disciple 'cause Jesus didn't have no women disciples, so's the closest she could get to Jesus was to play Mary Magdalene.

If they had allowed women to be disciples, she'da been one, I said.

That ain't what I mean, she said.

Well, you coulda played somebody's disciple, I said. They's got to be other holy mens and holy womens whose disciple you coulda played.

That was Catholic school, Nadine, she said. And we were just putting on one play and that one play didn't have but one holy man in it. And there was only two roles for women, Mary and the other Mary, the Magdalene. So you know they weren't going to let me play Mary.

Well, I'd've played somebody's disciple, if it was me, I said. Even if it wasn't in the play. I mean as long as I discipled myself to somebody who were good. I mean as long as they allows you to discipline yourself to them.

Sometimes, Nadine, you don't make any kinda sense. Then she said, You know, Mosquito, calling me by my other name, what I mean to say is you don't make the kinda sense I thought you'd make.

I start to tell Delgadina about the woman that wrote that other book and how I knowed her. Years later when I would tell her how as a little girl when I would visit my cousins we'd go to the home of a certain woman. She was middle-age then, but still very beautiful. People had said of her that she was chronically ill, and sometimes we didn't know if we would find her bedridden or up and about. When she was up and about, she'd sometimes play the piano for us and sing songs or tell us stories or read us stories or poems. And she'd have a poem for everything. If you did or said something, she'd have a poem for it. If you'd ask her a question about something your child-hood self didn't understand, she'd have a story or poem for it. Some-times I'd go to visit my cousins just so's we could go to the home of that certain woman.

And she was the one that discovered my hidden talent, I said when I finally told Delgadina about that woman.

What talent? asked Delgadina.

My talent for remembering everything I hear. I don't remember everything I read. But I remembers everything I hear. She would re-cite poems or tell stories to us and I could recite them back word for word, that is when I wanted to recite them back word for word. I'd heard about peoples they says has photographic memories, but she said I had what's called a auditory memory.

Delgadina looked at me.

I remembers everything I hear, I said. But I don't repeat it all. And then even after she told me about my hidden talent, she even had a story for that.

Years later, in the days when both Delgadina and I would begin to refer to her as our Spiritual Mother, we would file a complaint on her behalf with the Daughters of Nzingha. We didn't know what the Daughters of Nzingha's strategies would be—ain't I told y'all about the Daughters of Nzingha?—but Delgadina and I would take our investigative selves. . . . But that's another conversation, maybe even a mystical one. And we weren't no Thelma and Louise neither.

But I'm talking about Ray now. He take the book and sit down on the couch and start turning pages. I ain't know whether he read-ing the same book I reads and rereads, 'cause a lot of times men can read a book different from the way a woman reads it. A man might open that book and decide that just 'cause he don't like the tale of Leola and the mighty John Branurn he don't like the book, even though there's plenty of good mens in that book to make up for that scene where the mighty John Branurn knock that white panama hat off Leola's head, and then some. And certainly Mag is enough bad woman to make up for any bad man in any woman's book. But me I likes the love of Charley and Wasetta myself, and the strength of Kate.

You ain't one of them speed readers is you? I asks. I starts to ask if he's read the part about the mighty John Branurn, but I don't. And it seem like Charley Hickman enough good man to make up for any bad woman in any man's book.

Not exactly. I've learned to read pretty fast, though. You have to when you've got to handle a lot of immigration documents and then I get so much correspondence from people, immigrants, you know, and people seeking asylum, and just my own personal correspondence.

You want some more hot chocolate?

No thanks. This is good hot chocolate, though. With the marshmallows on top.

How long *la mujer* supposed to stay here?

Just for tonight. I'm working on getting someone to transport her to Canada.

I hope you ain't signifying for me to do that. It's okay here in Texas City and around the Galveston Bay area, 'cause I can work around transporting them refugees and my industrial detergents. I been to Canada, but I don't want to start driving them refugees up there to Canada.

Oh, no, we've got other interstate workers.

Yeah, 'cause I hope you ain't signifying for me to take that woman all the way to Canada, I says, though I'm trying not to sound like that petty demon.

I go and gets him another blanket and puts it over the back of the couch, and then I clears away them hot chocolate cups and saucers. When I comes back I thinks he be sleeping, but he still reading that novel. Just speed-reading them pages. I don't know if none of y'all speed-reads, but I likes that book like I said 'cause it got people in it just like the peoples I knows.

Well, goodnight, I says.

Goodnight.

When I wakes up in the middle of the night, I thinks he be sleeping, but I can hear him on the telephone, but it sounds like he's talking to himself. Now I know you can talk to yourself, but if he's talking to himself he's talking on the telephone, but then I realize it must be the other Ray he's talking to, the one called Ray Mendoza, who I ain't met:

Yeah, Ray, so you'll drive her as far as the farm. . . . Yeah, they've got a farm near the Canadian border. Somebody said it usedta be a real stop on the Underground Railroad. Someone else can take her across the border, okay? . . . No, that's why I'm calling you on this phone, it ain't likely that it's bugged. She's one of the greenlings. . . . Sure. . . . No, it's better if she settles in Canada. There's too many former revolutionaries who know her here. . . . The concubine. Yeah, he's taking a rest cure up near Toronto. She might be able to stay there with him for a few days. . . . Sure. Well, it's just that women are always judged by the company of the men they keep, you know. . . . Ray, you oughta know that. How many women are wrongly judged by keeping your company? If you keep the company of *generales*. . . . You know, refugees fighting among themselves. . . . Well, you know if you tell her about our deportation, everybody else'll know. Might as well put it in the funny papers. What about the gringa? Well, she could drive them, couldn't she? I don't think she'd get any hassles. . . . Naw, Ray, I don't mean to Canada, just up to the border. I'm talking about the ones from Chiapas. We've already got someone to drive the woman to Canada. . . . No, I am not going to introduce you to Nadine. . . . How'd you hear about her anyway? Naw, Ray, she ain't your type . . .

Then they says something in Spanish. Or maybe that's 'cause Raymond know I'm listening. When I gets up in the morning to fix the two of them breakfast, they's already left. Raymond has neatly folded the blankets and put the book back on the shelf. I opens the book to reread about some of them Kentucky people. Then I open one of them other African-American books that's got quotations in it. One of them quotations ask, Why does a black man have to do with love? It supposed to been asked by a Afro-Arabian poet in the Middle Ages, I think. Maybe even in them days they was telling black men they wasn't supposed to write about love?

CHAPTER 12

I COMES BACK TO MY APARTMENT AFTER TRANS-
porting some of them Chito Chitons. I ain't gonna tell y'all where
I transported them, 'cause the new Underground Railroad like
the old Underground Railroad. The people who transported people
on the old Underground Railroad didn't tell people everything. I
can't reveal to y'all everything, even them of y'all that is worthy listeners, or tell you all the strategies of the new Underground Railroad, at least the strategies I knows about, 'cause I don't know who
might be listening to this conversation. And like I said, I don't know
which of y'all is true spies and only pretending to be worthy listeners. Like every story, I gots to decide how much to tell y'all and
how much not to tell, but added to the fact that I'm talking about
a fugitive group, 'cause these undocumented immigrants is modern
fugitives, I's got to tell y'all as much as I should tell, but less of the
story than I know. I know that there is a lot of y'all that thinks that
this is a fabricated truth, and that even the names that I says is my
own might not be my true names. I got to talk to y'all more about
that, 'cause y'all keeps asking me this and that about my story. It ain't
that I don't trust y'all—I means the ones of y'all that is worthy listeners—but you can't trust everybody with every story. You can't

trust people with every story. You don't tell everybody every story. Even them stories that is satires ain't to be told to just everybody. You don't even tell everybody everything in the same story. Even during freedom them people knew not to tell every story and knew who were worthy to hear them stories and who weren't. There is people who says, I's free, I can tell any story I wants to tell. But even us government knows that they is confidential stories and secret stories and top secret stories. They has the freedom of information, but that is only a ruse.

I'm too tired to go to the cantina, and ain't even transported the industrial detergents I'm supposed to be transporting. I usedta park my truck at one of them warehouse-type places I rented owned by a trucking company. I didn't work for that trucking company, so I had to pay them to park my truck there. But then they got in trouble with the union 'cause somebody told them I wasn't union, so then I had to rent me a apartment that got its own parking lot that's big enough for me to park my truck, but still the apartment owner makes me rent it. I mean, makes me rent my space. Anyway, I parks my truck, then comes in the hallway and checks the mail. I know it a letter from Monkey Bread 'cause it postmarked California, though now she ain't writing in her handwriting, she type all her letters. She tells me she wants me to get e-mail so's she can e-mail me. Be telling me I better come into the modern world. But I know it Monkey Bread.

I takes the letter out of the mailbox, some bills and invoices and goes upstairs. I takes off my sneakers, gets me a Bud Light out of the refrigerator and some of them new chocolate pretzels I done bought for myself, and sits down in the living room and opens up the letter. I know it Monkey Bread 'cause Monkey Bread the only one that call me Nadine. I mean, on a regular basis. To tell the truth, I ain't know which one of my own names I prefers. I don't know what I'd call myself. Sometimes I feels like I'm Nadine, other times I feels more like I'm Sojourner. Sometimes I'm Jane. When I started reading Nefertiti Johnson's romance novels, I wanted to put Nefertiti in my name, though I don't think I'm nobody's Nefertiti. I likes Mosquito. I ain't nobody's Mosquito, and they calls me that. What? Where I say I was when I was reading that letter? Well, I gets so many letters from Monkey Bread. Some I takes with me to the cantina and reads. Sometimes I even rereads them. Contradictions don't

mean you ain't telling the truth. I did read it in my apartment first,
then I took it to Delgadina's cantina. I mean, Mr. Delgado's cantina
where Delgadina work at.

Dear Nadine,

Thanks for telling me about Nefertiti Johnson, the Afromance
novelist. I likes them comic romances. You asked me about John
Henry Hollywood? Sometimes I writes to John Henry in Covington, but I don't write to him on a continuous basis, 'cause he got himself a wife now. I think they might move to Kansas City. I know she
be, Who that woman writing you from out in California? We's
childhood friends. That's who I am.

Hey, Nadine, I think you's the only one who likes my stories and
poetry, except some of the Daughters of Nzingha. I got a author for
you to read. Somebody sent our star a script based on a novel by
Danny James who writes satires of African-American modernism,
least that how my star describes it.

Who is the new man you won't tell me about? I know you's in
love, Nadine, on account of your phraseology. I can't imagine no
man worthy of you. My star has got her a publicist who want to make
her into a Bo Derek–type sex symbol. I don't think she play that,
'cause she want people to think she a actress.

I hope John Henry has his ideal of a woman and I hope she realizes who she do got, and ain't be a fool. I ain't going to say nothing
'bout you and John Henry or you and that ex-husband of yours out
in Tasmania.

I thinks some of us is just fools, Nadine. I know my star is a fool.
Every time she gets drunk at some cocktail party she telling everybody about her and some Russian count. My star thinks I'm schizophrenic. Don't play Nadine when you're around me, she say. I told
her all about you, Nadine, and she thinks I plays Nadine sometimes.
Some of these directors is still trying to get me to play roles in they
movies. This director comes up to me and tries to get me to audition
for his new movie called *Kingfish*. I think he talking about Amos
'n' Andy, but it some movie 'bout the former governor of Louisiana,
Huey Long hisself. I'm supposed to play a maid in the governor's

mansion. I reads for the role, but they says I don't sound like no maid.

Do you realize, Nadine, that we have never had one of them my man conversations. I've had plenty such conversations with my star, 'cept she won't talk about that Russian count. Since she is becoming a bigger star, though, I has had to sign one of them I-ain't-going-to-talk-about-you-to-them-tabloids agreements. I ain't joking. Ain't nobody from no tabloid interested in my star's ass. She collects old copies of *Hollywood Confidential*.

I loves Nefertiti Johnson. I knows us New World African womens is romantic. Gotta be romantic. Don't let them tell you you ain't supposed to be romanced and them romancing every other woman, including them Desdemonas.

Thanks for photocopying that book that you's only got one copy of. I knows you don't trust me, Nadine, but I loves that tale about Leola and the Mighty John Branurn knocking that white panama straw hat off that woman's head. Course like you I loves that Charley Hickman and Wasetta love. This grown-up woman's book. I am including a little romantic story about me and John Henry. What did you say that Delgadina said about the burden of being an exemplary man?

Don't you let that Delgadina patronize you. Or treating you like you's supposed to be her disciple. She ain't no holy woman. Detective school sounds interesting, though. There's a lot of private detectives here in Hollywood, between acting gigs. Having your own private detective must be in vogue.

But yes, Nadine, I likes being the housekeeper of this Hollywood star and traveling to exotic places like Scandinavia. I am more than a glorified maid but her personal assistant. We have been to every continent except Africa, and have even been to the Pacific Rim. Hong Kong is a glorious place.

Read Zora Neale Hurston's book and the story of Big Sweet.

My star enrolled me in culinary school, although she has already got her a nutritional gourmet restaurant and gets to sit at the chef's table. You know the elites out here sits in the kitchen of some of these fine restaurants and it's called the chef's table.

Nzingha, our priestess, says that we should call each other womanfriend not girlfriend. But there is a lot of bizarre, eccentric, neurotic, and scandalous women out here in Hollywood. I ain't talking about Nzingha but pure of ass women like in that *Hollywood Babylon*. When you're rich you can be as wild of ass a woman as you wanna be, and don't nobody refer to you as no hoochie. Even the elite of the white trash variety as I heard somebody say in a movie.

I'd like to know more about that Miguelita and her Mr. Delgado. She sounds like a debutante my star says she knows whose father is a comic book artist—I mean he draws cartoons for the comic books. She says the Miguelita she knows looks like a comic book character herself. She sounds like another eccentric.

My star is playing a rocket scientist's dumb blonde in her new movie. Bimboism is they feminism and how they displays they feminine hubris. I guess if they's masculine hubris they can be feminine hubris. I mean for a lot of these movie stars.

I likes a good Brated movie myself, though. The only difference between a Brated movie and an Arated movie is the type of stars. Her next movie is one of them Japanese science fiction movies where she gets to play an intergalactic *gaijin* bimbo. *Gaijin* means foreigner in the Japanese language.

If your friend Delgadina do decide to become a detective, tell her to come to California. Girlfriend, you have started sounding like a regular commercial for Bud Light. I hope you ain't become no drunk and intemperate colored girl. I advise niacin to reduce the craving for alcohol.

I don't think my starlet is a natural blonde 'cause I seen pictures of her as a brunette, but Glamourtown is Glamourtown. And you know how these peoples is about they white aesthetic.

Anyhow, she is working on a improvised movie by a female producer and filmmaker. The film is sorta like jazz, you know, where they talk about the melody being a framework around which the jazz musicians improvise. Like what that Wynton Marsalis said talking about that jazz on television. She gets to play the hoi polloi.
Sincerely,
Monkey Bread
P.S. Girl, my star is making a movie about Australia and they wants

me to play one of them aborigines. I think they still calls them aborigines, don't they? Or is they native Australians? I told them I ain't got no design on being no actress. Every time they gets a role like that, they wants to hire me. They also wants me to play a African pygmy. I likes them pygmies and I'm flattered to have their stature. And this is Hollywood.

Dear Monkey Bread,

Thanks for you letter. I got one of them entertainment magazines and read about that Australia movie, *Love's First Green Language.* It don't sound like no B-rated movie to me. The daughter of a carnival sideshow owner who seduces a aborigine, but the aborigine is accused of seducing the daughter. I suppose Hollywood can turn it into a B-rated movie.

Sincerely,

Mosquito a.k.a. Nadine

Dear Nadine,

You's right about Hollywood. I got that novel and read it for myself, and it ain't no B-rated novel. The blurb say that the novel is considered to be politically subversive in Australia, but no Australian film company would make it 'cause it mixes too much politics and sex. It is a very voluptuous novel, but it ain't no B-rated novel. I wouldn't mind playing the aborigine woman if I was the love interest of the aborigine man as he is depicted in the novel. However his love interest is the carnival daughter. It is a B-rated movie, and Hollywood have turned the film script into a jungle of clichés, but it's my star's first star-quality role. They got a Puerto Rican to play the aborigine, though, one of them Rico Suave types. But in the movies he looks like a true aborigine. And got they syllables and rhythms in his language. My star has started collecting aborigine art.

Sincerely,

Monkey Bread

P.S. What name are you better known as in Texas? I have always preferred Nadine, you know, but remember when you be nicknamed Big-girl? And then everybody started calling you Mosquito, which seems incongruous to me. But it's like that little guy in that Brazilian movie that they call *Big Otelo* and it should be *Little Otelo*. But everybody still calls me Monkey Bread.

Dear Monkey Bread,
    Does your star call you Monkey Bread?
Nadine

Dear Nadine,
    My star used to call me Monkey Bread, but received a letter from one of them African-American organization, a member of whom overheard her on national TV referring to me as Monkey Bread and so she has started calling me by my true name, or what she believes to be my true name.
P.S. Nzingha is encouraging all us colored girls to tell our stories. How do you like my new word processor? I'm also learning exotic fruits like star apples and a Brazilian drink called cachaca, made with sugar cane. My star thinks Brazil is sexually stimulating and indulges in the aphrodisiac. I likes Brazil, but I don't consider it as exotic as Scandinavia.

Then in her next letters she tell me more about them Nzingha's Daughters. To tell the truth, I wants to hear more about them than I does about her star. She say they is still trying to get her to be her own woman and to leave the plantation, which they call working for that star. They calls her star the Abyssinian cat, though in her movies she look more like a Persian cat. She say she told them Daughters of Nzingha about me and they's quite delighted about me being a truck driver and seemingly my own woman.

Dear Monkey Bread,
    What you mean my own woman? I hope them Nzingha's Daughters is in favor of love. Is they just a political type of group?
Sincerely,
Mosquito

Dear Nadine,

Sure we's in favor of love. You can be your own woman and be in favor of love. Us priestess says that love is the essence of being human. One of the Nzingha's Daughters basic concepts, though, is that African women should be economically independent if possible. They's a lot of basic concepts, some to do with economics and others with culture. They promotes diversity amongst us African womens and we ain't all got to be the same woman. We should have diversity but we should recognize common interests. We's got working-class and intellectual-type womens and we's even got the Afro-womanist Development Bank. We uses womanist rather than feminist 'cause that Alice Walker's word, you know.

But you would like the Daughters of Nzingha and I would enclose some of our literature but we presently do not send out brochures and shit like them other organizations. We ain't no secret society or cultural fantasy and we don't recruit in the streets or at factories and political rallies. They is worker-intellectuals among us as well as pure intellectuals. I got me some books pan-Africanism and Garveyism so I can understand some of what Nzingha is talking about. I figure the priestess must be a pan-Africanist and Garveyite or one of them Ethiopianists.

They's a lot I could tell you about my priestess, but I'd have to write me a whole book.
Sincerely,
Monkey Bread

Dear Monkey Bread,

Thank you for your letter and the photo of you and Cooter and Nyam-Nyam of the Daughters of Nzingha. They both looks like girls and you looks younger. It must be that root tea you mentions. If they's from the Sea Islands, they must speak Gullah, don't they? They do look kinda like West Indians. Cooter kinda looks like this woman that works in a warehouse where I sometimes loads my truck up with industrial detergents and Nyam-Nyam looks kinda like a migrant. You's write about diversity.
Sincerely,
Mosquito

Dear Nadine,

The Daughters of Nzingha have started visiting the detention camps. Theys are all obsessed with the desire to escape, however, like they's modern fugitives. All we does presently is bring them hygiene stuff and foodstuffs and contribute sometimes with their legal defense, especially the priestess says we have a obligation to the Haitians and African Diaspora–type people. Because in the beginning the group would just meet and watch *Oprah* and every time somebody come on the screen one of us be saying, I thought I was the only fool, or we be saying, At least us ain't the only fool. Now we's beginning to see usselves as modern emancipists—ain't that the word?—though we ain't exactly emancipated nobody.

My star heard of our little group and called us racist in reverse. Or maybe some type of cult. You must know that I didn't tell her about our group, but she's a snoop. I think she had her private detective investigate us.

The priestess is kinda eccentric, but I don't think she crazy. I don't have a photo of our priestess, but she got a most African nose. Nyam-Nyam is sly-eyed and Cooter is the plump one with the innocent eyes. In truth, Cooter is kinda sly and Nyam-Nyam is the innocent type. The priestess say Cooter is as plump as a tinamou, which is some kinda bird, and she call me the secretary bird though I ain't no secretary, but I know the secretary bird a African bird, and Nyam-Nyam she just call Nyam-Nyam.

Sincerely,
Monkey Bread

Dear Monkey Bread,

You say you ain't a cult, but you sounds like a cult. I wants to learn more about the Daughters of Nzingha, but I don't want to join no cult. I read about some group out there that teaches women how to milk an untamed cow and new words like *fescinnine.* Is that the same group?

Sincerely,
Nadine

Dear Nadine,

Thank you for your letter. No, you must have been reading about some other organization. We don't refer to usselves as a organization. The reason I likes the Daughters of Nzingha is that they makes me think I am free, Nadine, even whilst I still works for that star. What do we study? Sometimes we study about the men be having their independence movements and the womens ain't free, but the men be trying to convince the women that their freedom ain't important. Our priestess says that all colonialists does that. She has her plenty of boyfriends and lovers, though.

Sincerely,

Monkey Bread

P.S. I probably do not have a talent for poetry, but here they are anyway. My nom de plume is also Monkey Bread. And here are also the stories that I promised you and a brochure about the International Trade Fair in Tokyo and one on an International Machine Tool Fair, since you like to collect brochures and I know you like them trade fairs.

Monkey Bread's Story

Do you take John Hollywood to be your lawful husband?

We was playing and so I said I took John Hollywood to be my lawful husband and promised to love and cherish him. We rented us a house because he was pretending to have himself a good factory job making business machines and I was pretending to have me a good job in one of them department stores downtown, and them was the years when they didn't hire African-American peoples to work as clerks in them stores, at least not in that part of the country. Them that owned they own little stores could work as clerks in them. He used his real name, John Hollywood, but me I renamed myself Casablanca, like the title of that movie, and I kept thinking it was a grand name, a grander name than Monkey Bread. John Hollywood wanted to call me by my true name, but I didn't think that my true name was a good enough name to be John Hollywood's wife. So I became Casablanca Hollywood.

We pretended like John Hollywood was a good Christian because in that little community good men was supposed to be good
Christians, and pretended that he was the best man in the world, and
who could marry better? Who couldn't be in love with such a man?
I don't know whether he pretended that I was the best woman in the
world. Even with my name Casablanca.

Then, after we was married, we pretended that we had us a short
weekend honeymoon to Mammoth Cave, Kentucky, where a lot of
newlyweds had honeymooned and come back telling glory stories.

We pretended a little neighborhood cave was Mammoth Cave,
and when we wasn't pretending we was husbands and wives, we was
pretending that we was guides in that cave, and we talked about how
we'd add more passages in that cave and would discover more passages in that cave, passages that hadn't been explored by any of them
other newlyweds. We had us a good time in that little cave and just
like newlyweds come back telling everybody how wonderful us
honeymoon, though we was telling imaginary people, and we was
telling them about how the Indians—cause we called them Indians
then—made that cave, and how they had that cave before the white
men come and commercialized it, 'cept we didn't use that word
commercialized.

Then, 'cause I'd never met John Hollywood's folks, we traveled
to his house to meet his folks, and pretended that they lived in North
Dakota rather than on the other street and pretended that they hadn't
been able to come to the wedding 'cause they lived in North Dakota
and there we was in Kentucky, you know. So we saved up money, or
pretending we was saving up money, so's we could go to North Dakota.

I don't know how long we pretended. I called him the good husband, and he'd sit on the porch with me at night and watch the moon
light up my face. We pretended it was the moon. I liked to comb his
hair with my fingers and kiss the top of his head, and I liked to tell
our imaginary people how wonderful a husband, and we'd pretend
we was drinking beer though it weren't nothing but root beer, Nadine. (I decided I'd put you in my story, although I don't think you
even knew John Hollywood in them days.) We'd drink beer which
was root beer and talk about Mammoth Cave. I don't know if they

Jim Crowed Mammoth Cave in them days, but that's where we pretended we'd honeymooned. We also pretended that we went up to Cincinnati to the zoo and to Louisville to the state fair. We even talked about having us some children, although they's imaginary children. I know what you's thinking, Nadine. Naw, we didn't do that in that cave.

Then we pretended that we traveled by bus to North Dakota, though we took us a bus ride all around the city. John Hollywood held my hand and I slept on his shoulder. We'd saved us a lot of money so's we could take that trip to North Dakota. We rode on the back of the bus, 'cause they Jim Crowed them buses in them days.

I asked John Hollywood, What your father do?

In the winter he work on the railroad, in the summer he a lumberman.

We held hands, and then we got off the bus and walked out into the country, though it was still the city, but we was pretending it was the country, you know, Nadine, and I pretended that I seen my first deer, you know, like they might have in the country of North Dakota. Then we walked on one of them little dirt roads, the dust sticking to our shoes. We walked across stones and seen a crab on its back in the sun. Then we come into the clearing, and they was three little girls with bowl haircuts playing on the porch. John Hollywood's sisters Lira, Lolly, and Lola. I couldn't tell them apart. John Hollywood introduced me to his parents as his new bride. They knew we was just play-acting so they shook hands with me and hugged me and called me pretty, 'cause you always calls new brides pretty.

We rested and ate there. We had us corn and venison stew and apple pie. Naw, Nadine, it wasn't no real venison stew, we was just play-acting that it was venison stew. I fell in love with John Hollywood's family and his little sisters and we all played us a game of catch in the yard. Then his daddy went to work and the little girls went off to school and John Hollywood went into town and I stayed with his mama who I thought was a quiet, beautiful woman, and she kinda reminded me of one of them Indian womens 'cause she had that long hair that she wore in braids, just like them Indian women, and she kept play-acting with us 'cause she said she wished that she could have traveled down from North Dakota to come to our wed-

ding, and then she told me that John Hollywood gave her a picture
of me and that she was pleased with his choice in a woman. I didn't
know that grownups could pretend so good as that.

Is he taking care of you? she asked.

Yes, ma'am.

And you take care of him? Yes, I see you do.

Then we washed the dishes together and went out to the garden
for tomatoes and set them on the windowsill, and she had all kinds
of plants in her garden and knew the names of them, just like you say
about Delgadina. And we took a walk together and she told me that
they had only one movie house in that little town, and figured that
my name being Casablanca that I must like movies. Do you swim?
There's a wonderful creek.

Course there wasn't no creek at all around there. When I told her I
didn't swim—which was a lie—she told me that maybe John would
teach me. Then she asked me how long we'd be able to stay, just like
I was a real newlywed, and wished I could stay and visit them
longer, and then we come back and sit on the porch, and John Hollywood returned from town. And his mama went back in the house to
do her housecleaning.

How was town? I asked.

Ain't a lot changed, he said. Then we pretended we was at the
movies and he sat with his arm around my shoulders like we'd see
the teenage boys do, then his mama bought us some hamburgers and
some of them little apple pies and some Coca-Cola. We had us a picnic and pretended it was us first picnic, which it was.

Even as a little boy John Hollywood were real muscular and
kinda remind me of a man. Didn't remind me of Dick in Dick and
Jane, but reminded me more of Dick in "Dick Tracy." Except even
more a manly man, but he weren't nothing but a little boy.

I don't know what else us pretended. I asked him if he'd ever
thought of settling in North Dakota, but he said it weren't nothing
there but the railroad and lumber.

Your mama look like a Indian, I says.

She is a Indian, he says. And then he told me 'bout his grandfather, a medicine man, and give me a belt of deerskin supposed to be
made by his grandfather. I still got that belt, Nadine, and sometimes
I thinks it's got real medicine in it.

I ain't know if that a true story he mama a Indian, but you know, Nadine, that's when I started to look at John Hollywood a little different, like they was something a little mysterious about him, even though he were the same John Hollywood. And he the same John Hollywood.

I know that some of y'all don't think that just them letters and even that story from Monkey Bread is enough and y'all want to see her for yourself. Well, stories ain't like them novels where there's plot unity and coherent scenes, when you's telling a true story, you don't always get to meet the folks you wants to meet. I know when Delgadina introduce a character in one of her stories, the teacher tells her that when you's writing a story, if you introduces a character you's got to do something with that character, especially if readers likes that character. I mean when Delgadina would take them creative writing courses. I told you about her taking them creative writing courses at that Community Center. She wanted me to take one of them courses myself and even read me some of the stories they had had to read for that class. I don't mean the stories that the students wrote, but they had to read stories that were published in anthologies. I remember she would sometimes read me some of them published stories. She know I like them storytelling types of stories and she would mostly read me them. Some of them stories was built around character and some of them stories was built around story. I mean, some of them focused on the characters in the story and some of them focused on the story in the story. I think Delgadina favorite were the story of an intellectual southern woman. She ain't say that that were her favorite, but she read me the whole of that story. I think the name of the character were Miss Leonora. They had colored people in that story, but I didn't identify with none of them colored people. Seem like whenever they is colored people in stories like that they is people of diminished humanity. Even that Faulkner that they talks about, and has got all them extraordinary stylifications in his storytelling and knows about all the stylifications and trickifications of the South and can hear the different peoples languages. Seem like the colored people in them stories has more diminished humanity than the whites in them stories, even though the stories themselves is written good. When that story say something about that Miss Leonora be an intellectual woman, Delgadina kinda paused at that line like it were a description of herself, although she were unlike Miss Leonora except for the portion of the story where it described her as being a beauty. And they were a description of her that I liked myself. That were where she were described as being a woman ready to talk about any subject except herself.

They's supposed to be certain rules to storytelling. Well, they ain't exactly rules. But you ain't supposed to tell written stories like people tell real stories. Like when I was coming out West I met a lot of different people, but if it were a novel I'd have to meet them people again or else it wouldn't be satisfactory as a novel. I mean, the most important of them people I'd have to meet again. I did get to meet that movie star, though, and I got to see Monkey Bread and them Nzingha people. But that were years later, when I decided to drive out there to California. I wasn't driving no truck then. I not only wanted to see Monkey Bread and them Nzingha people, that Nzingha herself and even her star, but I didn't like the fact that I'd just got as far as Texas City. I know when her star made a movie out there in New Mexico, Monkey Bread had written for me to come out there. She said, My star's making a movie out here in New Mexico, Nadine, so why don't you drive out here. She's playing a Indian, I mean a Native American. She didn't think she oughta play the Native American when they's real Native American actresses and even some woman named Sally who she believed would have made a better star for that movie, but she insisted that most of the other actors be true Native Americans, I mean true Navajo and Hopi and Zuni and Cherokee, 'cause they prefers to be called they true names like everybody else. The filmmaker thought that the American audience would still only come to see the movie if my star was in it playing Native, so she decided she would go ahead and play Native. She's a modern Native American woman who owns a hotel in Gallup, New Mexico. They's a lot of Mexicans in the movie, and I get to play the role of one of the women who stays at that hotel. At first they wanted me to play the cleaning woman and I told them I wasn't going to play no cleaning woman, so I gets to stay at the hotel. It ain't no glorified hotel, but just a little tourist-type hotel. Anyway, I thought you might like to come out to New Mexico whilst we's making that movie, plus my star got to have her own trailer and they treated her more like royalty making a movie in that little town than they do when she's in Hollywood and just a star amongst stars. And ain't got that blond hair neither, but got her hair looking like Elvis.

When I do go out there to meet them in California, she got her blond hair again. She a more diminutive little woman than the way she seem in them movies. She got blond hair and a real fair complexion. I don't think it a natural fair complexion. I think she uses them creams. And she say, So you're Nadine. I've heard so much about you, Nadine. Monkey Bread talks about you all the time. And she shakes my hand, and she got them little tiny hands, and they's well manicured.

That movie where she got to play Native made her more of a star than her other movies, but she ain't acting the diva, though. She got on blue jeans and a white sweatshirt and treating me like real people. And even treating Monkey Bread like real people. 'Cause I'm thinking she gonna be treating Monkey Bread like a glorified maid or some shit or maybe even her pet monkey, but she ain't. Or maybe she's one of them sorts that treats they pets like they's human beings. So maybe she is treating Monkey Bread like a pet, but she's just one of them sorts that treats they pets like they's human.

Monkey Bread got her own office that a combination of studio, office, bedroom, but a whole wing of the mansion is hers and she got her own entrance and can even invite her own guests up there, 'cept they's got to use her entrance, though. 'Cause her star got her own security people, and she got her own security person. Her security person kinda remind me of them Muslim, but she say he ain't no Muslim, though. He kinda fine, ain't he? she say. And he my own security person.

I even gets to go to one of them Hollywood-type parties, just little cocktail party, with some of her star's friends, a coupla starlets, a model from New York via the Caribbean, an investigative journalist, a chef at a Hollywood club, 'cause them Hollywood chefs they's supposed to be celebrities theyselves, a director of independent films, and me and Monkey Bread, and we's sitting at the table with them, and they's treating us like we's human. Well, they's kinda treating me like I'm Monkey Bread's pet.

Didn't I see you in that new Robert Townsend movie? one of
them asks.

I'm nibbling on some caviar and drinking a can of Budweiser.
Monkey Bread say the star ordered that Budweiser especially for
me. The others got champagne. The room they's having the cocktail
party in is one of them modern rooms, with colorful geometric furniture, which make the room look like it belong in one of them modern
paintings. It's kinda like a room inside a room. It got one of them
geometric-type rugs in the center of the room, and all the furniture is
arranged in geometric patterns on the rug, so that the room outside
the rug is free for the cocktail people to roam around in, like they's in
the margins. Then if they want, they can go into the room inside the
room. It's a room full of greens and oranges and yellows, and the
movie stars is wearing them same colors, and the dresses they's wearing is geometric theyselves. I tries to think of the name of that painter
that paints like that. Everything supposed to be geometry, so everything in the paintings is geometry. Everything in them paintings is
abstracted into triangles and circles and squares. They's got paintings on the wall that look like them kinda modernist art. Some of
them is prints of art by some of the famous painters and some of them
is supposed to be the original art itself. Her famous artist, though, is
a contemporary painter named Gillette Viking. I ain't never heard
of that painter myself. The star say she supposed to be a descendant
of them real Vikings, though. Least that's what she have in her pub-
licity brochures.

Naw, I says. I owns a little restaurant in Cuba. . . .

And before I can tell him it's Cuba, New Mexico, he's thinking I
mean that other Cuba. He a angular-type man, tall and slender, with
straight black hair and could be geometry hisself. Somebody say he
from one of them southern states, but his accent sound like
California.

Well, a lot of Americans are going down there, aren't they? he
asks, 'cause you know he know I ain't Cuban myself, though I've
seen Cubans that looks like me. I wanted to make a movie in Ha-
vana, but you never know what the State Department's policy is.
Well, I wanted to have a few scenes down there, then we ended up
using some stock footage. . . .

So I don't tell him Cuba, New Mexico, 'cause the real Cuba

sound more romantic. Then the star comes over and starts talking to that director. I ain't sure who's brownnosing who. Then they starts talking about the American movie as a genre. While they's talking the star acts like she wants to draw me into the conversation. But I can say for that movie star, she ain't as dumb as she looks.

Everybody wants to make the American movie, she says. Well, not everybody, but a culture's has got to be pretty strong to keep its own ethos, all the global standardization, all the talk of the international mind. I've got this friend who's a German filmmaker, you know, and he says if one of his movies doesn't duplicate the American movie, then his German audiences don't like it, say it's a second-rate or third-rate movie. But the truth is, he first wanted to be a filmmaker when he saw an American movie, then he saw *Rashomon* and the Italians and then realized it was the German movie he wanted to make, the truly German movie, not anything nationalistic, you know, but just the truly German movie. . . .

Isn't he the one making the movies based on Brecht's plays?

Brecht? He thinks Brecht is superficial, poetic, but superficial. . . . Anyway, he thinks you can't make a truly German movie without something about the war years. He wants to do something with German resistance, though, the Germans that resisted Nazism. He considers them the true German heroes. But he doesn't believe the Germans want any true movies about the war years. He might get an American production company. You should hear him tell you about the war because he's got a lot of stories that don't get in the history books. He wants to do this other movie about jazz, because he considers it the music of resistance, you know. Because they banned jazz in Germany during the war, so it was like a music of resistance, anyone who listened to jazz, you know. So he wants to make a movie about this subversive German who would listen to and play jazz. Then she's talking to me. Telling me about how a lot of the resisters would listen to jazz. Says he never understood jazz himself, can't decode it, but he still wants to do this movie about jazz. I love jazz. That's the thing about jazz, you're not supposed to be able to decode it. . . . Look at her. You're just supposed to love it.

She combs her hands through her hair. It that silky-type blond hair. I ain't know if she a natural blonde. Seem like Monkey Bread say she ain't no natural blonde. Monkey Bread say it the fashion in

Hollywood now amongst some of the true blondes for them to color they hair a color other than blond so's that they can prove they's true actresses.

I gots to say that she is the stereotype of the movie star, 'cause I ain't see no flaws even up close. Seem like see the aesthetic of perfection. I ain't know if they's tricks that them movie stars uses, I mean the ones that plays the movie stars, to obtain that aesthetic of perfection, at least the aesthetic of perfection based on they own standards of perfection. I ain't want to ask that woman her beauty secrets, though. I kinda would like to see her at one of them movie studios, you know, but Monkey Bread didn't invite me for no tour of none of them movie studios. But she say a lot of them stars' movies they ain't made in them studios, they's made on location. Still I think us coulda toured one of them movie studios.

Years later, though, I asked her how come when I come out to Hollywood she didn't invite me for no tour of none of them Hollywood studios.

Nadine, I didn't think you wanted to tour none of them Hollywood studios. If I'd thought you wanted a tour of one of the studios, we'da toured them. But I just ain't imagined you to be one of them people with that type of interest.

Of course when peoples tells you shit like that, you wants to imagine that you's the type of person they imagines you to be.

Well, I did want to kinda tour one of them studios to see if it would interest me, I said.

Then, of course, she were not in the employ of that star, but she did have somebody in the Hollywood studio tour business that she met when she were in the employ of that star to send me some brochures that stated I could get me a free tour of any one of them Hollywood studios. Before you could get your free tour, though, you had to see a certain number of Hollywood-produced movies and include your sales receipt. Since most of the movies that interested me wasn't produced in Hollywood, I didn't use none of them free tour brochures. To tell the truth, knowing Monkey Bread, I ain't know whether them was real brochures or confabulatory. I might see all them Hollywood-produced movies, go out to Hollywood to get my free tour and somebody tell me it a confabulatory brochure, or that brochure was just good for during the days when Monkey Bread was still in the employ of that movie star. Plus if y'all looks at the fine print, it says Monkey Bread Hollywood Promotions International. Or maybe I ain't know the true Monkey Bread and just think she a trickster.

Then they's looking at me like they wants me to join in that con-versation, I mean the star and the independent film director, and tell them what I thinks about American movies or German movies or some kinda movies or maybe that conversation about jazz. I kinda wish that Monkey Bread were standing over there to talk to them, 'cause she could tell them all about that jazz, 'cept she's over there talking to some other stars and starlets. And there's even a colored starlets that y'all's probably seen in some of them movies. To tell the truth she kinda look like the star, but brown-skinned. But she do have a similar quality of perfection, even by the aesthetic standards of Hollywood. They both looks like they middle name could be Venus. Or one of them goddess of love and beauty. I wants to go over and maybe ask her her beauty secrets, but Monkey Bread standing over there talking to her. I don't know what they's talking about. But the colored star standing there looking like from slavery to freedom, then she look towards me, then she look back at Monkey Bread. Monkey Bread must be talking to her in Ebonics or something, 'cause she like to do that with the colored elite, especially when they's at places like Hollywood cocktail parties. I did hear a earlier conversation between them, but they was talking about the star's boyfriend:

Naw, Monkey, he's part Japanese and part African American, from Tokyo, but he's got USA citizenship. His father was over there in Japan during the American Occupation of Japan after the war helping to rebuild the Japanese cities or whatever and met this beau-tiful Japanese woman. . . . A braidmaker. That's supposed to be some kind of art over there in Japan. The Japanese can make art out of everything. . . .

I know exactly who you's talking about, 'cause we've got some of his art around here somewhere. I saw somebody on MTV looked just like him. I mean, it was BET not MTV. He was dressed up like a rapper and interviewing one of them rappers, looking Japanese, but talking like a rapper. I thought it was him and asked my star whether that was the same one who art she collects but I know he wouldn't be on MTV or BET. . . . Well, he might be on BET but not on no video.

Then the star asks me if I'd like some more caviar, and I ain't even tasted the first caviar, but I would like another Bud Light. And she go over and get me Bud Light her ownself and brings it, and I'm standing there feeling like I'm the one supposed to be serving the caviar. The independent film director is nibbling on some caviar and talking to me again about the possibility of playing a role in one of his new movies.

But they's all acting like they's real nice people. Ain't even none of them catty scenes like in the movies. They might be brownnosing each other a little, but there ain't none of them catty scenes. And they ain't even got Monkey Bread to serve them. I thought Monkey Bread be serving them but she ain't. They's treating her like she's one of the stars. In fact, the only one I seen Monkey Bread serve were that colored star. She went over and got her some caviar and oyster crackers, but she musta told her to get her own champagne, 'cause the colored star went over and got her own champagne. They ain't got nobody to come around and serve the champagne, you's got to go up to the bar to get your champagne, and they's a man behind the bar that's serving the champagne. He ain't no colored bartender, like on the *Love Boat*, though. To tell the truth, he kinda looks like the mens you see on the covers of them romance novels. Maybe he out here in Hollywood trying to become a star hisself, and so he works the various Hollywood parties. Monkey Bread says they's a lot of them types in Hollywood. Then I think she's going to talk to me about the type of Hollywood that you reads about in them tabloids, but she ain't. Kinda like I'm supposed to be a naive in Hollywood, and she ain't want to tell me no Hollywood Babylon stories, not the Hollywood Babylon of the stars theyselves, but the Hollywood Babylon of them that wants to become stars.

I'm standing there thinking 'bout Hollywood Babylon when I realizes that the colored star is the same woman that I met once at one of them trade shows that I'm addicted to. I ain't think she know me, though, 'cause she probably see all kindsa peoples at them trade shows. I remembers her, though, 'cause I'm looking at her perfection and I'm thinking I've seen that perfection before, and then I remembers it that trade show. I starts to go over there and to specify her about that trade show, but then I'm thinking maybe she don't want these peoples to know that she usedta be a trade show actress, 'cause now she a starlet, and maybe she ain't even got it in her portfolio that she were a trade show actress, and maybe she do know me but don't want me to specify her, and tell the folks her origins at the trade shows. So I don't go over and specify her about meeting her at one of them trade shows. I do wants to ask her have she been to any trade shows, because since I has been working with the Sanctuary peoples I haven't been to as many trade shows. But then if I asks her about them trade shows she'll think I'm trying to specify her in front of them peoples who knows her as a starlet.

I know some of y'all wants me to identify that star as a true racist and have one of them scenes where them Hollywood peoples reveals they true selves, or asks me to dance or sing for them, or acts like them people in that movie where Burt Reynolds play the Indian and the people asks him to do a war dance or rain dance and he got to tell those fools he don't do no rain dance unless they wants some rain and no war dance unless they wants to go to war, and they's displaying their racism, but displaying it more to be fools than the true racists they probably is, you know, them scenes that pretends that them racists is just innocents. I know some of y'all wants one of them Hollywood scenes, but it weren't like that. Maybe there was some patrons amongst them, but they was trying to serve me caviar. And don't think I'm no fool. I knows they's just treating me the way they's treating me 'cause of that star, 'cause I met a joker look just like this film director once when I was driving my truck. I'm dealing with this new company, so this joker tries to give me the bum's rush till he finds out I'm with the Mosquito Trucking Company, but I decide not to let the fool know that I'm Mosquito herself. Course it was just a little trucking company but it had got a good reputation amongst some of his suppliers. I knows the only reason they wasn't giving me the bum's rush were because of that star and the only reason the star weren't giving me the bum's rush were because of Monkey Bread.

Even gives me one of his independent film productions cards.

They's real nice people, ain't they? say Monkey Bread when we's back in her wing of the mansion. She's got brocaded furniture that looks like it's out of a movie and even got gold threads in the sofa and chairs. I love champagne. I still don't like caviar, though. My star

didn't use to like it herself, till she made that movie that made her
famous. Course they're nicer to us now than they usedta be. That director usedta think my star was a bum.

Say what? I ask. I'm drinking me a Budweiser and sitting on that
sofa that musta cost thousands of dollars.

Well, he didn't think she was a good actress till she was in that
movie playing the Navajo. I remember she usedta audition for all of
his movies. Now he wants her in all his movies. She the same actress
it seem like to me. If she wasn't no good before that Navajo role, she
the same actress now. But that's the thing with these stars and starlets
out here, they's all the same seem like to me. I don't see no difference
between them that is stars and them that ain't. 'Cept them that is stars
gets treated like stars, people fusses over them and wants to please
them. They fusses over me and wants to please me too. But I know it
ain't me. I know it ain't me they wants to please. It's just 'cause I'm
in her light, and they thinks 'cause I'm her personal assistant that
they can get from me to her. It ain't like that. And they was fussing
over you too. I was wondering how they was going to treat you,
'cause if anything you sho ain't Hollywood. But I was pleased to see
them fussing over you and trying to please you. 'Cause that's what I
wanted for you, Nadine. I wanted you to come out here and have
people fuss over you and try to please you, so's you'd know what it's
like.

I think she's going to go on and make some meaning out of it, but
she don't. Or maybe explain to me that they's just fussing over me
'cause they knows I'm close to her, and if she's in her star's light, then
I might have some influence with them too. And wasn't her star telling everybody, I want you to meet Nadine, I want you to meet Nadine, and treating me like I'm somebody? Well, I'ma show you your
guest bedroom, say Monkey Bread.

You mean I got my own guest bedroom? I says. I thought I was
going to bunk with you.

Naw, girl, this is a mansion. Everybody got they own guest bedroom. This is a mansion, girl.

When she show me to that guest bedroom I think I'm dreaming,
'cause it remind me of something out of the Arabian nights. Got one
of them canopied-type beds with that mosquito curtain. I think they
call it mosquito curtain. And everything else look like it real silk,

and there's those thick Arabian-type carpets, those Oriental carpets, those Persian-type tapestries, and loveseats that looks like they's out of some Arabian dream.

Ain't that mosquito curtain, I asks.

Yeah, I think that's what they call it.

Y'all got mosquitoes?

Naw, girl, we ain't got no mosquitoes. That's just for the decor. That's a reproduction of a bed they used I think in one of them original Valentino movies. I know one of them old movies. This bedroom supposed to look like it belong in the palace of a sheik. All the bedrooms has got they own theme, but I thought you might like this one.

Yeah, I do, I do, I sho do.

We know who we are, though, don't we, Nadine?

What?

I still know who I am, said Monkey Bread.

That don't mean you don't belong here, I say. I starts to tell her about the trade show actress, but I don't want to specify her even to Monkey Bread, 'cause Monkey Bread be telling everybody she a trade show actress before she become a starlet, and like I said, maybe that ain't in her portfolio.

I ain't talking about that, I'm just talking about, you know what I'm talking about. Sometimes I think I'm the only person here who do know who they are.

I got to admit I did like being out there in Hollywood and having them fussing and trying to please me. Course I know if I'd gone out there not in the company of Monkey Bread's star, they'd've given me the bum's rush. I mean the same people who was fussing and trying to please me. 'Cause I did stop in one of them fancy stores, just so's I could tell Delgadina I been in one of them fancy store. I mean they's people in there buying thousand-dollar shoes. I'm there watching this woman put on these silver shoes that's thousand-dollar shoes. She pretend she ain't notice me, but this security guard starts watching me real closely. When I starts out of the store seems like I hear him say into that cell phone of his, The one in the blue with the French braids. Now I ain't bothered nobody in that store 'cept to be there. And already they's got me under surveillance. 'Cept these ain't no French braids, fool.

Now y'all know I ain't going out to California just to meet them movie stars. I tell Monkey Bread to take me to her temple.

Temple?

You know where Nzingha preach at.

It ain't exactly a temple, Nadine. Unless her home is her temple.

It a nice house, but a modest house. It got a large living room, though, one of them long living rooms, and there's nothing but African-American women in that living room. They's a lot of rooms in that house, though. When Monkey Bread show me through them rooms, I feel like I'm in one of them Italian movies I seen once, where you keep going through these different rooms. In one of them rooms, they's womens sitting at a computer, in another they's sitting around a table making a quilt, in another they's reading, not just books but a lot of bound and unbound manuscripts and Monkey Bread say that some of her writings is in that room. She refers to it as the New African Women's Writing Room. Then there's another room that's got nothing but papers in it, a computer and some of them computer files, you know, and Monkey Bread stops in that room, lifts up some papers and gives them to me. One is The Daughters of Nzingha Complaint Form and the other is The Daughters of Nzingha Not for Members Only Membership Card. I won't provide y'all with no copies of they complaint form, but y'all can read they Not for Members Only Membership Card. I ain't included their complaint form 'cause y'all has got to have a guerrilla personality to fill out them complaint forms and I ain't know which of y'all has got a guerrilla personality. Y'all that believes y'all has a guerrilla personality can contact the following organization for a copy of their complaint form which is similar to The Daughters of Nzingha Complaint Form:

For more information, call, write, or e-mail us:

The New Guerrilla Lawyers
P.O. Box 444
Las Vegas, Nevada USA 89119
Tel: 1-800-NEW-GLAW
info@ngl.com

I ain't sure whether they is the same guerrilla lawyers that works with the new Underground Railroad, whether they is guerrilla lawyers that works with the Daughters of Nzingha, or whether they is independent guerrilla lawyers.

And there's a kitchen where the womens is cooking. Few of them even reminds me of Aunt Jemima but I ain't want to say that. And there's a room that's got sculptures and pictures in it. One of them pictures have got two fists joined together. They's a man's and a woman's fists, but they ain't fighting each other, they's joined together. Monkey Bread say that that the logo of Nzingha's Daughters, that although it's a women's group, that picture is the symbolism of they ideal. Now I'm wondering why they's got to be fists. Now you know I ain't got to explain that, says Monkey Bread. And they's several other rooms that Monkey Bread shows me. One they calls the Catapus Playroom which is a room for the children's to play in. They's got girl and boy childrens playing in that room. They ain't just got toys in that playroom, though. They's got things like computers and learning-type toys, and some of them children's is even teaching each other how to speak languages, like Swahili and Japanese. They's a room called the Hidden Talents Room where womens can go to find out they different talents. They's another computer room, and then they's a room called the Truth Room. I got to tell y'all the truth. When I opens the door to that room expecting to see lots of people in it, they ain't nobody in it. I gots to tell y'all the truth even about the Daughters of Nzingha. Monkey Bread says they's a few people in there sometimes, though. She say you don't just have to be a Daughter of Nzingha to go in that room, and that even mens sometimes goes in that room. It ain't a well-frequented room, though, she says. It seems like it's got all kindsa communications equipment in it, but the center of the room is a table with books on it. They's only a very few books, though, that Monkey Bread calls the Truth Books. I didn't go inside the room myself, so I can't tell y'all the titles of them books. One were a large black book, seem like it were about eight and a half by eleven inches, a couple of inches thick. The strange thing about that book were it didn't have no title written on it nor the name of its author. Monkey Bread said you had to open the book to read it and you couldn't judge it by its cover. When you opened the book, you couldn't just read it, you had to keep reading it. [Note to reader: The Daughters of Nzingha bookstore assures you that it is not the book you are currently reading.]

And even upon reading it you didn't always understand it. And most people weren't even wise enough to open it. Then there was a thick green book and a pamphlet-size green book. There was a red book. Though these had titles on them, I couldn't read the titles. There was another book that was beige and tan and green. I couldn't read the title of that book neither. There may have been a few other books in that room, but there were very few Truth Books. Monkey Bread said most of the Daughters of Nzingha, when they wanted to do some reading, would go to the Daughters of Nzingha library or the Daughters of Nzingha bookstore. These places contained the Truth Books but also had other types of literature, which, to tell the truth, didn't always tell the whole truth.

I asked Monkey Bread whether she'd read the books in the Truth Room.

I reads them and rereads them, she said, but I ain't grown in spiritual wisdom enough to fully understand them. Sometimes I listens to the tapes, though, and looks at the videos, and gets on to the Internet. A lot of the womens goes in there when they first becomes members, but they don't stay, 'cause they's expecting to learn truths about everybody else, and finds out them books teaches them more truths about theyselves. I mean it tells you truths about other peoples and truths that ain't about peoples at all, but I think it's the truths about theyselves that keeps a lot of even us Daughters of Nzingha womens out of that room. To tell the truth, Nadine, a lot of us still thinks that this is a political organization or a social club, and though Nzingha don't exclude the fools amongst us, a lot of us has got to grow to significant wisdom to enter that room. We ain't all gots to be Mrs. Wisdom, though. 'Cause Nzingha don't play that.

She said other things about that Truth Room, but y'all got to be a member to hear it. We went into the Daughters of Nzingha Library and she got she other papers that she give me. The papers said Not for Members Only and like it said were only for those that weren't members. I suppose members had they own secret literature. However, she give me the *Not for Members Only Daughters of Nzingha Newsletter*, the Not for Members Only Daughters of Nzingha brochure which described the organization and its mission and the Not for Members Only Daughters of Nzingha membership card. Y'all ain't supposed to share even the Not for Members Only Daughters of Nzingha literature with just anybody. Then they was Our Inspiration Room, which contained portraits of peoples of color. It weren't one of them rooms there they puts portraits of all the firsts like in a lot of them exhibition, where even they tells you that Beethoven were a person of color. A lot of them portraits in that room I ain't never seen before, 'cept there were a portrait of Malcolm X, Garvey, and Martin Delany. There was a portrait of Nzingha, the original Nzingha, someone who looked like a Hawaiian queen, Sojourner Truth. And they were portraits of other womens I ain't never heard about. So it weren't like one of them typical exhibitions, like I said, that has everybody you's ever seen in the media no matter who they is. But you know me, I keeps looking around for the folks I've seen on television or read about in them books telling you about the first colored people to do this or that thing. Even the first colored person to play Jim Crow is in exhibitions like that. Didn't even see no entertainers in that room, 'cept as soon as Monkey Bread got in there she started singing. But y'all know how Monkey Bread is. She is who she is.

To tell the truth, I thought there would be just women in that Our Inspiration Room, as I thought there would be just books by women in the Daughters of Nzingha Bookshop, 'cause I knew there were a lot of African-American women reading groups who had started to read just books by other African-American women. But the Daughters of Nzingha Bookshop contains books by men and women, and even books written by children themselves. And it contains a lot of what the Daughters of Nzingha refers to as the noncanonical literature, which is literature by persons of color which is often not written about by academics nor even reviewed in the mass media. Which ain't to say it excludes the canonical literature, though it has a few buyers that only buys the noncanonical literature, though knowing the Daughters of Nzingha the way they does, they knows a lot of them ain't gonna read a book unless they's heard about it in the mass media. They also has a section containing all of Oprah's favorite books, whether or not they's written by persons of color. In fact, that section of the bookshop even have a banner that say OPRAH'S FAVORITE BOOKS.

They're not all my own favorite books, said the manager of the bookshop, but I value several of them and they gets the ones of us to come in here who would not ordinarily read a book but believes that everything they need to know they can get just by asking somebody. Course the men who frequent our bookshop, the few that realize that this is a shop for them too, and who don't devalue the Nzingha name and know that we carries their own canonical and noncanonical literature and wisdom books, don't go over to that section of the bookshop at all. I suppose it's because they've seen too many fools amongst them on the *Oprah* show. . . .

But I've seen fools amongst us women on the *Oprah* show, said Monkey Bread.

Yeah, but we're always presented as being fools for men, whilst the men are presented as being fools for who they are themselves, at least that one one of the gentlemen who don't go to the Oprah section told me. And you very rarely see men on there who are fools for some woman.

Well, I still gots to watch my *Oprah*, says Monkey Bread. Although Nzingha prohibits it now whilst we has our meetings. But I notice she don't schedule no meetings whilst the *Oprah* show is on, 'cause she knows that there is many of us, I got to speak the truth, that wouldn't come to the Nzingha Center, and there is still those of us that when we gets here still spends us time telling everybody how we came to the realization that we ain't the only fools amongst usselves. I don't think we should stop watching *Oprah* myself, 'cause there's some that says we's been infiltrated by the FBI and the CIA and that even some of the womens that comes here trying to help us to assist them to get off welfare is actually on the payroll of one of them groups or the ones who claims they is using us organization as a bridge between jail and the world, or maybe even it's the bankers amongst us.

What do you mean, Monkey Bread? asked the manager of the bookstore.

I mean, maybe it might be best for us to continue to watch *Oprah* doing us meetings or even Sally Jessy Raphael, because it will inspire the FBI and CIA to think our mission is to be a social club. I'm glad you've got some music in this bookstore, though, 'cause I can't even buy me Oprah's Favorite Books unless I got the opportunity to buy Erykah Baduh, Mary J. Blige, Queen Latifah, and Anita Baker. Did you see the video where Mary J. Blige is dressed up to look like all the womens of color in the world, looking like a Cherokee and then like one of them Indians from India and then like one of them Asian women and then like her own natural self.

While Monkey Bread and the bookshop manager are talking, I open some of the Not for Members Only Literature. I gets their Not For Members Only Membership Card:

The Daughters of Nzingha
Not for Members Only Membership Card

Membership Name:

The above membership card is valid only if unsigned and guaran-tees that the above unlisted member is a card-carrying Not for Members Only Member of the Daughters of Nzingha. Full mem-bers of the Daughters of Nzingha are not required to carry member-ship cards, because they know who they are.

Then there is a licensing agreement that allows even Not for Mem-bers Only Members to start their own Daughters of Nzingha Book-shops, Banks, Computer Stores, and Guerrilla Law Centers.

Part of the agreement reads: The Daughters of Nzingha is an un-registered trademark of New Africa Incorporated. It may be used only by descendants of the victims of the African Diaspora Ho-locaust.

That kinda surprised me, 'cause at first I thought they were going to allow just anybody to use the trademark, and it seemed to me that they would register that trademark if they didn't want just anybody to use it, but only descendants of the victims of the African Diaspora Holocaust. I also thought that they would say only those people who were the true Daughters of Nzingha. You know, the spirit of Nzin-gha. Nor did they limit the use of that unregistered trademark only to the women descendants of the victims of the African Diaspora Holocaust. I also noticed that they did not simply say African Amer-ican or New World African, and I supposed by using the term Afri-can Diaspora that they meant Africans everywhere. I hoped as I scanned their literature that no one would mistake me for being with the FBI or CIA. In fact, I was wondering that when I looked up and noticed a book called *A Bear for the FBI*. I wanted to purchase it,

but I didn't want anybody to think I was so interested in the FBI.
Then I went over and purchased one of the books from Oprah's Favorite Books. One of the books by Maya Angelou. Then after I purchase the Maya Angelou book, I felt a little more comfortable in
who I knew I was myself not to care if I was mistaken by someone
else as being who I wasn't that I purchased the Melvin Van Peebles
book *A Bear for the FBI* which someone had filed among the noncanonical books, although I had always thought it to be one of the
canonical books myself. I also purchased *I Am a Spy for the FBI*
which was actually a satire about someone at a small New England
college during the 1960s who is mistaken as being a spy for the FBI
because rather than majoring in Sociology, Anthropology, or Political Science is taking the following courses: Theoretical Chemistry,
Botany, and Environmental Journalism. I ain't sure if those are the
subjects, but it seemed as if the person signed up for all the courses
that weren't considered socially relevant, so that somebody decides
that she must be FBI. The novel turns out to be written by one of the
leading campus revolutionaries who is also a former member of the
FBI. Then we discover the novel itself is a fiction, written by a Theoretical Botanist, who is being followed by the FBI while working
on the Cactus Project in sub-Saharan Africa. Then we find out that
the novel is not really a novel but a journal. Then we find out that the
journal is really the journal kept by the spy following the theoretical
botanist throughout sub-Saharan Africa and who has only been
quoting from the theoretical fiction to prove that the theoretical botanist is a modern-day subversive who is still a true believer in the
revolution, and that the Cactus Project isn't really a botanical project
at all.

They's got a lot of rooms that's got books and papers in them,
'cause she took me into yet another room and give me some incorporation Papers and said that I should consider incorporating my trucking company. I thought that the papers would request that I pay the
Daughters of Nzingha thousands of dollars and that maybe that was
their ruse, but it said I didn't have to pay them no upfront fees to fill
out and file the incorporation forms; however, to incorporate the fee
was less than $100 and I would be provided with my own guerrilla
business lawyer and financial advisor. It also listed other Not for
Members Only members who had incorporated their businesses via

the New Africa Corporation on Turtle Island a.k.a. America, although the forms themselves were reprinted by the Daughters of
Nzingha Press in association with the Garvey Center, with which
they were supposed to be linked, although the Garvey Center was
maintained by African-American men, and they were also linked to
another organization which consisted of both African-American
men and women. The latter organization sounded to me more ap-
pealing, but when I asked Monkey Bread the name of it, she refused
to tell me who they were, except to say that they weren't any of the
organizations that I would read about in the newspapers. And unlike
the Daughters of Nzingha, they didn't recruit. You got to already
know who you are.

You mean who they are, I said. Don't you mean the only way you
can join them is if you already know who they are? One of them secret societies?

She didn't reply. She handed me a book of proverbs. I opened that
book expecting to find some African proverbs in there like at least
the one about it taking a village to raise a child or other often unac-
knowledged African proverbs but there weren't no proverbs, 'cause
she said you's supposed to put your own proverbs in there. Then she
lead me into that large living room where there's more women. I
think they's all going to be dressed up to look like Africans, but they
don't. They's got some African-looking women and them in African
clothes, but a lot just looks like everyday women. Some is even wearing blue jeans. There's old women and middle-age women and
young women. Some of them women got little girls sitting beside
them or sitting in their laps. Some is wearing scarves or got Afros or
wearing braids or straightened hair. They's every range of complexion. Some looks like they's just got off welfare or out of jail, others
looks like they's everyday working women, some looks like professional women, schoolteachers and bankers. I say bankers 'cause
Monkey Bread say one of them owns her own bank and is teaching
some of them other women the banking business. I know one of
them is in the computer business 'cause she the one taught Monkey
Bread about them computers. Few of them looks like they's in the
entertainment profession. I'm wondering which of them is Nzingha.
She's introduced me to a lot of them. There's that Cooter and Nyam-
Nyam and her other friends that I recognizes from her descriptions

of them in her letters. One of them women is named Asia and another is named Africa. I'm wondering how you can name a woman
after a whole continent myself. There was one named Canada, I suppose because of the history of New World Africans fleeing to Canada. One of them women Monkey Bread say is named Kultur.
Strange thing is these womens is also fussing over me and seem like
they's trying to please me, and fussing over each other and seems like
they's trying to please each other. They don't offer me no Budweiser,
though, 'cause they's all drinking some kinda herbal-type tea, which
Monkey Bread call they root tea and it supposed to have a lot of
healing herbs in it. I don't know what she call the name of them
herbs, but the drink do taste good. Drinking it I feels like I'm having me some type of communion.

Nzingha is here, someone says.

And I'm looking around, waiting for Nzingha to enter, but she
don't.

Nzingha is here, the women say.

And I'm still looking around like a fool, waiting for Nzingha to
enter. Now I know Nzingha a real woman, 'cause in all her letter
Monkey Bread say she real and I even seen a photograph of her.
Ain't I seen a photograph of her? But I'm the only one of these
women looking around for Nzingha and they's telling me she's here.

Where Nzingha? I ask, when Monkey Bread and me returns to
the mansion. I was hoping I'd get to meet Nzingha.

When you are one of us, you will, she said. She is shy to meet
anybody. She does not meet just anybody. But she is very fond of you
and I have told her all about you. She knows who you are.

Why they saying she's there.

Because she is. She is everywhere. There is Nzingha and there is
our priestess, Nzingha. She is everywhere.

That night I slept in the African room. I was surrounded by African masks. I was surprised that the star would have an African room.
Except for the masks, though, and the African sculptures, it looked
like a modern bedroom, an American bedroom. Did I dream of
Nzingha? I dreamt that an African-looking woman came into the
room wearing a mask. I could not tell which of the women she was.
Was it Monkey Bread herself? I only know that she began talking
to me and that it was in a voice that was mightier than Monkey

Bread's. And she seemed to speak in the accents of Africa America, of Caribbea, of Africa itself.

I salute you, Mosquito. I am Nzingha, warrior queen. Do not think of me as your leader. There are no leaders here. We are here to serve each other.

I laugh because I think of the stereotypes. Then I think of a science fiction movie in which aliens come to each to serve man bringing a strange book written in their alien language, and it turns out the book is a cookbook. They take humans back to their planet, fattening them up while they're on the spaceship.

There are no leaders among us, she repeats. We may if we choose elect a leader among ourselves.

I didn't want to listen to what she had to say. I kept asking, Who are you?

I am who you imagine me to be, she said. Perhaps I'm your own exemplary self.

I knew what she meant. She didn't mean that I was exemplary. Monkey Bread had said in one of her letters that Nzingha believed that everyone had many selves and that one of their selves was an exemplary self. A self that contained one's exemplary nature. Monkey Bread said that her philosophy of selves rather than a self was from African philosophy, though I didn't understand shit about it myself.

But you know who I am, she said.

Who?

I am Nzingha. I am here.

So I didn't know if I had dreamed her or if Monkey Bread's security person had let her into Monkey Bread's entrance and she'd actually come to meet me. Or was it Monkey Bread herself? I didn't think it was Monkey Bread. Well, she was taller than Monkey Bread. I cannot tell you if I merely dreamed her. I don't know for certain. Sometimes even now I think I hear her. But if it is her, it is in the form of my own thoughts talking to me. Nzingha? I ask. I am here, she says. We know who we are, don't we, Sojourner? I should not tell you this. For some among you will think I'm a nut.

Except Delgadina. When Delgadina came out to visit me when I had my restaurant in Cuba, New Mexico, I tells her about Nzingha.

I thought you said you never got to meet Nzingha, she says. I thought you said you went out there to California and met everybody but Nzingha. I got to tell y'all that Delgadina has started her own private investigations company, that she got her own private investigations company. Maybe I shouldn't tell y'all that, 'cause that's beyond this story. But I gots to tell y'all she weren't no bartender when she come out to visit me in Cuba, New Mexico. She don't look like no private investigator, but that's what makes good private investigators. She comes bringing me a copy of a new novel by Charlotte Carter, an African-American woman mystery writer, a novel called *Rhode Island Red*. And one of her own published stories written under a pseudonym. The editor of the little publication calls her a subversive intellect. They don't know I'm Chicana, she said. If they knew I was Chicana, they wouldn't say nothing about my intellect, even subversive. When I write as a Chicana, the closest they come to saying anything about intellect is to say I'm witty. She don't look like a private investigator, though, like I said. It ain't like in the movies where you just looks at them and knows they's a private investigator. And she don't just private investigate for anybody. She's got to believe in the people.

You can't believe in that many people, I says. I don't see how you can stay in business.

I ain't like you, Mosquito, is all she'll say.

I ain't sure what she mean. Maybe she mean I'm more stingy with belief than she is. 'Cause to tell the truth if I were a private investigator and used Delgadina's rules of private investigator, wouldn't be many people at all I'd investigate for. Not many people at all. Maybe Delgadina be one of them. Maybe Ray. Maybe Monkey Bread. Maybe a few others.

But you learn more about people, especially predatory types of people. I try to keep my wit, but you know, you get to learn about the evil passions. I mean, you learn about them being a bartender, but it ain't the same. But I've got a pretty good reputation as a private investigator. Like when I tended bar. People know me. They know I don't take nobody's shit. But there's a lot of devils in the world, Nadine, and a lot of them is the so-called people in authority. I always knew that. I mean, I knew it intellectually. Well, I didn't just know it intellectually. But now I'm learning so many new ways of investigating these bastards. There's rogues everywhere, Nadine.

Rogues everywhere. But I'm learning all kinds of new means and methods of investigating the bastards. If you ever need you a private investigator, you come to me. I can investigate all classes and types of people. And they don't even know I'm investigating them. All I got to do is play who they think I am. I usedta think there wasn't any real virtue in being who I am. But this is the perfect profession for me. Even when I'm amongst them that don't favor Chicanas, I can still do my work.

Of course I couldn't imagine ever needing no private investigator. Then it seemed kinda contradictory her saying that she played who other people thought she was, and then at the same time had the virtue of being who she is.

So then I'm sitting at the table in my restaurant with Delgadina and I'm drinking some root tea that Monkey Bread sends me sometimes from out there in California—I'd like to serve it in my restaurant, but it's especially blended and ain't really supposed to nobody drink it but members of Nzingha's group—and she's eating some of our restaurant's famous pancakes. They's more like tortillas, though, 'cause they's thin pancakes wrapped around apples or cherries or peaches or other types of fruit.

These are good, Mosquito. And then I'm telling her about Nzingha, that I think I met her and that I sometimes think I hear her voice in my thoughts. Am I a nut? Do you think I'm a nut?

Naw, Mosquito, you ain't no nut. That's sorta like a mystical experience that you had. You ain't no nut. Well, you might be a nut in America, but in some people's worlds what you had is normal. In some worlds people have mystical dreams all the time. I know sometimes when I travel through Mexico, the tales I hear. Not just the tales for the tourists, but the true Mexican stories. Why some of them would seem like fantasies to most Americans. Most Americans read Latin American literature like they're reading fantasies, but a lot of that is reality. Naw, you ain't no nut, Nadine. I wish some Mexican Nzingha would talk to me. Of course, she wouldn't be an Nzingha. She'd be somebody else. I wasn't going to tell you this, but the man that owned the cantina, Mr. Delgado, he didn't want you in his bar. He just had it in his thought that you were a drunk and a nut, and he didn't even know you. I told him you weren't either one of them. After a while, he figured you weren't. 'Cause he knows I don't suffer fools. Naw, you ain't no nut, Mosquito. Don't let nobody try to tell you that.

Some of y'all listeners confuses me when I'm talking to you. You wants me to clarify this and wants me to clarify that and wants me to clarify where I am and wants me to clarify who I am. And many of y'all don't know who Mosquito is from Nadine, and who Jane and Sojourner is when I'm telling y'all I'm all of them. Ain't I told y'all that? Contradictions in reality don't mean it ain't real. Maybe it's some of y'all who don't know who y'all is and needs to clarify yourself. I'm just kidding with y'all. I don't mind clarifying what peoples needs to know. Maybe modern stories just looks at theyselves, but I always prefers the storytellers that looks at them they's talking to, and acknowledges what other peoples needs to know. I ain't gonna tell y'all all my business, though. I don't play that. Even Nefertiti Johnson don't play that, and she's writing true confessional romances. Here they are. I've got the whole Nefertiti Johnson collection, but y'all got to read them for y'allself. Naw, I ain't gonna loan none of y'all that one. But Nefertiti Johnson can be bought anywhere.

CHAPTER 13

YOU'RE A STRANGE BIRD, DELGADINA SAY. WE'S in the cantina. This the real time of my conversation, 'cause I know there's a lot of y'all that ain't used to hearing conversations that jumps back and forth between real time, the past, the future, and virtual time, it be Monkey Bread be telling me about that virtual time, 'cause this the modern world, and that virtual time could be any one of them times. I think them Nefertiti Johnson romance novels is written in virtual time, 'cause they reads kinda like jazz in they rhythm, and sometimes I don't know where I am in them novels, or where the reader's supposed to be. To tell the truth, I be wondering how they publish them novels like that. 'Cause a lot of them novels you reads, them narrators always explains to you where they is. I mean, I'm explaining to y'all where I am myself, though I would really prefer to converse with y'all like in them Nefertiti Johnson novels. Even explaining to some of y'all where I am, y'all's still asking me where I am. Y'all claims y'all understands everything you read in them Nefertiti Johnson novels, but I guess that's 'cause she's telling y'all only what y'all wants to hear. When I ain't reading Nefertiti Johnson, who I like to read, I likes to reread that book I told y'all about. I gots me a tape of Ernest Gaines reading that Monkey Bread sent me and who she say her favorite writer, though I think he probably reminds her of one of them men she were in love with myself. Or maybe after she heard that rumor say he suppose to like fast womens. Ain't no rumor, say Monkey Bread, 'cause I read it myself in a book where he says himself that he likes fast womens. Man got a right to like a fast woman without being a bad man. Y'all know all that mythology y'all'self. Some men says I'm a fast woman, some men says I'm a slow woman, but I ain't met a man that ain't told me who they thinks I am. And I lets them tell me who they thinks I am. 'Cept I heard Delgadina say, Don't you tell me who I am. You don't know who I am. But me I likes to hear them tell me who they thinks I am. Well, I ain't going to say that. I don't always likes to hear them tell me who they thinks I am. 'Cause most the time it ain't who I think I am myself. But I lets them tell me. Delgadina say that a flaw in my character. Seem like to me if you know who you are, you can let people tell you from time to time who they thinks you are. And I told Delgadina that.

Mosquito, you don't mean that, she say. She even looking at me like I ain't the Mosquito she think she know. She know I am that Mosquito, but she looking at me like I'm a different Mosquito.

I'm talking 'bout men that loves me, I say, drinking my Bud Light, while she's wiping off the counter. I ain't talking 'bout them others. I ain't talking political, I'm talking love. Even my ex-husband had his own idea of who I am. I weren't his ideal for a woman, though he coulda been my ideal for a man. But he do got his ideal woman now.

Even love's political, say Delgadina. But I'm not talking politics either. I don't want some man to come claiming he loves me and then telling me some idea of myself that's a low opinion. Like there's men that see me working in this bar that's got a low opinion of me till I sets them straight as to who I am. I mean, men don't just have to tell me who I am that's got a high opinion of me. But that's a flaw in your character, Nadine.

I'm not talking politics, Delgadina, I'm talking love. If a man loves me I want to hear who he thinks I am. I don't think it would be some low thing.

You're naive. Drink your Bud Light. I don't want somebody telling me who I am even if it's some high thing.

I ain't so naive that I believes that. Anyway, I don't think most
men is raised to know a whole woman. And I ain't so conceited in
being a woman myself to think that we womens is raised to know a
whole man. That's why there is so many fools in love.

I likes the stories myself, the Ernest Gaines stories, I mean the
stories he tells. I likes to listen to that tape and them storytellers on
that, 'cause they sounds like true storytellers, and they don't tell nobody nothing that don't need to be told. I remember listening to one
of them stories and the only way he describe this woman be saying
she a Creole woman with a pile of black hair. Now that's the only
thing needs to be said to describe that woman, 'cause the listener can
take that and figure out who she is. You's got to be a man to know
something about whole womanhood to even be able to describe a
woman like that. And when you hears them stories you knows the
whole self of the women in them, as much for a man to know. Ain't
like them nineteenth-century novels where the writer take a whole
page or maybe several pages describe that woman, who she is, who
she think she is, what she look like, what other people think she look
like, as if the listener can't figure out none of that for they ownself.
And you don't need to know all that about that woman in that story.
Maybe in the nineteenth century they needed to know all them
things about them people. Suppose I tell y'all that the throw pillows
I've got on my sofa looks like they's made from a court jester's hat.
What that tell y'all about me? And then what if I tell y'all that on
the wall I gots me one of them posters that kinda a collage with them
historical figures in the collage, but the central figure in it is Malcolm
X, and that poster were made before the movie. 'Cause you know a
lot of peoples they is buying them posters on account of the movie.
What else that tell y'all about me? And suppose I tells y'all that I
likes to mix a little cinnamon in my Bud Light? What else that tell
y'all about me? I ain't know how to describe my hair. I still wears
it like the Afro weren't just a hairstyle but a statement of faith.
Sometimes I wears it underneath a scarf. Sometimes I braids it like
Whoopi, though she ain't the only one that wears them braids y'all.
Sometimes I puts it in a French roll, or puts it in them little rolls like

you see on some of them African women. I'm told my progenitors usedta wear their hair in every one of them fashions before they dis-covered the straightening comb, which ain't to say there some of us Johnsons got that good hair. Maybe that another reason I likes that Nefertiti Johnson, 'cause her romantic women might be over there in Italy sipping champagne but they's got they natural hair.

Anyway, it's after hours in the cantina restaurant and Delgadina sweeping up. I be reading one of Monkey Bread's letters and a story. She musta forgot to enclose that poetry and the photograph of herself and Cooter and Nyam-Nyam, though she did include the brochures on the international trade fairs, and she know I got dreams of at-tending one of them international trade fairs maybe even in Tokyo, though I ain't sure I can picture myself in that Tokyo, though them Pacific Rim countries is supposed to have the most modern trade fairs, like that Hong Kong.

I don't know how I got hooked on them trade fairs. I was trans-porting them industrial detergents when I seen me this giant pavilion and I asked folks what's that and they be saying it's a trade fair and I ain't never seen so many newfangled technologies, so I got hooked on them trade fairs and got one of them magazines that tells you where all the trade fairs are. So now I'm dreaming about that Tokyo trade fair. They's African Americans in Tokyo, though, 'cause I re-member seeing this documentary on Tokyo and they interviewed some Americans including some African Americans working in To-kyo. Ain't just them professional people in Tokyo either, they's them bar hostesses and factory workers. Seem like them African Ameri-cans had better things to say about that Tokyo than them European Americans, 'cause them European Americans they be complaining about them Japanese the same way that the African Americans is al-ways complaining about the European Americans; they be talking about discrimination 'cause they's Westerners and be talking about that glass ceiling in them Japanese companies and be sounding just like they's the niggers in Japan. The same ones who in America be telling the African American they don't know what they's complain-ing about. But I ain't heard none of them African Americans even them bar hostesses and factory workers say nothing about the glass ceiling.

They got them minorities in that Japan, though, that they treats like niggers, too, them Koreans and them other minorities that they got a special name for them that ain't pure Japanese, though them Japanese minorities be saying that the Americans they don't know the difference between the pure Japanese and them minorities. And them minorities they be having them their demonstrations 'cause they don't want to be the niggers of Japan. That's why a lot of them peoples comes to America. 'Cause they's the niggers in they own countries, but in America they gets to play white. One of them they interviewed, one of them African Americans, a expert on Japanese film, and be talking about the films of one of them minorities and be saying how it seem like every group or culture has got their niggers and the niggers of one group or cultures is the masters in another, and the different groups and cultures be jostling each other so's not to be the niggers, but the niggers in one country the masters in another, like them freed slaves that returned to Africa, they supposed to made them native Africans into they niggers. And them Koreans they's got they own whole country where they ain't the niggers, though I guess them Koreans they be having they own minorities, they own nig-gers, and maybe they's Japanese in Korea that's niggers. At first she say she study the pure Japanese films, then she got interested in the films of the Japanese minorities. I have always dreamed of those in-ternational trade fairs, though, like I said, but I've only attended lo-cal and national trade fairs. Except for the trade fair in Canada which you could call international and where I met my first African.

So I'm rereading that letter from Monkey Bread and rereading them stories and wondering whether that Vietnamese African-American woman a real woman or whether she Nadine pretending to be a Vietnamese African-American woman and wondering whether Vietnamese Americans would consider her a stereotype and then I'm looking through that Tokyo International Trade Fair brochure and dreaming of Tokyo while Delgadina is sweeping. I can't tell y'all about Delgadina sweeping, though, till I lets y'all read that newsletter from the Daughters of Nzingha. I don't exactly re-member when I received that newsletter, I just know that once I opened my mailbox and there was a newsletter from the Daughters of Nzingha, which Monkey Bread had sent me:

THE

Daughters of Nzingha

N E W S L E T T E R

NOT FOR MEMBERS ONLY EDITION

PUBLISHED BY THE DAUGHTERS OF NZINGHA

FREE SPEECH PRESS

In this newsletter, Daughters of Nzingha writers from around the world will find an opportunity to express themselves and publish their works. We publish everything. What you do not find published here is kept in our archives in Zurich, Morocco, Brazil, and other countries where there are Daughters of Nzingha. If you have a manuscript in any genre, please send it to us for excerpting. We publish manuscripts in the following formats: Nzingha Free Press Publications, Bound Manuscripts, Electronic & Print Archives. We are especially interested in works by unknown and noncanonical African Diaspora authors. We are always seeking keepers of our archives, information on which you will find in this newsletter. However, the following are the qualifications for archives keeper:

1. Must be seekers after knowledge, wisdom, and learning, including self-knowledge.

2. Must conquer your own ignorance.
   (Not the same as number 1.)

3. Must not submit to your own ignorance.
   (Not the same as numbers 1 & 2.)

4. Must have a guerrilla personality.

5. Must have the facilities to maintain an archives.

6. Must have a long memory.

7. Must be a hidden agenda and conspiracy specialist.

8. Must not be an apologist for the race, since not all of the documents contained in our archives are "praisesongs."

9. Must be independent. (Required reading: *Essays in the Literature of Rebellion* available in the Daughters of Nzingha Bookshop.)

10. Must be a Daughter of Nzingha or be sponsored by a Daughter of Nzingha.

(Other qualifications are unpublished.)

Invitation

We invite you to read this newsletter only if you are a Not For Members Only Member of the Daughters of Nzingha.

Dear Not for Members Only Daughter of Nzingha,

This is the newsletter for every Not for Members Only Daughter of Nzingha. This newsletter was suggested to us by our Free Speech editor Monkey Bread—y'all know who she is from her regular stories and poetry in our *For Members Only Newsletter,* in stories and poetry that offer simple explanations for the essential nature of the Nzingha woman, many written in unedited free speech. Monkey Bread offers us theories of everything, but in the form of stories. She does not tie the loose ends of any of her stories together, for that is not the nature of free speech. It was Monkey Bread's idea that we begin to collect anything and everything written by the descendants of the African Diaspora Holocaust, collect all stories, novels, poetry, and other literary documents, including works not only by our women but our men as well. The Daughters of Nzingha knows that this is a great responsibility, but it could also be a great achievement. Monkey Bread is becoming known among us as one of our teachers, at least in the area with which she is most familiar. (We wish she would "leave the plantation," though, and stop working for that movie star!— Amanda, woman-friend! If you allow her, this womanfriend will have you listening to "Jim Dandy to the Rescue" more than attending to the purposes of the Daughters of Nzingha.) We value her however as a good storyteller. She also helps us to maintain the Romance Section of our Daughters of Nzingha bookshops with books by the leading African-American writers of romance. We are also, because of her advice, starting our Angela Section. For you politicos, we don't mean Angela Davis, although we do have all her publications here. We mean the nonconfabulatory former engineer turned romance writer. Ain't she from Georgia

427

somewhere? Now y'all can find all her books in the Daughters of Nzingha bookshops. We kinda wish she would send us some engineering manuscripts for our archives, though.

How Can We Help You?
If the Daughters of Nzingha can help you, contact us.

No More Meetings
The Daughters of Nzingha is no longer holding meetings. Daughters of Nzingha members have turned our meetings into a social club, so we are no longer holding meetings. Daughters of Nzingha may now contact us only via Mrs. Cosmic Bigbee, mrs@bigbee.com.

Daughters of Nzingha Demonstrate
Some Daughters of Nzingha have been demonstrating and giving speeches outside of our centers for the right to hold meetings. Daughters of Nzingha management declares again: No more meetings!

Monkey Bread, Our Featured Writer
Monkey Bread was born in Covington, Kentucky, in ———. She was educated at a public high school and sometimes attended classes at Kentucky State College. She currently resides in California as the personal assistant of one of the leading Hollywood stars. She has an uncompromising and magnetic personality (when asked to salute even the Daughters of Nzingha's flag, she stated, I don't salute nobody's flag), a strong appetite for root tea and is a leading advocate of the African chewing stick and sponge rather than Western dentifrice. She is the ex-wife of Danny James, the Afromodernist writer (it was a secret marriage) and refers to herself as a former lover of John Henry. ('Cept you don't stop loving John Henry, she always adds.) She's a good cook. (You should taste her guacamole. It is featured in one of our restaurants, Chitlins con Carne with Poi. Do you know of any other race of women that can have a restaurant that serves such a combination of foods except for some of the secret societies in New Orleans?)

A Plea
Leave the Plantation!

An Artistic Event
The Mada and Coliene Gallery of Greenwich Village, New York, is exhibiting the works of the

renowned New World African Artist and Artist's Agent Paul Condor.

Jim Dandy to the Rescue

Monkey Bread is having another one of her famous Jim Dandy to the Rescue parties on her star's yacht. All Not for Members Only Daughters of Nzingha are invited. Monkey Bread says, This is a good, old-fashioned party and is not for the Negrophobics. We're going to have Native African watermelon, fried chicken, pork chops, turnip greens and grits! There will be numerous opportunities to party with the local coloreds as the yacht cruises the historical towns and villages of peoples of African descent. Monkey Bread has created a Jim Dandy to the Rescue Web site so that all partygoers can make their reservations online. You may also make your reservations at the Chitlins con Carne with Poi Restaurant in Oakland, California.

Recreated Settlement

Some members of the Garvey Center are recreating the Palmares Settlement, the seventeenth-century settlement of fugitive slaves in Brazil. Those who wish to become part of the New Palmares Settlement should contact your

Garvey Center. We especially want engineers and those with skills. Joan Scribner Savage, minor rock star, is one of the financiers of the new settlement; however, even Joan Scribner Savage says, We do not just want singers and dancers; this is a real settlement not a Broadway show. Note: You should easily find the settlement once you are in Brazil. We cannot print its whereabouts for security reasons.

Visitors' Center

The Daughters of Nzingha (Oakland) is starting a visitors' center for those women who are descendants of the victims of the African Diaspora Holocaust. Now you do not even have to be a Not for Members Only Member of the Daughters of Nzingha in order to learn more about the Daughters of Nzingha.

Archaeologist

Catherine Shuger's adopted daughter has her degree in archaeology and is now in Egypt where she is translating hieroglyphs and the *Papyrus Eber*. (This is not the same Papyrus Eber who is a member of our group.) She is also a leading professor at the Nzingha University.

Tour of Movie Studio

Monkey Bread is inviting some of us for a tour of the movie studio where *The New Confessions of Othello* is being filmed. Her star is playing the role of Desdemona in the neo-African modernist movie version of the novel. Bring your box lunches and root tea.

Herb Garden

We are seeking a new herbalist for our herb garden. You must be familiar with ancient African herbal plants and be familiar with Sophia Esmond's *Ethnoherbology*. Contact Sophia at her Ivory Coast address.

Retreat

(Censored for all but the *Members Only Newsletter*.) A refuge for New World African women.

Professors Sought for the Nzingha University

We are seeking professors to teach at Nzingha University. Please send us your course proposals. Currently we have an interest in teachers of the following:

- Theoretical Chemistry
- Afrocentric Biology
- Maritime History
- Lighthouse Management
- Afromodernist & Free Speech Literature

Argentine Tango

Dine at the new Argentine Tango, owned by Tita Rodriguez, Afro-Argentinean member of the Daughters of Nzingha.

Our Womenfriends Get off Welfare

Several of our womenfriends have started a new Daughters of Nzingha bookstore. They specialize in Afromance novels and say that so many New World African women have been purchasing their publications that it has enabled them to get off welfare.

Think Tank

The Garvey Center for the Advancement of Science in the African Diaspora is starting a new think tank. All New World African scientists interested in joining this new think tank should contact the Garvey Center or Prof. Dr. Naughton J. Savage, Esq., of New Guerrilla Thinkers Inc., a subsidiary of Savage Thinkers Inc. (additional information available on request).

Note: You all know Dr. Savage, the husband of our own Joan Scribner Savage.

NEWS ABOUT DAUGHTERS OF NZINGHA MEMBERS

Note: Some Daughters of Nzingha names are not printed for security purposes.

Ethnobotanist Sophia Esmond has started *Ethnoscience* magazine.

So-in-so is senior editor with our archives and is eager to receive manuscripts for our womenfriends. She is also the editor of Nzingha Online.

Joan Y'all Can Print My Name Scribner Savage is the new director of the Nzingha Foundation.

Y'all-know-who-we-mean's new book *Remix* is now on sale. It is the first volume in a series of books remixing Western literary tradition. She is the author of the wildly satirical *How to Build a Negro, Fuck the Fucking Fuckers and Their Fucking Fuckery: A Neo-Caribbean Novel, The Colored People's Book of Architecture and Urban Design,* and *Steppenwolf and Step 'n' Fetchit: Afro-eccentric Essays.* She has been doing a tour of all the Nzingha bookshops and says her book *How to Build a Negro* is still her most best-known and popular novel. I'm surprised by the extent to which New World Africans ourselves are still interested in the Negro. We are still very much interested in the Negro no matter how often we change our names. I'm a New World African of multiracial and multicultural descent myself, but it is also good to know that peoples of color are wise enough now to know that they are the primary audience for my satirical novels.

OUT OF THE COUNTRY IN SOMEBODY ELSE'S COUNTRY

California Association of Nzingha and the Association of Nzingha of Northern Canada are in the Caribbean on a new strategy which cannot be printed here for security reasons. They are said to be setting up protected areas for persons of color and the other disenfranchised peoples of the world who consider themselves natives.

The San Pedro River People of Color Birdwatchers Association are watching birds along the Nile.

The author of *The Mysterious Rendezvous in the Congo* is in the Republic of the Congo.

One of our editors is traveling in China and learning Chinese herb medicine.

The designer of our Daughters of Nzingha T-shirts, a noted sculptor, is holding a workshop for Not for Members Only in Prague. Most of us don't know why she considers herself a Daughter of Nzingha, since she spends most of her time in Europe. (If any of y'all other neo-African Cosmopolitan Artist Types Seeming to Prefer Neo-Nazi Europe for Europeans–Only Europe to You Know There Are Still Slaves There in Africa or even the It's So Hot It Makes Even My Chemically Straightened Hair Nappy I Should Start Wearing an Afro Again Girl I'm Glad I Never Stopped Wearing an Afro It Never Was Just in Vogue Styling the Natural What Kinda English is This Caribbean Y'all Must Be Reading Apollinaire You Know Them Stories That's Set in Prague Colored Girls in Prague who are interested in learning how to sculpt contact Shuger@aol.com.)

INTERVIEW WITH MONKEY BREAD

What made you get the idea that we should just publish anybody and everybody?

Well, I do limit it to the descendants of the African Diaspora Holocaust or various peoples of color who identify with Africa.

But doesn't that mean we don't have any standards?

Well, we do say that our standard is free speech. That's our standard.

When did you first get the idea, though?

When I was drinking root tea. And also sometimes when I write letters to my womanfriend who is a Not for Members Only member of our group. She collects my letters and my stories which I've written over the years and reads them, you know. So I thought our organization could do that. Nadine is sorta like my own personal archives.

432

Have you changed your approach to writing over the years?

Well, I keeps trying to get freer. You know, mixing my words with whatever I wants to mix them with. I think there's a lot of limitations in print. That's why I would really like to use all forms of audio and video. If there could be a book that contained not only the book but other forms of communication as well. Where when people opens the book it ain't just a book, but can contain a CD or a video, a newsletter, a press release, all kindsa forms of communication.

You should go on the radio.

Now, you know they'd just think I was Aunt Jemima. At least the Daughters of Nzingha claims they know who I am and that's why I considers y'all along with Nadine to be my primary audience. I don't mix my words or change my words around none. I don't have to explain none of my meanings to y'all. And I don't negotiate my identity with nobody. Even our own peoples. I am who I am. I do writes for peoples who knows how to hear me. I writes with as many words as I wants and digresses as much as I can to get the ideas to the listeners. I think that is so important. Not only to tell the readers what happens in a story but to get your ideas to them, your opinions, and to also tell the reader how you feels about the events in the story. And also to be able to create characters who have different ideas and opinions from the ideas and opinions that you yourself has. Some peoples thinks when you creates a character and the character expresses an idea or a opinion that that is your own idea and opinion but I likes to create characters who are they own true selves, and I thinks that only the Daughters of Nzingha and Nadine knows what I'm doing. Somebody says that they's essentially three kinds of readers: them that participates in the stories that they hear, them that just listens, and them that asks, What story was that I just heard? What was that story about that I just heard? You know what I mean? Ideally, a story should make them listen to all them kinds of listeners in one story.

What else do you have to say about the kinds of characters that you create?

I believes that there is several kinds of characters: they is the characters who does what they ain't supposed to do, characters that does what they is supposed to do, characters who does what they'd like to do. You can create characters as people ain't supposed to be and create characters as you thinks people is, create characters as you thinks people should be, and create characters as you thinks peoples should want to be. They is all types of characters. But you's got to have readers that knows what types of people that you is creating. Suppose you have created characters as they ain't supposed to be in order to tell peoples that they ain't supposed to act that way, but the readers thinks that you is creating characters as you thinks that people is, or they thinks that you approves of the behavior of them types of characters. But characters has to be they own free and true selves. I don't believes that you can come into the book and say to the readers, I approves of this character, this character I don't approve of, I believes that people is like this and they ain't like that. I suppose they is some authors that does that, but I believes that characters has the right to they own thoughts and opinions, even if they is my inventions, but I knows that Nadine knows that, that's why she my primary audience along with the Daughters of Nzingha, though Nzingha herself prefers the heroic types of characters.

Who is your favorite writer?

Ernest Gaines.

I would think that being a Daughter of Nzingha, you'd choose a woman-friend writer.

Naw. I likes the way that his characters narrates them stories, although some people thinks that he is conventional when compared to the more experimental-type writers. Writers like Clarence Major or Ishmael Reed or Steve Cannon or Trey Ellis. And I likes the man's name. He's got a perfecting name. I ain't a member of the Perfectability Baptist Church like Nadine. I'm a Catholic. But I think that Ernest Gaines has got a perfecting name. I believe that is his true name, though he has got the name of somebody that has named theyself. Equally important is the types of characters that he creates. And what he says about how we's got to tell our own histories, 'cause you can't find our true histories in them news stories. Well, he was talking about going around to the newspapers trying to find the story about a murder that he knew about, and it wasn't in none of the newspapers, 'cause they wouldn't put it in them newspapers and magazines, but the folks would talk about it, so that's how it became known to history, because the folks themselves would talk about it.

Of course Ernest Gaines could write about it.

Yes, he could write about it, but he can't write about everybody's stories. That's another reason for my idea. 'Cause it's us got to give worth to us own history and stories. Plus there is the factor of them people protecting themselves, so there is a lot of us history and stories that we's got to tell us ownselves. We protects usselves too, 'cause there's stories us don't want each other to tell. Course we wouldn't mind telling them if they wasn't overhearing them, 'cause that's African folklore. In African folklore, there's folklore they wouldn't tell them collectors at all. And a lot of them collectors they didn't understand about digressions, so they'd edit a lot of them folklores so that it weren't the true folklores. And they didn't always know the worth of a story. And a lot of the story in them folklores ain't just what you hear. But them Africans they tells all kindsa stories when they's telling they ownselves stories. They's Africans in America that only wants you to sing praisesongs. But in Africa they is all kindsa songs and stories.

How do you tell a story?

When I tells a story I starts with the story.

What do you mean?

I starts with the story. A lot of these modern-type storytellers the people keeps listening and still don't know what happens in them stories. But I starts with the story itself. I know a lot of times even when Nadine tells stories she don't start with the story. Sometimes she starts with everything but the story, but me I starts with the story.

I don't exactly understand you.

'Cause I ain't started with no story, that's why. I starts with the story, but the listeners themselves has got to decide whether the story is worth hearing and how much of it they wants to hear. A lot of my stories only the Daughters of Nzingha thinks is worth hearing. Some of my stories only Nadine thinks is worth hearing. And I's got other stories that only me myself thinks is worth hearing. Then I's got stories that I don't think is worth telling, and I's got other stories that I thinks is worth telling, but I ain't found nobody, not even Nadine, that I thinks is worth telling the stories to or that I thinks is worthy listeners. I mean, there is people that you thinks is worthy people, but that don't have to mean that you thinks that they is worthy listeners to every story that you has got to tell. Nadine is worthy to listen to almost every story I gots to tell, 'cause I's been telling her my stories and opinions since preschool. I tries to keep the peoples knowing where they is in my stories, not just where the characters is, but where the listeners is in my stories. I wants all my listeners to keep listening, but I don't require that they listen to the whole story, just what they thinks is worth hearing. Sometimes I even writes stories that I don't want the readers to hear all of.

Yes, I've read some of those stories of yours.

Some peoples thinks that that's a flaw in the story, 'cause they's used to stories where the writers wants you to hear all of the story. I might not want to tell all the story in that story. I might want to tell it in another story, or I might want someone else to tell the rest of the story, or I might not think that that story is a story that readers is supposed to or even needs to hear all of, but there's them that thinks that that is a flaw and ain't the storyteller's prerogative. Or I might introduce a character in one story, but you don't meet that character again till another story. Or maybe a minor character in one story is a principal character in another story. For example, I met a woman out here in Hollywood who started telling me a story about herself and she mentions somebody named Nadine. Nadine is my friend Nadine, and I knows it the same Nadine, but when she mentions Nadine Nadine is just a minor character in her story, 'cause she just met Nadine once and ain't know Nadine, but if I tells my own story about me growing up in Covington or even about me in Hollywood Nadine would be a principal character and personality in my story, but in this other woman's story she is only a minor character, though I wouldn't say that Nadine is a minor personality in anybody's story, though they is probably people who ain't know Nadine who could create Nadine as a minor personality. I knows they is probably white people that has met Nadine and if they even mentions her in they story it is probably as a minor personality type and maybe even a stereotype.

That's because in most Western fiction. . . . I forgot what I was going to say about Western fiction.

I do set some of my stories in the West, but I don't tell no cowboy stories. That don't mean no cowboy can't be a component in none of my stories. Cowboys can sneak into almost anyone's stories. Cowboys and cowgirls can be metaphors in almost any story. I likes to hear what peoples thinks of my stories, so that's why I always likes to send copies of them to my womanfriend out in Texas City, I mean St. Mary's, Texas.

I've never heard of St. Mary's, Texas.

It's another St. Mary's named after St. Mary of Egypt, you know, the other Mary. I likes to have her tell me what she thinks about my stories. That's Nadine. She's in St. Mary's, Texas. [Y'all knows I ain't in St. Mary's, Texas. I'm in Texas City, Texas. And Monkey Bread knows it.]

You keep your stories simple.

Most of them, yes I does. 'Cause there usedta be this woman that sometimes my womanfriend and I would visit when we was visiting her cousins in Lexington and she would sometimes read us very simple little stories and poems and then she'd say, Think deep, so I calls my simple stories *Think Deep Simple Stories,* though they ain't all simple stories. She wouldn't just read us simple stories and poems, but when she would read us simple stories and poems and we thought we understood them just because they was simple, she'd say, Think deep. That would let us know that they was Think Deep simple stories and poems. 'Cause they's people that thinks that if stories and poems ain't got a lot of literary allusions and ain't read like T. S. Eliot that you ain't have to think deep about what you's reading or that it ain't literature. So they thinks that T. S. Eliot is more literature or knows more about literature than them who writes Think Deep simple. My womanfriend I sends my stories to is the only one I know can think deep enough that even when I sends her silly stories she knows what I'm saying. Other people they be saying this is silly. We usedta be in love with the same man, so she probably knows me better than anybody else. You can't go higher in a story than who you are or how you defines yourself. Even a simple story can tell you who you is. Plus she supposed to have one of them auditory memories, I mean Nadine, so she knows to read my stories aloud so's she can remember them. And even if Nadine don't think deep enough for some of the stories I tells, she remembers them. When I can't find none of my stories, Nadine's got them in her long memory herself.

Is she a writer, your friend Nadine?

She tells peoples stories. 'Cept sometimes she tells peoples everything but the story. This might be her inspiration to write some of her stories and send them to us. I think she can go higher than who she is myself. Or who she thinks she is. When I writes stories, I can't go no higher than who I am. But I think Nadine can go higher than who she is. I advise everybody receiving this newsletter to send us their stories, though, whether or not the tellers of the story can go higher than who they is.

Not everyone.

I mean, the descendants of the victims of the African Diaspora Holocaust who's got stories to tell or the peoples of color who identify with Africa. And don't dumb 'em down. A lot of y'all thinks when y'all send out y'all's stories and especially from past experience with the mass media that y'all has got to dumb 'em down. Or when y'all thinks that y'all is writing for colored people, I mean for the common colored person. Don't send us no dumbed-down fictions. Y'all can write in Ebonics if y'all wants too, if y'all thinks that Ebonified English is more creative than standard English, which some of y'all fools just associates with them that ain't people of color, but that don't mean y'all's got to dumb down y'all stories for us. And I'm also talking about y'all from the South, though there is people from the South who writes a more refined English than standard. We would like to receive free and confidently written stories. Y'all can also send tape recording and e-mail fiction. If you ain't Erykah Baduh don't send us no videos unless you's telling a story in it. Let us know where the story is taking place, describe the peoples and scenes that needs to be described. Remember that listeners have got imaginations and sometimes their imaginations are richer than anything that they can hear. Tell your stories right and the listener tells as much of the story as you do. Fact, the listener might tell the better parts of the story.

Directory

Some of the Daughters of Nzingha have asked for a directory listing all the Daughters of Nzingha internationally. Although we would like to accommodate you, for security reasons we are unable to do so. If we were a social club or a political organization, we would print a directory and send it to everybody. The FBI and CIA probably know who we are anyway, but we believe that your unsigned membership cards are sufficient. They are color-coded so that only we know who you are. Please note that your membership cards are valid even if you do not choose to carry them, that is, you do not have to be a card-carrying member of the Daughters of Nzingha to be a Daughter of Nzingha.

Guidelines for Submitting Stories

Send us only the stories you want us to hear.

Note: Your story may already be on file with us if you told it to anybody who might be a Daughter of Nzingha or even a Not for Members Only Daughter of Nzingha.

Notes from the Secret Membership

If you have any ideas for Daughters of Nzingha, please let your Daughters of Nzingha representative know.

Daughter of Nzingha T-shirts are available in all sizes.

Sophia, are you in Russia?

The Fundamental Nature of the New World Africa Woman Lectures. Please send us lecture topics. We also like controversy. You scientists out there, what lecture topics do you have? We do not just want to be lectured to by social sociologists. All lectures are kept in our archives.

The Official Guide to the Daughters of Nzingha is not being published for security reasons.

Ulysses Johnson, write to your girlfriend c/o the Nzingha Bookshop in Kansas City.

Whoever sent us the Spiritual Mother Project documents, we are keeping them in our archives.

🐿️

Along with the newsletter there was another publication which contained information and an excerpt from the Daughters of Nzingha archives:

FROM THE

Daughters of Nzingha

ARCHIVES

Our archives contain novels, novellas, short stories, journals, plays, poems, screenplays, film treatments, nonfiction and various other documents. The following is an excerpt from one of the manuscripts included in our archives. Our archives contain other Electra manuscripts.

THE MYSTICAL AND PROPHETIC
WRITINGS OF ELECTRA

In her "native cultures" (Native Hawaiian, Native American, Native African, Native Spanish, even Native Irish—her maternal grandmother was Irish, born at a time when the Irish were also "niggers" in America, before being allowed to "play white") Electra might have been considered a mystic or a shaman in such cultures that allow women to be shamans. She had visions, heard voices, had prophetic dreams and intuitions, even practiced an intuitive form of Chinese feng shui—is it a form of Chinese household philosophy? You have probably heard it talked about as it is more well known in the West now and even Western corporations sometimes hire feng shui specialists. It is where things in a household or building must be arranged in a certain order to promote household harmony and well-being. She would have chronic pains. She would be misdiagnosed once as having epilepsy. She would be put on a drug for epileptics, which would do her more physical harm than good. It would be discovered she was not epileptic. Yet, epilepsy was a "name" for what she had. When she was no longer an "epileptic," no longer taking the drug for epilepsy, there was no longer a name for what she had. Was she just crazy? Was she neurotic? She would be diagnosed as being schizophrenic. There was no way for Western culture to deal with a woman such as Electra but to label her these things. She would defend her own so-called schizophrenia by naming intelligent people who were schizophrenics.

I do not know if she was really schizophrenic or whether this was another misdiagnosis from a culture who couldn't categorize a woman such as herself in any other way. And schizophrenia was a way not to take her chronic pains seriously, to give her drugs. Could she have healed herself if she had been born into one of her "native cultures" or among their "alternative healers," or even stayed in the country where she was born in a country town among the healing plants and flowers? Fresh air, spring water, sunshine. I read once of a culture who lived in a certain valley in Mexico, who drank a certain water rich in minerals and nutriments, who breathed unpolluted air, who ate natural and fresh foods and fruits and vegetables and herbs. People in that certain valley were always healthy. It was only when people from that valley would go into the city that they would become sickly and would have to return to that valley to be made well again. Even their bodies, used to the natural medicines, became sick when taking the artificial city medicines. The so-called medicines that made the city people well, or supposedly made the city people well, actually made them sick. They were only made well when they took their own natural medicines and were in their own natural environment. Because my mother's mother, my grandmother Amanda, for whom I am named, grew her own fruits and vegetables, kept an orchard and a grape arbor, got mineral-rich water from Spring Station or from a well, Electra was mostly well when she lived in the country. Her bouts of sicknesses would seem to occur whenever she'd move to the city. She tells of once living in the city so she could go to school. She became sick. I do know when we moved from the country to the city, she became sick. It is then that she began to develop chronic pains. Was it the city water with its chlorination, was it the polluted air, was it taking Western medicines—Standbacks for headaches, Ex-Lax for constipation, etc.—rather than natural medicines that Amanda knew about and used. (Amanda never took aspirin or other Western medicines, except for Fletcher's Castoria occasionally. She would probably use such things as codliver oil and other essential, healing oils.) Electra lived for a couple of years as a baby in Indiana with her mother and father, a Native Hawaiian who was also intermixed with Spanish.

Amanda my maternal grandmother (who wrote plays herself and song lyrics, but never published; whose father or grandfather, after Emancipation, founded his own town, purchasing the land from his former slave-owner—I do not say "master"—but who herself worked as a housekeeper and "domestic" to support her fourteen children, except for a time in Indiana during the First World War when she worked at the roundhouse polishing engines) had when I was a baby wanted to adopt me to keep me in the "healing" country. She had not liked our "city house." Perhaps she had presaged my mother's physical miseries there, her development of uncontrollable, chronic pains. Her misdiagnoses by medical doctors, maybe even what the medical doctors would eventually do to her. (I had my own mystical experience involving my grandmother, but I won't detail it here. The Daughters of Nzingha have asked me not to include other details, including human rights abuses, for security purposes.) My mother would not have known about environmental pollutants. Did my grandmother know about them? When such things were even suggested to her Western doctors as possibilities for my mother's chronic illnesses, they would laugh or dismiss them and prescribe their medicines. Or say the cause was schizophrenia, or even hypochondria. This is not the essay of "Electra's Adventures with Western Medicine," although I believe that such an essay should be written. This is told only as a background and context for her prophetic and mystical writings. I have mentioned that Electra's Native Hawaiian father was intermixed with Spanish (hence her love for both the ukulele and the guitar). I do not know about the other "native cultures," but I do know that the Spanish have been said to have produced more mystics than any other culture, thousands and thousands of them. There are surely mystics from her other native cultures. The Spanish, of course, because they had "literary mystics" we know more of them, while other cultures' mystics and mysticism are seen as an indication of their primitiveness rather than an indication of culture.

There are other things that I could say about Electra's mysticism, but I would probably be labeled schizophrenic myself. Some other things I say in fictional or poetic form in an epic poem for Electra.

A poor black woman born in the South near the beginning of the century—even if that was not her own sense and vision of herself—would not have been called a mystic or a shaman, but would have been called just plain crazy, or epileptic, or schizophrenic, or whatever. But I think her writings reveal otherwise.

The Prophetic Writings

There are at least four of Electra's writings, a novel, a screenplay developed from the novel, a short story (listed in *New African Women in Literature* and available from the Daughters of Nzingha Archives), and an experimental poem. There is still a strange sense of prophecy in these writings and in their very vocabulary and setting. (Additional details omitted for security purposes.)

The Mystical Writings

This section discusses mostly the poetry and song lyrics and the poetics of Electra and their mystical quality and subject matter. It also considers some of her unpublished and unrevised writings that suggest the mystic in their language and vocabulary or in Western tradition "the schizophrenic." Electra is from the generation of African Americans who would study such things as Latin and recite Latin and Greek literature and the classics. In the structure of some of her poetry and her use of rhyme and subject matter one can see some of these traditions. Her chronic illnesses kept her from pursuing much of her learning and even developing and revising her writing in ways that it could have been developed. However, there is a high-mindedness and love for learning and "cosmic" subject matter that is revealed in her poetry, creative nonfiction, and unrevised writings. There are also the folkloric novels that show the range of her cultural intelligences.

As a student in Middle America and the southern commonwealth, Electra was considered the top student. (She was also noted for her great beauty, which transcended mere physical beauty to Beauty Itself, but our concern here is the intellectual.) She even tells in her autobiography of classes, such as her Latin class, where certain teachers would send her to the library to study, since she already knew the material. In other classes she frequently heard the teachers remark, "Go to the board, [her maiden name]." Having the responsibilities of wife and mother as well as being chronically ill, much of Electra's intellectual and literary ambitions were unrealized except for the encouragement of editors, readers, listeners, and various others. One has the "sense of possibility" in many of her writings and subject matter, her often apparently simple but deep style. (Electra has an experimental autobiographical book called *Think Deep* which is an expression we'd often hear her say when things seemed simple at interpretation or surface meaning.)

Some of the works included here are also discussed in a book-length literary study of *The Writings of Electra*.

The Writings of Electra, in the Daughters of Nzingha archives, include novels, novellas, stories, poems, song lyrics, plays, interviews, screenplays, and film treatments. Photocopies are available from the archives on request. Selected works may also be viewed on the Internet at our ftp site.

Do you have questions about your Nzingha membership? Want to receive another newsletter? Looking to start a business? Want to know when is the next Daughters of Nzingha meeting? Want to buy a T-shirt? Contact:

You-know-who
Secret Statement of Faith Mission
Zurich, Brazil, Morocco & Georgia

Dear Daughters of Nzingha,

Although you may not be a member of the Daughters of Nzingha, which is not an organization nor do we hold meetings, we want to thank you for your spiritual support and for being a womanfriend of one of our members who is featured in the newsletter which we are sending you. We appreciate you.

We hope you like this newsletter. If you have stories, please send them to us. You can also send us stories on behalf of others. (Unsigned for security reasons; we are not just being paranoid.) Should you wish to reach us, please contact your Daughters of Nzingha representative. (Only you know who your Daughters of Nzingha representative is.)

Dear Nzingha Booksellers,

Thank you for your support. We are sending you a copy of our new newsletter and promotional material. You will understand why we have decided not to print our directory. Please freely order books from us and also bound manuscripts and prepublications from our archives.
(Unsigned for security reasons; we are not just being paranoid.)

Dear Monkey Bread,

Here is your copy of the newsletter, which you may forward to your womanfriend. We don't want to send the newsletter to her directly. Some of our womenfriends went to your party and said the watermelon was the best watermelon they'd ever tasted. They were sure it must be a true African watermelon. However, please be advised that the *Daughters of Nzingha Newsletter* no longer publishes party announcements; these however may be sent to the numerous organizations. If you know of anyone who would make a good keeper of our archives, please let us know. We are especially seeking those who are hidden agenda and conspiracy specialists with a long memory. You may contact me via my e-mail address.

You-know-who-I-am

P.S. The books that you are interested in purchasing are not yet being sold in our bookshop, but you can purchase them from almost any mainstream bookshop.

We cannot answer the questions that you sent us on issues of class and social status as we are not sociologists. However, you may forward your questions to the National Association for Socioeconomic Research or "the New Class Bigots" radio show.

The Goodest Gal in Tulsa by Amanda Wordlaw may be purchased here.

We have on order *My Sweet Alabama Newspaperman, Telling Good Love Stories, Sweet Sweet's New Lover,* and *Dreaming Denzel.*

We are unable to provide you with additional information on *The Writings of Electra* other than the information available in our Archives or on our ftp site. Yes, we do have certain documents on file, but they are only available to our guerrilla lawyers. Is she someone you think you know?

The organization that you are looking for is:

International New World African Writers and Artists Association

New Africa Corporation of Turtle Island a.k.a. America

Atlanta, GA 30324

Note: This is not a confabulatory organization, so only send them real letters.

Yes, we have received letters from the League of Campus Revolutionaries Reunion Committee asking us not to admit you to the Daughters of Nzingha. They mistook us for an organization and thought that we hold meetings to which you should not be admitted. However, we believe that you are a reformed person now. Even if you aren't, you do good work with our archives and we like your stories and poems. And so far, you're the only Daughter of Nzingha who reads and rereads the wisdom books in the Truth Room.

For light reading, however, this is a list of the New World African romance titles we have on order:

Temptation's Serenade, Forever Sweet Thang, A Beguiling Fugitive Slave's Refrain, Sweet Sweet for Always Rapsong, Devoted Sincerity Rap-

song, Seasons of Love's Night Magic, Hidden Agenda Conspiracy Love, Intimate Rapsong in Neo-African Ecstasy, Jim Dandy in Love, and Nefertiti Johnson and the Nefertiti novels:

- *The Passion of Nefertiti*

- *Nefertiti's Promise*

- *Valentino's Kiss*

- *Nefertiti's Moon*

- *Sweet Neferiti's Seductions*

- *Nefertiti Incognito*

Monkey Bread, don't bullshit us. If you are not requesting this list of books for yourself but someone who is not a Daughter of Nzingha, please let us know.

Also, we know you have been asking about the true identity of Electra. We cannot provide you with that information, nor can we tell you the true identity of Nefertiti Johnson, whether you want this information for yourself or someone who is not a Daughter of Nzingha.

We are adding some of Electra's maxims to our wisdom books. We are also seeking a curator for the Electra manuscripts. Our curators should have the same qualifications as our archives keepers. Most of our curators are also archives keepers. Monkey Bread, you are the most eclectic of our readers, but we think you are bullshitting us about Nefertiti Johnson. No, Nefertiti Johnson is not Amanda Wordlaw, as she writes all her romance novels using her own name.

Note: The Rapsong novels were originally rhapsody novels.

All books may be ordered by calling 1-800-NWA-4444.

❧

I ain't as eclectic a reader myself as that Monkey Bread, but that newsletter have kinda whetted my appetite to know the true identity of Electra, 'cause it seem like from reading about her I've read her work myself. And like every fan of African-American romances, I wants to know the true identity of Nefertiti Johnson. Anyway, so Delgadina's sweeping. That was before the time of me receiving that newsletter, but I still wanted y'all to read that newsletter, and if it's a real newsletter some of y'all might want to send in y'all's stories. Even if it's a confabulatory newsletter it might inspire some of y'all. I think it's a confabulatory newsletter composed by Monkey Bread and pretending to be from the true Daughters of Nzingha myself. I do know that while some of them romance titles by African-American women authors is real, I ain't never been able to find none of them other titles. To tell the truth, I think it's a confabulatory newsletter and that it's really a story written by Monkey Bread but in the form of a newsletter, and that she added that seemingly real letter to herself to make it seem like it were a more realistic story when it is probably more surrealism than reality. And another reason I think that newsletter is confabulatory is because she mentions people in it that I know to be confabulatory theyselves. Them is Mada and Coliene and Paul Condor, 'cause I played them in a play. I played Mada in a play and Monkey Bread played Coliene. That Paul Condor's name were Paul Konder, but it's still the same individual. That were the time that I went to Lexington to visit with my cousins and I brought Monkey Bread with me. We went to visit the neighbor woman that wrote poetry and stories and played the piano. She weren't feeling well, so we told her that we was going to the movies. I don't remember what movie, but when we told her what movie, she told us we could make our own movie. You know in them days there weren't mens like Denzel Washington and them other variety of New World African men in the movies, except for Sidney Poitier, whom the girls amongst us all adored—we had all just turned teenagers, you know—even though he were an "older man" we still adored him, although he were never loving any women who resembled us in them movies. I don't know what movie we said we was going to. We was waiting for her to give us maybe one of them movie cameras, so's we could pretend we was making us own movie, but instead she give us the script for a little movie. It were really a play, but she said that we could use the words in the dialogue of the play and go out on the patio and pretend we was making us own movie. We didn't have all the props for the movie, but them we didn't have, she said, we could pretend was there. We did two movies. One were about a man that kinda reminded me of my uncle Buddy, 'cept his name was Luther, and he weren't exactly like my uncle Buddy, 'cause he weren't going about searching for no Unicorn Woman to romance. He were on furlough during the Second World War and he come back to this little town to romance his girlfriend, who had the same name of the neighborhood woman who wrote the play, except the character were a character in a play which we made into an imaginary movie. I believe the name of the play were *Luther*. I believe my uncle Buddy had a friend whose name was Luther though I don't believe he were the same Luther as the Luther in the play. Monkey Bread and me got to play love interests in that play, and we got a couple of good-looking boys in the neighborhood to play Luther and Joe who were the principal male characters in the play.

But I'm talking about Mada and Coliene and Paul Condor. That were the other play which we made into a imaginary movie. I played Mada, Monkey Bread played Coliene and one of them good-looking boys played Paul Condor and pretended he were an international artist. In both them plays which we made into imaginary movies I got to be the director because of my hidden talent for having a auditory memory where I remember everything I hear. So's all everybody had to do was to read all they lines to me, so's I just would remember everybody's lines. A lot of them that couldn't remember they lines, I would remind them of they lines. But in that play it were Monkey Bread played the love interest of Paul Condor. I played the director of the play reimagined as a movie and I also played the character of Mada. There was a white character talked about in that play, but since there weren't any whites in that neighborhood on account of segregation, he had to be a imaginary character. The play were supposed to be set not in the South but in Greenwich Village among African-American intellectuals and artists, although they weren't referred to as African Americans in them days and one didn't see plays and movies about African-American intellectuals and artists. This the play which we made into a imaginary movie:

Blessings for Coliene: A Play

Scene: The stage has a multiple setting in modernistic/surrealistic style: CO-
LIENE's *luxurious living room, a cafe in Greenwich Village, and* PAUL's *art stu-*

dio. In her living room, COLIENE *is sitting at a piano composing music,* JO JO SPAIN *is sitting in the cafe drinking and flirting with* FRANCIE, *a waitress, and* PAUL *is standing at a canvas working on a painting of* COLIENE. *The play is set in the 1950s or it may have a contemporary setting. On the wall of* COLIENE'S *living room is a mural painted by* PAUL KONDER. *There is a large coffee table which* COLIENE *made and painted herself. Before the play begins* OCONNER *is seen painting the stairway.*

CHARACTERS

COLIENE, *a young African-American woman, a composer and writer*

JO JO SPAIN, *a young African-American man, very fair-skinned, an auto mechanic*

PAUL KONDER, *a young African-American man, an artist*

MADA, *a middle-age African-American woman*

OCONNER, *a middle-age white, a handyman*

FRANCIE, *a blond waitress*

COLIENE: [*at the piano, writing something on composer's paper; then she starts playing the piano and singing*] Hello, lover, Wouldn't you like to hear my song? Pull up your chair and listen I been a-singing all along,

I got plenty money, I've got rhythm and song, I've got a lot of something, That it takes to get along,

I've got a lot of loving I've been saving just for you, I've got a lot of everything that it takes for me and you.

I got the world if you want it Just say the words, I do, Then we'll both be married, lover, me and you.

[MADA *enters and hands her a drink.*]

COLIENE: Thanks, Mada. Don't you want anything for yourself?

MADA: Naw, I'd best be getting back. But I sho like your new house, Coliene. It's gracious luxury, that's what it is. It's wonderful. I knew you always wanted a house like this. A large brick house with a upstairs. Them large windows and gold-colored fine drapery. Large mirrors. Three bedrooms and two bathrooms. And them walls is true blue and royal. Shrubbery and trees all around it and flowers on the lawn. A house with a garden. That porch is like those porches down South, you know those porches the grand ladies court on and gossip, and that big old garage. Two Ford automobiles. I didn't know they built showers in garages.

COLIENE: I want to use it as a guest room, so I had Oconner build a room and shower above it. And Paul might want to use it as a studio instead of that little studio he has.

MADA: I know your secret. [*Pause.*] It's like art, though, ain't it? Well, they say architecture is a form of art. That's what Paul studied, but he couldn't find much work in it, so he took up painting. Rainbow hue in splashes to enchant. Ain't that what one of them art reviewers said of Paul's pictures? A stream of enchantment. Well, Paul could paint a picture of a house and it wouldn't be as beautiful as this one. Thank God for such graciousness.

COLIENE: I am grateful and happy. I have been blessed. It's just what I've always wanted.

MADA: And that beautiful grand piano, that must be your prize possession. Play me another of your melodies.

[COLIENE *plays another melody.* MADA *sings.*]

MADA: [*singing*] You may make me do, What you want me to do, You may make me strain When I want to gain, and You may do anything that you want to, But you can't Make me look down your road.

You may wrap me in rags, Make me pack up my bags And promise to take me away someday, And whatever you do, I'll still be true, But you can't make me look down your road.

You may even hide me, try me, hypnotize me, You may even lock me in chains, You may even bug me, You may even slug me, But you have nothing to gain, For whatever you do You'll make me blue, For you can't make me look down your road.

You may even beat me, Get someone to mistreat me, Bribe them to compare Wheel or deal me, But you'll have to kill me to take away my heart.

So you can do what you do, Say what you say, For I'll always be the self-same way, looking ahead, When you want me to look down, But you can't make me look down your road.

So whatever you do, Whatever you say, I'll always be, the self-same way, So do what you do, Say what you say But you can't make me, look down your road, Oh no, You can't make me look down your road.

I want to hear some more of that opera you're working on, the one set after the Emancipation. Sing me some of that.

[COLIENE *searches among the composer's paper*
and then starts playing and singing.]

COLIENE: Paul should really sing this part, or Jo Jo.

Out of bondage, Crackerwhip high! Precious story moving by. Great advancement, time to heal, gracious moments linger still.

Love, honor, honor bright. Lovers come from dark to light, travel onward, upward go, greet me sweetie, let me know. This I give, in dedication, to the sweetest girl I know.

Born of bread and sweet butter, sorghum molasses, cider and honey. Restless waiting, crossing line, blood brow sweat, but now bondage's over, and now, she's mine. Goodness, gracious, mercy, me. Sweetest little diddy I ever did see.

Mountains, valleys, hills and dales, wishes, longings, princelings, whales. High intentions, for this I adore. Pleasure, pleasure, make it more.

Hello, baby! I say to her. Well, I finally got enough nerve up. Can't compete, them other girls, sir, When Brown Sugar comes.

Brown Sugar comes, Sugar and me. We will have love, thanks be God above. Well! Won't take long, time grows near, I'm sort of crazy about that dear.

When a man's getting married, Sort of out of his mind, Just like a woman, if she loves, anticipating the moment, when it comes. Bride and groom, just give me room.

Richard, let me in. Move over, Dolly, I'm back again.

When Brown Sugar comes, Minds made up, Pretty as a speckled pup, Love that woman, my oh my, Wonder why I let them days go by.

Should have married her time ago. Well, now I just don't know. She's young and so am I, We just let some time go by.

Trying to save money, takes a lot; to keep chickens in a pot. She's got her hope chest for wedding fair. She's in luck, she's got my ever-loving care.

Wonderful woman, oh so sweet, a sunshine face, want you to meet. She comes into town, comes Sunday morn. All pretty, all adorned. Wedding day, man you guessed, Sunday, that day of rest.

Me resting? Be nervous as a clown. Still wishing yet, Sunday soon come around. Wearing my tails and all of that, Won't be long before I see my pet.

Best man is my brother Billy, Bridesmaid is her sister Milly. Got bridesmaids, wedding's in church, I'm anticipating, who goes first?

Suppose I'll be the first inside? Can't hardly wait to see my bride. Lives two hundred miles away. Can't hardly wait until that day.

She's got a head full of curly locks, beautiful brown eyes, high cheekbones that reach the skies, A peachy shape, I dare to tell, Me a salesman I got to sell.

Bought us a house on Fairview Way, Bright and pretty and Sweet and gay.

When Brown Sugar comes, I'll be around no more Fooling in this town, Settling down, and I'm going to stay, And nobody can keep our love away.

Love that woman, man, you've guessed. Come Sunday, day of rest. I'm taking Sugar in my arms. My how I need her charms.

Charming woman, with skirt up high, cutest legs, you'd ever spy.

When Brown Sugar comes, Sugar and me.

This I must confess, I'm sort of good-looking, when I'm dressed, got nice hair, an intelligent smile, my white teeth can shine, for miles. Kind of a fellow, what keeps in style, gonna live it up awhile.

Like that house on Fairview Way, Just right for Sugar. It's like her in every way. Bright and pretty and gay.

Got a nice green lawn, and round a fence, a stall for horses, and a house immense.

Pretty future, I agree, this sweet Freedom, and Sugar and me.

MADA: It sounds like they had ideals of men in them days. Of course it wasn't a ideal time. Where I'm from there's still little towns that got signs that say: "Nigger read and run, and if you can't read, run anyhow." And where they ain't got the visible signs, they've got the invisible ones. [*Pause.*] You and Paul have your very own art, though. That Jo Jo Spain ain't anything like y'all.

COLIENE: But I love Jo Jo.

MADA: I know you think you do. And you and Paul are "just friends." That Jo Jo, you're blind to his ways. He declares his love for you and you let him romance you. You're a fool, girl. You've got admirers, good men, even rich ones. Of course, I'm partial to Paul Konder. If I were a younger woman, I'd admire him for myself. I do admire him, but not for romancing.

[COLIENE *goes over to the coffee table and picks up a package of cigarettes, takes a cigarette out and lights it with the table lighter.*]

MADA: I really like that mural. That's Paul's. What in here is Jo Jo's? I bet he ain't give you nothing for your new house. Did he make that coffee table for you?

COLIENE: I made it myself. [*Pause.*] Jo Jo gave me this lighter for Christmas.

MADA: As tacky as he is.

COLIENE: Well, I cherish it very much.

MADA: 'Cause it's just about all he ever give you.

COLIENE: Jo Jo and I are getting married.

MADA: No. [*joking*] Does he know it?

COLIENE: [*sitting back down at the piano, smoking*] We've always talked about marriage, Jo Jo and I. It's just that we've always been so poor, like I told you. I didn't wanna marry him till we had more money. So we saved. . . .

MADA: You saved. Jo Jo couldn't save a penny. And I mean that both ways.

COLIENE: Why are you so hard on Jo Jo?

MADA: 'Cause I know his kind. Not like Paul.

COLIENE: We're the same kind. We both grew up so poor. Being poor doesn't add up to a full and happy life. [*Pause.*] Then I sold a few of my songs.

MADA: I grew up poor as a church mouse myself, but that don't mean I'm the same kind as Jo Jo Spain. [*Pause.*] I bet Oconner built that stairway, didn't he?

COLIENE: Yes.

MADA: It looks sturdy. You can tell he's a man that loves beautiful things, and likes to make the flowers grow, like Paul. I wish he were more like Paul.

COLIENE: What do you mean?

MADA: You know what I mean. [*Pause.*] I went out with him.

COLIENE: You told me he asked you out several times and you wouldn't go out with him.

MADA: I acted kinda silly, Coliene. Oconner, white and all. But, honey, as soon as we drank our first highball, I forgot he was white.

COLIENE: I told you he's a nice man. [*laughing*] You're his type, Mada, he told me so.

MADA: Well, I like him, but I can't get over the fact that he's white. [*whispering*] Wish I was like you, Coliene, you don't know no difference.

COLIENE: Oh, Mada, I know the difference. It's just that I lived so long with white, I'm used to them. I've never dated any one of them, though.

MADA: I thought Jo Jo was one when I first seen him, he's so fair-skinned and light-complected. Looks like one of those old-time movie stars with that slick hair and mustache of his. I've always had my suspicions about them. [*Pause.*] I've always liked mahogany-colored men like Paul. Tall, dark and handsome. Or short, dark and handsome, as long as they treats me right. [*Pause.*] But Oconner . . . I've always been a little withdrawing. Where I'm from, men like him sneaks around with women like us, but don't treat us like a proper lady.

COLIENE: Well, you'll get used to him.

MADA: [*laughing*] Yeah, if he gets me some more highballs.

COLIENE: Mada, you won't do.

MADA: He told me once he had money but he lost all his money in the stock markets and now's got to work as hired help. I thought he looked more distinguished than he is. You know, I'm a couple of years older than him? But that doesn't matter these days, does it? They say over there in Europe, women my age romances any man they wants. Just like them movie stars.

COLIENE: Mada, you know you could live right here with me now. Why not? I've got plenty of room. And I know you could use the money.

MADA: It ain't about money. You're a good friend, Coliene. I told Paul that I'd help you at least twice a week, Coliene, but I'll never leave Paul. He's the one saved me. He helped me when I needed help. Paul brought me up here from Virginia. I know, I know that I'm welcome here, but I can't leave my boy. My boy would be lost without me. [*Pause.*] My husband had run off and I lost my home, and I was staying at a little rooming house. I won't tell you all my story, 'cause you don't need to know it. And being a woman, you probably know it anyway without my telling you. But he helped me, so I in return help him. He's the first true man I ever met. And you know, the first true painting he painted was of me. He said he'd been looking for a woman of my kind and looks to pose for one of his paintings. Paul painted me and called the painting *Mother*. He decided to keep that painting for hisself. He wouldn't sell that one, not even to Mr. Tyrone, who sold some of his paintings in France and Germany. He keeps it in his drawing room. I traveled with him in Virginia, and then I come back here with him to work as his housekeeper. And you don't need me to stay here, Coliene, 'cause you and that Jo Jo are getting married.

COLIENE: Jo Jo is a worthy man.

MADA: [*Pause.*] I'll be back over in an hour. I gotta go see about Paul's dinner.

COLIENE: We can all have supper together here tonight to celebrate the new house.

MADA: Well, now, that's a good idea.

COLIENE: We'll make a foursome. I'll call Jo Jo and see if he can come. Sure, that's what I'll do, Mada. We can play Keno.

MADA: Jo Jo don't know how to play Keno.

COLIENE: All right, Mada. [*Pause.*] Jo Jo should love living here. I called him and told him that I wanted him to come over, but he wasn't in.

MADA: Probably out flirting. I know his type of man. And I know your type of woman. When they meet men like Jo Jo, all they do is share problems with me. Jo Jo is the kind of guy that likes to big time. Working all week just to spend his money. Never saves a penny. And I know he's stood you up plenty of times to date other women. Paul ain't well-to-do, his apartment ain't all that elaborate, but that studio he works in is sunny and bright, and he's a good man, and he wouldn't lead you a dog's life.

COLIENE: Jo Jo is just a friendly person.

[MADA *exits.* JO JO *exits the Greenwich Village café,
and* PAUL *leaves the studio and goes and sits down at the café table.*]

[JO JO *enters* COLIENE'*s living room, looking at the mural.*]

JO JO: Paul paint that?

COLIENE: Yes. It's lovely, isn't it?

JO JO: How much he charge you for that?

COLIENE: He didn't charge me for it, Jo Jo. It's a present.

JO JO: Sure, he wants something in return.

COLIENE: Not all men are like that.

JO JO: That Paul's a faker. [*looking around*] You've got every color of the rainbow in here. A pink record player. You really like lots of color.

COLIENE: I'm a very colorful person.

JO JO: I just seen Mada's rickety car, that old convertible, drive out of the driveway.

COLIENE: She won't use Paul's car.

JO JO: She been bad-mouthing me again? I know her type of meddlesome woman. I think her ex-husband musta looked like me 'cause I ain't done a thing to that woman. [*Pause.*] Now with all your money you can help her get a new one.

COLIENE: A new husband?

JO JO: A new car. [*mimicking Mada*] Honey child, some people sure have done come up in the world. Yes, they sho have. [*sitting down on the couch*] No wonder you all need help. I better give you three days, honey, 'ceptin two. You got more house than I thought. What you gonna do with it, honey?

COLIENE: [*playing herself*] Well, when Jo Jo and I get married, we can have children and we need all of the space that we can get.

JO JO: That's right, honey. But I sure wish that it was Paul you was setting your cap for. You know he's always taken a liking to you.

COLIENE: I know. Paul's a good friend. I'm very fond of Paul. But Jo Jo saw me first.

JO JO: Yes, honey. I sure wish that he hadn't. You and my Paul is just like my son and daughter. Why I could always have a family if you all was to hitch up.

COLIENE: I'm going to marry Jo Jo and that's that. [*Pause; to Jo Jo.*] How about a beer?

JO JO: Sure, child, always. That artist's studio you added onto the house is a waste of money. [*Pause.*] You sure must love your friends.

COLIENE: It's not Paul's. It's mine. I like it myself. I can write in that studio. Or sew.

JO JO: Sure. [*Pause, looking around.*] You're too much for me now.

COLIENE: No, Jo Jo. It's for us. Whatever I have become, it's for us.

JO JO: Are you sure, or is it for Konder?

COLIENE: Why, Jo Jo. Of all the mean things to say about me and Paul.

JO JO: Sorry. I used to like the guy. But not anymore.

COLIENE: Come on in the kitchen.

[*They exit.* COLIENE *returns and picks up the telephone.* JO JO *returns to the Greenwich Village café to drink a beer and flirt with* FRANCIE. *In his studio,* PAUL *picks up the telephone.*]

PAUL: Mada says it's a beautiful home.

COLIENE: I told her she could stay here and make it hers, but she won't leave you. Did Mada tell you I want you to come to supper?

PAUL: I'd be delighted. Any time that I can be around you, I want to.

COLIENE: [*laughing*] Mada thinks we're meant for each other. [*Pause.*] You know who's coming too?

PAUL: I don't care. I'll still be with my girl. Mada's crazy about your house.

COLIENE: Jo Jo in it will make it a home. [*Pause.*] Paul, you know you shouldn't joke like that around Mada. She overhears you telling me I'm your girl and thinks you really mean it. And that picture you painted of me and called *My*

Girl. I tell her that's just art. That's the way artists are, that if we had as many lovers as in our love songs and paintings we wouldn't know what to do with them, but she thinks you mean it. She thinks that painting is a special message for me—that you're in love with me. I tell her *My Girl* is no specific woman.

PAUL: Maybe I do mean it? Maybe I am in love with you?

COLIENE: I know you, Paul. You paint Love, but you've no specific woman in mind. You play us all. Jo Jo still doesn't like the idea of me going around with you, but I tell him we're friends, that's all. He knows we're just good friends. And he's a flirty guy himself and likes to have his women friends, so why shouldn't I have you for a friend?

PAUL: You remember how I stared at you when I first saw you? In Greenwich Village. I like beauty, and so I stared. You looked up at me and smiled. You weren't being fresh with me. I knew you weren't a pickup. It's just your way. You're a nice girl, Coliene. I smiled back and the rest is history.

[*In the Greenwich Village café,* JO JO *kisses* FRANCIE *and exits the café.*
COLIENE *enters the café and sits down at the table and is waiting
for* JO JO *to arrive. She's dressed cheaply, but in good taste.
This should be played as a flashback scene.*]

FRANCIE: What'll you have to drink?

COLIENE: Nothing now, thanks. I'm waiting for someone. He's supposed to meet me here.

[PAUL *enters, sits up at the bar and orders a drink, then spots* COLIENE
*and stares at her as if she's a "true beauty." She notices him and smiles.
He smiles back, then he walks over to her and stands at her table.*]

PAUL: Would you like a drink?

COLIENE: Not now, thank you. I'm waiting for a friend.

PAUL: Oh, I'm sorry. I'd like to know you. My name's Paul Konder. You have such a beautiful face. I'm not trying to be fresh, but I'm an artist and I'd like to paint your picture.

COLIENE: Oh. My name's Coliene.

PAUL: Coliene. What a beautiful name.

COLIENE: I'm interested, that is, concerning your painting me. I mean, if you're for real.

PAUL: Good.

COLIENE: How much do you pay?

PAUL: It depends.

COLIENE: I need the money. I'll be glad to pose for you. At your house?

PAUL: Of course, I need lots of light and I have it there.

[JO JO *walks in and spots them together, looks suspiciously at* PAUL, *and comes over to the table.*]

COLIENE: Jo Jo, meet Paul Konder. Paul Konder, meet Jo Jo Spain.

PAUL: Glad to know you, Spain.

JO JO: Likewise.

COLIENE: Paul's a painter. He's going to paint my picture.

PAUL: Sure thing.

JO JO: Yeah? Nice fellow, eh?

COLIENE: Yes, he is nice.

JO JO: How long have you known him?

COLIENE: Not long.

JO JO: Just some new man you've met? [*To* PAUL.] Sit down, man.

PAUL: No thanks, anyway. Three's a crowd.

COLIENE: It's all right, Paul. We're sort of used to crowds.

[PAUL *laughs and sits down. They order rum and Coca-Colas.*]

PAUL: I didn't want you to think I was trying to pick her up, man.

JO JO: I think what I think. Coliene's a pretty girl. No wonder you want to paint her. I'd paint her myself, if I could paint.

[COLIENE *hugs* JO JO.]

COLIENE: I've been trying to talk Jo Jo into going to night school.

JO JO: Heck, Coliene, I'm beat when night comes, and what energy I have left, that's for me and you.

PAUL: What kind of work do you do?

JO JO: Garage mechanic.

458

PAUL: Honest work.

JO JO: I know it's honest work. Coliene's a writer. Composes songs. Theme's her aspirations. Thinks I ain't got no ambition, the kind of man that'll get ahead, get to the top of the ladder, amount to anything. So she pushes me.

COLIENE: Jo Jo, you know that's not true.

JO JO: I'm good-looking, sure enough, but I've got no ambition. Are you a man of ambition?

[PAUL *says nothing.*]

JO JO: I love Coliene. I believe she loves me.

COLIENE: You know I do. I'm enchanted with you.

JO JO: Put that in a song. [*Pause.*] Pose for him. It'll help you with your savings. [*Pause; to* PAUL.] I know you ain't jiving her, 'cause I know who you are.

PAUL: What do you mean?

JO JO: I just know who you are, man.

[JO JO *exits.* COLIENE *and* PAUL *leave the café and go into the studio. She stands posing for him as he paints.*]

COLIENE: This is such a little studio, but there's plenty of light. I bet you'd like something more roomy and spacious. Did you do all those paintings on the wall?

PAUL: Yes.

COLIENE: They're nice. [*Pause.*] You must love this room. It's not how I imagine an artist's studio. But I bet in your dream house your studio is roomy and spacious, isn't it?

PAUL: You compose songs, Spain said?

COLIENE: Yes.

PAUL: Does Spain like your songs?

COLIENE: I don't know what Jo Jo likes. He's not really creative. With Jo Jo it's, This crate can do a hundred, that buggy I overhauled, now it's really a ready buggy. I cleaned and sparked about ten cars today. Forgot to put oil in Maxie's can. Honey, look at them sidewall tires, I painted them for Poby.

PAUL: But you love him?

COLIENE: Yes. Sometimes I wonder why the heck I do. I don't really share my work with him, though. He's not really interested in my music. [*Pause.*] You're real handsome. You should do a self-portrait. Thick beautiful hair. You don't wear a mustache like Jo Jo, though.

459

PAUL: Sometimes I do. I'm glad you came to let me paint you. Come back again Saturday. We'll get started early. I can't bear to wait until Monday to continue this painting. I'd like to finish it as soon as possible. I know that you're tired.

COLIENE: Yes. I've never had to sit this long posing before. It's quite an experience.

[MADA *enters the studio and looks at* COLIENE.]

COLIENE: Hi. I'm Coliene Cross. Mr. Konder's painting me.

MADA: Yes, ma'am. I thought I heard a lady in here.

COLIENE: You don't have to ma'am me.

MADA: Yes, ma'am.

PAUL: This is Mada, Coliene. She keeps house for me.

MADA: How you, ma'am?

COLIENE: Fine. But please, just call me Coliene.

MADA: And me, I'm just plain Mada.

COLIENE: I used to work as a domestic myself. I went to school at night and studied music and journalism. I first came to New York with Mr. and Mrs. Mix who were moving to the city and wanted me to help with their two children. I stayed with them a couple of years, still studying nights. Mr. Mix was a building contractor and went wherever there was work. They moved to Nashville and wanted me to move to Nashville with them, Mrs. Mix practically begged me to leave with them, but you know I prefer New York to Tennessee. Mrs. Mix knew I wrote songs and thought I might try to sell my songs in Nashville, but you know they wouldn't be buying my songs. I had to find lodging. Jo Jo, that's my boyfriend, wanted me to move in with him, but I moved into Mrs. Murphy's apartment for girls. She only had one apartment left, a basement apartment, three rooms and one bath, and this was not at all private. I share the kitchen and bathroom with two other girls, Anistine and Claudia. Anistine's an African American and from the South. Arkansas, I think. Claudia claims she's Italian. But if she's Italian, so is Jo Jo. I've been saving money so I can get a real apartment of my own. A full bath of my own would be great, my own kitchen. That's what you need to be yourself. I've been crowded up all my life.

MADA: Maybe Paul'll bring you luck. [*Pause.*] She's a pretty girl, Paul.

PAUL: Sure, she is.

[PAUL *covers the canvas and washes his paint-stained hands in the washbasin.*]

MADA: Paul needs a pretty young lady around. Mr. Tyrone'll probably like that picture, what I seen of it. He sold one of Paul's paintings over there in Europe. I got a pretty piece of money from that myself. Whenever Paul sells a painting, he gives me something to show his appreciation when it's me to show my appreciation to him.

PAUL: She just spends it back on me.

MADA: I buy little necessities. I like to go to the beach, though. Sometimes I go to Coney Island. I like to swim. So do Paul. We oughta take you to Coney Island with us.

COLIENE: Every time I think of Coney Island I think of Francie Ware.

MADA: Say who?

COLIENE: That's my boyfriend's other girlfriend. He likes to take her to Coney Island. He's got another girlfriend, Lea Bowman. He says we'll be seeing enough of each other after we're married, so he likes to take other girls out. And I'm to be a sport, you know. A good sport. Let him have his free time now. He's still sorta wild. We'll get married, I know he loves me, but I want to wait till we get some money, you know. He's proposed to me and everything. But I've had such a mean and poor childhood, you know. Jo Jo says I'm afraid of being poor, and I am. I've been engaged to him for two years. He's given me a ring. Well, I had to buy it myself. He's always moody and on nettles. I love him, though. It's just one of those things.

MADA: You can't calm down wild men. You don't love him. You're stuck on him. Women don't know the difference between love and being stuck on a man. What about Francie? Then let him be jealous of Paul. You and Paul can be good friends, and Jo Jo can be a good sport. Let you have your free time now. Paul's my very best friend. He got me out of that rooming house in Virginia.

PAUL: Oh, you'd have gotten yourself out of Virginia all right.

MADA: Paul got me a job modeling for different artists around New York and got me a job advertising some soap, and I even sing a little jingle about that soap, but mostly I works here for him. He's my dearest friend. What did Francie ever do for your lover boy? What's his name?

COLIENE: Jo Jo.

MADA: He sounds like a Jo Jo. I don't even know him, and you don't know yourself, but I know you deserve better. I know they say a woman's supposed to make herself happy, and I don't mean to meddle, but he just don't seem to be the right guy for you.

PAUL: If he knows how to play Keno, she'll like him.

MADA: We might play Keno together, but I'll still know his kind. Always at a bar, going from one bar to another, drinking, fooling around with a lot of no good supposed to be friends that don't mean theyselves any good or anyone else. Poker and card games. 'Cept Keno. You know this ain't no good and you think after you's married, he'll settle down, but you know he won't. Then he start to change your personality and even your purpose in life, till you don't even know who you are. And they just don't care. He'll lead you a dog's life. But when I was your age, I was like that myself. If some young women could see farther than her nose they'd see the better men, the men who really love them.

[COLIENE *and* MADA *leave the studio and return to the living room.*
COLIENE *sits down at the piano.*]

COLIENE: [*rising*] I'd better call Jo Jo again. I'm not sure he's coming over tonight.

MADA: I hope he don't.

COLIENE: Ah, Mada.

MADA: Well, I don't, honey child. He just ain't right for a sweet little thing like you. [*Pause.*] I was a sweet little thing like you myself. I wasn't as pretty as you is, but I was sho as sweet. [*Pause.*] You told me 'bout how when you and Paul went for a drive and stopped at that café, and seen Jo Jo with his Francie, hugging and kissing.

COLIENE: I never told you that.

MADA: Paul's sorry you seen that, but I'm glad you seen Jo Jo with his Francie. When y'all started to leave, Jo Jo shoved Francie and headed for you, half high with liquor. He coulda been my own. He coulda been my own. "Mada, Baby, I didn't know you was coming." Come on, baby. And Francie high as Jo Jo. They make a great pair. Two of a kind. How could Jo Jo be so common? Now take it easy, sweetheart. Jo Jo Spain ain't worth it. Paul's your friend. Jo Jo's the foolmaker. Share your dreams with Paul. Jo Jo just wants you where he can show you off. When you get old and he can't show you off, he'll. . . . Men is all alike. They'll turn you into a fool if you'll let them. Except Paul. . . .

COLIENE: I know. I know it's Paul. I know it's Paul I love, not Jo Jo. It's just. . . .

MADA: Good. It's just good, that's what it is. I'm glad you can see further than your nose.

COLIENE: I'll have to tell Jo Jo. I don't want to hurt him.

MADA: You won't. Just tell him, and good riddance. Talking about good.

[MADA *exits and* PAUL *enters.*]

PAUL: How's my girl?

COLIENE: Fine, Paul. I'm so glad you came.

PAUL: So am I.

COLIENE: Dinner's ready. We worked hard to fix this meal.

PAUL: Sure am hungry.

[PAUL *kisses* COLIENE *on the cheek, then he takes her in his arms and kisses her on the lips.*]

PAUL: I'm sorry, Coliene. I know you're Spain's girl. Has Spain come?

[JO JO *comes in to see them in each other's arms. He clears his throat.*]

JO JO: Well, I guess I know when to bow out. So long, Coliene. I always thought Konder was your man. Or you was his woman.

COLIENE: Oh, Jo Jo, I'm sorry, I . . . .

JO JO: Don't be. Good luck. Y'all women is all alike, though. Play a man for a fool.

[JO JO *exits.*]

PAUL: Now you won't have to tell him. He knows.

COLIENE: Oh, Paul, my sweet love. I do love you. But I don't like what Jo Jo thinks I am. I didn't play him.

PAUL: I know.

COLIENE: Come and see your studio.

Like I said I were Mada in that movie. The things that were be-yond our capabilities we had to imagine we was doing. But that's why I says that when I read about them imaginary people in that newsletter that's when I thought it were a confabulatory newsletter. Of course Monkey Bread might have put a confabulatory announce-ment in a real newsletter, so that it could be a real newsletter from the Daughters of Nzingha, but with a confabulatory announcement that Monkey Bread herself put into that newsletter, 'cause she know I would remember playing Mada in that play and would even remem-ber the play itself. Then they could be a real Mada and Coliene and

Paul Condor—or Paul Konder, as his name is in the play—in New York.

But they's a lot in that newsletter I don't believe. I don't believe that star of hers owns no yacht, and wouldn't let Monkey Bread's womanfriends be partying on it even if she did own one. They also includes some of Monkey Bread's stories in that newsletter, but y'all's already read the stories they includes. And all that talk about not printing people's names for security purposes, I just think that's Monkey Bread 'cause she ain't come up with the names for some of them characters, so she just says she ain't print they names for security purposes. Anybody can start they own newsletter. I think she just oughta call it *Monkey Bread's Newsletter* and ain't pretend she sending out no unofficial official newsletter of the Daughters of Nzingha organization.

But I'm talking about Delgadina sweeping. I tells her they ought to hire somebody to sweep up in the evenings, but she say that the bartender's job. They should oughta hire them another bartender, though, and ain't just Delgadina. Like in that movie, they had theyselves a coupla bartenders. It ain't one of them factory-made brooms but one of them handmade brooms she got at this craft festival. Delgadina, like I said, is one of them artsy people, and she like to go to these craft festivals the same way I likes them trade shows, where they got them people that makes pottery and stain glass and metalwork. And she even reads some magazine that tells you where all the art and craft festivals is. At them trade shows they got them newfangled inventions and technologies. I guess that the difference between the craft festival and the trade show, one got the technological inventions and the other got the artsy inventions, but sometimes there's artists that be combining that technology in they art. Some of them is just craft festivals and others is art and craft festivals, but artists from all over the country and I suppose all over the world come to them art and craft festivals, though some of them might just restrict theyselves to American art and craft people, but Delgadina say they got international art and craft festivals. The art and craft festivals they also got them regular artists that paints pictures and sculpts and shit, and even got cartoonists and caricaturists that can caricature anybody 'cause them caricaturists they be having they booths like the regular artists and displaying they caricatures and invites people to be caricatured 'cause Delgadina she got her a caricature of herself, in fact she got a couple of caricatures of herself, but I watched that caricaturist caricature some other African Americans on his sketch pad and they all looks like Sambo, so I didn't want me none of them caricatures, but sometimes I've seen me some African-American artists at them festivals with they art and craft, and even African-American caricaturists, though a lot of they caricatures look like Sambo too, though a lot of times I ain't sure what the difference between a art and a craft (is a caricature a art or a craft?), 'cause sometimes them craft people looks pretty artsy and a lot of times them artists looks pretty crafty. Delgadina ain't told me why she got them two caricatures of herself, but I know the reason. 'Cause the first caricaturist thought she were African American and so they's a Sambo look to that caricature, and the second caricaturist knew that she's Chicana so they's a different look to that caricature, though I don't know what the Chicana equivalent to that Sambo. I know them Chicanos gots they Sambo, though.

Anyhow, she bought this handmade broom from one of them craft people and say it sweep better than them factory-made broom and even if it don't sweep better than them factory-made broom, she just say she like them handmade brooms better. And she also bought some handmade Native American jewelry made of turquoise and a miniature tepee. She would like to buy her a full-size tepee, but say she ain't got no room to put no full-size teepee in her little apartment, and she say it okay for her to have a tepee 'cause they's as much Native American in her as Mexican, though she don't like it that a lot of them gringos have got tepees and she say it's popular among certain gringos to have tepees in their backyards. She say that a lot of them jewelry and tepees ain't made by authentic Native Americans, anyway, but by gringos wanting to commercialize on that Nativism, and even Miguelita she says knows how to make tepees, or at least the gringo version of a tepee, though she say a lot of them's got the conceit that they makes them tepees better or just as good as the native tepee makers, so she always like to buy her Native American arts and crafts at them craft festivals because then she can see that they's authentic Native Americans that make them. Though not all Native Americans looks like Native Americans, or the stereotype of the Native American, and she's even seen gringos that

most people mistake for Native American, but she say she can always tell the true Native Americans. And she also wants to buy her
one of them totem poles. You know them totem poles, 'cause she say
she have always had a interest in that totemism, and she even be saying how my name Mosquito influence her to have a character in one
of her stories for her writing class that have a totem in they name and
a trickster too, 'cause she say a mosquito could be a trickster just like
some of them other trickster animals, which is usually always the
smallest animals, although she say she ain't never heard about no
trickster mosquito, though she ain't exactly explained what she mean
by that totemism and tricksterism in a name, plus Mosquito my
nickname it ain't my real name. But she be saying in some cultures
women ain't supposed to know that they totem is only men. I wonder if that star of Monkey Bread's be calling them totem poles primitive and simplistic art, like she be calling that art of them aborigines.
I wonder if she calling it primitive and simplistic because the art is
primitive and simplistic or the way she see the art is primitive and
simplistic. Except they's some of them artists Delgadina says that deliberately cultivates the primitive, 'cause I be saying one of them artist can't paint worth shit and if that art then anybody a artist and she
be saying it because that artist a primitivist and be deliberately cultivating that primitivism but she do be saying in some of them so-
called primitive cultures everybody a artist 'cause every culture got
its idea or ideal of the artist and I be wondering how you can tell the
difference between the artist that be deliberately cultivating the
primitivism and the artist that can't paint worth shit and then she let
me read one of her art books and some article about some primitivist
artist and be making him sound like he a real artist even though the
painting don't look like shit, but that supposed to be modern art and
she be saying how she envy the modern artist because modernism
ain't triumphed as much in literature as it have in art. But, like I told
you, Delgadina herself sometimes makes them art and craft and she
know more about that primitivism, so if she say the artist a primitivist I figure she know what she talking about. She sculptures and she
paints and embroiders blouses and I be wondering how come she
don't set up her a booth, 'cause her art and craft look about as good
as the art and craft at them booth and certainly better than that prim-

itivism. But she be saying they professional art and craft people even the primitivist and she a amateur. Then I still be wondering what a amateur is if her art and craft looks as good as them professional art and craft.

Anyway, I'm sitting at a table with a Bud Light and the rest of the pretzels from the bar and rereading that letter from Monkey Bread, like I said. And then I'm rereading them stories again and wondering what sorta story I'd write if I were to write "Mosquito's Story." And then I'm thinking it would be a different story if I used any other of my different names, 'cause that's how stories is. I ain't thinking 'bout Delgadina or the bar, though, or even Monkey Bread or her star, or even that Tokyo, I'm thinking 'bout that Raymond and that African I met in Canada and that John Henry Hollywood, our John Henry Hollywood, Monkey Bread be calling him, and wondering if that little story about they imaginary marriage be a true story and wondering little bit 'bout my ex-husband. And then I'm thinking about that time Delgadina and me was playing this game— I'll tell you about my ex-husband if you'll tell me about yours. We was sitting at one of them umbrella'd tables outside a drive-in restaurant eating burgers and fries with salsa and Delgadina seen this guy with this woman and was just a-looking at him, you know. Looking like a fool actually. In fact I ain't never seen that Delgadina looking foolish at no man like that, 'cause there's plenty of good-looking men that come in that cantina, 'cause a lot of them Chicanos is good-looking at least by African-American standards. I'd just returned from that trade fair up in Canada and was telling her about Canada and starting to tell her about that African from Portuguese Africa and which movie star he kinda remind me of or which combination of movie stars when Delgadina seen this guy with this woman and like I said just start a-looking at him like a fool. And I seen plenty men in that cantina that's just as handsome or handsomer. And I be thinking that ain't Delgadina to be looking at a man like a fool no matter how handsome he is. Although I consider John Henry Hollywood and my ex-husband handsome men, I don't believe that I've been a fool for handsome men either.

What? I asks.

Nothing, she say, picking up a french fry and dipping it in salsa. I be telling her about them new curly french fries, but these is ordinary french fries. He just looks like my ex-husband. I thought that was my ex-husband for a minute. He looks just like my ex-husband.

And she be looking like she trying to hide from him behind her menu and then when she discover this ain't her ex-husband at this umbrella'd table with his new woman she still be looking at them like she a fool, though she put her menu back on the table. A guy with one of them oversize mustaches. One of them bandito-style mustaches actually. But he don't look exactly like no bandito. Not even one of them social banditos that Delgadina be telling me about, though in the American movies they'd probably have his type play-ing the rogue or the lover or the roguish lover. Look like he could be Juan Hollywood or whatever the Chicano name for Hollywood. Ain't got the roguish look to me though, not even a rogue in love.

Oh, yeah?

But he were with some other woman, like I said—one of them blond Hispanic. You could tell she a Hispanic, but her hair blond as a gringa's even them California gringas and look like it had been bleached more blond by the sun like them gringas on them Califor-nia beaches. In fact, her hair blonder than Miguelita's. And I guess by certain standards you could call her a beauty—shoulder-length blond hair, green, almond-shaped eyes, full lips (almost African lips, but they don't call them African lips, they call them full lips), and she painted her top lip a little darker red than her bottom lip, which mighta been the style. Actually, her top lip look like the top of a valentine. In fact, they both got shoulder-length hair, the man and the woman, 'cause he the sorta actor-looking type, that Hollywood type, like I said, or the artist or musician type. Broad shoulders, though a little more rounded than Egyptian shoulders and them Valentino-type eyes, which ain't to say I'm the Valentino generation, just that he the mold for that type, like them Hollywood blondes, like that Marilyn Monroe and them other Hollywood blondes the model for that other type, I mean the type that woman is. And she buxom, too, like them Hollywood blondes. And him he look like the kinda hero you see in them movies and even in them comic books, especially them heroes that's molded on the Valentino type and maybe even that Superman molded on that Valentino type. She look like she a natural blonde. But then maybe she ain't none of them blond Hispanics. Maybe he got himself a gringa like Mr. Delgado got him his Miguelita. They was talking so close to each other that they noses was touching. He's got one of them Roman-type noses and her nose is slightly flattened, but it a upturned nose, which supposed to be the ideal gringa nose. Sitting at another one of them umbrella'd tables. He glance around lynx-eyed at Delgadina and me and then look back at his girlfriend. Them men with long hair always reminds me of wild goats, though.

Tell you about my ex-husband if you'll tell me about yours, she say, dipping another french fry in that salsa. She scratch the back of her head and then reach for another french fry.

Course I don't like talking about my ex-husband to anybody, even Delgadina, but I still says okay, 'cause I want to hear about her ex-husband, so she starts talking first. Dipping a french fry in that salsa every time she want to punctuate her sentence. And I were expecting for her to tell me that her ex-husband were some real macho abusive-type son-of-a-bitch, you know, one of them mb and dtk's, *hijo de puta* types, but it turn out she were the abusive one. A real *puta*?

Not physical abuse, she saying. Mental abuse. Talking 'bout being mad bad and dangerous to know. I was always accusing him of doing things he wasn't doing. I knew he wasn't doing 'em, but I just couldn't stop myself from accusing him of doing 'em. I guess I wanted a divorce, you know, but didn't have the sense enough to just say I want a divorce, so I guess I just kept accusing him of doing shit, you know. At least this psychologist told me that mighta been why, 'cause I went to this marriage counselor for a while. It was after we were divorced, though, that I went to this marriage counselor, who said that mighta been my strategy. She has this idea that a good marriage is like the comity of nations, you know. . . .

The comedy of nations?

Comity of nations. We have our commonality but recognize each other's sovereignty at the same time. You know, for a harmonious marriage or some shit. I'm not really sure what the fool meant now, but I was impressed at the time. She's the one told me about ginseng and ginkgo biloba. I've always been too easily impressed by intelligent women, though. Intelligent men you tend to take for granted. She's writing this huge book on marriage, not one of those girlie pop psychology books they have on Oprah and Sally, but more of an intellectual sort. Sort of psychology and intellectual history of marriage. The comity of nations. That's her metaphor for the good marriage. . . . She's never been divorced. She's a Greek Catholic. She looks kinda like a Chicana but she's Greek. She's got this novel she appears in, one of those romans à clef, you know. . . . I kept thinking we'd get back together, you know, my husband and I, but then I decided to move to Texas City. He's still in Houston. He's got a girlfriend, maybe several girlfriends. I felt like a caged bird, though, while we were husband and wife. And not one of them canaries neither.

I try to picture her a caged bird and be thinking of them 1960s movies where they always got the womens dancing in cages. You know them 1960s movies they's always womens dancing in cages. I don't think you ever see men dancing in them cages, not even dancing in them cages with them women, though sometimes one of them drunken fools be trying to climb into one of them cages. And can't imagine Delgadina to be seeking the advice of no marriage counselor either.

You don't remind me of nobody caged bird, I says. I pours some salsa on my burger and take a bite. It good salsa. Delgadina made some salsa once with that Hermitage wine. I think it Hermitage wine, some kinda French wine, and I be thinking that salsa be a international dish if you can make it with French wine, like Delgadina put roasted cactus on her pizza. Kinda taste like that salsa, 'cept I don't think it got wine in it. This is pretty good salsa, ain't it? And you don't seem like the abusive sorta woman. You seem like the sorta woman not to take shit, but not the abusive sort. Course they's men if you the sorta woman that don't take shit considers that abuse.

She dip a french fry in that salsa and nibble. She take a gander at that couple, you know they's lovers, then back at me. Yeah, that's today. But then I felt like a caged bird, you know, Mosquito. I was in my twenties anyhow and naive as shit. I had this friend usedta call me Butterfly Shoulders 'cause of my nerves, you know. She dip another french fry in that salsa and nibble. Now tell me about yours.

I scrapes some of my french fries onto her plate. *Muchas gracias,* she say.

You ain't really told me about yours, I says.

She stir a french fry in the salsa. What do you mean?

You told me about yourself in relationship to yours. I dips a french fry in the salsa and pours some more salsa on my hamburger.

Naw, you just wanna get outta telling me about your own. Where'd you meet?

She already gobbled her french fries, even them new french fries I give her, and now grabbing more of my french fries, 'cause she know I don't like them french fries that much anyhow. She start to order one of them taco instead of a hamburger, but she don't really like them American-style tacos. She made me some of them Mexican-style tacos, authentic Mexican-style tacos, them soft tacos instead of them hard-shell tacos. Taco Bell–type tacos, she say, ain't authentic Mexican tacos. But I guess American-style pizza ain't authentic Italian pizza. I wonder if they got American-style Chinese food. Seem like I heard them Chinese makes Chinese food different for Americans than they does for theyselves to appeal to the American taste.

The Derby, I says.

Oh, yeah?

The backside.

Say what?

I think they calls it the backside. It the part where the grooms and the people that takes care of the horses resides. Ain't that called the backside? You know, a lot of them grooms sleep right inside the stable with them horses. They got they bunk beds set up right in the stable with them horses. The exercise people and trainers and shit. I remember hearing some of them talk, them exercise people and grooms and shit and it sounded like modern slavery, like them peach pickers in Georgia. I met me this woman who was like a peach picker in Georgia, said she had to escape from this place where she were picking peaches and sounded just like one of them fugitives back there in slavery times. But them grooms they sleep right inside the stables with them horses. I used to think that them people that traveled with them horses had theyselves a glamorous job, but it sounded like slavery times.

He a groom? But she looking at them lovers. I glances at them. Monkey Bread be talking about me having a pigeon for romance. I think that Delgadina got more of a pigeon for romance than me. Lovers. Them perfect-type lovers. Like I say, them movie lovers, even them television movie lovers, them mini-series lovers. I always prefers them lovers that comes on them talk shows, though, 'cause they more interesting.

Naw. He's sorta a jack-of-all-trades, I guess. But it was during the Derby and he were working there, actually working with them peoples who were setting up this exhibition of black jockeys, you know, 'cause most all of them original jockeys was African Americans. . . .

Yeah, I know. Now they got a lot of Hispanics. . . .

I wonders why she use that word *Hispanics* 'cause she always be correcting people when they call her Hispanic and say Chicano. Anybody say Hispanic she be correcting them and say Chicano, it ain't Hispanic it Chicano, she be saying and now she be saying Hispanic her ownself. She be always saying she ain't no Hispanic, she a Chicano, and she be even correcting me when I be saying she the first Hispanic I met. You the first Hispanic I met, I says. Which ain't exactly true 'cause they was a couple of Hispanics at that truck driving school. Don't call me Hispanic, I'm Chicana. Well, I guess she say Hispanic 'cause they ain't just Chicano Hispanics, they's Puerto Ricans, and Cubans, and Latin Americans and other Spanish-speaking peoples.

Yeah, and so he were there working on this exhibition, you know, 'cause you can't have the history of horse racing, you know, without the celebration of the African-American jockey. That's where I met him anyhow. He say some of them early races all they would have in them were them African-American jockeys, even in slavery time they had them slaves jockeying them horses, 'cause a lot of them jockeys went over to Europe, 'cause they were a lot more freedom over there and not that Jim Crow. He real ambitious, though, my ex-husband. Now he done gone back to college, you know, one of them business colleges, to study that ecological tourism, what they call that ecological tourism, you know, and in the tourist trade or some shit.

Ecological tourism?

You know, a lot of them modern tourism people call theyselves ecological tourism people 'cause a lot of them tourists, you know, destroys the ecology, you know, so the new tourism supposed to be ecological tourism. The more enlightened tourism people is supposed to be ecological tourism people. Anyway, he in Tasmania.

You mean Tanzania? She says some words that I knows is Swahili, but I ain't know what they mean. She even had her a class in Swahili at the Community Center. Telling me Swahili a simple language and that I should learn it. I remembers the Swahili word for buffalo, *nyati*. And I knows enough Swahili to tell this friend of mine who heard the word *nyani* not to name none of her childrens that 'cause it means baboon. She be telling me, Nadine, I heard the prettiest African name that I wants to name one of my childrens. What African name? I asks. I think she is going to say *osani*, which is the pygmy word for love. And she says *nyani*. I say, fool, *nyani* is a baboon. *Nyani*, that is so pretty, though ain't it? say this fool. And that fool probably have named one of her childrens Nyani, 'cause she knows that most of us that is learning other peoples languages is learning French rather than Swahili. *Are you Miss Nadine Johnson of the Covington Johnsons? Yes, and whose little girl are you? I'm little Nyani Worth Peacock, Sheila Worth Peacock's little girl. My mama talks about you all the time, Miss Nadine, say that you is the principal one who helped her to name me. Say she didn't have a name for me till you told her about a pretty little African name. And that I'm named Nyani on account of you, Miss Nadine, and everybody that hears my name say it is the prettiest little name that they know.*

Naw, Tasmania.

Tasmania! She say it loud enough so's the lovers look toward us like we's Tasmanians and then they continues courting.

Yeah. We amiable and all, you know. He sent me a coupla postcards about his wonderful adventures in Tasmania, but then he met some aboriginal girl, you know, got him a new wife and some kids, so he don't send postcards like he usedta, you know, but we's still amiable. . . . I usedta think that Tasmania were a imaginary country, on account of the Tasmanian devil in that cartoon you know, but it ain't. Tasmania's a real country, though I think he say it sorta like a state of Australia rather than a whole country it ownself. It a island, though. Tasmania a island. He a travel consultant—I think that what he call hisself—for people interested in that ecological tourism. . . . Supposed to be plenty of people interested in that in Tasma-

473

nia and Australia too, which is close to Tasmania or Tasmania is a
part of Australia, I ain't sure which. . . . He say a lot of people think
he a aborigine and surprise when they learn that he a African American and be wondering what he doing in Tasmania. . . .

   She looking like she don't know whether to believe me or not.
Like I'm one of what she call them unreliable narrators. She be looking at me like I'm talking shit, you know how bartenders looks at
you when they think you talking shit, though she ain't tending the
bar, but probably what they calls the unreliable narrators is the ones
telling them true stories, and it the so-called reliable narrators talking shit. But she still dipping her french fries—or rather *my* french
fries—in salsa. And she still glancing at them lovers. You know, them
furtive glances. But they's just studying each other. Noses almost
touching, like I said. Them's probably what you'd call lover's lovers.

   But you ain't actually told me what he's *like*, she say. Why'd
y'all divorce?

   I lifts both my eyebrows but don't say nothing. Ain't I told her
what he like? I know I said he ambitious. And gotta be adventure-
some to be over there in that Tasmania, whether it a part of Australia
or it own whole country. I think she waiting to hear some abusive
tale too. Some real son-of-a-bitch or some shit. At least seem like
most of them tales you read or hear from the point of view of a
woman, and not just African-American womens neither, is always
some abusive son-of-a-bitch. Then I'm wondering why they don't
have some name equivalent to bitch for a man. I guess that's bastard,
but then both son-of-a-bitch and bastard ain't call a man the thing
his ownself, being independent of a woman. Ain't no word that set
aspersions on the man he own whole self. If she waiting to hear some
son-of-a-bitch story, though, I ain't telling one, and never even
liked them kinda stories even when they is true. I knows I has sometimes been sitting in a nightclub drinking Budweiser and listening
to jazz and some woman I don't even know comes up to me and starts
telling me a son-of-a-bitch story about some man. I don't know her
and don't know the man, but she telling me her son-of-a-bitch story
like it the only type of story they is. Even them blues singers got them
a repertoire of other types of songs. I remember I went with Delgadina to hear this African-American woman novelist woman give a

reading. She say that the novel that she were reading from were based on the art form of the blues and that were why the woman was telling a son-of-a-bitch story. She didn't call it a son-of-a-bitch story. So she reads some of the story and the women in the audience they thinks it a good story. So I'm standing there with Delgadina talking to the woman.

Why the man in that story got to be such a son-of-a-bitch? My daddy ain't like that and none of the Johnson mens is like that. Why you write a story like that? Is you a feminist?

This is a blues novel and it uses the subject matter of the blues? explains the woman. Imagining a woman singing the blues, this is what she'd sing about, wouldn't she? Isn't this what she'd sing about? Then she sings me one of them blues songs, singing about different wrongs, you know. She says that that is not her idea of how men are, but if you're going to write a blues novel, sung by a woman, then that is the subject matter.

But why every man in that novel got to be a son-of-a-bitch. Delgadina gave me that novel and every man in it is a son-of-a-bitch. You should have some good mens in that novel. I knows when I watches movies, they's got plenty of sons-of-bitches in them, but they is always a man who's a good man who is a counter to the sons-of-bitches. I knows that the Johnson men is all good men.

This is a blues novel, Nadine, says Delgadina. Now she always calls me Mosquito, but talking with that woman novelist, she call me Nadine. And then she reiterates what that woman have said about the subject matter of the blues.

Y'all ain't listened to no true blues singers, I says. 'Cause that ain't the whole of the blues repertoire. I have heard people tell that lie about the blues before. You have chosen one type of blues song to sing, but if you listens to a true blues singer that ain't the whole repertoire. The true blues singer don't just sing one type of blues. If you listens to a true blues singer, it ain't just about who done who wrong. They sings about work, they sings about the railroad, they sings about the whole world, they sings about sweet honey, they sings about the rooster. They is evil and mean men and women in the blues. They is the boll weevil blues. They is good men and women in the blues.

I'm just a little country girl, off the cotton farm.
If I mistreats you baby, I don't mean you no harm.

There is people sings about working the turpentine farms and
them that sings about working in Detroit in Mr. Ford's factory.
They is blues that sings about St. Louis, Mississippi and Chicago.
They is blues that sings about Mr. President and the WPA. They's
blues songs about womens being glad for they sweet honey mens and
mens being glad for they sweet honey womens. No, they is not just
one subject matter to the blues. There's I'm tired of Jim Crow songs
and songs about the Good Lawd's children. There's I am what I am
songs. And some people singing the blues just 'cause they know the
song blues. I think you is writing them blues novels just 'cause you
knows the song.

Nadine, you don't mean that, say Delgadina.

She's right, say the woman. She's absolutely right.

There's Western Union blues and Mae West blues. There's
women is so tricky blues. There is my hair is so nappy blues. There's
gonna get me a yeller woman 'cause black women is so evil blues.
There's but I still love you the same old way blues.

You're right, you're right, you're right, you're right. What you say
your name is?

Nadine. The man I love is just as sweet as he can be. That's in the
blues too. What in the world made him love me so?

Girl, I shoulda talked to you before I wrote this novel, 'cause
you's so right.

There's I ain't gonna be nobody's slave for love blues.

Yeah, girl.

About the Peach Tree man.

Yeah, girl.

There's the I'm too good a man blues.

Yeah, girl.

Sometimes the blues seems like jazz to me.

Yeah, girl.

There's even people that tells the blues about itself.

What do you mean?

I don't tell her what I mean. I just tells her that the true blues
singer got a whole repertoire.

But I suppose most every woman got her a son-of-a-bitch tale like most every man got him a bitch story. A lot of them blues it seem like the woman be singing her son-of-a-bitch tale while the man be singing his bitch story. Of course that ain't all of the blues. And they's a aspect of the blues that's more humorous than a lotta peoples hears. And they's also the blues where a man sings about his good woman, and a woman sings about her good man.

How'd he propose?

I sip on my Coca-Cola. He didn't.

He didn't propose?

Naw.

Did *you* propose?

Didn't neither one of us propose. We was drinking them mint juleps in the backside, you know, and the next thing I know we's driving to the justice of the peace. I starts to tell her that we was sitting in the backside drinking them mint juleps and watching a couple of them jockeys shoot dice but that sound kinda like a stereotype, even though it the truth. I know a lot of y'all don't even want me telling y'all that, 'cause then y'all be thinking it just make more peoples you's got to explain that all us don't shoot dice like in them old Jim Crow movies. They probably wasn't shooting dice at all, y'all be saying, they was probably playing a game of bid whist or even poker, but because Nadine have seen so many Jim Crow movies with us playing dice she thought she seen them playing dice, which don't mean that she is lying, but mean that she is like them witnesses that they gives the psychological tests and they has white mens shooting dice and black mens playing bid whist and asks the people which one of the group of mens was shooting dice and they always say, even the colored peoples amongst them, that it were the black mens that was shooting dice and the white mens that was playing bid whist. So I don't say that about them jockeys shooting dice, I just says we was drinking them mint juleps 'cause nearly everybody at the Derby drinks mint juleps, them that frequents the backside, the ordinary folks in the stands as well as them VIPs. I don't remember seeing none of them jockeys drinking them mint juleps, though, but I guess them jockeys drinks them too. Can't be drinking them mint juleps, though, when you got to ride them horses. And maybe them jockeys all got to be teetotalers. Unless they got them nonalcoholic mint juleps for them teetotalers. I know you can buy you that mint julep syrup. She scratch her forehead and peek at me up over her designer eyeglasses. When she in the bar, though, she wear her them contact lenses.

No wonder y'all got divorced, she say. At least mine proposed, one of them real chivalric-type proposals too. Put his jacket down on the ground, got on his knee and shit, one of them old-fashioned proposals. Of course it was in his garage, but it was still a proposal. And in Spanish too, chica, which made it much more romantic. *¿Quieres casarte conmigo?*

To tell the truth, I ain't never been proposed to, except this one fool come up to me on the street and asked me if I wanted to marry him, but I thought the fool was joking, you know, or drunk. I ain't tell Delgadina I ain't never been proposed to, though, 'cause Delgadina she look like the kinda woman's probably got several proposals, though maybe not all chivalric. They's probably other womens ain't never been proposed to, but I ain't never sent out no questionnaires. We watches the man and woman that talking so close to each other it look like they noses is touching.

You pulling my leg, aintcha? she ask.

I won't tell her if I am or if I ain't. She get out her notebook 'cause she like that line about Tasmania. But in her notebook, the fellow ain't just in Tasmania, she gotta add something about them other devils. Then she look like she trying to hear what them lovers or what them lover's lovers is saying so's she can put that in her notebook. I guess all women divorce for the same reason, she say.

What reason? I asks, dipping into the salsa.

We just want more say-so, she say. Maybe the best women stays in the marriage and tries to work out some compromise. I think I'm a good woman but I ain't one of the best. She scratching her head now and then her elbow. Turn out she allergic to salsa but eat it anyway. After a moment, she be scratching her arm where you can see them little hives break out from that salsa. Just the tiniest hives she say form on the inside of her arm, near the elbows.

What do your ex do? I asks.

He's a steel sculptor, she say, scratching. He sculptures with steel. Well, I guess he can sculpture with all kindsa shit, but he prefers to sculpture with steel. He got this garage full of steel sculptures, you

know, the same garage he proposed to me in, amid all his steel sculptures and shit. Really romantic and shit. He a real good sculptor.
That's what he does for desire. For a living, he makes these steel
trellises you see on buildings. Steel trellises and gratings and shit.
He's got this sculpture that I think he should be famous for, it's sorta
the sculptural equivalent of the Klein bottle, I guess. You know that
confabulatory bottle which that glass that seem like it curves inside
itself but you can't really find out where them curves originates.
They always includes that Klein bottle in them books that tests
people's IQ and that shows the different inventions of peoples that is
supposed to have a high IQ like them Mensa books and them books
that's got mazes and puzzles in them and you's supposed to have to
solve the Klein bottle. He says it's not, but I think so anyway. He
sculptures more for desire, though.

No wonder she be liking them art and craft people, I be thinking.
Wonder if he one of them crafty artists or one of them artsy artists.
I be thinking about that metalwork on them buildings in New Orleans. 'Cause my girlfriend work for the Hollywood star went down
to New Orleans with her when she made one of them movies set in
New Orleans and be saying somebody be telling her how it African
artists made them metalwork on them buildings 'cause them African artists they supposed to be metalworkers. But they them slave
artisans, but she be saying how them Daughters of Nzingha be
telling her not to call them slaves anymore but just Africans, and
them Daughters of Nzingha they don't want her to keep working for
that Hollywood star and be her own woman, her own African
woman, but she be keep working for her anyhow. I guess all them
places she get to travel and maybe she wouldn't get to travel all them
places if she her own woman, even her own African woman. But me
I tell her not to tell me anymore about what them Daughters of
Nzingha be saying, 'cause I be thinking they just a cult, just like her
star said, or maybe it because I be starting to believe some of that cult
talk and wants to join up with them Daughters of Nzingha. Anyway,
that probably what she mean by them steel trellises, though, like
in that New Orleans. Delgadina, I mean. She scratch inside her elbow that got the hives, and then she scratch inside the one that ain't
got the hives. She still watching them lovers like a fool, like a romantic fool, and then I starts thinking not about my ex-husband but

about that John Henry Hollywood. Thinking about sitting on the bank of the Kentucky River fishing with John Henry Hollywood when I shows him one of them letters from Monkey Bread, one enticing me to come to California. Like I said, they been boyfriend and girlfriend they ownself, Monkey Bread and John Henry, but that was before she went out there to California, anyway he telling me even when they was going together he consider Monkey Bread only his sometimes girlfriend.

That girl always had her mind on Hollywood, he be saying.

His own name Hollywood, like I said, but he don't mean hisself, of course he mean that other Hollywood. Glamourtown. We both of us barefoot sitting on the riverbank, like I said, and got our dungarees rolled up and sitting on a log we pulled up close to the riverbank. He done caught more fish than me. In fact, he the best fisherman I met. I been thinking about going out to that California myself, I says. Even before Monkey Bread ask me. I don't say just Hollywood, 'cause that California more than Hollywood.

It don't surprise me, he say. 'Cause both of y'all is wild womens, I mean wild as in freedom-seeking womens. 'Cept I think you more freedom-seeking even than Monkey Bread.

Why don't you come out to California with me? I asks.

He don't say nothing. He take his fishing rod out of the water and lean it against one of them horsetail plants that grow along the riverbank. You just seeing California from the woman's point of view, he saying.

I don't know what he talking about and he don't explain it to me. They probably got a lot of pianos need tuning out in California, I says. And you know they probably more open-minded in California than they is around here. You be saying they let you move they pianos but don't want you to tune they pianos. All them African-American musicians, I bet they needs good piano tuners, anyhow.

You just looking at California from the woman's point of view, he say.

I be looking at the Kentucky River and at one of them riverboats, then one of them barges, then across the bank at Ohio, at the Cincinnati skyline, which were the tallest skyline I'd seen before I seen New York, then at the bridge stretching across the river, then at the horsetail plant. Now the first time he say that I didn't know what he

mean, but the second time he say that about my looking at California
from the woman point of view I understand what he mean, or least,
I think I understand what he mean—that if he the one ask me to go
to California with him then we go to California, but if I the one be
asking him to go to California with me he ain't going to no California. Leastwise that what I think he mean. 'Cause they a lot of mens
like that. They might have California dreams they ownself, but they
ain't going to California on a woman's desire.

You told Monkey Bread we going together, ain't you?

Out to California? I ask.

Naw, I mean us going together. Boyfriend and girlfriend.

Yeah, I says. I told Monkey Bread we's going together, 'cause I
ain't no fool. I mean, I am a fool, but I ain't that sorta fool. My mama
didn't raise that sorta fool. Of course, she say she didn't raise no fool.
What fool I am I gots to claim credit for myself.

He won't say so, but he probably thinking that why that Monkey
Bread be tempting and enticing me with that California, 'cause
womens is like that. I be thinking about what men is like, even them
good men, and he be thinking about what womens is, even, I suppose, them good womens, 'cause at least I don't think that John
Henry Hollywood be going with either Monkey Bread or me if he
didn't think we was good womens, though I guess they's mens that
go with womens that they don't think is good womens, at least they
idea of good womens. But if I be seeing California from the woman's
point of view, ain't he be seeing womens from the men's point of
view. He pick up his fishing rod and put it back in the water. I guess
them rivers in California be making this mighty river look like a
creek, he be saying.

But them fish, though, them fish, though, seem like they be treating his pole like they think it the only one in the water. And he even
be catching fishes, he tell me, ain't even native to this stream. And
he be catching them big fish. The fish I catches they all looks like
pollywogs. He one of them large, muscular-type men with big hands
and feet and one of them deep, melodious-type voices. Broad-
shouldered as them Egyptians in them sculptures. Broad forehead
and sorta Eskimo eyes. Or Inuit eyes 'cause they call theyselves Inuits. High cheekbones, dark complexion, full kinda reddish lips, but
that they natural color. I think he right handsome myself, though

Monkey Bread she think he ordinary-looking, 'cause she say she
don't like them pretty mens. I think he closer to handsome than ordinary-looking myself.

Delgadina and me, we watch them lovers lean toward each other,
whisper something and then they rise.

You a strange bird, she saying now. She standing near the bar
holding that handmade broom and spying at me. Running her other
hand through her Sean Young hairdo, except her hair more kinky
and curly than Sean Young's. Delgadina got a thick head of hair but
delicate, finely arched eyebrows.

I just sips my Bud Light and chews another pretzel. I just drinks
Bud Light and not when I'm driving. When I'm driving I drinks
one of them beer substitutes, one of them nonalcoholic beers. The
kind the commercials say your mouth can't tell it ain't beer, but it
sure can tell it ain't Bud. I oughta write me one of them commercials.
I guess everybody be thinking they can write them commercials
though. And I should start taking that niacin, though, that Monkey
Bread told me about.

I'm on my way to see that Melvin Van Peebles cowboy movie.
They say that one outta three cowboys was a spliv. Course in them
cowboy days people didn't wanna be a cowboy. Cowboy s'posed to
be a derogatory term. But then when they start to glorifying the cowboy they only want to paint the cowboy white. I done ask Delgadina
if she wanna go see that movie about the Southwest, but she got her
creative writing class at the Community Center. Started to ask Father Raymond, but he couldn't pretend to be no priest and come to
the movies with me. Still I guess priests go to the movies same's regular people do, but priests probably only go to the movies with other
priests or with monks. Be good to see some different-color cowboys,
though. And cowgirls too. I don't know if that movie supposed to
have spliv cowgirls in it, but I know it got spliv cowboys and they's
the heroes of the movie. I think they got a African-American woman
in that movie as the love interest, one of them mulatto types. In them
real cowboy days you had you a range of African-American womens
the same's African-American mens, and probably not just mulatto
womens the love interest.

Anyway, I'm sitting there drinking my Bud Light, thinking cowgirls and cowboys and the Southwest, and Raymond, and that Afri-

can, and John Henry Hollywood, and my ex, and Delgadina still telling me I'm a strange bird. I'm waiting for her to tell me I'm a strange bird how, but she just keep repeating the fact that I'm a strange bird. Strange bird how? I be thinking. I sucks on one of them pretzels and then eats it. Small crunchy pretzels mixed in with those large soft pretzels. And I'm wondering where them pretzels originated. Pretzel, that sound like a German word, though I think Delgadina said that pretzel supposed to come from a Latin or Greek word, but that pretzel sound German, though, or Dutch.

Strange bird how? I asks. I nibbles one of the small crunchy pretzels and then dunk one of the large soft pretzels in my beer.

You just a strange bird, she repeat.

Then she finish sweeping up, put that broom in the corner behind the bar, wipe off the counter, and then come and sit down at the table and drink a little of that Bud Light, drink a sip outta my bottle.

You don't drink, I says.

She a strange bird herself, being a bartender that don't drink, though I guess there's probably plenty bartenders that don't drink. First I thought she one of them allergic to alcohol, but she ain't. You a strange bird yourself, I says. But I guess it good to be a bartender that don't drink. Probably plenty bartenders that don't drink, ain't they? 'Cept you eat up all the Neapolitan ice cream. Maybe the best bartender is them that don't drink.

Yeah, but I'm kinda nervous. Gotta read my story to the writing class.

And Bud is moral support? I asks.

She look at me a moment, scratch her forehead. I glances toward someone peeking in the window of the cantina. Right, she say, and then she repeat that thing about me being a strange bird and scratch herself again like she do when she eating that salsa. You just pretend like you a *borracha,* though. I see how you just be sipping that Bud. I don't think you come to no bars to drink, I just think you come for the atmosphere. You a strange bird.

At least I know a bird from a mosquito, I says, nibbling a small, hard pretzel and then getting one of them large, soft pretzels.

Then Delgadina take another sip of that Bud Light, straight outta my bottle. Don't wipe the bottle off with her hands or nothing. Even in them cowboy movies when they drinks from each other's bottles they always wipes off the bottle. Just drink straight outta it. And then she wipe her lips with the back of her hand, like that girl with the nose-ring that me and Raymond seen in that Italian restaurant. Maybe that girl what you call a primitivist. And then she scratch the corner of her mouth and start saying that prunes and prisms; she read in one of her books one of them nineteenth-century novels that if you say prunes and prisms it give you nice-shaped lips. But she probably also be saying it 'cause she gotta read her story to that writing class.

When I drives up to the Community Center, I see Father Raymond in front of the center stamping out a cigarette. He ain't wearing priest's robes but priest's trousers and priest's tunic and that backward collar. If he didn't have that backward collar, he look like any ordinary man, good-looking man, but ordinary. But that the point of them backward collar. Except but he got on cowboy boots. I guess them modern priests can wear them cowboy boots. Modern priests in Texas anyhow. Otherwise people see them cowboy boots and say for sure that not a real priest. But this is Texas. And I just seen that cowboy movie and here another cowboy.

He told me he ain't no priest, I'm thinking. But maybe this a real priest. Suppose this a real priest telling me he ain't no priest? I thought he was truthful in telling me he ain't no priest. But a lot of y'all knows me for the fool that I am. *Is you is or is you ain't my baby?* I ain't no Catholic, but I still don't think no decent woman should be loving no priest. 'Cept of course he ain't no true priest. Or unless they changes them laws of celibacy.

Didn't know you smoked, I says, getting out of the truck. I just seen me the best cowboy movie. Melvin Van Peebles.

At first he look like he don't know me and ain't studying no cowboys. Like I'm some strange, forward woman. Maybe even one of them mad bad and dangerous to know types. Then he looking at me like I'm Mosquito. And then like Sojourner.

What are you doing here? he ask.

I'm picking up Delgadina, I says. She has her creative writing class at the Community Center.

Who's Delgadina? Delgadina who?

My bartender. My friend Delgadina. You know I'm always talking 'bout Delgadina. My bartender friend.

Monkey Bread? That the one you call Monkey Bread?

No, Delgadina, my bartender friend, not my California friend. Monkey Bread's my California friend. She the housekeeper for a movie star. Delgadina's the bartender.

Oh, yeah?

You know Delgadina, my bartender friend. I'm always talking 'bout Delgadina. She got a creative writing class in there in the Community Center and I promised to pick her up after it. I just been to see that Melvin Van Peebles cowboy movie, and I said I'd pick her up after her class. That's the best cowboy movie I seen. I don't think it's just 'cause it gots splivs in it. What about you?

I was supposed to meet someone here, but they didn't show. When I spotted you, I thought. . . .

I'm spying on you? You want me to drive you anywhere?

Naw.

You get your friend to Canada? *La mujer.*

He lift a eyebrow. Yeah.

Them refugees ever give her any more trouble?

Naw. We've resettled them in different places. They've settled in Miami and she's in Canada.

You like that love novel? You don't see many African-American love novels.

He lift another eyebrow. Yeah, it's pretty good.

I seen you read that quotation about what a black man got to do with love. I think the point must be that a black man can have everything to do with love like any other man. I thought you might like that book 'cause you be talking about that subversive love and shit. And that book supposed to be a love story. I like me tales about men and women. My friend Monkey Bread says I'm a romantic. They say it takes a romantic to know a romantic. Seems like I read that somewhere. Or maybe that's Delgadina quoting one of them writers she's always reading for that creative writing class.

Nur der Dicter versteht den Dichter; nur ein romantisches Gemut kann eingehen in das Romantische. . . .

Say what?

Hoffmann's *Don Juan.*

Yeah, Delgadina likes them Germans. She say them Germans don't got as long a literary history as a lot of them other Europeans, but they's still got some of the best writers in the world, that Kafka, that Hesse, that Mann. That Goethe. That Goethe he supposed to be some type of genius. I read somewhere if they was giving them IQ tests in Goethe's time he be some type of genius. I heard of that Hoffmann, but I didn't know them *Tales of Hoffmann* was tales of romance. I don't think I'm as half a pigeon for romance as Monkey Bread thinks I am, though.

He acting like he want to light up another cigarette. I glances in one of the windows and sees one of them karate classes. Sometimes they got them they karate classes in there, other times it aerobics. But you starts to see more and more women in them karate classes, and more and more men in them aerobic classes. I be thinking about that karate myself before I decide on that stun gun, 'cause, like I said, I never did like them classrooms. I wouldn't mind learning that karate if you could learn it in one of them courtyards, like in the movies. They call them karate teachers masters, though, don't they? I watches them in the window, they be kicking ass and then be bowing and shit. And women be looking like they kicking ass as good as them men and better than some of them. Usedta be a elementary school, the Community Center, but when the elementary school moved into a new building, they turned this one into a Community Center. 'Cept the true karate expert they supposed to prefer making peace to making war, like that wolf woman be talking about, *la loba*.

I starts to ask him more about that *la loba* when Delgadina come out of the Community Center. Hi, Mosquito.

Uh, this is Father Raymond, I says.

We's almost standing too close for him to be a true padre, so I backs away a little bit.

Hello, I'm Delgadina, she say.

Hello.

Good to meet you.

See you around, say Father Raymond as Delgadina and I start toward my truck. Good to meet you, Delgadina.

Same here.

Of course, I'm imagining they already know each other, that maybe Delgadina she be a secret worker for the Sanctuary movement her ownself, and maybe even it Delgadina been spying on me telling them I'm somebody they can trust. And maybe even Delgadina be the one he suppose to meet here. 'Cause that Delgadina she do seem a lot more intelligent than most bartenders, and maybe a bartender just her camouflage, or maybe I'm just stereotyping them bartenders. Maybe all the time she be coming to the Community Center she be doing that Sanctuary work, though. But if they does already know each other, they pretends they don't. But then if she were doing that Sanctuary work she wouldn't always be inviting me to that class.

That the Carmelite priest you was telling me about? ask Delgadina as we get in the truck.

I glances at Father Raymond, who peeking in the window at them karate people, then he turn and watch us. They still be kicking ass and then bowing and shit. The instructor he a real Asian, but he got every kinda people in his class. Father Raymond he light up another cigarette, but don't puff it, though. Maybe that lit cigarette a signal or something.

He a Benedictine, I says. Did you get butterfly shoulders?

What? She scratch her forehead. Say what?

Nerves. Your reading? I'm watching them karate people kicking ass and then bowing.

Naw. They liked the story mostly. 'Cept a few of 'em said I'm too preoccupied with being a Chicana, you know. And I should write universal stories or some shit. Gringo stories, that's what they mean by universal, or gringa stories, even gringa stories can be universal now. We Chicanos are *la raza cósmica*, the cosmic race. We're already universal. Some rangy girl in the class read this story about a mustached fish and everyone's like praising it for its universality and I write about *la raza cósmica* and it ain't universal. Someone even had the nerve to ask me why don't Chicanos ever write about centaurs and unicorns and fauns and nymphs and Proteus and shit. But stories about adolescent sexual frustration, they're supposed to be universal. Plus we got our Proteus and they call *nayatl* and they ain't imaginary, they real.

Anyhow, I think she be saying *nayatl* or maybe she be saying *nahuatal*. I want to tell her about that wolf woman, *la loba*, or maybe she already know about her. *La raza cósmica*. I used to think exploitation began with the Spaniards, though, she says. With the Europeans.

Don't it?

The Aztecs, they were exploiters too, I mean, the way they treated the Totonacs and the Tlaxcalans.

Oh, yeah? I guess everybody they be exploiting somebody.

Like even that documentary on Australia we seen, even them kangaroos exploiting each other—one kangaroo fighting another kangaroo. Looked kinda like that karate. But human beings ain't kangaroos. And still you be wondering whether that instinct make them fight like that or whether that the intellect. What them kangaroos be thinking when they gains control. But then one of them kangaroo don't think of hisself as exploiting them other kangaroo. And wonder if them kangaroos makes a distinction between them aborigines, the original Australians and them immigrants. But Australia that supposed to be a prison, though, so most of them white Australians ain't true and orthodox immigrants. Or whether them kangaroos makes a distinction between theyselves, 'cause they's got them red kangaroos. But human beings ain't kangaroos. I be just a-looking at that Australia 'cause it close to Tasmania.

Yeah. They used to rape their women—the Totonac and Tlaxcalan women—and have the Totonacs and Tlaxcalans pay high taxes and tributes and shit. Indians exploiting Indians and then the Spanish came and they treated the Aztecs like they'd treated the other Indians. Treated *all* the Indians like shit. That ain't to say that you gotta excuse the Spaniards. But, you know what I'm saying. . . . What started me to talking that exploitation shit anyhow? But you know what I'm saying?

Yeah.

Everybody colonizes somebody.

Yeah.

But a gringo's a gringo. A *gabacho's* a *gabacho.* I like writing fiction, but my favorite stories are true ones, like the one about La Beata, the Blessed One. And the heroines of the war of independence and the revolution of 1910. Sor Juana Inés de la Cruz, Santa Teresa de Ávila. . . .

La Beata?

A *curandera,* a healing woman and a revolutionary too. . . . The opposite of machismo is *hembrismo.* . . . The Aztecs usedta have women priests, you know. *Cuiatlamacazqui,* they called 'em. In the beginning, the Aztec universe usedta be feminine . . . healers and midwives. . . . Then the masculine gods. . . . I guess maybe a lot of universes usedta be feminine, you know. I guess it depends on who's in power how the universe looks, whose interpretation of the universe. . . .

She be talking about them Aztec women priests and I starts to tell her about the Daughters of Nzingha and they priestess, but I don't, I just listen. I don't know if them Daughters of Nzingha consider theyselves a true secret society, though. 'Cause if they was a true secret society, Monkey Bread wouldn't be writing about them in her letters, and I wouldn't even know they a Daughters of Nzingha. Or maybe they's a Daughters of Nzingha they wants peoples to know about and a Daughters of Nzingha that is secret.

I met this guy in the class who knows more about Chicano history than anyone. He likes my stories. He's not really Chicano, though, he's a Mexican. In Mexico he usedta be a mining engineer, but he's really a part of the Chicano community now. He works in the community, you know. He's always going into the factories and the migrant camps and working with the *huelguistas,* the strikers and shit. And union organizers and shit. He's part Indian, part Yaqui. He told me all about the Tomochi war when the Yaquis revolted, you know. And the Tarahumara Indians. He says I've got features like a Tarahumara Indian. . . . They're supposed to be the Indians the gringos couldn't subdue. . . .

You sound like you're in love.

Do I? Naw, he's got a wife.

You still sound like you're in love.

I don't play that, Mosquito, plus I ain't no fool. . . . He says I'm very *hembrismo.* That's like machismo except a woman. In Mexico his wife usedta be a doctor, but here she works as a pecan sheller. They both work in the same factory. Jovita. Jovita and Joaquín Vasquez de Agüello. Actually, she was born in Rio Abajo, New Mexico, but says that where she went to school they punished her one time for speaking Spanish on the playground and so her father took his family to Mexico—so she grew up in Mexico. In Hornitos. . . .

Say what?

Hornitos, a mining town, that's where she met Joaquín. They came here as refugees, all legal I mean, but he almost got deported, though, 'cause they tried to brand him a communist agitator or some shit or socialist or some shit, but he calls himself a labor defender. Anybody who defends workers, you know. He considers me a real *trabajadora*, a real working woman, 'cause I've worked in canneries, in clothing factories, packed crackers, worked as a seamstress and shit. Even worked in a mirror factory. But he's the first man I've ever met who I think genuinely believes a woman should be as free as a man. Maybe he's just jiving me, you know how men do, but I don't think so.

You're in love, girl.

You know I don't play that. There some people that says all's fair in love and war, but not me. If a man's got a wife, then I don't play that. But he don't call me Delgadina, he calls me Isabella—that's my middle name. Delgadina Isabella Rodríguez, or he calls me Isabellita but I prefer Isabella, that's more equal. But I ain't no fool, girl.

She pinches her cheekbones till they blush, then she straightens her do-rag.

I don't play that, she repeat. Plus, I ain't no fool.

I be thinking about them people that protest too much. She keep saying she don't play that probably mean she be thinking about playing with some wife's man. I don't play that myself, though. Course John Henry Hollywood were Monkey Bread's John Henry, but she ain't he wife and I didn't start going with John Henry till Monkey Bread moved to California. I puts the key in the ignition and we head away from the Community Center. I'd been watching Raymond to see if he'd meet somebody, but he just lit another cigarette. And I don't want him to think I'm spying on him.

This friend of mine says myth is a race, I says as we head away from the Community Center. Like you say that racial purity a myth, he say that myth itself is a race.

You mean race itself is a myth.

What I say?

Myth itself is a race.

She open my glove compartment, push aside my stun gun and flashlight, and take out some of my Jungle Jerky and start chewing. She must be allergic to that Jungle Jerky too 'cause she be scratching.

Race is a myth, I say.

Race ain't no myth, chica girl, whoever told you that was shitting you. She offer me some of my Jungle Jerky.

Muchas gracias. Oh, he didn't say it hisself, he said somebody else said it.

Whoever told him was shitting him. . . . Probably a gringo. Probably a *gabacho.* They be telling you race is a myth when it in they interest, otherwise they don't treat race like no myth. I signed up for detective school. They be having us take one of them karate classes too. I seen you watching them kicking ass. You oughta sign up for that class, chica. I know a little karate. I think every woman should know how to kick ass. I be learning to work with computers and learning about those miniature surveillance devices and shit, I mean for detective school, but I might have to kick some ass too, chica girl, so you gotta learn karate, but I was talking to the karate teacher, and he says the object of karate is to not kick ass, but to know how to kick ass if you have to. Anyhow, chica girl, I signed up for that detective school. Wanna celebrate?

Sure. But he ain't no gringo, or *gabacho* either, I says, defending Ray, though it ain't Ray she calling the gringo and *gabacho* it the somebody else said it. Plus, ain't gringo and *gabacho* the same thing?

I heads in the direction of her bar.

Not my bar. You ever been to a storefront cantina? A real cantina. You ever had any pulque?

I stops at this truckstop restaurant. They's a waitress there looks just like Miguelita. I sits down in one of the booths and orders breakfast.

Soapjourner? How come they call you Soapjourner? asks the waitress, looking just like Miguelita and acting just like she know me. She holding the steaming pot of coffee in one hand and straightening the strap of her bra with the other. Got on one of them bright yellow waitress outfits. Butterfly yellow. And she got yellow hair too. She say her grandfather a Tasmanian aborigine, but she don't look nothing like no Tasmanian aborigine herself, she look just like that Miguelita, except she a older woman and she ain't acting like no loca, though I don't think that Miguelita as loca as everybody say she is.

She as friendly as Miguelita, and she tell me the reason she be

*gawking when she seen me drive my truck up is they ain't no
women truck drivers in Tasmania and certainly ain't no other
African-American women truck drivers on this route. But she say
they is another spliv on the route. Don't you African Americans call
yourselves splivs? Where you from?*

South Texas.

So how come you a trucker?

You know, the romance of the road.

*I'm looking at the menu and she start advising me about that
menu. Advising me not to order any of they stew, 'cause she be calling it slumgullion stew. Some of these galoots likes slumgullion
stew, though, she be saying. You tell some of these gents it's slumgullion stew, they orders it anyhow. Not that they all gents.*

*Name's Sojourner, I says. They calls me Soapjourner on account I
carry industrial and ecological detergents.*

*Then I explains what a ecological detergent is and she be saying
that's the kinda detergent they uses, 'cause the dishwasher be allergic to them chemicals, plus that ecological detergent it clean them
dishes better, except but they uses that liquid ecological detergent
and me I carry that powdered ecological detergent. I don't tell her
'bout my other names, Jane and Nadine. I don't tell her 'bout that
Mosquito either. But she look like she ain't never heard the name
Sojourner neither. And then she start talking about how that Tasmania believe in all that ecological tourism and promoting them ecological detergents.*

*That a right unusual name, she say. Ain't got no Tasmanian
names like that.*

*I starts to ask her whether Tasmania is its own whole country or
whether it a part of Australia. I sips my coffee and bites into my
french toast—they got french toast in Tasmania—and taste them
eggs and then he come in, one she been telling me about, the other
spliv on the route. One of them tall men, six-four maybe, sorta dark-
complexioned from the Tasmanian sun but maybe butterscotch underneath the suntan. But I know who he is: he my ex-husband. He
spot me and we nod to each other, then he go sit down at one of the
booths and waitress she go over and pour his coffee and take his order. Pile of pancakes, maple sugar syrup, scrambled eggs, sausage on
the side, orange juice.*

At first I thinks maybe he don't recognize me, but next thing I know he's bringing these plates over putting 'em on my table. He don't say nothing, he just put couple plates down on my table, then go back get 'nother coupla plates, then get his coffee, then take the sugar off his table and put it on mine, then he sits down. He pours a little bit of that sugar in his coffee and stirs. I be wanting to tell him about that sugar, 'cause I seen one of them documentaries on that sugar, and me I always uses one of them natural fruit sugars.

You the one they call 'journer, aintcha? Heard about you even in Australia. They kept telling me you in Tasmania now and you and me was on the same route.

I didn't know if you'd recognize me, I says.

You know I always recognize you, Jane-Nadine.

Him, he say he don't carry just one sorta product, like I do. Sometimes he might have him a load of them Tasmanian bananas, other time he might be carry some heating fuel product to the folks in the outback—I be thinking they just calls it the outback in Australia, but he be talking about the outback—even palm oil, other time he might be the Tupperware express. Make me laugh when he say that. Didn't know they be having that Tupperware in Tasmania.

You got a nice laugh, he say. Thought you be older by now, but you look the same to me.

I'm older, I says. Did carry something other than soap once, though, I'm telling him.

What?

Had me this pregnant Mexican woman.

Say what? He be chewing and drinking coffee. He sop a little bit of his eggs up with his toast.

I didn't know she was there or nothing. Stopped along one of them border roads, you know, that Dairy Mart Road, then heard me a sound like this commotion, thought maybe some coyote back there, you know, or one of them prairie foxes, or one of them horny toads, got my stun gun and my flashlight, and she hiding back there behind one of them detergent crates. She don't come out of hiding till I shines that light on her. I think she going to have her baby there and then. It ain't labor pains, though, it hunger pains. I gives her something to eat. Yeah, she thinks I'm gonna turn her in but I don't. I didn't even think about turning her in. When she have her baby, she name him Journal 'cause she think that my name. Name him Sanctuary after the movement and Journal after me, or what she thinks is me. Me, I calls him S. J. Ramírez. He a half-Indian baby. One of them Tarahumara Indians. They supposed to be the fiercest Indians. Them Spaniards they supposed to be able to subdue all them Indians except them Tarahumara Indians. She came north to the States and he went south to Chiapas. I think it called Chiapas. He wrote her he want her to return to Mexico, though. And then I think he got involved in that rebellion down there, and then she got a letter from him wanting her to return to Mexico and then she heard from her cousin who were in jail in Middle America. We went out there, but I think her cousin went down there to Cholula or somewhere back in Mexico, so she thinking herself of maybe returning to Mexico, though I don't think she want to go to Cholula with them rebels on account of Journal and maybe they stay in Mexico City or one of them little border towns just across the border, 'cause he a American citizen. If she do return to Mexico, though, she say she might hire me to drive her cross the border. They's got a rebellion down there in Cholula, so I told her myself I ain't think she should take Journal to no rebellion, though I knows when peoples rebels they's got to rebel. I knows when peoples rebels they's got to rebel. Course they's every kind of rebellion. I ain't no rebel's rebel, though. Maria say sometimes you's got to become a rebel's rebel. She speak real good English now. She thinks I joined the Sanctuary movement or what they calls the new Underground Railroad. I be Ray's rebel, I be Maria's rebel, I be Monkey Bread's rebel, I be Delgadina's rebel, I be little Journal's rebel. Maybe I add some more to my list of rebellions, but them is people I know. You know that Ray receives solicitations for rebellion all the time. I think that's what I means by a rebel's rebel. I ain't reformed to rebellion Itself. You's got to put a name to my rebellion. They is rebels for abstractions. But that Delgadina, she know what I'm talking about. I ain't told her 'bout Maria and Journal, though, or even about us adventures with Maria's cousin in Middle America. But that be really funny if I drives her across the border back to Mexico, you know. She ain't made up her mind yet, though. If she do go back to Mexico, it be for love. It be for that rebel in Cholula. That the first baby named after me, though, or name they thinks is mine. Even she know it ain't

mine, she keep him that name, 'cause that the name she originally
think is mine. And her, Maria Ramírez her name. She be a trickster
and a jokester, you know, telling me her name Maria Barriga, 'cause
barriga that mean belly in Spanish. She think I'm a good woman.
Mujer buena. All I knows is all the time I travels along these border
roads, the border patrol they stops me and makes sure I ain't smuggling nothing. Might be two or three other trucks and real smugglers
and they stops mines. So that time I really am smuggling somebody
and don't know it. She think I'm a good woman 'cause I took her to
the Sanctuary priest. Truth of the matter is I took her to 'em as much
for them border patrol as for her. You know what I mean? That be
funny if I drive her back across that border to Mexico.

    Are you?

    If she makes up her mind about going back to Mexico. But Chia-
pas—I think it Chiapas—that supposed to be one of the poorest
Mexican states. In southern Mexico. That's where Cholula is. She
turned the front of her house into a store, you know, so I come to buy
one of her dolls, you know, so she starts telling me about her rebel,
and she thinking of going to that rebellion. I ain't actually come to
buy one of her dolls, though I usually buys one of her dolls when I'm
there. 'Cause they's superior to factory dolls, and sometimes I use
her dolls as promotional items, you know. But mostly I likes to collect them for myself, 'cause they is like art, you know. So I'm the one
convinces her not to take Journal to that rebellion. Now if it were her
her ownself, I could consider driving her to southern Mexico, but
they wouldn't let us get close to no rebellion in my truck, and anyway now they's contained a lot of them rebels, but they's still rebels
in them mountains down there. And she knows where they is. But
us ain't no professional rebels. Some people is supposed to help her
rebel to escape north. I believe they's always helped him to escape
north. So the thing is he don't trust America, he don't want to cross
the border into America, so we's got to decide on Mexico, I mean
she's got to decide on Mexico. But I already told her I'd drive her to
Mexico City.

When I come to see Maria and Journal she is packing her suitcases.
She's got her big suitcase and Journal's little suitcase. I think maybe
she has found out where her cousin was, the one that they'd jailed in

the Middle American commonwealth on account of her being a illegal alien and claimed it 'cause they ain't no what else to do with no illegal alien. Least that was their first claim. Then nobody claimed anything, and there weren't even any documents to prove Maria's cousin had even been originally arrested.

You found your cousin? I asks. Is she in Mexico somewhere?

She continues packing her suitcase with mostly blue jeans and sweatshirts, the skirt I first saw her wearing and several blouses, but points to a bunch of newspaper articles on her doll table. I calls it her doll table, 'cause that's the table where she make her dolls. I stands reading them articles and they's all about some kinda rebellion in Chiapas which somewhere in southern Mexico and talking about how some of them rebels have escaped into the mountains. They say something about the Zapatistas the same people I heard Ray talking about. The government have some of them rebels and some of them others have escaped. She ain't sure which rebels they have and which rebels escaped, but seem like she know everybody in Chiapas who might be amongst them rebels. I don't know if it's the same rebellion that Ray was talking about or whether this is a different rebellion. I ain't sure what that rebellion is about, but most all rebellions is for the same reason, for some kinda freedom, or some kinda power to help create freedom, but seem like one of them rebels is connected with Maria, her husband and lover or maybe the daddy of Journal, 'cept I ain't exactly sure. Seem like she going back to Mexico to that rebellion and taking Journal. She ain't say that, but her pointing to them newspapers when I ask why she packing make me think that.

Naw, you ain't taking my baby to no rebellion, I says.

Your baby? She still packing to go to that rebellion.

I know he your baby, Maria. I know Journal is your baby. But he name after me, or the name you thinks is mine, and when you says his name you invokes the name you thinks is me, and you ain't taking him to Mexico to no rebellion. They tells me that I has a man named Big Warrior in my ancestry, who fought the powers, who didn't even war chant first, but he didn't take his babies to war. He didn't take his babies to no rebellion. Least I don't think so.

The baby looking like he ready to go to the rebellion. Like he a little Big Warrior hisself. He got on little baby dungarees and she got his baby clothes and everything packed, and he standing up saying,

Jiba jiba jiba jiba jiba. And the way he saying it it sound like some rebel song. Yeah, he sounding like he ready to go to that rebellion, even though he just a little baby.

Then I gets the story that it seem like her husband and lover who the daddy of Journal sent her North on account of her going to have that baby and didn't tell her about the rebellion, though it was only a proposed rebellion then, but now she know about the rebellion and able to read them newspapers for herself, which tell about that rebellion and she on her way back to Mexico.

Naw, you ain't, I says.

Yes, I am.

Then we reasons about it. *You's got to talk to Ray's people first, I says. You's got to talk to Ray's people first. I think they has all the logistics on that rebellion.*

Ray? she asks.

Father Ray. I think he has all the logistics on that rebellion. You've got to talk to Father Ray first.

I calls up Ray's people from the number he give me and talks to somebody. It might be one of them guerrilla lawyers, but I ain't sure who it is, then Ray's people sends the other Ray, the Ray name Ray Mendoza. Ain't I described for you the other Ray? He the one looks like a Aztec god. He look like some type of Aztec god, 'cept he's wearing blue jeans and a sweatshirt. I introduces him to Maria.

I know Ray Mendoza, say Maria. But I'm interested in knowing more and learning more. How are you Señor Mendoza?

Jiba jiba jiba jiba jiba.

¿Cómo estás, mi hijo? say Ray to Journal. And then he and Maria they says something to each other, but that also in Spanish. Then they starts talking English. Then they put little Spanish with they English. I ain't know what they mean, but I remembers what they says: con la esperanza de la libertad y todos por su voluntad, ninguno forzado. *But years later I learned that them was code expressions that was actually from a Spanish epic, the same as when Maria started praying and talking about her* Padre espiritual *which is a name for* Dios. *Maybe that Maria a Nicodemus her ownself, and maybe that cousin weren't her real cousin but her confabulatory cousin. Course Maria ain't ask me to go with her nowhere else to defend nobody else's rights and freedoms, so maybe that her real*

497

cousin. I ain't ask Maria all that though, 'cause if she a real Nicodemus she ain't want to tell me she a Nicodemus. I'm thinking how
many other members of the new Underground Railroad she know
when Ray Mendoza notice them dolls of hers and say things like
fantástico and other fabulous words in Spanish, and then she give
him one of them dolls, and I'm thinking if even them dolls have got
codes in them and messages that she sends across the border, 'cause
ain't she told me that now they is mail order peoples even in Mexico
that buys them dolls? For all I knows, they is people in the rebellion
that has Maria's dolls. And y'all can't tell me that that line. But I'm
interested in knowing more and learning more, ain't no code for
something. Then I wants to ask her how she know Ray, I means the
other Ray, this Ray, but I don't. I tells him 'bout Maria's rebellion
and how I ain't want her to take Journal to no rebellion.

I believes them peoples has they right to rebel, I says, and if Maria want to go to a rebellion I drive her down there myself, but I ain't
going to allow her to take us Journal to that rebellion.

It ain't yours to allow, Journal, she say.

She know my true name, but she likes calling me that name she
originally thought was mine, and she likes keeping Journal with the
name she originally thought was mine.

And it wasn't his to send me up North and ain't tell me about the
rebellion, she say.

Then it Ray Mendoza who reasons with her talking to her like
he always know her and telling her that he knows some people that
knows some people. Then he tell Maria not to go down there to the
rebellion till he come back, and then when he come back he give us
more information than in them newspapers, which is the fact that
some people is helping her husband and lover to escape North, and
that if she want to go to Mexico, she can wait for him in Mexico
City and don't have to travel to the rebellion. And there's other
things about the rebellion and them rebels now that ain't in them
newspapers, 'cept I ain't going to tell y'all. I ain't going to tell y'all no
more about Maria's rebellion than I'm telling y'all. But while Ray
Mendoza was there, Maria says, I want to tell you more of my story,
Sojourner. But then before she started telling it I thought I heard a
little red bird say, I can tell, I can tell your story, Mommy, I can tell,
I can tell, I can tell, I can tell, I can tell. I ain't want to say nothing,

'cause I know that Ray and Maria ain't heard that little red bird. But Journal start saying, Jiba Jiba Jiba Jiba Jiba. And to tell y'all the truth, I ain't sure whether Journal say that or the little red bird.

I can't tell you more about Maria's rebellion, I says. I calls it Maria's rebellion, 'cause I first learned about it from Maria, except I could call it Ray's rebellion because I overheard Ray talking to someone about logistics, but it's Maria's people's rebellion, or it's the rebellion of them that made that rebellion. That's the thing about them rebellions, though, you's got to keep them confidential. I don't think modern rebels keeps their rebellions that confidential, 'cause I heard about they rebellion before I knew it was a rebellion. I do know that when they were having the rebellion some of Ray's people interviewed the rebels. I don't know if it was the same rebellion, the Chiapas rebellion. Maybe there are some other people that call themselves the Zapatistas or maybe they are the same Zapatistas. Them newspapers pretends they's telling you the whole rebellion, but they ain't know the whole rebellion, and a lot of what they does tell you is what the governments wants them to say. They pretends they's the free press, but ain't none of them the true voice of the people. I knows more about the rebellion than you reads in the newspapers. Ain't nobody know the whole rebellion but the rebels themselves. And they knows enough not to tell them newspapers what they do know. And I don't believe they even told Ray's people everything.

I mean are you in the Sanctuary movement? he asked. The new Underground Railroad?

How can I be in the Sanctuary movement or the new Underground Railroad in South Texas when I'm here in Tasmania with you? So anyway if I do decide to go down there to Mexico, I mean if Maria and Journal decide to go to Mexico, that be another adventure I can tell you about. I ain't no rebel's rebel, though, but I likes them that is.

He sop up some more of his eggs and chews his toast. He kinda remind me of Raymond and he kinda remind me of John Henry Hollywood, and even kinda remind me of the man in the storybook, and he kinda remind me of his ownself, and he looking like he be wanting me to say he his ownself. Wanting me to think of himself as himself. And making me think I'm my ownself too.

They's plenty thinks I am. But the border patrol usedta search my truck as much before I smuggled 'em as they do now. Course I didn't know I was smuggling 'em. But they got laws, you know, even against unknowingly smuggling aliens. And I think I know this girl, this woman, I mean, that's in the Sanctuary movement. I think she like a scout for the Sanctuary movement, you know, not the main-stream Sanctuary movement, but they still Sanctuary workers, 'cause Sanctuary is Sanctuary. My intellect tell me she just a ordi-nary working girl like me, a ordinary working woman, but my in-stinct tell me that she also a scout for the Sanctuary movement, you know. Her name Delgadina. I believe it were Delgadina that re-cruited me for the new Underground Railroad and I ain't even know it. 'Cause if she come asking me to be in the new Underground Railroad, she know I ain't going to, but if she put that Maria in the back of my truck or tell that Maria how to get into the back of my truck and I finds her in there, then I am going to be in that new Un-derground Railroad, 'cause she knows me almost like I knows my-self. Naw, I ain't told her what I knows. I just plays her game as she plays it. And it Maria told her to come to that play, and pretend she ain't know her. And I think I even know her signals, and she wear this ring just like this priest that in the movement. Maybe it just a coincidence, but I think she even done recruited this crazy gringa for the movement, 'cause the border patrols don't give her any has-sles, you know, and I overheard this priest be talking about some Mexican woman look like a gringa, though she a real gringa and I'm sure that Miguelita. I guess if you look like her all the borders is free. At least that's the story I think I know, I mean from bits and pieces of conversations I've overheard; I've overheard her, not the crazy gringa, I mean this friend this Delgadina I thinks a scout talking to people I thinks in the Sanctuary Movement. And a lot of them scouts, they never do reveal who they is. 'Cause that's the only way that they agrees to work for the new Underground Railroad they ownselves. Of course I ain't so ignorant to let her know that I know that she a Nicodemus, or at least I think I know that she a Ni-codemus.

He don't ask me what a Nicodemus, he just sop up some more of his eggs, sip some of that coffee, then pour syrup on his pancakes. Then he look up and ask, Nick who?

I want to ask him if he still married to that Tasmanian woman,
but I see he still wearing a ring and it ain't mine, so it must be hers.
And Miguelita she standing there with another hot pot of coffee and
looking romance—the other romance—but me I don't play that.

I'm in the cantina, drunk on Bud Light, when I almost ask Delgadina whether she a Nicodemus. I might even said the name Nicodemus, but she were reading one of them books of hers, and rather than
continue that Nicodemus conversation she start telling me about the
book she reading. That book called *The Confessions of Othello.*
Then when she holding that book up I notices that the name of the
author ain't just any author. 'Cause Monkey Bread mentioned him
in one of her letters and say her star making a movie from that same
book. That he supposed to be a famous neo-African satirist. I talks
about him like I really knows him, though I just knows him from
Monkey Bread's letters. I forgets to ask her about that Nicodemus
and starts talking about Othello.

Othello? That's Shakespeare, I says. How come him use that
name?

'Cause this is a satire and a parody, she say. He sorta write in a
style that's a combination of Clarence Major and Ishmael Reed.

Oh, yeah? I heard them names, but I can't say that I knows them
personally. My friend Monkey Bread has started reading all of his
novels. They is satires on neo-Africanism, and any neo-African can
appear in his novels, even Diana Ross and the Supremes or Pearl Bai-
ley. He is not a professional noblifier but a satirist. So what's that
book about? How do he parody Shakespeare?

But Delgadina don't tell me what the book's about, she gives me
the book so's I can read it for myself. Least that's what she says. But
then when I'm sitting there holding the book she starts telling me
about it anyway.

The Confessions of Othello, Nadine, is a parody of the classical
Renaissance play but written using twentieth-century values, I guess
that's how you'd describe it, because Shakespeare even though he
was a great playwright and all and depicted Othello as noble he was
still an individual and he was still the myth of the black man and the
kinds of imagery and associations he used were like animal imagery
and hell and evil, you know, all those kinds of images which are part

of the popular consciousness, I mean the popular European consciousness. So the title actually combines *The Confessions of Nat Turner*, you know, Styron's book. . . .

I heard about that William Styron's book, I says, although I couldn't remember what it was I'd heard about it. I knew it wasn't considered to be the true confessions of the true Nat Turner. I even remember reading an article by an African-American writer who confessed that he hadn't read the book, then he proceeded to tell why it wasn't a true confessions of the true Nat Turner. So it's a parody of that whole thing, the black-beast-beset-by-uncontrollable-passion-white-woman-crazy-religious-fanatic myth, you know, Nadine, like Faulkner and even Eudora Welty, I mean Flannery O'Connor, with her artificial nigger make an appearance in the book you know where there this huge black woman in the doorway and she can only be a symbol for sensuality and then there's Joseph Conrad there with his white superiority complex, you know the author of *Lord Jim*, I know you saw the movie, yeah, so he's writing a colonial novel within the anticolonial parody of *Othello*, except in certain parts of the novel he reverses all the imagery so that people are always talking to Othello about the prestige of his race, the African race, you know, and then some parts of it you can't tell whether it's a historical book or a futuristic book, and then in that *Lord Jim* . . .

Lord Jim, I says, and then I remember ain't I heard Monkey Bread say that. Lord Jim and talking about that other Jim himself.

. . . chapter it ain't the Malays but the whites that are described as the sensitive people that got to be treated with patience and kindness and then that made me think of Miguelita but I don't think that's the truth actually except for maybe Miguelita, then it's the whites and not the Malays that have the head-patting ceremony, and they go throughout the book patting people's heads. So instead of Othello condemning his blackness and trying to compensate for it, it's Desdemona condemning her whiteness and trying to compensate for it and talking about the vices of her race, and then there's the Hama of Japan, they appear in the book, and they're like the blacks in Japan, you know. The Japanese might have a good regard for individual Hama. There's a lot of quotes from LeRoi Jones.

That is a man to quote from, but he ain't LeRoi Jones.

I mean when he was LeRoi Jones in the novel, 'cause some of it is set in the 1960s and Desdemona is the one who is depicted with the exotic history and there's a lot of plays on her name, because she's the metaphor for the things that in Shakespeare's *Othello*, Othello is a metaphor for. Desdemona is depicted as the exceptional white, you know. If all whites were like you, Othello is always saying. But you know the whole color scheme is different. And Othello is always pondering about the meaning of Desdemona, you know. He's always telling Desdemona she's far more African than white. There is the assumption throughout the book that African is right. The narrator of the novel or rather the multiple narrators make clear that they are not condemning Desdemona but only her whiteness, and they keep trying to build her up as a heroine even though she's white. I still kept thinking of Miguelita, though. The book kept reminding me of Ishmael Reed . . .

He in the Daughters of Nzingha bookshop, 'cause they's got men's books too. Monkey Bread say she make sure them Daughters of Nzingha bookshops purchases all of his books, even though he makes satires of us Daughters of Nzingha types of African-American womanhood.

. . . you know, though it ain't by him. But whiteness is a flaw in the novel, and Desdemona keeps having to defend her whiteness. Or sometimes she doesn't defend it at all. You're white, says Othello. Says who? she replies. The traditional preconceptions that people have about what African is, they have in the novel about what white is. The assumption is that although one can be heroic with white skin, white is not synonymous with heroism, or, although Desdemona can be good with white skin, white is not synonymous with goodness. You know. So Desdemona is constantly trying to prove that she's only white without, that she's as dark and heroic as Othello.

That Othello supposed to be a true Shakespearean hero. I think we's got a Othello Johnson somewhere amongst the Johnsons. I know there's an Othello.

Even Othello comes to the defense of Desdemona. He says, She's only white on the outside. To the imagination white represents evil, but is white necessarily evil? Why can't Desdemona be white without and within? So throughout the book Desdemona refuses to acknowledge her whiteness, and wants to be as dark and good as

Othello and the rest of his tribe and thinks she has to be the same color as him in order for him to truly love her. So she's always traveling down to the Caribbean and to Africa to get some color, you know. But he's always telling her he so in love with her that most of the time he forgets she's white. But this ain't enough for Desdemona.

What about Iago? Is he in the book? I seen that play *Othello* myself, and I know you can't parody Othello without Iago being in that book.

He's somebody she meets in the Caribbean and then again in Africa. He's just got a minor role but instead of reminding Othello of his blackness he's always there reminding Desdemona of her whiteness. Why forget you're white? he keeps asking her. That's absurd. And he's also always reminding her of her inferiority. He's white himself but he sees himself as superior. Sometimes Iago appears as a bondslave, other times a pagan, other times a statesman. And he always likes to talk to Desdemona of the superiority of Othello's tribe and the inferiority of her tribe. He refers to Othello as a black pearl richer than all of Desdemona's tribe. Either that or it's his wife Emilia that tells Desdemona that. Then there's a scene where Desdemona confides in Emilia. Need I become dark to become virtuous? They're in the Caribbean sipping banana some kinda drinks made with bananas I forgot the name naw I make those myself. But white represents barbarism, madness, chaos. Everyone must overlook Desdemona's color rather than look at it.

Has Miguelita read that book?

Naw, I don't think so. All the gods in the novel are repainted dark, even Jesus. And Desdemona is the one with the double consciousness except the narrators don't call it double consciousness they've got another word for it. Sartre appears in the book and tells Desdemona that she's the victim of language, that all she's gotta do is change the language and white can be right. 'Cept Desdemona keeps justifying her whiteness even to Sartre. Even Shakespeare appears and tries to convince Desdemona who she is. Language is the only way people perceive nonobjective and metaphysical realities, he says. He tells her that although Othello may glorify the woman Desdemona he'll always condemn her whiteness, so he tries to get her to return to his play where she can be her true white self. It's okay if Othello stays in the neo-African novel, which is what the narrators

call the novel. He tells her that as long as she inhabits that neo-
African novel that the darkies in the novel—that's what he calls
them—will continue to develop attitudes toward her skin color and
continue to order their religion on the basis of it and also to justify
their behavior toward her with complex theories and even more
complex theories. But I is who I is and I belongs with my Othello,
says Desdemona.

Is you is or is you ain't my baby? I sings. That's what he's signifying on there.

So Shakespeare tries to coopt Othello to try to get him to come
back to the play and offers him so cowries or shit, and also tries to
convince him that European civilization is superior to the African
world because of the innate superiority of European languages, and
that especially French is the greatest language in the history of mankind. Othello starts speaking some Eskimo I mean Inuit language
to Shakespeare or some sorta of non-European native language that's
supposed to be more complex than any European language. Maybe
it ain't Inuit. I think Shakespeare returns to his play with Desdemona and Iago and they keep trying to convince Othello by playing
him all kindsa European music especially Mozart, you know, and
trying to convince him that he's the true savage beast that they're trying to tame. And then they's got a lot of subliminal messages in the
music. Trying to convince Othello that only Mozart is the music of
essential humanity. They even have Mozart compose music for the
Barbary horse, as they call Othello. And another piece of music
called "The Lascivious Moor." Except all this is subliminal.

Monkey Bread say he don't just write satires, though, he writes
about subliminal love, I think. No, sublime love. But that kinda
sound like subliminal love, don't it? Sometimes he mingles subliminal love into his satires of the neo-Africanists. I'm a neo-Africanist
myself, at least from the way that Monkey Bread describes it, but I
still appreciates a good satire of who I am.

And they even get Desdemona to record some of the subliminal
messages, because although these are historical figures it's also a
modern book. But they give Desdemona some of Iago's lines. So she
asks, Are you a man? Have you a soul or sense? But instead of the
music convincing Othello to return with Desdemona to the play,
Desdemona behaves as if she's still in love with Othello. And so

Shakespeare thinks that Othello's charmed her again with some of his African magic, 'cause he can't believe she's really in love with Othello. He thinks that Othello is just more cunning than even he imagined him. For Desdemona to naturally love an African to him seems inconceivable. Maybe in his play that he has control over, but not in the neo-African novel. He decides that if Desdemona truly loves Othello then love must be some type of cult rather than the true religion. Shakespeare furthermore decides that he'll just let Desdemona stay in the neo-African novel because her character is too flawed to return to his play, that he need someone who lets their reason rule over their passions. Then LeRoi Jones appears. . . .

I knows he has a new name.

. . . Yes, but he uses his original name and talks about the sensuality usually associated with the white woman and wonders why there isn't an African woman in the book. Then it's discovered that Iago's wife has only been pretending to be white, 'cause she thinks that whites have an aura of mystery and are more wildly sensual than her own tribe. I's just been pretending to be one of whitey's treasures, she says, quoting LeRoi Jones, I think. 'Cause I's always hearing tales of these big muscular beasts of unbelievable passion. Iago blames Shakespeare and Shakespeare professes that he's just an artist. Then he tries to seduce Desdemona by promising her the eternal glorification of white ladyness. I do confess my vices, says Desdemona, and returns with Shakespeare. Othello tries to get to know Emilia a little better. And Iago tells the audience that the book has been a farce and a parody and that the European readers can continue idealizing themselves and that the book and that the novels moves too swiftly and is too modern and is not classical enough and besides the relationships of all the characters are clearer in Shakespeare and that if they want to read the true story about Othello and Desdemona they oughta read Shakespeare. He also tells the reader that Desdemona belongs in Shakespeare because if she stayed in the neo-African modern novel she could never free herself from African notions of what the universe is. And that she would have to continue to deny her whiteness, and therefore her own humanity. Then Othello reappears and tells the reader how to make a certain kind of medicinal chewing gum.

I don't know him personally except from Monkey Bread's letters but that does sounds just like him. Monkey Bread said she met him at one of her star's cocktail parties when they was discussing making the movie and having her star to play Desdemona and when he met Monkey Bread he referred to her as a naive representative of the race or something like that and told her he would put her into one of his books. I don't know whether he called her a naive representative of the race or a native representative of the race, 'cause you know I don't know if that were a typo of Monkey Bread's, 'cause she uses them word processors now, you know. She says he's one of them intellectual types of African-American mens but that he treated her like his own countrywoman. I mean he didn't make her feel like a native, although he referred to her as a native.

Say what?

I orders me another Bud Light and starts nibbling on them chocolate pretzels and dipping them in salsa.

He said that he could relate to some of his other womenfriends intellectually, but he related to Monkey Bread emotionally. Or something like that. I can't remember all that Monkey Bread said in her letter. When I reads them aloud I can remember them, but when I just reads them I gots to read them again to remember them. Course Monkey Bread thought that was just his way of telling her that he thought she was kinda dumb. But I knows exactly what he means myself. I think when you just relates to somebody intellectually you is more limited. I mean the intellect is a grand thing, but when you relates to someone on the deep level, then you relates to them with everything you is.

Kinda like Claude McKay.

Say what?

Banjo, you know. Banana Bottom.

Say what?

He considered you "the masses" but he didn't relate to you as "an abstraction" like a lotta intellectuals. . . .

And ain't too many intellectuals that even know who Lawdy Miss Clawdy is.

Say what?

Monkey Bread say that when her star introduced her to him and she started talking to him he said, Lawdy Miss Clawdy. Then he start telling her how he was imagining somebody like her, you

know, for one of his books, and there she is. That must be strange for
a author to invent a character and then to meet somebody that is just
like the character that they invented.

What?

Monkey Bread said he usedta write this real obscure poetry about
Gurdjieff and shit, but ain't nobody heard about him till he started
writing them neo-Africanist satires.

Dear Nadine,

I gots to tell you more about Danny James. I's in love, girl. I mean
we ain't lovers or nothing, but I met him again at one of my star's parties 'cause they's thinking of making his Desdemona book into a
movie, you know. The way they is in Hollywood is they spends a lot
of time developing these creative properties. But he's telling me that
his true love is writing obscure poetry about the harmonious development of man, you know about somebody named Gurdjieff, and
quoting from Lord Byron and them kindsa people, but seem like as
soon as he started writing his satires like his first novel, *A Pickaninny's Stories,* then they started referring to him as a member of the
neo-Africanist tradition and turned him into a marketable author
and then everybody started to buying his novels, *The Panther Man,
Natural African Magic, Turkish Hash with Picasso.*

He took me out to a club and we listened to some freejazz musicians and then he sat with some of his musician friends talking about
Albert Ayler and the Congo, the New Republic of the Congo. One
of them musicians kinda reminds me of a rajah. They usedta all
know each other in Paris. But say that Paris today ain't like the old
days and talking about Wilfredo Lam and Ahmed Yacoubi and
even somebody named Cleopatra who ain't the historical Cleopatra
but some woman that they all knowed in Paris who usedta congre-
gate at Port Afrique which were formally known as Bwana's Table
but that were not politically correct so they renamed it Port Afrique.
I told him I didn't know none of what they was talking about, so he
gived me a copy of a book called *From Harlem to Paris* by a French
intellectual who writes about Richard Wright and other writers and
intellectuals of color and which tells about all the Negroes that

usedta go to Paris. Danny James say he been to Paris, but he ain't in that book, though, 'cause he ain't considered one of the canonical authors.

Then we went to some Bizarre little café and ate croissants and pretended we was in Paris, though I was telling him that my star might do a film in Paris. We ain't slept together 'cause he's got a girl-friend. We's just friends. He's writing about a character who's a sleepwalker. He says I reminds him of Bastet and the Venus Hotten-tot combined. He ain't mentioned pygmy like them movie directors that wanted me to play a pygmy. He's glad I didn't get that role to play Huey Long's maid. He knows Nefertiti Johnson, who is us fa-vorite romance writer. He say she ain't at all like the books she writes and that she don't write the kinds of books she is capable of writing. But you know how mens is about romances. I am sending you a copy of her newest romance set in Marseilles. I'm glad that you introduced me to the works of Nefertiti Johnson. I knows that this book is not in the bookstores yet, but because my star is a star I can order copies of all novels before they gets in the bookstores. And I'm also sending you a new satire by Danny James set in the Latin Quarter of Paris, New Orleans, and Morocco. He taught me how to dance the be-guine and to do the Argentine tango. I was telling him about Delga-dina who knows how to do the Argentine tango and so he taught me how to Argentine tango. He says when he was in Argentina he had him a class with a master of the Argentine tango.

He says that I'm the freest woman of color that he's ever met. Course you know the Daughters of Nzingha don't agree with him 'cause they says I'm still on the plantation. *Mais oui,* Nadine. He created his own martini that he refers to as the Elephant's Fountain 'cause it a real big martini and I felt kinda like Mada in that play ex-cept I don't be having to drink no big martinis to want to be with this man. He got a girlfriend, though, like I said. I don't play that. Anyway he's interested in me 'cause he thinks I'm the character that he's imagined for his novel, which is about a truly free woman of color.

We went to a jazz opera and stayed at a hotel owned by Ethiopi-ans (we didn't sleep in the same room). I have met his girlfriend who is a African woman from London. I thought when he introduced us that she was going to play that game that womens play with each other, but she didn't. She's a writer herself and we was all sitting in one of them restaurants drinking the Elephant's Fountain which Danny James taught the bartender how to make and they was talking about Bricktop's in Paris and the Bal Colonial and the Nardals and Prince Kojo and Claude McKay, Jessie & Nella, Dorothy & Anna & Emanuel's wife, who supposed to be crazy, and Angela Davis in Paris reinventing herself. They was all in that book by the French intellectual so it wasn't like they was talking Greek to me and I even said a few things about Langston Hughes in the Luxembourg Gardens myself, though I ain't never been to Luxembourg. His girlfriend's name is Djamila who was named after a famous resister during the Algerian war.

He knows Clarence Major and Ernest Gaines and Trey Ellis and other different African-American writers. He always satirizes the works of African-American women writers 'cause he don't believe that none of them knows how to portray a man. I showed him my story about John Henry, but he say that that a story about John Henry as a boy, not as a man. He do say that my boy John Henry is a lot more complex than a lot of these women's mens, though. I'm trying to learn as much as I can about storytelling. Danny James is always talking to me about them cultures where the peoples learns by listening to the wise old men and womens. He don't just see hisself as no storyteller, though, but as a literary man. He also give me a brochure that I'm sending you that is put out by this neo-African writers group that gives pilgrimages to Paris so's that people can see all the places where Richard Wright and them other writers went to when they was in Paris.

I asked Danny James what the themes is in his works, 'cause every works got to have themes. He say his principal theme is the ethics of ambiguity. But I really likes his African-American characters, even his womens. I was going to say that he is like them African-American male authors that complains that we don't create complex mens, and then when you reads they works they don't create complex womens. He satires everybody, though, the mens and the womens, but at least we gets to go with them to the Algiers Café or to eat fried chicken in Amsterdam or to listen to jazz in Skanderbourg or to discuss the metaphysics of ethical morality or to paint astronomical symbols on oyster boats. His books is all metaphors of the African Diaspora and us search for mythological, metaphorical, and metaphysical archetypes.

The professionals who noblify the race don't like his books 'cause he got a character that he calls the cosmic pickaninny. This is a character who appears and reappears in all his novels. She is a minor character in some novels and a principal character in other novels. But she's kind of a female surrealistic type of character and kind of in the Spanish picaresque tradition. He don't refer to it as the Spanish picaresque tradition, though, he refer to it as the African picaresque tradition. Sometimes he enters his novels himself. He even put his own mama in one of his novels and they went to Argentina together and learned how to tango 'cause he know all of the master tango dancers in Argentina or in a science fiction story went for promenades on the planet of Venus. I think that she's a New Orleans Creole or that some of her people is from New Orleans.

He also makes use of the myth of the noble savage. And has Savage Noble at the Negresco Café or listening to Bird playing jazz on the Rue Fontaine. Most of his characters is African Diaspora types that he tries to reassemble culturally in his novels. He give me a copy of Claude McKay's *Banjo* and I'm sending you a copy. I knows that I have always liked mens like Banjo and you have always liked mens like Ray. Read Claude McKay's description of the port of Marseilles.

He don't much like America, 'cause he says in America they makes color a crime. The only white people that appears in his novels is literary figures or them ethnic whites who ain't Americans. Sometimes he might include a American of the John Brown type, or them types who is always writing books about they participation in various nonwhite movements. I know in some of his early novels he usedta include white people, but he ain't really explained to me why he don't include them now. He satirizes everybody in his novels, but he says whenever he satirizes white people they think that his motives is political. And they says he don't know how to portray white people. I think they is just usedta having white people glorified. I don't think he should segregate his novels like that, though, but I guess he figure white people got so many writers to write about them or maybe he just prefers to write about African Diaspora peoples. Seem like he would want to include more American whites in them satires, though, because they always satirizes peoples of color, though most of the time they portrays them satires as if they is the reality of who we is. I have always considered "Amos 'n' Andy" to be a satire, but they is still peoples even in Hollywood that believes that is the true us.

I am also enclosing a copy of Maya Angelou's new book, and a copy of a book about a entertainer who used to entertain at Chez Inez in Paris and a book by a poet who says that jazz must be a woman. Here's a little except from one of his poems. I knows you don't like obscure poetry, but I don't think these few excerpts is too obscure:

> The panther woman paints
> Revolutionary ambiguities of
> African heritage
> Can Josephine Baker dolls
> Be purchased here?
> They think I'm Algerian.
> I read *L'Album Littéraire*.
> The plays of Victor Séjour.
>
> James Weldon Johnson
> Whispers to me
> Of Paris & freedom
>
> Is this the Rue Bourbon-le-Château
> Where Malcolm X visits Himes?
>
> Is love among my possibilities?
>
> I eat highbrow oysters
> And lowbrow chestnuts
> On the Venus Promenade
> Dreaming of Breton's canary
> In Moscow's red zone.

I read Van Peebles in French
I drink to the surrealists
And the internationalists of color

As if I were Emanuel's wife
On the Rue Bourbon

To tell you the truth, I thinks he is better at satire of the African Di-
aspora than obscure poetry myself.
Sincerely,
Monkey Bread

CHAPTER 14

WE'RE IN ONE OF THOSE SCENES LIKE IN THE movies, you know them romantic scenes in the movies, the man and woman in the bathtub together and all these bubbles. 'Cept we ain't making love now. We's just sitting across from each other. I've just told him something, and then the camera zooms in on him for a closeup. I imagine all the women in the audience thinking they's in love. Who that? they be asking and think he a new idol of the screen. Especially now that they is colored mens beside Sidney Poitier that you can refer to as screen idols. I'm always saying Denzel, but I also likes to watch them old Sidney Poitier movies. Of course, if I had made them movies for him, I woulda given him some love interest of color or made it like them fantasy-type movies, where a group of us womens of color decides that we don't like the scripts that they has given Sidney, so we enters the celluloid world and rewrites the script for Sidney with us in the movie. And even though we realizes that Sidney have got to continue to play the role of a credible man, 'cause he got to distinguish hisself from Kingfish and Bojangles, we still tries to coax him to a little playfulness and good humor, least when he's with us. He don't become so playful that peoples confuses him with the stereotype, though, like them characters personified by Martin Lawrence y'all know on the television. That Martin Lawrence have a complex personality, but it is so on the side of playfulness that the peoples don't know the difference between a complex clown, a buffoon, and the stereotype. I tries to think of them actors that refuses to add any playfulness into they roles, 'cause they knows how the audiences is and can't distinguish between playfulness and a clown. Do you suppose they is more peoples that knows who Step 'n' Fetchit is than knows who Denzel Washington is?

In fact, though, Ray do kinda remind me of a combination of all the beautiful gingerbread men I've seen, all of them, even kinda like some Indian from India I saw once on a music video from the Caribbean—'cause they's Indians from India who is immigrants in the Caribbean and has they own communities—and my first thought was, He looks like a Indian god. 'Cause he really did look like one of them gods. And then I started thinking it must be nice to be a people that looks at each other and sees they own gods and ain't have to look at other people's gods. I thinks of Maria with her Jesus looking like a Mexican, but that still ain't the same as they own Mexican gods, 'cause they's Mexican peoples that looks like they own Mexican gods, even if they has adopted the Catholic god and saints. And they's even got they saints, though, that looks like theyselves and is the patron saints of they towns and villages and has miracles stories about theyselves.

But that Ray he looks like hisself and a combination of all the beauty I've seen. So I'm thinking of that camera zooming in on him, and then the camera pans and looks at me and the peoples starts laughing, 'cause I ain't the kind of woman they generally sees in the movies, not as a object of desire or delight. And then they starts laughing 'cause they expects the woman to look like Vanessa Williams or somebody, you know the gorgeous type of mulatta African-American beauty. Or depending on the movie's politics, or its hidden agenda, he might be with some white woman, like when they give the beauteous Raquel Welch, considered their most beauteous white woman, to Jim Brown for a lover. I guess you could call that the Pocahontas mode in reverse, like they's always talking about racism in reverse. I guess if I was more sophisticated politically, I could have more to say 'bout that.

What is it about me that you like? he asks. I'm talking about Ray.
What is it about me that you like? What is it that attracted you to
me?

Seems like it's me supposed to ask that, I says, reaching over and
putting soap on the tip of his nose, 'cause I seen them do shit like that
in the movies. 'Cept he don't do like the movies and put suds on
the tip of my nose. You know, in the movies the woman puts suds on
the tip of the man's nose, then the man puts suds on the tip of the
woman's nose, and then they starts throwing suds at each other and
laughing and then they's making love. Instead of putting suds on the
tip of my nose, Ray looks at me like I'm a fool, then he takes a washcloth and wipes the suds off his nose.

What woman wouldn't be attracted to you? I asks. You's beautiful. You's intelligent. And you's got a secret life.

Secret life? What do you mean? What do you mean, Nadine? He
still wiping his face with the washcloth. It my Bugs Bunny washcloth, though. When I come to his apartment I bought him a Bugs
Bunny towel and washcloth set. I started to bring him some wine,
but then I seen that Bugs Bunny washcloth set and Bugs Bunny my
favorite cartoon character. Of course, he looked at them like they
was the present from a fool, but we is using them. I's also got a matching Bugs Bunny towel and washcloth set for myself and it's the same
Bugs Bunny. If y'all watches them early Bugs Bunny cartoons it ain't
the same Bugs Bunny. The early Bugs Bunny look more like he a
villain than a hero. There is something more cunning in that early
Bugs Bunny.

Usually he don't call me Nadine, so I wants to ask why he call me
Nadine, and what do he see the difference between me as Nadine
and me as my other names, but I says, I mean I knows you when you's
with me, Ray. But I hear all this talk about you, like you going down
to Latin America and different places when people's having they
revolutions. And you going to *el centro* to free different people. And
that story you told me about you getting deported from Mexico, you
know. And then there's the secret assistance you provide to different
peoples. And there's all your guerrilla lawyers and your friends
who's guerrillas. I believe that y'all is fighting the right fight, 'cause
y'all is for the oppressed peoples. And y'all is teaching different
peoples how to discipline and revolution theyselves. I have taught a

few individual peoples how to discipline and revolution theyselves, but I knows that is like child's play compared to what y'all does, and y'all's idea of a abundant revolution for the world. I knows that you knows enough about me to know what my capacities are, and you's got sense enough to know that I don't belong in none of y'all's strategy meetings. Of course, Monkey Bread would probably say that y'all undervalues my true worth. I'm thinking of this man that come to the Perfectability Baptist Church with his gun, and the preacher asked him why he was bringing a gun to church, they hadn't had nobody to bring no gun to that church since 1919 when they was fighting them white fools in Memphis that had just seen *The Birth of a Nation* and thought that colored people was who that movie portrayed us to be, that we was the nation's villains and they was its heroes and saints, and all the colored peoples gathered to the Perfectability Baptist Church to defend theyselves with they guns, and so the man says that he's bringing his gun to church 'cause he heard the sermon was on soldiering for the Lord, so the reverend tells him that every soldier in the Army don't carry no gun, that some peoples in the Army does other things than carry guns, and that there is even such a thing as Spiritual Warfare. So the man say, You can fight your Spiritual Warfare, Rev, and these others can do the things that don't require no guns, but I'm gonna keep my gun, Rev. The Reverend couldn't convince him that the sermon were a metaphor, so the man just sat in the back with his gun, being a soldier for the Lord. I knows that y'all is right, though, not to try to make no guerrilla warrior out of me, unless I could go to y'all's guerrilla war with some type of glorified stun gun, like in them science fiction movies. 'Cause to tell you the truth, Ray, when I'm transporting revolutionaries that fought on different sides of the same revolution, I can't tell who is who. I mean especially when they's from them countries where it ain't just black and white and they's all the same color and looks like the same people and fighting each other over the purity of an idea or the purity of a religion. And some of them fools even tries to start a revolution in the back of my truck. Now you know if I don't let no undisciplined peoples drink hooch in the back of my truck, I ain't going to let nobody start no revolution in the back of my truck. If some of these people don't learn how to revolution theyselves, I'm going to get back in my truck and revolution them myself. At least that's what

I'm thinking. But you knows me better than I knows you, Ray, because I tells you everything I am and most of who I'd like to be. I
don't tell people much about my childhood, 'cause that the only
child I feel I's got, the girl baby I usedta be, and for some strange
reason I've always felt that I's got to be her protectress. I know it
sounds like a stupidity for someone to make they child self they own
child and to protect her like they would they child. I remember Delgadina wanted to know why I don't talk about my childhood. I
wouldn't even tell Delgadina that and I tells you, Ray. You don't
know my childhood, Ray, but you knows the full woman that I am
and most of who I wants to be. And look at all the muscles in your
arms. You don't see muscles like that on most intellectual men. You is
a macho-type man as well as a intellectual. You's got all them books,
but you still rolls up your sleeves and fights the true fight. You is a
man of action as well as a thinking man. You romances me, but then
you's got friends that is genuine guerrillas, and even guerrilla women
friends, some of whom is gorgeous, I means like *la loba*. 'Cept I guess
what's secret to me, other people knows. A lot of them peoples that
knows you south of the border. I wonder what you'd be like if I went
across the border with you.

Do you want to come?

I starts to make a joke out of that, but I knows he means across
the border.

I've got to go down to Chiapas. Some of us are driving down
there. Do you want to drive to Chiapas with us? We're taking the
jeep, but we can take the Land-Rover if you want to come along.

Naw. Plus I wouldn't be going there just with you. I'd wanna just
be with you.

You can't build a revolution on just two people.

That what y'all doing—building a revolution?

I go where I'm needed, where I think I can do some good.

Working with different revolutionaries?

Most of the time it ain't the revolutionaries that need you. It's the
ordinary people.

Yeah, Delgadina was telling me about the Mexican Revolution
where the people, the ordinary country-type people in the little
Mexican villages they was as scared when the revolutionaries came
into their little villages as they was when the *federales* came, 'cause

they treated them the same. I mean, they didn't see no distinction between the way the revolutionaries was treating them and the way the *federales* was treating them. I mean, maybe they liked the ideas of the revolutionaries, but the revolutionaries created havoc in them little villages the same as the *federales*. . . .

We's got that type of soap that floats, so I'm playing with that soap. I ain't going to tell y'all what kinda soap 'cause I don't want to be no advertisement for me. And Monkey Bread say I'm already a advertisement for Budweiser.

I wrote this book called *Pure Revolution* and it dealt with that idea, says Ray. Actually, it's a philosophical novel, not a polemical novel. It imagines a universe where ideas fight each other. Not like here, where people fight each other over ideas. Oh, there are ideas worth fighting for. I don't mean that. Anyway, in my novel, there's something called the Revolutionary Idea, in its pure sense. But people pervert it to mean what they want it to mean, just as they pervert all the ideas in the novel. Yet, it is the ideas that fight each other, and the truest ideas triumph. In most revolutions, the revolutionaries end up becoming the devils that they fight. I mean, once the revolutionaries are in power, they become the oppressors. That doesn't mean I'm not for revolution. I had so many people misinterpret my book. But when I'm in countries that are having their revolutions, it is like you say, the ordinary people, they just want to get out. I haven't just been in Latin America, I've been in Indonesia, China, the Philippines. . . .

That's what I means, Ray, I don't know your secret self.

And most of them still believe in the American Idea. I mean, the true idea of America. I think the America Idea is everywhere but America. I mean, those who have the idea of what America really means. . . . You know, you've started seeing these signs they've started putting up on these border-town businesses—American-owned—I make it a point not to patronize any of those businesses 'cause they don't know what an American is. . . .

They think an American is just white people.

Well, I wasn't going to say it exactly like that. There are a few whites in our group who seem to know what an American is. But they're the exception. They're not the rule. And even with them, they believe that they . . .

That they's supposed to be the strategists. Like in them multi-racial-type movies and shit. They's got people of every race in them, but it's just the whites supposed to be the strategists and the idea-makers.

To tell the truth, they become fewer and fewer. I mean, those who know what America is. That's why I told you we're not the mainstream Sanctuary movement.

Una unión fuerte incluye a todos, I says, thinking of that union line.

Exactly, says Ray.

How come I ain't never heard of you? A lot of people who do what you do, they'd wants people to know about them. I mean you, Ray. They always gets on television and advertises theyselves. At least *Essence* magazine knows who they is and gives them awards, and they makes them stars who don't do nothing but be stars, look like stars that don't do nothing but be stars, or they appears on them television documentaries, like when they first did that documentary about the Nation of Islam, not that y'all is a Nation of Islam. Or at least somebody like Bryant Gumbel knows about them and puts them on TV. They might be minor leaders, but television knows about them. To tell you the truth, when that nun sent me to you, at first I thought you'd be white, and then when I saw you was colored, I thought at least you'd be somebody colored I had seen on television.

Ray takes the floating soap out of my hand and puts it in the soap dish. He says nothing, then he says, I guess I have this idea that the purest revolutionary is the one who is less known. I guess I've thought of the others as celebrity revolutionaries, you know. I don't mean all of them. Some of them are true. But that's the way the media work, to confuse people, even about their true leaders.

'Cause I wouldn'ta knowed about Malcolm if he wasn't on no television. I was just a little girl when I seen him on television. But he's the first black person I heard to call the white people that pale thing and to tell us we was golden. And if we hadn't seen them revolutionaries on television, them people who was playing Malcolm and el Ché at the revolution would have been playing. . . . I ain't know who they be playing. . . . I usedta be thinking that myself, though. I remember I usedta see some of them minor revolutionaries and they be having their strategy meetings televised and it seem like they enemy would always be there knowing who they were and taking notes and shit. I usedta always have that idea myself, how could them be true revolutionaries and televise they strategy meetings or even have them in them school auditoriums, you know, I mean them revolutionaries on the different campuses, them student revolution- aries. Maybe they had other strategy meetings that they didn't tele- vise or didn't have in them school auditorium, but seem like they was telling plenty of strategies to the general public. Then the people learn they strategies and develop counterstrategies. Seem like that's why they's so many counterstrategies 'cause all they strategies on television. Maybe that's why they even give Raquel Welch to Jim Brown to try to confuse the people. Me and Monkey Bread we used to watch them strategies on television all the time and that inspired Monkey Bread to have her revolutionary party. But then I know there's a lot of people who wouldn't let nobody lead them if they didn't know who they are. They'd be saying, Who are you? 'Cause I don't know who you are. I ain't seen you on TV.

I don't lead people. I help people acquire the knowledge to lead themselves. I'm still acquiring knowledge myself. We have advisors, spiritual, economic, political, legal, all kinds.

I've heard some people call you the General.

Those who feel they need a general. But I've never believed that everyone has to be a warrior, like you've acknowledged. When you look at societies, they have the warriors, the intellectuals, the work- ing people, the artists.

You tries to be everything, I says. I means you lets us others pick and choose who we wants to be, but you tries to be everything.

He said nothing, then he said, I don't mean a caste system where you make the people be one thing or the other. Or even a de facto caste system, where it's usually the poor who fight the wars. So we allow people to do what's in their capacity to do. We have people with us who just teach English as a foreign language, for example, who've never even been to a detention camp. I know you don't like going to the detention camps.

Naw, Ray. And I ain't like you, Ray, trying to be everything. I just drives my truck. They's got people sitting out there all day in the hot sun and treating them like cattle. It looks like them Nazi concentration camps. I'm having dreams about them detention camps and it's me sitting in them. God, Ray. You ain't supposed to treat people like that, that's human beings.

That's why we need more people like you.

What do you mean?

'Cause you identify with people on the human level. I mean, we need the grand theorists, the strategists like Alvarado, who have the grand ideas about humanity in general, defending rights and freedoms, as principles. . . .

I starts to ask him why Alvarado they grand theorist, but then I ain't heard him at none of them strategy meetings, so I can't ask why he the grand theorist. Then I'm thinking 'bout some story that Delgadina read to me once, some Russian story. One of the characters was just a ordinary sailor, he didn't have no ideas about humanity in general, but he were always going around showing his concern with peoples on a little, individual basis; but then there was this other sailor who were the intellectual and he had all the grand ideals for humanity, but he had no tolerance for peoples on the little, individual basis. So I guess that what Ray means, that his group need both them kinds, the kind that ain't tolerate no fools like Alvarado and the kind like me that tolerates every kind of fool they is. Which ain't the exact truth. I tries to discipline the hooch drinkers. I drinks Budweiser, but that ain't hard liquor. And now that Monkey Bread is sending me that root tea from the Daughters of Nzingha I don't drink as much of that Bud. I'm thinking all that, though, while Ray talking. If peoples could tell a polyphonic story, then y'all be listening to me tell my thoughts whilst y'all's is also listening to Ray's talking. I knows they is those amongst y'all that has got the conceit that I can't think and listen at the same time, but that is another hidden talent that I has. And can even watch TV whilst I'm listening and thinking. This is the only bar in town that caters to the Indians, someone says on my little pocket TV that's perched against the bathroom door.

Warriors like the other Ray. You say I try to be everything, but. . . . And you've met the other people in our group, our artist who helps with the documents, our guerrilla lawyers, our other refugee workers.

Y'all's even got y'all's own comedian. Then I think he's going to tell me his own idea or ideal that he has of hisself, but he don't.

So we need people like you, he says. I need someone like you.

I needs you too, Ray, I says. I means it, but I'm also thinking if that's what we'd say if we was in the movies and whether we's supposed to reach for each other now and start a-kissing. I knows that in the movies the peoples don't spend all they time in a love scene just a-talking to each other. Then I says, I don't go with y'all to them detention camps, though. I went to one with Maria when she was trying to get her cousin out of one. But that wasn't no detention camp. They had jailed her and Maria and Journal and me went there and had to prove that she would have resources if she got admitted to America, and so Maria says she could work with her making dolls and showed them her bank account. And I had to prove that I'm a resourceful person even though I ain't even her cousin, just 'cause I went there with them, and had to sign some kinda affidavit that I knew Maria. I don't know what that was about, I just said that I knows Maria and told them that she is a young woman of substance. I think Maria's cousin returned to Mexico, though. But if Delgadina becomes a private detective, then Maria can hire Delgadina to search for her cousin.

Yeah, I know about Maria's cousin.

Maria still ain't got citizenship, though, 'cause they's got a different type of law, seems like they is always changing them immigration laws, you know.

Yeah, I know.

But I don't go with y'all to them detention camps.

He starts lathering with the soap and soaping me and then I starts lathering with the soap and soaping him.

Yeah, I likes y'all's group. Y'all is like the union in that y'all don't let me participate in y'all's strategy meetings, but y'all does have these sessions where y'all listens to what everybody got to say. At first I thought y'all was having some kinda revolutionary parties where you got the peoples together, then I realized that that is part of y'all's strategy, that that is one of the ways that y'all communicates with each other and gets y'all's messages back and forth to each other, and hears what everybody has got to say and lets us all be heard, like

what Puff Daddy say about even them people that ain't no heroes
have got to be heard, 'cause like somebody else say us all can't be
like Noble Drew Ali. Even when I thinks y'all people ain't doing
nothing but talking shit, I'm learning. Y'all just lets me do what it's
in my capacities to do. I mean y'all nudges me, and even though y'all
knows me for the fool I am, that don't mean y'all wishes for me just
to remain a fool. I learns from Maria. Like I didn't even want to go
to jail with Maria and Journal to get they cousin. I mean, I wanted
to. But it seem like every time I'm in the presence of the police, they
starts looking at they wanted posters. And they's a lot more women
on them posters nowadays. They's gotta be somebody on them that
looks like me. And they photocopied all my identification. So they's
got me in they files. I mean, when I give the affidavit for Maria, they
photocopied all my own identifications.

Yeah, I know. We appreciate the help you do for us.

Well, I was just doing that for Maria and Journal, not y'all. And
for Maria's cousin. Even though I don't know her, she's Maria's
cousin, and if Delgadina becomes the detective that she has the capacities for becoming then she can hunt for Maria's cousin. And
there is even work that I has for Delgadina myself. But I likes y'all.
Y'all is sorta like that movie I seen where these revolutionaries, I
mean, it's during a war, so's they's legal revolutionaries, anyway so
they comes to Jane Fonda I mean the woman that Jane Fonda is playing and asks her to do something for them, it's something dangerous,
but the woman that wants her to do it say that if she feels she can't do
it that it's okay if she don't do it, I mean it ain't one of these things
where she's got to do it. I mean they still considers her to be someone
worthy. Of course, she does it, out of her own love.

Yeah, I know the movie.

I was thinking, though, if they would really still have considered
her someone worthy if she hadn't done what they wanted her to do.
I mean because she really did what them legal revolutionaries
wanted her to do. I mean they was illegal in Hitler's Germany, but
legal because it were a war. But I was thinking suppose it were a
different scenario, would they still think she were worthy?

Ray don't say nothing.

*I pictures Monkey Bread in us scene, 'cept she the director of the
movie. She be saying, Action y'all. Don't y'all know how movies is*

made. We ain't paying y'all y'all's exorbitant star salaries just to sit around and talk. Americans likes actions in they movies. This ain't no Swedish movie, excuse my French. Give us a French kiss. John Henry appears and him and Monkey Bread demonstrates the French kiss. Ain't y'all going to follow my directions? Is y'all casting aspirations on me and my integrity as a member of New Negrofied Directors Guild? I might not be amongst the legendary New Negrofied Directors, but I knows how to direct y'all in French kissing.

Pure Revolution, I says. I think I seen that book. I know I seen a lot of books dealing with Revolution, 'cause Delgadina got a lot of them books. She ain't just got revolution books, though, she got all kindsa books. That's what Delgadina's dream is herself is to be a writer. She wants to be a writer-detective, though, because the writing will be her avocation and the detectiving will be her vocation. I think she's read everybody books that's ever been written. Seem like it anyway. I tell her she should be in a book and represent the true Chicana, 'cause she ain't like none of them Chicanas they puts in the movies. She is more like Rita Moreno than Rosie Perez, but she ain't exactly like Rita Moreno neither, because she is of a deeper hue. I mean she's done her share of union organizing and boycotting but that ain't all she is. I boycott if Delgadina tell me to, 'cause she know what's to be boycotted, but I ain't organized no unions, and can't even Delgadina get me to join no union. I usedta belong to the union, though. I paid my union dues but I didn't attend no meetings. And when I did go to one of them meetings it didn't seem like it was the people's meeting. They didn't want to hear what I had to say. And somebody even tried to say I wasn't at the right union meeting, that I was at the wrong union meeting, that I belonged to some other union, when I knowed I belonged to that one and paid my dues the same as them and's gots the right to be heard. They throwed me out of that union meeting and I ain't been back to none. Course they tried to pretend they ain't throwed me out of the union when someone informed them I were a loyal, card-carrying member of that union. But they'd already throwed me out of that union. I works independent now. There's them that don't like it, and the same folks that throwed me out of that union that I rightfully belonged to in the beginning is trying to unionize me and is pretending that they'll allow me to even let my voice be heard. And they is always giving me they union flyers and pretending that they truly believes they motto that a strong union includes everybody, you know how they is when they thinks they can use you. But I know who they is now. And when you goes to them union meetings you can't count on there always being people there that knows you. And that ain't right. It should be the people's meeting. I bet Delgadina's probably read your book on pure revolution, though, 'cause she reads everybody. Sometimes she brings me books. But she knows I don't read everybody. 'Cause they's some folks out there who ain't writing for you and some you ain't meant to read.

We needs us some props, John Henry. She and John Henry leave the bathroom and comes back with a watermelon, fried chicken, and a couple of Budweisers. I think they's going to serve them to us but they sits in the director's chairs, one with Monkey Bread on it and the other John Henry and eats the food theyselves. Action y'all, says Monkey Bread between bites of fried chicken.

What do you mean? asks Ray.

I ain't one to destroy books, but I think they's some books that destroys people's souls. If they's holy books, they must be unholy books. I ain't mean them books that them religionists is telling you is unholy 'cause they's got bad words and sex in 'em, 'cause they's all kindsa books that is written to spiritualize people. They's books that spiritualizes peoples by telling them how they shouldn't be as well as how they should be. I likes to read books that makes you better for reading them. I don't mean that they's got to have just good people in them. Even saints in the storybooks often start out as sinners. So you can't even read about saints without learning something about sin. And I ain't amongst the people to be come asking what sin is. Sin is sin. I remember reading a book about a woman that was the sorta woman I never would want to be. But I also likes reading them books about the sorta woman I would like to become or that I could imagine myself as being. I ain't read no book yet about the woman I am.

You'd have to write your own book.

That ain't the woman I am. Least that ain't the one I am now. I likes to tell people stories but me I don't just like to tell anybody my tales. Seems like with writers just anybody can read your tales and make out of them what pleases them, and maybe what they interprets your tales as being might not please you at all. Or if I did write

stories, I'd imagine writing for the people who understood my
stories. Or I'd imagine just writing for people who I'd want to hear
my stories.

Who'd you write for?

Well, I'd write for you, Ray, though Delgadina was telling me
about all this feminist literature here if a woman imagines writing for
a man, then she ain't a liberated woman.

Who else would you imagine writing for? You couldn't just write
for me.

Well, Delgadina and Monkey Bread, that's my friend out in
Hollywood.

Hoochies and gents, the one and only Monkey Bread! says Mon-
key Bread, standing and prancing about. I feels like a banana, John
Henry. John Henry leaves the bathroom and comes back with a
bunch of bananas.

Sing me that "Banana Boat Song," John Henry, says Monkey
Bread.

John Henry obliges by singing "The Banana Boat Song."

Daylight come and me want Monkey Bread, sing John Henry.

Banana ain't nothing but Monkey Bread, say Monkey Bread.

I think y'all is the only ones I'd trust with my stories, I'm telling
Ray. I mean, y'all is the only ones I'd imagine telling my stories to. I
mean, other people might read them and have their own interpreta-
tions. It seems like I'm always around people that's writing. Mr.
Freeman, Delgadina, Monkey Bread, she's always sending me little
stories and poems. They say everybody wants to be in show business. But seem like I'm always around peoples that wants to write.
Stories and poems and plays. They is even people that calls me Mada
because of a role I played in a play when I were a young teenager. I
played a woman called Mada so they is a few peoples in central Kentucky that don't know my true name and whenever I goes to visit
my cousins in central Kentucky—I'm from northern Kentucky myself—but when I goes to central Kentucky they calls me Mada.
How you, Mada? And they don't know me by Nadine or Sojourner
or Jane or Mosquito or even Johnson, they just knows me by Mada.
Sometimes I think that Mada shoulda been the true name of Eve.

What?

'Cause when you spells Eve backward it's still Eve. But when you spells Mada backward it's Adam. And men always thinks that womens belongs backward to a man, 'cause that's biblical. They's people in central Kentucky that calls me Mada.

Ray don't say nothing.

We is trying to have us a interesting movie, y'all, says Monkey Bread as she and John Henry shares the same watermelon. They's eating different watermelons, but they's eating them like they's the same watermelon.

Or maybe they just wants to tell they stories, I mean them peoples that writes stories. I likes to tell my stories, 'cause then you knows who's hearing them. And all them written books has got a lot of rules. I wouldn't abide by them people's rules. I don't think a Mosquito-crafted novel would abide by any of them people's rules. And then they'd be telling me it weren't no novel. I guess they's people, when you tells them stories, they tells you they ain't no stories. But you still gets to tell your stories. Well, them union people didn't get me to tell what I had to say, but I gets to tell you about them, I gets to tell somebody about them, so I'm telling a story anyway. I guess most writers gets somebody to read them, but that ain't the same as talking. Them readers seems like choosy people, though. 'Cept Delgadina. Sometimes I think books chooses her to be read.

I've never heard you tell any stories. I've heard you express opinions.

Ain't I told you no stories?

No. You've told me a lot of what you think, a lot of your opinions.

Maybe I just think an opinion is a story. I know they's books that's built on opinions. 'Cause Delgadina's got herself a book called the opinions of somebody, except it's a novel.

It must be Sterne's book, *The Life and Opinions of Tristram Shandy.*

Yeah, that's the name of that book. 'Cept it's got a gent on it?

What?

It say, *The Life and Opinions of Tristram Shandy, Gent.* Gentleman, you know. That would be my book, *The Life and Opinions of Mosquito.* 'Cept I wouldn't be no gent.

Gentlewoman. They have gentle women. I think you're a gentle woman, Sojourner.

You's the only one.

528

There's a lot of meanings of gentle. You have an essential tender-ness. You're like some grand being, sure of strength, self-contained, but so sure of your strength that you don't overwhelm a man. A woman like you could overwhelm a man. You don't overwhelm a man's strength.

I just think that you ain't the sorta man to be overwhelmed. I'm all woman, but there's mens that don't know what a full woman is. You must know who I am. That's why I loves you. Tell me what pure revolution means.

He reached toward me for a kiss, then he leaned back on his side of the tub. I swiveled in the tub, glad for his king-size tub, 'cause I'm a king-size woman—I would say queen-size, but I'm bigger than that; and don't y'all be depicting me as fat neither, 'cause I know how a lot of y'all is; I can describe myself with every word in every-body dictionary and even them that don't have dictionaries and y'all still have y'all depiction of me; there is those of us who really is big and ain't fat—and sat with my back to him. He kissed the nape of my neck as he told me what pure revolution meant. Then he told me he liked my proportions and the smoothness of my skin and my hair and my color and my scent of vanilla. Then he whispered all my names.

Monkey Bread is busy photographing us. She the director, but she also the one holding the camera. John Henry continues eating fried chicken, watermelon, bananas, and drinking Budweiser.

Is there anything you do wrong? I asked, rising. I was thinking of the teachings of Delgadina. When she'd come back from them cre-ative writing classes she'd tell me different things she learned. For characters to be true, they had to have some flaw.

Well, I knows that you's a wrongdoer in the sense of the govern-ment's laws against immigration, but y'all's done explained that, and I believes that myself that there is divine human rights, that there is divine rights above the laws of individual governments. 'Cause if we obeyed the laws in slavery time there wouldn't be nobody free. Course there was some that worked within the law. They wasn't all Nat Turner or John Brown. Some was Salmon P. Chase.

What do you know of Salmon P. Chase?

Daylight come and me want Monkey Bread, sings John Henry.

I had turned around back toward him now. He looked as if he wasn't sure of the name of that man. I wasn't sure of his middle initial

myself. Delgadina told me about that man when I told her I woulda
gone along with John Brown or Nat Turner if there was women in
that group. Of course I was in one of my moods when I said that.
You don't know if you woulda gone along with John Brown or Nat
Turner or not unless you was there. Like them Christians that claim
that they wouldn't have called for Barrabas, when most of them
Christian is calling for Barrabas every day or reinterpreting Jesus to
be Barrabas. Ain't that the name of that man? Barrabas, I mean.

I know that Salmon P. Chase usedta work within the law. They
called him the attorney general of the fugitive slaves, 'cause he usedta
represent them fugitive slaves and also them abolitionists like a certain farmer that was a member of the Underground Railroad.

You read about him in some of our literature?

Naw, Delgadina told me about him. She musta read about him in
somebody books. When I come back from that jail with Maria who
went to get her cousin, I told you about that, I told Delgadina that
if I was back in the day with Nat Turner I'da gone along with him.
Then she told me about Salmon P. Chase. He didn't get a lot of business from other white people 'cause he was always defending them
fugitives and abolitionists, so them so-called respectable white
people wouldn't even come to his law offices and he didn't make
much money neither. But weren't none of us in no position to be no
Salmon P. Chase. The best we could do was try to get away from
them devils by any means necessary, and they wouldn't even let
black people testify against whites in them days or file complaints. It
ain't much different today. They'll tell you it is but it ain't. So anyway I was talking talk like that with Delgadina who had never heard
me talk that kinda talk. She know I don't take no shit from them
gringos that comes in the cantina, but that the first time she heard me
talk that kinda talk, after we got Maria's cousin outa jail. We does
wrongs, but seem like they does organized wrongs. Maybe they does
organized rights that they boasts of, but them organized rights don't
cancel they organized wrongs.

I remember when I was a little boy, I usedta play with these little
white boys, you know, 'cause we lived in this white neighborhood
near the Canadian border. All these little boys they usedta remind
me of the little boys I usedta read about in Mark Twain, you know,
so of course I favored them when I saw them and wanted to play with

them. And we played together. Cops and robbers, cowboys and Indians.

I bet they always had you playing the Indian. I wants to tell him about Leonora Valdez, the reservation Native American woman, to ask him about her and whether that were really her I seen, but I knows that were really her, and I knows I ain't supposed to ask questions about who is Nicodemuses.

I preferred playing the Indian, 'cept I liked to outmaneuver the cowboys. I didn't play Indian by their scenario.

I bet they didn't like that.

Naw, they rather liked having an Indian that was more ingenious than when they'd played cowboys and Indians amongst themself. Well, we didn't have problems playing together when we was boys. Lotta them don't know me now that they's grown men. Well, there was one time when they were playing policemen, though. And then another said that they didn't have any colored policemen, 'cause they didn't around there in those days. 'Cept they referred to it as cocoa police. Then the little boy that was my favorite among them and the one that most reminded me of one of the little boys in Twain went and made badges for us that said THE COCOA POLICE and he wore it too, though he was Irish I think.

They really do have cocoa police.

Oh, yeah.

There's a place called Cocoa, Florida, and all the police are Cocoa Police.

We is the Cocoa patrols. We patrols Florida for all you Negroes and Seminoles, says Monkey Bread. We was patrolling y'all's asses throughout slavery times and we is still patrolling y'all. We is the Cocoa patrols. We patrols all the Cocoa around South Florida. Nadine, I does believe that you is the runaway slave Aunt Blossom. We does believe that you is the same Aunt Blossom on this runaway slave poster. We is quite convinced that you is the same Aunt Blossom that ran away from Master Bwana. We knows that you is the one who is active in the Underground Railroad. We knows you ain't no Harriet Tubman, but everybody can't be Harriet Tubman. Rub-a-dub-dub get out of that tub. We is taking you back to South Florida, Aunt Blossom. Hush. I wants to hear this subversive conversation.

John Henry leaves the bathroom and returns with a funnel so's he can hear the conversation.

Oh, yeah? asks Ray. So anyway, we were the cocoa police and they played the other police, and we outmaneuvered them all the time. So when we were playing those child's games, well, I didn't feel any different from them, and those games allowed me to show my cleverness. Well, that's the best they'd called me was clever. The mother of the Irish boy when she was serving us milk and cookies said that she'd heard I was very clever. But the thing that happened that made me realize the consequences of being different was. Well, all the boys usedta run across this woman's lawn. It was a nice long lawn and the boys just liked to run across it. I'd always be respectful, so I wouldn't run across it. But one day I decided I'd be like the other boys and run across this woman's lawn. So the next thing I know she's out on the porch scolding me. Telling me that I'm a bad boy, that I'm the most despicable boy in the neighborhood. Now she'd seen the other boys run across her lawn plenty of times, even been out there and watched them run across it and just smiled at them. But me I did the same thing and I was a sneaky, bad, and despicable boy. So I stood there and let her scold me. I thought that would be all of it. Then the next thing I know this policeman comes to my house, not a cocoa police, and he's got a warrant for me to be brought into juvenile detention for trespassing on this woman's property, and I'm branded a juvenile delinquent and get the reputation for being the bad boy in the neighborhood, even though I was no different from the other boys.

You said you were more clever.

I mean, in my essential humanity I wasn't different from the other boys. When I read Twain I saw myself too, not Jim, but the clever boys. My cleverness then became referred to as cunning. I was a cunning, sly, sneaky little boy. I stopped playing with the little white boys and just sat on my porch. I read or played Chinese checkers or games like that. I'd watch them still run across the woman's lawn, and there were no consequences. But I was the juvenile delinquent of the neighborhood. They brought me before a judge and everything. I had been trespassing, but what was boyhood behavior with them was a criminal act with me. It was then that I learned what law was. In the abstraction. And in the enforcement.

I know what your story means.

Yeah?

That's what you's doing now. That childhood memory is what you's doing now. I mean, they lets the white boys and girls, all the peoples they consider white, run across the American lawn, but then when the colored boys and girls, the peoples they considers non-white, run across it, then they starts enforcing the laws. I mean the laws is there, but they enforces them at they own discretion. Or they makes laws that say little colored boys and girls can't run across they lawn. . . . Delgadina is interested in that, though. She is always reading these books about how racism, sexism, and classism influences the law. I knows one of them books that she got talks about that. But she say she ain't just got book knowledge of that. She say that she usedta belong to this group that usedta go and monitor the court-rooms, and they usedta monitor these places where people takes complaints. She say a lot of times people of color would come and give they complaints and that the peoples supposed to take com-plaints would discourage or even refuse to take they complaints, but then when gringos would come, especially if they had complaints against peoples of color, the peoples that takes complaints would al-ways be ready to take they complaints. She ain't say what that group of hers did besides just document and monitor all them abuses. Some of them books that she got say the same thing, but she have got more than book knowledge. I knows that on television I were watching one of them cop shows, and this female cop pulls these white young-sters over and discovers that they has drugs and she lectures them and scolds them and then sends them on they way and tells the audience that they'll remember that lecture and scolding and won't do drugs. She don't book them for possession or take them to the court or nothing. Then I'm watching another show and they gets this person of color with the same amount of drugs and ain't even have all the drug paraphernalia as them white youngsters—which suggests that maybe they ain't just possessors of drugs but dealers, and they don't lecture him and shit, they charges him with possession of drugs and he become part of the criminal justice system. I think he a Chicano. But when you study them law, you learns that they is just discretion-ary. Them white youngsters they have a different idea of the cops than the peoples of color. But that's why Delgadina tell me not to believe them when they says that peoples of color is a criminal people, 'cause every group is just as criminal. Some they just lectures and scolds. She have monitored with this group the criminal justice systems all over the world and it is always the dominant group that has the less peoples in the criminal justice system, and it ain't because they is less criminal-minded peoples. Why she say that even if you goes to Mormon country, where the Mormons dominates the other white Christians, you would think that them other white Christians is criminal peoples. She even read to me the depiction of non-Mormon whites in Mormon country from a book that she have, and it sounds just like peoples sounds when they is describing peoples of color. They is depicted in all of the same stereotypes, 'cause the non-Mormon whites don't dominate in Mormon country. So I knows what you means from book knowledge and more than book knowledge. I wish us didn't have to spend all us time thinking and talking about race, though. But this country were built on race. And there is always something in America to remind you that race matters. Personally, I think that is one of the controls the peoples has is to keep you thinking and talking about race so's they can think and talk about everything else. Sometimes they thinks and talks race, but they considers it marginal, whereas for us it's primary. Sometimes I refuses to think and talk race. But to tell you the truth, whenever I even goes to my trade shows, race is there, 'cause they is peoples that looks at me like I not supposed to be interested in the modern and newfangled electronics. So the story you tell me about that white woman is just the story of America. It is like one of them leitmotifs that Delgadina talks about. I think even Delgadina wanted to become a lawyer once, but when she discovered the true meaning of the law, 'cause she monitored it for herself, it just made her cynical. If she do decide to become a private detective I think that that is how she might use her knowledge of law. And I think she would have more freedom than she would have being a lawyer. That Delgadina she is like them Renaissance women 'cause she know about everything. Most peoples they don't imagine no Chicana like her. Even when I watch *Comedy Central* on BET, all they Chicanas is just hoochie women. I laughs at they accent myself. In fact, I laughs at my own accent when I hears them comedians using it. When I hears Shuckie Duckie, I think that his name, and some of them other southern-style comedians using my accent I laughs. It would be interesting to hear a intellectual type of comedian to use my type of accent but to do intelligent humor. You know the type of humor that is generally associated with intellectual humor. But they still makes humor out of everybody's accent, though. Shuckie Duckie were talking about playing his comedy act in Japan where they referred to him as Shucka Ducka, you know, making comedy out of the Japanese accent. Shucka Ducka-san. I probably couldn't imagine Delgadina myself if I didn't know her. But that white woman turning you into a childhood criminal for just running across her lawn that is just the story of America. I likes to collect the stories of America, especially the colored people's stories of America. I knows all the white people's stories of America. I has always been more interested in the colored people's stories of America, 'cause they ain't all in the books. All the white people's stories of America ain't in all the books neither, but they gets more opportunity to get in the books than the colored people's American stories. I means us own whole voices. I's traveled all over America and any person of color who has got a story to tell, I listens. They is a lot of people of color who is used to telling white people they stories, but they ain't usedta telling another person of color they stories. They is peoples that has to relearn how to tell other peoples of color they stories, 'cause they is things they don't have to explain. But they is so used to explaining theyselves and they motives to white people that they thinks they has to explain to me. I knows who they is without them telling me. 'Cause I has learned to listen. I knows the story of America. But the story of America is everybody's story. Another thing I don't like, though, is even us is deluded into thinking that the significant events of us history is only when it have to do with white people, that us can't be significant independent of white people. As if peoples of color don't have a story unless it converges with the white man or the white woman's story. Perhaps sometimes you'll tell me the story of your whole boyhood.

Ray look at me but don't say nothing. I know I ain't told him the story of my whole girlhood. I know I ain't told him my whole story neither. I ain't know why I said that, 'cause I know peoples don't tell you they whole story.

The strange thing about it is that years later that woman discovered she was colored too, say Ray. It was during the years of *Roots* and she decided that she'd trace her roots and traced them back to Jamaica. Well, she thought they were some old wealthy British Jamaican family, maybe owners of some large cane plantation, you know, so she goes to Jamaica to find the patriarch of her family. And when she goes to the little village she finds out the patriarch of her family is a little black man. They took her up a little goat path to the little black man's house. . . .

I've heard that. A lot of rumors where *Roots* influenced white people to trace they roots, and a lot of them when tracing they roots discovered that they own roots led them to Africa. That not all they roots led them to Europe. Some of they roots even led them to Asia. Maybe that's why they's whites who wants a new definition of whiteness, 'cause they knows that they themselves can't maintain themselves as white with the old definition of whiteness. They's them that say all peoples has they origins in Africa, though. But white people themselves in America is discovering the colored world. A lot of the peoples that they thought was white they is discovering resembles more the colored people of America than the so-called whites. They might coopt them for white and allow them to play white, but they is colored peoples. They still believes in the supremacy of whiteness, it just seems that they is in the process of modifying the old definitions. Even us African Americans is modifying us definitions, 'cause we sees all the colored peoples who resembles us but claiming they's white, or claiming they is neither black nor white. I knows who I am myself. What did she do?

People say she went insane. The people that were with her came back to the States. They say she stayed in that little house. All the family had moved to America, but they still had that little house there. And she stayed there, they say, and just went insane.

She coulda still played white in Jamaica, 'cause Delgadina said she went to Jamaica once and they thought she was white. She didn't have to go insane. She coulda just stayed in America and played white.

Yeah. Except she knew what that little black man meant in America.

Well, I still think she coulda continued to play white. Wasn't no cause for no insanity. Or she coulda gone out there to California, 'cause Monkey Bread says there's so many mixed people out there that they's got different rules for whiteness than everywhere else in America. I mean if discovering the nigger in her woodpile as the old people usedta say were enough to make her crazy.

Nigger in her woodpile?

You know that old expression the old people usedta have. They'd see certain white people and say they must have a nigger in they woodpile.

Naw, I never heard of that.

I think everybody's got a little nigger somewhere in their woodpile myself. Even them that claims European. They just tries to make you think that Othello was the only Moor over there. Delgadina say them Moors was over there for centuries. And more Moorish knights than Lancelot. And there weren't just one Desdemona fond of them Moors' good looks. And them enchanted Moorish princesses was the ideal of beauty. They knows they's got them in they woodpile, that's why they prefers to call them Moors. But don't nobody want that nigger in they woodpile.

What do you mean?

I mean 'cause they always gets the best of theyselves to represent theyselves and always gets the worst of us to represent usselves. And the worst of usselves is that nigger. That's the worst of usselves. So don't nobody want that nigger. . . . But I don't wanna talk that talk with you. You's my seventh love, well, you's my sixth love and my seventh love.

Say what? Now you know he's giving me that look that men give women.

I mean, there's this woman in our neighborhood that usedta write poetry and she'd sometimes read her poetry to me. Well, she would write plays and poetry and stories and all kindsa writings. A lot of good poetry, and better poems than this one, but my favorite one was about the seven loves.

My Seventh Love

My first love was puppy love,
My second anticipation
My third was the love of movie stars,
My fourth Imagination

My fifth a stronger love
termed infatuation
My sixth was a greater love
A mature situation

Along came my seventh love
That Cupid must have shot
And Cupid must have shot me too
For that Love hit the spot.

I was a little girl, that little poem helped me to understand the different kinds of love. I mean, little girl love and mature love. So I knew that every love wasn't love. Course when I seen that little figurine of Cupid I didn't think he were the proper representative for love, so that's why I calls you my sixth and seventh love. That's just a little poem to make children understand about love. She's got adult people's poetry too.

There's some adults I know that need a poem like that, he said.

Yeah, 'cause we's only got one word for love. 'Cause I knows when I wants your loving, that ain't all I mean. I mean, what the peoples thinks I mean. Or wants to think I mean. When I recited that poem for Delgadina and told her that poem helped me to understand love, except for that Cupid, then she said, We ain't all got the same Cupid. So that's still my favorite poem about love. 'Cause I know I ain't got the same Cupid as that little plaster of paris figurine. You know them little plaster of paris Cupids that people likes to put amongst they whatnots?

Yeah.

We of the Cocoa Patrol knows that you is Aunt Blossom and this must be that rebel that got our aunt Blossom the bestest Aunt Blossom on us plantation involved in that Underground Railroad, 'cause we knows that Aunt Blossom on her own would not have participated in liberating nobody. Now that we has learned, Aunt Blossom, about your connection to the Underground Railroad, we knows that you is a good storyteller, tell us all about it, Aunt Blossom, describe everybody, you writing this down, John Henry? Name names and describe hideouts, and how exactly did y'all escape us best Cocoa Patrols. You is the most cocoa of the cocoas.

While we is bringing you back to South Florida you can tell us some of your stories. Why, Aunt Blossom, it'll be just like Chaucer when he's got them pilgrims on they pilgrimage, and name names make sure that you names names 'cause you can't tell no good story, Aunt Blossom, and if you is good at drawing maps we'd like a few maps as well and provide us with all the details, yes Aunt Blossom, we knows how suggestible you are and that Ray have got you convinced that you should be liberating people instead of fixing us our favorite of your cornbread and cornpone and corn pudding and quality protein cornflakes and corn-fried potatoes and yam sandwiches and corn candy and Peruvian watermelon salad....

Then Monkey Bread seem like she become Gladys Knight of Gladys Knight and the Pips, 'cept she a combination Gladys Knight and a preaching woman. She say, Aunt Blossom, don't you listen to them patrollers, escape from them Cocoa patrols, Aunt Blossom, and keep on keeping on, you is too strong, Aunt Blossom, not to keep on keeping on, we is too strong, Aunt Blossom, not to keep on keeping on, you is too strong, Aunt Blossom, not to keep on keeping on, we is too strong, Aunt Blossom, not to keep on keeping on. And while she singing that, John Henry is singing, Too strong not to keep on keeping on, keep on keeping on, keep on keeping on, keep on keeping on.

Nadine, that ought to be the motto of your new trucking company, Keep On Keeping On. When you ships via the Mosquito Trucking Company you knows that you is shipping with a company that'll keep on keeping on. Then she becomes a preaching woman again:

I comes before you this morning to tell y'all that y'all is too strong a people not to keep on keeping on. People has asked me to know the true doctrines of the Perfectability Baptist Church. I ain't going to lie to y'all, but rumor has it that Perfectability Baptism is a combination of African Methodist Epicopalism, Scientific Christianity, Holy Roller Theology, Southern Baptist Theology, and Gladys Knight and the Pipism. We is too strong a people not to keep on keeping on. We is too intelligent a people not to keep on keeping on. We is too wise a people not to keep on keeping on. We is too sound a people not to keep on keeping on. We is too spirited a people not to keep on keeping on. I ain't going to lie to y'all and tell y'all that y'all is a perfect people, like some peoples tells they peoples. I ain't going to lie to y'all 'cause y'all would know I'm lying. We has spiritual perfection and we has the capacity to reverse the fables that the enemies of our peoples says about us and to attain the truth of who we is and who we wants to become.

Tell it like it is, Rev, say John Henry.

We has spiritual perfection and we has the capacity to reverse the fables about usselves and to attain the truth of who we is and who we wants to become.

Tell it like it is, Rev.

We has spiritual perfection and we has the capacity to reverse the fables about usselves and attain the truth of who we is and who we wants to become.

Tell it like it is, Rev.

> *We's too strong not to keep on keeping on.*
> *We's too strong not to keep on keeping on.*
> *We's too strong not to keep on keeping on.*
> *We's too strong not to keep on keeping on.*
> *We's too strong not to keep on keeping on.*

Tell it like it is, Rev.

We might not be a perfect people, but we is a perfectable people.

Tell it like it is, Rev.

Monkey Bread and John Henry rises in the air and flies about the room like they is in a magic show. I knows that Monkey Bread wants to quote from Maya Angelou, but so many people quotes from Maya Angelou that she resists quoting from Maya Angelou. They rises to the ceiling and starts dancing on it just like in the videos.

We is a sane people. Don't let nobody try to tell you you is crazy, say Monkey Bread. They racism makes them crazy fools. They racism makes them schizophrenic, not us. We is a sane people. John Henry to the rescue, John Henry to the rescue, John Henry to the rescue, John Henry to the rescue, John Henry to the rescue, John Henry to the rescue, High John the Conqueror Henry. How come you don't use your whole name, John Henry?

'Cause ain't everybody that knows who I is.

Then they parades around the walls and the ceilings, traveling the whole bathroom.

Too strong not to keep on keeping on. We's too strong not to keep on keeping on. Ain't we, y'all? Sing with us, congregation. Too strong not to keep on keeping on. Say we too strong not to keep on keeping on? Yes, we's too strong not to keep on keeping on. Halleluia. We's too strong not to keep on keeping on. Say it again. We's too strong not to keep on keeping on.

We rose from the tub. We dried each other. I put on my jeans and sweatshirt and wrapped a towel about my head and he put on a royal-looking robe and we went into the living room. I sat on the sofa. He went into the kitchen and came back with two cups of hot chocolate with marshmallows floating on top like floating islands. He sat beside me and put on his glasses. He looked through some letters that were on the table that had postmarks on them from around the world and looked like they were written in different languages of the world. Then he sat back on the sofa, drank his hot chocolate and looked at me.

The Revolution

You know I ain't recited that seventh love poem since the Revolution, I said, sipping hot chocolate.

What do you mean?

Well, that was when Monkey Bread and I was ostracized.

You got your recorder, John Henry? asks Monkey Bread.

John Henry reaches into his pants pockets and takes out a miniature recorder.

I don't know what you're talking about, says Ray.

Well, when Monkey Bread and I were in high school everybody was talking about the revolution so Monkey Bread had a party. A lot of people came to it, even John Henry Hollywood. Monkey Bread said she wouldn't believe in the revolution till she saw it, and since everybody was just talking about it, she decided that she would throw a party that she would call the revolution. So we had the party in the basement of Monkey Bread's house. People who come to the revolution had to come dressed up to resemble they favorite revolutionaries. So there's a lot of people that came as el Ché more than anybody, there was a few of the Black Panther heroes and the Black Panthers' wives and girlfriends, 'cause the women thought they could only come as the wives and girlfriends of the revolutionaries. A few of them women come as Harriet Tubman or claimed they was Harriet Tubman. A few men come as Marcus Garvey, though some of them that come claiming to be Marcus Garvey looked more like W. E. B. Du Bois. There was one Frederick Douglass and a few Nat Turners. Seem like the man that wrote that book *The Confessions of Nat Turner* had published his book, so they was denouncing that book and claiming to be the true Nat Turner. One brought his girl-friend that at first I thought was a white girl. There was one that come as Martin Luther King, but they sent him back home and he returned as Nat Turner. Some people came as Brazilian revolution-aries. There was a lot of Malcolms. A lot that only thought they looked like Malcolm, a few that really did resemble him. Some of the young women came as Malcolm's wife. There was people dressed up to look like the Black Muslims. They let Gandhi stay, though he was supposed to be a nonviolent man. One guy was sup-posed to be some Algerian that had fought in the war against the French. I don't know the names of all of them. There was even a John Brown. I wasn't sure why Monkey Bread had that party my-self. I do know that a lot of the people didn't get to the party on time. And she said a lot of them wouldn't even be there on time when the revolution did come. And there was one guy that didn't get there till the party was over. He peeked his head in the basement door and said, I thought somebody said they was having a party in here, and Monkey Bread says, Do we look like we's having a party? But by then they had ostracized the both of us.

How did they ostracize you? What do you mean?

I was dressed up to look like Sojourner Truth, wearing a scarf on my head and one of them type dresses they usedta wear back in them days, but didn't nobody know I was Sojourner Truth, and then after I read that poem about love, they starts calling me Aunt Jemima and handkerchief head and names like that and saying that love ain't the proper subject matter for a revolutionary. So Monkey Bread she gets up and starts cussing everybody out and telling them about they-selves and then she leaves and comes back dressed up to look like a cannibal with a bone pasted to her nose and still cussing all of them for calling me Aunt Jemima when I supposed to be Sojourner Truth. And telling me the least thing I knows who I am and they don't even know who they's supposed to be and shit like that. So they ostracized the both of us. You know, we went all through high school being ostracized, and there's still people in Covington that calls me Aunt Jemima. They don't even know me by Mosquito or my true name.

What about John Henry?

Daylight come and me want Monkey Bread, sing John Henry, and him and Monkey Bread comes out of the bathroom and into the front room where me and Ray is. Monkey Bread is dressed like a cannibal, the same cannibal costume she wore at the Revolution. She dances around with John Henry as he sings, Daylight come and me want Monkey Bread. Then they does the Argentine tango together.

We thinks that we has got enough for us movie. Come on John Henry, these fools don't know nothing about making no American movie. I knows y'all knows that this is not ideal cinematic form. Come on, John Henry. John Henry goes into the bathroom and comes back with the bunch of bananas. Then Harry Belafonte starts singing, you know like people starts singing in the movies. He sing the true "Banana Boat Song."

Me and John Henry is going to Florida, say Monkey Bread. Maybe they is got some Seminoles that wants to rebel. Come on, John Henry.

Daylight come and me want to rebel, sing John Henry.

Yeah, they ostracized him too, I said. 'Cause he grabbed Monkey Bread and took that pasted bone off her nose. And tried to calm the fool down. Then she looked up at him and started singing that song about John Henry. So they ostracized him for protecting us. I mean, I looked like a fool after I'd read that poem about love 'cause I thought sure everybody knew I was Sojourner Truth. I thought they knew my true name was Sojourner and would naturally know that I would come to the revolution as Sojourner Truth. So John Henry rescued us from the revolution. Least from that party. Plus somebody had seen me come in the door with a plate of watermelon and some fried chicken. I didn't know I wasn't supposed to bring watermelon and fried chicken. I didn't know they'd mistake Sojourner Truth for Aunt Jemima. But they's always peoples who looks at you and don't know who you is. I did have a white person to put an umbrella in my hand and to photograph me at the Derby to try to make me look like Sambo. One of them multicolored, rainbow-type umbrellas. I thought it was pretty till I realized they thought I was Sambo. And published my photograph in the newspaper 'cause I was the only jiggaboo at the Derby that wasn't serving mint juleps. Except the time Whoopi Goldberg came there. And I would still come to the revolution dressed as Sojourner Truth. I know I didn't like what I seen them do to Maria's cousin. I seen pictures of her since that time, and she ain't never looked helpless and hopeless in none of them early pictures of herself.

I starts to boast how when I was standing there with Maria and her cousin I imagined myself like Stallone in them movies, but even they ain't like Stallone in they movies. In reality they organizes themselves. Like that poem by Sterling Brown say. Them people don't come at you in ones. Then they tell you you ain't supposed to blame them all for what a few of them do. Now I seen them. And my impression is the same as his. I'm sitting there imagining I'm Stallone coming back to that place where they held Maria's cousin. Course there's those of you thinking that Maria's cousin ain't my cousin. How I'm supposed to be so concerned about how they treated her. But then I ain't telling my story to y'all. I'm telling my story to them that know what I means.

You didn't tell me who Monkey Bread came as, said Ray, looking at me from over the top of his glasses. And in that royal robe.

Herself.

And John Henry?

His natural self. To tell you the truth, when I seen Monkey Bread dressed up to look like a cannibal I wanted to ostracize her myself. I mean if them high schoolers hadn't ostracized me first. I mean I brought fried chicken and watermelon to the party, but I didn't do it with evil on my mind. I stopped eating watermelon till I learned it was a true native of Africa.

Now he's looking at me like he don't know whether I'm telling him a true story or whether I'm signifying myself 'cause he said I ain't told him no stories. You know, maybe he thinks I'm just telling him a story, 'cause he said I ain't never told him no stories. I gets up like I'm getting ready to go, but he slaps the seat beside him. I sit back down, but he don't say nothing to me. He starts reading them letters on the table. Course you know I'm wondering whether I told him too much about myself than he need to know. Or even if it is a confabulatory story, maybe it ain't the type of confabulatory story that he thinks I would tell. You know, like when Delgadina create them characters, they has got to do and say things that is consistent with they personality. And then mens has got they own ideas and preconceived notions of a woman. They's got one idea of you till you expresses too much. I likes people to express too much about them-selves myself. I won't lie and say I ain't got no preconceived notions.

That's a true story, I said. Monkey Bread did have a party and call it the revolution.

He don't say nothing. He continues looking at his correspon-dence. I think he going to be playful with me, you know how mens is in the romances when they's in love. But to tell y'all the truth he be acting more like them exemplary types of men. I remember Del-gadina be reading one of them books called Blakes, or the Huts of America, 'cause she were taking a class in African-American litera-ture, and she say it were an interesting book, as a historical book and the types of ideas it contained.

'Cept Martin Delany has the burden of having to make a exem-plary man, she said. It doesn't mean it's not the man's true self in this book. But people like Blake, they have the burden of being exem-plary men. I'm thinking what his personality would be like if he had the kind of freedom, well you know, if he had the kind of freedom.

I be sitting there and think whether Ray got the burden of trying to be a exemplary man.

What you need is a personal assistant, like Monkey Bread's star, I says, watching him with that correspondence. Them movie stars they's got personal assistants who answer they correspondence. You sho got a lot of correspondence, Ray. The only one who corresponds with me is Monkey Bread. I don't correspond back to her as much as I should. She say I must think it still slavery time and a crime to write, 'cause I sho don't write no letters. Or ain't as many as she would want. You should have yourself a personal assistant, though. One of them Sanctuary workers oughta assist you in answering cor-respondence.

545

There ain't really a lot of people that I trust—not with my personal correspondence, he said, and opened one of the letters that looked like Greek to me. But he read it.

I liked your story about the revolution, he said. But he still don't say whether he think it a real story or a confabulatory story.

I think he's going to say something else, but he looks back at them letters. This one looks like it in Chinese. He read that. Then he gets a little notebook on the table and starts jotting down notes. 'Nother letter got swiggles. He read that one. Then all the rest of the letters is English letters. I ain't try to read them, though.

I'm just sitting there sipping my hot chocolate. I'm sitting there thinking about that song about somebody getting upon that train that ain't got no ticket. Y'all know that song. Somebody singing about getting upon that train without no ticket. But you gets to ride some. I'm sitting there feeling like I ain't got no ticket to ride a lot of people's trains. And getting to ride some don't seem like it enough. Then I'm sitting there scolding myself like a fool. How come I'm there thinking 'bout ain't got no ticket to ride no train, when I gots me my own means of transportation. Get you a mule, fool, I heard somebody say when listening to that song. I ain't got no ticket to ride nobody's train. But I get where I wants to go just the same.

What are you humming?

Song about a train. I rose up and said I had to get back to work.

Stay, he said. Then he realized how that sounded. Stay with me.

I thought he wanted to make love again, but he didn't. I sat there thinking about what Delgadina said about the burden of being an exemplary man and watched him read letters, then I got up and made us some more hot chocolate. When I comes back with the hot chocolate, I do spy on one of them letters. It begins, As a man of integrity, I appeal to you. . . . I think it's one of them foreign people trying to write in English, so I don't know whether he calling hisself the man of integrity or Ray. 'Cause y'all know about them dangling modifiers.

Then I'm thinking of Delgadina. She reading that *Blake* and then she look up at me. I'm thinking what it would be like if Martin Delany put a character like you in a book with a man like Blake. I know one thing, you'd be freer to express yourself, 'cause you don't have the burden of being an exemplary woman.

Now I know some of y'all women of color wouldn't want her saying that about y'all. But I know what Delgadina mean, so I ordered me a Budweiser. 'Cept I wouldn't be talking no explicit sex scenes like some of them in the novels you reads, I said. I might not be exemplary, but I ain't evil.

Aw, Mosquito, this is modern fiction, this ain't the nineteenth century.

Then I'm sitting there watching Ray with them letters. He read them letters, and then he underline certain words in them letters and put certain words in his notebook. I knows what he's doing 'cause them letters have got codes in them. I gots to tell y'all a little bit more about them codes, but I ain't going to tell y'all everything. I sat there drinking hot chocolate whilst he read them letters.

You's as manly as Luther, I says, watching him. But you ain't as playful. That's 'cause you's got the burden of being an exemplary man.

He looked at me. Who's Luther? Is that John Henry's real name?

No.

Your ex-husband?

No. He a man in a play us children put on when we was childrens. I usedta go visit my cousin and there was this neighbor woman that wrote plays and we performed one of them called Luther. I remembers the description of him: Six feet tall, brown eyes, dark-complexioned, handsome, well built, strong and muscular, black hair in a crew cut. You ain't as dark as him and you ain't got no crew cut, but you's as well built and manly. 'Cept he could be more playful 'cause he didn't have the burden of being no exemplary man and no revolutionary personality. He's a good man like you is, though. He returns from the Second World War on a furlough to romance his girlfriend. They's truly in love and everything, but they's a game and playfulness to they romancing, even though it is set during the Second World War.

PLAYING A GAME OF ROMANCE

Listen to the radio,
And the lights are turned down low,
Grab your partner, and let's go,
A-playing a game of romance.

Take me to the picture show,
Still the lights are turned down low,
Light from the picture, make a glow,
A-playing a game of romance.

It's time this game got started,
The folks are getting tired,
A-waiting on you partner,
Now it's time to play our part.

Now you take me by the hand,
And a kiss on me you'll land,
Dance a jig to beat the band,
A-playing a game of romance.

Hoochie, Coochie, Cancha, Ochie,
A peck, a hug and a kiss,
Hoochie, Coochie, Cancha, Ochie,
Take me in your arms, like this.

Grab me partner and let's go,
Listen to the radio,
While the lights are turned down low
A-playing a game of romance.

That the little song in the play. Monkey Bread got to play the love interest, though, 'cause me I ain't no songstress. The play ain't about love being no game, it's about true love, though, except the woman in it sings different songs about love, I mean different songs about different kinds of love. I ain't going to do the whole play for you. But the woman that wrote the play is the one who helped me to learn my hidden talent.

What's your hidden talent? he asked.

I gots what they calls a auditory memory. It something like a photographic memory, except I remembers everything I hears, whereas them photographic memory peoples remembers everything they reads or in photographs.

He said nothing for a moment. But now y'all know why he don't allow me to come to none of they strategy meetings. Not that he don't trust me not to repeat things they says in them meetings, 'cause it's against the rules to repeat them strategy meetings. But maybe he thinks I won't know what to repeat and what not to repeat. 'Cept the first time when I asked about them strategy meeting he had him another reason.

How come I don't get to go to none of y'all's strategy meetings? I asked.

We was in the basement of one of them houses. I was supposed to wait there to load some of them refugees to take them to a certain farmhouse. Then I heard somebody say, Strategy meeting. Saying it to different people. Saying it to Al. Saying it to Ray. Saying it to the other Ray. I thought Ray be the one to tell people about the strategy meetings, but it weren't. Saying it to the woman claimed not to be the guerrilla lawyer. Saying it to the Grand Panjandrum, who I think the woman works the comedy clubs in South Texas. Or maybe it the woman deny being the guerrilla lawyer the Grand Panjandrum. Anyway I starts in with them to this part of the basement that looks like a classroom. Ray's standing at the door.

Where are you going, Mosquito?

Strategy meeting, I says.

No you're not. I don't want you to come to the strategy meetings. I don't want you involved in that.

'Cause I'm a greenling.

We need you to do what you do, to transport our refugees. It's better you just have your assignment when the border patrols stop you. You've got a lot to learn about the border patrols and you don't need to come to our strategy meetings.

I would like to sit in on a strategy meeting just to know what y'all's strategies is.

I don't want you involved in all that, Mosquito.

Don't you trust me with y'all's strategies?

He said nothing. Then he said, Anyway, I thought you would prefer not to come to our strategy meetings.

Why would you think I'd prefer not to come to your strategy meetings? I asked.

I don't want you to come to our strategy meetings, he said.

But why would you think I'd prefer not to come to y'all's strategy meetings?

I'd prefer that you don't come to our strategy meetings, he said. Then he said, You can start going to class if you want.

What class? I asked.

To become one of our, well, we call them hidden agenda conspiracy specialists. It's kind of a joking name, but what you do is you review letters. Sometimes we receive letters from various people, but because of the regimes, the lack of free speech, we have to be able to decode what's in the letters. You would read of course the translations into English and the letters written in English. Do you want me to sign you up for one of those classes?

Is it at the Community Center?

What? No, one of our people teaches it. This same strategy room. I'll sign you up for it.

Okay. I ain't know whether I wants to be no hidden agenda conspiracy specialist. Will that make me grow in wisdom so's I'll be able to attend y'all strategy meetings?

You are far more useful to us in the work that you do, Mosquito. I don't think you need us to grow in wisdom.

Yes, I does. You needs everybody and everything to grow wise, least that what my mama say. You needs the whole universe and everybody and everything that in it. My daddy has his say on wisdom. He used to tell me the story about wisdom itself, the story about how wisdom itself first come into the world and were dispersed amongst all the world's people. That ain't one people got a right to claim wisdom for theyself. I don't tell anybody that story of wisdom. Perhaps that is a flaw in my character, because I keeps that story of wisdom for myself. Of course there is people all over Africa that knows that story of Wisdom, so whether I keeps it to myself or not, there's them that knows it. And what else do my daddy say about wisdom? He say that everybody have got the right to wisdom, but they is some people that just do not know how to handle wisdom. 'Cept if you's a true Daughter of Nzingha you gets to also read from they wisdom books. I mean, if you is one of them that has enough wisdom to read them wisdom books.

Say what?

Daughters of Nzingha.

Oh, yeah?

But he ain't say what he mean by that oh yeah, he just let some more of the peoples come into the strategy room, gives me a map with my assignment, a newspaper and documents that I'm supposed to give to them border guards if any of them stops my truck, and then he stand at the door of the strategy room looking kinda like he a border guard hisself, then he go into the strategy room. Y'all know I wants to cross that border and go into that strategy room, but I don't. I stands near the door of the strategy room, though. It a soundproof strategy room, so I can't lie and say I overheard nothing. I started to tell y'all about my learning how to be a hidden agenda conspiracy specialist, but y'all gots to remember that I can't tell y'all everything for security purposes. If this were just my own story and I ain't become involved with the new Underground Railroad as well as the Daughters of Nzingha, I could tell y'all everything, except for all the love scenes, 'cause I don't believe in being too sexually explicit. But this new Underground Railroad have got to be maintained like the old Underground Railroad. When y'all is reading them slave narratives, y'all that reads them slave narratives, them fugitive and escaped former slaves don't tell y'all everything.

I already told y'all you don't tell everybody every story, and you don't tell everybody everything in the same story. Even that Frederick Douglass didn't tell y'all everything in his first narrative which were written when there was still slavery. He comes to a point in the narrative where he tells y'all that he can't tell y'all everything because if he tell y'all everything he be giving the slaveholders advantage, 'cause they would learn all them fugitives' secrets and it would prevent some of them other fugitives from escaping. There is some fugitives that tells everything, 'cause they wants to tell a interesting narrative, and there is probably some others that will write about the new Underground Railroad and even take y'all to one of them strategy meetings, but I ain't one of them. Of course my excuse is that Ray didn't allow me in none of them strategy meetings, and especially when learning that I have a auditory memory which has even been certified by the Church of Perfectability in Memphis, none of Ray's people wants me in they strategy meetings. I guess if y'all wants to go into one of them strategy meetings, y'all has got to join the new Underground Railroad for y'allselves and prove that you is reliable and truthworthy peoples. And even then they might not allow y'all in they strategy meetings. If any of y'all has got photographic memories and is a descendant of the victims of the African Diaspora Holocaust, the Daughters of Nzingha might be interested in having y'all work in they archives. If y'all has all the other qualifications. They likes peoples with auditory memories also, but the peoples with auditory memories has got to read all the documents in they archives aloud.

I does have the permission of the teacher of my hidden agenda conspiracy specialist class to read for y'all the letter that we uses to learn about how we uses letters to become specialists in hidden agenda conspiracies. We also uses other documents that seems like real documents but is just confabulatory documents. But here's the letter I has permission to quote. Y'all ain't going to understand everything in this letter, and I'm still decoding it myself, but y'all has probably heard some of the names mentioned already in various conversations amongst the new Underground Railroad conductors.

Dear Ray,

Are you somewhere being a revolutionary? I saw your guerrilla girlfriend in Quebec with another general. Or the same general. All generals look alike. Still it was good to speak another language. You remember when I used to love English. I used to love "my language." Now I prefer any other language. Sometimes I go to Miami just so's I can speak Spanish. Cathy is teaching me Japanese. You know, she spent some years there and still writes to her sensei of Japanese aesthetics. I've learned a few phrases in Chinese and a little Swahili. I've begun to write a little in French, although that's the same as English. The French don't understand my French, but Quebec French is freer. My Quebec friends understand me. Madame la Sagesse is there. From the islands. I wish I still remembered the Indonesian you taught me when we were kids. *Apa kabar?* And *ya* I still remember. But that could be *ya* in any language. Even Russian, ain't it? And some of those Scandinavian languages. Except I remember you said that *ya* in Indonesian sometimes means no. Very Kafkaesque. Can you imagine being in a country where you don't know whether the people are saying yes to you or no? But I guess it really is like that.

Re my principal reason for writing to you. We're trying to get national maybe international legislation which we hope to call Electra's Laws. Right now, these sorts of people, they're above the law. You hear about the rule of law. But there's no such thing. It's all discretionary. And jury nullification? This controversy about jury nullification. What about the nullification they practice from the get-go? I remember listening to a Geraldo's special called "The Color of Justice." Some of the things he said, he oughta know better. Remember when we usedta watch the old Geraldo, his investigative reports, and him reminding you of that Nicaraguan friend of yours. Nullification begins from the get-go. And the nullifiers? Well, you know what I mean.

I won't go into detail, because my mail is probably being opened and I don't know who to trust. I'm trying to think of the Chinese philosopher who said he'd meet trust with trust and even distrust with trust. Lao-Tse, yeah. I would meet trust with trust: I would likewise meet suspicion with trust. I used to think that was quite how I wanted to be. But now I just distrust. Especially so-called official information. The voice of authority. I remember Cathy used to tell me about things like that, but I just had that ideal of the Chinese philosopher, you know. Anyway, we've recorded, well you know how many constitutional, civil, criminal, citizen's, and other abuses, I won't list them here, including the laws, the statutes, and the local officials are still saying they can find no wrongs. Kafka? I know one of us must have written a book like that, so I don't have to keep calling it Kafkaesque. Aren't there some scenes in *The Invisible Man* like that? The official lie? But you know about official lies, I don't have to tell you.

Cathy and Ernest are somewhere in the Caribbean with the mosquitoes. One of those little islands. I think Cat Island again. I think they honeymooned there. On account of Sidney Poitier. I mean, that's how she first heard of the island, and he's her favorite actor. She still wishes . . . well, you know the eternal complaint of the colored woman. I shouldn't say that. Love's love, right? I know Cathy sends love and kisses. Ernest, I think, is your alter ego. 'Cept he's Cathy's revolutionary. I guess, if you're married to a woman like Cathy, and

you want to be a revolutionary, you've got to be a revolutionary devoted to the cause of Catherine herself. But he's still his own man.
He still don't take nobody's shit. He's still his own Ernest. Though
you remember when there were all those rumors about Ernest and
me when Ern and Cathy and I were all staying on the island of Ibiza?
Love's love, right?

I know you won't understand all this letter, Ray. You haven't read
all my books, so there are probably things in this letter that only
Cathy and Ernest would know what I mean. But give it to the people
you know. Someone should also forward a copy to the Daughters of
Nzingha. I don't trust to send a copy directly to them for security
reasons. I know one of your people has their address.

My cause is Electra. Cathy usedta say my problem was I didn't
have a cause. Fool don't know me. We've known each other for de-
cades, before Ibiza, and the fool still don't know me. But my cause
is Electra. Cathy's designing some buttons for us and some slogans.
Some say, Only in America. You know, Don King's famous slogan,
but with our double-entendre meaning. Or maybe his double-
entendre meaning. He's a sly one. They think he's saying one thing
and he's saying another. They're sly themselves. . . . They're human
rights abuses whatever the name. You know, to put them in their real
context. They're human rights abuses. And then Cathy's doing a
new sculpture. Good she's got something else to work on besides
"The Birdcatcher." Should I call them birdcatchers? Our little red
bird? Working with that image I told you someone gave us, about
the wagons circling, it ain't historical, the wagons always start circling, except they could never convince us, could they, that the true
savages weren't the ones inside the circle, not the Indians. We always
played Indian. Never them cowboys. Or in South Africa—they've
got the same cowboys and Indians motif, except it's the Zulu. . . .

Little Panda—well, she ain't exactly little now—says hi and so
does Lantis. We're back together, you know. I thought my name for
my daughter was unique, then I was surfing the Net and found out
there's another Panda, a writer of science fiction stories. I remember
when my little Panda said that's what she wanted to do. Got back
together in Cuba, when Panda was there for the Americas games,
representing "her" country, and I was trying to get an interview
with Castro, the man himself, although my Miami friends. . . . Well,

you know my Miami friends. They tell me their stories and I tells them other stories. At least tales from those still trying to keep their faith in the Revolution. But they're polite about it, my Miami friends, not like those you told me about when some of your friends were trying to get foods and medicines into Cuba. Panda says hi. Did I say that? Well, she says to tell you hi every time I write to you, Cousin Ray, so I am. I think you're her ideal, next to Lantis. You know, our little athlete-intellectual. She's returned to Miami now, where she teaches astronomy. She's making a new chart of the stars, a new chart of the heavens, calling the stars by their true names. At least our names for them. She flirted with Oceanography for a while, but didn't like the idea of being the only "colored girl" on those expeditions. She's still the only "colored girl" in her Astronomy Department. Now they're wondering how she got hired, writing astronomy articles for "colored magazines" and not those prestigious journals. I think she still writes a few articles for those prestigious journals. She doesn't like being middle class and doesn't look like a professor, is wearing braids or one of those new-style Afros—not our Afros, but that new style; least we combed our Afros, most of us— and has started going to her classes looking like a rap artist, or at least like that young woman in the Fugees, who she kinda resembles. The first time I saw one of those videos with the Fugees I said, Panda? Thought maybe she was moonlighting as a rap artist or something. Don't like being middle class, though. I think she's read too many satires. Some of my own. I tell her every race gotta have a middle class. And even some mandarins like her. Africa's got nobility. I don't just mean them elites you think I know. It's just what you do with it.

I have much more to say, much more, but only when I can talk to you in a secure place. Are you in love? I hope you are.

As for our Electra, our little red bird—I've been editing some of her writings. Some of them now seem quite mystical and prophetic. The Daughters of Nzingha are keeping copies of all of her writings in their archives and publishing selections on their ftp site on the Internet. (Our little Panda works with them on the Internet.) I'm dreaming of some of the characters she created. And those that I've created. They want in on this too. Like a certain private investigator. Even a character named Nadine. I don't have a book for her yet. I've

been working on my Sojourner Truth book. But I've been dreaming
of a character named Nadine. In the dream, she is quite real. I know
she is only a character who wants to be in one of my books, but in the
dream she's quite real. And maybe little Electra herself. You know,
the writings she did about when she was a little girl. It seems like just
when we almost forget who the enemy is, they remind us, don't
they? Dear Electra. Our dear Electra.

Your cousin,

Amanda Wordlaw

P.S. I just received *The Guerrilla's Notebook*. Well and good that
you send me your friends' books on the other regimes. But this is the
regime now, Ray. This is the regime. Don't let them sweet-talk you
that it isn't. Even that Viking woman, that friend of Cathy's. You
know, when I wrote you what Cathy said of her and I found it impossible to believe. I know who she is now. I know who they are
now. But I needn't tell you, Ray. You know who they are yourself.
What I need is a good group of legal guerrillas who can't be coopted.
(Even de facto.)

P.P.S. I was almost named Iris, you know. Not the flower. In Greek
mythology, Iris is the daughter of Electra and a messenger of the
gods. Maybe Electra meant to almost name me for the flower and
didn't realize she was also almost naming me, her own daughter, for
her own mythological daughter. . . . But why should I think she
didn't know when "colored people" had to read all that Latin and
Greek literature in those days. You know, those little colored schools
in the South had them learning all that Latin and Greek literature,
all that Latin and Greek mythology and shit. And all that colored
people's mythology of who they were supposed to be themselves.
Who am I. . . . I mean, in our own African mythology? Cathy said
when she first met me she thought I was named after that South African freedom word, Amandla! Or Ananda. From the Buddhist. You
know Ananda, don't you? Buddha's favorite disciple. Where does
Amanda come from? I know it means worthy to be loved. Maybe
she thought better to name me the name that means someone worthy
to be loved. Messenger of the gods? Me? We spend so much time
wanting to be worthy of others. Sometimes we just need to learn how
to be worthy of ourselves. Of course being a woman worthy of
Lantis ain't so bad—or other worthy men. I mean, or other women

and other worthy men. Anyway, Cathy's convinced that the only thing I still like about the Caribbean is they call me Mrs. Wordlaw. You know, instead of the feminist's Ms.

P.P.P.S. Sophie writes from Paris that she saw Old Man Johnson and his Algerian wife. What's her name? Mila? Just in Paris for the intellect, he says. He still prefers Spain. He spent enough time in France after the war. Sophie thinks he knows the French better than they know. Anybody colored knows the French. Anyway, Sophie and Old Man Johnson and his wife sitting at one of those little café tables when right on the boulevard these France for the French group were having one of they manifestations. Wanting all the immigrants out of France. Old Man Johnson and Mila just watched them. But you know how Sophie is. She pretended she was from one of the islands, Martinique, and started calling them all of their names. Speaking French, but with a Martinique accent, you know. Old Man Johnson and Mila had to rescue the fool. She's one of those little French women you can't tell what she is, anyway. I thought she was Algerian myself when I first met her. You know, Sophie, the little French girl. Well, woman, if you must.

P.P.P.P.S. Somebody wrote me thinking I'm Nefertiti Johnson. Can you imagine? You probably don't know her writings, so you don't know what I mean. I've stopped writing romance novels, but when I was writing them, well, I'd like to think my readers knew they were satires. But Nefertiti Johnson and her readers believe all that. With them romance is like a secret statement of faith. If you can think of anyone else to send a copy of this letter, please do so, even your guerrillas. Even Nefertiti Johnson if you think this letter will reform her. But it's our little red bird, my purpose in writing this. Electra.

Y'all has probably heard some of the names mentioned in this letter. I don't know whether this is a real letter from Ray's cousin or whether they hired the novelist Amanda Wordlaw to write a letter that could be used by our hidden agenda conspiracy specialist class. I believe that it's a true letter asking for the assistance of Ray's legal guerrillas. I believe that she really wanted the assistance of Ray's real guerrillas but decided on his legal guerrillas. So when I thought them people at them meetings was talking shit and gossiping about different people, they was really getting messages and codes to each other. Even when Ray was telling everybody about getting deported down in Mexico, even though they really did get deported in Mexico, they was also in the conversation messages from Al and Ray Mendoza. That is, Ray hisself had already gotten out of Mexico, but he needed someone to go down there and get Al and Ray Mendoza out of Mexico. So he was able to tell the people who knew the codes to go down there and get Al and Ray out of Mexico 'cause they didn't believe that Al and Ray's documents was legal. And even when them women was talking about talking shit and talking loud in front of them refugees they was giving each other messages. And even the names of Amanda Wordlaw and Cathy and Ern and Koshoo hisself is a code. Because I was wondering myself why they was mentioning them names when we ain't supposed to mention names. I kinda confused them by mentioning my name Johnson, though, 'cause Old Man Johnson is one of they codes as well as the name of a real man with a real Algerian wife that might even be my own uncle Buddy Johnson. That's why them women didn't say anything when I mentioned Johnson, 'cause they'd been told that I was a greenling and wasn't supposed to know the codes. Then one of them thought I might be a spy or was telling them that there might be a spy amongst us. Even love is a code amongst these people. So when that woman was talking about loving Ray I ain't know whether they was talking about true love or they code. That's all I'm allowed to tell y'all, though, about my hidden agenda conspiracy specialist class. 'Cept we are required to read and reread that letter and I still ain't discovered all the hidden agendas and conspiracies in it.

Read the letter for us, Nadine.

I reads the letter for the class.

What does the letter say?

Don't it say what it means?

I mean, what do you think is the letter's hidden agenda?

I didn't know it had no hidden agenda.

This is a hidden agenda conspiracy specialist class, Nadine. Every conversation and document and letter we review in this class has a hidden agenda or is the revelation of a conspiracy. Even the name Amanda Wordlaw is a hidden agenda. I'm going to give you a copy of our code manual. It's thumbnail size, so you can hide it anywhere. We continuously change the codes, but we always keep this letter as a point of reference.

Nefertiti Johnson I reads her romance novels, I know they can't be no hidden agenda conspiracy in her name.

She don't say nothing. I still ain't been able to decode what Nefertiti Johnson mean. I'm a fan of her romance novels, but now when I reads them I don't just read them for literature or entertainment, I tries to discover hidden agenda conspiracies. I does know that they is translated into numerous languages in the world. And maybe she writes them novels that people thinks is just romances in order to disperse the new Underground Railroad's own hidden agendas to the world. Either that, or the hidden agenda conspiracies of the Daughters of Nzingha, 'cause they has got more of her novels in they bookshop than that of anybody, except for Oprah's Favorite Books.

We don't just learn how to decode letters, though, like I said, we learns how to decode conversations. There is also another code strategy that I can tell y'all about. They uses ordinary books that they calls they code manuals. These is books that might be written by them that ain't even in the new Underground Railroad, but they builds codes around the names and conversations, so that they might send you a copy of a certain book and all you's got to do is get out your thumbnail code book which looks like a little dictionary to decode the book. For example, one of their official code manuals is a ordinary book of poetry called *The Cat Island Poems*. If I were to send Monkey Bread, for example, a copy of that book she would read it just as a book of poetry, but if I was to send one of us hidden agenda conspiracy specialists that book of poetry along with an ordinary-seeming letter, then that hidden agency conspiracy specialist could read that book of poetry along with the letter and then with the use of they thumbnail code book and the knowledge that they have learned from they hidden agenda conspiracy specialist class to read the messages and hidden agendas and even conspiracies in the book.

I won't quote from that book of poetry for y'all, but those of you that has read *The Cat Island Poems*, I knows that most of y'all think that them is just poetry and that them is just the names of people, I mean the people that is introduced in the book of poetry, but if y'all was hidden agenda conspiracy specialists that wouldn't just be a book of poetry. (If I'm allowed to quote them poems for y'all I'll quote them here. If I ain't, y'all can read my discussion of them.)

And a lot of it sounds like ordinary language and ordinary people's talking, but to tell y'all the truth they is even hidden agenda conspiracy specialists that can't decode that book. Along with the letter from Amanda Wordlaw to Ray, *The Cat Island Poems* is the principal book that I learns from. When they mentions star that's supposed to be a code word, and crazy supposed to be a code, and magic a code, and Mandinka a code, and even love, like I said, is a code. The way it works is they always keeps the same official code manuals, but they changes the codes in the thumbnail code book, so that the codemaster can use the same book to decode different messages. That also allows us to use almost any book as a official code manual, so that if a certain regime confiscates certain books, we can use books that the regime don't confiscate, and even them writers whose books is banned in they countries can send they books out to us just by sending us copies of books that ain't banned. Or the peoples in them regimes that don't got the freedom of speech, they can get they free speech to the new Underground Railroad. They says that it is okay for me to tell y'all this, unless they is countries that starts banning every book and newspapers. But the countries always allows official books and newspapers, but we can even make official books and newspapers subversive. We's even supposed to practice writing coded letters usselves and sending them to peoples we know as if they was ordinary letters. This the code letter I sent to Monkey Bread, though it is also a real letter to Monkey Bread which I wrote when she asked me to describe my truck.

Dear Monkey Bread,

You have told me to send you a description of my truck. I wished that you had asked me to describe my truck when I first got my truck. You know how much I would like to tell you all about my truck. You know how I tries not to be a materialist and to rise above materialism, but I does like my truck and it has proven to be useful not only to me but to other peoples. But they is security reasons that I can't describe my truck. I can't tell you the reason for even the reasons for they being security reason is a security reason. It's a big truck, though, and it's got a 800 number on the side of it for them that wants to learn how to drive a truck just like my truck. It also is painted with my favorite colors, and I painted it myself. Don't tell nobody my favorite colors. It used to have Mosquito Trucking Company printed on the side of it in big letters, but I don't print nothing on it now. Them that knows Mosquito knows my truck. Sometimes I has apprentices to ride with me, so's they can learn about the type of transporting that I does, which, if you has forgotten, is industrial detergent. There is still them that thinks I shouldn't be driving my truck, and whenever I has a male apprentice with me they thinks that the male is the driver and I'm the apprentice. Of course the only apprentices I gets is them that has the capacity to drive my truck. So that even though they is named apprentices they has the same capacities that I has. And there is some apprentices who has greater capacities in other areas, but they is still learning from me how to drive a truck. I've got several mirrors on my truck to make sure that everybody sees my mirrors and to make sure that I can see everybody. You know how my mama likes mirrors, so that is the best thing on my truck according to her lights. (She asked me to describe my truck before but for security reasons I am unable to describe my truck 'cause I don't take my truck when I goes out to Covington, 'cept for that time I took Maria and her baby Journal to Middle America, which is really a part of the southern commonwealth but people refers to it as Middle America. She had to go there to get her cousin out of jail. They don't know what to do with immigrants there like they do in South Texas. So they put her cousin in jail like a common criminal and denied her even more rights than they denies peoples in the detention camps. I am still angry about Maria's cousin. They's people that tell me I ain't supposed to be angry, 'cause it ain't like she my cousin.) I have learned more about the true meaning of America since I began driving my truck. When we was in this warehouse where I goes sometimes to get my supplies. Well, we has American and we also has foreign buyers that buys them industrial detergents. So this man says, All the American get in one line and all the foreigner get in the other line. So this Asian-American man gets in the line with the Americans. And this man gets angry and he repeats, I said all the American buyers get in this line. I said all the foreign buyers get in the other line. So this Asian American says, I am an American. And this make the man more angry. There is people who still don't know what America is.

Sincerely,

Mosquito

P.S. I gots to tell you the truth. When the man got in us line, I started to tell him, He said the foreigners in the other line, mister. But then I realizes for myself that he a American just like I am. I was glad I realized it for myself, rather than tell the man to get in the other line with them foreigners, and be the fool of that other fool. But you know the further truth, when I seen that man again at one of them other warehouses—they didn't have no line there for the foreigner and the Americans, 'cause we all stood in the same line—he asks me, What African country are you from? Except when I told him, I'm an American, he nodded and said, For sure, for sure. (I started to tell him a African country, though, but they is customs fees, and I didn't want to lie to the man, however I coulda told him like you Daughters of Nzingha "Africa in the New World.")

P.P.S. Delgadina is writing what she calls a border novel for her border art project. She has a long and involved first chapter because she wants it to be like the people who reads the novel has to cross a border to get into the novel. I tells her that they's a lot of people that ain't going to want to cross that border to get into her novel. I tells her that she can make that first chapter a little intricate but ain't too intricate so's the people won't want to cross the border to read the novel. But she wants the novel to be in the form of you know like them immigrants moving back and forth across the border and dodging them border patrols and moving from one border to another. So the reader is always coming to different borders in the novel and has got to cross them borders. But I tells her that she has still got to make them borders sincere. I ain't mean sincere, I means honest, the word that the man used in that play I told you about, that Rubén Sierra, when he talk about one scene moving honestly into another scene, or something like that. I reminds her what he say about one scene got to move honestly into another scene. I think she going to contradict me, but she say, You right, Nadine, I mean Mosquito. I guess honesty a form of sincerity, though, and sincerity a form of honesty. 'Cept with them fugitive slaves, though, they had to be sincere about they desire for freedom, but at the same time they couldn't be honest with them slaveholders. I mean when them slaveholders would come and ask for they free papers, and if they had falsified free papers they had to show them they falsified free papers. I think that Delgadina is going to revise the beginning of the novel so's that it's intricate like crossing a border but still is interesting for the reader to want to cross that border.

P.P.P.S. I am enclosing a copy of *The Cat Island Poems* which I think you'll like. Please let the Daughters of Nzingha bookshop know about this book of poetry. I think they might like it for they catalogue.

Now I knows that that is a ordinary letter, but Monkey Bread said that she gave a copy to her priestess and they reprinted it in the *Daughters of Nzingha Anthology of Noncanonical New World African Literature*, which has been translated into a number of different languages, including Japanese. I ain't know what they means by noncanonical literature myself, said Monkey Bread, when I asked her, but our priestess says that there's plenty to reprint the canonical literature so that at least in her anthologies she is committed to reprinting the noncanonical literature. Some of them *Cat Island Poems* is also reprinted in *The Daughters of Nzingha Anthology of Noncanonical New World African Literature*.

I wanted to tell Monkey Bread everything about the new Underground Railroad, but y'all know I ain't even tell Monkey Bread everything, so y'all know I ain't going to tell y'all. I got to kinda brag, though, 'cause they is designing for me a custom truck. I told y'all I wanted me a custom truck. I was telling Ray about when them immigration officials stops me all the time and they examines my truck and wishing I had me one of them custom trucks that a magician could help design, so's when they opens my truck whatever is in my truck disappears, and when they closes the truck they reappears, so the new Underground Railroad people is getting me a custom truck that sorta works like them magicians. I ain't got that custom truck yet 'cause they ain't found the magician to work on the design. I uses documents, they've provided me with and a folded-up newspaper. They don't stop me all the time, but when they does stop me, it like this.

Your name and registration.

I tells them my name and gives them my registration.

What are you transporting.

Farmworkers, sir.

That's when they looks like farmworkers and they's all dressed to look like farmworkers and they's all got they documentation to prove that they is migrant laborers. They's all got to get out of the truck and show they documentation. The ones you can't convince them is farmworkers is my apprentices.

I can't tell y'all where they is in the custom truck.

Or when I ain't got them farmworkers it's them Industrial Detergents.

I gots to know the exact name of them farms. I gots to know what them farmworkers is going to them farms to do. I can't say that they is going to that farm to pick potatoes when it a pecan farm. I gots to know the exact names of all them farmworkers.

There is some of them border patrols that when they stops me and asks me my name and registration I'm supposed to give them that folded-up newspaper. When they receives that folded up newspaper, then they don't open the back of the truck. There are others that I must never ever give that folded-up newspaper. I must know exactly who they is. They's others that when they asks for my name and registration I'm supposed to take out a map and pretend like I'm asking them how to get to a certain farm. And after they shows me how to get to the farm, I'm supposed to give them the map. And the new border patrols, the border patrols I ain't never seen before or them gringos that decides they's going to pretend to be border patrols when they ain't, I gots to use my own imagination and reason and judgment, say Ray, to learn how to handle them border patrols.

Ray say some solutions come from the imagination, and others you's got to use reason and judgment for.

Seem like I have learned more about using my imagination and reason and judgment driving my truck for Ray's fugitives than driving it for myself.

Ray, I'm going to tell you a story about my girlhood. It were when I was four years old. Most people thought that I was around seven years old, but I was four years old. They wanted me to sing this spiritual at the Baptist church, 'cause even though I were a little girl I had one of them full, deep voices, so I gets up in front of the church and sings them my favorite spiritual. There is even peoples that had convinced me that I had such a beauteous voice that I should become a singer of spirituals. So I gets up in front of the church and starts singing.

> I'm gonna lay down my sword and shield
> Down by the riverside down by the riverside
> I'm gonna lay down my sword and shield
> Down by the riverside
> Study war no more

Anyway, so I sings my then version of that spiritual and the peoples they oohs and ahhs and murmurs 'cause you ain't supposed to applaud in church. I calls it my version of the song 'cause I always sings it "Study war no more," like it a command, when the true song says, "I'm gonna study war no more." I remembers I always usedta sing it to say "Study war no more." But then this woman they calls the root woman, Mizz Cajun, gets up in the aisle and points her finger right at me. The peoples hushes, 'cause even though they is people believing in the gospel, they knows Mizz Cajun to be a woman of power and when she points her finger at somebody that means she is about to read them. I ain't going to describe Mizz Cajun, 'cause where they is people that don't like to be photographed, Mizz Cajun don't even like to be described. She have admonished people not to describe her to nobody. If somebody don't know Mizz Cajun, then they won't know her. If somebody don't know me, then they won't know me, is what she usedta say to everybody. And they is people that usedta say that didn't even segregation keep Mizz Cajun out of places. If she wanted to sit up at the counter at Woolworth's in Louisville, Kentucky, she would sit there. If she wanted to stay at the Phoenix Hotel in Lexington, Kentucky, she would stay there. If she wanted to sit downstairs instead of the balcony of the Palace theaters anywhere in the southern commonwealth, she would sit there. I ain't know if that is just the tales that peoples would tell about Mizz Cajun and that were just they metaphors for

*power, but that is what they would say about Mizz Cajun. And
there is white peoples that grew up on Mizz Cajun stories as well as
colored peoples. Now my mama she don't want Mizz Cajun to read
me, and although she knows the power of Mizz Cajun from all the
narratives in which Mizz Cajun is the force and power, and although she is a delicate type of little colored woman, I mean my
mama, and I were almost as big as her even at four years old, she gets
up to shield me from Mizz Cajun. She tells Mizz Cajun that she
don't want Mizz Cajun to read me. Now although my mama is a delicate woman she is a brave and bold woman and has a boldness of
spirit. So she stands there to shield me from Mizz Cajun's reading,
but Mizz Cajun gives me my reading anyway. She says to me, Sojourner, I'm going to tell you who you was back in Africa. I didn't
know who you was myself till you started singing that song, then I
remembered who you is. You is the one who usedta do battle back
there in Africa, you is one of us warrior womens that usedta do battle back there in Africa when they was trying to bring us over here
for slavery. I knowed you before the Middle Passage and I know you
now. I'm going to tell you who you is and I'm going to tell all these
people who you is. That's who you is. You is the warrior class. You
don't take no shit. You is the warrior class. You don't take no shit. You
is the warrior class. You don't take no shit. You is the warrior class.
You don't take no shit. You is the warrior class. You usedta battle the
white people when they come over there to try to get us to make
slaves of usselves. They made slaves of us and they got us to make
slaves of usselves. Course you had to battle some of us own peoples
'cause we was over there doing mischief to us ownselves. But you
was a warrior woman to keep us from slavery, to keep the white
peoples from enslaving us and to keep us from enslaving us ownselves. I didn't know that they had captured even you, Sojourner, till
I heard you singing that song. But they is going to come a day, Sojourner, and this is the truth, when you is going to have to pick up
your sword and shield and study war again.*

*Sojourner is going to do what she has to do, say my mama, but I
don't want her to study war. I wants her to study the word and to
mind the word. I don't want her to study war.*

Now the peoples looks at my mama like they thinks that she is a fool, 'cause this is Mizz Cajun. They knows the power of Mizz Cajun. You don't just talk to Mizz Cajun like you talks to ordinary peoples.

Then Mizz Cajun start singing, like she teaching me a new version of that song.

> I'm gonna pick up my sword and shield
> Down by the riverside down by the riverside
> I'm gonna pick up my sword and shield
> Down by the riverside
> Got to study war some more

Naw, say my mama, don't be reading that to my Sojourner. The word is mightier than the sword. Words is mightier than the sword.

Only when you controls the medium and the message, say Mizz Cajun.

When you takes the s off the beginning of sword and puts it at the end you's got words, say my mama.

The peoples in the church starts to murmur like they ain't never thought to take the s off the beginning of sword and put it at the end of sword till Mizz Cajun looks around at them, then they hushes. 'Cause whether or not what my mama say is clever, Mizz Cajun is still Mizz Cajun.

You say dat de words is mightier dan de sword? ask Mizz Cajun with a laugh.

Peoples knows that laugh, 'cause they says the first name of Mizz Cajun is Sheha. Peoples thinks that it's Sheba but it ain't. It's Sheha Cajun. Shehahahahahahahahahaha, laugh Mizz Cajun. You say dat de words is mightier dan de sword? Years later when I would learn the Swahili language, I would learn that Sheha means a village councillor. I ain't know if the peoples that named her knew that meaning of the word. All I knows is although they is peoples that says that Mizz Cajun's first name is Sheba her first name is Sheha.

> Shehahahahahahahahahaha
> Shehahahahahahahahahaha
> Shehahahahahahahahahaha
> Shehahahahahahahahahaha
> Shehahahahahahahahahaha

I say that Sojourner will do what she has to do, says my mama. But I would prefer that she study the word and mind the word.

I don't know if she say word with a small w or a large W. If she say it with a large W then it the word of God she talking about. Course I didn't know the difference at four years old between a small w and a large W.

Now my mama she usually talks in real proper English, but trying to shield me from Mizz Cajun she speaks in the language of the people, and even Mizz Cajun starts saying dis and dat although she don't usually say dis and dat. They has got different versions of who they wants me to become.

If she is going to have to mind de word she is going to have to remember all of dem dat she hears, say Mizz Cajun.

> *Sojourner? Peacemaker? Warrior?*
> *A little bird told me*
> *What she shall be*
> *When the words come forth*
> *Enough is Enough*
> *Then she'll do her warrior stuff*

Mizz Cajun turn around looking like them whirling dervishes and then it look like she were transforming herself into all the different colored peoples: Africans, Native Americans, Chicanos, Indians from India, Asians, Pacific Islanders, Hawaiians, Australian aborigines, Inuits and all the other different colored peoples.

> *Heya Heya Heya Heya Heya*
> *A little bird told me*
> *Peaceable she'll be*
> *Until the words come forth*
> *Enough is Enough*
> *Then she'll do her warrior stuff*

Y'all know that Enough is Enough! is that expression of them Chiapas rebels. How she know them Chiapas rebels' language all them many years ago?

> *Heya Heya Heya Heya Heya*
> *Heya Heya Heya Heya Heya*

Heya Heya Heya Heya Heya
Heya Heya Heya Heya Heya
Heya Heya Heya Heya Heya

When she say that, she ain't whirling like them dervishes but her ownself again, and then that Monkey Bread comes up and stands in front of my mama and me, like she is shielding my mama and me. So you's got me standing there, my mama standing in front of me to shield me, and Monkey Bread standing in front of my mama to shield my mama and me.

What is you doing, little pygmy girl? ask Mizz Cajun. I remembers you with your little pygmy spear and little pygmy shield too. Osani. Little pygmy girl, who's protectress do you think you is? Don't you try to work me, little girl. I will say, Mizz Johnson, for a little colored woman as delicate as you is, you has got a boldness and bravery of spirit. You makes me proud.

Then Mizz Cajun march out of the church singing her new version of the song, and she sang it real proper.

> *I'm going to pick up my sword and shield*
> *Down by the riverside down by the riverside*
> *I'm going to pick up my sword and shield*
> *Down by the riverside*
> *I'm going to study war some more*
> *Study war some more study war some more*
> *I'm going to study war some more!*
> *Nimekasirika!*

There is people that say that the reason that Monkey Bread is still a pygmy is on account of trying to work Mizz Cajun. They say that if she hadn't been standing up there trying to work Mizz Cajun, she mighta growed up to be the size of a natural woman. Others say that her people have always been a pygmy people and it don't have nothing to do with Mizz Cajun. You've heard of people saying, Don't play me, don't you try to play me, don't you play me. But when you is dealing with root women, you ain't playing them, you is working them. And they don't tell you not to play them, they tells you not to work them. I remember that that is when I started remembering every word and Monkey Bread started writing as her way of minding the word. She were only four years old herself, but she started asking the schoolchildren to teach her to read and write, so by the time we got to school she already knew how to read and write. (Monkey Bread didn't even know how to say school *and referred to it as* shule. *Teach me what y'all learns in* shule, *she'd tell the little children. Teach me to read and write and everything y'all learns in* shule.) *My mama have stayed the delicate type of colored woman, but she have kept the boldest and bravery of spirit that Mizz Cajun told her about. I knew she already had it coming up to protect me from Mizz Cajun, but then Mizz Cajun told her she bold and brave of spirit and seem like that boldness and braveness of spirit become more manifest. But there is even peoples that say there were more to Mizz Cajun's new version of the old spiritual that she turned into a war song, 'cause it were around that same time that all over the world the colored peoples started new freedom movements and they wasn't all them nonviolence neither. I mean, they was having freedom movements, but it seemed like they was renewed. There is even people that claims that whenever Mizz Cajun sings that song, whether it is in church or elsewhere, the colored peoples starts to pick up they swords and shields and to study war. To tell you the truth, whenever I hear about colored peoples anywhere saying* Enough is Enough! *like them peoples I heard you talking about, I thinks that Mizz Cajun must be somewhere singing that song.*

Ray and I, us go into the bedroom and play some. Then we's like figures dancing in a dream, then we's like surfaces, then we's the deep thing itself, then we's doing the African tango, the real tango, then we's circles and each the center of each circle, then we's what Delgadina call that radiuses, then we's the same being, circumferences—what Delgadina call them when she taking that class?—then we's all things and each other. What my mama say about you's got to learn from everything in the universe? What my daddy say about claiming wisdom? Well, there's all kindsa wisdom. We's the entire universe and usselves. Am I dreaming 'bout love? I'm the root and the tree, the spring and the river itself. Is that love? What did Zora say 'bout the flowering pear tree? Is Ray the one? Is Ray the absolute one? It's like we's in slow motion, powerful and precious, pure radiance.

Then I'm dreaming, talking to Ray in my dreams.

Ray, what your idea of love? Love supposed to be something make you feel perfect, make you feel like a full and perfect person?

Tell me your idea of love, say Ray.

I ain't never had no idea of love. I seen in a book, though, 'bout there being such a thing as separate parts but the same whole. Maybe that's what true love is, when peoples in true love, they's separate parts but the same whole.

Then we's listening to Miles. I'm telling Ray he's kinda like Miles. You's kinda like Miles, I'm saying.

I like Miles, but I'm not like Miles, he's saying. What do you mean?

Delgadina and me was listening to Miles and I told her I likes Miles but I likes the personality of Satchmo and then she told me I ain't supposed to like the personality of Satchmo 'cause he a stereotype, and then she go to her library and get a book that talk about how Miles and his generation of jazz musicians rejected the demeanor of Satchmo.

The sense of humor and playfulness? ask Ray.

The demeanor of Satchmo and some of them would even turn they backs on they audience. I likes to face my audience myself and play with them, even if they does think I'm a stereotype.

Then I'm telling Ray 'bout Delgadina giving me the whole history of why them men rejected they humor and playfulness so's not to be confused with the stereotype of the nigger entertainer or just the stereotype itself and talking about Sidney Poitier and even talking about the minstrels and Mr. Interlocutor and then talking of "Amos 'n' Andy"—I ain't supposed to like them neither—and then talking about a poet named Sterling Brown and what he say about plaster of paris saints and Langston Hughes and his character Simple and even another Ray Claude McKay's Ray and the difference between Ray and Banjo and asking him if he heard of that other Ray and something about Martin Delany and then Bojangles and that other Martin the comedian Martin Lawrence. What's the difference between comedy and stereotyping? ask Delgadina. And all got to do with rejecting or not rejecting one's sense of humor and playfulness so's not to be confused with no stereotypes. I tells Ray he is like Miles turning his back on his audience.

All I knows is if I was a jazz musician I would face my audience and play with them, I says, even if they does think I'm a stereotype. Facing your audience and even playing with them don't mean that you is just there to entertain them. They might look at me and think that I'm an entertainer or even that I'm entertaining them, but I ain't. I don't believe in being no entertainer myself, though I knows they is peoples that finds me amusing. They finds me amusing just because I'm who I am. Others has ostracized me for being me. I don't believe in us being no entertainers myself, 'cause the first thing they does in the movies when they captures people is to make them they entertainment. I seen that in a Civil War movie and I also seen it in a Nazi movie. The captured people always provided the entertainment.

I also seen it on a reservation where these native peoples was dancing for the tourists. When I seen them native peoples dancing for the tourists and not for theyselves, I said that is just like us peoples. It ain't to say that all the native peoples dances for the tourists. Or it mighta been a war dance and the tourists thought it were entertainment. I knows peoples who is entertainers and I tells them the same thing, that I don't believe in it. I likes good jazz, though. But you's like Miles, Ray, and you's like the other Ray, I don't mean your other Ray I mean Claude McKay's Ray. He is the intellectual in the book *Banjo* and the one named Banjo is just who he is. I guess they is both who they is. You can be a intellectual and be who you is. 'Cept you's different from the Ray in that book 'cause you's got your guerrillas.

Is you is or is you ain't my baby?

Then I'm with Monkey Bread and her star and we's eating caviar and drinking champagne, except we ain't in Hollywood, we's sitting in the Galileo in Covington. Then I'm at some museum and Ray and I is looking at a painting. The painting is blue and green and red and yellow oval shapes that seem to rise above the surface of the painting so that one dimension seems three dimensions. I tries to describe that painting like Delgadina would describe it. Nothing in the painting forms a straight line but seems to shimmer sometimes at a different angle. You can't tell it's painted colors or blue and green and red and yellow light as if the painting is made of light not color. Sometimes the painting seem smooth, at another angle full of textures, at another angle them colors has a greater intensity more shimmers of light revealing other colors, but some colors is perceived at some angles not at others.

Who painted that picture? I asks Ray.

You Mosquito, you Sojourner.

Then I'm reading one of Delgadina's books, 'cept the book is describing my painting.

Then I'm in Tasmania.

CHAPTER 15

I DON'T KNOW WHY RAY HAS BROUGHT ME TO THIS canyon. We're riding donkeys, not horses, along the Rio Grande. We're in Big Bend National Park, in the South Texas brush country. I ain't been to Big Bend National Park, but I seen it on television. At first I thinks it's the Laguno Atascosa, which a national wildlife refuge and reserve, but Ray say it Big Bend National Park. I tells Ray that this is my first time in Big Bend National Park. Ray tells me they's got everything in this park and in this part of Texas: mountains, deserts, rivers. It's like a whole other country, Ray says. And that's exactly the same thing that them tourism peoples says about Texas when they's trying to get people to come to Texas. People thinks that they knows America, but when they gets to Texas it's like a whole other country. I'm carrying cornstalk dolls that I bought at a ranch so's I can show Maria how to make cornstalk dolls, though her dolls is better than these cornstalk dolls.

Don't believe the government officials, and don't believe the military people, Ray is saying. I'm thinking why we riding donkeys when they's so many horses in the area, but Ray says it's because he's a *sacerdote*, a priest, and then we rides into a part of the park that is a reserve for wildlife. They's birds and ocelots and Ray starts telling me how secretive ocelots is, and then he shows me some of their habitats and trails. I'm not the resident biologist, he says, but you can ask me anything about ocelots and I can tell you. First, you must know that they are very secretive creatures.

Then we rides into Texas hill country and then we goes on a river cruise, except the river cruise takes us from America to Mexico and we're in one of them little Mexican villages. They ain't nothing to do in this village but to go around and talk to the villagers and take their photographs, but there's this woman named Valdez who doesn't want her photograph to be taken, but them other villagers lets us take they photographs. We also photographs a hawk and some deer and some wild Mexican goats.

Have you ever seen wild Spanish goats? asks Ray.

I thought they was Mexican goats, I says.

Things not resolved by the imagination are resolved by reason and judgment, says Ray. You're a valuable acquisition for the Sanctuary movement, for the new Underground Railroad. I don't mean to say it like that.

You sound like a pamphlet, Ray. You remember when you were first trying to recruit me, you sounded like a pamphlet, Ray. Are you the absolute one?

I mean, we treasure you, Mosquito.

We photographs some white pelicans fishing and a eagle and Ray talks about the pueblo architecture and Native American influences in this little Mexico village. I tries to photograph the woman named Valdez again, but she won't allow herself to be photographed. Ray gives her some documents and she returns with us on the Texas river cruise until we reach America. Then we rides some donkeys into Galveston. The woman named Valdez wants to see the Moody Gardens because she's heard that it's inside a pyramid, so we takes her to the Moody Gardens where Ray says there is thousands and thousands of species of plants and animals and gives us a guided tour, except it's all on television, I'm watching television, I'm watching us on television on the Animal Channel, and then Ray is telling us about America and the Americas, and Ray calls it a rain forest pyramid, then I tell Ray and the woman named Valdez that I've got to go to Tasmania, that I want to get me a horse and I knows exactly where I can find me a tamer of Australian wild horses, though I don't know why they're called Australian wild horses when they should be Tasmanian wild horses. I don't even know if he's a tamer of wild horses.

How do you tame a wild horse? I ask.

Calling them by name is required, he answers. Calling a wild horse by name is the best method I know of taming a wild horse.

If it a wild horse, have it got a name? I asks. I'm thinking Tasmania kinda looks like the mountains of New Mexico or the brush country of South Texas. I ain't convinced that this Tasmania. I think I hear somebody say something about the Chiapas project, the Chiapas defense.

Say what? I asks. I'm thinking about getting me a custom truck with a skylight, then I'm telling Ray I would prefer not to attend the strategy meetings. I'm a person of peculiarities, Ray, I'm saying. Then I'm in Tasmania riding donkeys 'cause I ain't want them to tame one of them wild Tasmanian horses just for me to ride.

Love is a curative power, someone is saying.

Tasman?

Mosquito, he whisper. Sojourner.

Yeah. Who's it? Tasman?

I'm on my sofa, curled up on one of them pillows that looks like them court jester's hats—yellow and green and red, whatever the color of them court jester's hats.

Say what? Raymond. This is Raymond. Who's Tasman? This is Raymond.

What? I'm dreaming 'bout Tasmania. I'm dreaming 'bout Tasmania. I'm dreaming 'bout Tasmania. I was thinking about us and then I started dreaming about Tasmania. Or maybe I was dreaming about us and thinking about Tasman. I know I was wearing that towel of yours again, but I thought I was Erykah Baduh, you know, 'cause it wasn't like no ordinary towel, I thought I had on one of them headdresses like I was an African queen, and I was sitting with you and you was reading your correspondences, except it was like when I was actually sitting with you and you were reading your correspondences, I mean you know, when we took the bath together, and then I was dreaming about Tasman in Tasmania.

Raymond. This is Raymond. Who's Tasman?

Tasmania. Raymond? I'm half-sleep and half-drunk, Raymond.

What you want? I'm dreaming about Tasmania. But I'm always dreaming about you. Raymond, *sacerdote, guerrero. Sagaz.*

Can you drive me to *el centro*? I'm at the center. Can you drive me to *el centro*?

Center?

Community Center. *El centro.* I'm at the Community Center. Can you drive me to *el centro*? Who's Tasman?

Drive you where you are?

El centro. I'm at the Community Center. This is Raymond. Who's Tasman?

El centro? That's in California, ain't it? Ain't they a detention camp in *el centro*? You gotta free someone from that detention camp, ain't you? I heard them talking about that detention camp at *el centro*. I thought you were taking that woman to Canada. That La Loba.

Guillermina?

Guillermina, who's Guillermina?

Can you drive me to *el centro*? Guillermina's in Canada, not *el centro*. I'm at the Community Center.

Naw, I'm half-sleep, Raymond. I been dreaming about Tasmania. You know, Tasmania. Not Tanzania. Except when we were at that cantina. I dreamed that we were at a cantina, but it was in Africa. You and me. That mighta been Tanzania. You heard about the Tasmanian devil?

Yeah. Can you drive me to *el centro*? Who's Tasman?

Naw, I'm half-sleep, Raymond. Half-sleep and half-drunk. Me and Delgadina been celebrating her signing up for detective school. Yeah, detective school. Can you imagine Delgadina a detective? I can imagine Delgadina a detective. Except she ain't call herself a detective, though, she call herself a investigative consultant or some shit. 'Cause a lot of these modern detectives they got a lot of fancy names for theyselves, you know with all the computers and shit. At one of them trade fairs they be telling you how them modern spies and detectives uses computers and shit. You know even them oceanographers they got them computers. I used to think if you a oceanog-

rapher you got to know how to scuba-dive but you don't, 'cause a
lot of them oceanographers now, they just sit at they computers and
explore the ocean. They can map the whole ocean and put that ocean
in them computers. Delgadina, I can imagine that Delgadina a detective. Says us women, Delgadina says us women, us *mujeres*
oughta all learn how to kick ass. We oughta learn how to kick ass, us
mujeres. Like at the Community Center. You seen them kicking ass?
They be kicking ass, and then bowing to each other and shit, them
Oriental bows, 'cept Delgadina say you ain't supposed to say Oriental you supposed to say Asian. Except a lot of the modern detectives
they don't have to kick ass, just turn on they computer and do they
detective work, like them spies them espionage people just turn on
they computer, like them oceanographers. My friend Monkey Bread
she's learning them computers, that word processing, ain't no oceanographer or no detective neither, she work for this movie star out in
California. I told you about that Monkey Bread. Anyway we been
celebrating Delgadina signing up for detective school. Drinking
pulque at a real cantina. Pulque, you ever had pulque? And palm
wine. You ever had any palm wine? Except we didn't have any palm
wine, just pulque. I guess pulque is the Mexican palm wine. Or
palm wine is the African pulque. Made out of that fermented cactus
juice. I don't think you got to ferment that palm wine, though. Don't
they drink that palm wine straight from the tree? That pulque looks
kinda like milk. We went to this storefront cantina—you ever been
to a storefront cantina?—and had some pulque. That a real strong
drink. You ever had pulque? It ain't Bud Light. It's the Mexican
palm wine. It's a real strong drink, but it looks like milk, though. I
can't drive boo to *el centro*. I might could drive you when I'm half-
sleep, but I can't drive boo when I'm half-drunk. Not to no *el
centro*. Who you got to free from *el centro*? Your old girlfriend? I'm
just kidding, Ray. Who's Guillermina? La Loba? Ain't La Loba
and Guillermina the same woman? I'm Mosquito and I'm Nadine
too. That the eternal revolutionist's old girlfriend, ain't it, La Loba?
I met me a real African in Canada. I ain't been to Africa but I been
to Canada. Guillermina your old girlfriend? Delgadina's boyfriend
thinks he's a drunkometer. The man from Hornitos. Guillermina's
your old girlfriend, ain't she? I'm just kidding, Ray. I'm half-sleep
and half-drunk. Did I tell you about Maria and her cousin? I took

them to Middle America to get her cousin free? Maria and her
cousin and me and Journal.

Half-sleep and half-drunk, I think he's gonna convince me anyhow, but he don't. He says, Fine, I'll get one of the others, and hangs
up the phone.

I'm dreaming he's on his way to *el centro* to free his old girlfriend
Guillermina from the detention camp, except in the dream his old
girlfriend is me. Then I be dreaming about Delgadina and Father
Raymond. Delgadina be coming outa the Community Center. Delgadina in her peacock skirt. But she got one of them karate outfits
under her peacock skirt 'cause she been learning how to kick ass. Be
kicking ass and then bowing and shit. And I'm either a mosquito in
the dream or an orangutan. Must be an orangutan. Like I thought
that Indonesian woman be calling me a orangutan. I forgot what Father Raymond say that orangutan mean. Maybe that just her word
for American.

Uh, this is Father Raymond.

Isabella?

Hello, I'm Delgadina.

Isabellita?

I'm Delgadina. Mosquito's bartender friend. Except I ain't a
mosquito in the dream I'm a orangutan.

Hello.

I be thinking Isabella must be her code name, her spy name. Or
maybe that Isabella the name of the other one—his true love. And
then I'm a woman—ain't no mosquito and ain't no orangutan—in
the back room of a shoe and saddle repair shop in Mexico City
mending one of them saddles. And then that Father Raymond—
Raymond—he come in the back room of the shop. After we mend
the saddle together—must be that labor theory of equality Delgadina be talking about—we put the saddle on one of our wild horses
and gallops along that border road. Galloping along that whole border, free as kings.

Ray, I be saying.

Don't call me Ray, call me Tasman, he be saying.

And then he turn into my ex.

Tasman.

Then we sitting in a cantina, a storefront cantina, except it ain't pulque we drinking, it's palm wine, and the storefront cantina ain't in Mexico it in Africa. Course I ain't had no palm wine, so it taste like pulque, but the dream say it palm wine.

And then I'm dreaming about being with Maria and Journal and Maria's cousin and Clara the guerrilla lawyer and that Haitian man who must be a guerrilla lawyer and then I'm with Delgadina in the cantina again.

We be drinking pulque and she be calling me amiga. Have some more pulque, amiga, and that pulque look like milk. And she be wanting to play that tell me about your ex I'll tell you about mine game. I be drinking that pulque, but be calling it palm wine.

What's pulque?

Pulque is pulque.

And then we be eating some of them tacos, real tacos, not them Taco Bell tacos. And I be calling them softail tacos, and she be call- ing them the great un-American taco. This the great un-American taco, she be saying and sipping on that pulque that I be calling palm wine. Then somebody seen her scribbling in her notebook a gringo that came in the cantina least look like a gringo and be asking her, Are you writing the great American novel and she answered, Naw, I'm writing the great un-American novel. Must be a gringo. And then Delgadina she be saying to me that she should call what she writing a un-American novel 'cause shouldn't just the gringos claim America for theyselves, 'cause America more than the gringos and all them other Americas, that Latin America and that Brazil. The other Americas, she be calling them, 'cause even me when people say America I be thinking of one America, but then she be talking about the other Americas. Maybe she ain't writing the great Ameri- can novel, she be saying, but she be writing an American novel, and be able to claim America for herself too. Or some shit like that. But I'm still sipping on that pulque and calling it palm wine. And she sipping on that pulque and scribbling in her notebook.

But don't tell Miguelita, that crazy mujer, she says. Women like us, Nadine, we ain't wifable woman. Crazy mujeres, that's what we are.

And then this other man come in the bar he ain't a gringo he a Chicano or Mexican and Delgadina get up and start just a-kissing on him. I think it that vato, *the one from Hornitos—did she say Hornitos?—I think it that* vato *anyway, the one she telling me about, the* vato *with the wife—or is it the wife from Hornitos?—the* vato *I know she in love with but maybe it a vato she don't even know, maybe it just any* vato, *maybe it just any* vato *from Mexico or one of them border towns. I know don't know that* vato *but I think I know that* mujer *comes in the cantina and Delgadina and that* mujer *pointing at each other and I'm kinda disillusioned 'cause Delgadina say she don't play that. I'm thinking that* mujer *Miguelita and the man Mr. Delgado who I ain't never seen but Miguelita a gringa and this* mujer *ain't a gringa then I'm thinking she Maria that this Maria and that man the Tarahumara Indian then I'm thinking she Guillermina and that man Raymond his ownself and then I'm thinking that woman is Delgadina her ownself. Ring on her little finger, just like Raymond's. Didn't I say so? Maybe she one of the Nicodemuses. Ring on they little finger, maybe that they signal so they know each other. Or ring in the nose.*

The next day, when I'm awake and sober, when I come in the cantina a man is standing at the bar talking to Delgadina. He look like a cowboy, got on cowboy boots, cowboy hat, cowboy plaid shirt, cowboy blue jeans, hair kinda long in the back. He one of those macho-looking men. He look part Mexican part Indian maybe Navajo. He kinda remind me of one of them country singers and his voice what I hear of it when I'm coming toward the bar sound like one of them country singers, maybe like that one whenever I see him I can't tell what race he supposed to be, 'cept all them other country singers treat him like he white, so I figure he must be white, though I know there's a lots of part of the South they would question his race.

Nadine, I mean Mosquito, this is Charlie T. Juárez, this my ex-husband.

Ain't she say he a sculptor? He kinda don't look like no sculptor. 'Cept they's a lot of artist don't look like no artist. I mean people idea of a artist.

How you doing, Nadine, he say. You the one they call Mosquito. Real polite-type man. Rugged. Kind you see on them ranges in the Southwest. I guess somebody like him could do that kinda iron and wire sculpture.

He look like he mighta wanted to say more to me, but he too involved with talking to Delgadina, so I sit down at the bar, kinda
away from them, so's they won't think I'm spying on them. I get me
some pretzels and dip them in salsa on the bar, and reach behind the
bar and get my own Budweiser 'cause I know where Delgadina
keeps them. She still talking to Charlie T. Juárez. He must like that
T. in his name for his own ex-wife to introduce him. Seem like she
said her ex-husband named something else ain't she? Or maybe she
had more than one ex-husband. He's got a mustache and he's got all
these papers with him that's he's got on the bar and holding toward
Delgadina. I think they's divorce papers, that maybe they ain't
legally divorced and he's handing her the divorce papers. When he
kinda smiled at me I seen a gold cap on one of his teeth, and he
smelled and looked like somebody been riding the range. Kinda
musky, you know.

Anyway, Delgadina, like I'm saying, my new wife don't want the
motel and we're moving back East, so you might as well take the
property. I'll sign my share over to you.

I don't know, Charlie T. I don't think I want that old motel myself. I don't want it unless I can afford to fix it up. I told you you
could have that property when we got divorced and you's still keeping my share. In fact, I told you Eden Pride could have my share.

She's a Juárez now, said Charlie T.

She's still Eden Pride to me, said Delgadina. Well, you looking
good. I can blame her 'cause you's looking good. You look like she's
taking care of you.

We take care of each other.

I don't think I want that property, though. I don't think I want
that old motel. You can sell it to somebody.

Naw, I don't want to sell it. Got a couple of Navajo gals who's
running it for us now. They might buy it. I think maybe they might
buy it. I might sell them my share of it.

Well, you can sell them my share 'cause I don't want it. I don't
think I want it.

I think you oughta keep it, Delgadina. I can have the Navajos
send you your share of the profit.

You know that motel don't make no profit. I ain't seen no profit.

That's 'cause you gave Eden your profit. I ain't gonna say that it made a lot of profit, 'cause Eden don't want the responsibility of that motel neither. Anyway, we's moving East, and you's closer to New Mexico than we are.

Yeah, I know but.

Well, you can keep the papers anyway. The Navajos got your address out here, and you's got their address. And you'll have better access to that motel than we will out East.

Where out East y'all going?

New York City.

I think she's going to ask him why they's going to New York City, 'cause I wants to know myself. She don't ask him, though. Maybe she already know him so well that she already know why he going out there. Or maybe that Eden Pride from New York City. Or maybe he like that artist I heard on TV who said you don't know if you's a true artist till you tries to be a artist in New York. Lotta artists thinks they's artists till they tries to be a artist in New York. I wants to ask him whether he's taking his sculptures to New York.

I don't get out there to New Mexico.

If you own you some property out there you might. The Navajos take pretty good care of it. But it does need fixing up. Lotta folks when they come out there and see it's Navajos running it they don't want to stay there. You know what I'm saying. I think you oughta keep your ownership but I'll sell the Navajos mine. They the managers. You don't have to go out to New Mexico to manage that motel.

If that's what you think is best, Charlie T.

Then he give her them papers, tip his cowboy hat to me, and stroll out of the cantina.

That's him, she said, like a fool.

I got me another Budweiser and took one of the stools that was closer to her.

He's looking good, she said, folding up the papers and putting them in her apron pocket. Last time I seen him he looked like he been through a season in hell. Course that was when he was married to me. I can't fault Eden Pride none. I wish I coulda kept him looking that good.

And you know I'm sitting there wondering if this the same Delgadina. Then one of those *vatos* comes in the bar and she serves him a whiskey, fritos and salsa.

You look like you been through a season in hell, she said.

I didn't know whether she was talking to that *vato* or remembering Charlie T. Juárez.

Now don't y'all ask me no more about that Charlie T. Juárez 'cause I only seen him once. Years later, when I was living in New Mexico my ownself, I seen someone, I thought was him. He was with a Chicana, though, and nobody coulda mistaken her for no Eden Pride. I mean with a name like Eden Pride. Naw, it wasn't Delgadina either.

Here's a letter somebody sent you from Paris, say Delgadina, and reach under the bar.

Paris? I asks, then I'm wondering who know me in Paris and how they know to write me c/o Delgadina.

Who I know in Paris? I'm asking myself, then I'm thinking maybe it my legendary uncle Buddy Johnson, but he wouldn't know nothing about my whereabouts or about Delgadina; then I'm thinking it Nefertiti Johnson, 'cause I did send her a fan letter; I thought maybe it were from Maria's cousin, that maybe she had immigrated from Mexico to Paris, but she ain't know about Delgadina neither.

CHAPTER 16

SIT UP AT THE BAR AND OPENS THE LETTER,
then I order me another Bud Light and goes to one of them booths
to read it. I don't sit near the crazy gringa, 'cause she be telling me
her crazy gringa stories whilst I tries to read it. Anyway she reading
her own mail from Paris, probably that Sophie woman.

Dear Nadine,

I is writing to you c/o Mr. Delgado's cantina 'cause everybody
know where that is. I forgot to bring my address book, and we's in
Paris.

Didn't I say come to California and see the world? My star and I
is in Paris, the City of Lights, girlfriend. (Even got Bud Light.) It's
just like the picture books, 'cept my star says she bored. Is we in the
same Paree?

She's doing a movie. She plays a seventeenth-century French
duchess who likes to collect specimens from Africa, like the Hottentot Venus, and put them on display in them intellectuals' saloons. I
plays one of the African specimens. My star wanted to play one of
the randy whores, but she the duchess. I'm sending you a book of

poetry about the Hottentot Venus by a African-American woman author.

They've even got a Rajpoot Indian frequenting the saloon. Anyway this Martinican man rescues the Hottentot woman from being put on exhibition in the saloon. I'm in love. In the movie, though, people pay to see my *steatopygia*, my buttocks. You know these Europeans has always been crazy. You look like the Venus Hottentot. They's got a lot of mosquitoes in Africa says the woman who plays the Hottentot, who's a real Hottentot. I told her you looks like her.

I ain't no private detective, but in my investigations, though, I have discovered the following about your true uncle Buddy:

After the war he spent some time in France where he was in love with this French woman who turned out to be a collaborator with the Germans during the war, but she was so beautiful that after they had her up to Cognac, they released her, but when they seen her with a Negro at least some of the French, because they believed all the American tales, wanted to send her up to Cognac again, so your uncle returned to America. He spent some time in the States and returned to France during the period of the Algerian war, when he was in love with an Algerian woman who the French claimed was a conspirator and he helped her to escape and they escaped to Spain, I believe. Either that's your uncle or somebody else's uncle, but they's got the same name. I met a woman named Madame la Sagesse who told me their story. She's rather disillusioned with Paris but still comes here, she says, to visit her African friends.

They's a lot more splivs in this Paris than you would imagine. They Jim Crows people over here too, though. Marseilles is the gateway to Africa.

A lot of the people you think is splivs here in Paris, though, is North Africans and Algerians and ain't even Afro-French, though they's got a lot of them Afro-French. Madame la Sagesse who claims to be descended from the real Venus Hottentot is from one of the islands, although when she's not in Paris she spends most of her time in Quebec.

The Luxembourg Gardens is beautiful. Our pension is on the Rue Bourbon-le-Château.

When he ain't acting, my Martinican friend teaches a course in stage design. He is also a watercolorist. He ain't like a lot of intellectuals who thinks they's supposed to lead you around by the nose. His name is the French word for *fisherman* but it sounds like the French word for *sinner* because in French the word for *sinner* and *fisherman* sounds kinda alike.

He wants to take me with him to Amsterdam. He don't like my nickname, Monkey Bread, and calls me by my real name Cricket, which ain't my real name neither. I think you and Mr. Freeman are the only ones who know my real name. He has a room in an Ethiopian hotel where I even met a real African prince. Can you imagine me roaming around Europe with some man I hardly even know? I might go to Amsterdam. My star supposed to be doing a movie in Amsterdam.

Yours,

Monkey Bread a.k.a. Cricket

P.S. You said you couldn't remember how I got my nickname Monkey Bread. 'Cause I used to be real light-skin when I was a girl—what they used to call yellow in them days—so first my nickname were Banana, but then this little boy be saying, Banana? Banana ain't nothing but Monkey Bread. Then everybody start calling me Monkey Bread. Course I don't look like Monkey Bread now, you know, but they still calls me Monkey Bread. And even you still calls me Monkey Bread. You know, I think I have figured you out, Nadine. I think you are like that Mrs. Wisdom. I think you are attracted to people who you think represents culture and superior intelligence. I don't mean always they culture, the European culture. I remember that we was always acquaintances growing up and we starred in plays together, but when we become real friends was when that English teacher told everybody that I wasn't as dumb as they thought I was. Then you started believing that you could learn from my intelligence. I'm not saying it's something that you knew that you were doing. I mean like that Delgadina in Texas City, and then that man that you won't tell me nothing about. I think they likes you because of your powerful personality and you is attracted to them because of what you can learn. The reason I likes you is because you is the freest woman I know. You tells people what you wants to tell them and refuses to tell them what you don't. You might lie a little and say that it is for security reasons, but that is because of the knowledge that you have acquired about people. You know how we is. You have certainly told me over the years more than I have needed or wanted to know. But you is also sort of my protectress. Do you remember when you and John Henry had to rescue me? Everybody was talking revolution. I think I wanted to start a revolution among our ownselves. There's a woman who belongs to the Daughters of Nzingha and every time anybody say something to her about revolution she say revolution yourself or talk about how people got to revolution theyselves or how you would say it revolution us ownselves. She believes in the other types of revolution 'cause the rumor is that she finances them, but I guess that is only for them peoples she is convinced have revolutioned theyselves first and that she can trust to revolution others. I think she must be a free woman, but peoples say she have psychological problems, so I thinks you is freer than her, Nadine, 'cause you is both sane and free. It's kinda easy to be free when you's crazy. But then you is a slave to your insanity or you manipulates it, like Mrs. Wisdom's cat in that poetry. Nzingha has the superior wisdom and is the wisest woman I know—do that make you want to join the Daughters of Nzingha—and has the freedom of her own womanhood, but she has the Daughters of Nzingha to contend with, and so has to be a example to us, but you don't have to be a example to nobody but yourself.

I puts Monkey Bread letter into my shirt pocket and go up to the bar. They ain't much business in the bar, so Delgadina sitting up there reading E. D. Santos. She a Chicana woman writer, I think Delgadina ideal of the Chicana woman writer or the educated Chicana or something. I don't think she known to the publishing establishment, though, 'cause Delgadina always got to order her novels.

Somebody come up to Delgadina and say something.

I'm reformed, she say.

I ain't know what she talking about. I'm wondering what Delgadina got to be reformed about—least the Delgadina I know. Then I think I hear her say something sound like, You better reform your own ass. 'Cept I ain't sure if that what she saying. Then she saying something in Spanish. And then she giving whoever the man is a copy of one of the E. D. Santos books to read. I ain't read them myself, so I can't tell y'all what they's got to do with reformation. Or maybe it's that people has got to reform they ownself.

I sits up at the bar drinking me another Bud Light. But I also thought the letter was from Ray. 'Cause I ain't know his whereabouts. I pays for them beers and gives Delgadina a tip—she say she ain't want no tip, but I always gives her a tip anyway, 'cause she the bartender, then I goes out, gets in my truck and heads for the mission school, 'cause I know if anybody know he whereabouts, the whereabouts of Ray, it be that nun. Got to call him Father Raymond, though. Got to remember he Father Raymond.

But she telling me that the immigration authorities is wise to him and he don't want to compromise the movement. We in her office in the mission school. I'm talking about the nun who first introduced me to Ray and them new Underground Railroad people. She ain't behind her desk now, that nun I'm talking about, but standing in her nun's habit looking out the window into the courtyard at them Mexican and Native American childrens. They's having they recess, playing kickball and other children's games. She a bigger woman than she seemed the first time I seen her behind that desk when she thought I'd come there to apply for that housekeeper job, and she a broader-shouldered woman. Talking about that John Henry Hollywood's having Egyptian shoulders. She got Egyptian shoulders. I don't know if the real Egyptians got shoulders like that or just them in them museums. Or maybe just the aristocratic Egyptians be having shoulders like that. At first I didn't think she were the same nun, though, but she got the same mannerisms as that other nun. She scratching underneath her wimple, and I'm thinking it must get hot and itchy and sticky underneath that wimple, especially in South Texas, and be wondering how them nuns be wearing all them habits in South Texas anyhow, but then I be thinking about them desert peoples in North Africa that wears clothes that looks like them habits. I be thinking she might take that wimple off, though, but she don't. Probably that's why they got a lot of them plainclothes nuns like they got them plainclothes detectives and shit.

They was in the classroom, her and them Mexican and Native American childrens, then when she seen me coming up to the mission school she come to the door of the mission school and motioned me into the classroom. Them Egyptian shoulders be looking almost as wide as the door of the classroom. So I come in the classroom and I sat in the back of the class till they did they geometry, that Euclidean geometry I think, then she send them out to play. But I be watching her drawing them circles and triangles and shit on the board and solving them theorems, and they be talking about different-type angles and shit. I didn't know that elementary schools learned that geometry and solved them theorems and shit; I thought that geometry were just high school. I be pretending it me up there teaching them that geometry, but I don't understand a lot of that shit, excuse my French, so I just starts rereading that letter from Monkey Bread, 'cause I don't much like classrooms anyhow like I said and that Monkey Bread letter transport me to Paris, France, and I be thinking that if that Delgadina do become a private detective maybe I could hire her to hunt up my uncle Buddy Johnson. Of course I couldn't afford to be sending her to that Paris, though. Delgadina she be talking about how they uses them computers, like I said, a lot of them modern-day private detectives and maybe she just put my uncle Buddy name in that computer and find out exactly what boulevard in that Paris he is and where he soul food restaurant, or maybe I go to that Paris and hunt for my legendary Uncle Buddy my ownself. You my legendary uncle Buddy Johnson? I be asking. And he be saying he didn't know he legendary. And I be telling him how he even in a storybook, at least somebody in a storybook with the same name as my uncle Buddy. But that nun, she real dexterous at that board teaching them kids that geometry and drawing them circles and triangles and shit. And them kids real bright too though some of that geometry look like Greek. When I glance up from Monkey Bread letter she drawing a circle without even using one of them machines. I thought you supposed to use them machines when you draw a circle. I try drawing a circle on Monkey Bread's letter but it don't look nothing like a circle. And she be talking to one of them kids who say he want to be a architect and she be saying them architect gotta know that geometry.

But that nun she be tugging on her wimple and be telling me about how she be getting one of them new computers for them kids so's they can keep up with the modern world. You can even learn you that geometry on them computers, she be saying, with that new computer software you be learning that geometry and all kinda math and science even that astronomy and she be wanting them kids to be able

to compete in the modern world, not just in their little villages in
Mexico or Mexico City or South Texas. She be telling me how some
of them Mexican kids come across the border to go to her school and
then they gotta go back across the border and they's some Americans, Norteamericanos, that don't even want them to come across the
border to go to school, 'cause they's some of them that's petitioning
the state government maybe even the federal government so's that
them kids won't be allowed to cross the border to go to school.

They be wanting to change the law so's the Mexican childrens
can't come across the border to go to school, you know, they be having to stay in Mexico. I be telling her about them trade shows 'cause
they has the most newfangled computers and shit, that a lot of the
most newfangled computers are at them trade shows even before
they's on the market, you can find every type of computer at them
trade shows, but I don't say "and shit" 'cause she a nun.

The kids both them Mexican and Native American kids you can
hear them talking that Spanish on the playground, though some of
the Native Americans they be talking some of them Native American languages, maybe that Navajo or that Yaqui, if them Yaqui Indians got them a language called Yaqui. First time I heard Yaqui,
though, I be thinking they said Yankee. The nun she be telling me
that the mission school is more enlightened than it used to be. They
used to ban the kids from talking they own language, even on the
playground. The Native American kids they weren't allowed to
speak they native languages and them Spanish kids they weren't allowed to speak that Spanish. 'Cept she say most of them Native
American kids they be speaking that Spanish with them Mexican
kids, and I know that 'cause like I said I be hearing them speaking
that Spanish, though she know some of them native kids they speaks
Navajo like I said and some of them other native languages. She be
saying she trying to learn some of them Native American languages
herself, but she be saying a lot of them native languages is more
difficult to learn than them European languages, though she say she
know a few words in Navajo and Nahuatl. I think she say Nahuatl,
'cause she be saying that Nahuatl a language too. And she be showing me a book with some of them native languages and a lot of them
do look like Greek and a lot of them native words is longer than them
German words. Especially one of them Canadian Indian languages

she show me, but she say she be specializing in the native languages of the Southwest. But in them old days before that mission were enlightened, them Native American and Mexicans and native Mexicans, they had to just speak English at the mission school, and even on the playground they had to speak English. But now they're more enlightened. On the playground the kids can speak Spanish or they can speak they Native American languages, but it's only in the classroom that they must speak English, except for Spanish class they can speak that Spanish. And maybe if they have one of them Navajo classes they be speaking Navajo, but I be thinking they should get them a real Navajo to teach that class or a real Yaqui if they be teaching them a Yaqui class. And then I be wondering if she not just the same gringa nun I first met, but is she a real gringa 'cause she ain't sound as gringa as when I first seen her and then I be thinking that maybe she one of them gringa-looking Mexican women or Mexican American women 'cause they's gringa-looking women in Mexico same as African-looking women.

Except for Spanish class, she say again, pulling on her wimple. But a lot of those kids teach me more Spanish than I teach them. I wish we could afford to hire someone to teach one of the native languages too. But then there are so many of them native languages and I wouldn't want to privilege one native language over another, though. Of course here in South Texas English is a privileged language, but when I teach my class I try not to privilege English over Spanish or Spanish over English.

Ain't I said she don't seem as gringa as when I first seen her? And me I'm wondering why they have Spanish class, though, when they already speaks Spanish and she be saying them kids speaks that Spanish better than she do, so I guess she must be a gringa, though Delgadina say they's Mexican Americans that don't speak Spanish they ownself or just know a few words in Spanish. And of course people has English class that already speaks English. Them English class they teach you one kind of English, so maybe them Spanish class teach them kids one kind of Spanish and maybe ain't even the Spanish that they speak and maybe teaching them what they consider the high-class Spanish, and maybe even that Spanish Spanish and not even that Mexican Spanish, though I know that Mexican Spanish different from that Spanish Spanish. I had me a dream about them kids, though. They was in the courtyard playing the Lone Ranger, except all the kids wanted to be the Lone Ranger, didn't none of them want to play that Tonto. Then all the kids spotted me and they be saying, Let her play Tonto, let Nadine play Tonto. And I be wondering how they knew my name Nadine and guess maybe that Carmelite nun told them my name Nadine. So I tells the kids I don't want to play Tonto or Tonta, so they ties me to a stake and starts beating drums, except but they beating them African drums, and be telling me that since I ain't a true native of the Southwest that I gotta play Tonta. I be thinking they going to say because I'm a African American I gotta play Tonta, but they be saying because I ain't a true native of the Southwest. Except them from Mexico be calling the Southwest the Northwest 'cause the Southwest of the U.S. is the Northwest of Mexico.

Them's African drums, I be saying. If y'all can be beating them African drums, how come I gotta play Tonta?

It's all the same drum, they be saying.

Lone Ranger don't beat no drum, I be saying.

Yeah, but we do, they be saying.

But one of them kids beating the African drum and be beating that drum just like a real African like he know the language of that drum he be saying he ain't the Lone Ranger nor that Tonto either, he Gregorio Cortez. I heard about that Gregorio Cortez 'cause Delgadina call them social bandits like I said which I guess make them different from them ordinary roguish bandits and different from that Frito bandito too. Some of them kids, though, they keeps beating the African drum though some beats it with more a South American or Caribbean flavor, others more Native American, while the others be playing basketball, except but they don't play it like basketball, they play it like soccer, and be kicking the ball with they feet. And they be letting the girls play soccer with the boys inside this dream, though outside the dream I don't remember seeing them girls in the courtyard playing that soccer with them boys or even girls playing soccer with other girls. Then one of the little girls say her name something sound like Nako or Sinako but it a longer name than that I just remember the "nako" or "sinako" part of that long name, little Native American girl, she come and untie me from that stake and say that even if I ain't a native of the Southwest I don't have to play Tonta and don't have to be tied to no stake neither. And then after that I be in another dream, I be that Maria climbing inside of my truck, and then that Maria be me, scrambling up into the back of my truck with that flashlight and that stun gun and shining that light on my gua-raches and my belly.

Sojourner.

But now we standing in her office, though, like I said, and that Carmelite nun talking in that voice again, like elementary school teachers talking to adults the same way they talks to children but she don't sound as gringa as the first time I seen her, like I said, and I be wondering again if she the same nun, but I know she the same nun, and maybe she sounding more gringa when I first seen her 'cause maybe she didn't know if I'm one of them immigration officers and didn't know whether she could trust me, me being a stranger.

We watching them childrens playing. All the childrens they got them dark eyes and I be wondering whether that teacher see wild animal eyes or wild people eyes or just people eyes. You know, that movie I told you that Delgadina and me went to and that man be saying that dark-eyed woman have them wild animal eyes, and me I didn't see no animal eyes just human woman eyes, and I be wonder-ing how come in that movie the woman with the dark eyes supposed to have animal eyes.

Say what?

He don't want to compromise the movement, she be saying. But she won't tell me where he is. But me I'm thinking maybe he's in Mexico with that girlfriend. He in Mexico? I start to ask her. I don't ask her that, though. And I'm still thinking about that woman in the movie supposed to have wild animal eyes and then I'm thinking about that woman he brought to hide in my apartment that night and then about that comparison being a petty demon shit. And then I'm thinking more about that other woman, the one he brought to my apartment, the one that them other refugees attacked on account of they remembered her as the general's concubine, the concubine of that tyrant, leastwise I think that the tale. Maybe it her he in love with now, I'm thinking, or maybe it her his original girlfriend, the original girlfriend he be telling me about, maybe he ain't told me the whole true story and maybe he up in Canada with her, his first true love, one say she always be picking her them strong men. I guess you can be a strong man without being a tyrant. But that comparison a petty demon, he be saying.

He ask me to drive him to *el centro*. He asked me or I dreamed it. He in *el centro*?

Or in Mexico with that girlfriend? I'm thinking. Or in Canada with that new girlfriend? Or maybe that new girlfriend the original girlfriend? And then I be thinking of Delgadina once she be telling me she like them modern stories with them open-ended resolutions where you don't know the whole story, you don't know the resolution of the tale, but me I always likes the solution to the tale. So I ask her again if he in *el centro*, if he in Mexico, if he in Canada, but again she won't tell me where he is and she just repeat that he don't want to compromise the movement.

I was half-sleep and. . . .

I don't tell her I was half-drunk too, 'cause she a nun. Drunk as a skunk on account of me and Delgadina celebrating her detective school. And in that cantina and her teaching me one of them drinking songs in Spanish. I don't remember the words to that drinking song in Spanish except we was singing about a jug of pulque and a good man and then she started singing one of them Mexican *corridos* and some woman in one of them named Delgadina just like herself, except she be saying the Delgadina in that song a bad woman and she try to see herself as a good woman. You and me is good women, she be saying, and us drinking that pulque. I ask her to tell me about the other Delgadina, the Delgadina in that song, but she won't tell me, 'cause she be saying that that Delgadina in that song, in that *corrido*, is one of them mb and dtk women, mad, bad, and dangerous to know and she try to be a good woman, we's both good women, she saying, but she do tell me that she ain't named after the Delgadina in that song, though. You and me is good women, she be saying, and I ain't named after that Delgadina in that song, and then we drink some more of that pulque and toast to the good women and the good men of them drinking songs.

I don't tell her about that pulque, 'cause she a nun. Leastwise, I think she a nun. Maybe them nuns drink pulque. But in Mexico that Isabella—I just name her Isabella my ownself—he say that Isabella she already got her this new boyfriend, some perfect Eden-type love. But maybe he decide to reveal hisself, decide that he wanna be that perfect Eden-type love his ownself. Yeah, he decide he want to be her perfect love his ownself. And maybe that story about her in Mexico ain't even true, 'cause maybe she the general's concubine. And I'm thinking I don't know which of them stories Raymond be telling me or that concubine be telling me is the true story.

You a real Carmelite nun? I asks. Leastwise I think she a Carmelite.

Yes, I am, she say. Why? She pull on her wimple—I think that's what you call a wimple.

I just thought maybe you was in disguise too, you know like the padre.

What padre in disguise? What do you mean?

Now I don't know whether she just say that 'cause she don't know or not to compromise the padre, but then I'm thinking—naw, I don't believe he no real padre pretending to be no padre in disguise—cause then he be too cunning. Talking about that trickster and shit. But I don't pursue that disguise thing 'cause maybe she do think he a real padre, though I wouldn't mind asking her if she know his old girlfriend. But then a real padre ain't supposed to have a girlfriend, except in them scandals. And then I'm thinking about that *el centro* again. Did I dream that *el centro* or did he call me about that *el centro*? I think about taking my truck and heading for that *el centro*.

But I leaves the mission school and goes back on my route, carrying that industrial detergents. Them border patrols they spots me and stops to see if I'm carrying any contraband.

What's this? he ask, waving his flashlight.

Industrial detergents. Look like powdered milk, though.

What?

Detergents. You know, industrial detergents. Look like powdered milk, though. The texture and color of powdered milk.

Well, ain't all of it the color of powdered milk. They be different colors, them detergents, but they all the texture of powdered milk. Well, come to think of it most detergents, I mean powdered detergents, look kinda like powdered milk, don't they? Except them liquid detergents. They got liquid industrial detergents, but I just like me the powdered industrial and ecological detergents. . . .

Open up one of them drums.

He raps on the drum with his flashlight. His border patrol uniform look shabbier in the daylight.

These detergents they ain't for everyday peoples, though, I explains, opening the drum. They's for industry, you know. Biodegradable. And them detergents they uses to sop up that oil on them beaches with. This ecological and industrial detergents. I guess that's why they prefers powdered detergents on account of sopping up that oil on beaches, I mean.

I'm still kinda hung over from that pulque and maybe them border patrol they don't trust you when you looks at them with hawk's eyes. They supposed to be looking at you with them hawk's eyes.

All this industrial detergents? he asks.

He shines the light on that detergent, sifts some through his fingers, sniffs it. I think he gonna taste it too but he don't. He put it back in the drum. All this industrial detergents? he repeat and shine the light on them other drums.

Yeah. That's all I does is industrial and ecological detergents. I ain't no contrabandista.

I be thinking he's gonna ask for my green card. I just seen me one of them documentary on them green cards on my pocket TV where they's these people make theyself a business of recruiting peoples so's they can get married to these aliens so's they can get theyself a green card. I don't know if them Nicodemus does things like that or not, though. I be thinking about harboring that fugitive Maria, but then I be thinking she ain't no modern fugitive Maria but one of them fugitive Africans them Daughters of Nzingha say call them fugitive Africans or captured Africans not slaves. And in them days them captured Africans desirous of freedom they be saying they be crazy, and them plantation psychiatrists they even have a name for it, and maybe even one of them Latin names, and then they send them to one of what they call them Negro asylums, 'cause that desire for freedom supposed to be a neurosis or some shit.

Show me your license and registration papers.

I be thinking he's gonna ask for my green card, but he don't. I shows him my license. He shine his light on my license, then on my face, then back on my license. I shows him my registration papers and then heads towards Texas City.

I know they's a lot of them modern-type stories, where I just be telling you I heads back to Texas City. And keep y'all wondering. Y'all be wondering whether me and Father Raymond gets back together, or whether I finds me some other man, 'cause a lot of y'all likes them romantic stories, even y'all that reads literary fiction. And a lot of y'all still be wondering whether Father Raymond a real priest pretending he ain't a priest or ain't a real priest pretending he a priest. All I know is when I gets back to Texas City they's a letter for me. First I thinks it's from Monkey Bread, but it ain't Monkey Bread's handwriting, even though she's using that word processor these days, and also it ain't postmarked California but Cuba, New Mexico.

Ms. Sojourner Nadine Jane Johnson (Mosquito)
c/o Delgado's Cantina
Texas City, Texas 77590
Dear Mosquito,

I hope you are well. I started to ask you to come with me, but I don't know how long I'll be here, working for the cause. Plus, it would seem rather strange, me being a priest, and having my woman with me. I am a real priest, you know. Not a real Catholic priest. One of the local shamans made me a priest of their faith, the old faith, before the conquerors. But we're allowed to have a woman. The old faith, before the conquerors.

Some of my mail will come to me c/o you. You're the only one I trust. Forward all the personal mail. It should be forwarded to my P.O. box in Cuba, New Mexico, and from there someone will forward it to me where I am. I won't tell you where I am. They only speak Spanish here, and one of the old native languages. I shall re-emerge and find you, Sojourner. Take care.
Yours,
Ray

EPILOGUE

MY MAMA DIDN'T RAISE THE SORTA FOOL THAT would tell y'all the whole story about Ray and his people and the workings of the new Underground Railroad in South Texas. In fact, most of Ray's people who is the subject of this story has relocated to different parts of the Americas, some in the USA, some in Canada, others in Mexico and Brazil, a few in Europe and Asia and Africa. Some even in Australia. Maybe even South Texas is just a metaphor.

I know there is those of you who wants to know more of various people in my story. Some of y'all wants to know more about Maria and Journal, others of y'all wants to know more about Miguelita, some of y'all don't think I've told y'all enough about Ray and still thinking why I be interested in a man like Ray, and thinking even John Henry more my type of man than Ray, and some of y'all wants to know more about John Henry. I know there is womens amongst y'all that wants to know more about various mens I've mentioned in my story, who their wives or lovers is, whether they's available. Some of y'all don't care if they ain't available but wants to know more about them anyway. Some of y'all wants to know more about my ex-

husband in Tasmania. Some of y'all wants to know more about Delgadina's ex-husband in New York. I've told y'all that them men ain't
available and has got they true loves, but y'all still wants to know
more about them. Some of the men amongst you thinks that y'all
would make more interesting men than the men in my story. Some of
y'all would like to retell the story so's that the men is more interesting
than the women and that it would be a better story if Ray had more
a role than Delgadina and that Ray would be even more interesting
if I had him tell me more about him being a guerrilla and all the
different macho types of things that he does when he goes there to
Latin America and also some of the other macho types of things that
Ray does that ain't in my story. I know there's lots of y'all that thinks
that Ray is a more complex man than I tells about in this story and
that I should've waited to get to know him better and to know men
better in general than I knows them before telling y'all my story.
I would like to know what y'all mens thinks about Ray, because I
would like to be able to learn more and know more about y'all's ideals of manhood and to conquer my own ignorance so's that I can
write about Ray from a perspective that is broader than my female
one. When Ray decides he wants to tell y'all his own story for hisself, he might tell y'all the type of complex and macho story that y'all
mens can identify with true manhood. I knows that I has got to become a better storyteller before I can transcend my female perspective. Delgadina would say that us females ain't got nothing to transcend, but I do know for a fact that the Charlie T. Juárez that I seen
for myself ain't the same Charlie T. Juárez that Delgadina describe
for me. And her specifying about me subduing myself around men.
Seem like she were subduing herself around Charlie T. Juárez. Unless she were seeing Charlie T. Juárez for his true self and feeling like
a true fool. I do know a little something about Eden Prine, and I will
say that Delgadina is a more intellectual woman than Eden Prine.

Some of y'all is thinking that even Ray is lovers with Maria.
'Cause I know I heard somebody say that Alvarado knows Quechua. Then why Ray say that he needed Maria to translate Quechua.
Or maybe Ray was working with her on something to do with the
Chiapas Rebellion, which she were only pretending she didn't
know anything about until she read about it in the newspaper. I am
prohibited from asking too many questions about people I suspect of

being Nicodemuses. Some of y'all is thinking whether or not Delgadina in the new Underground Railroad. I myself thinks that she is
and has offered clues that she might be. 'Cause I know before Maria
got in my truck that Delgadina was asking all kindsa questions about
the latch on my truck and I know she ain't never been interested in
the latch on my truck. She even practiced unlatching my truck herself, like she was testing to see how easy it was to unlatch. Pretending
that she thought I should get a better latch for my truck, which actually I think that she was glad that it had a easy latch. I believe that
Delgadina has an active role and is engaged in the new Underground
Railroad but she prefers to work as a Nicodemus. Now that she is in
detective school and learning how to be a detective I think that is
just to help her to work better for them and maybe even work for
their guerrilla lawyers investigating. 'Cause I knows they have they
own private investigators 'cause I heard Alvarado on the telephone
with somebody.

We've got our own private investigators, he said.

I ain't going to tell y'all what else they's got of they own, but it
sounds like they's started they own independent government and
they own powers and own diplomats and own constitution. I ain't
going to say that that is the true truth. But I knows that Alvarado
kept saying what they had of they own, and it sounded like he was
talking about a whole independent government.

I's told y'all the true truth about most of the peoples in this story,
although I ain't told y'all the whole truth about none of the peoples
in this story. Or perhaps I've told y'all the whole truth without telling y'all the real truth. Like I said, my mama didn't raise the sorta
fool that would tell y'all the whole story, 'cause that would be like if
I was a fugitive during the time of the old Underground Railroad I
got myself free, then I comes telling everybody all the secrets. I gots
to defend the rights and freedoms of them that ain't got they freedom
yet. I'm only telling y'all as much as I am telling y'all because this is
supposed to be kept in the archives of the Daughters of Nzingha.
The archives keeper is supposed to be truthworthy, but being a hidden agenda conspiracy specialist I have still employed everything
that I've learned. My first love is the love of language, though, and
whilst I defends the rights and privileges of the new Underground
Railroad and maintains as much of they secrets that they ain't re-

vealed they ownselves, I wants to maintain they privacy, conquer my own ignorance, and to tell y'all a story about South Texas.

For y'all who wants to hear more about Miguelita, I prefers not to tell y'all more about Miguelita. There is plenty of people to tell y'all about Miguelita, 'cause like I said, she is the kinda white girl that can cross any borders. She is crazy, so the peoples in the cantina that knows her and that knows she is the wife of Mr. Delgado protects her and don't allow people to call her out of her name, even though Miguelita ain't her true name. I will say that I had a longer conversation with her during the time that Delgadina didn't want to talk to her. That was when Delgadina had discovered that even the gringo that she thought wasn't a gringo because he wasn't a part of American history was still a gringo. You know, the Welshman that she thought respected her for her intellect and she discovered that all he saw was a hoochie woman. Or maybe he just thought she resembled a Bond girl. Delgadina ain't told me whether he tried to kiss her or just revealed his true gringo self in his conversation with her. Anyway, so like I said, Delgadina would just see Miguelita as the gringa and not "our gringa" and said, You go talk to Miguelita. She'd served her some Mexican beer and Miguelita wanted to talk, but Delgadina come and asked me to go talk to the gringa, so I took my Budweiser over to her table and sat down. Now I thought she would be telling me about Sophie or about the consonance of wines or about some general, but she started telling me about herself.

She let me know that she ain't one of them crazy peoples that thinks they's sane. I'm schizophrenic, she said, sipping her beer.

I knows, I said, 'cept I told her that I didn't know exactly what that meant to say about her. Anyway, I knows from them documentaries that there is peoples that says my whole race of peoples is schizophrenic. So I told her that I didn't know exactly what that mean to say about her.

I usedta have these episodes where I would run away and assume other identities, she said. I didn't know I was doing it. I mean, when I have these episodes I don't know I'm doing it, I think I really am the people I say I am.

I gots to tell y'all that although Sophie a blonde she ain't got that silk-type blond hair of Monkey Bread's star, she got that real kinky type of blond hair. She got thick and kinky type of blond hair. And she one of those types of women that you can't tell her age. Sometimes I think she younger than me and Delgadina, sometimes I think she us age, other times I think she one of them old white women that just looks like she young. You know the kind that poses in *Playboy* when they middle-age but still got them girlie figures. I be wanting to know myself how they keep them girlie figures. I be wanting to know they secrets of beauty myself. I prefer to read they secrets of beauty in something like *Cosmopolitan*, though. Delgadina has started subscribing to the *New Yorker*, 'cause she seen an article about her ex-husband's sculpture in one of them. I don't read the *New Yorker* myself, though, 'cause I prefers the types of magazines that has articles on beauty in them. I don't subscribe to all them people's notions of beauty, but I would like to know how them womens keep they girlie figures. I prefers not to read them types of magazines that fabricates too much of the truth or insults people's intellect. Some people can tell stories that insults your intellect, though, and they is still interesting stories. I know that whenever I meets Cayenne Goodling at the Perfectability Baptist Church, the one in Memphis, that she can insult my intelligence telling me all kindsa stories about Elvis and the Church of Elvis, and although I can't claim to be the true fan of Elvis that Cayenne Goodling is or them who describes him as looking like a Greek god, nevertheless Cayenne Goodling is such a good storyteller that sometimes I goes to Memphis just to have her insult my intelligence, 'cause it seem like Cayenne Goodling is not only a good storyteller but has created a whole new genre to insult people's intelligence. I don't mean that the subject matter of Elvis is a insult to people's intelligence—cause I knows how Elvis fans is—I means the way that Cayenne Goodling recontextualizes the subject matter of Elvis to create a new storytelling form whose express purpose it seems is to insult the intelligence. I don't just go to Memphis to have my intelligence insulted, 'cause I don't have to go all the way to Memphis for that. I also goes to attend the Perfectability Baptist Church, 'cause they ain't got no Perfectability Baptist Church in the Southwest. Monkey Bread says that if I wants a Perfectability Baptist Church in the Southwest I oughta form one myself.

Like when you was in Paris pretending to be Sophie? I asks. I'm talking about Miguelita. Y'all know I told y'all about Miguelita.

She sip her Mexican beer and then look at me. No, Sophie's a real
woman. When I was in Paris I was sane. Sophie only knows me as
sane. When she writes letters to me from Paris, she is always writing
to me as if I'm sane. She usedta be my roommate when I was in Paris.
She's a real woman. I thought she was Algerian when I first met her,
though, because the room that we rented is in an immigrant neighborhood of Paris, and she prefers the immigrant neighborhoods of
Paris. She has dark hair and a dark complexion and I thought she was
Algerian, but she's a Frenchwoman. She still thinks I'm the same
woman that she met when I was her roommate in Paris. You know
how you meet people you hope to resemble. That's what Sophie's
like. She's the ideal sort that you hope to resemble. Most of her
friends are immigrants. I remember Sophie introduced me to one of
the immigrants and he said, America, that's my dream. Sometimes
we'd sit in the cafés with the intellectual types. They didn't like
America or Americanism. And some of them considered me a white
devil, but they respect and admire Sophie so much. But every time
America would do something that got into the newspapers, the intellectuals would always want me to defend America. Then once
America did something and I said, How can I defend that, that's in-
defensible? They liked me more, but they could never adore me as
much as they adored Sophie. And how could they adore Sophie
more? Sophie's a Frenchwoman. And look at how the French behave? How could they adore Sophie more than me? How could he
adore Sophie more than me?

Who adore her more? The immigrant who called America his
dream? Mr. Delgado? Who adore her more?

She won't tell me which who she means. She sips her Mexican
beer, then she says, She knows the rules of the game, though. Sophie,
I mean. But she has her own stratagems. Sophie is real. Sophie is not
a product of my imagination or who I pretend to be.

She reaches into her jeans pockets and hands me a letter. I open it
and read, but it's in French. It's postmarked Paris and it's signed Sophie. But I don't know what the French in it says. She puts it back in
her pants pocket.

It wasn't until I returned to America that I started having these
episodes, schizophrenic episodes where I'd run away and assume another person's identity but actually believe it was my own. I went to

Mexico and became someone. I was in Canada and became someone else. My father would hire different detectives who would find me, and they'd put me in an asylum for a while, and then I'd realize my true identity and they'd free me again. Then I'd have another schizophrenic episode and run away and become someone else. I wanted to tell Delgadina who I am.

Well, Delgadina don't want to know who no gringo or gringa is right now. She don't care who the shit y'all is. She don't want to know none of y'all 'cause she thinks she knows y'all's true selves. She believes she knows who you are now, and she doesn't want to know any of you. None of you have anything to say that she even wants to hear. She says that I can talk to you, but she don't want to talk to you.

Miguelita don't say nothing. She looks into her Mexican beer, then she drinks it. Then she looks around the cantina. Then she drinks more of her Mexican beer, then she looks at me. What about you? she asks. I gots to tell y'all she didn't ask it in English, she asked it in French, but I knew that's what she was asking even though I ain't know what the French say. Who do you think I am?

I knows you's a gringa, but it seems like every other time you's ready to talk about anything except yourself. Now that you's ready to talk about yourself I wants to hear what you's got to say. Delgadina thinks you gringos are all guilty of war crimes anyway. And she thinks all of y'all oughta be tried as war criminals for what y'all not only have done but is doing to the colored peoples of the world. She was making an exception of you, and maybe Jimmy Carter because of his work amongst the Africans and other different colonized peoples, and even the poor whites that don't know that they's colonized, she knows they's gringos, but they's still fools that don't know they's colonized, and maybe a few others, whose names she ain't revealed to me, but that were while she still had some conceits about y'all. She just come back from protesting something at the University of Texas anyway and she don't want to talk to no gringo.

I protested that myself, said Miguelita.

Well, I don't know what y'all was there protesting, only thing I knows is Delgadina usedta think you was a rare breed of gringa. But she is in her nonnegotiable mode right now. In fact, I wanted to watch *Jane Eyre* with her on television and she wouldn't even watch *Jane Eyre* with me and Jane Eyre is her favorite Jane, especially when Jane Eyre say that she is not a bitch, she is Jane Eyre. She was writing up something to say at the protest. You know if she is in the mode not to even want to know who Jane Eyre is, and would prefer to write up something to protest about than to watch *Jane Eyre*, then she is not in the mode to want to know who any other gringa is. Then after that even though *Jane Eyre* was still on, she read E. D. Santos rather than watch the movie. She wanted to know if I was coming to the protest, but I told her I had some industrial detergents to take to Galveston. So I just watched *Jane Eyre* myself and then come back to my own apartment, made me some hot chocolate, ate some of them chocolate pretzels, watched the news on television. I think there was a little something about that protest that Delgadina were talking about. I kinda thought that maybe I should go protest. But I know Delgadina be there protesting, and I didn't think that protest would get these industrial detergents to Galveston. Plus, I had a prior commitment to take some industrial detergents to Galveston. I gots as much race pride as Delgadina, though. Course being a member of the Perfectability Baptist Church, I has got to temper my pride with wisdom. We is who we is, we does what we do, and we knows who we is capable of becoming. We don't submit to us own ignorance nor do we submit to the ignorance of other people. There's more to the Perfectability Baptist Church. I don't know everything about Perfectability Baptism, but I does try to know more and learn more. I wants to know more about you and Mr. Delgado, though. I knows that he is a secretive man.

He's the one who helped me decide who I want to be, said Miguelita. Sometimes I think I'm going to run off again and become someone else, and then I just go to Delgado and then I know who I am and who I want to be and where I am and where I should be.

You sounds almost like you's a Perfectability Baptist, 'cept we just allows colored people in us church and them that claims they's colored. And we always says we, excuse my French. We says we a lot, but we has the independence of us ownselves. But what you says about Mr. Delgado, that's how I feels about. . . . I starts to tell her Ray's name, but I ain't. I wants to tell her Ray's name. But I knows I can't be telling her Ray's name. That's how I feels about the man I feels that way about. Except I knows who I am and decides who I wants to be. I knows where I am and where I should be.

I ain't sure how much I'm telling her is from what I've learned being a member of the Perfectability Baptist Church and how much I've learned working with Ray's people and how much I've just learned being Mosquito, transporting my industrial detergents, going to trade shows and being who I think I am.

I wants to ask Miguelita if she in the new Underground Railroad, but I don't. To tell y'all the truth I'm thinking they's all Nicodemuses. I ain't no private investigator or private detective neither, but this what I thinks: I thinks that Leonora Valdez, the reservation Native American, is the first one that thought I might be useful. She the one seen me get out of my truck and come into the pueblo-style McDonald's, started talking to me and telling me she were a student at the University of New Mexico and on her way to Albuquerque, you know the one that say she don't let nobody photograph her. She mighta told Ray and his people about me or maybe she told Delgadina about me and Delgadina say she already knew me but didn't think I were the kinda person that would want to be in anything like the new Underground Railroad, that's why she ain't tried to recruit me for it herself, 'cause I'm too much of a independent type of person, and she mighta even specified me and saying that the only community I'm responsible to is the community of me myself and I, 'cause Delgadina liking me don't mean she don't acknowledge my flaws of character, plus she don't even believe I'm a member of the Perfectibility Baptist Church, or maybe she thought I was too much of a fool to be in the new Underground Railroad and would be telling everybody about it. Then they decided to test me with Maria, you know to test whether I were a person to be trusted or whether I was like them slaves that were always running to the master to tell them everything the other slaves was doing. And because I ain't told even Delgadina about Maria, and I tells Delgadina almost everything, they be thinking maybe I'm to be trusted. They musta known more about my psychology than I know myself, 'cause how they know I would even ask about the Sanctuary movement once I discovered Maria in my truck. I coulda just drove her to the immigration people and turned her in as a illegal alien. How they know I would go to the nun and ask her about the Sanctuary movement. I guess they knew my route and knew that I knows about that mission school. Or maybe they know that Maria would be able to convince

me not to take her to immigration. Well, I don't know all they stratagems. Maybe if they had seen me trying to take Maria to immigration, they woulda stopped my truck, pretended they was immigration police, then got Maria free. But since I proved that I weren't
that type of fool, they decided to learn more about me. So they still
wants to find out more about me, so after I introduces myself to Ray
and has Ray to show Maria to the secret rooms in they cathedral,
they has Ray interview me whilst the woman who originally scouted
me, Leonora Valdez was listening on that radio that weren't a real
radio, and then she handed Ray her assessment of me in that newspaper that was a real newspaper but had her coded assessment of me,
and because I didn't even tell Ray that I knew Leonora Valdez or
that she even looked like somebody I thought I knew, they figured
I were a little more truthworthy and then they decided that I were
truthworthy enough to transport them refugees, and truthworthy
enough to become a hidden agenda conspiracy specialist and to
memorize documents, but not truthworthy enough to be one of the
peoples that helps to form the strategies, 'cause they still don't allow
me into none of they strategy meetings.

And Miguelita I think she a Nicodemus that were recruited because she one of them type of white girls that can cross anybody's
border and they ain't question her, 'cause I was even telling Ray that
myself, and because she crazy she can kinda endear herself to peoples
and camouflages even the fact that she a gringa. 'Cept I gots to tell
y'all that although I likes Miguelita I don't fully trust her and think
that she might also be a spy for one of them secret government organizations like them secret-type government organizations that they
portrays on television and that decided they would recruit the John
Brown in her—cause there is always a John Brown type in every colored story—even though she's a *mujer*, they would recruit the John
Brown in her to work for them, 'cause they's people that says that
John Brown were supposed to be crazy, 'cause whilst they don't
mind the mainstream Sanctuary movement they had started hearing
about some new type of new Underground Railroad that colored
people themselves was the leaders in and decided to recruit their
most endearing white crazy woman and have her infiltrate Delgado's
cantina. Or maybe she ain't even know that she is working for this

secret-type government organization and just think that she is being Miguelita.

Y'all can decide who Miguelita is for y'allselves. I don't want to study Miguelita, but y'all that wants to study her can come to Delgado's cantina in South Texas. There's a lot of *vatos* there to protect her, though, and she is the revered wife of Mr. Delgado, so y'all had better not get too inquisitive about her identity.

After I got through talking to Miguelita I did go back up to the bar and try to tell Delgadina her story, about her schizophrenic episodes, but Delgadina didn't want to hear it. She's just a lying gringa, she said. I might be the biggest bitch in my old high school, but she's the biggest bitch in this cantina.

That the first thing she said, then she said, Take my advice and don't start spending too much time thinking about the Miguelitas. I don't know who she is and don't want to know who she is. I know I've not seen Mr. Delgado at all and he's the one I'm truly interested in. Sometimes I think that even Mr. Delgado is a fabrication of Miguelita's.

I tells her that I saw a *vato* with Miguelita at her play when she were doing that play *La Raza Pura* and that I'm pretty sure that was Mr. Delgado. She were too busy courting that *vato*. You know, the *vato* that were singing about the Argentine tango, so I didn't ask her if that Mr. Delgado.

Delgadina don't say nothing, she just wipe off the counter. Some *vatos* come in the cantina and she takes their order, then comes back and sits at the counter and starts writing in her notebook. I asks her what she writing.

A praise poem for my people, she say. It's about an intelligent people. I'm going to tell them how intelligent they are, how good their spirit is, how balanced their minds are, how sane they are when everybody's trying to tell them they're not, how. . . .

And she just be praising her people, telling me what a great people they is, and specifying them to they origins, 'cept it the good specification, 'cause it specifying they greatness. Course Delgadina the kind that don't praise the people all the time. She prefers to praise the people, but she ain't got no immitigable rules, and don't praise every *vato* and *chica* that comes in her cantina. Sometimes she tells me what she likes about me, other times she describes me for the fool that I am.

It a while before she starts talking to Miguelita again. First she lectured her on the war crimes of her people, then she asked Miguelita to tell her the story that Miguelita had told me. Miguelita told her the same story, except she revealed to her the different identities that she had assumed when she was assuming identities. And then she told Delgadina all that about Mr. Delgado helping her to decide her true self. I thought Delgadina would specify her about that, but she didn't. Then we all gets in her rented Land-Rover and goes out into the desert so's she can show us her new house. I mean, Delgadina's new house. She got one of them adobe houses, you know in the pueblo-type style, in the Native American and Mexican style, she say she prefer that to her little apartment in Texas City, plus she don't have to just grow them container plants but can grow real plants in her own garden, 'cause I have told y'all how Delgadina is about buds and blossoms, and she probably be growing a lot of them flowering cactus-type plants, and it exactly the same house that Alvarado told me where to find. Y'all know I told y'all about the house in the desert that Alvarado described to me as being a stop on the new Underground Railroad. At least, I assumed that was what he was telling me, I mean when I wasn't assuming that he was trying to get me to come out to that house for hoochie purposes. I knows it the same house, though, and I knows that it were purchased from Alvarado, but I ain't tell Delgadina I knows. Delgadina and Miguelita and I sits upon the roof of her new house and looks at the stars.

The next day, though, I got to drive Maria and Journal back to Mexico. I ain't supposed to drive them to the rebellion. I'm just supposed to drive them to the northern part of Mexico and they's supposed to meet with Maria's husband, who a Quechua-speaking Mayan Indian or Native Mexican. There's a lot of story about Maria that I can't tell y'all for security purposes. I could tell y'all everything about Maria and her Mayan lover. Some of y'all thinks that them Mayans is just people of history, but they is people of today, and they has they own language. I ain't going to tell y'all none of that, for it is Maria to decide if any of y'all is worthy to hear her story. I don't think that Maria would tell anyone, and not even me, the whole story, though, because it has to do with Chiapas rebels. True rebels don't tell everything. True rebels is not who you believes them to be or who you decides them to be, but who they is. And they true identity, they true self, is nonnegotiable.

The other Ray is coming along with us. He supposed to pretend to be my husband and Maria our daughter and Journal our grand-baby. Them border people might believe all that going into Mexico, I tells them, getting into Nuevo Laredo, but what about when us tries to come back to the Laredo in the USA. They's got strategies for getting back in the USA that they don't share with me. As for now, though, I's got all the documents proving I'm Mrs. Mendoza. I know them Mexicans be wondering what an Aztec god sees in me.

Muy mujer, says Maria as we get into the Land-Rover. I know it's the same Land-Rover that Delgadina rents all the time, but I don't say so.

Ray Mendoza sits in the front with me, Maria in the back with Journal who's in his baby's seat.

Muy mujer, says Maria as we head first east toward Laredo. I've already written to Ray to tell him that I'm only playing Mrs. Mendoza. I used everything in the letter that I learned in my hidden agenda conspiracy specialist class, 'cause I don't know who would be opening my correspondences to Ray. The spies amongst y'all can read all the correspondence I writes to Ray. Y'all'll only know what I says. It be Ray that knows what I means.

Dear Ray,

I has started the Mosquito Trucking Company which is a worker-owned company. The motto of our trucking company, as suggested by Gladys Knight and the Pips song is "The Mosquito Trucking Company keeps on keeping on." ("Keeps on keeping on" is printed on many of our trucks.) Mosquito trucks travels throughout the USA, Canada, and Mexico. We is also considering having us fran-chises internationally. We has all-new, custom-made trucks that is streamlined and solar-powered. They also runs on gasoline. They is strong and powerful trucks, and we believes they is the sound-est trucks they is. The trucks have many different components and changeable colors, though my favorite trucks I always keep with my own favorite color. I designed them myself, with the assistance of an

African magician and astrophysicist, and they uses all the new international knowledge that I learned from years of my addiction to
trade shows. All our trucks ain't named Mosquito, because many of
our independent owners likes to name they trucks after theyselves or
even they favorite peoples, including movie stars. Denzel, Sidney,
Billy Dee. 'Cept some of the movie stars don't want us trucks named
after them because they names is they trademarks, so us just nicknames us trucks after us favorite movie stars or even us favorite revolutionaries and guerrilla personalities.

I hopes that this letter reaches your village. The other Ray and I
has purchased a motel-restaurant in Cuba, New Mexico, and is in
business with some Navajos who manages the motel while we manages the restaurant. We purchased the motel-restaurant from Delgadina. It were formerly a motel-restaurant owned by her and her
ex-husband Charlie T. Juárez, the famous Chicano artist. When he
married Eden Prine (Delgadina calls her Eden Pride) and moved to
New York, he gave the property to Delgadina. Since Delgadina prefers to be a private detective and no bullshit private investigator, she
sold the motel-restaurant to me. She was going to give the motel-
restaurant to me, but we decided on a sale price that also includes her
maintaining equity in the motel-restaurant.

People thinks that I am Mrs. Mendoza. Ray and I encourages the
thought and likes to tease peoples. Everybody that comes in the restaurant I praises Ray to them and tells them he's like a Aztec god,
and he's always telling peoples I'm like a African goddess. I has seen
photographs of some African goddesses and they does kinda resemble me, or I should say I kinda resembles them. I kinda likes the
fact that they is goddesses that I resembles. However, I am still a
Perfectability Baptist. All my peoples is Baptists except them who
is Catholics, and the ones who ain't Catholics is African Methodist Episcopals and there is a few Witnesses for Jehovah amongst us,
and they says that some of us ancestors was Mohammedans and us
mighta even had some Buddhists. My uncle Buddy Johnson, rumor
has it, were the first amongst us to become a Perfectability Baptist.
We have even added Gladys Knight Pipism to the church. Originally Perfectability Baptism combined only Southern Baptism, Hol-
ler Roller Theology, Scientific Christianity, and African Methodist
Episcopalism.

"Do not submit to your own ignorance"; the motto of the Daughters of Nzingha is actually derived from a speech given by Malcolm X. That is what is different about the Daughters of Nzingha. They don't just include wisdom derived from Afro-womanhood but also includes Afro-manhood wisdom books in they archives, books which I has in my memory. I first heard that quoted by the Daughters of Nzingha, though, in a newsletter as one of the requirements for being an archives keeper. To tell you the truth, I am an archives keeper and I have been submitting to my own ignorance since preschool. I still submits to my own ignorance unless I'm in the presence of someone who refuses to allow me to submit to my own ignorance. I try not to submit to other people's ignorance, but I have certainly been known to submit to my own ignorance. Of course, once I knows it for the ignorance it is, I stops submitting to it. Perhaps that is why they allows me to be a archives keeper.

Some members of the Perfectability Baptist Church are Negroes, others is colored people, others is blacks (with a small *b*), others is Blacks (with a big *b*), others is Afro-Americans, others is African-Americans (hyphenated), others is African Americans (unhyphenated), others is Just Plain Americans, others is New World Africans, others is Descendants of the Victims of the African Diaspora Holocaust, others is Multiracialists, others is Multiethnics, others is Sweeter the Juice Multiracial Multiethnics (these are people like myself who have other races and ethnic groups, like Mexicans, Irish, Greeks, and Italians in they ancestry but who resemble pure African gods and goddesses), others is Cosmopolitan Neo-Africans, others is African-Internationalists, others is African Memphians from the Republic of New Africa Memphis and drapes theyselves in the Africa Memphis flags, 'cause when I give them some of my Republic of Texas literature that talked about gringos freeing theyselves from imperial Mexico they decided to form they own Independent African Republic in Memphis, not the whole state but just they own city, though like the Texans they still considers theyselves to be Americans but not citizens of the "corporate United States."

There is some members of the Perfectability Baptist Church, though, who don't believe that we should keep Gladys Knight Pipism as part of the official church doctrine. They don't want people to think that we are the William Faulkner Stereotypical Colored Peo-

ples Southern Baptist Church. They don't want people to think that
we're silly, even if they do believe in Keep on keeping on. Cayenne
Goodling wanted us to add some of the doctrines of the Church of
Elvis, but we ain't that silly. There is some members of the church,
myself included, that believes we should add to us church doctrine
Mama Didn't Raise No Foolism. Since I don't have any children of
my own, they have made me a Official Mama of the Perfectability
Baptist Church, which ain't the same as a matriarch, 'cause they is
also Official Papas of the Church. I ain't allowed to tell other peoples
children Mama Didn't Raise No Fool, though. We is modernists
and you can't just be telling other people's childrens they ain't been
raised to be a fool.

Ain't James Brown have a song say "Papa Don't Raise No Fool"?
I think that you can acknowledge that they is a subtle difference to
Mama didn't raise no fool and Papa don't raise no fool. When
peoples talks about the difference between masculine and feminine
languages, I thinks you can see the difference in saying Mama didn't
raise no fool and Papa don't raise no fool. Papa don't raise no fool is
the language of command. Mamas just tells they children that they
didn't raise no fool. I am glad they have named me one of the Official
Mamas of the Church and not the Official Fool.

The church still don't allow no women preachers but they lets us
along with the mens who ain't official preachers to assume the role of
griots in our various African Diaspora communities. I am the official
griot to the small New World African community of Cuba, New
Mexico. We might tell warrior stories or culture stories or children's
stories or whatever stories we wants to tell. We are not required just
to tell stories that have to do with Perfectability Baptist theology,
though most of us have at least got to mention the Perfectability Baptist Church. We is also required to be as much listeners as we is storytellers. And if peoples asks us questions while we is telling stories,
we's got to answer them questions. If we prefers not to answer them
questions or ain't got no answers for them questions, then we has got
to say so and include it in us stories. As storytellers we has got to
know that the listener is as important to the story as the storyteller.
As for the other Ray being a Aztec god and me being a African goddess and us being married, we just gets playful with the peoples. I
uses my name Nadine for the restaurant name and the other Ray uses

his whole name, so the restaurant's name is Nadine and Ray Mendoza's. That is why the peoples thinks that I'm Mrs. Nadine Mendoza when my true name is who I am.

Most people still calls me Mosquito, and they don't know my full name. You know a lot of people don't even know what your full name is, either Ray, even the other Ray, and I had to tell him your full name is Ray Guerrero Sacerdote Ku'oko'a-Maikai. I know it is because you have the same name as your aunt Electra, whose story I know as well as my own because of all the documents that Amanda Ku'oko'a-Maikai Mariner Wordlaw has sent me to read aloud and keep them in my memory. I have in my memory all the mystical and prophetic writings of your aunt Electra and all of her other writings and all the documents. I have also in my memory all of the documents of the Spiritual Mother project. I has got so many auditory memory obligations: to you and your people, to Monkey Bread and the Daughters of Nzingha, and even to being an Official Mama of the Perfectability Baptist Church. I gots to keep the official doctrine of Mama and Papa Didn't and Don't Raise No Fool in my auditory memory to keep us childrens from becoming fools and to help them that is fools already, as well as all the stories and histories of everybody of color who sends they stories and histories to the Daughters of Nzingha archives, and to be able to distinguish between the stories that is wisdom stories and them that is trickster stories, and also to be able to think deep. Monkey Bread refers to me as the worthy listener when she is not calling me Nadine. Even though I am a griot for the Perfectability Baptists, Monkey Bread still prefers to refer to me as a listener.

I know how people of color is about stories, though. If the African traditional story about wisdom and its many variations can come all the way from Africa to America and be told to me by my Papa Didn't Raise No Fool Neither Daddy, who has as much Mexican in him as African, and my mama, whose maternal grandmother looks just like Miguelita, the crazy gringa I told you about but my maternal great-grandmother was sane and "went for black," as my mama says, with a sane mind, can tell me stories of an uncle Bud and aunt Blossom, escaped slaves from slavery times, and stories about my granny Jane, who looked just like a African and who kept on keeping on and who kinda remind me of Kate Hickman in one of my favorite books

615

I reads and about John Free who fought in the Civil War and also
wrote letters for colored soldiers and Big Warrior the Seminole African who fought with the Seminoles in Florida and about Africans of
the warrior class; this letter would be too long if I tells you their
story, including all the other stories in my auditory memory—not the
same Uncle Bud as the Uncle Bud World War II Uncle Bud but
Aunt Blossom's Uncle Bud of slavery times, but Mama says they is
many Buds and Blossoms in us family—then I knows that in your
African-Mexican village you can hear tales about a Mrs. Nadine
Mendoza of Cuba, New Mexico, so I wants you to know the truth
of the story, for the purposes of the revolution, you know what I
mean, Ray, even though I know that you more than anybody knows
me for who I really am.
Sojourner Nadine Jane Nzingha Johnson

AUTHOR'S NOTE

I have included in this novel characters (among them Saturna the Indian, his horse Chew Sue, and Jo Jo Cushoff), a song ("Playing a Game of Romance"), and a poem ("My Seventh Love") written by my mother, Lucille Jones, as well as her play, *Blessings for Coliene*.